Digital Signal Computers & Processors

OTHER IEEE PRESS BOOKS

Digital Signal Computers & Processors

Edited by
Andres C. Salazar

Member, Technical Staff
Bell Laboratories

A volume in the IEEE PRESS Selected Reprint Series,
prepared under the sponsorship of the IEEE Acoustics,
Speech, and Signal Processing Society and the
IEEE Computer Society.

The Institute of Electrical and Electronics Engineers, Inc. New York

PRINTED IN THE UNITED STATES OF AMERICA

IEEE International Standard Book Numbers: Clothbound: 0-87942-099-5
Paperbound: 0-87942-100-2

Library of Congress Catalog Card Number 77-82295

Sole Worldwide Distributor (Exclusive of the IEEE):

JOHN WILEY & SONS, INC.
605 Third Ave.
New York, NY 10016

Wiley Order Numbers: Clothbound: 0-471-03968-3
Paperbound: 0-471-03969-1

Contents

Introduction

Digital signal processing has now become an established field, and its importance as a method of manipulating waveforms grows daily as the new technology in circuitry evolves. Electronic technology, with the advances in integrated circuits with respect to lower price, increased speed and reliability, and enhanced capability, has made practical the processing in real time of signals whose spectra exceed the voice bandwidth. Applications of digital signal processing techniques to digital communications, radar, sonar, geological sensory systems, and speech signal analysis and synthesis are now commonplace. The publication of two IEEE Press volumes on digital signal processing by the IEEE Acoustics, Speech, and Signal Processing Society represents, in a way, the proliferation of interest and attention being given by researchers and applications and development engineers to these techniques.

In the past, new digital methods for processing waveforms were implemented on large, expensive general-purpose machines where virtually unlimited memory, processing capability, and time were available readily. Real-time implementation of these techniques was more a theoretical concept than a reality for all except a few basic and simple algorithms. As electronic technology matured and more became known about the limitations of digital signal processing, machines which were stand-alone, operating in real time, and implemented a digital signal processing technique became known as "digital signal processors." At first, these machines ranged in size from a room-full of equipment such as the FDP (at M.I.T. Lincoln Laboratories) which was general purpose in nature to nothing more than a rack which contained a programmable second-order section.

The role of computer architecture became increasingly important as more complicated applications were considered for digital signal processors. Speed, complexity, power consumption, computing capability, and cost were all factors to be considered in the design of these machines. It has been only in the last few years that the technology in integrated circuits has made feasible and viable the consideration of these machines for a myriad of applications. The advent of the general availability and large variety of low power Schottky devices and high-speed ALU chips, including the new bipolar microprocessor families, has generated an enormous amount of interest in the digital implementation in real time of many algorithms previously considered too costly. The burgeoning low-speed MOS microprocessor system market which, at present, by and large is dedicated to control and bookkeeping applications is starting to move towards higher speeds and more arithmetic capability. The multiply operation was long considered a costly, bulky, cumbersome, and time-consuming element. Again, new LSI bipolar technology has now produced single chip 8×8, 12×12, and 16×16 bit multipliers with less than 200 ns typical execution time. These chips are available now, and future improvements will likely include reduction in power consumption, higher reliability, and reduction in cost. An element which was somewhat expensive for many years was the A/D converter with reasonable conversion time. Developments in the last three years have also drastically reduced the price of this key element in a digital signal processor.

Memory elements, whether random access or read only, had been of medium density and cost. New production methods, especially in MOS technology, have permitted increased density, cost reduction, speed enhancement, and in general have contributed to the overall reduction in parts count, power consumption, and component cost required for implementing digital signal processors.

The architecture of the digital signal processor has traditionally depended on the application one has in mind for the machine. However, it is likely that with the advent of new cheap key elements, machine architecture will become more general purpose in nature. As a natural consequence to this trend, a digital signal processor, possibly with a switch-selectable sampling rate and easier memory and program control, will be offered on the market. It may be possible that the microcomputer revolution, which has recently come to encompass the fast minicomputer market, will spread to the digital signal processor field. As yet, micro- and minicomputer system manufacturers have provided only medium-speed hardware multipliers as additional peripherals, and have done little to modify architecture or software features in order to facilitate high-speed convolution, FFT's, or filtering. It is only when both hardware and software implementations of digital signal processing techniques are taken into account that a serious and viable digital signal processor product can be put on the market. An important consideration in working with a digital signal processor is the construction of a flexible and user-oriented interface or support system. This system permits the user to create, edit, assemble, load, probe, and monitor the program execution in the processor.

It is unfortunate that no software papers could be included in this volume. The few that were suggested to me considered general-purpose computers and were not involved with digital signal processing at all. Many workers in the digital signal processing field, including the Editor, consider themselves primarily "software types" with, of course, a serious interest in implementation and hardware. It is a curious phenomenon that the circuit design aspect of the machine evokes the most interest and generally gets the larger share of the patent and publishing limelight. Experience in software implementation of digital signal processing algorithms gives one a better perspective as to the advantages and disadvantages of a particular machine architecture. The vertical or horizontal microprogramming word organization, the number and sizes of memory registers, instructional branching, and looping capability are all machine features which can be better evaluated from a programmer's point of view. Management of the machine's resources in implementing an algorithm requires a considerable amount of planning and insight into both machine capability and algorithm understanding. Programming also inevitably requires careful manipulation of the signal data in order to minimize roundoff noise, aliasing, overflow, and other impairments peculiar to digital signal processing. We hope to see more papers in this field solicited and published in the future.

This volume is intended to serve as a reference source for those engineers and scientists who have determined that digital signal processing techniques can prove useful in their projects and are convinced that real-time execution is imperative for handling the signal data base. This book also serves as a companion volume to the two previous IEEE Press collections, entitled *Digital Signal Processing and Selected Papers in Digital Signal Processing II*, both compiled and sponsored by members of the Digital Signal Processing Committee of the IEEE ASSP Society. The present volume is co-sponsored by the Computer and ASSP Societies of the IEEE since the elements and the architecture of digital signal processors are unmistakably computer-like, and much of the literature on high-speed processors can be found in the former Society's TRANSACTIONS. The application and purpose of the machine is digital signal processing, and it is this field which is of great interest to ASSP TRANSACTIONS readers.

The present reprint collection is organized into four parts, the first of which is an overview of general-purpose processors either custom-built or commercially available. In Part II five articles are reprinted which stress architectural points about such processors. Part III consists of four sections: A. Computing Units, B. FFT Computing, C. Multiply Configurations, and D. A/D or D/A Conversion. These sections include papers which have dealt with individual elements of a digital signal processor. It has been breakthroughs or improvements of these elements which have played a key role in the real-time implementation of digital signal processing. In Part IV we have chosen five papers which are more specialized in nature in that they discuss a specific application of digital signal processors. The highly disparate field of application illustrates just how widespread the interest in such machines is at present.

It should be mentioned at this point that a large number of papers were considered for inclusion in this volume. Some papers, although they ordinarily would have been included here, were left out because they had been reproduced in one of the two above-mentioned IEEE Press volumes.

ACKNOWLEDGMENT

It is my pleasure to acknowledge the help and advice of Joe Fisher, President of Signal Processing Systems, and Larry Rabiner of Bell Laboratories who encouraged me from the beginning to carry out this editing effort.

The LX-1 Microprocessor and Its Application to Real-Time Signal Processing

GARY D. HORNBUCKLE, MEMBER, IEEE, AND
ENRICO I. ANCONA, MEMBER, IEEE

Abstract—LX-1 is an integrated circuit prototype of a microprocessor which is being used as a design vehicle to study the problems associated with the design and implementation of a similar computer constructed with large-scale integrated circuits. The organizational simplicity of LX-1 is emphasized and the supporting microprogramming and simulation facilities are discussed and examples are given.

The major portion of the control of the microprocessor is implemented in a 256-word by 64-bit control memory, and the remaining logic is partitioned into a very few unique functional logic circuits. There are 16 general-purpose 16-bit registers and a 256- by 16-bit scratch memory. The cycle time is 70 ns, and logic is provided for addition, bit logical, array shift, and array multiply operations.

To demonstrate the feasibility of using small, general-purpose, microprogrammed computers for real-time digital signal processing, the application of LX-1 as a digital vocoder was investigated. The advantages of using a microprogrammed processor rather than special-purpose hardware for this application are the lower cost of such a general-purpose computer and the flexibility provided by the ability to change the microprogram.

An implementation of the spectrum analyzer portion of the vocoder and its operation on the LX-1 simulator is described. The results show that real-time operation of the spectrum analyzer on the LX-1 prototype could be expected with minimal additional hardware, e.g., a 200-sample input buffer. Moreover, the proposed LSI version of LX-1 could be operated in half duplex mode for both analysis and synthesis, or to process several input channels.

Index Terms—Computer design, LSI computers, microprogramming, real-time digital signal processing, spectrum analysis, vocoders.

INTRODUCTION

THERE is currently much interest in machines designed to take advantage of large-scale integrated circuit (LSI) technology. This paper discusses a microprocessor which was designed and built at the M.I.T. Lincoln Laboratory. The organization and regularity of layout were central considerations because of the constraints posed by large-scale integration. The major portion of the control of the microprocessor is implemented in a control memory and the remaining logic is partitioned into a very few unique functional circuits. The technique of control implemented in a control memory (often read-only memory) is well known and is called microprogramming, and such processors are referred to as microprocessors.

The paper describes a prototype processor, called LX-1, which has been built primarily to test the applicability of microprogramming, as well as the particular design, to a variety of problems. However, the prototype was constructed from commercially available emitter-coupled logic circuits which are similar to those anticipated for an LSI version. The logic was partitioned as nearly as possible in the same manner that an LSI version might be. This paper emphasizes the organizational simplicity of LX-1 and discusses the supporting microprogramming and simulation facilities that have been programmed on the TX-2 computer at the M.I.T. Lincoln Laboratory. Specifically, it discusses in detail the application of LX-1 to the problem of real-time, digital encoding of speech.

LX-1 is a processor intended for use in a multiprocessor environment with a hierarchical, general-purpose memory system. It has three levels of memory—register, scratch, and control—but has no core or bulk memory as these are treated as I/O devices. LX-1 can be used in a variety of ways. For example, it can be used as a digital controller, such as a drum or tape controller, or as a special-purpose processor to rapidly compute such functions as Fourier transforms, floating point arithmetic, or trigonometric functions. The more common use for microprocessors has been in the role of a Central Processor to interpret (or emulate) so-called machine languages, such as is done in several models of the IBM System/360, and microprocessors have been proposed which could interpret higher level languages such as LISP [1] and Euler [2]. A wide variety of applications is made possible by changing the contents of the control memory, i.e., the microprogram. In a general sense, LX-1 is like other processors if one considers the (read-only)[1] program to reside in the control memory. With this view, LX-1 is a four-address machine with limited (read-only) program memory. The four addresses contained in a typical microinstruction are the location of two operands, the location of the result, and the location of the next instruction.

HARDWARE DESIGN

Partitioning

In the design of LX-1, the emphasis was placed upon simplifying the backpanel wiring, minimizing the number of different kinds of circuits, and simplifying testing, since these are major considerations in large-scale integration. The processor was not designed to simplify microprogram-

Manuscript received September 18, 1969; revised January 25, 1970. This work was sponsored by the U. S. Advanced Research Projects Agency.

G. D. Hornbuckle was with the Massachusetts Institute of Technology, Lincoln Laboratory, Lexington, Mass. He is now with Applicon Inc., Burlington, Mass., 01803.

E. I. Ancona is with the Massachusetts Institute of Technology, Lincoln Laboratory, Lexington, Mass. 02173.

[1] Read-only is placed in parenthesis here to emphasize that microprogram memory need not be read-only. The control memory of LX-1 is read-only with respect to the microprogram, but is externally writeable.

Reprinted from *IEEE Trans. Comput.*, vol. C-19, pp. 710–720, Aug. 1970.

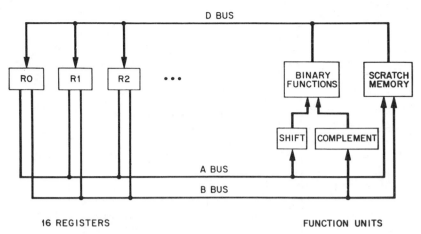

Fig. 1.   Simplified block diagram for the LX-1 microprocessor.

ming, although considerable attention was given to making it possible to concisely write and conveniently debug microprograms.

The three major components of LX-1 are the control memory, a set of 16 16-bit registers, and several function units which perform operations on the data in the registers. The function units realized in LX-1 include a logic and adder unit, a scratch memory, and a multiplier unit.

To simplify the backpanel wiring a three-bus structure was used. Fig. 1 gives a simplified block diagram, Fig. 2 is more detailed. Each of the 16 registers is connected to the A- and B-bus which are the data paths from the registers to the function units, and each register is connected to the D-bus which is the data path from the function units to the registers. These 48 bus wires consume one layer of parallel wiring on the backpanel. The remaining wires, which consist of selection lines, input/output lines, and other control wires, cause all the backpanel wiring crossover problems. An attempt was made to minimize the number of these wires by suitable partitioning of the logic and by simplifying the basic design.

The number of different kinds of circuits was minimized by partitioning all flip-flop memory into identical registers, one-half register per card or LSI chip. The logic and arithmetic function units are partitioned into three types, each of which is iteratively repeated for the function. One type implements four bits of a function unit which can generate the arithmetic sum or Boolean sum or product of two operands. A second type implements one-eighth of an array shift function unit. A third type generates the arithmetic product. The remaining two frequently used logic circuits are a select circuit which selects one of eight inputs or decodes three inputs into eight outputs, and a select circuit which is used to select between pairs of inputs such as for the B-bus complement function.

The remaining miscellaneous circuits, such as bus drivers, either would be fundamentally different for LSI or would be added to the frequently used circuits to avoid new circuit types. The circuits directly associated with the control memory would also be different for LSI. The scratch memory of LX-1 is constructed from one printed circuit card

type which contains 16 16-bit integrated circuit memory elements. A similar LSI scratch memory circuit would contain 256 memory bits with decoding. Table I gives the number of each circuit type used and Fig. 1 shows where they are used.

Register slice, rather than bit-slice, partitioning was chosen for reasons of expandability. It was felt that it would be desirable to be able to increase the number of registers and function units with only minor revisions in the layout. With bit-slice the number of bits per register could be expanded easily, but this was considered to be of secondary importance, although with LX-1, the number of bits could be conveniently increased in four-bit increments. Another important reason for using register slice partitioning was to isolate all sequential circuits, that is, all flip-flops, to one circuit type. All other circuits, other than the scratch memory and control memory buffer, are combinational, and well developed techniques for diagnosis of combinational circuits are applicable [3].

Operation

During a typical microinstruction, the contents of one of the 16 registers is placed on the A-bus, the contents of the same or another register is placed on the B-bus, an operation is performed in a function unit, and the result which appears on the D-bus is stored in the same or a third register. This entire sequence occurs within a single 70-ns clock cycle; the clock is only used to strobe the function results from the D-bus into a register and to strobe the results of control memory read cycles into the control memory buffer. The control memory, which is constructed from the same circuit as the scratch memory, acts as a combinational circuit during reading, and the read cycle is generally overlapped with the register operations.

The data on the A-bus can be shifted or rotated from zero to 15-bit positions, right or left, and the data on the B-bus can be complemented, prior to the arithmetic and logic function operations. The latter include binary addition and bit-by-bit AND, OR, and EXCLUSIVE-OR. Subtraction of the B-bus data is performed by complement addition. Both one's and two's complement arithmetic are made possible

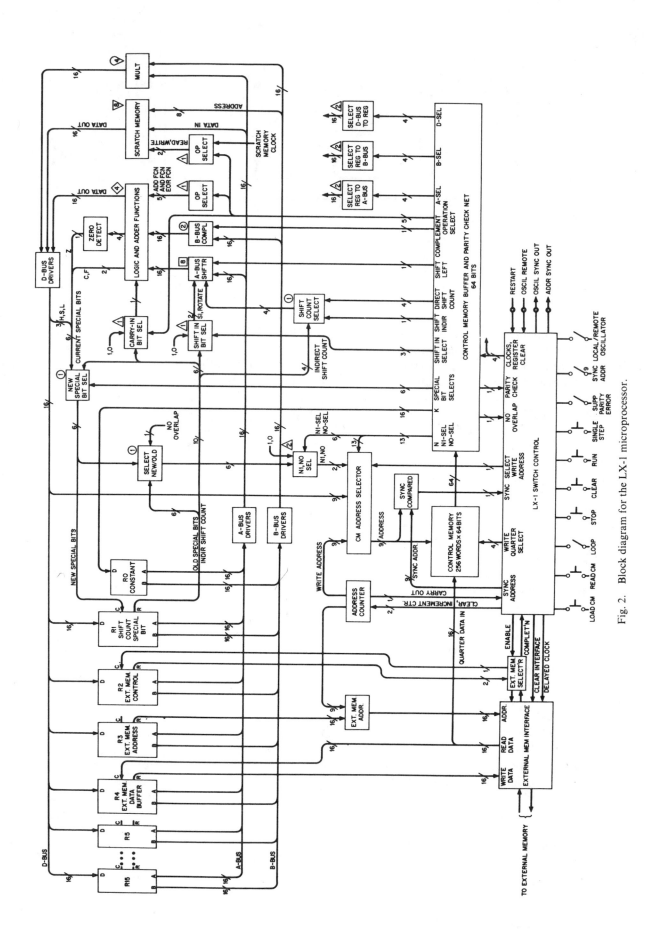

Fig. 2. Block diagram for the LX-1 microprocessor.

TABLE I

LX-1 CIRCUIT TYPES

Circuit Type	Fig. 1	Circuits Used	Gates per Circuit	Gates Used	Signal Pins per Circuit
Register		32	72	2304	47
Adder/Logic	◇	4	71	284	21
Shift	□	8	75	600	24
Select 1	△	12	13	156	26
Select 2	○	4	49	196	33
Multiply	▽	4	103*	412	57
Scratch Memory	△	8	37†	296	20
		72		4248	

* Includes 64 full adder circuits.
† Excludes 256 memory bits.

by allowing the carry-in to the lowest order adder position to be a logical one, logical zero, or one of six special bits. All types of shift operations, such as arithmetic and logical, are possible because the bits shifted into the vacated bit positions can be selected from logical one or zero, one of five special bits, or the bits shifted out (for rotate or cycle shifts). Also, the shift count can be stated explicitly in the microinstruction or can come indirectly from register one.

The second function unit of LX-1 is a 256-word scratch memory. In a single microinstruction, a word can be read from or written into the scratch memory. The data to be written come from the A-bus, and the address comes from the low-order eight bits of the B-bus. The write-clock is derived from the basic machine clock.

A third function unit, an array multiplier, generates the high-order or low-order 16 bits of the product. Two instructions are required to store the results for full precision. The multiplier is attached to the A-, B-, and D-buses in a manner similar to the other function units.

All overflow, carry indicators, and condition bits used for carry-in, shift-in, and conditional branches are stored in six bits of register one. These special bits are as follows:

H—high-order bit of D-bus
C—carry-out of add operation
Z—zero detect from adder/logic unit
L—low-order bit of D-bus
S—second-from-low-order bit of D-bus
F—overflow from add operation or multiply operation.

By selecting any two of the special bits, a logical one, or a logical zero, one can cause absolute, two-way conditional, or four-way conditional branches. All next-address selection bits are included in every microinstruction and a program counter is not used. The address counter shown in Fig. 2 is for external loading of the control memory. In each microinstruction, one can elect to save any subset of the special bits just generated or to save the old values. The conditional branch can use the old values or the newly generated values of the special bits. In the latter case an extended cycle is caused because overlap of control memory reading

and function execution is not possible. Since an extended cycle is also used for addition to allow for worst-case carry propagation, long extended cycles can occur. A special case of the next-instruction bits allows the next control-memory address to come from the D-bus. This extended cycle feature allows microprogram subroutines and branch tables.

Sixteen bits of each microinstruction are reserved for an immediate constant. The constant will appear on the A-bus or B-bus if register zero is selected. A standard register circuit is used for register zero to allow uniform gating onto the A- and B-buses, although it is wired to act as a non-storage data transfer circuit.

Each register, in addition to its A-, B-, and D-bus connection, has 16 output and 16 input lines, one for each bit. These connections are used internally in the processor in the case of register one, but the remaining 448 leads can be attached to external equipment. For an LSI version some rather small connectors will be required. Although a multiplexed I/O bus would avoid these connections, the timing problems and complexities of such logic would be greater. Even if one were to construct an I/O bus, further logic would be needed to tap onto the bus for each external device. If such logic were to be constructed with LSI, one would have a problem similar to connecting 448 leads to the microprocessor. Furthermore, for LX-1 most of the timing problems associated with input/output equipment can be solved in the microprogram. It is unlikely that all 14 registers will be attached to I/O equipment, although at least two are required if an external memory is connected to the processor. The interconnection of two processors can be made by simply attaching the input leads of a register in one processor to the output leads of another, and vice versa. Communication control can be handled with the microprograms.

FIRMWARE DESIGN

A programming package has been created on the TX-2 computer that allows a user to write and run microprograms written in a symbolic assembly language. Statements in this language, called ML, correspond to the control instructions for the LX-1 processor. ML programs are free-format text files. The language allows symbolic labels, register names, literal and address constants, and is highly readable. The ML programs are compiled by the ML assembler, which is implemented in VITAL [4], into files of control memory bit patterns. Side-by-side formatted listings are produced. The control memory files created drive the LX-1 simulator. Eventually, they will be read into the LX-1 control memory or be used to determine read-only memory bit patterns in subsequent LSI versions. The syntax and description of the language are included in the Appendix.

The LX-1 microprogram checkout and debugging package (LXSIM) provides a cycle-by-cycle simulation of the LX-1 prototype processor. The simulator was designed to allow maximum user flexibility. Snapshots of the current machine status are given via an on-line display. Breakpoints can be put on microinstructions or on memory locations. Individual instructions can be altered or the whole program can be edited and recompiled. Memory locations can be examined and filled. Conditional execution or single stepping of the simulator is possible. New control memory or main memory files can be loaded at will. Different versions of the simulator, corresponding to various machine configurations, can be selected.

Since its purpose is to assist in debugging microprograms, the simulator is controlled interactively in a very flexible way. This flexibility is achieved because the simulator is designed to accept a large number of low-level text-encoded commands. If desired, the user can enter lists of these commands directly, via the outline keyboard, but to do so is quite tedious. These basic commands, though quite flexible, are relatively primitive. For example, 72 characters must be typed to clear the 16 general registers. To combat inevitable user fatigue, a run-time command package has been written to allow the directed expansion of user-defined succinct commands into primitive commands.

User commands are defined by procedures written in the DOMEX (Display Oriented Macro EXpander) language, which has been based on the TRAC language [5]. Like TRAC, DOMEX is a language for text manipulation. Strings of characters may be named, parameter markers inserted, and strings called by name with argument lists. Character strings can be treated arbitrarily as executable procedures, names, or as text. Recursive function calls are also possible.

Unique to DOMEX is its ability to use the on-line display and Sylvania tablet [6]. Pseudo light buttons can be defined and given procedural value. When a light button is pointed at, the procedure is executed, at times producing a new selection of light buttons. The procedure executed may also send strings of commands to the simulator. It can interrogate the status of the 16 registers in the simulated machine and use this information to control the generation of the command sequence sent. The procedure may also choose to demand characters from the tablet. The character recognizer [7] will be called and its output made available to the procedure.

Part of the flexibility of DOMEX commands is their run-time definition. When the simulator package is first called, the only defined DOMEX command is one that will read and execute text files. An initialization text file might contain a DOMEX procedure which, when executed, defines other commands. Different users may have different initialization files. The user is free to drop or edit old definitions or to create new ones. DOMEX procedures can define new ones or be self-modifying. New initialization files can be written out at any time.

Typical simulator control procedures that can be defined might include:

1) single step until a selected register contains a given value,
2) load one register from another,
3) remember the machine status so it can be restored later—even at a different session,

4) print read-only memory in symbolic format,
5) trace a register, typing the value and the microprogram instruction counter every time it is changed,
6) edit, recompile, and reload the control memory file,
7) write out a text file which, when read in, redefines all strings currently in use,
8) trace an instruction, printing out selected register values every time it is executed.

The selection and form are, of course, up to the user. The command package can be tailored as desired.

APPLICATION TO REAL-TIME SIGNAL PROCESSING

The usefulness of the LX-1 design to real-time digital signal processing was investigated to demonstrate LX-1's capabilities and flexibility. In particular, its application to the spectrum analyzer and coding portions of a digital channel vocoder was investigated. The vocoder algorithm was designed by Anderson [9] and Bially [10]. This particular application was chosen because of the current interest in digital signal processing and also because the computational load and real-time constraints imposed by the spectrum analyzer algorithm are well-matched to the microprocessor's capabilities.

The advantages of using microprogrammed processors rather than special-purpose hardware are twofold: first, general-purpose LSI processors like LX-1 are potentially less expensive than special-purpose devices. Second, the flexibility provided by the microprogrammed control enables designers to alter their algorithms by changing only the control memory contents.

The LX-1 Simulator

The vocoder spectrum analyzer and coding were simulated using the LXSIM package on the TX-2 computer. Except for input/output, and input buffer maintenance, the vocoder simulator microcode is identical to that of the real vocoder microcode. The above operations, however, do not add significant overhead to the computations, and thus the values obtained from simulation are reasonable.

Channel Vocoder

The overall vocoder analyzer and synthesizer structure is shown in Fig. 3. The input to the analyzer consists of 10-bit samples of speech entering at a 10-kHz rate, or every 100 μs. Speech bandwidth compression in the vocoder is achieved by coding two parameters of the speech: the first parameter is the pitch period, which is a measure of the excitation to the vocal tract. The second parameter is the spectrum, which is a measure of the characteristics of the vocal tract. The spectrum analyzer calculates the magnitude of the response of the vocal tract at 32 frequencies. These two parameters are coded into 2400 bits/second and are transmitted to the synthesizer.

There, the impulse response of the vocal tract, or the inverse discrete Fourier transform of the spectrum, is con-

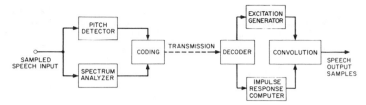

Fig. 3.   Digital vocoder system.

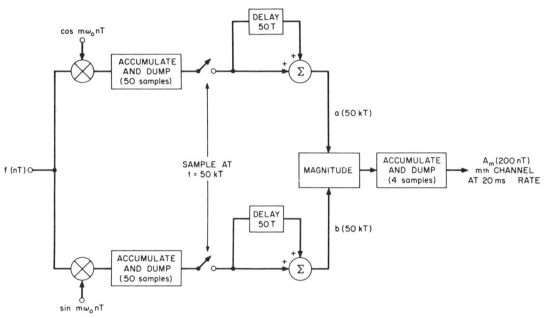

Fig. 4.   Simplified mth channel of vocoder analyzer.

volved with an appropriate excitation to produce speech. Only the spectrum analyzer and coding portions of the vocoder are described here in detail and the results of simulation on LXSIM will be discussed. The reader is referred to Gold [11] for a description of pitch detection and to Anderson [9] and Bially [10] for a description of the synthesizer.

Vocoder Spectrum Analyzer

The spectrum analyzer consists of 32 bandpass filters centered at 100, 200, $\cdots$, 3200 Hz. Each bandpass filter is of the form shown in Fig. 4. The 10-bit samples of speech are input into each channel at a 10-kHz rate and are modulated by a sine and cosine function at the center frequency of the bandpass filter in question. Fifty successive samples are accumulated and saved, and are then added to the sum of the previous 50 samples. The magnitude of the function is then taken. Thus, every 5 ms the magnitude of the discrete Fourier transform at the center frequency of the filter for the last 10 ms of input has been found. This corresponds to

$$\sum_{n=0}^{99} f(nT)e^{jm\omega_0 nT}$$

for channel m (center frequency $m\omega_0$), where $\omega_0 = 2\pi \times 100$ Hz.

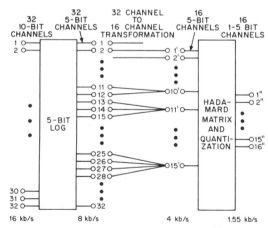

Fig. 5.   2400-bit coding of 32 vocoder channels.

The second portion of the spectrum analyzer's function is to take the average of the last four 5-ms outputs and to code the output of the 32 channels to enable transmission at 2400 bits/second, as shown in Fig. 5. First, the 5-bit logarithm of each of the 32 10-bit channels is taken. Then the 32 channels are converted to 16 by means of a linear combination of less significant channels, and finally the channels are multiplied by a Hadamard matrix to decorrelate the channels and quantized to 1 to 5 bits per channel. This coding yields a total of 1550 bits/second. The remaining 850 bits/second are used for pitch information.

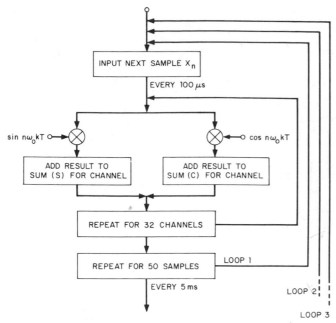

Fig. 6.   Loop 1 of microprogrammed analyzer.

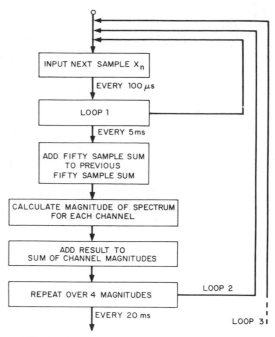

Fig. 7.   Loop 2 of microprogrammed analyzer.

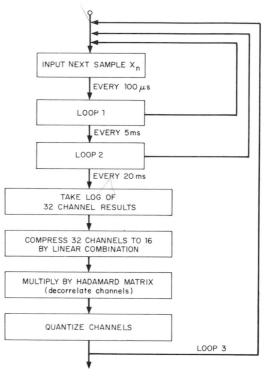

Fig. 8.   Loop 3 of microprogrammed analyzer.

Microprogrammed Analyzer

There are three main loops in the microcode.

Loop 1: Every 100 μs, the discrete Fourier transform of the current sample at the 32 frequencies is computed. Next, the running sum over the last 50 samples, as shown in Fig. 6, is computed as follows:

$$\sum_{n=0}^{49} x_n \sin m\omega_0 nT, \tag{1}$$

and

$$\sum_{n=0}^{49} x_n \cos m\omega_0 nT \tag{2}$$

where m is the channel number and ω_0 is the base frequency (100 Hz). The first quadrant of the lowest frequency sine wave (100 Hz) is stored in 25 words of the read-only control memory. Each value is coded into 6 bits. All other sine and cosine values may be obtained from this table by appropriate functions for the sign and table lookup. The multiplication is done by means of the array multiplier mentioned earlier. Thus, the input to Loop 2 is the 64 sums of the form shown in (1) and (2).

Loop 2: Every 5 ms, the 64 sums are added to the sums of the previous 50 samples, which were stored in the scratchpad memory, and the magnitude of the spectrum for each channel is calculated (see Fig. 7). Next, the sum of four spectrum magnitudes for each channel is calculated. Thus, every 20 ms, the input to Loop 3 consists of 32 10-bit spectrum magnitudes.

Loop 3: Every 20 ms, the logarithm of the sum of the spectra is calculated and the 32 channels are compressed to 16 by appropriate linear combinations of the logarithms. Finally, the 16 results are multiplied by a Hadamard matrix

to decorrelate the channels and the channels are appropriately quantified to yield a total of 32 bits every 20 ms (see Fig. 8). The magnitude of the Hadamard coefficients is always one and their sign is calculated by means of

$$h_{ij} = \alpha_1 \cdot \beta_4 \oplus \alpha_2 \cdot \beta_3 \oplus \alpha_3 \cdot \beta_2 \oplus \alpha_4 \cdot \beta_1$$

where $i = \alpha_1\alpha_2\alpha_3\alpha_4$ and $j = \beta_1\beta_2\beta_3\beta_4$ are the row and column indices, respectively. If $h_{ij}=1$, the sign is negative. If $h_{ij}=0$,

TABLE II
RESULTS OF SIMULATION

	Length (μinstructions)	Best Time (μs)	Worst Time (μs)
Loop 1 (every sample)	50	55 (55 μs/sample)	80 (80 μs/sample)
Loop 2 (every 50 samples)	30	45 (1 μs/sample)	50 (1 μs/sample)
Loop 3 (every 200 samples)	120	650 (3.2 μs/sample)	700 (3.5 μs/sample)
Overall (per sample basis)	200	60	85

the sign is positive. Note that · is logical AND, and ⊕ is logical EXCLUSIVE-OR.

Results

The results, using a 70-ns cycle time for LX-1, are shown in Table II. All times marked "per sample" assume a 200-sample input buffer. This buffer is necessary because, as shown in Table II, the 5-ms and 20-ms calculations take a considerable amount of time. The 100-μs calculation is fast enough, however, to enable the analyzer to catch up with the input every 200 samples at most. Depending on the values of the speech input samples, the computation times vary within the limits described in Table II.

The above implementation shows that the analysis of input speech can be done in real-time. Two factors, however, have not been taken into account. One is the maintenance of the input buffer and the other is the section of the analyzer dealing with pitch detection which operates in parallel with the spectrum analyzer.

It can also be seen that Loop 2 and Loop 3, even though they are long, add at most a 10 percent overhead to the overall calculation if a 200-sample input buffer is assumed.

CONCLUSION

In summary, the simplicity of organization of LX-1 lends itself to large-scale integration, yet the instructions are complex enough to be interesting and useful. The price for simplicity appears to be in the long words required in the control memory. All attempts to date to decrease the number of bits per microinstruction have resulted in rather ad hoc and cumbersome additions to the present logic. For example, the 16-bit constant field could be eliminated by referencing a second read-only memory indirectly. This would eliminate approximately ten of the 64 bits. With a hardware program counter one could also eliminate about eight bits from the next-instruction address. However, program counters must be incremented, and if the adder is used in order to avoid a new chip type, the cycle time might increase. One could also allow fewer operations per instruction. Rather than allow a shift followed by an add, these could be separate instructions. In fact, if one were to attempt to decrease the number of bits in each microinstruction to 16, he might be led to an instruction set typically found in 16-bit minicomputers. The 64-bit microinstructions of LX-1 are, on the average, four to six times more powerful than typical 16-bit instruction sets.

There appear to be many possible applications of LX-1. Microprograms have been written to simulate two small machines; the Digital Equipment Corporation PDP-8, and the Hewlett–Packard 2115A. Both took approximately 100 microinstructions and ran at real-time with respect to the machine being simulated. A 64-terminal communications line multiplexer has been coded. It also required less than 100 microinstructions and took about 1 μs per bit input or output (all serial/parallel conversion was done in the microprogram).

The usefulness of the design to a vocoder analyzer has been demonstrated, and the only required hardware addition is a 200-sample (slow) input buffer memory. The LSI version, which should be five times faster, could be used with no hardware modifications and should be fast enough to handle both analysis and synthesis simultaneously.

Thus, real-time digital signal processing is feasible in small microprogrammed computers, and the expected performance of LSI technology should make this method of operation even more attractive because of the potential cost advantage and the flexibility provided.

APPENDIX

Syntax for ML

The syntax for ML is based upon the extended BNF notation developed by Cheatham [8]. The metasymbol ⇒ is equivalent to the BNF ::= and means "is defined as" or "consists of." Upper case alphabetics and all other characters (other than metasymbols) are terminal symbols, whereas strings of lower case alphabetic characters (in some cases separated with dashes) are used to define nonterminal syntactic elements. Exceptions are that space, tab, and cr stand for the obvious terminal symbols. The metasymbol | is used to separate and specify alternatives, brackets enclose alternatives, and brackets with subscripts and superscripts mean the following:

[ ]$_j^i$ choose at least j but at most i of the alternatives
[ ]^i choose none or at most i
[ ]$_j$ choose at least j with no upper limit
[ ] is equivalent to [ ]^1
{ } is equivalent to [ ]$_1^1$.

The following example means that a jwak is defined as a snex followed by at most 3 zats followed by exactly one carriage return:

$$\text{jwak} \Rightarrow \text{snex}[\text{zats}]^3 \{\text{cr}\}.$$

In general, the microprogram source text may be liberally sprinkled with separators; only those places where separators are necessary are indicated in the following.

Preliminary

alphabetic-character $\Rightarrow$ A | B | C | $\cdots$ | Z | 1

alphanumeric-character $\Rightarrow$ alphabetic-
character | 0 | 1 | $\cdots$ | 9   2

separator $\Rightarrow$ space | tab   3

comment $\Rightarrow$ * [any-character-but-cr]$^\infty$ 4

lname, cname, rname $\Rightarrow$ alphabetic-character
[alphanumeric-character]^{15} 5

General Program Structure

microprogram $\Rightarrow$ definition-section assignment-
section END cr   6

definition-section $\Rightarrow$ [definition-line cr]$_1$ 7

definition-line $\Rightarrow$ comment | definition [comment]   8

assignment-section $\Rightarrow$ [assignment-line cr]$_1$ 9

assignment-line $\Rightarrow$ comment | assignment-
statement [comment]   10

Definitions

definition $\Rightarrow$ register-declaration | constant-
declaration   11

register-declaration $\Rightarrow$ rname = octal-number-
modulo-16   12

constant-declaration $\Rightarrow$ cname $\equiv$ octal-number-
modulo-2^{16} | cname $\equiv$ label   13

Assignments

assignment-statement $\Rightarrow$ [label] [separator]$_1$
assignment [/[goto]]   14

assignment $\Rightarrow$ left-side [$\rightarrow$ right-side]   15

right-side $\Rightarrow$ [dregsel] [, special-bit]^6 16

left-side $\Rightarrow$ [aregsel [shiftop] logop] [$-$]
bregsel | 17

aregsel [shiftop] + [$-$] bregsel
[, carryin] | 18

aregsel [shiftop] $-$ bregsel | 19

[aregsel] λ bregsel | 20

aregsel $\{\bar{x} | \underline{x}\}$ bregsel   21

bregsel, aregsel $\Rightarrow$ rname | cname | octal-number-
modulo-2^{16} 22

dregsel $\Rightarrow$ rname   23

logop $\Rightarrow$ $\vee$ | $\wedge$ | $\forall$ 24

shiftop $\Rightarrow$ $\{/ | *\}$ {octal-number-modulo-16 | #}
[, {special-bit | 0 | 1}]   25

carryin $\Rightarrow$ {special-bit | 1 | 0}   26

label $\Rightarrow$ lname [({1 | 0} [, {1 | 0}])]   27

goto $\Rightarrow$ lname [({special-bit | 1 | 0}
[, {special-bit | 1 | 0}]) [|| |]]   28

special-bit $\Rightarrow$ C | Z | H | L | S | F   29

Description of ML

A microprogram consists of a set of definitions (or dec-larations) and a set of assignment statements. The defini-tions allow the use of symbolic names for register identifi-cation and literal constants.

Example: Define register 5 to have the name XYZ:

TABLE III

MICROINSTRUCTION BIT ASSIGNMENTS

Key Syntax Line	Fig. 1 Name	Number of Bits	Function
22	A-Sel	4	Select 1 of 16 registers for A-bus
22	B-Sel	4	Select 1 of 16 registers for B-bus
23	D-Sel	4	Select 1 of 16 registers for D-bus
17	Operation-Select	5	Select 1 of 32 operations
16	Special-Bit-Select	6	Update or ignore 6 special bits
28	N	6	Select next address modulo 4
28	N1-Sel	3	Select second bit of next address
28	N0-Sel	3	Select low-order bit of next address
25	Shift-Indir	1	Select indirect shift count
25	Dir-Shift-Count	4	Direct shift count
25	Shiftin-Sel	3	Select shift-in
25	Shift-Left	1	Shift left or right
18	Complement	1	Complement B-bus
13	K	16	16-bit constant
—	No Overlap	1	Execution dependent next address
—	Parity	1	Control memory parity
	Spare	1	
		64	

$$XYZ = 5 \qquad [SX - 12].^2$$

Each assignment statement is translated into a 64-bit microinstruction for which the bit assignments are given in Table III. The basic form of an assignment statement is:

$$\langle \text{A-bus select} \rangle \, \langle \text{operation} \rangle \, \langle \text{B-bus select} \rangle \rightarrow$$

$$\langle \text{D-bus select} \rangle / \langle \text{next instruction select} \rangle.$$

Example: Store the binary sum of the contents of regis-ters ABC and XYZ into register XYZ:

$$\text{ABC} + \text{XYZ} \rightarrow \text{XYZ} \qquad [SX - 15, 16, 18].$$

If the next instruction field is missing, the next sequential instruction is assumed and the appropriate bits are filled in by the assembler.

Of the 16 addressable registers, register zero is wholly dedicated for immediate constants, register one is partly dedicated for the special bits and indirect shift count, and the remaining 14 registers are available for general use.

Example: Define the immediate constant PQ and load it plus register ABC into register XYZ. The three statements following the definition are equivalent.

$$\text{PQ} \equiv 177326 \qquad [SX - 13]$$

$$\text{ABC} + \text{PQ} \rightarrow \text{XYZ} \qquad [SX - 15, 16, 18]$$

$$\text{ABC} + 177326 \rightarrow \text{XYZ}$$

$$\text{PQ} + \text{ABC} \rightarrow \text{XYZ}$$

Of the 32 possible operations selectable, eight are for addition (eight different carry-in options), three are for the

---

^{2} SX—12 refers to syntax line 12, above. Only the key syntax lines are referenced. Numbers used in programming examples are octal; numbers used in the text are decimal.

logical operations AND, OR, and EOR, two are for reading and writing the scratch memory, two are for the multiply operations, and the remaining are unassigned.

Example: Form the logical OR of ABC and XYZ and put the result in register XYZ.

$$ABC \lor XYZ \to XYZ \qquad [SX - 17].$$

Example: Increment register ABC. The first increments with a carry-in, the second with a constant. The third adds one or two to ABC depending on the state of special bit H.

$$ABC + 0, 1 \; \to ABC \qquad [SX - 18]$$
$$ABC + 1 \quad\;\; \to ABC$$
$$ABC + 1, H \to ABC$$

Example: Subtract ABC from XYZ assuming 2's complement encoding:

$$XYZ - ABC \to XYZ \qquad [SX - 19].$$

Example: Multiply ABC and XYZ and place the low-order 16 bits of the product in UVW:

$$ABC \underline{x} \, XYZ \to UVW \qquad [SX - 21].$$

Any subset of the special bits which are generated each cycle can be ignored or saved in register one. In the latter case, the old values are lost.

Example: Save the carry (C) resulting from the addition of ABC and XYZ, and also save the low-order bit (L) of the sum.

$$ABC + XYZ \to XYZ, C, L \qquad [SX - 16].$$

Program sequencing information is contained in each microinstruction. The location of the next instruction, modulo 4, is given explicitly, and the low-order two bits which complete the next instruction address may be given explicitly or selected from the special bits. Unconditional branches, two-way branches, or four-way branches are provided.

Example: Clear register ABC and branch to L1:

$$0 \to ABC \, / \, L1 \qquad [SX - 14].$$

Example: Test the sign bit (H) of ABC and branch to L2(0) if the sign bit is 0, or branch to L2(1) if the sign bit is 1:

$$ABC \to , H \, / \, L2(H) \qquad [SX - 14,28].$$

Example: Test the carry bit (C) and branch to L3(0, 1) if the carry bit is 0, or branch to L3(1, 1) if the carry bit is 1.

$$ABC \, / \, L3 \, (C, 1) \qquad [SX - 15,28].$$

The data on the A-bus can be shifted or rotated, right or left, up to 15 positions, and the data on the B-bus can be ones complemented prior to the addition or logical operations.

Example: Shift XYZ left three bits (shifting in zeros) and AND with the complement of ABC:

$$XYZ * 3 \land - ABC \to PQR \qquad [SX - 17,25].$$

Example: Divide the 2's complement number in ABC by 16:

$$ABC \to , H \qquad *save \; the \; sign\text{-}bit$$
$$ABC \, / \, 4, H \to ABC.$$

Example: Rotate ABC left an amount equal to the number of zeros in XYZ. Assume COUNT is register 1 where the indirect shift count must be stored:

$$0 \to COUNT$$
$$- XYZ \to TEMP, Z, L \, / \, L3 \, (L, Z)$$
$$L3 \, (0, 0) \quad TEMP \, / \, 1 \to TEMP, L, Z, \, / \, L3 \, (L, Z)$$
$$L3 \, (1,0) \quad COUNT + 1 \to COUNT \, / \, L3 \, (0, 0)$$
$$L3 \, (0, 1) \quad ABC * \#, F \to ABC \; *shiftin = F \; causes \; rotate.$$

The low-order eight bits of data on the B-bus select the word to be written into or read from the scratch memory. For writing, the A-bus contains the data to be written, and for reading, the scratch memory output appears on the D-bus.

Example: Swap word 26 of the scratch memory with ABC:

$$ABC \to TEMP$$
$$\lambda \, 26 \to ABC \qquad [SX - 20].$$
$$TEMP \, \lambda \, 26$$

A special case of the next microinstruction selection bits has the effect of causing an unconditional branch of the microprogram to the location whose value is on the D-bus. This feature makes branch tables and subroutines possible.

Example: Call subroutine SINE. The subroutine will return to L2:

$$L2 \equiv L2 \qquad [SX - 13]$$
$$L2 \to RETREG \, / \, SINE$$

*Subroutine return within SINE

$$RETREG \to / \qquad [SX - 14].$$

ACKNOWLEDGMENT

The authors wish to express their gratitude to the many members of the Digital Computers Group who contributed to the LX-1 project. In particular, they wish to acknowledge the work of R. Kalin, who was responsible for the simulator and DOMEX, and S. Pezaris, who was responsible for the engineering.

REFERENCES

[1] H. Webber, "A microprogrammed implementation of Euler on IBM system/360 model 30," *Commun. ACM,* vol. 10, pp. 549–558, September 1967.

[2] G. D. Hornbuckle, "Representation, generation, and manipulation of computer graphical information," Ph.D. dissertation, Department of Electrical Engineering and Computer Sciences, University of California, Berkeley, Calif., 1967.

[3] G. D. Hornbuckle and R. N. Spann, "Diagnosis of single-gate fail-

ures in combinational circuits," *IEEE Trans. Computers*, vol. C-18, pp. 216–220, March 1969.

[4] L. F. Mondshein, "Vital: compiler-compiler systems reference manual," M.I.T. Lincoln Laboratory, Lexington, Mass., Tech. Note 1967-12, February 1967.

[5] C. N. Mooers, "TRAC, a procedure-describing language for the reactive typewriter," *Commun. ACM*, vol. 9, pp. 215–219, March 1966.

[6] J. F. Teixeira and R. P. Sallen, "The Sylvania data tablet: a new approach to graphic data input," *1968 Spring Joint Computer Conf., AFIPS Proc.*, vol. 32. Washington, D. C.: Thompson, 1968, pp. 315–321.

[7] J. E. Curry, "A tablet input facility for an interactive graphics system," *Proc. Internatl. Conf. on Artificial Intelligence.* Washington, D. C., May 1969.

[8] T. E. Cheatham, Jr., "The theory and construction of compilers," Massachusetts Computer Associates, Inc., Wakefield, Mass., 1966.

[9] W. M. Anderson, Jr., "Specification of a digital vocoder system," presented at the Acoustical Society of America, Cleveland, Ohio, November 19–22, 1968.

[10] T. Bially, "Structure of a digital channel vocoder," presented at the Internatl. Conf. on Communications, Boulder, Colo., June 9–11, 1969.

[11] B. Gold, "Computer program for pitch extraction," *J. Acoust. Soc. Am.*, vol. 34, no. 7, pp. 916–921, July 1962.

The FDP, a Fast Programmable Signal Processor

BERNARD GOLD, SENIOR MEMBER, IEEE, IRWIN L. LEBOW, SENIOR MEMBER, IEEE,
PAUL G. McHUGH, AND CHARLES M. RADER, MEMBER, IEEE

Abstract—This paper contains a description of the architecture of the fast digital processor (FDP), a general purpose digital attachment to a UNIVAC 1219 computer facility. The main purpose of the FDP is to enhance the capability of the UNIVAC facility for performance of digital signal processing operations such as digital filtering and discrete Fourier transforms. The structural design evolved during a series of discussions among the four authors. The FDP is presently being constructed under the supervision of one of the authors, P. McHugh, and should be completed in late 1970.

Index Terms—Digital filtering, digital signal processing, fast Fourier transform, general purpose computers, parallel processing, pipeline processing.

I. INTRODUCTION

THERE are a variety of techniques whereby general purpose digital computers may be modified or extended to increase the operating speed. For example, modest speed savings may be attained by attaching fast multiply and divide hardware or by having separately addressable memory modules so that instruction cycles and data cycles can be overlapped. Further increase in speed results from attaching arithmetic hardware which performs high speed special operations such as digital filtering and discrete spectrum analysis. If this arithmetic hardware is augmented with some high speed memory, very large speed increases (of the order of 50 to 100) can be expected in performing operations such as the fast Fourier transform. However, a great variety of problems include an appreciable amount of "overhead," that is, programming which is not easily structured. Thus, for example, the simulation of a speech communications device such as a vocoder may be speeded up by only a factor of 3 given an attachment capable of doing the spectrum analysis one hundred times faster than could be done by the conventional computer.

Such a result focuses attention on the need to incorporate more general purpose features into a signal processing computer structure. A great variety of architectural changes have been proposed to augment the speed of repetitive arithmetic operations for signal processing; these can be crudely categorized as 1) the incorporation of "scratch pad" memories, 2) pipeline schemes, and 3) parallel processing.

The fast digital processor (FDP) being constructed at the M.I.T. Lincoln Laboratory makes use of all the above techniques to increase speed. The FDP is expected to be able to perform signal processing simulations close to two orders of magnitudes faster than modern, conventional, digital computers. A vocoder simulation, for example, which typically requires about 200 times real time on a standard computer, could be programmed to operate close to real time on the FDP.

The FDP should be completed by the end of 1970. Its main applications are expected to be in the areas of communications, radar, and speech processing, although it should be of use in many other areas, notably biology, medicine, seismology, and sonar.

It achieves speed advantage through the use of fast commercial integrated circuit elements and a logical structure which permits each main unit of the machine to operate at maximum speed. Specifically:

1) The arithmetic section is designed to perform very efficiently the sum-of-products operations which are central to recursive digital filtering, the fast Fourier transform (FFT) and correlation operations.
2) The data memories are structured so as to exchange data with the arithmetic section at optimum efficiency.
3) The control uses a separate memory for storing instructions. Its structure, in particular the way it performs indexing, permits the data memories to operate at maximum speed.

In the remainder of this paper, the main features of the FDP structure are described and its signal processing capabilities are illustrated with a few examples.

II. FDP STRUCTURE

Fig. 1 shows the important transfer paths of the FDP. Programs are run from memory M^c, which controls the main data flow from memories M^a and M^b to all places shown in Fig. 1. Since M^c is conceived to be a small memory, longer programs can be stored in M^a and M^b and block-transferred to M^c when needed. M^a, M^b, and M^c are addressed independently and can therefore be operated in parallel. Except for block transfers from M^a and M^b, the control memory M^c cannot be written into; thus programs are almost non-self-modifying.

The parallelism inherent in the FDP is partially indicated in Fig. 1; for emphasis we will list some special speed-up features:

1) four arithmetic units, each including a multipler which can operate in parallel with the main arithmetic registers;

Manuscript received June 15, 1970; revised August 6, 1970. This work was sponsored by the Department of the Air Force.

The authors are with Lincoln Laboratory, Massachusetts Institute of Technology, Lexington, Mass. 02173.

Reprinted from *IEEE Trans. Comput.*, vol. C-20, pp. 33–38, Jan. 1971.

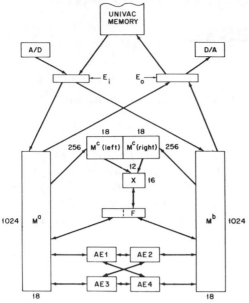

Fig. 1. Structure of the FDP.

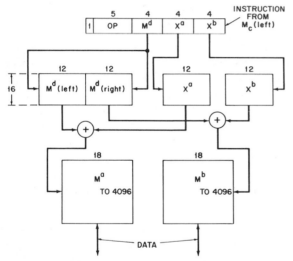

Fig. 2. Memory addressing.

2) two independently addressable integrated circuit memories, M^a and M^b with read and write times of 150 ns;

3) a separate instruction memory, which allows overlap of instructions and data cycles;

4) a double length instruction word which enables two instructions to be simultaneously executed on the FDP.

Although the size of M^a and M^b can be extended, in principal, limitlessly, we have restricted it to 4096 words by designing the addressing circuitry with 12 bits. Present plans allow for M^a and M^b to be 1024 words, which corresponds to a 10-bit address. Addressing is indirect, via M^d, a 16-register 24-bit integrated-circuit memory, as shown in Fig. 2. The indexed address for M^a and M^b is formed by adding the contents of the two 12-bit portions of M^d to X^a and X^b, respectively. Writing into M^d requires no special instructions because addresses 0 through 15 of M^a and M^b are

wired to control M^d as well as the data memories on a write cycle.

The input–output capabilities of the FDP were deliberately kept low, on the grounds that the UNIVAC 1219 already supplied most of the necessary in–out control. In order to make the FDP useful for some real-time applications (for example, speech processing) an analog–digital and digital–analog converter will be connected. The only other in–out path is to and from the mother computer, UNIVAC 1219, which, in addition to supplying medium size core storage (32K, 18 bits, 2 μm) will also be needed for assembling and editing FDP programs.

The FDP is an 18-bit fixed point machine. Floating point routines must be programmed, as must multiple processor arithmetic, the latter being facilitated by 4 link bits which allow the carries from an AE to an adjacent AE.

III. The Arithmetic Elements

Simply building four AE's, rather than one, does not insure a fourfold increase in the processing speed. In addition, the data transfers between memories and AE's must be matched to the computational speeds of the AE's. Further, since multiplications take longer than other operations such as additions, indexing, and memory transfers, it is important that the AE's be substantially free during the execution of the multiply. Referring to Fig. 3(a), this is accomplished by separating the multiplier hardware from the basic AE structure. Thus, a multiply instruction begins with transfers from I and Q to buffer registers in the multiplier, leaving the AE free to obey the next instruction. When the multiplication is complete (usually several instructions later), its output can be transferred to R.

Instructions controlling the four identical AE's are arranged as shown in Fig. 3(b). Each 4-bit operation code controls a given AE, independent of the action of the other AE's. The mode bits 01 cause the 4-bit operation codes to be interpreted as one of the possible register transfers indicated by the communication lines shown in Fig. 3(a). (This format includes the multiply instruction which, structurally, is merely a transfer of I and Q to the multiplier.) It is legal, for example, to call (using op 1) for a transfer from R^2 to R^1 and simultaneously (op 2) to call for a transfer from R^1 to R^2; the result will be a correct exchange of the data due to the simultaneous execution of the two instructions.

The mode bits 00 cause the 4-bit operation codes to control arithmetic operations. As in the transfer case, different AE's can simultaneously perform different arithmetic instructions, but, since all AE's are under the same mode bit control, a single instruction cannot simultaneously command one AE to perform a transfer and another AE to perform arithmetic. This is not an arithmetic but a control limitation and in fact, since the FDP is simultaneously controlled by two 18-bit instruction words, simultaneous transfer and arithmetic is permissible.

In addition to the three full length registers and the multiplier, each AE has an activity bit, an overflow bit, and a link bit. The activity bit is controlled by the activate instruction which, at the programmer's option, can be set unconditionally or conditionally. Turning the activity bit off "freezes"

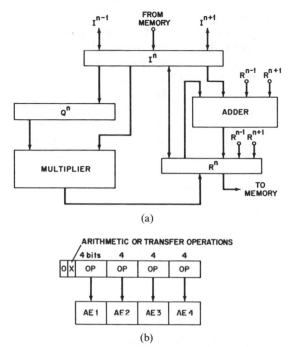

(a)

(b)

Fig. 3.   The arithmetic element.

the AE until the bit is changed. The overflow system is not unlike that of other computers except for the fact that there are 4 possible overflows, one for each AE. Thus, the jump on overflow instruction allows for a jump on various logical functions of the four overflow conditions. The link bit links contiguous AE's to facilitate multiple precision programs, by allowing the propagation of carries to the adjacent AE.

The number system used throughout the FDP is 2's complement. The multiplier is of the array type, purely combinational. Present specifications on the multiplier execution time is 450 ns or 3 instruction cycles. There is no hardware interlock on the handling of the multiplier output; if the program calls for a transfer from the multiplier output gates to the R register sooner than the third instruction after a multiply instruction, the transferred result will generally be in error. A possible advantage of this lack of interlock is that it permits possible future incorporation of higher speed multipliers without necessitating any additional modifications.

IV. CONTROL MODE INSTRUCTIONS

When the first mode bit of the instruction words is a ONE rather than ZERO, the instruction word no longer controls the AE's. Our rule is that such instructions in the left half of M^c are generally interpreted as M^a and M^b instructions, leading to the addressing scheme of Fig. 2 while the same mode bit in the right half of M^c is interpreted to be a control instruction, which, in turn has several different formats. Since the simultaneous execution of either two memory or two control instructions is not permitted because it would greatly complicate the control of the overlap, we feel that the above constraint causes no great loss of generality. Some aspects of the control mode instruction set will now be discussed. These can be categorized as index register manipulation, indexed jumps and skips, arithmetic jumps,

input–output and nullify instructions. Because of the overlap requirement mentioned in item 3 of Section II, an instruction is already being fetched before the preceding jump has been interpreted by the instruction decoding hardware. This leads to a somewhat different program design than in more conventional computers; as a simple example, a single loop of an FDP program would have the terminating conditional jump as the *next to the last* instruction in the loop. For more complicated conditions, a programmer could easily get into trouble; for such cases, a special instruction is provided which avoids this difficulty, allowing the programmer to insert jump instructions as he would in conventional single address computers.

To perform index register arithmetic without compromising the memory overlap features of the FDP, it was necessary to include the F register system (Fig. 1). Via F, index registers can be controlled in a general way from the data memories. Further, F allows facile addition, subtraction, and scaling of the index registers. Special logic attached to F allows bit-reversed counting carry propagation from left to right (instead of the usual right to left) which speeds up the bit reversal often needed for FFT programs.

V. BLOCK TRANSFER

As presently constituted, M^a and M^b each contain 1024 words and the instruction memory M^c contains 256 double length (36-bit) words. If a program is longer than 256 dual instructions, part of it can be kept in data memory and transferred to M^c when needed. In this way, the FDP is capable of running programs longer than 1000 dual instructions *provided* that the data base is small. Via the UNIVAC 1219 (32K of core) much longer programs can be run at the cost of programming complications; pieces of the program must be transferred into M^a and M^b via the in–out system and then transferred to M^c via the block transfer.

All FDP instructions are 18 bits long except for block transfer which is 36 bits. The left 18 bits specify the beginning of the blocks in M^a and M^b which are to be transferred while the right 18 bits control the run-down of an index register which determines the block length. Also, the index register contents added to the 8-bit base address of the right 18 bits determine the location in M^c of the transfer. When the block transfer instruction is complete, the following instruction, which has been saved in an external buffer, is executed.

VI. INPUT–OUTPUT

We felt that the FDP design would be made appreciably more complicated if it were given the full input–output capability expected from most commercial general purpose computers, namely, connectability to large numbers of diverse peripheral devices. Digital tapes, paper tape reader and punch, drums, display, etc. are handled by the UNIVAC 1219. We restricted the number of FDP connections to four:

1) output to UNIVAC;
2) input from UNIVAC;
3) real-time output to a digital to analog converter;
4) real-time input from an analog to digital converter.

These connections allow for the following modes of operation:

1) The FDP running as an independent real-time processor (it is required that a binary program be transferred from the UNIVAC 1219 to FDP; then the 1219 may be disconnected).
2) The FDP as a real-time preprocessor for the 1219. In this mode, the A/D converter and the 1219 are the peripherals.
3) The FDP as a real-time post-processor. Here the FDP is presumably performing real-time processing and receiving its control signals from the 1219.
4) The FDP as a fast processing attachment. Data enters the FDP from the 1219, is processed, and the result sent back to the 1219.

Transfers between FDP data memories and its peripherals are performed one datum at a time; there is no block transfer in–out mode. The sequence of operations is as follows.

The in–out control instruction (IOC) alerts the desired peripheral unit. When a unit is ready to deliver or accept a datum, it sets the IN or the OUT flip-flop. The subroutine which actually performs the datum transfer is reached via one of the instructions JPINR (jump on input ready), JPOUR (jump on output ready), JPIOR (jump on input or output ready), all the conditions depending completely on the states of the IN or OUT flip-flops. The transfers take place between the E register (the in–out buffer register) and M^a or M^b. There are separate E registers for input and for output.

The input–output instruction format permits the possibility of multiplexing 16 peripheral devices on each input and output line; to accomplish this would require some additional hardware.

VII. BOOTSTRAP/CONSOLE AND OPERATION

Initialization of an FDP program begins with a small wired program that transfers an intermediate binary code from a variable UNIVAC position to a fixed location in M^a and M^b via the in–out system and thence to a fixed location in M^c via a block transfer. The intermediate program contains all the necessary parameters to transfer any FDP program or data residing in binary form in the 1219 to the desired positions in M^a, M^b, and M^c. Once this is done, control resides in both 1219 and the FDP as determined by the various programs in each computer.

Preliminary plans for running procedure include the ability to stop the program at a binary location in M^c as determined by a toggle register, to continue without resetting initial conditions, to start afresh from any location in M^c, and to enter binary data manually from toggle registers to M^a, M^b, and M^c. Lights will be provided on the console which allow inspection of the various important registers.

VIII. REMARKS ON FDP HARDWARE

The FDP is designed with Motorola MECL II, ECL dual-in-line integrated circuits. This was the fastest commercially available logic line when we made hardware decisions and we chose it for this reason.

We are mounting the MECL circuits in the arithmetic and control sections on relatively large wire-wrapped boards (8 inches by 17 inches) which hold up to 180 dual-in-line packages. Each arithmetic element contains 10 boards with a total of 1200 packages; the control contains 28 boards with a total of 2800 packages. The principal reasons for using this technique were 1) to save the time and manpower necessary to develop a line of printed circuit boards, 2) to increase the reliability of the completed product, and 3) to construct the machine so that it could be accessible to engineers for easy maintenance and change.

The memories are designed around the MECL II 16-bit memory integrated circuits mounted on multilayer printed boards. We have chosen printed circuits here because of the inherent modularity of the memories which allows them to be constructed from only five board types.

IX. DATA EXCHANGE PROGRAM

The elementary program shown in Fig. 4 illustrates some basic FDP features. First we note the two simultaneous fetches from M^a and M^b and the fact that the timing of the execution is always fixed by the instruction and does not depend on surrounding instructions. This condition greatly simplifies the FDP control hardware. The structural constraint which made this simplification possible is embodied in the rules that 1) two simultaneous control mode instructions are prohibited and 2) two simultaneous memory instructions are prohibited.

The overlap feature is seen more explicitly in the timing sketches of Fig. 4. We notice that the memory instructions consist of three parts: 1) the instruction fetch, 2) address computation, and 3) reading or writing. The total time required for all three parts is 400 ns. In order to limit the effective time per instruction to 150 ns, careful consideration had to be given to the precise time at which each instruction was to be executed relative to the fetch. The timing we achieved insures that, despite the overlap, the action of a given instruction is not perturbed by neighboring instructions.

Instructions 3 and 5 (from M^c (right)) illustrate the parallel capabilities of the AE's. Because of the paths shown in Fig. 3(a) and because 4 AE's can be simultaneously activated with a single instruction, good arithmetic flexibility is attained.

Instructions 4 and 5 constitute the inner loop and it can be seen that these instructions suffice to perform the necessary exchanges involving two memory reads, two memory writes, a conditional jump, and the necessary data exchange between AE's. It is interesting that two cycles suffice for the inner loop despite the lack of an explicit exchange instruction and despite the fact that the paths between M^a and M^b must be routed through both I and R registers. On the debit side, instructions 1, 2, and 3 were necessary to "prime the pump," that is, to set up the initial conditions in the various registers so that fast data flow became possible.

X. DIGITAL FILTERING AND FOURIER TRANSFORM ON THE FDP

In order to understand the underlying stimulus of the FDP design work, it is necessary to comprehend the princi-

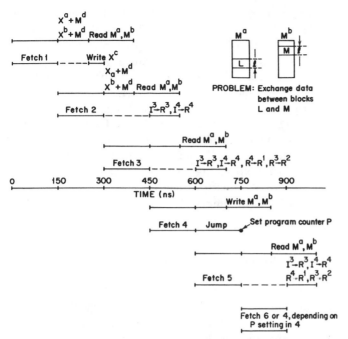

Fig. 4. Program for exchanging data between M^a and M^b.

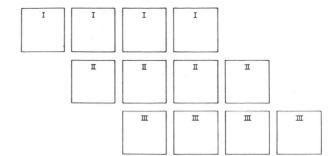

Fig. 5. Efficient recursive filter.

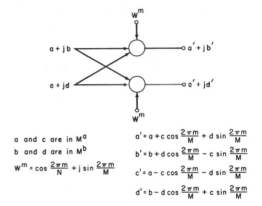

a and c are in M^a
b and d are in M^b
$w^m = \cos \frac{2\pi m}{N} + j \sin \frac{2\pi m}{M}$

$a' = a + c \cos \frac{2\pi m}{M} + d \sin \frac{2\pi m}{M}$
$b' = b + d \cos \frac{2\pi m}{M} - c \sin \frac{2\pi m}{M}$
$c' = a - c \cos \frac{2\pi m}{M} - d \sin \frac{2\pi m}{M}$
$d' = b - d \cos \frac{2\pi m}{M} + c \sin \frac{2\pi m}{M}$

Fig. 6. Fast Fourier transform "butterfly."

ples of digital signal processing theory. In this section we will show how the FDP can be used to program two algorithms which play an important role in digital filtering and discrete Fourier transform, respectively. Since much signal processing makes use of these operations, our remarks should help create insight into the original motivations which led to the present FDP design.

1) Linear difference equation with constant coefficients: The equation,

$$y(nT) = (2e^{-aT} \cos bT)y(nT - T) - (e^{-2aT})y(nT - 2T)$$
$$+ Ax(nT) - Bx(nT - T) \quad (1)$$

represents a one-zero-two-pole digital resonator with resonant frequency $b/2\pi$ bandwidth and an $a/2\pi$ anti-resonance frequency (zero) located at B/A. By cascading or paralleling such resonators, sophisticated filter designs can be synthesized.

2) A fast Fourier transform "butterfly": The pair of computations

$$x \pm y e^{j(2\pi M/N)} \quad (2)$$

(where x and y are, in general, complex numbers, N is the number of samples being transformed, and M is a parameter which varies with the location of the computation in the FFT array) is often called a "butterfly" and is one of the basic algorithms leading to evaluation of the discrete Fourier transform, defined as,

$$X_k = \sum_{n=0}^{N-1} x_n e^{-j(2\pi nk/N)}. \quad (3)$$

Further information on these computations is contained in [1].

We will now show how to perform the computations indicated in (1) and (2). Only the inner loop will be shown, since thereby a simple guess at the FDP speed can be made.

It is interesting to note that both (1) and (2) require 4 multiplications. Thus, efficient use of 4 parallel hardware multipliers could result in a four to one time saving in implementing a digital filter or FFT.

As our first problem we consider a bank of parallel digital resonators, each obeying a form of (1), with different center frequencies but equal half bandwidths. We simulate the n resonators on the FDP using the next-state technique whereby the difference equations for all of the filter banks are performed for each new input datum. An efficient way of arranging the program is shown in Fig. 5. The three subsets of the complete algorithm are labeled I, II, and III.

I	II	III
Enter coefficients of filter $n+1$ in Q registers, enter states of filter $n+1$ in I registers.	Perform the four multiplications shown in (1) for filter n.	Perform the additions shown in (1) and store result for filter $n-1$.

Each triplet of subsets comprise the algorithm for one of the n filters. Because of the 4 AE's of the FDP, because of its ability to execute two instructions simultaneously, and because of the separation of the multiplier from the AE, the FDP is nearly capable of performing all of the suboperations simultaneously on different filters, as indicated by any column in Fig. 5. It turns out that 5 instructions suffice to perform these three operations; because of the instructions and data memory overlap feature, the inner loop time is 750 ns.

The FFT "butterfly" computation is illustrated in Fig. 6. This computation perhaps best illustrates the speed gained by the FDP architecture. For a conventional computer structure with a single AE, a single memory, and nonoverlapping data and instruction stream, about 80 memory cycles are required per butterfly. For the FDP a straightforward count of the arithmetic, memory, and indexing operations needed should yield about 40 cycles (since overlap results in a 2:1 savings). However, 4 multiplications and 4 additions can each be done in a single cycle in an 18-bit instruction word. Also memory speed is doubled because of the two parallel memories. All indexing can be done in parallel with the arithmetic operations. Part of the next butterfly can be set up during the present computation. We have investigated several different butterfly algorithms and have succeeded in programming them in 6 to 10 machine cycles, depending on the extra tasks (such as in–out and overflow checks) included in the inner loop.

XI. FAST FOURIER TRANSFORM THROUGHPUT ON THE FDP

The running time of a practical FDP program will, of course, depend on the specific problem conditions as well as the programmer's ingenuity. The following two examples will serve to give the reader a feeling for throughput rates.

1) The largest FFT data base that the FDP can presently handle in real time with maximum efficiency is 256 input samples (which, in general, may be complex numbers). This limitation is caused by the present memory size of 1024 registers for M^a and M^b. It is assumed that data enters directly through the analog to digital converter and is buffered in M^a and M^b while the previous block of data is being processed. In this program, the FFT butterfly takes 8 FDP instruction cycles. Thus, the total butterfly time is $8 \times 150 \times 128 \log_2 (256)$ ns, or 1.2288 ms. The computed running time of the complete FFT (excluding bit reversal) will depend on the number of times that overflow conditions must be checked and corrected. If the signal is such that this never happens, the computed FFT running time is 1.7 ms; in the worst case of overflow at each step in the $\log_2 N$ iterations, the FFT running time is 2.25 ms. Bit reversal time is less than 0.4 ms.

2) Performance of an FFT with a data base of 1024 or more samples requires the use of the main computer core memory, and a consequent increase in the processing time. The example programmed begins with a 1024 sample in the UNIVAC 1219 memory. If the larger FFT is broken into 4 blocks of 256 samples each, it is possible to process each block without too much data transfer between FDP and UNIVAC memory. Assuming the same 8 FDP cycles per butterfly as in example 1, the total butterfly time is 6.144 ms. The program running time was estimated by breaking the program into subprograms, computing both processing

and input–output time, and using the larger of the two numbers. The resultant time was 23.72 ms. In this program, UNIVAC uses the FDP as a high speed peripheral and the final answer appears in UNIVAC. Since, from example 1, it appears that for a 256 point FFT the total time is double the butterfly time, we see that the insufficiency of FDP memory has led to a loss of about 2:1 in speed. Provided that the 18-bit register length of the FDP causes no undue error, the above reasoning may be extended to larger FFT sizes, up to $(256)^2 = 2^{16}$, and the claim can be made that a complete FFT up to that size can be accomplished using the FDP as a peripheral with a running time of about 4 to 5 times the butterfly time.

Other programs which have been written for the FDP include: 1) solution of 8 simultaneous linear equations, 2) a real-time high-speed autocorrelation function routine, 3) a set of elementary mathematical subroutines (such as sine, cosine, exponential, etc.) using polynomial approximation, and 4) a set of floating point routines. In all these cases, it is estimated that the FDP performs these programs about 50 times faster than the UNIVAC 1219.

CONCLUSION

The FDP is a programmable processor which can speed up signal processing algorithms by as much as two orders of magnitude as compared to conventional computers. This is accomplished by a structure which allows for a degree of parallel processing, pipeline methods, and the use of high speed circuits. This combination of techniques has resulted in a structure with flexibility and generality. As a consequence, overhead operations as well as signal processing computations are performed very efficiently. We, therefore, expect that the FDP will be fast and efficient for a broader class of computations than that for which it was designed.

ACKNOWLEDGMENT

The authors gratefully acknowledge the contributions of A. McLaughlin, P. Blankenship, A. Huntoon, M. Mullo, and S. Weinrich to the hardware design and construction of the FDP. An FDP simulation program developed by J. Drinan and H. Frachtman has proved of great value. The authors also thank J. Allen for useful programming advice, and S. McCandless and D. Johnson for contributions to the fast Fourier transform programs cited as examples.

REFERENCES

[1] B. Gold and C. Rader, *Digital Processing of Signals.* New York: McGraw-Hill, 1969.
[2] G. D. Bergland, "Fast Fourier transform hardware—A survey," *IEEE Trans. Audio Electroacoustics*, vol. AU-17, pp. 109–119, June 1969.

A Research-Oriented Dynamic Microprocessor

ROBERT G. BARR, JEROME A. BECKER, WILLIAM P. LIDINSKY, AND VERNON V. TANTILLO

Abstract–A horizontally structured microprogrammable processor (AMP) designed as a tool for microcontrol, language, and processor design research, is described. The machine employs a minimally encoded microcontrol word, a very general multiple bus structure, high-speed local storage, several arithmetic/logic units, and completely asynchronous memory referencing. These features combine to yield substantial low-level parallelism and a highly versatile microinstruction. In addition, hardware modification is easily accomplished, further supporting the experimental nature of the processor.

The paper first establishes a frame of reference, after which the processor organization and implementation is discussed. Next a brief description of the software is provided. Finally, initial work with the machine is discussed and related to the design of microcontrolled processors and associated languages.

In addition, AMP is also used in an experimental raster graphics system called MIRAGE.

Index Terms–Computer architecture, horizontal microcontrol, low-level parallelism, microprogramming, performance evaluation, processor organization and design.

I. INTRODUCTION

AN important trend in the design of computing systems is the implementation of the CPU as a horizontally microcontrolled processor containing a multiplicity of ALU's, local stores, buses, etc. Microcontrol offers a variety of advantages such as machine-level compatibility between computers, variable architecture and organization, and the ability to program at a level much closer to the actual hardware. In addition, if the control store is easily modified, systems and languages may be tailored to the application at hand and microprograms may be dynamically controlled. The multiplicity of resources and the horizontal structure of the control provide the advantage of low-level parallelism.

Many unanswered questions exist in horizontal microcontrol, microprogramming, and low-level parallelism. The proper organization of these machines, the effective use of parallelism, instruction stream optimization, implications of dynamically alterable microstores, the direct implementation or support of higher level languages in microcode, the consequences of user microprogramming, microlevel interrupts, difficulties in horizontal microprogramming, and microdiagnostics are just a few.

This paper describes the Argonne Microprocessor (AMP), which was designed and constructed at the Argonne National Laboratory as part of the Laboratory's microcontrol research effort.[1] This paper also describes the results of initial work using the machine.

Manuscript received July 6, 1972; revised December 12, 1972, and May 7, 1973. This work was performed under the auspices of the U.S. Atomic Energy Commission.

The authors are with the Applied Mathematics Division, Argonne National Laboratory, Argonne, Ill. 60439.

[1] AMP is also used as part of the MIRAGE system [1].

The motivation for building AMP rather than buying a machine stems primarily from three facts. First, no commercially available, horizontally controlled microprocessor with a sufficient degree of low-level parallelism and asynchronism[2] was available. Also, the possibility of having a machine constructed to our design specifications appeared to be economically unfeasible. Second, it was felt that, in the case of microprogramming and microcontrol, a machine's usefulness as a research tool would benefit greatly from the ability to experiment with hardware as well as software. There appeared to be no other way, outside of construction, to obtain this capability. Third, the advent of medium- and large-scale integrated circuits, convenient integrated circuit mounting techniques, the availability of automated wirewrap services, and the ability to write diagnostic programs for the hardware made the process of constructing a machine much less of a task than commonly assumed.

II. FRAME OF REFERENCE

A substantial body of literature exists in the area of microcontrol and microprogramming [3]. With it comes a variety of different terminologies and definitions. It is desirable, therefore, to first establish a frame of reference with respect to the literature in order to resolve some of these ambiguities.

A. Definitions

1) Assembly Instruction: A mnemonic instruction that is mapped by an assembler into one or more machine instructions.

2) Machine Instruction: A bit pattern that is interpreted by the executing control hardware in a wired control machine or by a microsubroutine in a microcontrolled machine.

3) Microinstruction: A bit pattern normally stored in control memory which controls, at a primitive level, the processor hardware. It specifies the microoperations to take place during one microcycle. The microinstruction may contain a single operation as is usual in a vertical microprogramming or specify several concurrent operations (horizontal microinstruction).

4) Microroutine: A sequence of microinstructions. A machine-level instruction is normally executed by a microroutine.

5) Microoperation: A primitive microprogram action (e.g., addition, shift, transfer, branch, etc.).

6) Microprocedure: A sequence of microoperations which constitute a meaningful whole, not necessarily in contiguous microinstructions.

[2] Husson [2] and others feel that without highly synchronous processor configurations, microcontrol is much less attractive. We felt that this was not the case.

Reprinted from *IEEE Trans. Comput.*, vol. C-22, pp. 976–985, Nov. 1973.

7) Control Memory: The high-speed memory in which microinstructions are stored.

8) Local Store: A small, very high-speed memory located within the CPU and operating synchronously with the CPU. It is the fastest of all memory types.

9) Manipulators (or ALU's): Entities within the processor that perform actual manipulations of the data under direction of the microinstruction (e.g., add, shift, logical AND, byte packing, etc.).

10) Buses: Multiple-source/multiple-destination paths by which data may be routed between registers, manipulators, memories, and I/O devices.

11) Microcycle: The cycle of control which performs the fetch and execution of a microinstruction. Microcycles are often overlapped. They can also be classified as being monophase or polyphase [4]. Monophase describes a microcycle with one execution control pulse, while polyphase implies more than one. The polyphase microcycle can further be divided into "simple polyphase" and "complex polyphase." In the simple polyphase approach there is a single set of control pulses during the time that the microinstruction is stable. In the complex polyphase approach, a set of control pulses is repeated several times [5].

12) Sequencing: The determination of the chronological order in which microinstructions are to be executed.

13) Current Word Sequencing: A scheme of sequencing where each microinstruction determines the addresses of the very next microinstruction.

B. Definition of AMP

AMP, in terms of conventional terminology and the above definitions, is a horizontally structured, simple polyphase microprocessor with the capability of performing several microoperations per microinstruction. It has a 1024-word control store and uses a modified version of current word sequencing with two different microcycle times. The microinstruction length is 74 b. All memory and peripherals are organized as parts of a single main memory space. The CPU consists of a 64-word local store, three ALU's, a variety of registers, and a very general multiple bus structure. A further important feature is the ease with which hardware can be modified.

III. Machine Description

A. Introduction

The AMP microcycle is complex, spanning a sequence of ten timing signals. This fact, coupled with the parallelism of the CPU and the large microword, yields versatile microinstruction. For example, a single microinstruction can fetch up to three operands, perform two data manipulations, store two results, perform a conditional microsequencing operation based on manipulation results, and execute a memory reference. This is in contrast to machines such as the one proposed by Cook and Flynn [6] which is designed to be simple in order to preserve speed.

The microprocessor is characterized by a multiple internal high-performance bus structure with several sources and

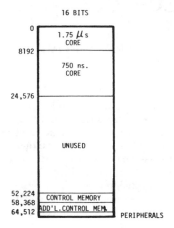

Fig. 1. AMP main memory space.

destinations for each bus. A similar but less parallel arrangement was used in the LX-1 processor [7]. This busing scheme differs from that used by several other existing or proposed machines with multiple bus structures [8], [9].

The 74-b microword which controls the processor uses judicious but minimal encoding to extend its capabilities. Microsequencing is done on a current word basis to ease the task of the microprogrammer. Two out of three data manipulators, an interleaved 64-word local store, and a number of other registers function simultaneously.

B. Memory Organization

As Cook and Flynn [6] point out, all processors have a hierarchy of memories going from the fastest (e.g., registers) to the slowest (e.g., tapes). AMP has four levels that are: 1) 64 local general-purpose registers of 16 b each; 2) the control memory which consists of 1K of 80-b words of which 74 b are presently used; 3) 16K of 750-ns core of 16-b words; and 4) 8K of 1.75-μs core of 16 b. The 64 general-purpose registers along with 12 registers for special use are integral to the CPU itself. The other levels of memory are contained within a single memory space as shown in Fig. 1. This main memory space also contains an area reserved for peripherals. Thus every peripheral becomes simply one or more addresses in main memory, and any memory reference action may, with equal facility, address any of the levels of memory or the peripherals.

The 64-register local store is normally used for temporary storage of operands which are either generated by the CPU or obtained from main memory. All CPU manipulations are performed on the contents of the local storage registers or the 12 additional registers.

Communication between the processor and the main memory space is fully buffered and completely asynchronous. Portions of the memory are segmented, allowing simultaneous cycling.

Since memory references are asynchronous, additional memory can be added to the unused area with ease. The microprocessor is capable of accepting memories of any access or cycle time.

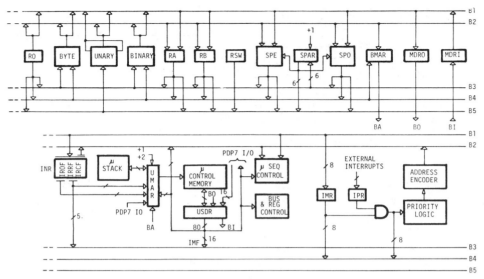

Fig. 2. AMP central processor.

C. CPU Organization

The microprocessor is shown in Fig. 2. Three manipulators (byte, unary, binary) exist within AMP for purposes of enhancing low-level parallel processing capability. The availability of these manipulators is a function of the mode of the current microinstruction (two modes exist) with the unary manipulator available to both modes. Its function is to perform operations on single operands (e.g., increments, decrements, shifts, etc.). The binary manipulator is available during "word" mode microinstructions. It performs arithmetic and logic operations on one or two operands. The byte manipulator is available to "I/O" mode microinstructions. Its purpose is to facilitate byte operations within the word-organized processor. It performs byte-to-word and and word-to-byte transformations (e.g., packing, unpacking, swapping, etc.).

The philosophy behind treating the manipulators on the basis of the number of operands with which they deal stems from the fact that the execution of code quite often deals with these two classes of operations simultaneously. Binary operations may be used for the actual processing of data while unary-type operations may be used for bookkeeping purposes. Manipulations on lists and arrays are typical examples.

One of the alternate schemes which was considered involved having two identical manipulators both having unary and binary capabilities. This approach was not used because the added complexity of the units contributed too greatly to propagation time and cost. Also considered was the elimination of the microinstruction mode feature. The mode approach ultimately prevailed for reasons of economy and because of the strong desire to maintain the ability for significant microinstruction expansion based upon further experimentation.

Schemes for the efficient use of multiple manipulators as suggested by Kleir and Ramamoorthy [10], or as described by Tomasulo [11], are not implemented in the hardware. This is, however, a fertile area for investigation.

The effectiveness of this particular arrangement of manipulators will be discussed later.

The three lower (usually source) buses and two upper (usually result) buses are compatible with manipulator availability which requires up to three data sources and provides up to two results per microinstruction. The buses may also be used for direct register-to-register transfers. In this case the simultaneous use of manipulators may be sacrificed. The multiple-input multiple-output feature of the buses allows a great deal of versatility. One can, within limits, consider the processor to be an array of resources (manipulators, registers, local stores, buses, etc.) which are allocated and connected in a specific fashion by the current microinstruction.

The local stores (SPO and SPE) are arranged as two separate 32-word scratchpads if addressed directly by the microinstruction, or as a single 64-word interleaved store if addressed by SPAR. This arrangement allows a single microinstruction to address up to three different locations within SPE and SPO. This local store arrangement plus the existence of two general purpose registers (RA and RB) makes available five possibilities for manipulation sources and results. The existence of additional specialized registers increases this number.

The address register (BMAR) and data buffers (MDRI and MDRO) allow complete asynchronism with the main memory space. Nonsynchronous operation is further enhanced by the ability of the microcode to manipulate the timing of the microinstruction cycle.

The μ STACK is a LIFO stack which is used in conjunction with the UMAR (micromemory address register) primarily to facilitate microsubroutine linking. The present depth of the stack (4 words) was dictated by hardware considerations and the general feeling that the ability to handle five levels of microcode in this fashion would be temporarily adequate. In any event, deepening the stack in hardware is so simple that the question of stack depth was felt to be best left to experimentation.

The INR is a register that is primarily intended as a machine-level instruction register. Since AMP is microprogrammable, the machine instruction format can be almost anything that fits within 16-b word boundaries or multiples thereof. However, the transfer and skewing of bits from the INR to the UMAR and the buses provide a convenient means of putting instructions into a specific 16-b format which consists of three fields. In this format the 6-b IROF field can be used for an operation code or for an extended operation code. The 5-b IRRF field can be used for an extended operation code or for passing parameters between the machine language and the microsubroutines which execute the machine code. The 5-b IRCF field can be used for passing similar parameter information. The field boundaries are determined by the fact that these three fields are independently routed from the INR register to the UMAR and the buses.

The use of the hardware-defined fields of the INR is a limitation on machine instruction generality. The implementation of variable field definition controlled by either the microinstruction or by mask registers was considered. However, the hardware required to select and skew fields was substantial. In addition, the cost (in microcode bits) of direct microinstruction control was prohibitive. The three nearly equal fields per word represent a good compromise between field capacity and number of fields per word and can be used effectively for multiregister variable word length machine languages. Of course, the microprogrammer need not use the INR since microcode can be designed to handle almost any format.

A conventional hardware priority interrupt scheme is used in the microprocessor. The microprogrammer has the option of using the hardware or creating his own interrupt scheme.

Registers RSW and RO represent a console switch register and a wired "zero."

D. Microcontrol Word

The microcontrol word organization shown in Table I has been minimally encoded so that most of the CPU resources are available during every microcycle. Encoding has been done on bits controlling those resources wherein exclusivity is a fact. For instance, the internal buses B1 through B5 are each controlled by 3 b that are fully encoded to provide eight sources to each internal bus. In order to conserve microcontrol word bits, a mode bit is used which determines the usage of bits 32 through 40. Microcontrol word bits 48 through 52 also have a dual role designed to minimize control word size. These bits are used for direct addressing of SPO or for an extension of the immediate field, which is normally 11 b. If this field is not explicitly used by the microprogrammer for SPO addressing, it is automatically used as an extension of the immediate field. With the exception of the above two double usage cases, all fields of the microcontrol word are available for allocation of resources during each microcontrol cycle.

TABLE I
MICROCONTROL WORD ORGANIZATION

FUNCTION	FIELD	FUNCTION	FIELD
MODE	0	UNARY MANIP. CONTROL	41–45
μ JUMP ADDR. OR IMMEDIATE FIELD	1–11	SPAR CONTROL	46–47
RA INPUT CONTROL	12–13	IMMEDIATE FIELD EXT. OR SPØ ADDR.	48–52
BMAR INPUT CONTROL	14–15	SPØ INPUT CONTROL	53–54
B1 INPUT CONTROL	16–18	SPE ADDR.	55–59
B2 INPUT CONTROL	19–21	SPE INPUT CONTROL	60–61
B3 INPUT CONTROL	22–24	LOCAL STORE ADDR. SOURCE	62–63
B4 INPUT CONTROL	25–27	JUMP CONTROL	64–66
B5 INPUT CONTROL	28–30	RETURN (POP STACK)	67
MDRØ INPUT CONTROL	31	SKIP	68–70
RB INPUT CONTROL	32–33	STORE RTN. ADDR. (PUSH STACK)	71
* INR INPUT CONTROL	34		
BINARY MANIP. CONTROL	35–40	UPPER BUS SELECT FOR SEQUENCE TESTING	72
I/Ø CONTROL	32–34	CONTINUE	73
* IMR INPUT CONTROL	35		
UMAR INPUT CONTROL	36–37		
BYTE MANIP. CONTROL	38–40		

*Field usage determined by MODE bit.

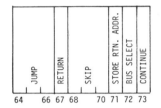

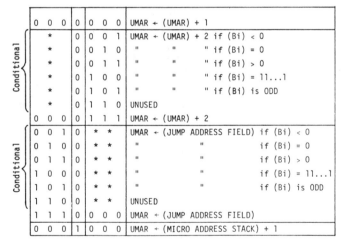

* = any code other than 1 1 1 or SKIP field code
** = " " " " " " JUMP " "

Bi = Bus 1 if (USDR(72)) = 0
Bi = Bus 2 if (USDR(72)) = 1

Fig. 3. Microinstruction sequence control bits.

E. Microsequencing

Fig. 3 details the possible sequencing states. Conditional sequencing defaults to an increment of the UMAR if the condition on the selected BUS is not met. Note that the conditional sequencing states can be merged to form a three-way branch.

This microsequencing scheme eases microprogramming somewhat. However, it is limited. Experience has shown, for instance, that the logical OR of certain of the bus conditions is very desirable. Likewise, it is desirable to set and test (under microcontrol) a special status register that can be held over microcycle boundaries. Present sequencing will be expanded to include some of these features. As Husson [2] points out, the specification of the address of the next microinstruction and the available conditional branch tests have profound implications on the performance and the cost of the system.

F. Timing Considerations

AMP executes either a fast cycle (430 ns) when unconditional sequencing is required or a slow cycle (700 ns) when the next microinstruction address is a function of the results of the execution of the current microinstruction. In addition, the microprogrammer can directly control the timing in a limited fashion by interrupting the microinstruction execution

---

Example 1:

```
SPE27<¬A&B>SPØ10–BI–>SPEØ,MDRØ      *NAND ØF SPE27 & SPØ10->SPEØ & MDRØ
INCREMENT SPAR                      *(SPAR)+1→SPAR
<ADD1>RA–B2–>RA,BMAR                *(RA)+1–>RA & BMAR
IF B1=0 GØTØ #FRED                  *CØNDITIØNAL JUMP
IF B1 ØDD SKIP                      *CONDITIØNAL SKIP
PUSH                               *CURRENT MICRØADDRESS TØ STACK
· · ·                             *MICROINSTRUCTION DELIMITER
```

---

in midcycle. This feature allows both manipulators and the main memory space to be handled in a completely asynchronous fashion.

Worst case design criteria were used in the design of the timing cycles. By simply adjusting the timing chain, a 10 percent speed increase should be possible. In addition, selective use of pin compatible Schottky logic and redesign of the timing generator would increase the machine speed by an additional 25 percent. Thus the microcycle times could be reduced to 280 ns and 455 ns [5].

G. Ease of Hardware Modifications

The processor was designed as a research tool; therefore, ease of hardware modifications and additions was considered to be of great importance. Hardware additions fall principally into two areas: additions to the CPU; that is, additional general-purpose registers, manipulators, buses, and local stores; and the area of additional memory and peripherals.

The internal buses are of prime importance in the addition of general-purpose registers, manipulators, or local stores, and therefore have been designed to accommodate this fact. Additional functional units will also require expansion of the microcontrol word. The control memory may be horizontally expanded to 96 b merely by the addition of plug-in boards. It may also be expanded vertically to 2048 words.

Peripheral devices may be added in any number limited only by the restriction of the number of available addresses in main memory assigned to peripherals. At present this number is 1024 words.

To facilitate hardware modifications and additions, an

average integrated circuit packing density on wirewrap boards of 75 percent was used as a design target. The physical structure will allow additional hardware such that the present machine could be easily doubled in size.

IV. SOFTWARE

The present software support for AMP consists of a microassembler and an expandable macroassembler for AMPMAC (a virtual machine defined on AMP). Both assemblers were written in PL1.

A. Microassembler

While the microassembler is the subject of another paper [12], it will be briefly mentioned here. This assembler has many of the capabilities of a conventional assembler, but also is capable of the multiplicity of specifications per microword which AMP requires. The microlanguage is at a level close to the actual hardware. The following is an example of a single microinstruction consisting of five microoperations.

SPE27 and SPØ10 are locations in the even and odd local stores, respectively. SPAR is the local store address register. SPEØ is a local store register as addressed by SPAR. The two conditional sequencing operations effect a three-way branch since the default condition is an increment of the UMAR.

All manipulators designations are enclosed by "<" and ">" symbols and the source buses are implied. Thus, <¬A&B> is a binary manipulator operation with SPE27 and SPØ10 routed to the manipulator over buses 3 and 4, respectively. The result is routed over bus 1 as specified. Similarly, <ADD1> is a unary manipulator operation with RA routed to the manipulator over bus 5.

B. AMPMAC Virtual Machine Instruction Set

Forty-two AMPMAC machine instructions have been implemented to date utilizing 248 control words and ranging in complexity from a simple load register from console switches instruction (LRSW) to a complex multiple record disk-core transfer instruction (XDC). Table II lists the instruction set and gives brief descriptions. The AMPMAC machine, its implementation, and its analysis, is the subject of a future paper. It is mentioned here to build a framework for the following section.

C. Machine Instruction and Microcode Linking

The scheme of implementation of the AMPMAC machine language at the microcode level involves the use of microroutines which are called by the machine instructions via branch and extended branch tables located in the control memory. Microroutine linking is performed via a micro-

TABLE II
AMPMAC INSTRUCTION SET

INSTRUCTION	MNEMONIC
Load Register(s) Immediate	LRIM R,Val 0, Val 1,...,Val N;
Load Register(s) Direct	LDR R,N,A;
Load Register(s) Indirect	LRIN R,N,A;
Store Register(s) Direct	SRD R,N,A;
Store Register(s) Indirect	SRIN R,N,A;
Move List thru Mask and Shift Right	MMSR R,C;
Move List thru Mask and Shift Left	MMSL R,C;
Move List thru Mask	MM R;
Set Memory Array	SETM R;
Add Registers	ADDR R1,R2;
Subtract Registers	SUBR R1,R2;
And Registers	ANDR R1,R2;
Or Registers	ORR R1,R2;
Exclusive Or Registers	XORR R1,R2;
Move List and Add	ADDM R;
Move List and Subtract	SUBM R;
Jump Direct	JMD A;
Jump Indirect	JMI A;
Jump and Store PC Direct	JMDS A;
Jump and Store PC Indirect	JMIS A;
Subtract and Jump if Less than Zero	SJLZ R,N,A;
Jump if Less than Zero	JLZ R,A;
Subtract and Jump if Greater than Zero	SJGZ R,N,A;
Jump if Greater than Zero	JGZ R,A;
Write Absolute Vector List	WAV Res,R;
Erase Absolute Vector List	EAV Res,R;
Write Incremental Vector List	WIV Res,R;
Erase Incremental Vector List	EIV Res,R;
Write Absolute Point List	WAP Res,R;
Erase Absolute Point List	EAP Res,R;
Write Incremental Point List	WIP Res,R;
Erase Incremental Point List	EIP Res,R;
Halt	HALT;
Skip	SKP N;
No Operation	NOP;
Core List to Printer/Plotter	HCD R;
Printer/Plotter Line Terminate	HCLT;
Printer/Plotter Form Feed	HCFF;
Printer/Plotter Remote EOT	HCET;
Printer/Plotter Finish	HCFN;
Core to Disk, Disk to Core Multiple Block Transfer	XDC R;
Load Register from Switches	LRSW R;

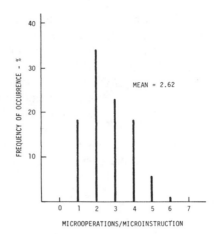

Fig. 4. Microoperation histogram.

supervisor which has the job of fetching machine instructions and handling interrupts. The microroutines have been coded for execution speed rather than control memory efficiency.

Another approach that was considered for microroutine linking was to eliminate the microsupervisor and allow each microroutine to fetch the next machine-level instruction. This scheme is likely to execute even more quickly than the previous one, but is also likely to be less efficient in terms of usage of control memory if implemented in a straightforward fashion. However, because of AMP's internal parallelism, a possibility exists within this approach for improving control memory utilization. By locating the necessary microoperations within the microroutine and taking advantage of the low-level parallelism of AMP, the microsupervisor functions may be able to be embedded in a distributed fashion within the microroutine without the use of additional memory or execution time. The effect would be equivalent to the overlapping of machine-level fetch, decode, and execution times.

The whole question of methods of microroutine linking and the relationship to machine instructions represents an important research area which is outside the scope of this paper. The present microsupervisor implementation was the easiest and quickest to accomplish, and represents a base point on which to focus further work.

V. EXPERIENCES

A. Applications Programs and Microcode Analysis

In order to be able to evaluate microcode support of the AMPMAC machine language and also to compare it to the direct support of a system at the microprogramming level, alternate programs were written in the AMPMAC language and directly in microcode for a graphics applications system now in use. Thus the graphic system was implemented in two ways: 1) via AMPMAC machine language; and 2) directly as problem-oriented microcode.

The total microcode provides a sample size of 350 microinstructions for statistical analysis. The two approaches allow some interesting comparisons to be made.

B. Microcode Analysis

The analysis reported on here is primarily static and is therefore subject to the limitations of this type of approach. It does, however, provide some insights.

Microoperations per Microinstruction: Fig. 4 is a microoperation histogram (see definition of "microoperation" in Section II). The number of microoperations in each microinstruction is, in a very real sense, a measure of the parallelism embedded in the microcode. Mean values of 2.72 and 2.58 were calculated for problem-oriented microcode and the microcode supporting AMPMAC. While the histogram of Fig. 4 is for the sum of all the code, the distributions for the two separate bodies of microcode did not differ significantly.

Microinstruction Bit Utilization: Another interesting statistic involves bit utilization within the microinstruction. Fig. 5 is a histogram providing this information. Bit utilization can also be thought of as a measure of parallelism but it is also a measure of the overall CPU resource utilization. The mean value for all microinstructions is 29.7 b per microword. The mean value for the problem-oriented microcode is 31.1, while the mean value for the microcode supporting the machine language is 29.2. As with microoperations, the problem-oriented microcode fares slightly better. However, there is no significant difference in either the means or the distributions.

Microprocessor Resource Utilization: The graphs (Figs. 6–9) examine functional unit resource utilization with an eye toward the question of low-level parallelism. Bus utilization is shown in Fig. 6. Upper bus utilization is high. Lower bus utilization is not quite so high, and B4 in particular is used less than 20 percent of the time. This is partially a consequence of the applications system analyzed. A system

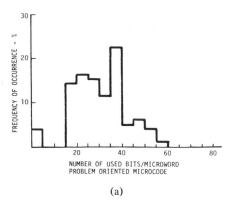

(a)

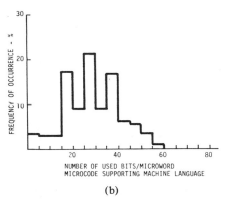

(b)

Fig. 5. Microword bit utilization.

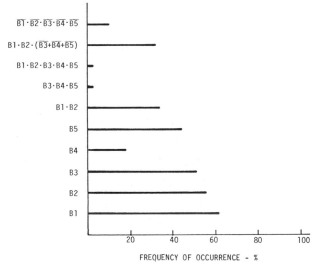

Fig. 6. Bus utilization.

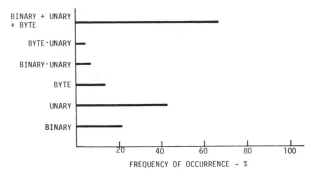

Fig. 7. Manipulator utilization.

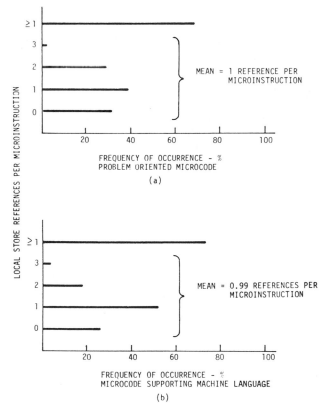

Fig. 8. Local store utilization.

utilizing the binary or byte manipulators more would improve B4 utilization. Note also that the simultaneous use of both upper buses is reasonably high and almost the same as the simultaneous use of both upper buses when at least one of the lower buses is not used. In fact, the ratio of these last two numbers is approximately 0.98. This is due in part to the fact that the upper bus B1 is used for data exchanges with main memory which then prevents multiple manipulations from occurring.

Manipulator utilization (Fig. 7) is another item of interest. About 30 percent of the microinstructions utilize no manipu-

lator at all. This is primarily due to the extensive linking in the microcode supporting AMPMAC.

Local store utilization is shown in Fig. 8. In both cases the distribution is about the same, with the problem-oriented microcode faring slightly better. Although Fig. 8 does not show it, the microcode supporting the machine language had a much higher utilization of local store addressing via the local storage address register. This is to be expected since the machine language is a multiregister type.

Approximately 30 percent of the microinstructions do not utilize local storage. Of those that do, however, about half require two or more locations. This indicates that AMP's method of local storage addressing is effective.

Investigation of microsequencing and especially conditional microsequencing shows that long cycles represent 16 percent of the microinstructions. Microinstructions which contain only sequencing operations and therefore in some sense are wasted, occur 3.5 percent of the time. Three-way branches are used less than one percent of the time as are microstack operations. The general feeling is that these figures are likely to improve with microprogrammer experience and with the addition of some hardware modifications that will improve stack accessibility and sequencing versatility.

Jump address/immediate field utilization (Fig. 9) shows a variation between problem-oriented microcode and the microcode supporting the machine language. Here the problem-oriented microcode needs a large number of constants but the microjumps are relatively few. For the machine language microcode the converse is true. This is not surprising. Significant numbers of parameters are passed between the machine code and the microcode; thus few constants have to be derived for the microcode. The large number of jumps is due to the fact that the microcode supporting the machine language consists of a branch table and a large number of small microroutines. With the program-oriented microcode the routines are few and no branch table exists; however, constants are not passed to the microcode and must be generated.

An Execution Time Comparison: Fig. 10 is a comparison of execution times for matrix addition problems. The subject matrices had 16-b integer elements and dimensions of 126 × 126. The execution times shown are for 1000 matrix additions. Care was taken to ensure that a linear relationship existed between the number of matrix operations and total execution time for each type of code.

The four cases shown are defined as follows.

Case 1: Direct microcode approach. In this case, the process is completely microencoded.

Case 2: AMPMAC code with "ADDM R" instruction.

Case 3: AMPMAC code without "ADDM R." AMPMAC routines coded to use indexing.

Case 4: AMPMAC code without "ADDM R." AMPMAC routines coded to use indirect addressing.

In order to interpret Fig. 10, some further definition is required. Let

T_t Total execution time.
T_c Actual time spent in computation.
T_i Microcode inefficiency due to nonexpansive machine level instructions.
T_f Machine instruction fetch time.

Then

$$T_t = T_c + T_i + T_f.$$

Furthermore, for the direct microcode approach (Case 1), it can be reasonably argued that

$$T_i = T_f = 0.$$

It can be seen that the machine instruction fetching overhead is substantial for the two cases where the language is not very expansive (T_f). In addition, however, code inefficiences exist due to microlinkage overhead, and also because the short microroutines associated with simple machine instructions prevent effective utilization of machine parallelism. (This inefficiency is represented by T_i.)

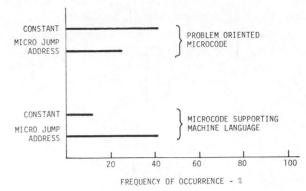

Fig. 9. Jump address/immediate field utilization.

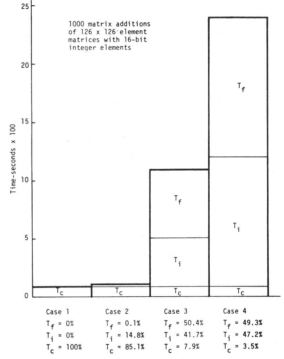

Fig. 10. Matrix additon execution times.

To provide a comparison, the same problem was executed by a fast assembly level program on an IBM 360/75. CPU time on the Model 75 was approximately 4 percent greater than the execution time of Case 1 for AMP.

VI. CONCLUSION

AMP is the result of initial research into low-level central processing unit parallelism and horizontal microcontrol. Its primary purpose is as a tool for further research in these and associated areas. As such, a design goal was to create a versatile and usable machine with easily modifiable and expandable hardware.

A number of design features contribute to the versatility of the machine. A multiple bus structure with each bus having multiple-input/multiple-output capability allows other resources within the CPU to be connected in a wide variety of ways. The low-level parallelism provided by the multiple ALU's, the register arrangement, and the local store addressing scheme, besides allowing parallelism, adds to the versatility of the microinstruction. The ability of the microcode to control timing as well as data paths, registers, and manipulators is a significant and somewhat unique feature. The main memory implementation—especially for peripherals, is also a contributing factor.

A primary design feature that makes the machine easily usable at a microcode level is the "microoperation" concept. This feature, however, in turn required a more complex (and consequently slower) microcycle than other machines either proposed or implemented [6], [8]. The main memory arrangement and its asynchronism makes memory referencing (and particularly I/O operations) very convenient for the microprogrammer. Another concession to ease of microprogramming was the concept of current word sequencing.

The machine was made hardware modifiable with the inclusion of expandable bus structures, expandable control word and memory size, the main memory scheme, unused data selection compatibility for functional units, and the construction techniques employed in building the machine. These features lead to the ability to easily add functional units (such as local storage and manipulators), change the possible routing to and from existing units, and modify microsequencing. Additional buses may also be added and microstack operations expanded. A variety of other modifications are also possible. Even the control word width limitation of 96 b is is not a real upper bound since more control memory can be added in parallel so long as cabinet space remains and wire lengths are kept reasonably short.

It should be noted that many of the design decisions were made either with an eye toward future modification based on experimentation or because of a finite research budget and limited manpower. For instance, with a larger microinstruction the "MODE" feature could have been eliminated or the number of buses and local stores increased. The versatility of the microsequencing could also have been improved by including a branch test register, a greater number of conditions on which to do microbranching, and providing such things as conditional stack operations. A faster microcycle would have been desirable. This would have required a faster control memory, a higher performance timing chain, and higher speed logic. The machine was designed, however, so that these as well as other changes could be made at a later date as the result of ongoing experimentation.

In general, microinstruction mode control which redefines the meaning of microcontrol bits represents a restriction on microinstruction flexibility and an increase in microcycle time due to necessary mode decoding. In AMP's case, there are presently 22 unused control bits (within the 96-b limit) which could, with full mode switching, provide up to 44 additional control lines. Absence of mode control would leave AMP with 15 unused bits. Mode control lengthens AMP's microcycle time by 5 ns.

Initial CPU resource utilization analysis tends to show AMP to be a "balanced" machine. That is, hardware resource utilization tends to be relatively even. However, utilization figures are not as significant as the degree of low-level parallelism that can be achieved. This is especially true today. With the low cost of CPU hardware, it is no longer as economically effective as it once was to maximize CPU resource utilization.

The concept of microoperations per microinstruction is a meaningful measure of low-level parallelism. The mean value of 2.62 can be increased. In order to improve this figure, microprocedure overlap must be increased. This, in turn, implies a greater level of interactions between microinstructions. Improved organization and expanded hardware can relieve limitations due to resource and location dependencies.[3] A number of changes are being implemented with this in mind. Microcode optimization strategies which consider such things as location and data dependencies are necessary to utilize the resources that are available.

It can be argued that with a 74-b microword, a considerably larger number of microoperations per microcycle should be able to be performed. For instance, if it is assumed that a single microoperation as defined in this paper is similar in power, on the average, to half a machine instruction of a 16-b minicomputer, then a 74-b microinstruction should contain a mean value of 9.2 microoperations. It must be remembered, however, that the 16-b machine instruction (like a vertical microinstruction) is highly encoded in order to maximize instruction efficiency. As was also pointed out, this encoding severely limits instruction versatility. Thus there is a tradeoff between versatility and instruction efficiency.

Experiences with AMP so far indicate that it is desirable to eliminate as many levels of intermediate language as possible and to design microcode to directly relate to more expansive machine instructions. This is due to the inherent parallelism of the CPU and the fact that dependencies may be more easily eliminated on larger blocks of microcode. The overhead associated with each machine-level instruction is also a contributing factor. In general, these facts are likely to be true for horizontally organized processors.

ACKNOWLEDGMENT

The authors wish to thank R. Clark who wrote the microassembler, W. Snow for the wirewrap and debugging program, E. Jones for his overall programming assistance, and D. Jacobsohn for many helpful suggestions. Their contributions have been significant to the overall effort.

REFERENCES

[1] W. P. Lidinsky, "MIRAGE, a microprogrammable interactive raster graphics equipment," in *Proc. IEEE Comput. Soc. Conf.*, Sept. 1971, pp. 15–16.
[2] S. S. Husson, *Microprogramming: Principles and Practices.* Englewood Cliffs, N.J.: Prentice-Hall, 1970.
[3] M. V. Wilkes, "The growth of interest in microprogramming: A literature survey," *Comput. Surveys*, vol. 1, pp. 139–145, Sept. 1969.
[4] S. R. Redfield, "A study in microprogrammed processors: A

[3] Location dependencies arise from the placement of information in registers or local store locations from which the data are not directly available for further processing. These dependencies may occur due to lack of forethought or because of conflicts between microprocedures.

medium sized microprogrammed processor," *IEEE Trans. Comput.*, vol. C-20, pp. 743–750, July 1971.

[5] R. Barr, J. Becker, W. Lidinsky, and V. Tantillo, "AMP, a dynamic microprocessor," Argonne Nat. Lab., Argonne, Ill., Rep. ANL-7988, to be published.

[6] R. W. Cook and M. J. Flynn, "System design of a dynamic microprocessor," *IEEE Trans. Comput.*, vol. C-19, pp. 213–222, Mar. 1970.

[7] G. D. Hornbuckle and E. I. Ancona, "LX-1 microprocessor," *IEEE Trans. Comput.*, vol. C-19, pp. 710–720, Aug. 1970.

[8] R. F. Rosin, G. Frieder, and R. H. Eckhouse, Jr., "An environment for research in microprogramming and emulation," Preprints 4th Annu. Workshop on Microprogramming, Sept. 1971.

[9] H. W. Lawson, Jr. and B. K. Smith, "Functional characteristics of a multilingual processor," *IEEE Trans. Comput.*, vol. C-20, pp. 732–742, July 1971.

[10] R. J. Kleir and C. V. Ramamoorthy, "Optimization strategies for microprograms," *IEEE Trans. Comput.*, vol. C-20, pp. 783–794, July 1971.

[11] R. M. Tomasulo, "An efficient algorithm for exploiting multiple arithmetic units," *IBM J.*, vol. 11, pp. 25–33, 1967.

[12] R. K. Clark, "Mirager the 'best-yet' approach for horizontal microprogramming," in *Proc. 1972 Ass. Comput. Mach. Conf.*, 1972.

[13] M. J. Flynn and R. F. Rosin, "Microprogramming: An introduction and a viewpoint," *IEEE Trans. Comput.*, vol. C-20, pp. 727–731, July 1971.

[14] M. J. Flynn and M. D. MacLaren, "Microprogramming revisited," in *Proc. Ass. Comput. Mach. Nat. Conf.*, 1967, pp. 457–464.

[15] E. W. Reigel, J. Faber, and D. A. Fisher, "The interpreter," in *1972 Spring Joint Comput. Conf., AFIPS Conf. Proc.*, vol. 40. Montvale, N.J.: AFIPS Press, 1972, pp. 705–723.

[16] A. B. Tucker and M. J. Flynn, "Dynamic microprogramming," *Commun. Ass. Comput. Mach.*, vol. 14, pp. 240–250, Apr. 1971.

LSP/2 PROGRAMMABLE SIGNAL PROCESSOR*

P. E. Blankenship   A. H. Huntoon   V. J. Sferrino

M.I.T. Lincoln Laboratory

Lexington, Massachusetts 02173

Abstract

A general-purpose, bus-organized computer proposed for high performance, real-time applications performs a radix-2 FFT "butterfly" at an average rate four times faster than the Lincoln Laboratory FDP computer.

LSP/2 Origin

In recent years, the advantages of digital signal processing (DSP) have become well established in radar, sonar, speech and seismic research. Programmable digital processing systems are inherently more flexible than alternative techniques: software alterations obviate massive hardware retrofits. Major digital shortcomings--speed, cost, reliability--have been overcome by fast, dense-digital integrated circuits (ICs) available commercially at moderate prices and by special design schemes.

Completion of the Lincoln Laboratory FDP[1] in 1971 was one of the first attempts at a medium-size state-of-the-art, programmable signal processor. Comprised of about 10,000 second-generation ECL devices, the FDP featured fourfold parallelism and 150-nsec cycle time. FDP performance and reliability inspired more compact, cheaper, and more easily programmed structures capable of at least

equivalent performance. The initial result, derived from the Lincoln LX-1,[2] was a 12-bit, bus-type computer optimized for complex arithmetic called Advanced Signal Processor.[3] But ASP was lacking in several critical areas: word length, general register complement, local cache memory and in-out. LSP/2, a re-thinking of the ASP, incorporates the latest digital technology, packaging techniques and architectural insights gained from high performance radar applications experience.

Architectural Overview

Conceptually, LSP/2 (Fig. 1) consists of three major components: 64-word general register file (M_c), 32-bit data bus system (A, B, D) and dedicated function modules. M_c serves as a high speed data source and sink receptacle that can be associated, under program control, with any functional element. Each component is devoted to a specific task or class of tasks. For typical arithmetic operations, the 32-bit data paths are considered divided into two 16-bit bytes providing simultaneous performance of identical 16-bit operations. Designed according to this convention, all function elements provide effective twofold parallelism for single-precision calculations. Some operations permit linkage of upper and lower bytes providing 32-bit, double-precision capability, but sacrifice duality.

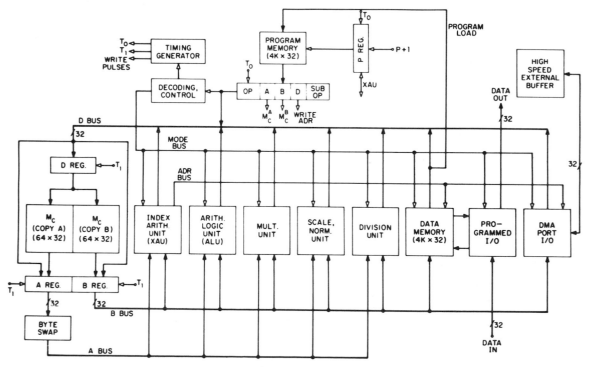

Fig. 1. LSP/2 processor architecture.

* The work was sponsored by the Departments of the Air Force and Army.

To clarify LSP/2 data flow, consider the arithmetic operation:

$$A_u + B_\ell \rightarrow D_\ell \; ; \; A_\ell + B_u \rightarrow D_u$$

where u and ℓ refer to upper and lower bytes, and A, B, D refer to the contents of the three distinct general registers. In words, the notation implies two simultaneous, 16-bit additions where the upper byte of register A is summed with the lower byte of register B and the result overlays the lower byte of register D. Similarly, the lower byte of A is combined with the upper byte of B and stored in the upper byte of D. LSP/2 carries out this sequence as follows: 6-bit addresses A and B are supplied as part of the command format and serve as pointers for accessing input operands from M_c. M_c is realized physically as two memory modules (M_c^A, M_c^B) whose contents are always identical, thereby permitting two independent registers to be accessed in a single memory-read epoch. A selects a location in M_c^A, B selects a location in M_c^B. Operand B is distributed to the function modules via the B bus, operand A passes through a "byte swap" multiplexer. This permits an optional exchange of upper and lower A bytes to enhance instruction flexibility. The selected function module derives the desired byte combination from the source buses, performs the desired operation, and feeds the results to the D bus. Conceptually, the D bus connects all function module outputs to M_c and the control permits only the desired output to be routed back for storage. The D address, also supplied in the command format, serves as a write address to permit the desired results to be recorded in both copies of M_c when machine timing permits.

This sequence typifies all arithmetic operations defined by the function module set. The modules are largely self-contained, independent, dedicated, and conceptually strapped in parallel from the source to sink buses. Nominal LSP/2 elements include:

1. Index arithmetic unit (XAU): branch related calculations
2. Arithmetic-logic unit (ALU): fixed point, 2s complement add/subtract, Boolean and constants manipulations, single or double precision
3. Multiplier: real and complex, fixed point, 2s complement multiplication

4. Shift matrices: end off/end-around shifts, floating-point normalizations and mantissa alignment
5. Division unit
6. Memory port: high rate data exchanges between M_c and external memories
7. Data memory (M): 4096 x 32 bit local cache memory connected to auto-interrupt in-out facility.

LSP/2 instructions are grouped in four classes according to type and format. Each group may encompass several function modules. Examples of operations belonging to each class are:
1. Arithmetic: $A \pm B \rightarrow D$, $A \times B \rightarrow D$, $A \div B \rightarrow D$, $A \times 2^B \rightarrow D$
2. Constants: $A \pm Y \rightarrow D$ (Y is supplied in command format)
3. Control: $Y \rightarrow P$ and $P + 1 \rightarrow D$ if $A > 0$ (P is program counter)
4. Memory: $A \rightarrow M(B)$, $M(B) \rightarrow A$

Code is supplied by a separate 4096 x 32-bit program memory (M_p) that is accessed in parallel with function executes. M_p is loaded via a special block transfer path from M and can be copied out, a location at a time, into M_c for diagnostic reasons.

Timing Philosophy

Three streams of events work concurrently (Fig. 2): accessing of M_p, general register file read and writes, and function module operations. Start of a machine cycle is defined by timing mark T_o when P is altered and a new instruction begins in M_p. When P is altered, instruction register (IR) is loaded with the instruction fetched during the previous epoch and the decoding process begins. In the sub-epoch defined by T_o to T_1, operands A and B are read from M_c and loaded into the distribution bus buffer registers. During the interim between T_1 markers, the selected function module operates on the buffered operands and reports results to the D-bus buffer register where they are saved for recording in M_c. Summarizing, in a T_o-to-T_o epoch, instruction fetches occur in parallel with M_c operations. In the period T_o-to-T_1, M_c reads out operands, and records results of the previous operation from T_1 to the next T_o. Offset by time T_1, but also occurring in parallel, are the actual function executes.

For maximum efficiency, M_p access time, M_c read/write cycle, and function execute epochs should all be matched. Calculations show good balance is achieved for nearly all instruction types if the nominal T_o-to-T_o epoch is set at 70 nsec. Some of the more complex functions, e.g., multipliers, require more time than the 70 nsec minimum, thereby requiring that machine timing be adaptive. This is accomplished in practice via linkage between the control decoder and the timing generator. In effect, T_1-to-T_1 spacing can be varied in discrete increments as a function of the instruction type being decoded.

Since related control class computations affect the potential status of P, they must be carried out in a T_1-to-T_o epoch rather than from T_1-to-T_1. In this sense they constitute a special case, although no particular difficulties are posed by such a requirement.

Fixed-Point Features

LSP/2 performs 2s complement arithmetic operations on calculated operand pairs, or with one

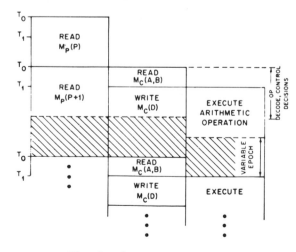

Fig. 2. Overlapped timing.

calculated operand and a stored constant. The machine's twofold parallelism permits single-precision computations to proceed simultaneously for dual 16-bit operand pairs, whereas double-precision calculations use a single 32-bit operand pair and do not proceed in parallel. In general, results may be halved under program control prior to storage. Overflow flags are provided for results appearing on both the upper and lower D-bus bytes.

In a fixed-point context, LSP/2 offers hardware add, subtract, multiply and divide capability, plus such Boolean functions as logical AND, INCLUSIVE OR, EXCLUSIVE OR, EXCLUSIVE NOR, and 1s complementation.

In the arithmetic/logic/multiplication unit (ALMU), which includes all major fixed-point computation sections except the divider (Fig. 3), two 16-bit ALUs perform the majority of single-precision arithmetic and logic operations, and offer double-precision capability when carry paths are linked. Multiplexers, used liberally throughout, manipulate operands to increase flexibility. Addition and subtraction may be performed in conventional single- or double-precision formats, or in double precision using sign-extended, single-precision operands.

Multiply operations include real integer, fractional, real extended, and partial complex options. Two 16 x 16 bit signed 2s complement array multipliers use special gated 2-bit adder circuits and carry look-ahead techniques to provide 32-bit products in less than 50 nsec.[4] The fractional or integer portion of each real multiply may be obtained simultaneously, together with overflow flags. Integer overflow is indicated when the upper 16 product bits do not agree, whereas fractional overflow is signified by disagreement between the two most significant product bits. Real extended multiplies use single-precision A- and B-bus operands, and provide all 32 product bits (integer and fractional portions) on the D bus. No overflow can occur.

High speed complex multiplications are often required in DSP and provide an incentive to package the array multipliers and ALUs together (Fig. 3). By so doing, a partial (half) complex multiply (two real multiplications plus a final add or subtract) can be executed using a single macro-instruction. Output halving may also apply to partial complex multiplications.

The ALMU provides a path for register-to-register transfers by adding the constant zero to a selected operand and applying the result to the D bus. Stored 12-bit (sign-extended to 16 bits) constants (signal Y) may be substituted for normal B-bus operands and are passed from the IR to the ALMU (Fig. 3). Boolean functions ($A+B$, $A \cdot B$, $A \oplus B$, $A \overline{\oplus} B$, $\overline{A}$, $\overline{B}$) do not set overflow flags.

The divider array, a separate functional module, provides signed 2s complement results in accordance with a nonrestoring algorithm. The application of a 32-bit dividend and 16-bit divisor produces a 16-bit quotient and 16-bit remainder. Integer or fractional division is permitted and operand multiplexers provide a multitude of input options. The quotient and remainder may be permuted on the D

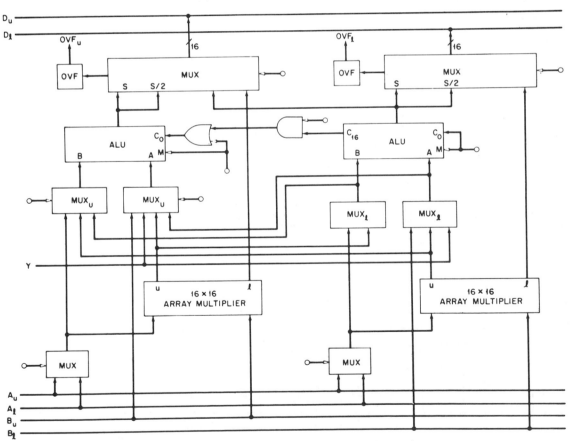

Fig. 3. Arithmetic/logic/multiplication unit.

bus, and provision is included for output sign extension and suppression of the remainder. For fractional division, the overflow flag is set if the numerator magnitude equals or exceeds that of the denominator. Overflow is indicated for integer division when the numerator magnitude is equal to or greater than 2^{16} times that of the denominator.

Shift/Rotate Operations

Shifting and scaling capability is useful for both fixed- and floating-point operations. For fixed-point calculations (Fig. 4), the number of bit positions shifted or rotated is specified by data either on the B bus or from the IR with negative quantities signifying movement to the right, and vice versa.

Conventions for end-off shifting of signed 2s complement operands are:

1. Right shifts: sign extension occurs along with loss of least significant bits
2. Left shifts: zeroes fill the least significant end of the A operand, and overflow is announced on the D bus.

Floating- to fixed-point format conversions may be accommodated using standard scaling instructions.

Floating-Point Features

Ordinarily, floating-point calculations on a fixed-point machine are made via software. In LSP/2, performance is enhanced and programming lessened by the inclusion of normalization and mantissa alignment hardware (Fig. 4) together with accompanying control instructions. Floating-point data are represented with an upper byte fractional mantissa and a lower byte exponent.

Multiplication and division are straightforward programmed operations that use fixed-point function units for mantissa arithmetic, and ALUs (Fig. 3) for calculating characteristics. Floating-point addition and subtraction are more unwieldy, requiring additional hardware to maintain computaional speed and programming ease. Floating-point addition and subtraction become simple fixed-point mantissa calculations that may proceed, after exponent alignment, via ALUs. Extra hardware is provided for exponent comparison, after which, the mantissa associated with the smaller of the two is scaled by the amount required to equalize exponents. Extra hardware centers around two subtractors and associated multiplexers (Fig. 4) that control one of the 16-place shift arrays previously discussed. A shift count word and control bit are formed that command the D_u shift array to send a properly weighted mantissa to M_c, and determines which of the original two mantissas should be retained for further processing. The appropriate exponent is placed on the lower D-bus byte.

On completion of floating-point calculations, as well as for fixed-to-floating-point conversions, normalization is appropriate and useful. LSP/2 uses a detector of leading 1s or 0s (detector K, Fig. 4) in conjunction with 16-place scaling units

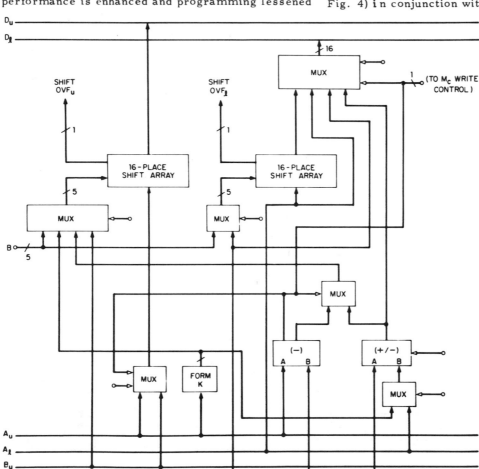

Fig. 4. Two 16-bit shift arrays for end-off shifts or end-around rotation of A-bus operands.

to left-shift the A_l operand while decrementing B_l a like amount, $K.^u$ In a floating-point context, operand B_l is ordinarily the exponent corresponding to the mantissa in A_u. If normalization is requested in the presence of mantissa overflow, automatic recovery is provided by right-shifting operand A_u one place (with sign reconstitution), and incrementing by one operand B_l.

Another feature related to radar bulk filtering is a bit-search option that permits index $K+1$ to be calculated (the number of leading 1s or 0s, plus 1), such that groupings of contiguous 1s or 0s within data words may be detected.

External Memory Port

Unique demands imposed on LSP/2 for such special applications as radar DSP include a series of high data rate exchanges between the internal structure and external memory modules via a "memory port" mechanism, a bus-oriented complex through which memory elements (4K x 16, typical size) connect to the processor. Management of these peripherals with their diverse specifications require their integration into the processing data stream without compromising processor speed. Integration was achieved by synchronizing data interfaces within a modest number of machine epochs for the slowest natural data rate of a peripheral. This required providing a small amount of fast intermediate data buffering to store arguments for pending data block transfers for a time period corresponding to the longest code block in the main processor that must be serviced without interruption. This artifice permits the main processor and addressed peripheral to minimize lost time associated with the normal request-acknowledge interface resulting in increased system efficiency.

External memory modules are selected by special instructions issued prior to the desired execution time. The addressed module can be interrogated for status and issued preparatory commands and arguments for subsequent data transfer. Address information obtained from the XAU is distributed,

along with data supplied by the B bus, to all peripheral modules.

In-Out Capability

A 16-channel in-out structure featuring automatic interrupts and an asynchronous priority arbitration mechanism is connected to M. Even-numbered channels are considered outputs and odd-numbered channels, inputs. Each of the four low ordered channels is attached to a 32-bit data buffer register (E registers 0-3) that permits word-at-a-time transfer of data to or from in-out peripherals as well as M. Through an 8:1 multiplexer these channels can communicate with up to eight peripheral devices on a time-shared basis. The remaining 12 unbuffered channels with controls identical to the buffered set (although data paths are omitted) transmit mode, status, and timing information.

Basic entry into the priority interrupt loop (Fig. 5) is via continuous monitoring of request-acknowledge lines from all peripherals simultaneously. Priority ranking for the 16 in-out channels is indicated by each channel's assigned number in descending order. Channels 12-15 are grouped as a set of high level channels, and the remaining channels (0-11, including the buffered set of four at the lowest rank) are grouped as low level channels (Fig. 6).

Encountering a channel requiring service, its group level is established and subsequent servicing is accomplished in either the right- or left-half sequences of Fig. 6. If a high level channel is encountered first, all other interrupts are locked out by high level lockout and channel arming logic. Simultaneously, the 16-channel priority encoder produces a 4-bit word (α) that is part of a hard-wired pseudo-op code to be loaded into the IR. This special instruction ignores the normal M_p output and is of the "jump to subroutine/save P" class, which causes in turn a branch to a preferred region of M_p. This region contains a jump table that engenders a second branch to the desired interrupt service routine. The table address for the artifical instruction is computed according to

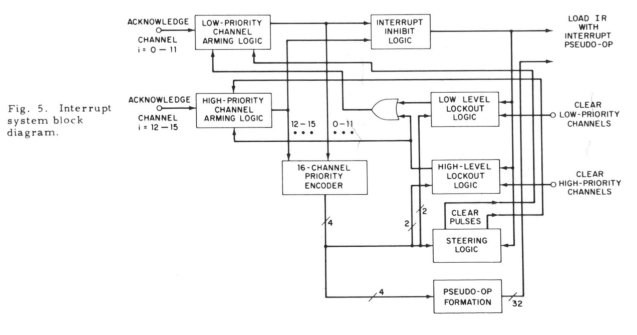

Fig. 5. Interrupt system block diagram.

$$M_p \text{ ADDRESS} = 7760_8 + \alpha$$

where α = the 4-bit address of the channel demanding service. Thus M_p ($7760_8 + \alpha$) contains a branch to the service routine associated with the αth channel.

If a low level channel is encountered first, the same sequence of events ensues except that only the remaining low level channel interrupts are locked out, and prior to servicing of the pending low channel interrupts, all high level channels are examined for status. A ready status on any of the channels results in a branch back to the high level sequence. Thus high channel servicing cannot be interrupted. Low channel servicing can be interrupted only when encountering a high level interrupt. This implies a service routine nesting of maximum level 2.

A further feature of the interrupt service loop is that the overflow stack is pushed down one level during interrupt and then restored after servicing or interrupt has been completed. Also servicing of pending interrupts is deferred while jump instructions are in progress. This feature is necessary to avoid construction of an erroneous return point from the stored return address.

Hardware

The MECL 10K line of high speed digital integrated circuits (ICs) used in LSP/2, coupled with a controlled impedance transmission line scheme of signal distribution by wirewrap over ground plane, controlled impedance cabling, and balanced line distributed buffers result in a basic computation cycle time of 70 nsec using overlapped instruction cycles.

Wirewrap boards housing some 2500 ICs for the basic processor (exclusive of external memory) accommodate 160-180 elements per board. Boards with output terminators that do not consume IC space presage a 15-18 board processor. Printed circuits are used where high speed performance-- internal memory, general register file, arithmetic elements such as the multiplier/divider complex-- is more critical. The MECL 10K line requires special thermal control effected with an average air flow of 500-600 lfm.

Performance Comparison

LSP/2 power vs that of other processors is compared realistically via specific tasks:
1. LSP/2 can perform a 16 x 16 bit complex multiply in 200 nsec; FDP requires 600 nsec.
2. LSP/2 performs a radix 2, decimation-in-time, elementary computation defined by relations

$$\underline{A}' = \underline{A} + \underline{B} \cdot \underline{W}^K \; ; \; \underline{B}' = \underline{A} - \underline{B} \cdot \underline{W}^K$$

where all operands are complex and $W = \exp(-j\frac{2\pi}{N})$ in 340 nsec; about four times faster than the FDP.

To get a feel for the effects of control overhead, a 16-point FFT might serve as a better comparative vehicle. Using straight line code, FDP can perform FFTs of this size at about 1.5 usec/point. Calculations show that LSP/2 can perform equivalent computations at about 0.42 usec/point, or four times as fast.

Because of size limitations of the general register file, the LSP/2 handles data most expediently in batches of 8 or 16 points. This suggests that larger transforms might be performed most efficiently using radix-8 or -16 algorithms in conjunction with a two-dimensional approach.

Summary

A bus-organized processor proposed for high performance, real-time applications derives its power from:
1. high speed general register file
2. dual parallelism
3. macro-function modules to reduce overhead
4. high speed combinational logic arrays
5. overlapped, adaptive timing
6. 3rd generation ECL technology.

In FFT operations, the processor is four times faster than the FDP while comprised of one-third as many integrated circuits. Utility is further enhanced by a flexible in-out and floating-point capability attained at little extra expense by taking advantage of the machine's duality.

Acknowledgment

The authors gratefully acknowledge the many invaluable contributions of Dr. Bernard Gold and the helpful comments during evolution of the current design of Dr. R. J. Purdy, J. M. Frankovich and P. G. McHugh.

References

1. B. Gold, et al., "The FDP, a Fast Programmable Signal Processor," IEEE TC, C-20, 1, 33-38 (January 1971).
2. G. H. Hornbuckle, E. I. Ancona, "The LX-1 Micro-processor and its Application to Real-Time Signal Processing," IEEE TC (August 1970).
3. P. Blankenship, et al., "Design Study of the Advanced Signal Processor," Technical Note 1972-17, Lincoln Laboratory, M.I.T. (27 April 1972).
4. S. D. Pezaris, "A 17 x 17 Bit Array Multiplier," IEEE TC, C-20, 4, 442-447 (April 1971).

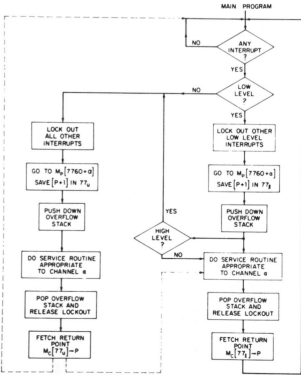

Fig. 6. Priority interrupt system.

A VERY HIGH-SPEED MICROPROGRAMMABLE PIPELINE SIGNAL PROCESSOR

Hideo AISO, Mario TOKORO, Shun-ichi UCHIDA, Hideki MORI,
Noriyuki KANEKO, and Motoo SHIMADA

Faculty of Engineering, Keio University 832 Hiyoshi-cho,
Kohoku-ku, Yokohama 223, Japan

This paper describes the functional characteristics of a very high-speed signal processor being implemented in hardware. This signal processor involves dynamically microprogrammable control designed for general purpose processing of a wide variety of known pattern information but also adaptable to new applications. A pipeline control has intentionally been adopted for real-time processing. Any type of functional unit can be attached to the signal processor which may be used either in conjunction with other computers or independently. A microprogram assembler and a microprogram simulator have been provided to facilitate microprogramming.

1. INTRODUCTION

As the necessity for pattern information processing grows, the technology of signal processing becomes more important. In particular, recent signal processors are required to provide the capability for real-time processing of a large amount of data. Therefore, several high-speed signal processors have recently been implemented in hardware [1] [2]. Described here is a very high-speed and general purpose hardware signal processor developed to fulfill the requirements of signal processing mentioned below.

1.1 Requirements of Signal Processing

(i) Capability of processing

In most types of signal processing, the Fast Fourier Transform (FFT) [3] is an essential arithmetic operation. The Inverse FFT (IFFT), Convolution, Correlation, Windowing, Transfer Function and so forth, all based on the Fourier Transform, are also important. Moreover, some applications demand the calculations of special functions in addition to conventional arithmetic and logic operations. However, it is extremely difficult to estimate the versatility of the operational functions that the signal processor has to provide. This trend leads to the conclusion that signal processors in the future should be designed to accommodate enough power for computation.

(ii) Data to be processed

It is imperative for a signal processor to effectively carry out the operations on a large, properly ordered set of data, which may be expressed in either real or complex numbers. Of course, it should also have the ability to treat a single piece of data. Signal processing of multi-dimensional array data should also be taken into consideration.

(iii) Speed of processing

With the expansion of application fields, much higher-speed signal processors may be necessary for real-time processing. Recent technology and applications demand that the signal processor carry out a 1 024-point FFT within 5 ms, and it is said that the number of sampling points of the original signal may often reach 8 192.

(iv) Flexibility of system configuration

Signal processors are expected to have enough flexibility to allow the organization of various system configurations depending on the application, the performance of any kind of computation, and moreover, a large number of sampling points. Any type of functional units, A/D and D/A converters, and even display units may be required. To achieve better system performance, it is necessary to have the capability of organizing an effective multiprocessor system using an external computer. An independent signal processor may also be needed for simple applications.

1.2 Main Features of the Signal Processor

The signal processor is generally expected to have both the capability for high-speed processing of large amounts of data and a flexibility of system configuration that does not require any modification of its internal structure. An attempt has been made to develop a signal processor to fulfill the requirements mentioned above. The main features of this signal processor are as follows:

(i) As a main functional unit of this processor, a very fast hardware FFT unit has been developed. This FFT unit is designed to be adaptable to various operations other than FFT.

(ii) The FFT unit can operate on complex data, and it is possible to handle two channels of real data simultaneously.

(iii) The signal processor has been designed to calculate a 1 024-point FFT in approximately 3 ms, and it has the capability to handle signals of up to 8 192 points.

(iv) A hardware mechanism, which automatically generates the necessary addresses to access the data in the main memories, has been provided.

(v) Any type of equipment of up to sixteen functional units can be used as the system components of the signal processor, and thus functional flexibility is guaranteed.

(vi) In order to make the total time for the processing of the data as short as possible, a pipeline control scheme has been adopted throughout the signal processor. All the functional units, including the FFT unit, are to be pipelined. Although the length of pipeline depends on the type of functional units to be attached, the address generator is designed so that the functional units are allowed to consist of any length of pipeline.

(vii) To provide the capability for the realization of any application-oriented system, a dynamically microprogrammable control has been employed and a residual control approach has been adopted throughout the system. Thus, the problems that the microprogrammable control may encounter in pipeline processing have been solved.

(viii) In order to achieve adequate response time in a real-time environment, a fast interrupt handling mechanism has been provided.

(ix) For better system performance and higher throughput, the signal processor has an interface to connect to a conventional computer. As an independent system, this signal processor may also be useful for some applications.

Reprinted with permission from *Inform. Processing 74, Proc. IFIP Congr. 74*, Aug. 5-10, 1974, pp. 60-64.

(x) A microprogrammed interpreter for an intermediate machine language has been provided, and a microprogram assembler and simulator have also been developed.

2. SYSTEM CONFIGURATION

As can be seen from fig. 1, the signal processor is composed of a Control Unit (CU), an Arithmetic and Logic Unit for Control (CALU), a Memory Unit (MU), an Address Generation Unit (AGU), pipeline Functional Units (FU's) such as an FFT Unit (FFTU), a Computer Communication Coupler (CCC) and an I/O Interface Unit (INTFU). The main characteristics of the system components are as follows:

2.1 *Bus Configuration and Data Flow*

This processor adopts the bus oriented configuration which enables to make the data flow uniform throughout the system and thus provides flexibility and expansibility in its configuration. It logically has four 32-bit busses named the Input and Output Busses (IB's and OB's) as shown in fig. 1. However, only two 32-bit bidirectional busses are really provided and used in an interleaved manner, to which the MU, CCC, INTFU, and any FU can be attached.

Before an operation begins, some of these units are selected by a microprogram and a data path is established. Namely, the units to be accessed in the MU and an FU to carry out the operation are determined and then they are connected to the IB's and OB's. This data path is pipelined and the length of the pipe varies depending upon the type of the operation and the FU being used. Besides the establishing of the data path, the address pattern being generated in the AGU and the type of the operation performed in the FU are also determined. In the middle of the operation on a set of data, the data are read out from the MU at the addresses supplied by the AGU and transferred to the FU through the OB's. The data processed in the FU are then sent back to the MU through the IB's. In this case, memory read and write operations are performed alternately.

2.2 *Control Unit (CU)*

The CU is composed of the following units: A Control Memory (CM), which is a RAM with the maximum capacity of 4K 32-bit words, a Control Memory Address Register (CMAR), a Return Address Register (RAR) to be used for do-loop operations and subroutine linkage, an Interrupt Address Register (IAR) to save the return address on receipt of an interruption, and Indirect Control Registers (ICR's) such as the Bus Control Register (BCR) and the Memory Control Register (MCR). The CU also includes the control logic for executing the microinstructions and handling interruptions. The CU itself is pipelined to speed up the execution of the microprograms.

2.3 *Arithmetic and Logic Unit for Control (CALU)*

The CALU is an essential unit in the basic configuration of the signal processor. It is used when the status of the processor is to be sensed, and its results are in turn fed back to the sequencing of the microprogram. The CALU holds only a 4-bit internal status, which is often used in interruption processing. The CALU provides the capability of performing Add, Sub, AND, OR, EXOR, 2's and 1's Complements, 1-bit Shift (arithmetic/logical and left/right), 1-bit Rotate Shift (left/right) operations on 16-bit operands.

2.4 *Memory Unit (MU)*

The MU is organized from four General Registers (GR1-GR4); three independent Main Memories (MM1-MM3), each of which has its own read and write Buffer Registers (MBR's); Bus Selection Switches (BSS's); and Skew Units (SU's). Each MM consists of 4K 32-bit words. Both MM1 and MM2 store the data to be processed, while MM3 stores tables of trigonometric functions (cos x and sin x for $0 \leq x \leq \pi/4$) and some other control information. Each 32-bit word usually contains a complex number, the left half of which represents its real part and the rest its imaginary part. The BSS's selectively connect the GR's and MBR's to the IB's and OB's in 32-bit width. The SU's are used to interchange the left half and the right half of the 32-bit data on the busses. The BSS's and SU's enable arbitrary connections between the busses and the MU in 16-bit width respectively. The bus connections are determined by the content of the BCR. The selection of the MM's to be accessed and the choice of either 16 or 32-bit width is specified by the MCR.

2.5 *Address Generation Unit (AGU)*

The AGU generates addresses for various computations and supplies them to the MM's, and it also has the capability for permitting to connect pipeline FU's of any length up to eight to the busses. The generation and supply scheme is as follows: The Data Counter (DC) is a 12-bit counter, which is advanced by a preset increment under the control of a bit in the micro-

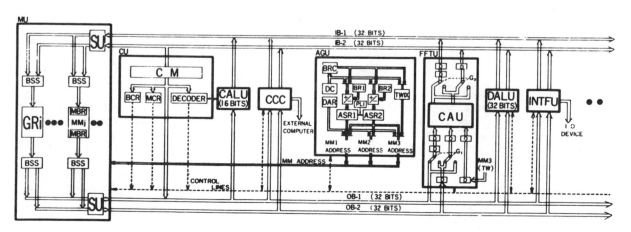

Fig. 1. CONFIGURATION OF THE PROCESSOR.

instructions. The Bit Reversion Circuit (BRC) converts the output of the DC to the bit reversed value depending on the stage of the FFT. The Twiddle Index circuit (TWIX) generates the addresses to obtain the twiddle factors and Hanning windowing coefficients which are stored in MM3, in compliance with the output of the BRC and DC respectively.

The Pipelength Indicator (PLI) indicates the length of the pipeline FU being used. Its content specifies the number of register in the Address Shift Registers (ASR1 and ASR2) to be used for the pipeline operation. Namely, these specified registers keep the addresses which have already been used to read out the data from the MM's until they are used again to write the data into the MM's. The ASR's enable the operations to be carried out "in place", and automatically supply proper addresses for read and write operations. Two Base Registers (BR's) are used for relocation.

The AGU has two Direct Address Registers (DAR1 and DAR2) which are used to construct an efficient microprogrammed interpreter, and to manipulate the control data, while the addressing scheme stated above is mainly used for the pipeline operations. Several microinstructions related to the DAR's are provided. DAR1 can be advanced by one by the microinstructions.

The increment of the DC, the contents of the BR's and the PLI, the choice of the input to the TWIX and ASR's, and the connection of the outputs of the TWIX and ASR's to the MM's are invariant during a pipeline operation. However, the timing for advancing the DC, and the timing for shifting and setting of the ASR's are dynamically controlled by the microinstructions.

In addition to the mechanisms mentioned above, the AGU has facilities to set flag-bits on, corresponding to the following three states to be detected by microprograms: The first state indicates that the Pipe Length Counter (PLC) has become zero. The PLC, which can be preset at an arbitrary value, is set back by one in synchronization with the timing for advancing the DC. This state is used to construct a small repeat-until-loop in microprograms mainly for the pre-process or the post-process of the pipeline operations, which are explained in the next chapter. The second state indicates that the content of the DC has become equal to the preset value of the Data Size Indicator (DSI), which is used to construct a larger repeat-until-loop primarily for the main-process, which is also explained in the next chapter. The third state indicates that the whole stage of the FFT or of the IFFT has terminated. This state is used exclusively for the main-process of the FFT and IFFT.

Having the powerful and flexible facilities stated above, the AGU can generate various address patterns, such as the following examples: 1) sequential order incremented by a preset increment, 2) bit reversed order incremented by a preset increment, 3) FFT index, 4) Twiddle factor index, and 5) Hanning windowing index.

2.6 *FFT Unit (FFTU)*

The FFTU, which adopts the Sande-Tukey algorithm [4], handles the complex number as a pair of 16-bit fixed-point real numbers. However, the set-floating-point 2's complement representation is used for the data to be processed, while the fixed-point signed magnitude representation for the trigonometric data. The set-floating-point representation means that every data is aligned so that the maximum value in the set of data lies in the range between 1 and 1/2, and thus the set has an exponent common to the whole data.

The FFTU is a pipeline FU with the pipelength of four, which is composed of nine registers (D's) to hold data, two switching gates (G1 and G2), and a radix 2 Complex Arithmetic Unit (CAU) as shown in fig. 1. The D's and G's are provided to supply data in pairs to the CAU, which have usually been read out from the same MM in two adjacent timings, and to store the calculated data into the same MM in two adjacent timings, in order to

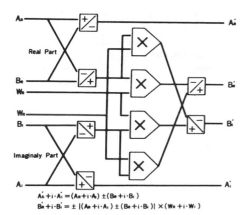

$$A_R + i \cdot A_I' = (A_R + i \cdot A_I) \pm (B_R + i \cdot B_I)$$
$$B_R' + i \cdot B_I' = \pm [(A_R + i \cdot A_I) \pm (B_R + i \cdot B_I)] \times (W_R + i \cdot W_I)$$

Fig. 2. Radix 2 complex arithmetic unit (CAU)

process "in place". Since the basic arithmetic operations can be summarized in the following formuli: A ± B and ±(A ± B) x W, the CAU consists of two complex adders and a complex multiplier composed of four 17-bit x 17-bit fixed-point multipliers including two 34-bit adders as shown in fig. 2. In order to reduce the multiplication time in consideration of cost, each multiplier employs an iterative logic which includes a 16-bit x 4-bit multiplication logic and a modified carry-save adder's array [5].

Since it is very important to minimize truncation error in arithmetic operations, an auto-scaling technique has been introduced and implemented in the FFTU by means of providing eight 2-bit overflow-save registers and four shifters to automatically produce the calculated data in the set-floating-point representation.

Under the control of microprograms, the FFTU is utilized to perform the following functions: FFT, IFFT, Convolution, Auto and Cross-Correlation, Hanning Windowing, Complex Addition/Subtraction/Multiplication, Double Precision (32-bit) Addition/Subtraction, Conjugation, Shift Right Arithmetic, and so forth.

2.7 *Computer Communication Coupler (CCC) and Interface Unit (INTFU)*

Both the CCC and the INTFU are connected in the same manner as the FU's, an example of which is the FFTU.

The CCC is used for all communication between the signal processor and the external computer. The standard data width of the CCC is 16 or 32 bits. In the data exchange with the external computer, the CCC operates as if it were an FU. In case of input of the raw data from the external computer, its DMA channel is used. It is triggered by the CCC on transferring a piece of the data. The input data are sent to the MU through the IB's and then written into it. In case of output transfer, the processed data in the MU go through the OB's and then are sent to the external computer via the CCC. In these cases, each transfer of a piece of data is controlled by the same microinstructions that are used for the pipeline operations. The addresses used are also supplied by the AGU.

Another data transfer between this processor and the external computer occurs when the microprogram is to be loaded into the CM. In this case, the CCC takes a role of controlling this operation with the help of the external computer. This function provides a unique capability for dynamic microprogram loading which permits overlaying the microprogram, as well as for initial microprogram loading.

The INTFU operates in almost the same manner as the CCC, as far as the data exchange with an external device is concerned. However, it has two functions for I/O transfer. One is the microprogrammed I/O transfer for high-speed devices and the other is the I/O transfer for low-speed devices which make use of interruption.

2.8 *Other Functional Units*

An ALU for complex and double precision Data (DALU), a Max/Min Data Sampler (MMDS), and a Variable Shifter (VS) have been provided. Also, FU's which calculate Division, Logarithm, Square Root, Arctangent, and so forth may be attached to the processor.

3. CONTROL AND MICROINSTRUCTION

3.1 *Microinstructions for Pipeline Processing*

For the benefit of microinstruction design, pipeline operations may be divided into three minor processes, namely, the pre-process, the main-process and the post-process as shown in fig. 3. Furthermore, these processes can be divided into the following steps: 1) Initial set-up of parameters, 2) Data transfer and operation, and 3) Index increment and completion checking. These steps can be determined so that step 1) specifies all the parameters needed for the operation and steps 2) and 3) are independent of the characteristics of the operation. Then the microinstructions which control these steps become independent of the functional unit. Such design can be realized by means of a sub-division of the control structure.

The control structure on pipeline process may be classified into two groups. One is static control, which is unchanged throughout the pipeline process on a set of data. The other is dynamic control, which varies during the process. Namely,

C1) static control
a) data path (selection of MM's, FU and busses), b) bit width (16 or 32 bits), c) operation to be performed in the FU, and d) address pattern to be generated;

C2) dynamic control
a) read or write of MM's, b) update of MM address, c) transfer of data on the busses, d) sensing of the status, and e) control of the FU in the process of the operation.

Group C1) is the one to set up a pipeline configuration in the processor. Group C2) dynamically controls the data flow in it. This processor employs a residual control technique [6] so that the ICR's control group C1). According to this analysis, the following microinstructions have been designed.

For static control,

11) EMIT   contains a 16-bit data in itself and sets it into a control register,

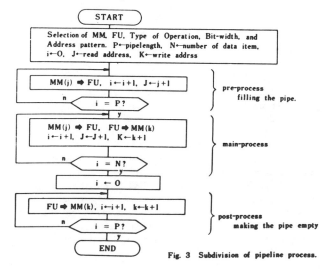

Fig. 3 Subdivision of pipeline process.

12) SS   sets the content of a GR or an MBR into a control register.

For dynamic control,

13) MD   controls the data transfer between the FU and the MU, the read or write of each MM, and the updating of the address; and checks the completion of the operation,

14) FS   transfers intermediate results, the status in the FU, and the I/O data to a GR or an MBR.

These instructions are mainly used to set up a data path and control the data flow.

3.2 *Processing of a Single Piece of Data*

A series of pipeline processes on several sets of data and the I/O operation require the capability of handling a single piece of data to analyze the intermediate results or the status so as to decide on the operation to be performed next. But the pipeline functional units are very inefficient for such operations because of their heavy overhead in terms of initial set-up, the pre-process, the post-process, and the saving of the status during interruption processing. For these reasons, the CALU is provided and controlled by the following instruction:

15) ALOP   performs arithmetic and logic operations between the GR's.

Two instructions are also provided for data transfer between the GR's and the MM's:

16) LR   transfers data from an MM to a GR,

17) SR   transfers data from a GR to an MM.

3.3 *Supports for Interruption Processing and I/O Operations*

Communication to the other computers and I/O operations require high speed response to interruption. However, there are crucial problems to harmonize this requirement with the pipeline scheme.

The problems are 1) How to sense interruption, 2) When to accept interruption, and 3) How to deal with the status in the pipeline units. For 1), this processor provides a hardware mechanism which transfers control to a particular address when interruption is accepted instead of sensing the interruption by microinstructions. In answer to the problems 2) and 3), to avoid saving the status in the pipeline unit, interruption could be inhibited until the operation is completed. However, this method would make quick response impossible. This processor compromises with these problems by having the limitation that the programs initiated by interruptions are allowed to use only the CALU. However, this is not seriously detrimental because all the communications with the external computer and I/O operations can be sufficiently performed by the CALU. In addition to the hardware supports, the following instructions have been designed to sense and analyze the status.

18) RFI   is used to return from the interruption.

19) JOT, JNT   conditional jump instructions, sense the status.

110) SKP   senses the status and branches to one of the five different addresses.

3.4 *Supports for Programming*

In order to implement a microprogrammed interpreter, a special microinstruction, which can attend to the finer details of the processor in cooperation with the SS and the FS, is provided.

III) AM   controls only the read and write operation of each MM.

4. PROGRAMMING

In this chapter the microprogram assembler, the microprogram simulator, and the signal processing oriented Intermediate Machine Language (IML) and its interpreter, including the interrupt handler, are described.

4.1 *Microprogram Assembler and Microprogram Simulator*

A microprogram assembler and a microprogram simulator have been developed to run on the NOVA DOS as aids to micro-programming and debugging. The microprogram simulator, which is the modified version of a simulator developed to check the validity of the design of the hardware, executes the sequence of microinstructions step by step. All the errors can be detected by this microprogram simulator. The microprogram assembler and the microprogram simulator have great extensibility for the attachment of a variety of functional units.

4.2 *IML Interpreter and Interrupt Handler*

It is tremendously cumbersome to assemble and debug micro-programs for every job. In order to avoid this cumbersome work, a signal processing oriented Intermediate Machine Language (IML) has been prepared for the users. This IML is a set of Intermediate Machine Instructions (IMI's), each of which is composed of an operation code and a certain number of the parameters, the number of which depends on each operation. A program written in IML is stored in the program area of MM3 to be interpreted by the IML-Interpreter which is coded in microinstructions. The IML-Interpreter is composed of a Do-Interpretive-Loop (DIL) routine, routines for individual operation, and an Interrupt Handler (IH). The DIL routine analyzes the op-code of the IMI and transfers control to the routine corresponding to the individual operation. After the completion of the operation, the control returns to the DIL routine.

The IH handles interruptions such as power failure, machine errors, program errors, and I/O requests. The IH can properly treat multi-level interruptions with an Interrupt Mask Register (IMR) in the CU, which controls the priority of the interruptions.

The typical usage of MM3 is listed as follows: The upper 1 025 words of MM3 are used to store the trigonometric function table, the next upper area is used as a stack for the IH, the next area is assigned to be the working space for the routines of individual operations, and the rest of the memory is dedicated to the program area.

5. CONCLUSION

The functional characteristics and the control structure of a very high-speed general purpose signal processor have been described. As the result of the full use of possibilities provided by microprogramming and the residual control scheme, the functional versatility has successfully been accommodated. By means of an extensive use of pipeline techniques, it can be applicable to future real-time applications.

With this signal processor having the main memories of 300 ns cycle time, a 1 024-point FFT can be performed in approximately 3 ms. It is surely possible to improve its computing performance by using much faster memories.

At the time of this writing, the design of the processor has almost been completed. Simulation has proved the effectiveness in most cases of the basic operations encountered in signal processing. Efforts are now under way to realize its hardware with reasonably available semiconductor devices at present.

It is believed that this processor will demonstrate what can be obtained from the techniques employed in itself, and contributes to the design of much larger and faster signal processor of the next generation.

ACKNOWLEDGMENT

The authors wish to thank the many people of the research and development group of Takeda Riken Industry Co., Ltd. for their enthusiastic discussion and patient endeavors for the implementation of the signal processor. They would like to greatefully acknowledge the encouragement, support, and counsel of Messrs. Ikuo Takeda and Mitsuo Goto, President and Vice President of Takeda Riken Industry Co., Ltd. respectively. The suggestions and assistance of their colleagues of Keio University are also greatly appreciated.

REFERENCES

[1] R.R. Shively, A Digital Processor to Generate Spectra in Real Time, *Digest of the First Annual IEEE Computer Conference*, Sept. 1971, 21-24.

[2] H.L. Groginsky and G.A. Works, A Pipeline Fast Fourier Transform, *IEEE Trans. on C.*, Vol. C-19, No. 11, Nov. 1970, 1015-1019.

[3] J.W. Cooley and J.W. Tukey, An Algorithm for the Machine Calculation of Complex Fourier Series, *Math. of Comput.*, Vol. 19, April 1965, 297-301.

[4] W.T. Cochran, J.W. Cooley, D.L. Favin, H.D. Helms, R.A. Kaenel, W.W. Lang, G.C. Maling, Jr., D.E. Nelson, C.M. Rader, and P.D. Welch, What is the Fast Fourier Transform?, *IEEE Trans. on AU.*, Vol. AU-15, No. 2, June 1967, 45-55.

[5] S.F. Anderson, J.G. Earle, R.E. Goldschmidt, and D.M. Powers, The IBM System/360 Model 91: Floating-Point Execution Unit, *IBM J. of Res. and Develop.*, Vol. 11, No. 1, Jan. 1967, 34-53.

[6] H.W. Lawson, Jr. and B.K. Smith, Functional Characteristics of a Multilingual Processor, *IEEE Trans. on C.*, Vol. C-20, No. 7, July 1971, 732-742.

A Microprogrammed Approach to Signal Processing

GARY L. KRATZ, MEMBER, IEEE, WILLIAM W. SPROUL, MEMBER, IEEE, AND EUGENE T. WALENDZIEWICZ

Abstract—This paper provides a summary of the design features of a microprogram controlled high speed signal processor referred to as an analyzer unit (AU). It provides an overview of the interrelationship between processing requirements, a language structure in which these requirements can be efficiently programmed, and an AU design that can efficiently execute the processing requirements. Particular emphasis is placed on the microprogram structure of the system computational unit, the Arithmetic Processor.

To the present, high speed signal processors have not been general purpose in nature. There have been a large number of high-speed digital filters and fast Fourier transform (FFT) analyzers designed but only a few designs have attempted to address high-speed systems capable of efficiently performing a wide variety of signal processing algorithms plus post processing and display formatting functions [1], [2]. The signal processor discussed herein brings a general purpose capability to this area through the microprogramming of a highly pipelined, paralleled processing system.

Index Terms—Computer architecture, digital signal processing, fast Fourier transform, microprogram, parallel processing, pipeline processing.

I. PROCESSING REQUIREMENTS

SIGNAL PROCESSING in an analyzer unit (AU) consists mainly of digital filtering and performing Fourier transformations on large blocks of sensor data. Numerous other support operations such as weighting, long term integration, and output formatting are also required. While not comprising the major part of the processing load, these operations require a general purpose capability in the AU. The processing requirements largely define three major parameters of the AU; storage, precision, and throughput.

The primary AU storage medium is the Bulk Store which for a range of applications may vary from 64 *K* words (32 bits) to 256 *K* words in size. Bulk Store requirements are largely defined by system requirements and are primarily independent of architectural consideration. Bulk Store requirements are minimized by packing data in the required number of bits rather than in a standard word length; 8, 16, 24, and 32 bit formats are provided. Separate storage is provided for microprograms and operational programs.

Storage requirements are comprised of data buffers used

Manuscript received September 7, 1973; revised January 15, 1974.
G. L. Kratz and W. W. Sproul are with the Federal Systems Division, IBM Corporation, Manassas, Va. 22110.
E. T. Walendziewicz is with the Federal Systems Division, IBM Corporation, Burlington, Mass. 01803.

to accumulate data for processing, temporary buffers used as working areas, coefficients used in computational algorithms, and system processing parameters. Generation of trigometric coefficients used in fast fourier transforms (FFT's) and heterodyning operations eliminates the need for additional storage for these coefficients.

Arithmetic and memory register lengths strongly affect system performance. Roundoff noise enters the data processing calculation when values are rounded, adding to the error variance in the computations.

The magnitude of this roundoff error strongly influences the choice of scaling in the system. Scaling is needed particularly in digital filters and FFT's to avoid overflow and provide maximum precision in the computation [3]. Because of the dynamic range of the possible signal processing output values, a fixed worst case scaling could reduce the variance of the sample values to the point where the roundoff noise variance substantially degrades the signal/noise ratio of the output. Signal dependent rescaling is therefore provided in the analyzer unit (AU).

Signal processing throughput requirements have been conventionally expressed in terms of a required number of multiples per second. The AU design modularly provides throughputs from 10 to 40×10^6 multiplies/s. The majority of processor loading is derived from filtering, FFT, and FFT weighting algorithms which tend to be multiply limited. However, an extensive number of post-FFT algorithms are required and these tend to be storage or adder limited, making loading expressions in terms of multiplies per second somewhat misleading unless a greater adder throughput and sufficient storage bandwidth can be demonstrated.

II. SIGNAL PROCESSING LANGUAGE

The AU has two distinctly different levels of machine programmability. Each of the two machine languages provides distinct benefits to either the system designer or the system programmer. Each of the two machine languages has its own set of objectives.

The first level of machine language programmability in the AU is the microprogram language. This is the system designer's language and is hardware data flow oriented. It provides programmable access to, and control over, the system's detailed hardware functions. There are two separate microprogram languages in the AU. One is associated with the general purpose controller, the Control Processor (CP), and the other is associated with the high

Reprinted from *IEEE Trans. Comput.*, vol. C-23, pp. 808–816, Aug. 1974.

42

speed signal processor, the Arithmetic Processor (AP). Microprograms in both of these languages are implemented in read/write control storages.

The second level of machine language programmability in the AU is the Signal Processing Language, or SPL. This is the system programmer's language. The SPL is problem oriented. Its architecture and instruction sets have been designed and tailored toward signal processing applications. The SPL is an emulated machine language, created by, and executed under, microprogram control routines.

The SPL architecture and instruction sets can be expanded, changed, and improved with no hardware changes in the system. The SPL architecture and its instruction sets could be completely replaced with a different problem-oriented machine language if required by new and substantially different applications.

SPL instructions are divided into four classes, General and Supervisory instructions, Data Transfer Instructions, Input/Output (I/O) instructions, and Complex Function instructions. The General and Supervisory instruction set provides the system programmer with the framework in which to structure the program flow. It is similar to the instruction sets found in state-of-the-art general purpose computers. The Data Transfer instruction set provides a command structure used for transferring data sets between Bulk Store and the AU processing elements. The I/O instruction set provides a command structure for control of peripheral devices. The Complex Function instruction set provides the systems programmer with the framework in which to command the execution of the signal processing algorithms which are referred to as complex functions in the AU. The Complex Function instruction set provides an efficient method of initiating the execution of a complex function or chain of complex functions in the AU. The complex function structure is designed to take advantage of the AU's ability to chain together a sequence of complex functions without program intervention, minimizing wait time and thus resulting in maximum system efficiency.

III. ANALYZER UNIT FUNCTIONAL ELEMENTS

The AU contains the following six functional elements which are organized as shown in Fig. 1:

1) Control Processor
2) Arithmetic Processor
3) Bulk Store
4) Storage Controller
5) I/O Channels
6) Input Signal Conditioner.

The following paragraphs describe the AU elements with emphasis on their function in the system. System processing requirements are partitioned among the processing elements in a manner designed to minimize idle time caused by one processing element requiring service from another element.

A. Control Processor

The CP performs the AU system supervisory and data management functions. The CP initiates commands to the other functional elements of the AU by communication with them via its External Data Bus. This gives the CP direct access to all the command and status registers of the AU which are addressed as a simple extension of the CP local store.

The CP is a microprogrammed 32-bit general purpose computer. The CP has a Program Store for SPL programs and data and a writeable Control Store for microprograms.

The arithmetic and logic area is a conventional 32-bit design providing operations on word, halfword, byte, or 4-bit operands. Operations on 4-bit operands enhance CP capabilities as a controller by providing an efficient means of manipulating device command words. Operands may be selected from 64 local storage words, 192 external storage words (External Registers) provided to facilitate control of external devices, or literals. Local Store register locations may be addressed directly or indirectly to provide efficient emulation of SPL general register operand specifications.

Program Store is nominally 16 K by 34 bits including 2 parity bits. It is modularly expandable in 8 K increments to 64 K words.

The CP Control Store is a 2 K by 34-bit read/write store with 32 data bits and 2 parity bits per word. The CP microprograms are executed from CP Control Store. The CP microprogram sequencing logic includes the capability to branch on any pair of bits in Local Store or External Register to permit efficient monitoring of external device status condition, and the capability to branch on an SPL op code to the start of an instruction execution routine facilitating the emulation of SPL.

B. Arithmetic Processor

The Arithmetic Processor (AP) performs the AU signal processing functions. The AP is organized with the Arithmetic Element Controller (AEC) controlling up to four high speed Arithmetic Elements (AE's) and their Working Stores in parallel. The AP is controlled by a microprogram stored in AP Control Store.

The AP is organized in parallel with up to four AE's; each AE is a pipelined processor with the computational and logical capability to process a wide variety of complex function algorithms. A single microprogram, interpreted by the AEC, controls both the parallel and pipelined features of the AP.

1) *Arithmetic Element:* The AE is the AU building block for performing the arithmetic operations of signal processing algorithms. The architecture and implementation of the AE's, as well as the entire Arithmetic Processor,

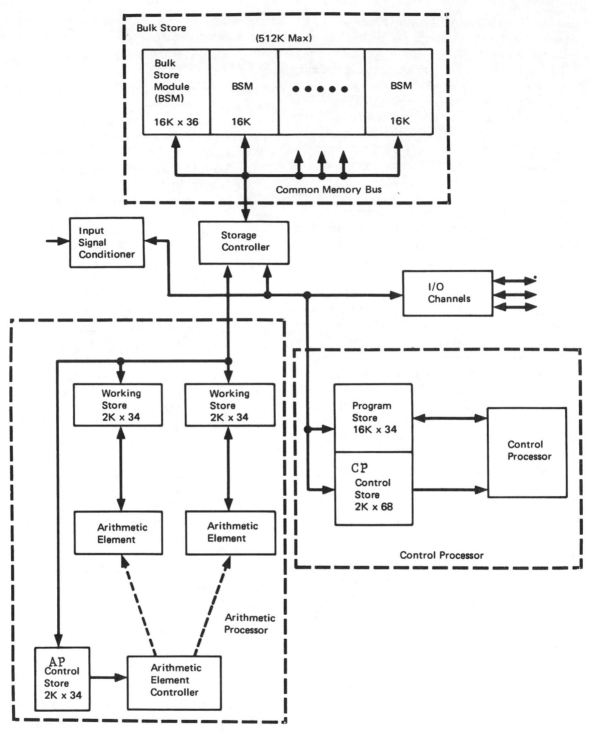

Fig. 1. Analyzer unit data flow.

was motivated by the objective of providing efficient high speed execution of many different signal processing algorithms. Fig. 2 shows a block diagram of the AE.

The basic elements of the AE include a 16 × 16-bit two's complement multiplier, a three input 32-bit arithmetic logic unit with independent scaling on each input, an output stage with post scaling and true-complement, round/truncate capability, and distributed local storage devices for temporary data and scale factor storage.

The AE operates in a pipelined fashion at a 100 ns staging rate such that new operands enter each stage of the execution pipe every 100 ns. There are a total of six stages from the multiplier input through the adder to the output registers.

The number of stages in the pipeline strongly influences the execution of an algorithm, particularly when recursive functions are involved. Six stages was chosen to provide balance between minimizing programming complexity

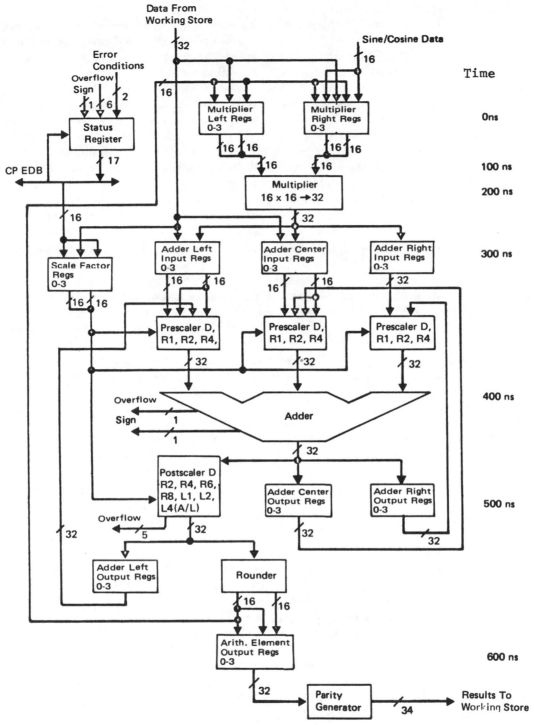

Fig. 2. Arithmetic element.

(minimizing the number of stages) and hardware implementation (optimizing the number of stages [4]).

Control of the adder input scaling and post adder scaling operations is by code words stored in the Scale Factor Registers (SFR). All other AE controls including addressing of the SFR and all other local storage elements, arithmetic operations, and I/O transfers are generated in the Arithmetic Element Controller from the stored micro-

instructions. The microinstructions are read and decoded every 100 ns and provide synchronous controls for all AE's in an AP configuration.

The local storage and processing areas of the AE are shown in Fig. 2 along with their interconnections. Each of the distributed local store register areas contains four 32-bit registers. The flow of data in the AE is either through the Multiplier to the Adder or directly to the

Adder. Adder output data may be looped back to either the Adder or Multiplier inputs or output from the AE Output Registers (AEOR).

The 32-bit data words from Working Store can be input to the Multiplier Registers (MLR or MRR), the Adder Input Registers (ALIR or ACIR), or the Scale Factor Registers (SFR). The SFR, which controls the three adder input prescalers and the postscaler, also has an input from the CP. 16-bit operands may enter the Multiplier Registers from the Sine/Cosine Generator or be fed back from the Adder through the Rounder. The input source selection, as well as read and write address and controls are provided by the AEC for these and all other local storage registers in the AE.

A read operation in the SFR, MLR and MRR selects one of eight 16 bit half words stored in each of these registers. The half words read from the MLF and MRR provide multiplier and multiplicand data inputs to the Multiplier. The full 32-bit Multiplier output is written into the ALIR, Adder Center Input Registers (ACIR), or Adder Right Input Registers (ARIR).

The three inputs to the Adder are selected from pairs of Adder Input and Adder Output Registers. The left input is selected either from the ALIR or Adder Left Output Register (ALOR) for feedback. The same is true for center and right inputs. Each of these inputs is then independently shifted by one of four scale factors: direct (no shift), right 1, right 2, or right 4. The vacated high-order bit positions are filled with propagated signs. Each input may also be inhibited (force zeros). When logical functions are specified by the AEC, the operands are not shifted.

The Adder output data is stored in the ACOR or AROR or is passed through the Postscaler operation providing shifts of direct, left 1, left 2, left 4, right 2, right 4, right 6, or right 8. The vacated high order bits are filled with propagated signs on right shifts.

The output of the Postscaler element can be stored in ALOR and also passed through a Rounder, which can round to 16 bits or pass the full 32. The resultant 16 or 32 bits are stored in the Arithmetic Element Output Registers (AEOR) for transfer back to WS. The rounded 16 bit word can also be fed back to MLR or MRR.

2) *Working Store:* Each AE is supported by a Working Store which consists of two separate $1 K \times 34$ bit $(32 + 2$ parity) memories whose data buses, both input and output, are switchable. This arrangement permits either memory section to communicate with Bulk Store while the other is supporting an AE. The data rate into or out of each Working Store half is 34 bits every 200 ns. Since the data rate from and to the Bulk Store is 34 bits at 100 ns, two Working Stores are interleaved on one Bulk Store data port.

3) *Arithmetic Element Controller:* The AEC controls the AE, as well as Working Store data transfers and the generation of trigonometric coefficients for use in signal processing algorithms. Up to four AE's are controlled by the AEC with all AE's executing a single program on different data sets in parallel. Variations in program execution is provided by conditional operations where each AE selects the function it performs based on a data dependent conditional status bit.

Except for AEC Initial Program Load and task initialization, which are controlled by the CP, the AEC provides full processing control over the Arithmetic Processor, including all AE–WS transfers, and the AP control Store. This frees the CP from signal processing tasks, allowing it to be utilized for supervisory and data management functions.

The AEC consists of three functional areas which combine to provide control over Arithmetic Processor signal processing. They include microinstruction decoding and AE control generation, address and control generation, and the Sine/Cosine Generator. The AP Control Store nominally contains 2048 68-bit instructions $(64 + 4$ parity), which are accessed at a 100 ns rate to provide controls for the Arithmetic Processor.

The address generation section receives Working Store (WS) address and control information from two sources: the decoded microinstruction for transfers to and from the AE; and the Storage Controller (SC) for transfers from the SC. The WS left/right half selection and address source selection are made on a priority basis. Working Store operates at an interleaved 200 ns cycle rate.

The Sine/Cosine Generator operates on a 200 ns cycle rate taking an incremented angle input and converting it to a trigonometric coefficient using a combination of table look up and interpolation techniques.

AEC Microinstruction: The 64-bit AEC microinstruction is divided into two sections. The first 48 bits control all the operations of the pipelined AE every 100 ns cycle. The remaining 16 bits control storage, branching, and Sine/Cosine generation. Since these operations occur at a 200 ns rate, the 16 bits controlling them can be interpreted differently on alternate cycles, effectively increasing the microinstruction length.

The AE control fields (bits 0–47) control the AE pipe of Fig. 2 as follows.

Left Multiplier Input Field (0-2)
  Selects 16-bit multiplicand from MLR.
Right Multiplier Input Field (3-5)
  Selects 16-bit multiplier from MRR.
Multiplier Destination Field (6-9)
  Destines 32-bit multiplier prodict to one of 12 AIR's.
Left Adder Input Field (10-15)
  Selects a 16 or 32-bit operand from ALIR or ALOR. Also controls True/Complement (T/C), Absolute Value and Inhibit functions.
Center Adder Input Field (16-21)
  Selects a 16 or 32-bit operand from ACIR or ACOR. Also controls T/C, Absolute Value and Inhibit functions.
Right Adder Input Field (22-27)
  Selects 32-bit operand from ARIR or AROR. Also

controls T/C, Absolute Value, Inhibit, and Conditional functions.

Scale Factor/Logic Select Field (28–31)

For arithmetic operations (bit 31) this field selects a 16-bit scale factor which controls the four shifters. For logical operations there is no shift and this field specifies the logical operation.

Adder Result Destination Field (32–34)

Selects which register group the adder output is to be destined.

Adder Result Register Field (35–40)

Selects which register within the selected group gets the result and if 16 or 32 bits is to be saved.

Rounder Field (41–43)

Controls the rounder function for output data formats of sign/magnitude, true, complement, and abs. value. Also rounds of 16-bit operands.

Control Field (44–45)

This field causes the setting of AE status and overflow bits.

The storage, branching and Sine/Cosine control fields (bits 48–63) control the remaining AP facilities as follows.

Even cycle

Storage Command Operation (48–52)

Specifies Working Store data transfers. In store operations also specifies the AE source register.

Increment Select (53)

Selects one of two increment registers that can be used to update the storage address.

Address Generation Control (54–55)

Specifies the operation performed to update the storage address.

Address Register Select (56–58)

Selects the storage address source and a pair of increment registers used to address Working Store and update the address.

Branch Operation (59–60)

Specifies the microprogram next address branching function to be performed.

Branch Control Register Select (61–63)

Selects the branch control register used to specify branch address and count on conditional branches.

Odd cycle

Read Destination (48–52)

Selects the destination for Working Store fetch operations.

Sine/Cosine Operation (55–56)

Specifies Sine/Cosine operation and angle update function.

Angle Select (57–58)

Selects the angle and delta angle sources for Sine/Cosine generation.

Sine/Cosine Destination (59–61)

Destines the Sine/Cosine result to one of the MRR's.

C. Bulk Store

Bulk Store (BS) is the primary AU storage medium, providing storage for data buffers, temporary buffers, coefficients, and program parameters. Bulk Store is available in sizes from 16 K to 512 K in increments of 16 K words.

Bulk Store is organized in 64-bit doublewords with 8 error correction code (ECC) bits associated with each doubleword giving 72 bits total per doubleword. The 8 ECC bits provide for correction of all single bit errors and detection of double bit errors.

The Bulk Store operated at an 800 ns cycle time with two 72-bit arrays operating interleaved to achieve an effective 400 ns doubleword rate per Basic Storage Module (BSM). Up to four BSM's may be operating concurrently, providing a total Bulk Store transfer rate of 100 ns per doubleword.

D. Storage Controller

The Storage Controller (SC) is a special purpose processor which transfers data and parameters between Bulk Store and other AU elements.

The primary function of the SC is to page blocks of data between Bulk Store and the AP Working Stores. The SC transfers are scheduled to use one half of Working Store while the AE processes data in the other half of Working Store. This concurrency minimizes AP idle time that would result if data transfers and processing functions were sequential.

During the transfer of data between Bulk Store and Working Store the SC can perform a variety of logical functions on the data. These functions include 1) compressing data when transferring from the AP to BS and expanding data when transferring from BS to AP, 2) scaling data during transfers to provide for maximum precision in data, 3) bit reverse addressing FFT data during transfer to eliminate bit reversal as a processing load, and 4) demultiplexing data during transfer from Bulk Store to AP.

The SC also provides the control capability to page microprograms into the AP and CP Control Stores or programs and data to the CP Program Store.

The SC also performs error correction operations on data read from Bulk Store and generates the error correcting code on Bulk Store write operations.

The SC queues up to four transfer commands and resolves conflicts over the availability of Bulk Store with its priority control logic.

E. Input/Output Channels

The I/O channels are special purpose devices designed to implement channel requirements for each specific application. Digitized analog sensor data from the Input Signal Conditioner is also received through the I/O area.

F. Input Signal Conditioner

The Input Signal Conditioner (ISC) provides the analog sensor interface for acoustic data for the AU. The ISC preprocesses acoustic data before transmission to the Bulk Store.

IV. AP MICROPROGRAMMING

The SPL complex function algorithms are performed in the Arithmetic Processor under microprogram control. Each algorithm or group of similar algorithms is implemented in a microprogram. When the Control Processor, as AU supervisor, determines that an algorithm is to be performed, it transfers the necessary initialization and control parameters for the AP microprogram and initiates execution of the microprogram.

This section presents the control and microprogramming parameters required for microprogram execution. It discusses how these parameters are used by the microprogrammer to implement algorithms. An example is given to show data flow in a signal processing algorithm.

A. Microprogram Parameters

There are a number of control parameters associated with the execution of every microprogram. These parameters are stored in the hardware registers of the AEC during the microprogram execution. This section shows how the microprogram uses the control registers.

1) Branch Registers (BR)

BR

22   31

There are eight 10-bit Branch Registers which give the microprogram addresses used on unconditional branch operations. Branch registers may be required for program sequencing or may be used to provide a means of sharing common code between several routines. Branch addresses are generated from microprogram cross referencing by the microprogram assembler.

2) Branch and Count Registers (BCR)

BCR

Count	Reset		Branch Address	
0	7 8 15		22	31

The eight Branch and Count Registers define microprogram addresses used on conditional branch operations. Branch and Count Registers are used to control loop operations. The Count field is specified by the SPL programmer define the number of points to be processed in a complex function. The reset field specifies a reset value for the Count field allowing a single loop to be reinitialized multiple times in a nested loop application. To process an algorithm N times Count is set to $N - 1$. If the loop is nested the Reset field is also set to $N - 1$.

Branch and Count Registers are also used to provide switches between segments of a program. For example,

the SPL programmer may set the Count field to zero or one to select between two ways of processing an algorithm.

3) Scale Factor Registers (SFR)

The eight SFR's provides the scaling factors for all operations. For some algorithms, the data characteristics are well known beforehand and the microprogrammers will always use a single set of SFR's. For other algorithms the data sets vary in magnitude and the scaling values must be generated just prior to microprogram initiation. These scaling factors are generated by the SPL program, dependent on such conditions as input AGC and AE status indicators for potential overflow.

The SFR has four fields, three for controlling the adder input shifts and one for controlling the output shifter. The input shift controls are data true or complement and shift direct, right 1, right 2, right 4, and inhibit. The output shift controls are direct, left 1, 2, or 4, and right 2, 4, 6, or 8.

4) Address Registers (AR) and Increment Registers (INCR)

The Address Registers and Increment Registers operate in pairs to provide pointers to data sets in Working Store or Program Store. There are a total of eight pairs of these registers.

Four of the AR's may be used for form angles for the Sine/Cosine Generator. Here the 16-bit AR expresses angles from zero to 360 degrees. The first 2-bits represent the quadrant and the remaining bits are 2^{14} divisions within each quadrant. The INCR contains an angle update value. The INCR can be an effective negative value by using a large positive value; for example $-\pi/8$ can be expressed as $+15\pi/8$.

The AR's and INCR's are used to store angles in the FFT process and in bandshifting during some digital filtering processes. For FFT's the initial values of these registers will always be the same at the beginning of a process. For bandshifting, however, the initial value will be the final value from the previous filtering of that channel. Thus the microprogram must store away these registers after some operations.

5) Sine/Cosine Destination Registers (SCDR)

There are four of these registers, one for each of the four AR–INCR pairs which may be used for angle registers. The bits of this register specify which of the AE's are to receive the sine and/or cosine values generated.

6) Decimation Register (DECR)

This register is used to select decimation values generally used after digital filters.

B. Program Phases

There are two phases of AP microprograms:

1) Initialization
2) Execution.

During the Initialization phase the CP loads its control registers in the AEC and the AE's. The microprogram uses a pointer to Program Store to access the list of parameters (i.e., complex function command) it needs for the program to be executed. One of the parameters loaded

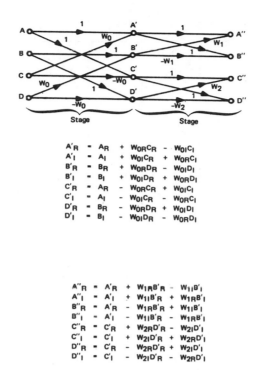

$$A'_R = A_R + W_{0R}C_R - W_{0I}C_I$$
$$A'_I = A_I + W_{0I}C_R + W_{0R}C_I$$
$$B'_R = B_R + W_{0R}D_R - W_{0I}D_I$$
$$B'_I = B_I + W_{0I}D_R + W_{0R}D_I$$
$$C'_R = A_R - W_{0R}C_R + W_{0I}C_I$$
$$C'_I = A_I - W_{0I}C_R - W_{0R}C_I$$
$$D'_R = B_R - W_{0R}D_R + W_{0I}D_I$$
$$D'_I = B_I - W_{0I}D_R - W_{0R}D_I$$

$$A''_R = A'_R + W_{1R}B'_R - W_{1I}B'_I$$
$$A''_I = A'_I + W_{1I}B'_R + W_{1R}B'_I$$
$$B''_R = A'_R - W_{1I}B'_R + W_{1I}B'_I$$
$$B''_I = A'_I - W_{1I}B'_R - W_{1R}B'_I$$
$$C''_R = C'_R + W_{2R}D'_R - W_{2I}D'_I$$
$$C''_I = C'_I + W_{2I}D'_R + W_{2R}D'_I$$
$$D''_R = C'_R - W_{2I}D'_R + W_{2I}D'_I$$
$$D''_I = C'_I - W_{2I}D'_R - W_{2R}D'_I$$

Fig. 3. Four point FFT equations.

into the Microprogram Address Register during initialization is the starting address of the algorithm to be executed. The final step of initialization is an unconditional branch to the algorithm microprogram.

The Execution phase accomplishes the signal processing functions. In microprogramming a pipelined processor such as the AE, there are generally a few microinstructions required initially to get the process started (get the pipe "primed") and at the end, a few final microinstructions to get the last results put away. But the main body of the microprogram is expected to be a compact, high-speed processing loop. The key to efficient AE microprogramming lies in keeping the pipeline fully utilized. Many signal processing algorithms, such as the FFT butterfly, inherently keep the pipeline full. This is usually the case whenever complex algebra is used in the algorithm because it generally has a high computational load and consequently is not very susceptible to bandwidth limitations. In other cases the pipeline can be kept full by interleaving related calculations. This technique is used in the recursive filter algorithms where calculations on points from successive filter stages are interleaved.

C. AP Microprogramming Example

The following section demonstrates the microprogramming of an algorithm in the AP. The execution phase is described using flow charts and AP microprogramming forms to illustrate data flow through the AE with respect to microinstruction execution cycles.

An example of a complex function which is extensively used in acoustic and other signal processing is the FFT butterfly. A four point butterfly is used. Fig. 3 lists the equations involved in the AU to generate all FFT's with an even number of stages. An eight point, three stage algorithm is combined with the four point algorithm to implement FFT's with an odd number of stages.

Exact details of initialization for this problem depend on the size of the FFT problem to be executed. An AP microprogramming form showing the first 32 execution cycles appears in Fig. 4. Note that the multiplier becomes fully loaded after 4 cycles and the adder after 8 cycles. This algorithm is an example of a complex function which makes maximum use of the AE multiplier and adder bandwidths. The first 16 microinstructions are required to completely fill the AE pipeline. The next 16 comprise the execution loop for this complex function. To perform a 1024 point FFT this loop would be executed 256 times on each of 5 passes. Between passes rescaling operations are performed to prevent arithmetic overflow during the next pass.

The inner loop execution time for a 1024 point FFT in a one AE configuration is 2048 microseconds plus an initialization time of 6.2 μs. A total of about 70 microinstructions are required to implement the complete algorithm.

The four point FFT butterfly has been programmed and simulated. Digital filtering, FFT weighting, gram thresholding, and bearing computation programs have also been programmed and simulated. Results demonstrate that the pipeline can be kept fully utilized.

V. CONCLUSION

Technology has evolved to the state where programmable processor designs can compete with hardwired implementations in real time high speed processing. The use of programmable processors in signal processing provides the user with the much needed flexibility to adapt to new algorithms and applications.

Cycle	Read WS	Load MLR	Start Multiply	Load ALIR	Load ACIR	Load ARIR	Start Add	Load ALOR	Load AEOR	Write WS
0	D(n)									
1										
2	B(n)	D(n)								
3			$W_{0R}D_R(n)$							
4	C(n)		$W_{0I}D_I(n)$	B(n)						
5			$W_{0R}D_I(n)$		$W_{0R}D_R(n)$					
6	A(n)	C(n)	$W_{0I}D_R(n)$			$W_{0I}D_I(n)$				
7			$W_{0R}C_R(n)$		$W_{0R}D_I(n)$		$B_R(n)+W_{0R}D_R(n)-W_{0I}D_I(n)$			
8			$W_{0I}C_I(n)$	A(n)		$W_{0I}D_R(n)$	$B_R(n)-W_{0R}D_R(n)+W_{0I}D_I(n)$			
9		$B_R'(n)$	$W_{0R}C_I(n)$		$W_{0R}C_R(n)$		$B_I(n)+W_{0R}D_I(n)+W_{0I}D_R(n)$			
10		$D_R'(n)$	$W_{0I}C_R(n)$			$W_{0I}C_I(n)$	$B_I(n)-W_{0R}D_I(n)-W_{0I}D_R(n)$			
11		$B_I'(n)$	$W_{1R}B_R'(n)$		$W_{0R}C_I(n)$		$A_R(n)+W_{0R}C_R(n)-W_{0I}C_I(n)$			
12		$D_I'(n)$	$W_{1I}B_I'(n)$			$W_{0I}C_R(n)$	$A_R(n)-W_{0R}C_R(n)+W_{0I}C_I(n)$			
13			$W_{1R}B_I'(n)$		$W_{1R}B_R'(n)$		$A_I(n)+W_{0R}C_I(n)+W_{0I}C_R(n)$	$A_R'(n)$		
14			$W_{1I}B_R'(n)$			$W_{1I}B_I'(n)$	$A_I(n)-W_{0R}C_I(n)-W_{0I}C_R(n)$	$C_R'(n)$		
15			$W_{2R}D_I'(n)$		$W_{1R}B_I'(n)$		$A_R'(n)+W_{1R}B_R'(n)-W_{1I}B_I'(n)$	$A_I'(n)$		
16	D(n+k)		$W_{2I}D_I'(n)$			$W_{1I}B_R'(n)$	$A_R'(n)-W_{1R}B_R'(n)+W_{1I}B_I'(n)$	$C_I'(n)$		
17			$W_{2R}D_R'(n)$		$W_{2R}D_R'(n)$		$A_I'(n)+W_{1R}B_I'(n)+W_{1I}B_R'(n)$		$A_R''(n)$	
18	B(n+k)	D(n+k)	$W_{2I}D_R'(n)$			$W_{2I}D_I(n)$	$A_I'(n)-W_{1R}B_I'(n)-W_{1I}B_R'(n)$		$B_R''(n)$	
19			$W_{0R}D_R(n+k)$		$W_{2R}D_I'(n)$				$A_I''(n)$	
20	C(n+k)		$W_{0I}D_I(n+k)$	B(n+k)		$W_{2I}D_R'(n)$			$B_I''(n)$	
21			$W_{0R}D_I(n+k)$		$W_{0R}D_R(n+k)$				$C_R''(n)$	
22	A(n+k)	C(n+k)	$W_{0I}D_R(n+k)$			$W_{0I}D_I(n+k)$			$D_R''(n)$	
23			$W_{0R}C_R(n+k)$		$W_{0R}D_I(n3k)$				$C_I''(n)$	
24			$W_{0I}C_I(n+k)$	A(n+k)		$W_{0I}D_R(n+k)$			$D_I''(n)$	$A''(n)$
25		$B_R'(n+k)$	$W_{0R}C_R(n+k)$		$W_{0R}C_R(n+k)$					
26		$D_R'(n+k)$	$W_{0I}C_I(n+k)$			$W_{0I}C_I(n+k)$				$B''(n)$
27		$B_I'(n+k)$	$W_{1R}B_R'(n+k)$		$W_{0R}C_I(n+k)$					
28		$D_I'(n+k)$	$W_{1I}B_I'(n+k)$			$W_{0I}C_R(n+k)$				$C''(n)$
29			$W_{1R}B_I'(n+k)$		$W_{1R}B_R'(n+k)$			$A_R'(n+k)$		
30			$W_{1I}B_R'(n+k)$			$W_{1I}B_I'(n+k)$		$C_R'(n+k)$		$D''(n)$
31			$W_{2R}D_R'(n+k)$		$W_{1R}B_I'(n+k)$			$A_I'(n+k)$		

Fig. 4. AP microprogramming form-four point FFT.

This paper has described the architecture of an acoustic analyzer unit that combines multiple parallel pipelined multiply-adder units into an efficient signal processor. The analyzer provides modular growth with throughputs of 10×10^6 to 40×10^6 multiplies per second. Microprogram control and careful attention to system organization provide a flexible processing capability and maximum utilization of existing hardware.

ACKNOWLEDGMENT

The authors wish to acknowledge the contributions of many individuals in the development and verification of the Analyzer Unit concepts. In particular the authors wish to acknowledge the work of R. B. Kmetz, director of the design effort; D. E. Wallis, principal designer of the Control Processor; K. B. Baxter, principal logic designer of the Arithmetic Processor; and R. L. Harper, who assisted in the microprogramming verification of many signal processing algorithms. Numerous other people contributed to the microprogramming and simulation of the Analyzer Unit design.

REFERENCES

[1] G. D. Hornbuckle and E. I. Ancona, "The LX-1 microprocessor and its application to real time signal processing," *IEEE Trans. Comput. (Special Issue on Computer Arithmetic)*, vol. C-19, pp. 710–720, Aug. 1970.
[2] B. Gold, I. L. Lebow, P. G. McHugh, and C. M. Rader, "The FDP, a fast programmable signal processor," *IEEE Trans. Comput.*, vol. C-20, pp. 33–38, Jan. 1971.
[3] A. V. Oppenheim and C. J. Weinstein, "Effects of finite register length in digital filtering and the fast Fourier transform," *Proc. IEEE* vol. 60, pp. 957–976, Aug. 1972.
[4] T. G. Hallen and M. J. Flynn, "Pipelining of arithmetic functions," *IEEE Trans. Comput.* (Short Notes), vol. C-21, pp. 880–886, Aug. 1972.

Parallel And Sequential Trade-Offs In Signal Processing Computers

BERNARD GOLD

M.I.T. Lincoln Laboratory
Lexington, Massachusetts

Abstract

Digital signal processing algorithms have already had a noticeable effect on computer design. However, efficient computer design is based on so many trade-offs that often a simple-looking structure is neglected in favor of a trickier, more elegant looking structure. For example, because of the parallel processing inherent in the FFT (fast Fourier transform), it seems natural to assume that a signal processing computer have parallelism. While this approach is justified in certain cases, it is not the best approach in all cases. It is the main intention in this paper to examine the effect of technology, money constraints, environmental issues, and, above all, application areas. By examining 3 specific designs and their conditions in some detail, it is shown how the situation greatly controls the feasibility of a given design. A part of this paper will focus on the evaluation of one specific device for use as a speech processing terminal. The results of this particular study indicate strongly that high speed circuits plus a very simple mainly sequential computer structure best fits a set of problems which heretofore were thought to require parallelism.

I. Introduction

Since computers are general purpose devices and are therefore capable of satisfying a variety of diverse needs, the art of specifying a 'good' computer structure becomes a 'black art', often dependent on the background and whims of a particular designer. In recent years, signal processing computers have been designed and constructed to speed up the processing of speech, sonar and radar signals with each designer going his own route with the result that a rather wide spectrum of architectures now exist. Since the design and successful construction of a sophisticated piece of hardware such as a computer is usually a costly and time-consuming effort, it behooves us to examine carefully the premises determining such work. Within the past five years, the author has been involved in 3 signal processing computer designs; one of these was constructed, one is being constructed, and the third has not yet been constructed. In addition, I have observed at close quarters the design and construction of a fourth computer at Lincoln Laboratory and have a passing familiarity with two or three other such efforts. I will try to sketch out as much background and technical details as seem reasonable, with the hope of drawing a few general conclusions from this rather small sample as to how this overall problem should be approached.

II. The Fast Digital Processor

In the mid 1960's there was sizeable activity in the field of speech bandwidth compression with much of this activity going into computer simulation of candidate systems. While many useful results were obtained via these simulations, the non-real time aspect proved disappointing and often led to erroneous conclusions. In 1967, I proposed that Lincoln Laboratory build a signal processing computer which, in conjunction with our existing computer facility, could serve as a real-time test bed for new speech processing systems. At that time, a great deal of interest had been aroused about two specific digital signal processing algorithms, recursive digital filtering and the FFT (fast Fourier transform). Since both algorithms were applicable to speech processors, they strongly influenced the computer structure. In addition, however, since a) there are a great many other algorithms related to speech and b) the 'home' for the computer was to be as part of a facility it seemed very desirable to include much general purpose capability in the design. The result was the FDP[1] (fast digital processor); its basic structure is shown in Figure 1. It's features were:

1. The use of the fastest commercially available logic family at the time, 4 nanosecond ECL (emitter-coupled logic).
2. 4 arithmetic elements, each with full array multipliers.
3. Instruction pipelining.
4. Two memories for data and a separate memory for instructions.
5. Dual instructions.
6. A cycle time of 150 nanoseconds.

In 1967, both the high speed circuits and the parallelism were necessary in order to fulfill the requirement that real-time simulation of speech systems be possible.

Thus far we can summarize the above experience by noting that to build a new computer one must have a) a specific goal, b) a 'home' for the computer and c) available components appropriate for the problem at hand.

The FDP was completed in 1970 and is presently still running as part of our facility. It is interesting to trace briefly the history of its use. About the time it was completed, interest in speech processing had fallen to a low point among the various sponsoring agencies. Thus, although the computer had a home, it did not immediately have a 'mission'. It turned out that the 2 largest projects for which it was initially used were both radar projects. It performed very adequately in these roles primarily because a) its general purpose nature and b) the

Reprinted from *Nat. Telecommun. Conf. Rec.*, Dec. 2-4, 1974, pp. 491-495.

prevalence of the FFT in radar signal processing problems. In 1971, the Advanced Research Projects Agency (ARPA) initiated an effort directed towards speech recognition and for the past several years the FDP has served as an acoustic processor for the system built by Lincoln for this project. In 1972, re-awakened interest on the part of various government agencies in speech compression systems made it possible for the FDP to play the role for which it was originally specified. At present, it is the central component of an existing real-time speech processing evaluation facility, as indicated in Figure 2. Through the teletype console, new speech processing programs can be accessed from the drum and entered into FDP program memory in several milliseconds; meanwhile, the speakers can continue to carry on an uninterrupted conversation with only a small 'glich' while the new program is being loaded.

III. The LX-1 Computer

Another computer built at Lincoln while the FDP was being built was the LX-1[2]. The primary motivation for this work was the furtherance of partitioning schemes for LSI development. There was an underlying premise that a general purpose structure led to a fairly regular logic layout and would thus be more efficiently partitioned. The 'home' for this device was the TSP (terminal support processor), an interactive graphical facility. ECL circuits were used because the designers had long range plans to develop LSI technology for these circuits. So far, no signal processing motives have appeared. It turned out, however, that the conceived structure was thought, because of its speed, to be applicable to a variety of signal processing problems, and as an exercise, Ancona programmed a vocoder analysis scheme on the LX-1.

The LX-1 configuration is shown in Figure 3. This machine features a 16 register bussing system with function boxes, such as adders, multipliers, etc. hung on the bus. Memory is treated like a function box with one bus going to the memory address register. The LX-1 was designed to be a micro-processor with control information residing in a fixed memory with 64 bit instruction length. Data word length is 16 bits. A single instruction normally contains 3 four-bit address fields plus a specified function; this means that 2 source registers and one destination register can be specified for a given operation (e.g., $R_n + R_m \rightarrow R_p$) where n, m and p each select one of the 16 registers.

The LX-1 has a faster instruction cycle than the FDP but less parallelism, despite the fact that the same logic family was used for both computers. This illustrates the point that computer speed decreases with increased parallelism. This point may seem to violate common sense, since, after all, the simplest case of parallelism is to have two identical computers. However, useful parallelism almost always involves some form of communications between the parallel components and this inevitably costs money and time.

IV. The Lincoln Signal Processor

A computer which was designed but not built is the LSP[3] (Lincoln Signal Processor). Although it was generally agreed that the LSP design was quite innovative and elegant, and an excellent vehicle for demonstrating 2 nsec ECL hardware, a brief discussion of its history may be educational. The original purpose of the LSP was as an airborne radar signal processor. This led to the notion that the word length should be 12 bits, for compactness. At some point in the project, it was decided to perform airborne experiments using a drone airplane with processing taking place on the ground. Thus, the mission and the 'home' disappeared and the computer design was halted. However, it is not really that easy to turn off a group of dedicated computer designers. Eventually, another mission was found, namely, to use the LSP as a flexible post-processor in a large radar digital signal processing environment for anti-ballistic missile defense. For a period of several months, intensive work was done on defining the appropriate post-processing algorithms and, in parallel, updating the LSP structure. What emerged was a most interesting computer design as sketched in Figure 4. The 12 bit byte was changed to 16 bits with a register consisting of two bytes. The function boxes were generally dual arithmetic devices (e.g., 2 16 bit multipliers). The general registers of the LX-1 were replaced by fast memory elements arranged as a 64 register by 32 bit memory. The three address structures of the LX-1 was kept. This, plus the two byte format resulted in an architecture which was about twice as efficient for performing the FFT as the FDP. Since the hardware was about twice as fast, this resulted in a four-fold increase of FFT speed compared to the FDP. Digital filtering was speeded up by about the same factor. It is interesting to note that this architectural speed-up occurred even though the number of effective arithmetic elements was reduced from four to two; the reason for this can be traced to the three address format for the fast scratch memory plus the three bus system.

A truly innovative feature of the LSP design was the use made of the two byte format for floating point computation. By using one byte for the mantissa and the other byte for exponent and by providing for simultaneous use of half of two separate function boxes, it was found that floating point arithmetic could be programmed very rapidly with almost no increase in dedicated floating point hardware. As far as we know, this is the first example of a computer design where the same hardware was configured to be especially efficient for both fixed point signal processing operations plus more general floating point operations.

Because of its proposed application to high performance radar systems, a fast input-output port was deemed a requirement; this was arranged as a bus-oriented connection with the stipulation that fast block transfers from the ports to scratch memory blocked other simultaneous uses of the machine. This resulted in a 320 megabit per second transfer rate.

Unfortunately, the LSP design did not turn out to be an optimum match to the radar post-processing algorithms, since these algorithms required very little signal processing or floating point programs. Therefore its construction was again deferred. It is our opinion that the LSP could be an appreciable improvement over the FDP as part of our laboratory facility since it is faster, cheaper, smaller, more easily programmed and more readily reproducible than the FDP.

V.   The Digital Voice Terminal (DVT)

The final computer design to be discussed derived from recent work done at Lincoln Laboratory in connection with the continuing need of various government agencies for narrow-band digital speech processors. At the present moment and probably in the foreseeable future, a variety of agencies, laboratories and algorithms will be competing for predominance in this area. Meanwhile, as new speech communication channels become available, decisions must be made on which algorithms to implement as hardware. It seems that these contradictory requirements of an evolving field and the need for fairly long term fixed decisions can best be met by incorporating flexibility into the hardware designs. There are some other good reasons for flexibility (i.e., general purpose capability).

1.   Speech processing consists of a diversity of algorithms; typically a given system may incorporate 14 to 20 algorithms each of which are quite different structurally and could lead to different hardware implementation.

2.   Special environments, such as the ARPA network, may require a speech processor which is adaptive to the traffic flow on the communication network.

Based on such considerations there presently exists a fairly strong bias in the speech processing establishments that any hardware device intended for field use should incorporate some programmability. We now come back to the very interesting question of the appropriate structure for such a device and bring forth the following arguments:

1.   If a versatile speech processor can be built which is fast enough to avoid parallelism, a great deal of benefits derive. A sequential machine is probably more cost efficient if it is required to program many diverse algorithms (and for speech this is the case). Sequential programming is always many times simpler than parallel programming. Since sequential machines tend to have greater logic regularity, LSI techniques should go further. To summarize , then, when we discovered that 2 nanosecond ECL hardware could be used to construct a flexible (programmable), sufficiently powerful (comparable to the FDP), sequential (thus easily programmed) machine for relatively low cost and size (about 500 dual-in-line 16 pin packages, parts cost less than $10,000) which could be foreseen to be reduced by 4:1 via LSI in 3-5 years we enthusiastically looked for and found support and are now in the process of building it.

The structure of the DVT[4] is given in Figure 5. The organization centers about a 2 bus system with four major registers (A the accumulator, X the index register, P the program counter and B the input-output registers). Also connected to the bus are a fast 512 register (by 16 bits) data memory and a 1024 x 16 program memory, and an ALU (arithmetic-logic unit). In addition, the machine can access a 200 x 16 somewhat slower memory as a peripheral device. One bus establishes a path from the outputs of the four major registers and the ALU to the data memory input. The other bus establishes a path between the ALU and the four major registers with the data memory output communicating to the registers through the ALU.

The machine cycle includes 3 levels of overlap. These are a) instruction fetch (53 nanoseconds), b) instruction decoding and data memory reading and c) ALU operations or data memory writing (53 nanoseconds). The timing can be better understood via several examples but in order to do this we must first define some of the instruction repertoire.

Instructions reside in 16 bit registers; with the exception of the input-output instructions, the format consists of a 6 bit OP-code, a one bit index control and a 9 bit address as shown in Figure 5. ALU instructions consist of transactions between data memory M_d and one of the major registers, with the Y field defining the memory address for x = 0 and with Y plus the contents of the X register defining the address for x = 1. For the set of jump instructions, Y represents the jump location in program memory and the x bit determines whether or not the contents of the program counter are saved at a fixed location in data memory. Also, jumps have an optional variation to either 'kill' or 'not kill' the next instruction.

A typical sequence of instructions is shown in Figure 6. An instruction generally consists of 3 major epochs a) the fetch from the program memory, b) decoding of the instruction and reading of data memory into a buffer and c) either an ALU operation or a data memory write. Notice that in Figure 6, instruction 2 is able to write the information generated by the ALU in instruction 1; also that the read in instruction 3 doesn't overlap with the write of instruction 2. Notice also that instruction 4, a jump conditioned on the contents of A, goes into effect with instruction 5.

There is no need for further details in order to make our main points. Simply stated, speech processing algorithms are composed partly of structure signal processing algorithms such as digital filtering the FFT and correlation. Such algorithms could benefit from some form of arithmetic and memory parallelism in a computer structure. But also they are composed of a collection of rather messy little algorithms which are difficult to categorize (such as pitch extraction, parameter coding, least mean square curve fitting, etc.) and are probably most economically handled through an old fashioned general purpose sequential machine. It has turned out in the DVT program that the most reasonable way to build a versatile speech processor is by designing as much raw speed as possible into a sequential structure. It is also true that increased speed and increased circuit integration supplement each other so that aiming for more speed helps direct one towards greater compactness and vice versa.

References:

1.   B. Gold, I. L. Lebow, P. McHugh, C. Rader, "The Fast Digital Processor - a Programmable High Speed Signal Processing Computer," IEEE Trans. on Computers, January 1971.

2.   G. D. Hornbuckle, E. I. Ancona, "The LX-1 Microprocessor and its Application to Real-Time Signal Processing," IEEE Trans. on Computers, August 1970.

3.   P. E. Blankenship, B. Gold, P. McHugh, C. J. Weinstein, "Design Study of the Advanced Signal Processor," TN 1972-17, MIT Lincoln Laboratory, April 27, 1972.

4. A. J. McLaughlin, B. Gold, P. E. Blankenship, "The Versatile Micro Processor, VMP" private communication.

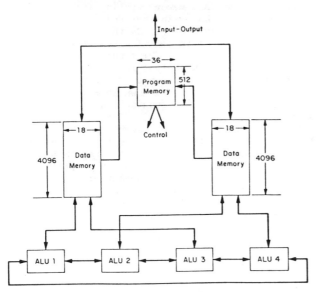

OVERALL STRUCTURE OF THE FDP

Figure 1

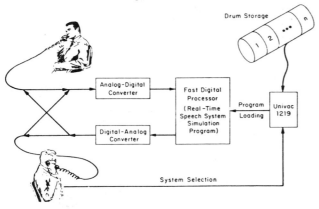

REAL-TIME CONVERSATIONAL EVALUATION OF SIMULATED SPEECH COMPRESSION SYSTEMS

Figure 2

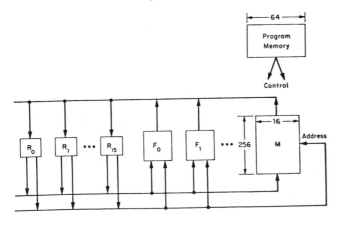

LX-1 MICROPROCESSOR

Figure 3

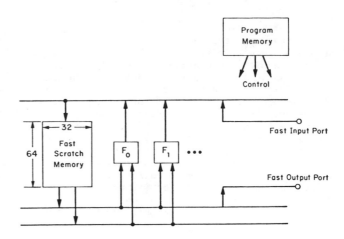

THE LINCOLN SIGNAL PROCESSOR

Figure 4

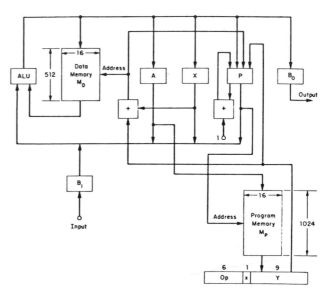

THE DIGITAL VOICE TERMINAL

Figure 5

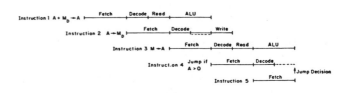

EXAMPLE OF TIMING OF COMPUTER CYCLES

Figure 6

Special-Purpose Hardware for Digital Filtering

STANLEY L. FREENY, MEMBER, IEEE

Invited Paper

Abstract—A tutorial summary of the basic considerations necessary for designing custom digital filter hardware is presented. Emphasis is placed on fundamental principles and not on promotion of a specific design approach. The paper begins with a review of quantization (finite-accuracy arithmetic) effects. This is followed by a discussion of the elements of digital filters and how they are constructed, a review of the important technologies available, and a discussion of how the elements are put together to make a system. As examples of recent vintage hardware, the final section discusses three multipliers suitable for use in digital filters.

I. INTRODUCTION

THE STEADILY decreasing cost of digital integrated circuits is causing more and more people to take advantage of the flexibility and the ability to realize complicated algorithms with high precision afforded by digital signal-processing techniques. At present, hardware for digital processing tends to fall into one of two categories: that which operates at medium speed, is flexible, and can be used to implement a variety of complicated algorithms; and that which operates at high speed, is efficient, and is dedicated to the implementation of a single algorithm. Equipment of the former type is almost invariably programmable. That of the latter may be programmable in a limited way, but is often hard wired. Undoubtedly, the future will see a merging

Manuscript received September 10, 1974; revised October 29, 1974.
The author is with Bell Laboratories, Holmdel, N.J. 07733.

of these two camps, but for the time being they are distinguishable.

This paper will confine itself to the latter category, i.e., hardware for the efficient and economical real-time implementation of simple algorithms. Specifically, the class of algorithms will be limited to that associated with digital filtering. This class is characterized by the input/output relation

$$y_n = \sum_{i=0}^{M} \alpha_i x_{n-i} - \sum_{j=1}^{N} \beta_j y_{n-j} \tag{1}$$

where x_n is input sequence and y_n is output sequence, and the α's and β's are the filter coefficients.

Clearly, from (1), the fundamental constituents of digital filter hardware are simply adders, multipliers, and delay elements. However, questions of what type of arithmetic to use, whether to use serial or parallel architecture, what technology to employ, how to handle overflow problems, etc., combine to make the job of building a special-purpose digital filter a complex one, indeed. In point of fact, clear-cut answers to these questions and others like them do not exist. This is due partly to the inherent complexity of the subject and partly to the fact that the field of digital integrated circuits is changing so rapidly as to make the establishment of any technological ground rules very difficult. Be that as it may,

Reprinted from *Proc. IEEE*, vol. 63, pp. 633–648, Apr. 1975.

this paper will attempt to review the general principles, rules of thumb, and points of view that do exist. There are two basic approaches to the construction of digital filters: 1) the completely custom approach, where all pieces of the hardware are explicitly tailored to a specific application; and 2) the "building-block" approach, where a small family of IC chips can be used to perform a variety of different tasks. If the particular application is sizable enough to require a high-volume production run, then, clearly, the first approach is warranted. In situations where high-production volume is obtained only by considering several different applications at once, then the building-block method will be of greater interest. Since these two approaches can lead to somewhat different conclusions concerning the hardware, a distinction between them will be made from time to time throughout the paper.

The general tenor of the paper is tutorial. It is meant to be of greatest use to those readers with a mainly theoretical or software background who desire to learn more about the hardware aspects of digital filtering. Therefore, much introductory material is included which can be profitably skipped by readers with greater familiarity with the subject. The paper is quite specifically not intended to give one a "cookbook" recipe for building a digital filter. The present rapid progress in digital technology would make such an attempt obsolete by the time it reached print. Emphasis is placed instead on a discussion of basic principles which are to some extent technology independent.

The paper begins with a number of important considerations not obvious from (1). This is followed in turn by a discussion of the elements of digital filters and how they are realized with digital logic, a review of the important digital IC technologies available, a discussion of how the elements are put together to make a system, and, finally, some examples of digital filter hardware of recent vintage.

II. Some Basic Considerations

If one were to draw from (1) a block diagram composed of adders, multipliers, and delay elements, the result would look like Fig. 1. This is known as the *direct* form of a digital filter.

But, strictly speaking, (1) does not apply to digital filters without modification; what it does describe are *discrete-time* or *sampled-data* filters, in which only time is discrete and the other quantities are continuous. When applied to digital filters, it is necessary that all the terms of (1) be expressed with digital words of finite length, i.e., they must be *quantized*. Were it not for this requirement, the order in which the airthmetic operations of (1) are performed would be immaterial and the direct form of Fig. 1 would suffice for all digital filters. Such is not the case, however, and in practice the number of bits of word length used to represent various quantities in (1) has a strong effect on the amount of hardware required to build the corresponding digital filter. Therefore, this section is devoted to a brief review of the consequences of quantizing the items of (1), with emphasis on hardware considerations.

A. Forms of Digital Filters

Because the order in which the computations of (1) are carried out matters, a surprising profusion of digital filter forms different from Fig. 1 have been suggested in which various forms can differ markedly with respect to the amount of hardware required to meet a given set of performance cri-

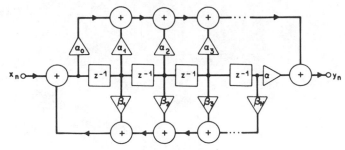

Fig. 1. Direct form.

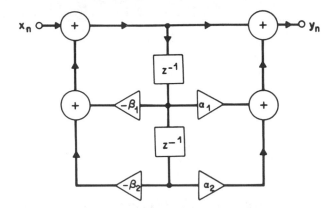

Fig. 2. Recursive second-order section.

teria. The study of different forms of digital filters is still being actively pursued and little in the way of general remarks can be made about the relative advantages and disadvantages of specific forms for particular applications. However, two generic forms deserve mention because of their extensive use, both in theoretical studies and in general-purpose computer and special-purpose hardware realizations. These are the basic second-order section (Fig. 2) and the finite-impulse response (FIR) filter. The latter is simply the direct form of Fig. 1 with the recursive coefficients (β's) set to zero. FIR filters are useful because they can produce digital filters with exactly linear phase and because FIR design techniques have been devised for a number of special applications [1].

The second-order section of Fig. 2 can be used to realize any desired filter by cascading (Fig. 3) or paralleling (Fig. 4) the basic sections. The filters so produced have proved in practice to be relatively economical of required coefficient and data word accuracy, and hence of required hardware. Moreover, such filters are not difficult to design since the values of the coefficients can be quickly determined once the pole-zero configuration of the transfer function is known. This allows classical analog filter design techniques to be easily adapted to the design of filters of the cascade and parallel forms [2]. For these reasons, the basic second-order section has assumed much importance in digital filter work to this point and will therefore be assumed, unless stated otherwise, in subsequent discussions that require reference to a specific form.

B. Quantization Effects

Let us now review in a bit more detail the results of quantizing the various terms of (1).

1) Coefficient Quantization: First, it is necessary to express the coefficients (α's and β's) of (1) with finite-length words and this places constraints on the locations of transfer function singularities. Coefficient accuracy generally enters the digital

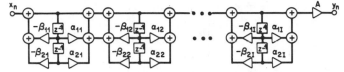

Fig. 3. Cascade form.

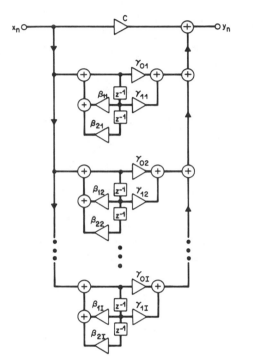

Fig. 4. Parallel form.

filter design procedure as follows. A design is first obtained which yields essentially infinite-accuracy coefficients. By whatever process is available (usually trial and error), the coefficient words are shortened until the minimum lengths are found which still satisfy the original filter specifications. Coefficient length is an important parameter since the amount of required multiplier hardware is more or less proportional to the number of coefficient bits needed.

Different filter forms can differ substantially in the amount of coefficient accuracy required to achieve a given filter transfer function within a specified tolerance. In particular, the direct form of Fig. 1 suffers in this respect when compared to other forms. For example, the parallel and cascade forms require the same number of adders, multipliers, and delay elements as the direct form, but they generally produce filters with shorter coefficient words for the same transfer function tolerance. Another form which appears to be particularly thrifty of coefficient word length is the wave digital filter of Fettweis [3], although this form generally requires more adders and memory elements than either the parallel or the cascade form. Typical (although not universal) values of coefficient word length are 8-12 bits for parallel, cascade, and FIR filters and somewhat less (perhaps as low as 1-4 bits) for the wave digital filters.

As already stated, a digital filter is customarily designed by first discovering the minimum order filter which will meet the transfer function tolerance specifications with exact coefficients. When the coefficients are shortened, there is quite often a tradeoff between coefficient accuracy and filter order insofar as the required total number of multiplier bits is concerned. For example, suppose a particular design produces

an eighth-order cascade filter with 10-bit coefficients. The total number of multiplier bits is

4 second-order sections × 4 multipliers/section

× 10 bits/multiplier = 160 bits.

It is quite possible that by increasing the order to ninth, only 8-bit coefficients will be required. In this event, the total becomes $4\frac{1}{2} \times 4 \times 8 = 144$ bits. This sort of result will generally produce a hardware saving in custom designs tailored to a specific application. It is less likely to produce a saving when using universally applicable chips where coefficient bits come in groups of perhaps 4 bits each.

2) Data Quantization: With regard to data word quantization (x's and y's of (1)), the filter input sequence itself must first be expressed by digital words of fixed length. If this sequence was obtained by encoding an analog signal, as is quite often the case, then an error (noise) of mean-square value $\delta^2/12$ (where δ is amplitude corresponding to least significant bit of data word) is incurred at the outset. This error is thus inversely proportional to the data word length, being reduced 6 dB by each additional bit used. However, a long initial data word length is gained only by using high-accuracy encoders (analog–digital converters), which can be quite expensive. On the other hand, the digital filter is often imbedded in a system where analog signals are converted to digital form for reasons other than to perform digital filtering; therefore, determination of the required encoding accuracy is not necessarily part of the digital filter design, nor should the cost of such encoding necessarily be considered part of the cost of the digital filter.

3) Roundoff Error: Not only must the data word be of fixed length initially, but its length must be controlled throughout the computations of (1). Since an M-bit word times an N-bit word produces an $(M + N)$-bit product, in all but low-order FIR filters the data word will grow unmanageably unless it is shortened by rounding or truncation after each arithmetic operation (or small group of arithmetic operations). In most applications it is found convenient to use a fixed data word length throughout the digital filter computations and to keep reshortening the word to this length as various arithmetic operations cause it to grow. Each time it is done, this shortening process produces an error which, regardless of whether it comes about from truncating or rounding, is called *roundoff error (noise)*. It has been found that under most circumstances, roundoff error may be safely modeled the same way as quantization error, namely, as an uncorrelated additive noise of mean-square value $\delta^2/12$, where δ is amplitude associated with the least significant bit of the retained data word [4]–[6]. In a complex filter involving many multiplications, the roundoff error will often increase the noise component manyfold over the initial encoding error. This is combated, as it is in any sequence of numerical computations, by temporarily increasing the length of the data word for the duration of the computations. The extra bits effectively absorb the roundoff noise and the filter produces an output in which the noise is not unduly increased over that which was present in the input.[1] The hardware cost to provide these extra bits manifests itself by an increase in the required

---

[1] It should be noted that in cases where the filter output word is made equal in length to the initial input word, the final rounding step which accomplishes this produces a roundoff error equal in mean-square value to that incurred in the initial encoding of the signal. Hence the overall noise after filtering can be no less than 3 dB greater than the initial encoding noise. This fact is often overlooked.

data storage capacity, by increased adder and multiplier hardware in parallel-data systems, and by an increased operating speed (clock rate) in serial-data systems.

As to how many extra bits are required in any given application, there is again a variation among different digital filter forms. It is difficult to make general statements about this. However, in the case of the often used cascade form of Fig. 3, the order in which the sections are placed generally has a strong effect on the number of extra bits required and algorithms have been devised to find the optimum ordering for a given transfer function [4].

4) Limit Cycles: Another consequence of rounding the data word after multiplication is that most configurations in which recursive terms of (1) are present (i.e., that contain feedback) are capable of producing a stable periodic nonzero output for zero or constant input. Such outputs are called *limit cycles* (often *small-scale limit cycles* to distinguish them from large-scale limit cycles to be discussed below).

Although the mechanism by which limit cycles are produced is essentially the same as that which produces roundoff error, and is therefore well understood, recursive digital filters of even modest complexity can produce limit cycles of surprising richness and variety whose magnitudes are difficult to predict except by direct simulation [7]. Although much useful work has been done to estimate and bound [8] the magnitude of limit cycles for particular classes of filters, the complexity of the subject has thus far thwarted the creation of any generally applicable theory. It has been this author's experience that in filters of practical interest, the magnitude of the limit cycles is rarely greater than that of roundoff noise and a solution for the latter (viz., lengthening the data word) makes the former negligible, too. It should be emphasized, however, that nothing like a mathematical proof of this assertion exists.

5) Overflow (Large-Scale Limit Cycles): Yet another consequence of using a fixed-length word to represent data samples is that the result of some arithmetic operation or other will occasionally call for a value which lies outside the allowed set of values. The outcome, called *overflow*, is that an incorrect in-range number is produced whose value depends on the details of how the arithmetic operation in question is performed.[2] For example, overflow can occur at the output of any two-input adder when the two inputs each approach full-scale value, causing their sum to approach twice full scale. In the case of the commonly used two's complement adder (discussed below), the result is an overflow characteristic like that depicted in Fig. 5(a), the so-called "wraparound" characteristic. It has been found that when this type of overflow occurs in the feedback loop of second-order sections with certain coefficient (β_1 and β_2) values, full-scale oscillations ensue which are stable and which persist regardless of what input sequence is subsequently applied to the filter [9]. These overflow oscillations are also called *large-scale limit cycles* and are clearly undesirable.

Although overflow can be prevented by providing several extra bits at the most significant end of the data word, this is a costly and unnecessary waste of dynamic range and is unsatisfactory in any case, since momentary overflow can still

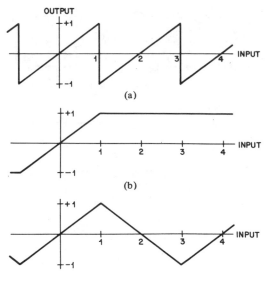

FULL SCALE DYNAMIC RANGE NORMALIZED TO ±1

(c)

Fig. 5. Overload characteristics.

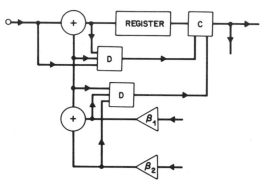

Fig. 6. Overflow detection and correction in recursive section.

occur due to a power turn-on transient or a digital error. Once the overflow oscillation has started, there is no sure way of stopping it short of turning off the power.

A more effective way of dealing with overflow is to bring about an overflow characteristic different from that of Fig. 5(a). One method of doing this which is applicable to filters made up of second-order sections is illustrated in Fig. 6. A storage register capable of holding one data word is inserted into the recursive portion of a second-order section as shown. The boxes marked *D* each compare the sign of an adder's two inputs with that of its output. If two positive inputs produce a negative output or two negative inputs a positive output, then overflow has occurred.[3] This fact is signaled to the *C* box, which then blocks the output of the holding register (which is otherwise allowed through) and puts out a full-scale positive or a full-scale negative number, whichever is appropriate. The holding register is necessary in serial-data systems since otherwise there is not enough time to substitute the full-scale word after the overflow decision has been made. (The register is not strictly necessary in parallel-data systems, but would probably be used anyway for reasons to be dis-

---

[2] Overflow can also occur during encoding when the analog signal momentarily exceeds the dynamic range of the encoder. This type of impairment is properly ascribed to the encoding process, however, since it is not augmented by subsequent digital filtering except insofar as the filter transfer function might enhance certain frequencies present in the error.

[3] For simplicity, it is assumed here that overflows occur only in adders. Multiplier overflows can occur also and are handled by a straightforward extension of the technique under discussion.

cussed in Section III-A.) This operation effectively creates the "saturation" overflow characteristic of Fig. 5(b), which has been shown to be oscillation free [9].

Another method of suppressing overflow oscillations is somewhat more flexible and works as follows. The data word is lengthened by one bit at the most significant end. As the word is passed through points where overflow can occur, the wraparound behavior of Fig. 5(a) is allowed to take place naturally. However, because the extra bit doubles the available dynamic range, the "period" of the sawtooth is now twice what it was before. At an appropriate point in the feedback loop, the two most significant bits (i.e., the extra bit and the normal significant bit) are examined. If they are alike, the word is passed unaltered. If they differ, all bits of the word except the extra bit are complemented. A little reflection will convince one that insofar as the original data word is concerned, the characteristic of Fig. 5(c) is produced. This characteristic has also been shown to produce stable operation [9]. This method is more flexible than the previous one in that it allows the signal to pass through several potential overflow points before resetting and is therefore applicable to more general configurations than second-order sections. It is merely necessary that one checkpoint occur in each feedback loop. (Feedforward loops have finite memory and overflows are "forgotten.")

C. Types of Arithmetic

Before the hardware realization of any digital filter can be effected, one must choose from among several methods of numerically representing the data and coefficient words of (1). Among the available choices, only binary arithmetic and logic will be considered since no truly viable digital alternative has ever been suggested.

Perhaps the most fundamental decision is whether to use the *fixed-point* or the *floating-point* numerical representation. In fixed point, all the bits are used to represent the amplitude or "mantissa" of the word (negative numbers and the necessity of a sign bit are ignored for the moment). In floating point, some of the bits are used for the mantissa and the rest for the exponent. For a fixed word length, the floating-point representation is capable of handling a much larger dynamic range than fixed point. Conversely, floating point can handle a given dynamic range with fewer bits than fixed point. This latter observation leads to the oft made assertion that, for the same dynamic range, floating-point multipliers are simpler than fixed point. For example, assume a situation that requires 24-bit data words and 12-bit coefficients. The 24-bit fixed-point word could be replaced by an 8-bit mantissa, 4-bit exponent floating-point word, and the coefficient by one with a 4-bit mantissa and a 3-bit exponent. The 24×24 fixed-point multiplier is thus replaced by a 8×4 multiplier, plus a 4-bit adder to add exponents. On the face of it, this would appear to be a considerable reduction in hardware; however, this sort of simple comparison can be quite misleading. Moreover, against this (apparent) simplification goes the observation that the floating-point adder is more complicated because it requires prealignment of the bits of the mantissas (according to the relative values of the exponents) before they can be added. Therefore, in practice, hardware comparisons between these two types of arithmetic are not clear-cut.

Further light can be shed on the fixed- versus floating-point argument by considering roundoff noise. Liu and Kaneko [10] have studied roundoff behavior in filters using floating-point arithmetic and Jackson [4] those using fixed point. Weinstein and Oppenheim [11] have compared the two results for a single second-order section and found the floating-point representation to be superior only for filters having very high Q. This is reasonable, since filters with high Q also have high gain, allowing the greater dynamic range capabilities of floating point to come into play. For cascade filters containing many sections, the overall gain can become quite high, thus indicating that floating-point arithmetic could be advantageous for such filters. However, it is customary to employ *scaling* (i.e., multiplication by a fixed constant, usually a power of two) between sections in a cascade fixed-point filter. This allows the use throughout the filter of much shorter length fixed-point words than would otherwise be required. This compromise permits realizing the generally better roundoff noise performance of fixed-point arithmetic within each section, while retaining much of the benefit of floating point for cascaded sections. Hence it would seem that the usefulness of floating-point arithmetic *per se* is confined to special filters having exceptionally high Q's.

Having thus settled on the use of fixed-point arithmetic, a decision must next be made as to how to handle negative numbers. The two principal methods of representing positive and negative fixed-point numbers are *sign + magnitude* and *two's complement*. As the name implies, sign + magnitude numbers are ordinary binary numbers with a sign indicating bit attached to the most significant end of the word (commonly a 0 for positive and a 1 for negative). Two's complement numbers are the same as sign + magnitude for positive numbers, but negative numbers are equal to

$$2^N - |X|$$

expressed as a straight binary number, where N is number of bits/word (including sign) and X is magnitude of number to be represented. The two number systems are best illustrated by an example. The 4-bit (including sign) representations of 5 and -3 are

	S + M	2'sC
5 =	0101	0101
-3 =	1011	1101

Sign + magnitude adders are complicated by the fact that inputs with like sign are added but those with unlike sign must be subtracted, and binary addition and subtraction involve different rules. By construction, the (algebraic) addition of two two's complement numbers follows the same rules regardless of sign; hence the two's complement adder is simpler. As far as multiplication is concerned, the sign + magnitude multiplier is somewhat simpler but the difference is not great (as will be seen in Section III).

III. Realization of the Elements of Digital Filters

A. Digital System Design

Having summarized the important consequences of the necessity of realizing digital filters with finite-accuracy arithmetic, we now undertake a more detailed investigation of how the building blocks of these filters are actually implemented. This will be facilitated by first reviewing some of the basic principles of digital system design. (This discussion is included as a brief introduction to the terminology of the subject for those who are not familiar with it. Readers interested in learning more are directed to one of the many thorough treatments of the topic, e.g., Peatman [12].)

The basic elements of digital systems are the familiar logic gates: AND, OR, NAND, NOR, and NOT. (The EXCLUSIVE-OR is a basic *logical connective* but not a basic gate in that it is customarily realized with combinations of the other gates.) It is possible to build digital systems using a mixture of all these gate types. This is rarely done, however, because in each digital technology—transistor–transistor logic (TTL), emitter-coupled logic (ECL), metal–oxide–semiconductor (MOS), etc.—some of the gate types are easier to build than others. Moreover, it is unnecessary to use a mixture, since, for example, the NOR gate is self-sufficient in the sense that entire systems can be (and are) built using this type of gate alone.

Digital circuits made up of combinations of one or more of these gate types interconnected in such a way that the output states are related to the input states according to the well-established rules of *Boolean algebra* (i.e., no memory of past states is involved) are called *combinational* circuits. Memory is introduced by the use of *flip-flops*, bistable circuits which assume one or the other stable state upon external command and remain in that state until the arrival of a command to change. Digital circuits containing flip-flops are called *sequential* circuits and are characterized by the fact that in general the present output states depend on past input and output states, as well as on present input states. The sequential circuits considered in this paper are *synchronous* in that a source of regularly occurring pulses called a *clock* is applied to all portions of the circuit at the same time and causes them to change state simultaneously.

The design of efficient sequential circuits requires a knowledge of how basic digital elements change state. For individual gates, the dominant feature which limits the speed of operation is usually the *propagation delay*, although in some designs *rise* and *fall* times must be considered also. In purely combinational portions of sequential circuits, the limiting factor is the worst case or *critical path* delay. Much of the effort in designing high-speed sequential circuits goes into discovering and minimizing critical path delays.

There are other ways of categorizing digital circuits which have been found useful. For example, there are the two basic methods of transporting the data word in systems which use a multibit word. In *parallel-data* systems, the different bits of the data word appear on separate (parallel) wires and the time interval associated with a bit and that with a word are the same. In *serial-data* systems, the bits appear sequentially, usually least significant bit first, on a single wire. In serial-data systems, the bit and word time intervals are different, the latter being as many of the former as there are bits in the word. In an analogous manner, various functions (subsystems) of a digital system can be connected in parallel, in which separate circuits perform many functions simultaneously, or connected serially, in which the same hardware performs several functions one at a time. (The terminology used for these ideas can be a bit confusing. Serial operation as defined here is also a form of multiplexing (discussed below), and is often referred to as such. Also, the term serial is sometimes used to mean the cascade connection of different circuits; however, the term pipelining (also discussed here) is generally reserved for this situation when the cascaded circuits are separated by retiming flip-flops.) The most obvious and important reason for choosing one or the other of these approaches concerns speed of operation. As we have just seen, a digital circuit realized with a particular technology

can be made to go only so fast. If greater speed is required (and use of a different technology not allowed), then parallel operation, with its attendant proliferation of hardware and interconnective wires, is the answer. Conversely, when some sequence of like operations does not tax the inherent speed of the technology being employed, it behooves one to perform them serially and save hardware.

Another technique often employed to make more efficient use of the speed capability of a technology is generally referred to as *pipelining* and works as follows. Suppose a group of digital functions can be done with a purely combinational circuit, but at the expense of a large critical path delay. An alternative is to divide the large circuit into a number of smaller circuits separated with retiming flip-flops. The composite function is now performed as a sequence of elementary functions. Each subcircuit has a much shorter critical path delay than the single large circuit and the pipelined version will therefore operate at a considerably higher clock rate. The desired function is thus performed in several shorter clock intervals rather than a single long interval. The overall time required to do the function may, in fact, be longer than before but this increased latency is of no consequence in many systems—the important improvement being the increased throughput.

Yet another technique which allows more efficient use of hardware is time-division multiplexing [13]. This term applies to the situation where a single circuit is time shared repetitively over several functions, each in its turn. It is customary to distinguish two types of multiplexing. The first occurs when the same function or algorithm is applied to many channels at once. The second takes place when the same piece of hardware is time shared over several functions in an algorithm being applied to a single channel. For the latter type of multiplexing, some parameter of the circuit is generally changed as each subfunction is performed in turn. Take, for example, a multiplier in a digital filter. For type one multiplexing, the multiplier coefficient is fixed (hard-wired) and is physically the same whether one or any number of channels is applied to it. When used with type two multiplexing, it is usually necessary to employ a different multiplier coefficient during each word time interval by reading successive coefficients from a read-only memory (ROM). It is possible of course for a digital function, such as the multiplier under discussion, to be subjected to both types of multiplexing at once.

As the following discussion of the realization of adders and multipliers will attest, the various techniques described in this section have all proved useful in the design of digital filter hardware. This is particularly true of multiplexing, since in situations where many channels must be filtered simultaneously it allows a direct reduction in the perchannel filter cost in a way which is not applicable to analog filters. The ability to multiplex digital filters thus makes them economically competitive in areas where their inherent complexity would otherwise prevent it.

B. Adders

The basic arithmetic element of digital filters is the adder. The rules for adding two single-bit binary numbers A and B are best summarized by the truth table given in Table I.

The circuit for performing this simple function is called a *half adder*. When a carry is present at the input, the circuit becomes a *full adder* and the rules are as given in Table II.

TABLE I

	A	B	Sum	Carry
	0	0	0	0
	0	1	1	0
	1	0	1	0
	1	1	0	1

TABLE II

A	B	Carry In	Sum	Carry Out
0	0	0	0	0
0	0	1	1	0
0	1	0	1	0
0	1	1	0	1
1	0	0	1	0
1	0	1	0	1
1	1	0	0	1
1	1	1	1	1

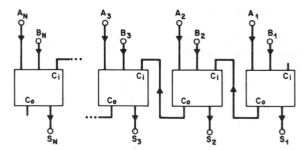

Fig. 9. Parallel-data adder.

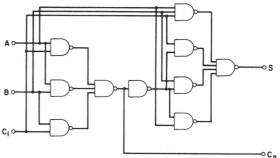

Fig. 7. Full adder.

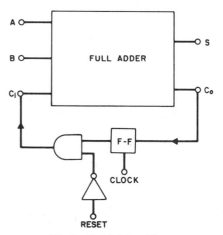

Fig. 8. Serial-data adder.

In common with all digital circuits of nontrivial complexity, there are many ways of realizing the single-bit adder function. An efficient design using all NAND logic is shown in Fig. 7. Adders are commonly classified according to whether they handle data in serial or parallel form. We will consider representative designs of both types.

1) Serial-Data Adder: An adder suitable for serial-data operation is easily made from the single-bit full adder of Fig. 7 by the connection of a flip-flop between the carry-out and carry-in terminals (Fig. 8). The two words to be added are applied to the input terminals in bit synchronism, least significant bit first. The flip-flop takes the carry from one bit

position and applies it to the next most significant position as required.

To prevent interference between words, it is necessary to inhibit the carry propagation during the arrival of the least significant bits of each new word by applying a reset pulse once per word cycle as shown.

Insofar as negative numbers are concerned, the adder of Fig. 8 will handle two's complement numbers as it stands. An adder suitable for handling sign + magnitude numbers directly is more complicated because the rules for addition and subtraction are different for this type of arithmetic. It is usually simpler to use the adder of Fig. 8 preceded by a sign + magnitude–two's complement converter [13].

2) Parallel-Data Adder: An adder for parallel-data systems can be created equally simply by connecting several single-bit adders, as shown in Fig. 9, in which the carry output of the ith stage is connected to the carry input of the $(i + 1)$th stage. There will be as many adders as there are bits in the word, including sign (again assuming a two's complement representation). Comparing this approach to the previous serial-data one, we see that for a basic system clock rate of f_B hertz and an N-bit word, the parallel adder does f_B additions/s, whereas the serial adder does only f_B/N. However, the higher speed is gained at the expense of N times as much hardware. This is an example of the tradeoff of speed versus hardware between parallel- and serial-data systems discussed earlier.

Unfortunately, there is a difficulty with the configuration of Fig. 9 which renders the foregoing comparison somewhat oversimplified. There exist input words A and B for which the most significant bit of the sum S_N is influenced by the carry C_1 generated in the least significant bit position. For C_1 to make such influence felt, it must propagate through all the intervening adder stages, with each stage contributing two gate propagation delays (refer to Fig. 7). Since this situation must be allowed for, the parallel adder clearly cannot operate at the same clock rate f_B as the serial adder, since the latter expends only five propagation delays per bit time. (This assumes the same technology for both adders and a word of nontrivial length.)

This flaw in the parallel-data adder can be a serious one in many circumstances and a number of solutions to it have been proposed and implemented. One solution involves the introduction of pipelining. In this method, one abandons time synchronism between all the bits of the same word and places all least significant bits in, say, bit time slot 1, all next least significant bits in time slot 2, and so on, up to all most significant bits in time slot N. The process would then repeat itself with the next word. Since the carry from any stage is now not needed at the adjacent stage until the following bit time, we are back to the situation of five propagation delays/ cycle and the two types of adders should now run at the same speed. For this scheme to work, however, flip-flops must be inserted between each carry output and the carry input of the adjacent stage, thus increasing further the hardware required by the parallel-data adder. Moreover, the inherent timing complications and the fact that the word time for the parallel adder is now the same as for the serial adder both tend to compromise the basic advantages of parallel-data systems.

Another approach which keeps the bit and word periods the same employs the so-called *carry look-ahead* technique [14]. In this method, extra logic is used to compute effectively all the carries needed for an N-bit addition in a small amount of time. The method works as follows. If A_i and B_i are the ith bits of the two words to be added and if C_i is the carry generated at the ith stage and C_{i-1} that generated at the $(i-1)$th stage, then the logical relation between these quantities is

$$C_i = A_i \cdot B_i + (A_i \oplus B_i) \cdot C_{i-1}$$

where $\cdot$ represents AND, $+$ represents OR, and $\oplus$ represents EXCLUSIVE-OR.

This relation can be verified easily by referring to the second truth table (see Table II). To illustrate the method, consider a 4-bit parallel adder. The three carries which must be generated within this adder are given by

$$C_1 = A_1 \cdot B_1$$
$$C_2 = A_2 \cdot B_2 + (A_2 \oplus B_2) \cdot C_1$$
$$C_3 = A_3 \cdot B_3 + (A_3 \oplus B_3) \cdot C_2.$$

As they stand, these relations merely illustrate the difficulty, since C_3 cannot be generated without C_2, which in turn cannot be generated without C_1. By making some obvious substitutions, however, these relations can be rewritten as

$$C_1 = A_1 \cdot B_1$$
$$C_2 = A_2 \cdot B_2 + (A_2 \oplus B_2) \cdot A_1 \cdot B_1$$
$$C_3 = A_3 \cdot B_3 + (A_3 \oplus B_3) \cdot A_2 \cdot B_2 + (A_3 \oplus B_3)$$
$$\cdot (A_2 \oplus B_2) \cdot A_1 \cdot B_1.$$

Using these relations, it is now possible to generate C_1, C_2, and C_3 directly from the A's and B's. The most complicated circuit, that for generating C_3, is shown in Fig. 10, from which it can be seen that fewer delays are now involved. If the method is generalized to adders of more than 4 bits, the number of gate propagation delays remains substantially constant regardless of the number of bits, but the required amount of hardware grows quite rapidly. The method is thus impractical for relatively long words. In practice, a compromise is made in which the full data word is divided into groups of perhaps 4 bits each and the carries to be propagated between adjacent groups are formed with a circuit similar to that of Fig. 10. In this way, an economical tradeoff is effected between extra hardware and the total number of gate delays encountered.

C. Multipliers

The multiplier is often the most complicated arithmetic element in a digital filter and some effort has therefore been made to discover efficient ways of realizing this function. We consider the more conventional approaches first.

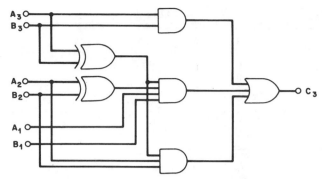

Fig. 10. Carry look-ahead circuit.

TABLE III

A	B	$A \times B$
0	0	0
0	1	0
1	0	0
1	1	1

The rules for multiplying two single-bit binary numbers A and B are as given in Table III, which is seen to be nothing more than the logical AND function. Hence a single-bit binary multiplier is simply an AND gate.

1) Serial-Data Multipliers: A useful way of constructing a multibit serial-data multiplier can be discovered by examining the process of doing a binary multiplication by hand. Consider the following example, in which the multiplicand and the multiplier are associated with the data word and the coefficient word, respectively (a fractional coefficient is used since an overflowed product could result otherwise):

$$
\begin{array}{ll}
1101 = & 13 = \text{data word} \\
\underline{0.101} = & 0.625 = \text{coefficient} \\
1101 & \\
0000 & \\
\underline{1101} & \\
1000.001 = & 8.125 = \text{product.}
\end{array}
$$

In this process, familiar since grammar school, the data word is multiplied by each bit of the coefficient in turn and the partial products thus generated are placed one below the other, with each successive partial product shifted one bit to the left. When one realizes that, in serial systems, left-shifting by one bit is accomplished by a one-bit delay circuit (flip-flop) and that the addition of the partial products can be done one at a time, rather than in a single step as is customary, then the circuit of Fig. 11 follows immediately. This is the basic form of the *serial-parallel* multiplier discussed by Jackson, Kaiser, and McDonald [13], and so named because it handles data words serially and coefficient words in parallel.

As it stands, there are two difficulties with this multiplier. 1) The serial connection of adders requires that, during each bit time period, signals be propagated through many gates in tandem; this is similar to the problem associated with the parallel adder discussed previously and poses a difficulty for high-speed operation. 2) The output word (product) has length equal to the combined lengths of the data and coefficient words, whereas it is desirable for input and output data words to be of the same length.

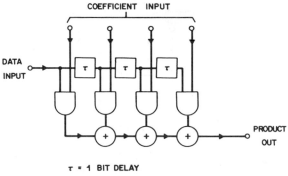

Fig. 11. Serial-parallel multiplier.

$\tau = 1$ BIT DELAY

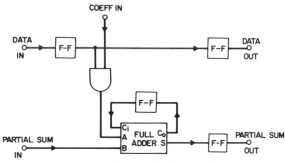

Fig. 12. Pipeline multiplier cell.

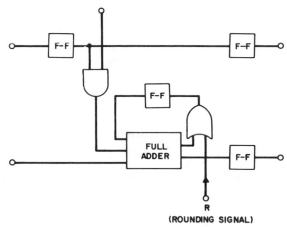

R
(ROUNDING SIGNAL)

Fig. 13. Pipeline multiplier cell showing rounding.

The first problem is again solved by the introduction of pipelining. An extra pair of flip-flops is added to the basic multiplier cell, as shown in Fig. 12. The extra delay thus inserted effectively doubles the total multiply time of the circuit but also, by breaking up the long strings of tandem gates, considerably increases the allowable operating speed and hence the throughput rate. The doubling of the multiply time is generally no problem since it is merely necessary to substract this delay from the total data delay intrinsic to the operation of the digital filter. This version of the serial-parallel multiplier is often referred to as the *pipeline multiplier* [13].

The second difficulty is resolved by introducing a special signal, usually called a *rounding signal*, which demarcates successive output words [13]. In its simplest form, this signal is propagated in synchronism with the final bit of the input word in such a way that it is used to block momentarily the carries in successive adders (refer to the discussion of serial adders in the foregoing) and effectively truncates the word to the desired number of bits. However, it is possible to use this signal to round off and not just truncate the word. This is accomplished in the following way. Up to now, the discussion has presupposed the multiplication of positive words only. However, sign + magnitude words are easily handled by performing an EXCLUSIVE-OR operation on the signs of the data and coefficient words in a separate circuit to produce the sign of the output word. The sign bit of the input data word is thus not propagated along with the other bits, leaving a vacant bit time within the multiplier. Now, in order to round the output word to the desired number of bits, it is necessary to know only the first bit to the right of the rounding point and not the remaining least significant bits. This is true since rounding a binary word is accomplished simply by adding a 1 to the word in the first position to the right of the rounding point. This being the case, it is thus

possible to use the vacancy left by removal of the sign bit of one data word to temporarily lengthen the following data word by one bit at the least significant end. In the final multiplier state (Fig. 13), a 1 is effectively added to the least significant bit and the word then truncated to the desired length. The sign bit of the preceding product word is then inserted by a circuit not shown.

The serial-parallel multiplier as described thus far is suitable for hard-wired (i.e., unchanging) coefficients only. It is possible, however, to implement a multiplier in which the coefficient is different for each input word. This is done by adding a coefficient holding register into which successive coefficient words are read from an external memory in such a way that the new coefficient bits replace the old in the correct sequence as the data word propagates through the multiplier. It should also be pointed out that, in custom fixed-coefficient designs, it is unnecessary to build a complete multiplier cell for coefficient bits which are zero; it is merely necessary to provide the proper delay in the data and partial product signal paths, thus reducing the total amount of hardware required for each multiplier.

The circuit as described so far handles data words in sign + magnitude form only. With slight modification it is possible to build a pipeline multiplier that will handle two's complement data words. To see how, assume a two's complement data word equal to $-13 = 10011$. Now suppose that this word is applied to the pipeline multiplier as it presently stands and suppose further that the two least significant coefficient bits are both 1. In this case, the sum performed by the first active adder in the pipeline chain is

$$X \ 1 \ 0 \ 0 \ 1 \ 1 \ = \text{data word}$$
$$+ 1 \ 0 \ 0 \ 1 \ 1 \ Y = \text{shifted data word.}$$

A difficulty is immediately perceived. In the sign + magnitude case, bit positions X and Y would be filled with zeros after sign bit removal and the correct sum would be obtained. With two's complement words there is no sign bit removal and X and Y are the least significant bit of the next data word and the most significant bit of the preceding data word, respectively. Clearly, an incorrect sum will result in general unless some modification is made. The solution is to lengthen the data word at the most significant end by one bit; in two's complement, this must be done, not by filling in a zero but by extending (replicating) the sign bit. (This action is identical to that for implementing the second overflow detection method described in Section II-B5). Hence, if this method of overflow control is employed, data words with the desired sign extension will automatically be applied to the multiplier.) With sign extension, the foregoing sum becomes

$$
\begin{array}{ll}
X\ 1\ 1\ 0\ 0\ 1\ \ \ 1 & = \text{data word} \\
\underline{1\ 1\ 0\ 0\ 1\ 1\ Y} & = \text{shifted data word} \\
|1\ 0\ 1\ 1\ 0\ 0|Z & = \text{first partial sum.}
\end{array}
$$

For this sum to be achieved correctly, the bit position X must be the extended sign bit of the data word. However, bit X is still the least significant bit of the following data word. Proper operation is accomplished by adding a circuit to the partial sum input to the multiplier cell which passes the input normally, except that it blocks the least significant bit of each word and transmits instead the repeated sign bit of the previous word. At the same time, the carry of the full adder is blocked so that the adder starts afresh (at the points marked with vertical rules in the foregoing sum) to produce a new partial sum. All this is caused to happen at the proper time by the rounding signal discussed previously. Each first partial sum is applied, along with the data word shifted once more, to the next multiplier, which produces the second partial sum, and so on, until the final output word is obtained. This procedure gives a truncated rather than a rounded product. However, in two's complement arithmetic, truncation and rounding produce the same amount of roundoff noise, except in the former there is a dc offset of one-half the least significant bit. In most applications this offset is quite negligible. To handle negative coefficients it is necessary to provide a complementing circuit after the final multiplier stage which negates the product word if the coefficient is negative.

2) Parallel-Data Multipliers: Efficient multipliers which handle both data and coefficient words in parallel form involve the use of cellular arrays [15] whose operation is again best understood by reference to the "pencil-and-paper" multiplication algorithm. Several types of cells have been proposed; the one given in Fig. 14, due to Hoffman *et al.* [16], is representative. An array of such cells that performs the example multiplication of the previous section is shown in Fig. 15. Information is passed vertically, diagonally, and horizontally in the array. The coefficient bits are applied as shown, one bit for each row in the array. Each coefficient bit controls the operation of its associated row of cells as follows. If the coefficient bit is a 0, that row passes the accumulation of partial products (vertical inputs) unchanged, i.e., without adding anything to it. If the bit is a 1, the data word (passing through diagonally) is added in proper position to the sum of partial products by the row of cells functioning as a parallel adder. In this way, the full product word is produced as shown.

As before, it will be desirable in most applications to round the product to the same length as the input. This can be accomplished here simply by presetting the initial carry input at the bottom row to 1 instead of 0 and then truncating the output word at the appropriate place.

As it stands, the array multiplier of Fig. 15 will handle positive numbers only. Sign + magnitude numbers can be accommodated as before by providing a separate EXCLUSIVE-OR circuit for the sign bits. Two's complement data words can be handled directly if the number of cells in each row is made equal to the total number of bits in the data word (including sign) and if in the top row (corresponding to the

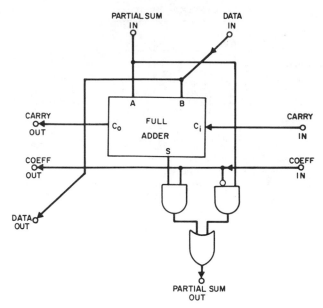

Fig. 14. Hoffmann cell.

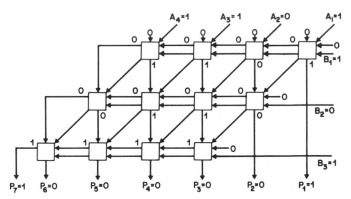

Fig. 15. Array (parallel-data) multiplier.

least significant coefficient bit) the sign is extended by connecting the vertical input of the leftmost cell of the second row to the most significant bit of the data word, rather than to the leftmost carry output of the top row. In this case it is not necessary to lengthen the data word by one bit as before, unless one employs the method of overflow control that requires it. To handle negative coefficients, it is necessary as before to include a circuit to complement the output word when the sign of the coefficient is minus.

3) Speed Comparison of Serial-Data and Parallel-Data Multipliers: A perhaps oversimplified but still useful comparison [17] between the array multiplier and the pipeline multiplier can be obtained as follows. Let

τ_p basic propagation delay of full adder used in parallel-data multiplier,

τ_s basic propagation delay of full adder used in pipeline multiplier,

M coefficient word length,

N data word length.

From the structure of each type of multiplier, it should be clear that, to a first approximation, the multiplication time required by the parallel multiplier is proportional to $M + N$, while that required by the serial multiplier is proportional

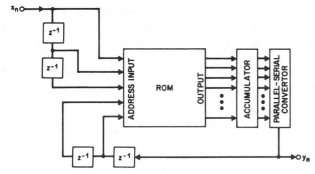

Fig. 16. Second-order section (due to Crosier *et al.* [18]).

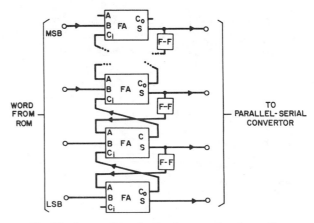

Fig. 17. Accumulator for Crosier second-order section.

only to N. Hence we may write

$$T_p = \gamma(M+N)\tau_p$$

$$T_s = \lambda N\tau_s.$$

The expression for the parallel-data multiplier assumes that the propagation delay through the basic array cell is the same vertically as horizontally. This is usually not true but the difference is not great enough to seriously affect the accuracy of this rough comparison. The constants of proportionality are not the same because in the pipeline multiplier the full adder normally contributes less to the overall cell propagation delay than in the array multiplier and also because the array multiplier structure allows greater advantage to be taken of statistical averaging of the random variation of gate propagation delays.

Typical values of word lengths and proportionality constants are

$$M = 10$$
$$N = 20$$
$$\gamma = \tfrac{1}{2}$$
$$\lambda = 3$$

in which case,

$$T_p = 15\,\tau_p$$

$$T_s = 60\,\tau_s.$$

This says that if the two types of multipliers were built using the same basic technology, the array multiplier would be something like four times as fast. However, this advantage is gained at the expense of something like twenty times the number of cells. Considering the accuracy involved, it is difficult to conclude anything from this comparison except that the two approachs offer the designer a tradeoff between speed and required hardware.

D. Other Approaches to the Arithmetic Operations

Many attempts have been made to find other ways of realizing the arithmetic operations in a digital filter which better utilize certain characteristics of large-scale integrated circuits. A noteworthy example is the approach proposed by Croisier *et al.* [18] and discussed by Peled and Liu [19]. It makes efficient use of read-only memory (ROM) and is applicable to the realization of second-order sections (Fig. 2) with fixed coefficients. To see how this approach works, we first consider the simple relation

$$w = Au + Bv \qquad (2)$$

where u, v, and w are considered variables and A and B constants. Consider further the relations between the quantities u and v and their constituent bits u_i, v_i, $i = 0, 1, \cdots, N-1$:

$$u = \sum_{i=0}^{N-1} 2^i u_i$$

$$v = \sum_{i=0}^{N-1} 2^i v_i. \qquad (3)$$

Substituting (3) into (2) gives

$$w = A\sum_{i=0}^{N-1} 2^i u_i + B\sum_{i=0}^{N-1} 2^i v_i$$

$$= \sum_{i=0}^{N-1} 2^i (Au_i + Bv_i). \qquad (4)$$

The important observation to make at this point is that for each bit pair (u_i, v_i) there are exactly four possible values which the expression in parentheses in (4) can take on: 0, A, B, and $A + B$.

Now the general relation between the input x_n and the output y_n for a second-order section is

$$y_n = \alpha_0 x_n + \alpha_1 x_{n-1} + \alpha_2 x_{n-2} - \beta_1 y_{n-1} - \beta_2 y_{n-2}.$$

Generalizing from (4), we can write immediately

$$y_n = \sum_{i=0}^{N-1} 2^i [\alpha_0 x_{ni} + \alpha_1 x_{(n-1)i} + \alpha_2 x_{(n-2)i}$$
$$\qquad\qquad - \beta_1 y_{(n-1)i} - \beta_2 y_{(n-2)i}]. \quad (5)$$

The expression in brackets now has 32 possible values:

$$0, \alpha_0, \alpha_1, \cdots, (\alpha_0 + \alpha_1 + \alpha_2 - \beta_1 - \beta_2)$$

made up of all combinations of each coefficient being either present or absent. Since the α's and β's are assumed fixed, these 32 different possibilities can be stored in a 32-word ROM. If the five quantities x_n, x_{n-1}, x_{n-2}, y_{n-1}, y_{n-2} are arranged to appear serially, the least significant bit first on the five address input leads of the ROM, then the output during each input bit interval is the correct value for the bracketed quantity in (5). The remaining details of this method can be understood by referring to Fig. 16. The output of the ROM is fed in parallel to a special accumulator, shown in Fig. 17,

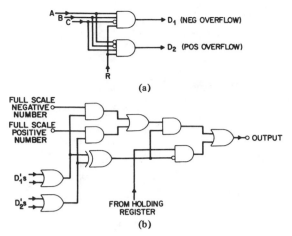

Fig. 18. Overflow detect and correct circuits.

which consists of the parallel adder of Fig. 9 to which some flip-flops have been added as shown. This accumulator functions by adding the present ROM output to the previous accumulated value shifted by one bit position toward the least significant end of the word. This shifting operation introduces the 2^i weighting factors of (5) and allows the correct accumulation of partial products.

As usual, the explanation has been made for positive numbers only. However, since the rules for the (algebraic) addition of two's complement numbers are the same as the rules for the addition of positive straight binary numbers, the extension of this method to handle two's complement arithmetic is straightforward.

E. Memory

The construction of digital filters requires two basic kinds of circuitry: 1) the digital logic used for the arithmetic operation discussed so far and 2) memory. The latter in turn divides into two more or less distinct groups: that used for storing past values of data samples and that used for various odd jobs such as timing shims, overflow correction, and scaling. For the latter applications, tandem connections of flip-flops (i.e., shift registers) will suffice. For the former, conventional flip-flop construction is too inefficient and other, more specialized, methods are used. A discussion of the different types of memory is more appropriate to later sections and is deferred at this point.

F. Miscellaneous Operations

1) Overflow Detection and Correction: The basic methods for performing these functions were illustrated in Fig. 6. However, it is appropriate to discuss in slightly more detail the contents of the D and C boxes of that figure. An expanded view of these boxes is shown in Fig. 18. For purposes of discussion, we assume a serial-data second-order section. The D box should produce the proper outputs when the adder inputs are of like sign but different from the sign of the adder output, and should produce no outputs otherwise. The R signal is the same as that used in the serial-parallel multiplier and enables circuit operation only when the sign bit is present.

The C box (Fig. 18(b)) accepts ORed correction signals from the two detect points and gates through the positive full-scale word for a positive overflow condition and similarly for nega-

tive overflow. In the absence of overflow, the held data word is allowed to pass. Also, if overflows of opposite types occur at the two detect points, they cancel and the held data word is passed.

2) Scaling: In a previous section, it was mentioned that the cascade form using fixed-point arithmetic greatly benefited from the use of scaling, generally located between cascaded second-order sections. Without scaling, inordinately long words would be required. It is not usually necessary to scale by anything more accurate than a simple power of two. This is easily accomplished in serial-data systems through the use of shift registers and in parallel-data systems by an intentional misalignment of bit lines. When scaling down (i.e., shifting toward the least significant end of the word), it is customary to truncate in two's complement after scaling.

IV. AVAILABLE TECHNOLOGIES

In the previous sections we reviewed the basic elements of digital filters and how they can be realized with digital logic. Before one can actually build a filter, however, consideration must be given to the type of digital logic to be used. Until recently, this choice was complex but manageable; today it is bewildering. The variety of IC families and subfamilies has grown enormously in the past few years and the number of possible approaches to digital filter construction is now very large. In view of the complexity and rapidly time-varying nature of this situation, no attempt will be made here to give anything like a comprehensive discussion of the available alternatives. Instead, it will suffice to make some general remarks about the basic proved technologies. These remarks, together with those in Section V, will hopefully serve to help the reader in making his own evaluation of the newer technologies as they emerge.

There are three attributes of each technology which are fundamental to their use in any digital system: 1) how small physically the basic devices can be made, 2) how much power they dissipate, and 3) how fast they can be made to operate. The first and second attributes together determine the packing density, i.e., the number of devices/chip that is possible. The second and third are usually variable but highly correlated for a given technology. That is, it is generally possible by design to increase or decrease the operating speed of specific device types with a corresponding increase or decrease in the power dissipated. Hence, for a given technology, the ratio of power dissipation to speed, called the *power–delay product*, is roughly constant and is often used as a figure of merit.

The two generic types of integrated circuits are the *unipolar* and the *bipolar*. The most commonly used forms of the latter, named for the way in which the constituent devices are interconnected to make gates, are transistor–transistor logic (TTL) and emitter-coupled logic (ECL). Representative circuits made from these two technologies are the TTL NAND gate (Fig. 19(a)) and the ECL OR gate (Fig. 19(b)). Variations on the TTL theme include high- and low-power versions, which differ basically in the amount of bias current drawn, and the newer *Schottky* series, which uses Schottky diodes to prevent the transistors from saturating and thereby reduces the power–delay product by about a factor of two.

The unipolar technology, better known as metal–oxide-semiconductor (MOS), again has several variations. The principal forms are p-channel and n-channel, so named for the type

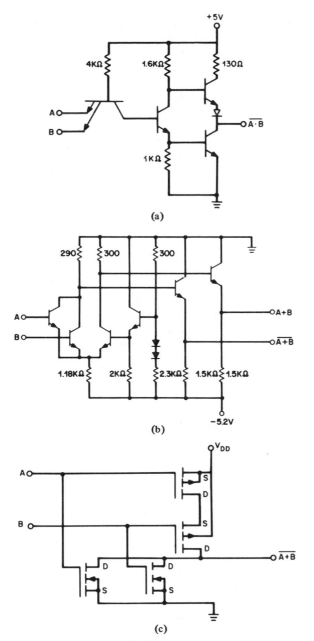

Fig. 19. (a) TTL NAND gate. (b) ECL OR/NOR gate. (c) CMOS NOR gate.

TABLE IV

	Power–Delay Product (pj)	Gates/Chip
TTL	100	200
ECL (10,000 series)	40	100
CMOS	20	>1000

devices to prevent punch-through and a sufficiently thick base region to give a reasonable collector junction breakdown voltage.

By contrast, MOS devices are intrinsically high impedance and, at higher frequencies, essentially all the power is dissipated dynamically in the charging and discharging of parasitic capacitances. In particular, the power/switching transition is proportional to $C_p V^2$, where C_p is the parasitic capacitance and V is the logic voltage swing. For F transitions/s, the dynamic power is thus proportional to $C_p V^2 F$. Since this dynamic power is proportional to F, it will sooner or later swamp out the static power as frequency of operation increases. In CMOS circuits, which employ both types of MOS transistors in such a way that the bias currents tend to cancel, the static power is very low and the total power dissipation follows the proportionality law over a broad frequency range. For this reason, CMOS devices have been employed extensively in low-frequency, very low power applications. Packing density limitations for unipolar devices are similar to those for bipolar devices, viz., power dissipation/unit area and limitations on device geometry [21].

One area in which unipolar devices have particularly excelled is that of dynamic (volatile) memory. Because of their inherently high impedance, it is possible to hold a charge on the parasitic capacitance long enough to make useful dynamic storage devices out of MOS circuits. Quite large single-chip shift registers and random-access memories (RAM's) have been made using this technique.

Table IV is presented to give those unfamiliar with present technology some idea of what can be achieved. The numbers are representative but substantial variation between specific designs is a general rule. Also, these are by no means the only technologies available; they are, however, the ones in common use.

V. System Architecture

Having learned what the elements of digital filters are and how they are constructed, there remains the task of putting them together to realize a specific filter. In this section we discuss various facets of this problem.

A. Partitioning

One of the most fundamental system architecture considerations is that of deciding what goes onto which chips (given that it is usually infeasible, or even undesirable, to put everything on one chip). We have seen that, conceptually, the basic building blocks are adders, multipliers, and delay elements. Are these the best units for the physical modules? So far this question has been answered in the affirmative (with the exception of the Croisier second-order section discussed previously), although no real proof has ever been given that this situation is optimum. However, a natural division does exist between

of current carrier used, and a combination form which employs both types—called complementary MOS or CMOS. An example of a CMOS circuit is the NOR gate shown in Fig. 19(c).

Bipolar devices are characteristic of low impedance and the power consumed in circuits which employ them is primarily the static power dissipated in bias and pull-down resistors and current sources. Dynamic power dissipation comes into play only in very high frequency operation for some designs. The frequency of operation is determined by 1) dynamic power dissipation (in some designs), 2) circuit time constants which in turn depend on static power dissipation via the impedance level of bias resistors, and 3) minority lifetime of base carriers in saturating circuits. Packing density is limited either by allowed power dissipation/unit area or by various factors which influence device geometry [20]. The latter include employing a sufficiently large isolation region between

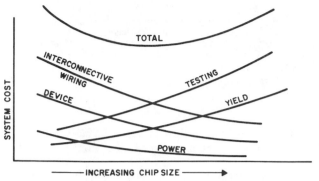

Fig. 20. System cost versus chip size.

memory and arithmetic logic since at this point they are efficiently realized with different technologies.

One approach to this problem is to consider the various factors which influence total system cost as a function of chip size. These are depicted in Fig. 20. It is assumed that the system is made of chips of uniform size of a given technology, which is almost never true. However, the general implications of Fig. 20 are still useful for systems using chips of varying sizes and types.

One obvious component whose cost increases with chip size is the yield cost. For a given technology, larger chips mean lower yield and this costs money. Balancing this trend, of course, is a decrease in the *cost/device* since larger chips contain more devices. Another factor whose cost increases with chip size is the cost of *testing*. The number of valid states which must be tested varies more or less exponentially with the number of devices/chip and the testing of large chips can become quite complicated. Two other quantities that decrease in cost with increasing chip size are *power* and *interconnective wiring*. The latter cost decreases simply because fewer chips generally mean fewer interconnective wires. In fact, the whole point of large-scale integration is to automate the interconnection of devices and thereby make that process much cheaper. The amount of power dissipated decreases with decreasing interconnective wiring because it requires more power to transmit signals over these wires than over the intrachip connections, which are much shorter and have less capacitance.

As can be seen from Fig. 20, the variation of these five factors conspires to produce a minimum chip cost for some particular chip size. Unfortunately, for any system of nontrivial complexity, the precise calculation of this minimum is virtually impossible because of the very intricate and highly nonlinear interaction of all the quantities involved. It is, nevertheless, quite helpful to know that it exists and what factors contribute to it.

B. Serial Versus Parallel-Data Word

Another facet of system architecture concerns the question of serial versus parallel orientation of the data word. Previous discussions have presented arithmetic units of both types with some comparison of their respective capabilities. It is appropriate to view these two basic approaches from the system standpoint as well.

The concept of providing a small set of flexible modules (chips) which can be efficiently used to construct a variety of filters plays an important role in this comparison. It is a characteristic of the serial–parallel multiplier that the amount

of hardware required to build it depends upon the coefficient word length but is independent of the data word length. However, the hardware to build a parallel multiplier depends upon both. Now, an argument such as the one presented in the previous section on partitioning, will convince one that for efficiency a serial–parallel multiplier module should contain more than one cell (bit)—for example, four appears to be a nice compromise with present technology. Use of such a module would thus restrict the realizable coefficient words to those whose length is a multiple of 4 bits, but no restriction is placed on data word length. With the parallel multiplier, both coefficient and data word are "quantized." This latter fact represents a certain loss of flexibility, although it is difficult to judge the seriousness of it in the abstract, without further knowledge of the system into which the modules will be imbedded.

There is also the matter of interconnective wires. If one assumed the "conventional" partitioning referred to previously, i.e., separate adder, multiplier, and memory modules, then the parallel system definitely uses more wires to interconnect its modules, other things being equal. Since these wires cost money, this is a clear disadvantage. However, it is quite possible that other nonconventional partitioning methods exist which mitigate this disadvantage considerably. More work is definitely needed in this area.

C. Memory

The alternatives for the data storage function are random-access and shift register memory. As already stated, either of these types can be realized quite efficiently with MOS circuits, although MOS speed limitations will require the use of some serial–parallel conversion in higher speed serial systems. Again, questions of modularity enter into the choice of which type memory to use. The basic delay unit in a digital filter must store a number of bits equal to the product of the data word length and the multiplexing factor. This number is likely to vary drastically from one filter to the next.

One solution to the problem is to use a small family of standard sized RAM's (e.g., 256 bit, 512 bit, 1024 bit, etc.). For each application, a RAM would be chosen which had the smallest capacity to do the job. In some applications, the waste would approach 50 percent, but this would probably still be less expensive than a custom design.

It is also possible to construct a similar family of shift registers, in which a variable length could be achieved with each chip via appropriate external connections. With present technology, however, this appears to be a more expensive way of doing things.

D. Testing and Fault Detection

A very important part of any digital system design involves provision for testing the finished product and means for discovering a failure when it occurs during normal operation. Many techniques for fault detection in digital systems have been discovered and proposed (see, for example, [22] and [23]). The majority of these techniques apply to combinational circuits only and, as we have seen, digital filters are highly sequential. However, much of the present effort in fault detection is aimed at sequential machines and new and more useful techniques applicable to digital filters are sure to be forthcoming.

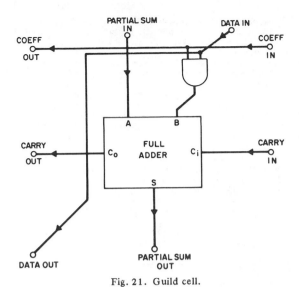

Fig. 21. Guild cell.

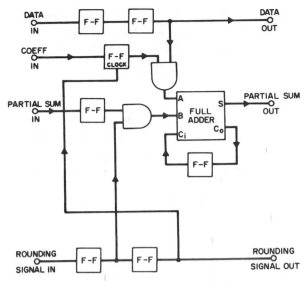

Fig. 22. Example of pipeline multiplier cell.

VI. SOME EXAMPLES

Since the previous sections consist mostly of generalizations based on a combination of fact and experience, it is appropriate to end the paper with some specific hardware examples of recent vintage. Three methods of realizing the multiplier function will be given: two serial–parallel realizations, one using ECL 10 000 and one using low-power Schottky TTL; and a full parallel realization using a new bipolar process called emitter-follower logic (EFL). These are by no means the only multiplier designs available. They simply represent a somewhat arbitrary choice from among those designs with which the author is most familiar.

The parallel multiplier is that described by McIver, Miller, and O'Shaughnessy [24]. It is a 16-bit by 16-bit array multiplier whose basic cell (Fig. 21) is a variation of that in Fig. 14. A moment's reflection will convince one that this cell, due to Guild [25], operates in the same way as the Hoffmann cell already described. This multiplier is realized on a single chip measuring 7.65 by 7.09 mm. It performs a full 16 by 16 multiplication in about 330 ns and dissipates approximately 3.5 W when operating at this speed. It contains the equivalent of some 3000 gates, giving a packing density of approximately 55 gates/mm². Other special features of the circuit are the following:

1) a special input circuit which is clocked twice during a single multiply time; during the first half-cycle, the two 16-bit inputs are accepted on 32 input leads; during the second half-cycle, the 32-bit product is produced on these same leads. This time sharing of input/output reduces the required number of leads from 64 to 32, a substantial saving.

2) a basic cell design such that the logic levels are not restored at the output; this results in the multiply time being proportional to $\sqrt{N}$ rather than N, the number of bits/input word. Although this operation reduces noise margin somewhat, it significantly increases the throughput rate.

The second and third examples are the realization of a serial-parallel multiplier with commercially available chips of the ECL 10 000 line and the 74 LS Schottky TTL line, respec-

tively. The same basic multiplier cell was used for both technologies and is shown in Fig. 22. The performance characteristics of these two realizations, together with those for the array multiplier, are summarized in Table V.

This comparison is not made with a view to choosing the "best" multiplier of the three, but simply to illustrate different design alternatives. In fact, insofar as the figure of merit of column D is concerned, the different approaches give much the same performance. The lower value for the array multiplier is due primarily to the fact that it is a truly large-scale design, whereas the other two are made up of small- and medium-scale chips.

TABLE V

	A	B	C	D
EFL array	3 MHz	330 ns	3.5 W	1.2
ECL 10 000	87	184	14.4	2.6
Schottky TTL	21	762	3.1	2.4

Column identification:
  A basic clock rate,
  B time required for a 16 × 16-bit multiplication,
  C total power dissipation for a 16 × 16-bit multiplier,
  D power dissipation per 10^6 multiplications (16 × 16 bit) per second (a useful figure of merit, the lower the better).

VII. CONCLUSIONS

This paper has attempted to review the important aspects of the design of special-purpose hardware for digital filters. It was seen that most of these aspects arise from the necessity of using finite-accuracy arithmetic. Emphasis was placed on discussing basic principles rather than on promoting a specific design approach. The field has clearly not matured and much work remains to be done.

In the near future, the area most likely to have the greatest impact is that of technology. Although this discussion was confined to the more or less proved technologies, subsequent digital filter designs are most probably going to make use of some of the newer technologies. Two of these deserve mention: the use of sapphire substrates with CMOS circuits and the bipolar technology called integrated-injection logic (IIL). These approaches promise a very low power–delay product combined with high packing density and a reasonable operating speed. With these and other ways of building digital IC's on the horizon, one can only conclude that the future for digital filtering is bright.

ACKNOWLEDGMENT

An attempt was made to bring together a number of diverse ideas and, therefore, the writing of this paper benefited from discussions with many people. In particular, the author wishes to thank S. K. Tewksbury, R. B. Kieburtz, and G. L. Baldwin for their sound advice and generous devotion of time to lengthy consultations.

REFERENCES

[1] L. R. Rabiner and C. M. Rader, *Digital Signal Processing* (Part C). New York: IEEE Press, 1972.

[2] B. Gold and C. M. Rader, *Digital Processing of Signals*. New York: McGraw-Hill, 1969, ch. 3.

[3] A. Fettweis, "Pseudopassivity, sensitivity and stability of wave digital filters," *IEEE Trans. Circuit Theory*, vol. CT-19, pp. 668–673, Nov. 1972.

[4] L. B. Jackson, "Roundoff-noise analysis for fixed-point digital filters realized in cascade or parallel form," *IEEE Trans. Audio Electroacoust.*, vol. AU-18, pp. 107–122, June 1970.

[5] B. Liu, "Effect of finite word length on the accuracy of digital filters—A review," *IEEE Trans. Circuit Theory*, vol. CT-18, pp. 670–677, Nov. 1971.

[6] J. S. Thompson, "An improved discrete model for quantization errors in digital filters," *IEEE Trans. Audio Electroacoust.*, vol. AU-21, pp. 125–127, Apr. 1973.

[7] R. B. Kieburtz, "An experimental study of roundoff effects in a tenth-order recursive digital filter," *IEEE Trans. Commun.*, vol. COM-21, pp. 757–763, June 1973.

[8] I. W. Sandberg and J. F. Kaiser, "A bound on limit cycles in fixed-point implementations of digital filters," *IEEE Trans. Audio Electroacoust.*, vol. AU-20, pp. 110–112, June 1972.

[9] P. M. Ebert, J. E. Mazo, and M. G. Taylor, "Overflow oscillations in digital filters," *Bell Syst. Tech. J.*, vol. 48, pp. 2999–3020, Nov. 1969.

[10] B. Liu and T. Kaneko, "Error analysis of digital filters realized with floating-point arithmetic," *Proc. IEEE*, vol. 57, pp. 1735–1747, Oct. 1969.

[11] C. Weinstein and A. V. Oppenheim, "A comparison of roundoff noise in floating point and fixed point digital filter realizations," *Proc. IEEE*, vol. 57, pp. 1181–1183, June 1969.

[12] J. B. Peatman, *The Design of Digital Systems*. New York: McGraw-Hill, 1972.

[13] L. B. Jackson, J. F. Kaiser, and H. S. McDonald, "An approach to the implementation of digital filters," *IEEE Trans. Audio Electroacoust.*, vol. AU-16, pp. 413–421, Sept. 1968.

[14] Y. Chu, *Digital Computer Design Fundamentals*. New York: McGraw-Hill, 1962, pp. 390–391.

[15] E. J. McKlusky, "Iterative combinational switching networks—General design considerations," *IRE Trans. Electron. Comput.*, vol. EC-7, pp. 283–291, Dec. 1958.

[16] J. C. Hoffmann, G. Lacaze, and P. Csillag, "Iterative logical network for parallel multiplication," *Electron. Lett.*, no. 4, p. 178, 1968.

[17] C. R. Baugh and B. A. Wooley, private communication.

[18] A. Croisier, D. J. Esteban, M. E. Levilion, and V. Riso, "Digital filter for PCM encoded signals," U.S. Patent 3 777 130, Dec. 4, 1973.

[19] A. Peled and B. Liu, "A new hardwave realization of digital filters," *IEEE Trans. Acoust., Speech, Signal Processing*, vol. ASSP-22, pp. 456–462, Dec. 1974.

[20] B. Hoeneisen and C. A. Mead, "Limitations in microelectronics—II. Bipolar technology," *Solid-State Electron.*, vol. 15, pp. 891–897, 1972.

[21] ——, "Fundamental limitations in microelectronics—I. MOS technology," *Solid-State Electron.*, vol. 15, pp. 819–829, 1972.

[22] H. Y. Chang, E. G. Manning, and G. Metze, *Fault Diagnosis of Digital Systems*. New York: Wiley, 1970.

[23] A. D. Friedmann and P. R. Menon, *Fault Detection in Digital Circuits*. New York: Prentice-Hall, 1971.

[24] G. W. McIver, R. W. Miller, and T. G. O'Shaughnessy, "A monolithic 16 X 16 digital multiplier," *Dig. Tech. Papers, 1974 IEEE Int. Solid-State Circuits Conf.*

[25] H. H. Guild, "Fully iterative fast array for binary multiplication," *Electron. Lett.*, no. 4, pp. 283–284, 1968.

On the Hardware Implementation of Digital Signal Processors

ABRAHAM PELED, MEMBER, IEEE

Abstract—An approach to the machine organization of dedicated hardware digital signal processors is proposed that is based on a specialized representation of the processing coefficients derived from the canonical signed-digit code. This leads to a realization requiring the minimum number of add/subtract operations to mechanize the required multiplications and additions.

The proposed organization is shown to be highly modular and well suited to integrated circuit implementation, and offers a significantly better performance when compared with existing realizations using prepackaged multipliers.

I. INTRODUCTION

THE increasing availability of computing power at continually decreasing cost has made real-time digital signal processing possible and cost-effective in many areas, including speech processing, seismic exploration, vibration analysis, and radar and sonar detection, to mention only a few [1]–[4].

There exists a large class of applications in which the digital signal processing is performed in real time by dedicated hardware. This paper addresses such applications, as opposed to applications in which general purpose computers are used to perform the digital signal processing.

In this paper we suggest a possible implementation of such dedicated hardware signal processors based on the use of the canonical signed-digit code [5] to represent the set of constants required for the processing. This canonical coding will permit the mechanization of the multiplications required, using a minimum number of add/subtract operations. This code was used extensively in the early days of digital computers to achieve fast multiplication. Later on, due to the inefficiency involved in the conversion, more restricted versions were used [6] that still achieved a speed compatible with other operations to be performed in a general purpose computer, and not making the arithmetic unit the bottleneck limiting the speed of operation. This is, though, not the case in many of today's real-time digital signal processing systems. These systems are essentially "number crunchers" requiring very high computation rates, and in many cases several arithmetic units operating in parallel will be needed. Thus the cost of the arithmetic unit will be a major contributor to the total systems cost, significantly affecting its cost effectiveness.

Another factor that makes the canonical signed-digit code a potentially attractive way of representing the processing coefficients is that without loss of generality, and only at the expense of some storage increase, we can maintain those

Manuscript received March 24, 1975; revised July 10, 1975.
The author is with the IBM Thomas J. Watson Research Center, Yorktown Heights, NY 10598.

coefficients in this code in our machine and eliminate the inefficiency of having to convert the multiplicand before each multiplication from the standard binary code to the signed-digit code that was present in general purpose computers.

We now proceed to propose an architecture for the machine organization of such real-time digital signal processors that will exploit this special representation of the processing coefficients to achieve a significantly better multiplication rate per hardware expenditure than is achieved with standard multipliers. Although in this paper we will mainly base our comparison on standard available TTL medium-scale integration (MSI) IC's, the same improvements can be expected when large-scale integration (LSI) and other technologies are considered.

II. REPRESENTING THE PROCESSORS COEFFICIENTS ON THE BASIS OF THE CANONICAL SIGNED-DIGIT CODE

The signed-digit code is well known, was especially prominent in the early days of electronic computers, and appeared in many publications in the 1950's with reference to fast multiplication. A complete treatment of the properties of this representation is given in [5] and a discussion of its use in fast multiplication is given in [7]. We repeat below, without proof, some of the more important properties of this representation.

Given an integer X in the range

$$-2^{B-1} \leqslant X < 2^{B-1}. \tag{1}$$

It can be represented in a 2's complement binary representation, or in a generalized representation by B signed binary coefficients β_i, according to

$$X = -x_B 2^{B-1} + \sum_{i=0}^{B-2} x_i \cdot 2^i = \sum_{i=0}^{B-1} \beta_i \cdot 2^i$$

$$x_i = 0, 1; \quad \beta_i = 0, \pm 1, B - 1 \geqslant i \geqslant 0. \tag{2}$$

The representation of X in terms of β_i is the binary signed digit code for X. This code has the following properties.

1) Minimality and Uniqueness: Let T be defined by

$$T = \sum_{i=0}^{B-1} |\beta_i| \tag{3}$$

and we require that

$$\beta_i \cdot \beta_{i-1} = 0 \quad n \geqslant i \geqslant 0, \tag{4}$$

i.e., no two consecutive digits are nonzero. Then there exists a unique set $\{\beta_i\}$ that satisfied (4) and there exists no other set $\{\beta_i\}$ for which T is less, that is, X is represented using a

Reprinted from *IEEE Trans. Acoust., Speech, Signal Processing*, vol. ASSP-24, pp. 76–86, Feb. 1976.

minimum number of nonzero β_i's. A representation satisfying (4) is called the canonical signed digit binary code.

2) Existence: For any integer in the range of (1) there exists such a minimal decomposition.

3) Average Number of Nonzero Digits: Assuming a uniform probability density for X on the range of (1), then the probability of occurrence of a nonzero digit is given by

$$\Pr\left\{|\beta_i| = 1\right\} = \frac{1}{3} + \frac{1}{9B}\left(1 - \left(-\frac{1}{2}\right)^B\right) \tag{5}$$

and, therefore, for moderately large B the average number of nonzero coefficients β_i will be $B/3$ as opposed to $B/2$ in the usual (nonsigned) binary representations.

The following identity is basic to understanding the reduction in the number of add/subtract operations required when the multiplicand is expressed in the canonical signed digit binary code

$$2^{k+n+1} - 2^k = 2^{k+n} + 2^{k+n-1} + 2^{k+n-2} + \cdots + 2^k. \tag{6}$$

This identity indicates that a sequence of add operations will be replaced by an addition and substraction (e.g., the number 15 instead of being written as 01111 which requires four additions will be written as 1000-1 which requires only two). Equation (6) is also the key to the conversion from a regular binary representation to the canonical signed digit. Starting from the least significant bit and progressing towards the most significant bit, let x_i, x_{i+1} be two consecutive bits in the binary representation of X, and c_i the carry generated by the conversion in the ith step ($c_o = 0$). Then x_i is replaced by β_i according to the rules given in Table I. The conversion can be done also in parallel, which is straightforward based on (6).

Tables II–V give representative examples of the representation of the filter coefficients for various nonrecursive filters using this code. All nonrecursive filters shown here are symmetric with $h_i = h_{N-i} i = 0, \cdots [N/2]_I$, where h_i are the coefficients. Therefore we list only $[N/2]_I$ coefficients in the tables ($[X]_I$ denotes the integer part of X). Figs. 1–4 show the frequency response of these filters as obtained with the quantized coefficients. Since we started with equiripple filters, it is evident from the figures that quantization of the filter coefficients destroys this property. In Table II a 27-tap low-pass nonrecursive filter is given and the average number of nonzero digits per coefficient is 2.36, and since $B = 12$, this is $B/5.08$. Next we see a 33-tap low-pass filter using 10-bit coefficients, and here we get $B/4.37$ nonzero digits. Table IV shows a 56-tap bandpass filter using 12 bits. Again, here the average number of nonzero digits is $B/4.95 = 2.43$. Finally, Table VI shows a 100-tap multiband filter. Here we get $B/6.2 = 1.94$ nonzero digits. Thus, as we see from these examples, for nonrecursive filters the average number of nonzero digits is far less than $B/3$, and will in most cases average less than $B/4.5$, the exact number depending on the attenuation required. This is very significant. To illustrate that we mention that the 100-tap filter of Table VI will require in the standard approach 50 multiplications and 100 additions per input sample, taking into account the coefficient symmetry (i.e., if data come in at a 10-kHz rate we have to

TABLE I
CONVERSION RULES FROM BINARY TO THE CANONICAL SIGNED DIGIT CODE

c_i	x_{i+1}	x_i	c_{i+1}	β_i
0	0	0	0	0
0	0	1	0	1
0	1	0	0	0
0	1	1	1	-1
1	0	0	0	1
1	0	1	1	0
1	1	0	1	-1
1	1	1	1	0

perform a multiplication and two additions every 2 μs), whereas if we use the signed-digit code we will be able to accomplish the same doing only 150 additions (50 + 50(1.94-1) + 50, see (7) and following text for explanation), which for the 10-kHz input rate means doing only three additions in 2 μs.

Table VI shows the results for the cosine coefficients required in a 64-point discrete Fourier transform (DFT), obviously the sine coefficients will be the same. Table VII shows the average number of nonzero digits per coefficient for various length transforms and number of bits used to represent the coefficients. It is easy to see that *irrespective* of these parameters we average $B/3$ nonzero digits, as could be expected.

Tables VIII and IX show the case of recursive digital filters, first a sixth-order notch filter, and a tenth-order low-pass filter. Here we average $B/3$ nonzero digits, since we are generally dealing with large numbers. The average for the numerator is lower, but that is due to the fact that every 2 out of 3 coefficients are 1, and we would not count those as multiplications.

After we have presented these representative examples, we now proceed to point out another property of many digital signal processors that makes additional savings possible. In many cases the operation to be performed is

$$z = a \cdot x + y \tag{7}$$

where a is a constant coefficient, and x and y are either data points or intermediate results. As we will show in the next section, by choosing a suitable architectural structure for the arithmetic unit we will be able to combine this operation and make the number of add/substract operations (with concurrent shifting) required to perform this multiply–add operation $B/3-1$. It follows therefore that we will average only 0.94 adds per multiply for the nonrecursive filter of Table VI (for $B = 12$) and 2.6 adds per multiply for the FFT coefficients (if 12 bits are used to represent the coefficients).

The question that we now address is what is the most suitable representation for the processing coefficients that will be based on the canonical signed-digit code and minimize the control logic required in the arithmetic unit to derive the following information.

1) The total number of add/subtract operations required to multiply by this coefficient—this information is mainly needed

TABLE II
Nonrecursive Digital Filter—27 Taps

FILTER COEFFICIENTS EXPRESSED IN THE CANONICAL SIGNED DIGIT CODE USING 12 BITS

Coefficient	Int												
8.14712050E-03	17	0	0	0	0	0	0	0	1	0	0	0	1
8.82963880E-04	2	0	0	0	0	0	0	0	0	0	0	1	0
-1.21095780E-02	-25	0	0	0	0	0	0	-1	0	1	0	0	-1
-2.33753820E-04	0	0	0	0	0	0	0	0	0	0	0	0	0
1.94129390E-02	40	0	0	0	0	0	0	1	0	1	0	0	0
1.22882030E-03	3	0	0	0	0	0	0	0	0	0	1	0	-1
-3.27448250E-02	-67	0	0	0	0	0	-1	0	0	0	-1	0	1
-6.95225080E-04	-1	0	0	0	0	0	0	0	0	0	0	0	-1
5.33999200E-02	109	0	0	0	0	1	0	0	-1	0	-1	0	1
1.54158240E-03	3	0	0	0	0	0	0	0	0	0	1	0	-1
-1.00243210E-01	-205	0	0	0	-1	0	1	0	-1	0	1	0	-1
-9.82600960E-04	-2	0	0	0	0	0	0	0	0	0	0	-1	0
3.15881190E-01	647	0	0	1	0	1	0	0	0	1	0	0	-1
5.01667680E-01	1027	0	1	0	0	0	0	0	0	0	1	0	-1

NUMBER OF NONZERO DIGITS IS = 33 I.E. AN AVERAGE OF = 2.36 PER COEFFICIENT

TABLE III
Nonrecursive Digital Filter—33 Taps

FILTER COEFFICIENTS EXPRESSED IN THE CANONICAL SIGNED DIGIT CODE USING 10 BITS

Coefficient	Int										
-1.70975850E-03	-1	0	0	0	0	0	0	0	0	0	-1
-5.66305590E-03	-3	0	0	0	0	0	0	0	-1	0	1
-5.16583400E-03	-3	0	0	0	0	0	0	0	-1	0	1
2.10548940E-03	1	0	0	0	0	0	0	0	0	0	1
1.05457450E-02	5	0	0	0	0	0	0	0	1	0	1
6.72016290E-03	3	0	0	0	0	0	0	0	1	0	-1
-1.04730800E-02	-5	0	0	0	0	0	0	0	-1	0	-1
-2.07911390E-02	-11	0	0	0	0	0	-1	0	1	0	1
-3.13848650E-03	-2	0	0	0	0	0	0	0	0	-1	0
2.97799370E-02	15	0	0	0	0	0	1	0	0	0	-1
3.30440400E-02	17	0	0	0	0	0	1	0	0	0	1
-1.68231520E-02	-9	0	0	0	0	0	0	-1	0	0	-1
-7.23012090E-02	-37	0	0	0	0	-1	0	0	-1	0	-1
-4.32102380E-02	-22	0	0	0	0	-1	0	1	0	1	0
1.08116830E-01	54	0	0	0	1	0	0	-1	0	-1	0
2.94427570E-01	151	0	0	1	0	1	0	-1	0	0	-1
3.80510870E-01	195	0	1	0	-1	0	0	0	1	0	-1

NUMBER OF NONZERO DIGITS IS = 39 I.E. AN AVERAGE OF = 2.29 PER COEFFICIENT

TABLE IV
Nonrecursive Digital Filter—56 Taps

FILTER COEFFICIENTS EXPRESSED IN THE CANONICAL SIGNED DIGIT CODE USING 12 BITS

Coefficient	Int												
6.28501640E-04	1	0	0	0	0	0	0	0	0	0	0	0	1
-2.06151510E-03	-4	0	0	0	0	0	0	0	0	0	-1	0	0
-3.59398960E-03	-7	0	0	0	0	0	0	0	0	-1	0	0	1
9.19772080E-04	2	0	0	0	0	0	0	0	0	0	0	1	0
2.20607590E-03	5	0	0	0	0	0	0	0	0	0	1	0	1
-6.09823270E-04	-1	0	0	0	0	0	0	0	0	0	0	0	-1
5.80978770E-03	12	0	0	0	0	0	0	0	1	0	-1	0	0
5.97883390E-03	12	0	0	0	0	0	0	0	1	0	-1	0	0
-7.19704110E-03	-15	0	0	0	0	0	0	0	-1	0	0	0	1
-8.88548790E-03	-18	0	0	0	0	0	0	0	-1	0	0	-1	0
6.15206550E-04	1	0	0	0	0	0	0	0	0	0	0	0	1
-6.92458820E-03	-14	0	0	0	0	0	0	0	-1	0	0	1	0
-4.96438520E-03	-10	0	0	0	0	0	0	0	0	-1	0	-1	0
2.29928050E-02	47	0	0	0	0	0	1	0	-1	0	0	0	-1
1.85523180E-02	38	0	0	0	0	0	0	1	0	1	0	-1	0
-1.06724430E-02	-22	0	0	0	0	0	0	-1	0	1	0	1	0
-1.29632090E-03	-3	0	0	0	0	0	0	0	0	0	-1	0	1
-2.72547170E-03	-6	0	0	0	0	0	0	0	0	-1	0	1	0
-4.70883700E-02	-96	0	0	0	0	-1	0	1	0	0	0	0	0
-2.18418840E-02	-45	0	0	0	0	0	-1	0	1	0	1	0	-1
5.14126720E-02	105	0	0	0	0	1	0	-1	0	1	0	0	1
2.70580350E-02	55	0	0	0	0	0	1	0	0	-1	0	0	-1
6.36695330E-03	13	0	0	0	0	0	0	0	1	0	-1	0	1
8.06371570E-02	165	0	0	0	0	1	0	1	0	0	1	0	1
-6.57089050E-03	-13	0	0	0	0	0	0	0	-1	0	1	0	-1
-2.41418060E-01	-494	0	0	-1	0	0	0	0	1	0	0	1	0
-1.29671340E-01	-266	0	0	0	-1	0	0	0	0	-1	0	-1	0
2.71040200E-01	555	0	0	1	0	0	1	0	-1	0	-1	0	1

NUMBER OF NONZERO DIGITS IS = 68 I.E. AN AVERAGE OF = 2.43 PER COEFFICIENT

TABLE V
NONRECURSIVE DIGITAL FILTER—100 TAPS

FILTER COEFFICIENTS EXPRESSED IN THE CANONICAL SIGNED DIGIT CODE USING 12 BITS

Coefficient	Int												
-2.2860471E-04	0	0	0	0	0	0	0	0	0	0	0	0	0
4.6663638E-04	1	0	0	0	0	0	0	0	0	0	0	0	1
1.7210505E-04	0	0	0	0	0	0	0	0	0	0	0	0	0
-5.8030523E-04	-1	0	0	0	0	0	0	0	0	0	0	0	-1
7.6657529E-04	2	0	0	0	0	0	0	0	0	0	0	1	0
-1.1722877E-04	0	0	0	0	0	0	0	0	0	0	0	0	0
-4.8267060E-04	-1	0	0	0	0	0	0	0	0	0	0	0	-1
-2.2867473E-04	0	0	0	0	0	0	0	0	0	0	0	0	0
-3.1130784E-04	-1	0	0	0	0	0	0	0	0	0	0	0	-1
-6.6404836E-04	-1	0	0	0	0	0	0	0	0	0	0	0	-1
-2.3507013E-04	0	0	0	0	0	0	0	0	0	0	0	0	0
1.2529874E-03	3	0	0	0	0	0	0	0	0	0	1	0	-1
-2.5075367E-03	-5	0	0	0	0	0	0	0	0	0	-1	0	-1
3.1966735E-03	7	0	0	0	0	0	0	0	0	1	0	0	-1
3.0965717E-03	6	0	0	0	0	0	0	0	0	1	0	-1	0
-2.8669307E-03	-6	0	0	0	0	0	0	0	0	-1	0	1	0
2.7194656E-03	6	0	0	0	0	0	0	0	0	1	0	-1	0
7.6879840E-04	2	0	0	0	0	0	0	0	0	0	0	1	0
-8.4809954E-05	0	0	0	0	0	0	0	0	0	0	0	0	0
-3.9028507E-03	-3	0	0	0	0	0	0	0	0	-1	0	0	0
-1.3038618E-03	-3	0	0	0	0	0	0	0	0	0	-1	0	1
-6.0564503E-03	-12	0	0	0	0	0	0	0	-1	0	1	0	0
-2.1930318E-03	-4	0	0	0	0	0	0	0	0	-1	0	0	0
8.7957976E-03	18	0	0	0	0	0	0	0	1	0	0	1	0
-1.4017522E-02	-29	0	0	0	0	0	0	-1	0	0	1	0	-1
5.8937761E-03	12	0	0	0	0	0	0	0	1	-1	0	0	0
1.4732715E-02	30	0	0	0	0	0	0	1	0	0	0	-1	0
3.3102010E-03	7	0	0	0	0	0	0	0	0	1	0	0	-1
4.5542629E-03	9	0	0	0	0	0	0	0	0	1	0	0	1
-4.4911820E-04	-1	0	0	0	0	0	0	0	0	0	0	0	-1
6.6324966E-03	14	0	0	0	0	0	0	0	1	0	0	-1	0
-9.0660192E-03	-19	0	0	0	0	0	0	0	-1	0	-1	0	1
8.7511428E-03	18	0	0	0	0	0	0	0	1	0	0	1	0
-3.6427930E-02	-75	0	0	0	0	0	-1	0	-1	0	1	0	1
-2.7088676E-02	-55	0	0	0	0	0	-1	0	0	1	0	0	1
3.4617051E-02	71	0	0	0	0	0	1	0	0	1	0	0	-1
-2.6491120E-02	-54	0	0	0	0	0	-1	0	0	1	0	1	0
-3.6131442E-03	-7	0	0	0	0	0	0	0	0	-1	0	0	1
7.6833963E-03	16	0	0	0	0	0	0	0	1	0	0	0	0
4.0290331E-02	83	0	0	0	0	0	1	0	1	0	1	0	-1
3.7547635E-02	77	0	0	0	0	0	1	0	1	0	-1	0	1
2.8115734E-02	58	0	0	0	0	0	1	0	0	-1	0	1	0
4.8965332E-03	10	0	0	0	0	0	0	0	0	1	0	1	0
-7.1911037E-02	-147	0	0	0	0	-1	0	0	-1	0	-1	0	1
1.3272513E-01	272	0	0	0	1	0	0	0	1	0	0	0	0
-9.9565414E-02	-204	0	0	-1	0	1	0	-1	0	1	0	0	0
-2.3473442E-01	-481	0	0	-1	0	0	0	1	0	0	0	0	-1
-9.3034059E-03	-19	0	0	0	0	0	0	0	-1	0	-1	0	1
-1.3260376E-01	-272	0	0	0	-1	0	0	0	-1	0	0	0	0
3.3612376E-01	688	0	1	0	-1	0	-1	0	-1	0	0	0	0

NUMBER OF NONZERO DIGITS IS = 97 I.E. AN AVERAGE OF = 1.94 PER COEFFICIENT

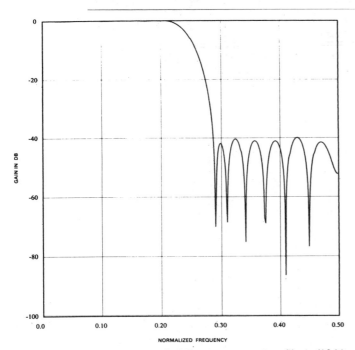

Fig. 1. Frequency response of 27-tap nonrecursive filter (12-bit coefficients).

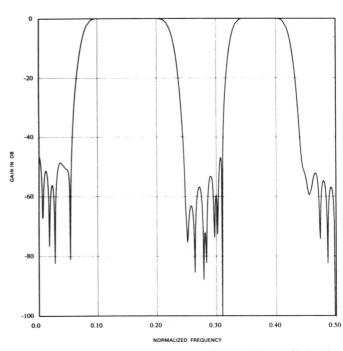

Fig. 3. Frequency response of 56-tap nonrecursive bandpass filter (12-bit coefficients).

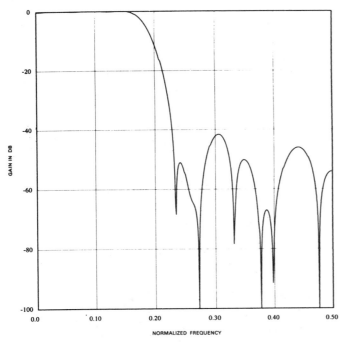
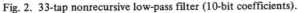

Fig. 2. 33-tap nonrecursive low-pass filter (10-bit coefficients).

Fig. 4. 100-tap nonrecursive multiband filter (12-bit coefficients).

by the microprogram to know when to get the result and continue processing;

2) the number of positions to be shifted before each add/subtract;

3) to control the type of arithmetic operation, i.e., should an addition or subtraction be performed.

A representation that will satisfy these requirements is to use a field of $[\log_2 (B/2)]_I$ bits as a header for each coefficient which will contain the total number a_N of nonzero digits in this coefficient, followed by a_N fields of length $[\log_2 B]_I + 1$

bits in which the first $\log_2 B$ bits will determine how many positions are to be shifted and the last bit will be 0 or 1 depending on whether we should add or subtract. Therefore, the average coefficient will require

$$N_B = (B/3) \cdot [[\log_2 B]_I + 1] + [\log_2 (B/2)]_I. \qquad (8)$$

Obviously, since only integer numbers are allowed for the fields, and furthermore, memory is usually available in fixed configuration, some inefficiency in memory allocation will result. Consider a specific example where B is between 9 and

TABLE VI
64-Point FFT Cosine Coefficients in 12 Bits

FFT COEFFICIENTS ARE EXPRESSED IN THE CANONICAL SIGNED DIGIT CODE

Coefficient	Integer												
1.00000000E+00	2048	1	0	0	0	0	0	0	0	0	0	0	0
9.95184779E-01	2038	1	0	0	0	0	0	0	0	-1	0	-1	0
9.80785310E-01	2009	1	0	0	0	0	0	-1	0	-1	0	0	1
9.56940413E-01	1960	1	0	0	0	-1	0	1	0	1	0	0	0
9.23879560E-01	1892	1	0	0	0	-1	0	-1	0	0	1	0	0
8.81921351E-01	1806	1	0	0	-1	0	0	0	1	0	0	-1	0
8.31469715E-01	1703	1	0	-1	0	1	0	1	0	1	0	0	-1
7.73010612E-01	1583	1	0	-1	0	0	1	0	-1	0	0	0	-1
7.07106866E-01	1443	1	0	-1	0	-1	0	1	0	1	0	0	0
6.34393513E-01	1299	0	1	0	1	0	0	0	1	0	1	0	-1
5.55570424E-01	1138	0	1	0	0	1	0	0	-1	0	1	0	-1
4.71397346E-01	965	0	1	0	0	0	-1	0	0	0	1	0	1
3.82683873E-01	784	0	1	0	-1	0	0	0	1	0	0	0	0
2.90285707E-01	595	0	0	1	0	0	1	0	1	0	1	0	-1
1.95091126E-01	400	0	0	1	0	-1	0	0	1	0	0	0	0
9.80176926E-02	201	0	0	0	1	0	-1	0	0	1	0	0	1
3.13973774E-07	0	0	0	0	0	0	0	0	0	0	0	0	0
-9.80160032E-02	-201	0	0	0	-1	0	1	0	0	-1	0	0	-1
-1.95059579E-01	-400	0	0	-1	0	1	0	0	-1	0	0	0	0
-2.90284216E-01	-595	0	0	-1	0	0	-1	0	-1	0	-1	0	1
-3.82683503E-01	-784	0	-1	0	1	0	0	-1	0	0	0	0	0
-4.71395969E-01	-965	0	-1	0	0	0	1	0	0	0	-1	0	-1
-5.55569700E-01	-1138	0	-1	0	0	-1	0	0	1	0	0	-1	0
-6.34392262E-01	-1299	0	-1	0	-1	0	0	0	-1	0	-1	0	1
-7.07106173E-01	-1443	-1	0	1	0	1	0	-1	0	-1	0	0	0
-7.73010075E-01	-1583	-1	0	1	0	0	-1	0	1	0	0	0	1
-8.31468621E-01	-1703	-1	0	1	0	-1	0	-1	0	-1	0	0	-1
-8.81920755E-01	-1806	-1	0	0	1	0	0	0	-1	0	0	1	0
-9.23879266E-01	-1892	-1	0	0	0	1	0	1	0	0	-1	0	0
-9.56939936E-01	-1960	-1	0	0	0	1	0	-1	0	-1	0	0	0
-9.80785672E-01	-2009	-1	0	0	0	0	0	1	0	1	0	0	-1
-9.95184600E-01	-2038	-1	0	0	0	0	0	0	0	1	0	1	0

NUMBER OF NONZERO DIGITS IS =127 I.E. AN AVERAGE OF = 3.969

TABLE VII
Average Number of Nonzero Digits for FFT Coefficients

B \ N	16	32	64	128	256	512	1024	2048
8	2.71	2.73	2.75	2.80	2.71	2.72	2.73	2.73
10	3.47	3.68	3.58	3.45	3.39	3.37	3.38	3.37
12	3.41	3.89	3.99	4.01	4.01	4.03	4.03	4.03
14	3.63	4.24	4.48	4.66	4.65	4.68	4.68	4.69
16	4.13	4.87	5.23	5.32	5.37	5.34	5.33	5.33

N = transform length; B = number of bits

16; 3 bits will be required for the header field and $4 + 1 = 5$ bits for each nonzero digit, making $N_B = 23$, which implies an approximate doubling of the storage capacity for the coefficients. Furthermore, if we assume that the memory is available in a 8-bit wide configuration, we will have to use $N_B = 32$ which corresponds to an almost tripling of the memory required for coefficients.

Table X shows the FFT coefficients of Table VI represented in the form described above. In the next section, dealing with the architectural organization of the processor, we shall discuss how to deal with the unequal lengths required for the different coefficients as illustrated in Table X.

III. An Architecture for the Machine Organization of Digital Signal Processors

Fig. 5 illustrates the functional block diagram of a digital signal processor. The basic units are as follows.

1) Random-access memory (RAM) in which the input data to be processed resides and where the output data are transferred.

2) An arithmetic unit capable of performing the operation $a \cdot x + y$.

3) High-speed scratch-pad storage for intermediate results.

4) A control section containing the string of microinstructions necessary to perform the required signal processing.

5) Memory in which the processing coefficients $\{a_i\}$ reside, which may be read-only memory (ROM) or RAM for programmable processors.

This structure is not unique. In fact it is quite similar to what is available today in microprocessors and minicomputers. The only obstacle to using these general purpose processors is that their computational rate is by far inadequate even for the more modest signal processing tasks.

For the sake of simplicity and clarity we proceed to define a machine organization in which the processing coefficients will have an accuracy of up to 16 bits, which is adequate for

TABLE VIII
SIXTH-ORDER RECURSIVE NOTCH FILTER

NUMERATOR COEFFICIENTS

FILTER COEFFICIENTS EXPRESSED IN THE CANONICAL SIGNED DIGIT CODE   USING, 12   BITS

Value	Int												
1.00000000E+00	1024	0	1	0	0	0	0	0	0	0	0	0	0
-1.61803461E+00	-1657	-1	0	1	0	-1	0	0	0	1	0	0	-1
1.00000000E+00	1024	0	1	0	0	0	0	0	0	0	0	0	0
1.00000000E+00	1024	0	1	0	0	0	0	0	0	0	0	0	0
-1.61803461E+00	-1657	-1	0	1	0	-1	0	0	0	1	0	0	-1
1.00000000E+00	1024	0	1	0	0	0	0	0	0	0	0	0	0
1.00000000E+00	1024	0	1	0	0	0	0	0	0	0	0	0	0
-1.61803461E+00	-1657	-1	0	1	0	-1	0	0	0	1	0	0	-1
1.00000000E+00	1024	0	1	0	0	0	0	0	0	0	0	0	0

TOTAL NUMBER OF NONZERO DIGITS IS =   21   I.E. AN AVERAGE OF =   2.33   PER COEFFICIENT

DENOMINATOR COEFFICIENTS

FILTER COEFFICIENTS EXPRESSED IN THE CANONICAL SIGNED DIGIT CODE   USING, 12   BITS

Value	Int												
-1.51803461E+00	-1554	-1	0	1	0	0	0	0	-1	0	0	-1	0
9.21598269E-01	944	0	1	0	0	0	-1	0	-1	0	0	0	0
-1.53713288E+00	-1574	-1	0	1	0	0	0	-1	0	-1	0	1	0
9.02500000E-01	924	0	1	0	0	-1	0	1	0	0	-1	0	0
-1.58713281E+00	-1625	-1	0	1	0	-1	0	1	0	1	0	0	-1
9.21598269E-01	944	0	1	0	0	0	-1	0	-1	0	0	0	0

TOTAL NUMBER OF NONZERO DIGITS IS =   25   I.E. AN AVERAGE OF =   4.17   PER COEFFICIENT

TABLE IX
TENTH-ORDER ELLIPTIC RECURSIVE LOW-PASS FILTER

NUMERATOR COEFFICIENTS

FILTER COEFFICIENTS EXPRESSED IN THE CANONICAL SIGNED DIGIT CODE   USING, 12   BITS

Value	Int												
1.00000000E+00	1024	0	1	0	0	0	0	0	0	0	0	0	0
-1.41961670E+00	-1454	-1	0	1	0	0	1	0	1	0	0	1	0
1.00000000E+00	1024	0	1	0	0	0	0	0	0	0	0	0	0
1.00000000E+00	1024	0	1	0	0	0	0	0	0	0	0	0	0
-1.37234500E+00	-1405	-1	0	1	0	1	0	0	0	0	1	0	-1
1.00000000E+00	1024	0	1	0	0	0	0	0	0	0	0	0	0
1.00000000E+00	1024	0	1	0	0	0	0	0	0	0	0	0	0
-1.22251130E+00	-1252	0	-1	0	-1	0	0	1	0	0	-1	0	0
1.00000000E+00	1024	0	1	0	0	0	0	0	0	0	0	0	0
1.00000000E+00	1024	0	1	0	0	0	0	0	0	0	0	0	0
-7.31235500E-01	-749	0	-1	0	1	0	0	0	1	0	1	0	-1
1.00000000E+00	1024	0	1	0	0	0	0	0	0	0	0	0	0
1.00000000E+00	1024	0	1	0	0	0	0	0	0	0	0	0	0
1.55649950E+00	1594	1	0	-1	0	0	1	0	0	-1	0	1	0
1.00000000E+00	1024	0	1	0	0	0	0	0	0	0	0	0	0

TOTAL NUMBER OF NONZERO DIGITS IS =   34   I.E. AN AVERAGE OF =   2.27   PER COEFFICIENT

DENOMINATOR COEFFICIENTS

FILTER COEFFICIENTS EXPRESSED IN THE CANONICAL SIGNED DIGIT CODE   USING, 12   BITS

Value	Int												
-1.50277710E+00	-1539	-1	0	1	0	0	0	0	0	0	-1	0	1
9.82435230E-01	1006	0	1	0	0	0	0	0	-1	0	0	-1	0
-1.49814610E+00	-1534	-1	0	1	0	0	0	0	0	0	0	1	0
9.36639790E-01	959	0	1	0	0	0	-1	0	0	0	0	0	-1
-1.50927350E+00	-1545	-1	0	1	0	0	0	0	0	-1	0	0	-1
8.57742310E-01	878	0	1	0	0	-1	0	0	-1	0	0	-1	0
-1.53313450E+00	-1570	-1	0	1	0	0	0	-1	0	0	0	-1	0
7.37310410E-01	755	0	1	0	-1	0	0	0	-1	0	1	0	-1
-1.55649950E+00	-1594	-1	0	1	0	0	-1	0	0	1	0	-1	0
6.26565930E-01	642	0	0	1	0	1	0	0	0	0	0	1	0

TOTAL NUMBER OF NONZERO DIGITS IS =   38   I.E. AN AVERAGE OF =   3.80   PER COEFFICIENT

most processing purposes. The arithmetic will be done in 16-bit wide registers, corresponding to multiplying and adding with a 16-bit precision. All arithmetic is in fixed point. Increasing the arithmetic precision can be easily done by using 20-bit registers and a 20-bit adder.

Let the processing coefficients be represented as described in Section II (see Table X) and assume we have a ROM 8 bits wide (e.g., Signetics 8205 512 × 8 bits or 8204 256 × 8 or 8223 32 × 8, depending on the number of coefficients required). The coefficients are stored sequentially according to their index. Each coefficient will be assigned as many locations as nonzero digits. The first location will contain the 3-bit field

TABLE X
An Example of Using a Specialized Representation to Facilitate
the Control of the Shift Matrix and Adder/Subtractor

FFT COEFFICIENTS EXPRESSED ON THE BASIS OF THE SIGNED DIGIT CODE

```
 1   001  00000
 2   011  00000  10001  10101
 3   100  00000  01101  10001  10110
 4   100  00000  01001  01100  10000
 5   100  00000  01001  01101  10010
 6   100  00000  00111  01110  10101
 7   110  00000  00101  01000  01100  10000  10111
 8   101  00000  00101  01010  01111  10111
 9   101  00000  00101  01001  01100  10000
10   101  00010  00110  01110  10010  10111
11   100  00010  01000  01111  10100
12   100  00010  01011  10010  10110
13   011  00010  00111  01110
14   101  00100  01010  01110  10010  10111
15   011  00100  01001  01110
16   100  00110  01011  10000  10110
17   000  00000
18   100  00111  01010  10001  10111
19   011  00101  01000  01111
20   101  00101  01011  01111  10011  10110
21   011  00011  00110  01111
22   100  00011  01010  10001  10111
23   100  00011  01001  01110  10101
24   101  00011  00111  01111  10011  10110
25   101  00001  00100  01000  01111  10001
26   101  00001  00100  01001  01110  10111
27   110  00001  00100  01010  01101  10001  10110
28   100  00001  00101  01111  10100
29   100  00001  01000  01100  10011
30   100  00001  01000  01101  10001
31   100  00001  01100  10000  10111
32   011  00001  10000  10100
```

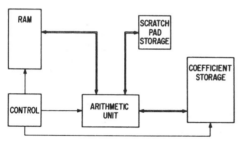

Fig. 5. Block diagram of a general purpose digital signal processor.

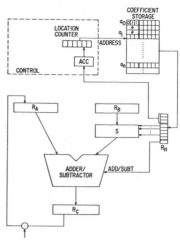

Fig. 6. Proposed organization of the arithmetic unit in a digital signal processor that uses a special representation for the coefficients.

indicating how many nonzero digits there are a_N (a maximum of 8 for 16-bit coefficients) and the first 5-bit field indicating how many positions should be shifted and whether an addition or subtraction is required. The subsequent $(a_N - 1)$ locations contain the rest of the $a_N - 1$ 5-bit fields of this coefficient. Thus, a serious inefficiency is caused by using an 8-bit memory to store 5 bits, a better storage efficiency could be achieved if we had available memory that is 5 bits wide, thus wasting only 2 bits on the first field of each coefficient.

This arrangement of the coefficients will make it easy for the control to keep track of where the next coefficient should come from. In the control there will be a location counter pointing to the address of the next processing coefficient, and each time a new coefficient is fetched the value of a_N (the first 3-bit field) is added to the location counter to give the address of the next coefficient. This is illustrated in Fig. 6.

Fig. 6 also shows the proposed organization of the arithmetic unit which consists of the two input registers R_A and R_B (each 16 bits), a shift-matrix S capable of shifting the value in B during one clock cycle the number of positions indicated by the control register R_H which is loaded from the coefficient memory. This shift matrix can be implemented either by custom IC's containing $B^2/2 = 128$ two-input AND gates and suitable decoding to implement a mask-skew circuit, or by using such a commercially available IC as the Signetics 8243 8-bit position scaler which performs exactly the required func-

tion for an 8-bit shift matrix (except for an inversion which will require an additional IC containing inverters) or Advanced Micro Devices AM25510 4-bit shifter. In general, such a shift matrix could be implemented using several levels ($\log_2 B$). The number of gates required will be proportional to $B \log_2 B$, rather than B^2. The arithmetic unit also has a 16-bit adder/subtracter who will add or subtract under the control of the last bit in R_H. This adder can be implemented using 4 standard 4-bit ALU's, however, they provide more functions than we need. Finally we have the output register R_C which can be loaded into either the RAM, the scratch pad, or wrapped around R_A or R_B to perform accumulation.

It is easy to see that the throughput rate of the arithmetic unit can be quite high since the shift operation is static and, depending on the number of levels in which it is achieved, will require as many gate propagation delays, which for Schotthy TTL gates will be some 20 ns for 6–8 levels, and the addition time using 5 IC's (4 ALU's as 74S181 and a look-ahead carry generator as 74S182) will require 28 ns, thus our throughput rate per shift/add will be easily 60 ns. Thus, in general, we will achieve an average multiply–add of a 12 × 16 bits with a 16-bit result in 240 ns and a 16 × 16 bits with a 16-bit result in 300 ns. This will require some nine IC's. An even higher throughput rate can be achieved by concurrent shift and add which will require a look-ahead fetch. This will double the speed to, respectively, 120 and 150 ns. Although we will give detailed comparisons later, we only mention here that using the Advanced Micro Devices AM2505 4 × 2 TTL MSI multiplier it is possible to perform a 12 × 16 bit multiplication in 275 ns using 18 IC's and a 16 × 16-bit multiplication again with a 16-bit result in 275 ns using 22 IC's. However, as we demonstrated in Section II, in many cases the average number of adds that will be required will be less than $B/3$ leading to even better results.

If large LSI is considered, since the arithmetic unit described above contains approximately 1000 gates, it could be fit on one integrated circuit. Depending upon the specific technology used, different speeds would be achieved.

It is clear that the proposed structure is quite general and can be used to implement any signal processing function we may require. The only difference from currently available processors would be to insert or convert upon input the processing coefficients, be they filter coefficients or FFT sine/cosine values, to the representation described in Section II. Since the insertion or modification of coefficients, even in programmable signal processors is done off line, or at least at a rate several orders of magnitude slower than the real-time processing speed, this will not affect the computational rate that can be achieved.

An additional important advantage of the proposed organization is the fact that we can easily mix coefficients with different word lengths, which is in many cases desirable, and gain a computational advantage from shorter word-length coefficients. This is not the case for systems using a general multiplier.

Although the exact savings that will be achieved in a particular application depend on the specific coefficients needed in that application, the comparison made above with a multiplier and the examples that we present in Section V for an FFT processor and implementation of digital filters, tend to indicate that the proposed method will indeed yield results superior to a standard approach.

IV. A COMPARISON WITH HIGH-SPEED MULTIPLIERS

In this section we attempt to compare the performance of standard high-speed multipliers [9], [10], with the equivalent multiply/add arithmetic unit described in Section III. This comparison does not take into account the increased storage required for the coefficients, since this depends on the number of coefficients and their specific values. The examples in the next section show that the comparison results are essentially the same when this is taken into consideration.

From [11] it follows that if Schottky TTL gates are used to implement high-speed multipliers using Wallace's scheme or Dada's scheme, the time required to multiply two B-bit numbers is

$$T_M = 18.84 \log_2 B + T_A(2B) + 20 \text{ ns} \qquad (9)$$

where $T_A(2B)$ is the time required for addition of $2B$-bit numbers, and the number of gates required is

$$M_G = 13B^2 - 16B \text{ gates.} \qquad (10)$$

The performance obtained from the arithmetic unit proposed in Section III is

$$T_{EM} = \frac{B}{a_N} T_A(2B) \text{ ns} \qquad (11)$$

$$EM_G = 33B + 3.63\, B \log_2 B \text{ gates} \qquad (12)$$

where a_N is determined by the average number of nonzero digits (usually 3). The number of gates corresponds to a $2B$-bit adder with carry look ahead and a B-bit shift matrix.

For the purposes of comparison we consider the multiplication rate over the number of gates required to achieve it for both cases and define an efficiency ratio as

$$E_{M/EM} = \frac{1/T_M/M_G}{1/T_{EM}/EM_G} = \frac{T_{EM} \cdot EM_G}{T_M \cdot M_G}. \qquad (13)$$

From (9)–(13) it follows that

$$E_{M/EM} = \frac{1}{a_N} \cdot \frac{T_A(2B)\,[33 + 3.63 \log_2 B]}{\left[13 - \dfrac{16}{B}\right][18.84 \log_2 B + 20 + T_A(2B)]}. \qquad (14)$$

Addition time will be $T_A = 28$ ns for $8 < B \leqslant 32$, and letting $a_N = 3$, (14) reduces to

$$E_{M/EM}^{(B)} \cong \frac{11 + 1.21 \log_2 B}{22.29 + 8.75 \log_2 B} \qquad 8 < B \leqslant 32 \qquad (15)$$

which would be the range of interest for B in digital signal processors. From (15) we find that $E_{M/EM}(16) = 0.28$ and $E_{M/EM}(32) = 0.26$, which implies that the proposed scheme is almost four times as efficient as the Wallace multiplier for the case of digital signal processors, where no conversion to the signed-digit code is required as described above.

Table XI lists the efficiency ratio as defined above based on a comparison with two standard multipliers; one the Advanced Micro Devices AM2505 that uses carry–save combined with examination of two multiplier bits at once, and the second a Texas Instruments implementation of a Wallace multiplier using SN74LS261, SN745275, and SN745274. It is worth mentioning that the AM2505 although slower, has the advantage that it does a multiply/add as in (7), and requires no correction for 2's complement multiplication.

V. IMPLEMENTING THE PROCESSORS—SOME EXAMPLES

In this section we present some examples of the implementation of digital signal processors using the organization proposed in Section III and compare it to existing realizations.

We adopt a figure of merit F_T which is defined as

$$F_T = R/N_{IC} \qquad (16)$$

where R is the data rate throughput in kHz and N_{IC} is the number of MSI TTL IC's required. F_T is a good measure of the cost of processing digitally, data coming in at a given rate.

A. A 1024-Point FFT Processor

For a radix-2 decimation-in-time algorithm [8], the arithmetic unit will repeatedly perform the operation

$$a_R' = a_R + (c_R \cdot \cos(2\pi k/N) + c_I \cdot \sin(2\pi k/N))$$

$$c_R' = a_R - (c_R \cdot \cos(2\pi k/N) + c_I \cdot \sin(2\pi k/N))$$

$$a_I' = a_I + (c_I \cdot \cos(2\pi k/N) - c_R \cdot \sin(2\pi k/N))$$

$$c_I' = a_I - (c_I \cdot \cos(2\pi k/N) - c_R \cdot \sin(2\pi k/N))$$

where a_R, a_I, c_R, c_I are the real and imaginary parts of the input to the "butterfly," a_R', c_R', c_I', a_I' are the outputs, k is an integer depending on how many steps of the algorithm have been executed, and N is the number of points, 1024 in our case.

We assume that $B = 12$ bits are used to represent the sine/cosine coefficients, 16 bits for the data, and 20 bits are retained in the arithmetic to allow a reasonable dynamic range and accuracy.

If T is the time required to perform the computation indicated in (10) then, assuming that fast enough memory RAM is

TABLE XI
EFFICIENCY RATIO FOR TWO STANDARD MULTIPLIERS VERSUS THE PROPOSED SCHEME FOR TWO VALUES OF THE AVERAGE NUMBER OF NONZERO DIGITS

B	$E_{M/EM}$ (AM2505) $a_N = 3$	$a_N = 5$	$E_{M/EM}$ (SN745761) $a_N = 3$	$a_N = 5$
8	0.14	0.08	0.30	0.18
12	0.18	0.11	0.32	0.19
16	0.15	0.09	0.28	0.17
24	0.13	0.08	0.27	0.16
32	0.11	0.07	0.26	0.16

used for the data to keep the arithmetic unit continuously busy, a $2/(T \log_2 N)$ complex data rate throughput will be achieved if one arithmetic unit is used. By adopting a pipeline architecture for the processor [12], [13] and using $\log_2 N$ arithmetic units, a complex data rate of up to $2/T$ can be achieved.

From Table VII we see that the sine/cosine coefficients for this case average 4.03 nonzero digits. Thus to compute (7) we require an average of 20.12 adds, making $T = 1207.2$ ns. To do this we need some 12 IC's consuming 6 W. To allow more flexibility in considering various speeds of operation and to permit a fair comparison with existing realizations, we include the IC's needed for storage of the coefficients. As evident from Section III, we need 30 bits for each coefficient (taking into account the inefficiency caused by using 8-bit wide ROM), thus requiring four IC's of 512×8 each for storage.

The throughput rate will be $R = \cong 165$ kHz, making the figure of merit $F_T = 10.31$.

If a standard prepackaged multiplier chip such as AM2505 is used, we will need 20 IC's to multiply the 12×16 bit numbers and it will take 275 ns for a multiply and add. However, since we need to add and subtract a_R from the multiplication result, we are faced with the choice of adding additional hardware (a 20-bit adder) or wasting two multiply cycles, just to perform two additions. Assume we add the additional five IC's for an adder, then T in this case will be 1100 ns. Storage for the coefficients is here only two IC's. Thus the throughput rate here will be 182 kHz, making the figure of merit for this case $F_T = 6.74$, i.e., nearly two times less than in our proposed implementation.

Since we did include the memory in the arithmetic unit, F_T will remain constant when adding arithmetic units to increase the throughput rate. A fully pipelined structure having 10 arithmetic units will in both cases permit a ~ 1.7 MHz complex throughput rate, however, in our implementation requiring 160 IC's versus the 270 needed by the standard approach.

Finally, we mention that although it is true that a stand alone FFT processor may be required to do multiplication by other than fixed coefficients (e.g., squaring to compute the power spectrum), usually the rate at which such multiplica-

tions have to be performed is significantly slower than the FFT computations, and they can be mechanized in the proposed machine as shift/add with skip across zeros.

B. Digital Filtering

Here we consider a processor that must perform a series a filtering operations on an input data stream, which would be either a high-frequency signal, or a stream derived from multiplexing several lower rate channels. One such useful processor (a digital frequency division multiplexer/demultiplexer) is described in [4], [14].

Let us consider, therefore, a hypothetical processor that will implement, the 10th-order low-pass recursive filter of Table IX, the 56th-order nonrecursive bandpass filter of Table IV, the 100-tap multiband nonrecursive filter of Table V, and the 6th-order recursive notch filter of Table VIII. For simplicity we assume that all coefficients will use 12 bits, and data 16 bits, with 16 bits rounded arithmetic results. For this processing task a total of 102 multiplications and 188 additions must be made for each incoming data point. (Taking into account the symmetry of the nonrecursive filters and not counting as multiplications the recursive filter coefficients that are unity.) From the aforementioned tables, we see that only 361 add/subtract operations will have to be performed in the proposed implementation.

Thus the throughput rate that can be achieved by a processor using the architecture proposed in Section III is $R = 1/(361 \cdot 60) \cong 46$ kHz and the arithmetic unit will have nine IC's consuming about 4.5 W. Storing the filtering coefficients will require only one 4096-bit IC, although we will use an average of 32 bits per coefficient. This makes the figure of merit of this hypothetical processor $F_T = 4.6$.

If we consider now implementing the same processor with the prepackaged multipliers, then 18 IC's are needed to perform the multiplications, one IC for coefficient storage, and four IC's for an adder to account for the 86 more add's than multiplies. The throughput rate $R = 1/(102 \cdot 275) = 36$ kHz, making the figure of merit for this case $F_T = 1.57$, which is nearly three times less than in the proposed realization. The even better performance here is due to the lower average of nonzero digits for filter coefficients than for FFT coefficients.

VI. CONCLUSION

We have proposed a machine organization for the implementation of dedicated hardware digital signal processors that is based on a specialized representation of the processing constants. This organization is shown to be highly modular and well suited to integrated circuit implementation. Upon comparison with existing realizations, the proposed implementation was shown to be significantly more efficient in terms of achievable computing power per hardware expenditure. This is done without any loss of generality, and only at the expense of a fixed increase in storage requirements for the coefficients.

Finally, we mention that a recent approach to the hardware implementation of digital signal processors that also does not require multipliers was suggested recently by B. Liu and this author [15], [16], and the approach proposed in this paper are essentially complementary. While the former approach

IEEE TRANSACTIONS ON ACOUSTICS, SPEECH, AND SIGNAL PROCESSING, FEBRUARY 1976

addresses mainly high-speed processing applications and the increase in speed is achieved at the expense of an exponential increase in coefficient storage requirements, the approach proposed in this paper is intended mainly for low- and medium-speed applications and requires only a constant increase in coefficient storage.

In the relatively short time that digital signal processing has evolved it has attracted increased attention and found ever widening applications. Numerous approaches to the hardware implementation of such processors have appeared, most notably the pioneering work by Jackson *et al.* [17]. These have opened up new options and widened the areas in which digital signal processing has become an effective and economical means of performing a variety of tasks. It is hoped that this paper will offer yet another powerful and efficient option to the system designer, whose ultimate responsibility it is to choose the most cost-effective approach to satisfy his specific requirements.

ACKNOWLEDGMENT

The author wishes to thank his colleagues J. Cocke and A. Chang for introducing him to the canonical signed digit code and the stimulating discussions on the subject matter.

REFERENCES

[1] J. F. Kaiser, "The digital filter and speech communication," *IEEE Trans. Audio Electroacoust. (Special Issue on Speech Communication and Processing–Part II)*, vol AU-16, pp. 180–183, June 1968.

[2] D. Silverman, "The digital processing of seismic data," *Geophysics*, vol. XXXII, pp. 998–1002, Dec. 1967.

[3] R. R. Shivley, "A digital processor to generate spectra in real time," *IEEE Trans. Comput.*, vol. C-17, pp. 485–491, May 1968.

[4] S. L. Freeny, R. B. Kierburtz, K. V. Mina, and S. K. Tewksbury, "Systems analysis of a TDM-FDM translator/digital *A*-type channel bank," *IEEE Trans. Commun. Technol. (Special Issue on Signal Processing for Digital Communications–Part I)*, vol. COM-19, pp. 1050–1059, Dec. 1971.

[5] G. W. Reitweisner, "Binary arithmetic," in *Advances in Computers*, vol. 1, F. L. Alt, Ed. New York: Academic, 1960, pp. 232–308.

[6] S. F. Anderson, J. G. Earle, R. E. Goldschmidt, and D. M. Powers, "Model 91 floating point execution," *IBM J. Res. Develop.*, vol. 11, pp. 34–53, Feb. 1967.

[7] H. L. Garner, "Number systems and arithmetic," in *Advances in Computers*, vol. 6, F. L. Alt, Ed. New York: Academic, 1965, pp. 163–168.

[8] B. Gold and C. M. Rader, *Digital Processing of Signals*. New York: McGraw-Hill, 1969, pp. 173–196.

[9] C. S. Wallace, "A suggestion for a fast multiplier," *IEEE Trans. Electron. Comput.*, vol. EC-13, pp. 14–17, Feb. 1964.

[10] R. C. Ghert, "A 2's complement digital multiplier the AMS505," Advanced Micro Devices, Sunnyvale, CA, Application Note.

[11] A Habibi and P. A. Wintz, "Fast multipliers," *IEEE Trans. Comput.* (Short Notes), vol. C-19, pp. 153–157, Feb. 1970.

[12] H. L. Gorginsky and G. A. Works, "A pipeline fast Fourier transform," *IEEE Trans. Comput.*, vol. C-19, pp. 1015–1019, Nov. 1970.

[13] M. J. Corinthios, "The design of a class of fast Fourier transform computers," *IEEE Trans. Comput.*, vol. C-20, pp. 617–623, June 1971.

[14] M. G. Bellanger and J. L. Daguet, "TDM-FDM transmultiplexer: Digital polyphase and FFT," *IEEE Trans. Commun. (Special Issue on Communications in Europe)*, vol. COM-22, pp. 1199–1204, Sept. 1974.

[15] A. Peled and B. Liu, "A new hardware realization of digital filters," *IEEE Trans. Acoust., Speech, Signal Processing*, vol. ASSP-22, pp. 456–462, Dec. 1974.

[16] B. Liu and A. Peled, "A new hardware realization of high-speed fast Fourier transforms," *IEEE Trans. Acoust., Speech, Signal Processing*, vol. ASSP-23, pp. 543–547, Dec. 1975.

[17] L. B. Jackson, J. F. Kaiser, and H. S. McDonald, "An approach to the implementation of digital filters," *IEEE Trans. Audio Electroacoust. (Special Issue on Digital Filters: The Promise of LSI Applied to Signal Processing)*, vol. AU-16, pp. 413–421, Sept. 1968.

Part I
Additional Reading

E. L. Cole and E. W. Beaver (Westinghouse Elec. Corp.), "Matrix controlled signal processing," in *EASCON 74 Rec.*, Washington, DC, 1974, pp. 592–599.

N. L. Tinklepaugh and D. R. Wilcox (Naval Electronics Lab., Code 5600, San Diego, CA 92152), "High speed processing with asynchronous modules, in *Nat. Telecommun. Conf. Rec.*, 1974, pp. 515–519.

Part II
Architecture

Architectural considerations of a signal processor under microprogram control

by Y. S. WU

International Business Machines Corporation*
Gaithersburg, Maryland

INTRODUCTION

The application of microprogramming to seismic, acoustic and radar processing is well-known.[1,2,3,4] The system architecture required to address wide bandwidth signal processing problems is of a general form shown in Figure 1. In order to provide the high throughput which is required by digital signal processing, parallelism is generally accepted as the proper design concept for the signal processing arithmetic element. A microprogram processor (or a host processor) could be used to control the arithmetic element which can be either an associative processor,[5] functional memory,[6] parallel ensemble,[7] matrix array processor[8] or a vector processor.[9] The efficient design of the microprogram processor is the key to insure the high duty cycle utilization of the expensive arithmetic element hardware. Parallel architectures fall far short of their expectations because of the control problem associated with keeping all the hardware usefully occupied all the time.[10]

This paper surveys basic digital signal processing algorithms. It proposes a signal processing architecture consisting of a microprogrammed control processor (MCP), a highly efficient sequential signal processing arithmetic unit (SPAU) and necessary buffer memories. Emphasis is placed on the MCP architecture because of its importance in enhancing the system performance. An application example, optimum processing[11] in frequency domain, is given to verify the applicability of the architecture.

Hardware technology surveys, and fabrication and packaging considerations are beyond the scope of this paper. The firmware and microprogramming support software discussions are also omitted.

---

* Presently employed at Naval Research Laboratory, Washington, D.C.

BASIC DIGITAL SIGNAL PROCESSING ALGORITHMS

A wealth of literature, including several very good text books is available in signal processing and digital signal processing.[12,13,14] A brief description of some of the processing algorithms is included here. In general, linear filter theory and spectrum analysis techniques form the basis of digital signal processing. Time-domain and frequency domain equivalence of processing is widely assumed. In practice, time-domain digital processing is only used in real time applications with relatively short sample data block. The fast Fourier transform (fFt) algorithm[15,16] provides the efficient digital processing link between time and frequency domains, and frequency domain processing is preferred for narrow-band analysis with fine resolution and large quantities of input data.

Time-domain processing

Consider a sampled signal $\{x(t_n)\}$, where $t_n = nT$, $n = 0, 1, \ldots n$ and T is the sample period. A linear digital filter is written as:

$$y(t_n) = \sum_{m=0}^{N} h(t_m) x(t_{n-m}) \tag{1}$$

where $\{y(t_n)\}$ are filtered outputs of $\{x(t_n)\}$ and $\{h(t_n)\}$ are sampled impulse responses of the filter.

Similarly, the correlation function of $\{f(t_n)\}$ and $\{g(t_n)\}$ can be written as:

$$l(t_n) = \sum_{m=-N}^{N} f(t_{m+n}) g(t_m) \tag{2}$$

Another type of time-domain processing, which is known as recursive filter, is commonly used for limited number of samples to compute successive value of out-

Reprinted with permission from *1972 Spring Joint Comput. Conf., AFIPS Conf. Proc.*, vol. 40, May 16–18, 1972, pp. 675–683.

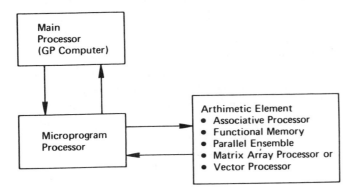

Figure 1—System organization

puts. Let $\{x(t_n)\}$ be the input signal samples, then the filtered outputs $\{y(t_n)\}$ are expressed by the linear difference equation:

$$y(t_n) = \sum_{k=1}^{N} W_k y(t_{n-k}) + \sum_{k=0}^{r} \lambda_k x(t_{n-k}) \qquad (3)$$

where $\{w_k\}$ and $\{\lambda_k\}$ are weighting or filter coefficients of the recursive filter.

For N sample points, time-domain processing requires N^2 multiply-sum operations. Therefore, real time application of time-domain processing is limited to short sample data blocks only. Typically, N equals 64 or less.

Frequency domain processing

Let $\{X(f_i)\}$ be the discrete Fourier transform of a signal $\{x(t_n)\}$ that

$$X(f_j) = \sum_{n=0}^{N-1} x(t_n) \exp(-i2\pi f_j t_n) \qquad (4)$$

where $i = \sqrt{-1}$, $j = 0, 1, 2, \ldots N-1$ and $f_j = j(1/NT)$.

This discrete transform involves a couple of assumptions. Equally spaced time samples are assumed. Also the sampling rate must be above the Nyquist rate, twice the frequency of the highest frequency in the waveform being sampled. When these criteria are met, the discrete Fourier transform has parallel properties to the continuous transform. The original waveform can be completely recreated from the samples. Transformations between the time and frequency domains are performed by using the discrete transform and its inverse. It can be shown that the equivalent frequency domain digital filter in equation (1) can be written as:

$$Y(f_j) = X(f_j) H(f_j) \qquad (5)$$

where $\{Y(f_j)\}$ and $\{H(f_j)\}$ are discrete Fourier transforms of $\{y(t_n)\}$ and $\{h(t_n)\}$ respectively.

Similarly, the equivalent correlation function in frequency domain can be shown as:

$$\Phi(f_j) = \bar{F}(f_j) G(f_j) \qquad (6)$$

where $\{\bar{F}(f_j)\}$ is the complex conjugate of the discrete Fourier transform of $\{f(t_n)\}$.

As a special case, the power spectrum density function is:

$$|F(f_j)|^2 = \bar{F}(f_j) F(f_j) \qquad (7)$$

It is seen that for N frequency domain samples, the equivalent digital filtering or correlation function requires N complex multiplications instead of N^2 product-sum operations in the time-domain. Tremendous computational savings for large N can be achieved if an efficient processing link between time domain and frequency domain is established. The fast Fourier transform algorithm is this missing link.

Fast fourier transform

Since 1965, a great deal of attention has been given to the fFt algorithm by the digital signal processing community. Interested readers can find detailed derivations and variations of the algorithm in references listed in the Bibliography.[13,15,16,17] A simple derivation is included below.

Let's rewrite the discrete Fourier transform expression shown in equation (4).

$$A_r = \sum_{k=0}^{N-1} x_k \exp(2\pi i r k/N) = \sum_{k=0}^{N-1} x_k W^{rk} \qquad (8)$$

where: $i = \sqrt{-1}$

$W = \exp(2\pi i/N)$

$N = $ number of samples

$r = $ harmonic number $= 0, 1, \ldots, N-1$

$k = $ time-sample number $= 0, 1, \ldots, N-1$

Thus A_r is the rth coefficient of the Fourier transform and x_k is the kth sample of the time series.

The samples, x_k, may be complex, and the coefficients, A_r, are almost always complex.

Working through an example in which $N = 8$ will illustrate some of the calculation short cuts.

In this case: $j = 0, 1, \ldots, 7$

$k = 0, 1, \ldots, 7$

To put these into binary form:

$$j = j_2(2^2) + j_1(2^1) + j_0$$

$$k = k_2(2^2) + k_1(2^1) + k_0$$

where: $j_0, j_1, j_2, k_0, k_1, k_2 = 0, 1$

Thus:

$$A(j_2, j_1, j_0)$$

$$= \sum_{k_0=0}^{1} \sum_{k_1=0}^{1} \sum_{k_2=0}^{1} \chi(k_2, k_1, k_0) \left[W^{(j_2 4 + j_1 2 + j_0)(k_2 4 + k_1 2 + k_0)} \right] \quad (10)$$

Now the W can be broken down further:

$$W^{(j_2 4 + j_1 2 + j_0) k_2 4} = \left[W^{8(j_2 2 + j_1) k_2} \right] W^{j_0 k_2 4}$$

$$W^{(j_2 4 + j_1 2 + j_0) k_1 2} = \left[W^{8 j_2 k_1} \right] W^{(j_1 2 + j_0) k_1 2}$$

$$W^{(j_2 4 + j_1 2 + j_0) k_0} = W^{(j_2 4 + j_1 2 + j_0) k_0} \quad (11)$$

Since $W^8 = \left[\exp(2\pi i/8) \right]^8 = \exp(2\pi i) = 1$, the bracketed terms equal one, and can be dropped from the computation. (Note that $\left[\exp(2\pi i) \right]^2 = 1^2 = 1$.) This saves many calculations.

Then $A(j_2, j_1, j_0)$ can be obtained by sequentially calculating the χs as follows:

$$\chi_1(j_0, k_1, k_0) = \sum_{k_2=0}^{1} (k_2, k_1, k_0) W^{j_0 k_2 4}$$

$$\chi_2(j_0, j_1, k_0) = \sum_{k_1=0}^{1} 1(j_0, k_i, k_0) W^{(j_1 2 + j_0) k_1 2}$$

$$\chi_3(j_0, j_1, j_2) = \sum_{k_0=0}^{1} = \chi_2(j_0, j_1, k_0) W^{(j_2 4 + j_1 2 + j_0) k_0}$$

$$A(j_2, j_1, j_0) = \chi_3(j_0, j_1, j_2)$$

Once these computation savings were found, one may generalize that for N point fast Fourier transform $\frac{1}{2}N \log_2 N$ complex multiplications and summations are required. For the equivalent digital filter operation in equation (1), $N(1 + \log_2 N)$ complex multiplications are performed including the fFt on input samples and the inverse transform to obtain time domain filtered outputs. Comparing with N^2 operations required for (1), this is a worthwhile saving in processing load, when N is large.

What are the basic operations?

Product-sum and complex multiplications!

A PROPOSED SIGNAL PROCESSOR ORGANIZATION

The basic arithmetic operation performed by a signal processor is the high speed multiplication in the form of product-sum for time-domain processing and complex multiply for the frequency-domain computations and the fFt algorithm. These operations are always performed on arrays or blocks of sensor data. In other words, signal processing deals exclusively with 'structured' data. A system architect faces:

1. The design of a high speed **Signal Processing Arithmetic Unit** (SPAU).

2. The problem of how to keep this arithmetic unit efficiently and usefully busy.

The latter poses a bigger challenge because it dictates the system through-put by collecting and controlling sensor inputs, and structuring the input data in a manner that can be most efficiently accepted by the SPAU. Typical functions are:

- I/O control
- Multiplexing or Decommutation
- Data conditioning
- Scaling
- Orthogonal addressing
- Format conversion
- Data buffering, blocking and packing.

The above listed preprocessing requirements for a SPAU are characterized by:

- Relatively simple algorithms
- Highly iterative operations
- Low precision

The advantages of using a **Microprogrammed Control Processor** (MCP) rather than special purpose hardware for these interface functions are the lower cost of such a general purpose architecture and the flexibility provided by the ability to change the microprogram. Furthermore, microprogramming implementation of these functions offers 5-10 times performance gain over a conventional general purpose computer of comparable technology.[1,2,3] In addition, macro signal processing functions can be provided by properly sequencing the SPAU under microprogram control. Some of these

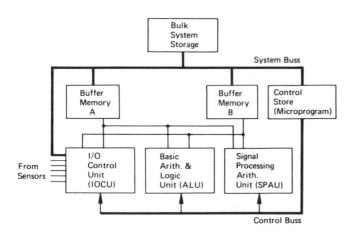

Figure 2—Functional diagram of a microprogrammed signal processor

macros could be:

- Convolution Filter
- Recursive Filter
- Beam Forming
- FFT
- Inverse FFT
- Correlations
- Power Spectrum
- Filter
- Unpack
- Matrix Operations

By requiring the system to be under microprogrammed control, the designer is permitting a single piece of hardware to be specialized to a particular type of signal processing calculation by allowing for the design of an optimum 'instruction set' for that calculation to be loaded into the control store of the MCP.

Figure 2 depicts the functional diagram of a signal processor under microprogram control. The major components are System Storage, MCP, and SPAU.

System storage hierarchy

The structured nature of signal processing requires a block (or page) of data to be operated upon by the SPAU. Therefore, SPAU performance specifications define the buffer speed requirements for each 'page' and the system through-put requirement determines the transfer rate between the system bulk store and the buffer memories. A system storage hierarchy is implied. As to the microprogrammed Control Store (CS), one may consider each signal processing kernel as a module (or page) with highly repetitive execution duty cycle.

If Writable Control Store (WCS) is considered, a dynamic paging hierarchy can again be established for the microprogram execution.[18,19] Since both data and the programs are sequential and block in nature for signal processing, no cache requirement is foreseen. For relatively long data blocks, buffer paging with respect to the system bulk storage can be accomplished through the MCP I/O control unit. No additional paging hardware will be required.

Buffer memories

At least two independent buffer memories will be required because of the over taxing demands on buffer memory cycles by the pipe-lined SPAU operations while MCP ALU and IOCU are preparing the next block of data for SPAU consumption. Two buffer memories in conjunction with MCP can only support a SPAU with a 4-cycle basic operation. If a 2-cycle SPAU is required, four independent buffer memories will be needed to achieve the desired performance.

A 64-bit buffer memory interface is proposed for the purpose of increasing real time instantaneous signal input bandwidth as well as enhancing the paging interface efficiency with the bulk system storage. Experience indicated that each buffer memory should be expandable vertically in 256 by 64-bit words increments up to 4K words. 1K to 2K 64-bit words buffer size is commonly seen. It is intended that the buffer memory is the same monolithic storage used for the microprogram control store for commonality and logistic simplicity. The speed of the buffer memory is defined by the operational requirement of SPAU.

Control store

A 64-bit wide control store compatible with the buffer memory is used for the microprogram storage. Each micro-instruction is capable of executing the following operations in parallel:

- Access the Buffer Memories for One or More Operands
- Manipulate Local Registers and Arithmetic Registers
- Perform Arithmetic and Logic Functions
- Decode and Status Sensing
- Decision Making
- Form Next Micro-Instruction Address
- Other Special Controls

Allowing multiple micro-instruction formats, one can easily reduce the micro-instruction width to 32-bit with a degradation of MCP performance by less than 15 percent. Double fetch of micro-instructions can be considered; however, microprogramming will be more difficult in this case.

Since writable control store is used in the system, dynamic paging of microprograms will be considered. Tight kernels are characteristic for MCP microprograms in the signal processing environment. Small page size (i.e., 64 micro-instructions) may be adequate for a dynamic control store size of not exceeding 1K 64-bit words.

Bulk system storage

Bulk System Storage can be provided as an I/O attachment to the MCP-SPAU signal processing system in the stand alone case. Or, the signal processing subsystem can be considered as interfacing through the bulk system storage with the central computer complex. In this case, bulk system storage can be a part of the shared CPU main memory or auxiliary large core storage (LCS).

The speed requirement of the bulk system storage is dictated by the type of processing performed in the MCP-SPAU. Assume a block of data with N points are first transformed into N spectral elements in the frequency domain and then filtered by N corresponding filter coefficients; the following are observed:

Data Transfers—
    Bulk System Storage to MCP-SPAU
        N Input Data Points
        N Filter Coefficients
    MCP-SPAU to Bulk System Storage
        N Filtered Outputs
Computations—
    $N + \frac{1}{2}N \log_2 N$ Complex Multiplications

If single cycle data transfer and 2-cycle complex multiply are assumed, the speed ratio between the bulk system storage and the buffer memories is obtained as $(2 + \log_2 N)/3$. When $N = 1024$, the speed ratio equals 4. This allows bulk system storage bandwidth to be 4 times slower than the buffer memory speed.

Local stores

Local storages will be provided in MCP and SPAU data flows for internal arithmetic operations. Further discussions are deferred until later sections.

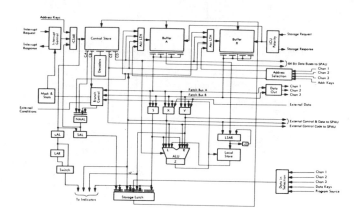

Figure 3—Microprogrammed control processor data flow (MCP)

Microprogrammed control processor (MCP) architecture

The architecture of the MCP is oriented toward its signal processing application as an interface and control processor. The salient features of the MCP required by this application are:

  a. High-speed buffer and channels
  b. Efficient interrupt scheme
  c. Simple external interfaces
  d. Ease of microprogramming

These design goals were achieved by:

  a. Using two independent monolithic storage units as buffer memories and linking them with a wide 64-bit channel interface.
  b. Using only three registers in the data flow and matching the storage cycle time with the internal processing time in order to permit the interrupt overhead operation (save and restore) to be performed in three micro-instructions.
  c. Using a monolithic read-write storage as a microprogram control store. A 64-bit microprogram instruction provides a control format that is 5 to 10 times more powerful than typical 16-bit instructions found in minicomputers and provides the computing power necessary to perform the interface tasks. A read-write control store provides the ease of program modification required to efficiently debug the operational microprograms. It also offers dynamic paging of microprograms through the system storage hierarchy.

The basic data flow is shown in Figure 3. The functional units include:

a. Sequence Unit. The sequence unit is that portion of the machine which controls the sequence of logical operations by determining the order in which control words are addressed from the control store. The sequence unit operations are controlled by the control store word, storage bus condition, data flow conditions, machine status, and channel conditions. The address for each control store word access is assembled by the sequence unit from the above controlling sources in the next address assembly register (NAAR). The save address latch (SAL) holds assembled addresses for storage during interrupt processing. The last address register (LAR) holds the previous cycle control store address register (CSAR) when a machine stop occurs.

b. Buffer Memory Control and Bussing. Each of the basic buffer memories has a word width of 64 bits, used as four 16-bit words in the data flow. The buffer control unit (BCU) serves as an interface between the buffer memory and the various devices that use storage, such as I/O channels, the MCP data flow, and any other direct access devices such as SPAU that may be connected to it. The BCU includes a priority determination unit, an addressing unit, a storage bus, and fetch busses.

c. Data Flow. The data flow includes three 16-bit registers that provide the necessary buffering between the storage bus and the arithmetic and logic unit (ALU). They are destination registers for data fetch and ALU operations. Input selection is under direct control of the control store. All three registers have connections to the storage bus to allow them to be saved following an interrupt. Selection of operands to the ALU is controlled by a control store field. The ALU is a conventional 16-bit parallel adder and logic unit that performs a function on the selected left (L) and right (R) operands. 16-bits represents a 96 db dynamic range. Physical measurements or control signals seldom require more than 16-bit precision. Microprogrammed double-precision can be used for rare exceptions. The ALU output (Z) is latched when the function is completed and held through the late part of the control cycle, when the result is transferred to the destination register. The registers are set late in the control cycle and are held for an ALU operation in the next cycle. The ALU functions include adding, shifting, and logical operations.

d. Local Storage. A 16 word Local Storage is contained in the data flow. The local store provides 16 bit inputs to the ALU. The local store write register has an input from the ALU latch. Local store is addressed from the Local Store Address Register (LSAR). The LSAR has inputs from the X register, the CD field, and the LSAR decrementer. The Local Store can be accessed and written in one MCP cycle. It can be expanded to 32 words. Or, a second local store can be added to achieve the operations of two independent register stacks within one MCP ALU cycle.

e. Literals. Two 16-bit literals are available to the ALU for generation of constants and buffer memory addresses.

f. Interrupt Processing. Interrupt processing consists of saving program status data that would be destroyed in processing the interrupt, and restoring conditions so that the interrupted program may be continued after the interrupt has been processed. The save operation is performed in one micro-instruction:

$$SCXYS(O)$$

This micro-instruction stores the CSAR, X register, Y register, S register, stats, and masks in four consecutive locations in both buffer memories beginning at address 000_{16}. The restore operation requires two micro-instructions:

1. $A(O) = X, B(1) = Y$
   This loads the Y register with the vaule to be restored into S and places the CSAR value to be restored into the X register.

2. $A(2) = X, B(3) = Y, Y = S, RTN$
   This restores X, Y, and S registers; RTN forces CSAR to be loaded from prior X register value returning to the next address of the routine that was interrupted and also restores stats and masks.

The restore operation is interruptable. Interrupts of MCP can be generated by I/O channels, program stats and SPAU completion. There are four programmable interrupt priority levels.

Signal processing arithmetic unit (SPAU)

In preprocessing, it is observed that there is no requirement for a hardware multiplier in interface or control functions. However, an extremely high duty cycle multiplier is necessary to satisfy signal processing requirements. Furthermore, a 'structured' multiplier will be needed in this case.

In order to accommodate both time domain and frequency domain operations, the SPAU is designed to execute the following basic operation with implicit addressing:

$$D_i \leftarrow \pm A_i * B_i \pm C_i$$

where $i = 1, 2, 3, \ldots 4096$ and A, B, and C are all complex numbers

Although the SPAU provides a basic 16×16 complex multiplier, it is hardware equivalent to four 16×16 real multiplier or one 32×32 fixed point multiplier. Under the MCP microprogram control, the SPAU can function as desired in various configurations when application arises. For special case fFt operations, block floating point format may be assumed with 12-bit mantissa and 4-bit scaling.

The SPAU buffered operations can be interrupted by the MCP when MCP ALU registers require a single multiply operation, i.e., MCP register mode has priority over the normal buffered mode of SPAU. The SPAU buffered operations are initiated by MCP microprograms and SPAU interrupts the MCP on completion.

The SPAU design includes the necessary pipeline to assume an asynchronous operational speed. The basic SPAU operation requires two to four buffer memory cycles dependent upon number of independent buffer memories used in the system. Some special functions are included in the SPAU design such as fFt address generation and conjugate multiply.

The parallel matrix multiplier logic of SPAU is very straightforward. However, the amount of hardware in terms of logic gate counts is probably twice the MCP ALU/IOCU combined. It is almost anti-climactic to state again the importance of the 'lean' MCP design in order to keep the 'fat' SPAU usefully busy.

AN APPLICATION EXAMPLE—ADAPTIVE SPATIAL PROCESSING

The function flow of the application example is shown in Figure 4. The mathematical computations required to achieve the 'optimum' processing are described below.

The sensor input signals $x_K(t)$ are first transformed into spectral elements in frequency domain that

$$\{X_k(f_i)\} = FFT\{x_k(i)\} \tag{13}$$

Then the frequency domain inputs are filtered to ob-

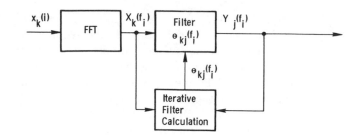

Figure 4—Adaptive spatial processing

tain the desired beam outputs

$$Y_j(f_i) = \sum_{k=1}^{k} \theta_{kj}(f_i) X_k(f_i) \tag{14}$$

Where $Y_j(f_i)$ is the jth beam output and $\theta_{Kj}(f_i)$ are optimum filter coefficients including spatial processing in the frequency domain. These filter coefficients are updated through iterative gradient search process to minimize the output noise power. The output power spectrum is then computed

$$\{P_j(f_i)\} = \{ \mid Y_j(f_i) \mid^2 \} \tag{15}$$

Notice the block array forms of data which are efficiently processed by the SPAU. The MCP will control the paging and I/O for the system.

The optimum gradient search algorithm first computes the gradient for minimization as an input-output cross correlation function $Z_{Kj}(f_i)$ that

$$Z_{kj}(f_i) = Y_j(f_{i_0 m}) \{ \exp(j2\pi f_i \tau_{jk}) X_k(f_{N-i})$$

$$- X_j(f_{N-i}) \} \tag{16}$$

where $X_j(f_{N-i})$ are average beam outputs computed much less frequency. Notice the spatial term $\exp(j2\pi f_i \tau_{jk})$ in the equation and $j = \sqrt{-1}$ in the exponent instead of subscripted j. In order to maximize the output noise power change between mth and $(m-1)$th iteration, an iteration step size $a_j(m)$ is chosen that

$$a_j(m) = \frac{\sum_{i=1}^{N} Y_j(f_{N-i}; m) Q_j(f_i; m)}{\sum_{i=1}^{N} \mid Q_j(f_i; m) \mid^2} \tag{17}$$

where

$$Q_j(f_i; m) = \sum_{k=1}^{k} X_k(f_i) \exp(j2\pi f_i \tau_{jk}) Z_{kj}(f_i) \tag{18}$$

then the iterative processing is completed by

$$\theta_{kj}(f_i;m) = \theta_{kj}(f_i;m-1) - a_j(m)Q_j(f_i;m) \qquad (19)$$

and

$$Y_j(f_i;m) = Y_j(f_i;m-1) - a_j(m)Q_j(f_i;m)$$

In addition to loop controls for the gradient search algorithm, the MCP will handle orthogonal addressing and organize the optimum filter coefficients in such a manner which can be efficiently retrieved from the bulk system storage.

The distributed processing load of this application to MCP and SPAU is normalized to MCP total processing load and tabulated below:

		Percent	
	MCP Load	4-cycle SPAU Load	2-cycle SPAU Load
FFT		9.7	4.9
Filter	9.8	69.7	35.0
Iterative Search	86.0	17.0	8.6
Power Spectrum	4.2	0.4	0.2
Total	100	96.8	48.7

It is noted that for the adaptive spatial processing 2-cycle SPAU will not be needed unless an additional MCP unit is included in the system. The 2-buffer memory configuration as indicated in Figure 2 will be applicable to this problem. The load balancing between MCP and SPAU is accomplished by the heavy involvement of MCP microprograms in the various processing loop controls of the gradient search algorithm to compute the optimum filter coefficients. For less demanding MCP control role in other signal processing applications, the 2-cycle SPAU with four buffer memories can handle higher through-put when needed. Additional MCP processing can also be applied to post detection computations which are not described in this example.

CONCLUSION

The Microprogrammed Control Processor and the Signal Processing Arithmetic Unit architecture presented in this paper blends economy, flexibility and performance in one design. It can truly be a general purpose signal processor. If ECL and bi-polar memories are used for implementation, 50 nanoseconds microinstruction time and 100 nanoseconds complex multiplication speed can be achieved for ground based applications. The hardware size in terms of logic gate counts is approximately one tenth of that of a commercially available general purpose computer with equivalent performance.

ACKNOWLEDGMENT

The author wishes to express his sincere gratitude to many people who participated in applying microprogramming to signal processing problems. In particular, he would like to thank R. G. Baron and S. G. Francisco of IBM for their pioneer work in seismic and acoustic processing, R. A. Rieth of Teledyne-Brown and J. W. Fisher of Bell Telephone Laboratories for their active involvement in radar processing and G. L. Kratz of IBM for general microprogrammed processor architecture work during the past five years.

REFERENCES

1 R G BARON W VANDERKULK S D LORENZ
A LASA signal processing system
IBM Federal Systems Division internal report Bethesda Maryland November 1965
2 *Large aperture seismic array signal processing study*
IBM Final Report—Prepared for the Advance Research Project Agency Washington D C Contract Number SD-196 July 15 1965
3 G D HORNBUCKLE E I ANCONA
The LX-1 microprocessor and its application to real time signal processing
IEEE Transactions on Computers August 1970 Vol C-19 Number 8
4 Y S WU G L KRATZ
Microprogrammed interface processor (MIP) and its application to phased array radar
Tech Note Spring Joint Computer Conference May 1971
5 J E SHORE F A POLKINGHORN JR
A fast, flexible, highly parallel associative processor
Naval Research Laboratory Report Number 6961 Washington D C November 28 1969
6 P L GARDNER
Functional memory and its microprogramming implications
IEEE Transactions on Computers July 1971 Vol C-20 Number 7
7 J A GITHENS
An associative, highly-parallel computer for radar data processing
In L C Hobbs et al eds "Parallel Processing Systems Technologies and Applications" Spartan 1970 pp 71-87
8 R S ENTNER
The advanced avionic digital computer
Ibid pp 203-214
9 *IBM 2938 array processor*
IBM System Reference Library 1967
10 J E SHORE
Second thoughts on parallel processing
To be published IEEE International Convention March 1972

is not needed.

11 B WIDROW P MANTEY L GRIFFITHS
   B GOODE
   Adaptive antenna systems
   IEEE Proceedings Vol 55 Number 12 December 1967
12 Y W LEE
   Statistical theory of communication
   Wiley N Y 1960
13 B GOLD C M RADER
   Digital processing of signals
   McGraw-Hill N Y 1969
14 F K KUO J F KAISER Eds
   System analysis by digital computer
   Wiley N Y 1967
15 G D DANIELSON C LANCZOS
   Some improvements in practical Fourier analysis and their application to X-ray scattering from liquids
   J Franklin Inst Vol 233 pp 365-380 and 435-452 April 1942

16 J W COOLEY J W TUKEY
   An algorithm for the machine calculation of complex Fourier series
   Math of Comput Vol 19 pp 297-301 April 1965
17 W T COCHRAN ct al
   What is the fast Fourier transform?
   IEEE Proceedings Vol 55 Number 10 October 1967
18 R W COOK M J FLYNN
   System design of a dynamic microprocessor
   IEEE Transactions on Computers Vol C-19 Number 3 March 1970
19 W R SMITH
   Simulation of AADC system operation with an E2-B program workload
   Naval Research Laboratory Report Number 7259
   Washington D C April 22 1971
20 S S HUSSON
   Microprogramming principles and practices
   Prentice-Hall Englewood Cliffs N J 1970

Architecture Of A Programmable Digital Signal Processor

Sperry Research Center, Sudbury, Massachusetts

Abstract

A good many digital signal processing applications
require high-speed computational capabilities in
order to operate in real time. The recent advances
in digital device technology have made it possible
for system designers to consider a distributive
processor approach as an attractive solution. In
addition to the speed requirement, many signal
processing algorithms present a complicated data
addressing problem when Random Access Memory (RAM)
is used for main storage.

This paper examines the architecture of a programmable digital signal processor with a distributed
configuration using semiconductor RAM for storage.
The buss structure of the processor accepts microprogrammable modules programmed to execute signal
processing algorithms. These modules receive
commands via a control buss and data (in an
a priori sequence) from another buss. As a solution to the addressing problem, a module called
the address processor is provided, which generates
all data addresses required by the various modules
and acts as the system executive.

Introduction

Applying general purpose computers to signal processing problems is quite often unsuccessful in
real time applications, primarily because of the
rate at which computation must be performed. In
many systems, input processing (A/D conversion,
digital filtering and frequency translation) must
occur concurrently with other computations such as
Fast Fourier Transform (FFT), phase detection,
windowing or weighting, to name just a few. Parallel processing is an attractive solution to gain
the necessary thruput; however, control problems
can overshadow the data processing problem in these
systems, particularly when the system is programmable. Once a system has been configured, keeping
the hardware usefully occupied all of the time is
difficult because the computational load varies
significantly over a given time frame. Programmability, quite often desired, presents another
problem, as the size and location of data records
and coefficients change in a random access memory.

A general distributed processor [1] approach to
signal processing is proposed and a specific sonar
application is discussed as a demonstration of the
architecture. The design objectives for this
architecture are as follows:

- Real time capability
  Sufficient thruput to process, in real
  time, signals in the audio range.

- Programmability
  Filter characteristics, operating frequency, and number of channels should
  be easily programmed.

- Modularity
  Additional capability or additional
  special functions should be easily added.

- Ease of check out and maintenance

Algorithms

Before proceeding to the architecture, a brief
examination of the more prevalent signal processing
algorithms will prove useful. A wealth of literature exists in the derivation [2] and application
[3,4] of these algorithms and hence only the results are presented here.

Two algorithms exist for digital filtering. First
the Infinite Impulse Response (IIR) filter

$$y_i = \sum_{n=1}^{k} \alpha_n y_{i-n} + \sum_{n=0}^{r-1} \beta_n x_{i-n} \qquad (1)$$

the output being a weighted sum of k past outputs
and r past inputs. Secondly, the Finite Impulse
Response (FIR) filter

$$y_i = \sum_{n=0}^{N-1} h_n x_{i-n} \qquad (2)$$

where the ith output is a weighted sum of N past
inputs alone.

Correlation is another candidate for frequently
used algorithms

$$y_i = \sum_{n=-N}^{N} f_{i+n} g_n \qquad (3)$$

and frequency translation

Reprinted from *Nat. Telecommun. Conf. Rec.*, Dec. 2–4, 1974, pp. 496–500.

$$y_n = x_n\, e^{j2\pi nk} \quad , \tag{4}$$

where k is the ratio of translation frequency to the sampling frequency.

Lastly, the FFT calculation should be included

$$A_r = \sum_{n=0}^{N-1} x_n\, e^{j2\pi \frac{rn}{N}} \quad , \tag{5}$$

where A_r is the rth frequency component of the transform.

Examination of Eqs. (1) through (5) reveals some important aspects from a computational viewpoint. First, complex multiplications and summations are the only operations required, excluding scaling. Secondly, the computations are data independent; i.e., no program modification or branching takes place as a result of the execution of the algorithm. As a result of these properties, functional units can be considered which, when presented data and coefficients, produce an answer in a fixed amount of time.

The computational rate required in many of the algorithms is proportional to the signal bandwidth (w) and sample rate. To be able to select a narrow-band signal centered at a programmable frequency f_c which can vary over a wide band requires a high sample rate if f_c is not restricted and the sample rate remains constant. The sample rate (f_i) into a digital filter must be two times the highest frequency present by the sampling theorem. Thus $f_i \geq 2(f_c + w/2)$.

In some cases where $f_c \gg w$ it is advisable to reduce the sample rate so that the computation rate may be lowered. Instead of frequency-translating the input spectrum at the high input rate (f_i), a bandpass filter may be implemented and output subsampled. Translation may then be implemented at the lower filter output rate. Craig and Crooke [5] have shown that FIR filters for sample rate reduction in many cases require less computation than IIR implementations. Memory addressing of data records for FIR filter consumption can prove to be troublesome, however. Consider data being stored sequentially in records in a Random Access Memory (RAM). The filter equation is given in Eq. (2). If the input data is real and the impulse response complex and symmetric, Eq. (2) reduces to Eq. (6)

$$y_i = \sum_{m=0}^{\frac{N-3}{2}} \left(x_{i-n} + x_{i-N+1+n}\right)(Re)h_n$$

$$+ \left(x_{i-n} - x_{L-N+1+n}\right)(Im)h_n$$

$$+ \left(x_{i-\left(\frac{N-1}{2}\right)} h_{\frac{N-1}{2}}\right) \tag{6}$$

Taking advantage of the symmetry of the impulse response has changed almost half the number of multiplications to additions and subtractions. However, a complicated addressing pattern now appears. Figure 1 illustrates the data points as stored sequentially in a RAM. Data points required by the computation are equidistant about the center of the filter, beginning with the newest and oldest samples. As computation progresses each pointer must be tested for the appropriate record limits and, once reached, must be reset to the correct address. Each time the computation is completed the pointers must be adjusted to reflect the sample rate reduction through the filter. Add to this, address generation, multiple channels, programmable filter lengths, relocatable records, and this computation becomes significant.

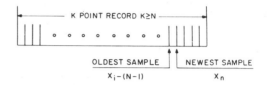

FIG. 1 Input data record.

Fortunately, the signal processing algorithms are data independent for the most part so that a separate address generation unit can serve several functional units.

Architecture

To obtain the thruput required and solve the addressing problem, a distributed processor is proposed as shown in Fig. 2. It consists of microprogrammable modules connected together by a control buss to an address processor, and a data buss to a main storage unit. The address processor provides all main memory addressing and acts as the system executive. Each micro-module is microprogrammed to perform certain signal processing algorithms. These algorithms are written as micro-subroutines, with the number of routines in a

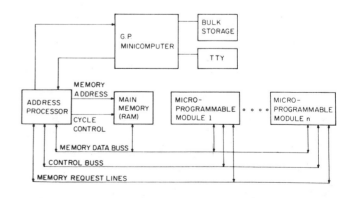

FIG. 2 Programmable digital signal processor.

module and the number of modules per system being dictated by the particular problem being solved, memory loading, and the degree of programmability desired. As the system executive, the address processor issued control words over the control buss to individual micro-modules requiring them to execute particular subroutines. All data to and from the modules come in on an a priori manner, the data address being calculated by the address processor before the module is allowed memory access.

Because this architecture allows all modules to operate concurrently, a very high thruput can be obtained, memory loading being the chief limitation. Elastic type input memories may be put in the micro-modules so that data in excess of that currently being used for computation can be stored. An even flow of data out of the main memory results, with memory overload due to uneven computational rates avoided. Internal scratchpad memories for certain micro-modules have advantages. First, traffic on the data buss is minimized in one respect since some nonessential data transfers do not take place (partial results stay in the micro-module). Secondly, algorithms that are performed in the same unit and follow one another in the signal processing sequence can pass data internally, again limiting data buss traffic. Thirdly, algorithms can be partially computed so that, by programming, an even computational load may be obtained. This last item results in a more complete utilization of the modules and permits the use of slower hardware.

A general purpose minicomputer is used to initialize the system and allow operator interaction via a teletype. Application programs and coefficients are assembled in the minicomputer and loaded into the digital signal processor. Additionally, this small computer may contain diagnostic programs to check out the entire signal processor to almost any level, provided the appropriate points within the modules are made accessible to the buss.

Check-out is greatly simplified because of the ease in which the system interface may be simulated; two busses and some memory request lines constitute the entire system interconnection. Besides acting as the rest of the signal processor, the test computer may provide the microprogram for the module under test. This test configuration will usually not allow the test module to operate at full speed; however, a majority of problems can be detected and a useful module provided for system integration.

By making all or a portion of the ROMs in each module writable, a dynamic microprocessor [6] arrangement may be configured, or diagnostic routines for each module may be loaded and executed.

Address Processor

Functionally, the address processor acts as a high-speed minicomputer with multiple program counters. Implemented as a pipeline processor with separate instruction and data memories, it executes instructions in excess of 8 MHz. Figure 3 is a detailed block diagram illustrating data and control paths.

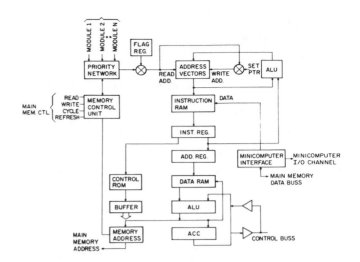

FIG. 3 Address processor block diagram.

Instructions are accessed from a file called "Address Vectors." This file contains a vector (or program counter) for each module on the buss and one for the address processor itself. Determination of which vector is selected to address the instruction memory is made in one of two ways. First, if the main memory has been cycled, the vector corresponding to the module that is getting access is selected to address the instruction memory, for a single instruction time. These programs are said to be foreground programs, and are analogous to single instruction interrupt programs in a conventional machine. Secondly, when not responding to main memory cycles, a flag register (containing one bit for each buss module) is decoded to select a vector for addressing program memory. Programs executed as a result of this second type of vector selection are termed background programs. Background programs run to completion so that only one vector can be processed in this mode. As a result, all other vectors are constrained to operate in the foreground mode, or wait until the current background program relinquishes control. This is done by resetting a bit in the flag register.

As memory requests come to the address processor, they are routed to a priority network which resolves conflicts and initiates the memory cycle controls concurrent with address processor operation. At the appropriate time the memory address file is gated to the memory address lines, and the selected module enabled to place/receive data from the data buss. The memory address file has a location for each buss module and is assumed to contain the next address required for the algorithm being executed. A foreground instruction is subsequently executed in response to this memory cycle and results in the memory address file being updated, or a flag being set indicating a background program requires execution. This method of interrupt handling, which in effect slips a single instruction into the current instruction stream, completely does away with the overhead usually associated with interrupts and allows the processor to respond in a minimum amount of time. Because of pipelining and considerations of just when a foreground instruction is allowed, the address processor with a 8 MHz instruction rate can support a main memory speed of 2 MHz. A penalty is incurred by having no interrupt overhead and that is in the class of instruction that may be executed. These instructions (foreground) may not change the state of the machine as observed from the background program in progress. They may, however, update the memory address file by incrementing or decrementing it or placing a new value from the data memory into it.

Other aspects of address processor operation are similar to a conventional minicomputer with the exception of its high speed. An oscilloscope display of the vector select lines gives a snapshot view of just what the address processor is doing at any given time. A module's background program appears as a single voltage level broken by interrupts from various other modules. This program viewing can be very useful in locating faults or in following system operation.

How many modules a single address processor can support depends upon many factors. Primarily because the system is memory limited, a good deal will depend upon the partitioning of the problem so that the distribution of algorithms to the modules minimizes main memory loading.

Application

As an example of the utility of this architecture, an active sonar processing problem will be discussed. Hardware for this application has been designed and developed at the Sperry Research Center and designated the SPAR receiver, an acronym for Sperry Programmable Acoustic Receiver.

A computational flow diagram illustrating the processing required is given in Fig. 4. Three analog signals are input to the system, one omnidirectional and two others proportional to the target's location in the north-south and east-west planes of the sensor. Each channel is analog low-pass filtered for band limiting, converted to digital and sampled at an adequate rate to preserve the spectrum and provide a guard band. Because the spectrum of interest is relatively narrow, a sample rate reduction of 16:1 can be realized through the bandpass filter. Each channel is next translated to baseband, low-pass filtered, and correlated

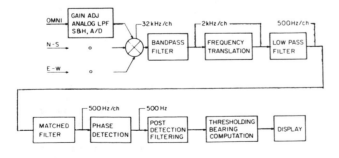

FIG. 4 Active sonar processing computational flow diagram.

against a replica of the transmitted signal. Through the low-pass filter a sample rate reduction of 4:1 may be accomplished A phase detection is next performed where the three channels are combined into a single complex signal whose magnitude indicates the degree of correlation and whose phase indicates the target bearing. Velocity can be determined by correlating several frequency-shifted replicas of the transmitted waveform against the incoming channels. Further processing for post detection filtering, thresholding, and bearing computation is required. This processing, however, need not be concurrent with the calculation required through the phase detection algorithm. Processing through phase detection continues until a data record spanning the range of interest exists in the main memory and, at this point, input processing is suspended until the post detection algorithms have been completed and a display presented to the operator. This entire process is repeated each time a signal is transmitted or a ping occurs.

A block diagram of the hardware constructed to implement this sonar processing is illustrated in Fig. 5.

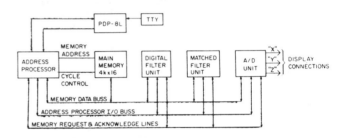

FIG. 5 Sperry Programmable Acoustic Receiver (SPAR) block diagram.

The microprogrammable module complement of this system was selected by partitioning the problem into categories of special function, computational rate requirements, and algorithms which would be performed in sequence. The A/D unit performs all the analog functions including a D/A conversion to drive a display unit. It is programmable in that the input sampling rate may be designated by the control word from the address processor. Because the multiplication rate required in the correlation process was approximately 50% of the total multiplications required, a separate unit (matched filter) was designated to perform this function alone. Lastly, a digital filter unit was assigned all remaining tasks.

Operation

Operation is initiated by the operator inserting various parameters into the PDP-8. These include minimum and maximum range, operating frequency, display parameters, etc. These parameters are converted to constants which the PDP-8 inputs to the address processor along with the operating program. Filter coefficients and the transmitted waveform replica are stored in the main memory. When a transmit interrupt is received by the PDP-8, a range gate process takes place and the address processor is started. It first calculates the input record address for the A/D, places it in the memory address file, and then commands the A/D to sample the input channels. By continually updating the memory address file as samples arrive from the A/D, the address processor can determine when to begin the bandpass filter operation. In this case every sixteen input samples requires a BPF. As the sixteenth sample arrives, the address processor commands the Digital Filter Unit (DFU) to execute its BPF subroutine. The micro-routine in the DFU is of a general nature, permitting the number of points in the impulse response to be programmable. The DFU requests data and coefficients (in a predetermined way) indefinitely, performs the required calculations, stores the result in internal scratch memory. As the address processor detects, by address computation, that the algorithm is complete, it changes the control word in the DFU to indicate the translation subroutine. This process continues, requiring the low-pass filter to be done by the DFU and the correlation to be done by the matched filter. The address processor program is such that one one-quarter of the LPF is done for each translated BPF output, yielding an even computational load on the DFU.

Conclusion

The distributed processor architecture presented in this paper is well suited for signal processing applications providing the thruput needed from relatively slow parts. Providing high-speed arithmetic units data in a fast and efficient manner has been accomplished by the address processor, which solved the addressing problem associated with random access memories and programmability.

Increased performance from this architecture may be gained from faster technology. However, this approach will not give the thruput required for multichannel or radar applications. Additional work is required in expansion of the architecture, perhaps with multiple address processors and multi-ported memories.

References

1. R. N. Nelsen et al, "Distributed-function computer architectures," A Summary of the 1973 Lake Arrowhead Workshop, Computer, vol. 7, no. 23, March 1974.

2. L. R. Rabiner and C. M. Rader, editors, Digital Signal Processing, a selection of digital signal processing papers, IEEE Press, 1972.

3. Y. S. Wu, "Architectural considerations of a signal processor under microprogram control," 1972 Spring Joint Computer Conference, AFIPS Proc., vol. 40, pp. 675-683.

4. G. D. Hornbuckle and E. I. Ancona, "The LX-1 microprocessor and its applications to real time signal processing," IEEE Trans. on Computers, vol. C-19, no. 8, August 1970.

5. A. W. Crooke and J. W. Craig, "Digital filters for sample-rate reduction," IEEE Trans. on Audio and Electroacoustics, vol. AU-20, no. 4, October 1972.

6. R. W. Cook and M. J. Flynn, "System design of a dyanmic microprocessor," IEEE Trans. on Computers, vol. C-19, no. 3, March 1970.

Acknowledgment

The author wishes to thank the many people at the Sperry Research Center who contributed to the successful completion of this project. In particular, A. Crooke and E. Ott who collaborated in the architecture and design; H. Sloate, B. Cashman and P. Schottler who provided invaluable programming; and R. Steel without whose skill a finished system would not have been a reality.

Digital Signal Processor Architecture
For Voice Band Communications

J. S. Thompson

Bell Laboratories
Holmdel, New Jersey   07733

Abstract

The relative complexity of the circuits required for digital signal processing and
the fact that many processing algorithms
have operations in common has encouraged
designers to consider modular or functionally partitioned architectures for digital
signal processors. In this paper attention
is directed primarily at the modular architectural requirements of digital signal
processors performing independent small
scale tasks found in voice band communications such as tone signaling, echo control,
data transmission and transmission format
translation. The major design choices
which must be made in a modular architecture are presented in the context of applications from this class of processes and
are illustrated with the description of an
experimental processor model which has been
built. A summary of experience with this
model is presented to demonstrate some advantages of modular architecture and to
point to areas for future investigation.

I.   Introduction

As the field of digital signal processing
has developed, an increasing amount of effort has shifted from theoretical analysis
of algorithms and structures to design techniques for real-time hardware implementation. To date, however, the bulk of the
attention in hardware realization or digital
signal processor architecture has been on
either special purpose custom designs or on
very high speed general purpose computers
and peripherals for conventional computers.
Very little thought has been given to the
problem of how best to reduce the total cost
of implementing a variety of different digital signal processing applications. As a
result it has often been assumed that if one
could not economically use a commercially
available general purpose computer or signal
processor then the only alternative was to
use a custom design and to retrace all the
steps of previous designers for each new
application. This same problem has arisen
for the case of digital processor design in
general and one suggested solution is the
use of standard functional building blocks.

The concept of digital processor design
based on a class of functionally partitioned modules is not new, in fact, may be
considered the logical extension of the
process of ever higher levels of integration
in digital circuits ([1]). In digital signal processing, however, the predominance
of common complex operations such as recursive filtering and fast Fourier transforms illustrates the need to examine carefully the major decisions which must be
made in the development of a modular architecture. The interrelations between a
class of applications and such architectural
characteristics as data path width, arithmetic organization, functional partitioning
and control structure must be understood as
a first step in the specification of an architecture well suited for these applications.

In the discussion that follows, an experimental digital signal processor is described
and its particular characteristis are used
as examples of design choices in a modular
architecture. Since a number of different
applications were to be investigated with
the processor, it has a rather general purpose capability but experience which has
been gained with it is also felt to be of
importance in more specialized situations.
In this respect the objective of this paper
is not only to describe a particular example of modular architecture, but also to
consider some of the possible advantages of
modular architecture that may not be immediately obvious.

II.   Processor Architecture

A.   General Form

Several objectives were adopted in the design of the experimental general purpose
signal processor. As with previous work on
modular systems ([1]), it was assumed that
the processor would be partitioned into
functional units that could be constructed
as individual physical units with standard
interfaces for data and control. In this
way modified elements could be substituted
in the processor without the need for modifications to other portions of the system.

Reprinted from *Nat. Telecommun. Conf. Rec.*, Dec. 2–4, 1974, pp. 501–506.

Since multiplexing is a prominent feature of digital signal processing hardware, an element may have to communicate data with several other elements including itself in the course of a processing cycle. A second objective, therefore, was to realize a general purpose system by switched interconnection of individual system elements using controlled crosspoints and shared data busses.

With these two objectives realized, the general form of the processor can be shown with the block diagram of Figure 1. The flexibility or generality of the particular processor configuration is determined by the number of independently controlled crosspoints which are actually implemented out of the class of all possible crosspoints. A specific block diagram of the experimental processor is shown in Figure 2 with specific indication of the implemented crosspoints and the functional modules.

For reasons to be discussed in later sections, synchronous data transfer was chosen and it became a further objective of the design to make all modules responsive to a single simple system clock sequence. This means that all modules send and receive data at the same instants. The realization of an algorithm on a processor of this form consists of a sequence of system clock cycles with a particular crosspoint control word associated with each cycle. With a given set of modules, data busses and crosspoints, the signal processing function is determined solely by the sequence of control words read from the control memory. In addition to crosspoint control function, it may be assumed that processing modules may have a variety of operating states which may also be under the direction of the control word. In general, then, the control word will have two portions, one for determining module interconnections and the other for determining module processing states.

B. Functional Partitioning

The detailed requirements for control sequences in a processor of the form shown in Figure 1 may only be determined when the functional elements are specified. This specification involves interaction and compromise between applications, algorithms, control complexity, data path width and arithmetic organization. In voice band applications where an operation as complex as a second order recursive section is used extensively, a functional partition based on that total operation would likely be appropriate ([2],[3]). In this case it is assumed that a permanently wired configuration of adders, multipliers, memories and other elements would realize the function directly and furthermore that this function could be multiplexed to realize higher order filters. If, at the other extreme, the partitioned

functions consisted of multipliers and adders as well as other necessary elements, the realization of the second order difference equation would require considerably more control supervision, especially if a single, higher speed multiplier was to be used in place of the individual multipliers used in the previous partition.

To further complicate the issue, if a physical size limitation is imposed, there is a definite limit to the operational complexity of a given partition when the data path width and arithmetic organization are fixed. The data path width in this context refers to the number of bits of a data word which are transferred and processed in parallel. At one end of the scale, serial processing or one bit data path width requires a minimum of hardware per basic arithmetic operation and so a partition as complex as a second order recursive section would likely be best implemented with a serial organization. Full parallel organization, at the other end of the scale, would likely restrict partitioning to the basic functions such as multiplication and data storage.

In the experimental processor, the arithmetic function $F = X \cdot Y + Z$ was chosen as a partitioned function and goes part way toward realizing not just recursive difference equations but also nonrecursive equations and numerous other potentially useful functions ([4]). With this function, isolated multiplications can be performed with greater ease and efficiency than can be done with a function which was configured primarily for second order recursive filtering and when such filtering is required, less control is needed to realize it than in the case of separate adders and multipliers. Additional elements were partitioned to provide data and coefficient storage and other special processing functions which are described in greater detail in the next section.

The data path width was chosen to be 4 bits as a compromise between signal connections and processing speed for the arithmetic unit. The choice of a relatively small data path width means that it is physically easier to implement a large number of data busses and consequently to support more parallel processing. In the experimental processor, parallel processing is quite limited since only a single arithmetic unit is used, but it should be obvious that additional units could be included in the same structure.

Data path widths less than full parallel require coordination for transfer of data words in parts between function modules. This requirement strongly suggests a synchronous or periodically clocked mechanism of transfer and this direction is further indicated for small data path widths of one or four bits where the process delay time of all functions is about equal. Asynchronous transfer can have significant processing speed advantage only when there is a great discrepancy in process delay times for different functions such as between addition and multiplication in full parallel organization. Asynchronous communication between complex or higher level processes does seem to be advantageous, however, and will be considered in a later section.

III. Function Module Description

A. Data Format

As a general rule, digital signal processing applications for voice band communications can be realized with fixed point arithmetic and data words that range in the size from 16 to 24 bits. The experimental processor was designed to operate with a 24 bit, two's complement, fixed point data word. Since the data path width is four bits, it takes a six phase clock cycle to transfer a full word between any two functional modules. All functional modules send and receive the full 24 bit word with the exception of the arithmetic unit multiplier input and the function generator input which effectively only use 12 and 13 bits, respectively, for processing.

B. Control Memory

While the control memory for actual specific applications would likely be read only memory, the experimental processor control memory is random access and may be loaded through a connection to a higher level support processor. Control words are read from sequential locations, one for each six phase clock cycle except when a special external address control line from the register unit is active. In this case a program transfer occurs and the next control word is taken from the address specified on the 12 bit external address bus shown in Figure 2.

There are actually two types of control words and they are designated type 0 and 1. Each word is 25 bits long and the format for both types is described briefly in Figure 3. The type 1 control word is of the general form mentioned earlier and includes 12 crosspoint control bits and 12 function state bits. The type 0 control word is devoted exclusively to changing function module states.

C. Data and Coefficient Memories

The data and coefficient memories are addressed incrementally with type 1 control words using a 4 bit two's complement increment for each of the coefficient read/write, data read, and data write addresses, as shown in Figure 3. Both memories may have their addresses reset absolutely with a particular type 0 control word and addresses applied to the 12 bit external address bus. The data memory holds full 24 bit words while the coefficient memory only holds 12 bit words which are output to other modules with the bits aligned with the 12 least significant bits of the system data format.

D. Arithmetic Unit

The arithmetic unit, as with all modules in the system, operates in a pipelined or overlapped fashion so that it accepts X, Y and Z inputs during one six phase clock cycle and returns the result during the next cycle while accepting new input. Selection of which 24 bits of the 12 plus 24 or 36 bit product constitutes a scaling function and since a variety of applications was under consideration, the selection of scale was provided as a state that could be set by a type 0 control word. The arithmetic unit consists essentially of a multiplexed array of six 2x4 bit two's complement multiplier circuits.

E. Register Unit

The register unit is built around a standard integrated circuit arithmetic logic unit (74181). In addition to the functions normally available from the ALU, the register unit provides various data conditions that may be tested for program transfer control. The least significant 12 bits of the data word currently in the register can be conditionally added to the external address bus to provide indexed control transfer or memory address reset. The register unit also has 15 words of storage which may be selected by type 0 control words and are often useful for holding process state variables not conveniently located in the data memory.

F. Function Generation

In many signal processing applications there are data manipulation operations, often nonlinear, which cannot be conveniently or efficiently performed by basic logic or arithmetic elements. For the experimental processor, interest in applications involving sinusoidal modulation and demodulation led to the design of a function generator that performs SIN or COS transformation on the input data word.

G. Input/Output Unit

To provide communication with external devices, a group (4) of the input/output registers has been provided for the processor. The 24 bit registers are accessed in full parallel by external devices and in the four bit byte serial format by the processor. As explained more fully in the next section, each register corresponds to a distinct processing channel or state of the processor so that several different processes may be operating on each of several different channels.

IV. Processor Programming, Performance and Experience

A. Program Structure and Operation

Digital signal processing algorithms are inherently cyclical with the algorithm cycle synchronized in some manner with the sample rate of channel supplying or receiving signal data. In the experimental processor rather than deriving the processor clock from the channel sample clock, a system was adopted which is similar to the interrupt mechanisms of general purpose computers and permits channel synchronization at the only points where it is really necessary, data input and output.

Each input/output register has a service request latch and program start address associated with it. Upon receipt of a service request pulse, the processor executes the control words of the program from the start address up to a halt instruction at a rate determined by its internal clock. Upon execution of a halt instruction, the processor is idle until the next service request is received. Simultaneous requests on different channels are treated on a fixed priority basis.

By making the program start address available for program modification, long programs which do not require the same real time processor attention as signal processing algorithms, may be segmented to avoid monopolizing the processor. Examples of such programs in voice band applications are start-up and recovery cycles for data modems, coefficient adaptation algorithms for channel equalization and signal length timing in tone signaling receivers.

B. Performance

The experimental processor has a clock phase length of about 100 nsec which means that 600 nsec are required to complete six phases or a single functional operation. Processing speed is often more meaningful expressed in terms of the rate for a common operation and in the case of digital signal processing such an operation would be the second order recursive filter section. The amount of time necessary to execute this function depends on its program implementation and for this processor a second order recuesive program generally requires from four to six program steps depending on the requirements for overflow oscillation protection and intersection scaling for higher order filters. Processing times are thus 2.4 to 3.6 μsec or, for an 8 kHz sampling rate, stated another way, the processor has

the capacity of from 34 to 52 second order sections of recursive filtering.

C. Operation Experience

Experience programming and operating the experimental processor has to a great extent reinforced a number of assumptions about modular architectures and has provided indications of benefits that may not be generally appreciated. The concept of interchangeability of function modules with improved or upgraded versions has indeed been verified as improved designs for arithmetic units, memories and register units were introduced to the system.

The ability to introduce improved module designs to existing systems and even the high volume manufacturing benefits of using standard function modules may be of secondary importance to some of the other capabilities of this approach to processor architecture. As an example consider maintenance and fault diagnosis. Since several programs can be resident in the control memory at once, control sequences which exercise and test individual modules have been written and can run concurrently with signal processing programs. Such programs could be designed to provide fault alarms in the same manner used by larger and more complex digital systems.

In many voice band applications, signal processing equipment must interface with higher level digital processors for supervision or control. The channel concept embodied in this modular architecture permits such communication to occur asynchronously. Furthermore, signal processors can communicate with one another in the same manner enabling complex functions to be assembled from several smaller systems. In this way the concept of modularity is extended to higher levels in a natural fashion.

All of the features mentioned above were, of course, based on experiences with the general purpose processor that was built. The extent to which these features are dependent on a general purpose capability is not known and is the subject of continuing investigation. It will also be important to determine if a processor architecture based on functional modularity and stored program sequence control can compare favorably with processors designed for very specialized tasks [(5)].

V. Conclusions

An experimental digital signal processor has been described and presented as an example of some of the design choices available in modular processor architecture. Many of the choices made in the design were compromises between extremes that would yield a more general purpose processing capability. The processor control structure based on interrupt driven, stored program sequence control was emphasized as the source of benefits in the processor architecture that go beyond those associated simply with the processor function modules themselves. It was suggested that even for special purpose applications, the architectural features which enhance maintenance, fault detection and flexibility may be advantageous. In this respect, a modular architecture of this type may be preferred even if it were not quite optimal in terms of first cost or power consumption alone.

References

1. N. L. Tinklepaugh and D. C. Eddington, "2175 Program: Quick and Easy Design (QED) of Systems Through High-Level Functional Modularity," Navel Electronics Laboratory Center, San Diego, California, Report Number NELC/TR 1904, January 28, 1974.

2. L. B. Jackson, J. F. Kaiser and H. S. McDonald, "An Approach to the Implementation of Digital Filters," I.E.E.E. Transactions on Audio and Electroacoustics, Vol. AU-16, September 1968, pp. 413-421.

3. H. S. McDonald, "Impact of Large-Scale-Integrated Circuits on Communications Equipment," Proceeding of the National Electronics Conference, Vol. 24, 1968, pp. 569-572.

4. B. V. W. Witte, "Utility Concepts of an ax+b Microelectronic Module," Proceeding of I.E.E.E. Region Six Conference, 1972, pp. 47-55.

5. S. L. Freeny, R. B. Kieburtz, K. V. Mina and S. K. Tewksbury, "Systems Analysis of a TDM-FDM Translator/ Digital A-Type Channel Bank," I.E.E.E. Transactions on Communication Technology, Vol. COM-19, Number 6, December 1971, pp. 1050-1059.

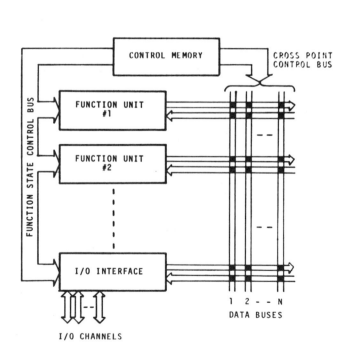

Figure 1

Block diagram of a general digital signal processor architecture based on functionally partitioned modules and stored program control.

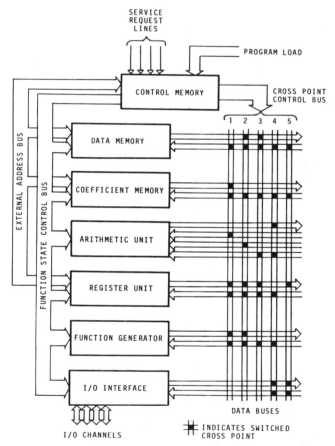

Figure 2

Block diagram of the experimental digital signal processor described in the text. Note that only a portion of the possible data bus cross points have been implemented.

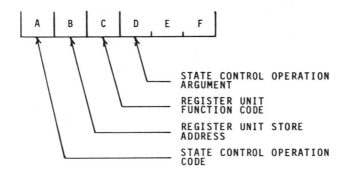

TYPE 0 CONTROL WORD

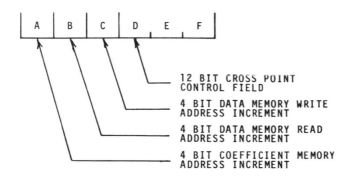

TYPE 1 CONTROL WORD

Figure 3

Explanation of bit field functions in the
two types of processor control words. 24
bits of the 25 bit control word are indicated above. The 25th bit designates the
control word type.

ARCHITECTURE AND APPLICATIONS OF THE SPS-41 AND SPS-81 PROGRAMMABLE DIGITAL SIGNAL PROCESSORS

JOSEPH R. FISHER

Signal Processing Systems, Inc., Waltham, Mass.

The SPS-81 is a programmable processor specifically designed for application to signal processing. This restriction to a very specialized class of computing problems has profound implications on the architecture of the processor. In particular it is possible to achieve very high speed with only modest system cost.

The character of signal processing operations as a class of computing problems and a design approach which takes advantage of this character will be described.

I   Introduction

The concept of a programmable digital signal processor evolved from the hardwired digital signal processor through the recognition that, in mathematical terms most signal processing problems bear a striking resemblance to one another and can be solved effectively with common hardware elements. For example complex multiplication and accumulation of real and complex products constitute a large fraction of all signal processing operations. Also many functions (e.g. direct convolution) require the intensive use of a small data base which is updated at a slower rate so that a small, high speed scratch pad memory may be used.

Another aspect common to signal processing problems is the need for the control of data input and output and buffering between devices each of which has its own particular interface requirements and asynchronous data rate.

Although signal processing problems have strong similarities, they also have important differences, so that flexible control and interconnection of hardware elements is required.

These considerations led to the design of the SPS-41 and the SPS-81 Programmable Digital Signal Processors manufactured by Signal Processing Systems, Inc. of Waltham, Mass. This paper describes architectural concepts applicable to high speed signal processor structures and their realizations in the SPS-41 and SPS-81.

The SPS-41 was designed to have the ability to perform signal processing operations at very high speeds--roughly 100 times faster than a typical minicomputer--and yet to have enough flexibility to do almost any function which might be required. The SPS-81 is architecturally identical and roughly twice as fast as the SPS-41.

II   Architectural Concepts

To achieve high processing speed without pushing the speed of individual circuits, some form of parallelism must be used. There are many forms of parallelism ranging from large arrays of relatively simple, identical processors (such as in the Illiac IV) to a single deeply pipelined processor with highly overlapped instruction execution. Here we wish to compare different architectures subject to a constraint on total processor cost. The SPS-41 and SPS-81 were designed to be produced at a cost which is low enough to find wide applicability and yet high enough to permit individualized customer support. This dictated a parts count roughly 10 times (for the SPS-41) that of a typical minicomputer. With the parts thus constrained, the question of structure can be addressed. One possible configuration would be an array of somewhat fewer than 10 identical simple processors plus interconnection hardware, but this would provide something less than 10 times the throughput of a minicomputer whereas an improvement of roughly 100 times was desired.

The key to improved efficiency is functional specialization in which different portions of the logic are specially configured to perform different portions of the signal processing task efficiently. One obvious approach to functional specialization would be to have an FFT processor, a filtering processor, etc., all interconnected. This approach is widely used for hardwired processors and is ex-

Reprinted from *EASCON 74 Rec.*, Oct. 7-9, 1974, pp. 674-678.

tremely efficient in dedicated applications where the capability of each subprocessor can be matched to the task and the interconnections between subprocessors can be designed so that no conflicts arise. But in a general purpose processor this approach is inefficient because in any given application one or more subprocessors could be expected to be used only a small fraction of the time.

A second approach is a deeply pipelined processor which is superficially like an ordinary minicomputer with a very high instruction execution rate. In such a processor, each instruction is executed as a sequence of small steps with different hardware used for each step. The hardware for consecutive steps is arranged in a pipeline so that a new instruction can be started in each clock period and many instructions are in successive stages of execution at any time. The classical weakness of a deep pipeline is that branching is difficult. It is also difficult to design a pipeline in which different types of instructions can be mixed efficiently.

A better approach to functional specialization is to find a way to decompose signal processing operations into a set of general subtasks which will almost certainly be required in any application and then to design a specialized processor for each subtask. These subtasks should be well-delineated and should have well-defined communications between them.

One such decomposition which is widely used in computers is to separate computation from input/output processing. This allows one processor to be optimized for computation while a second nearly independent I/O Processor is optimized to handle the idiosyncrasies in timing and control of peripheral devices. This decomposition (along with others to be discussed later) is used in the SPS-41 and SPS-81. The Input/Output Processor of the SPS-41 has roughly 4 times as many parts as a minicomputer and executes instructions in 200 nanoseconds or roughly 10 times faster than a typical minicomputer. Moreover the IOP's instructions are 3 address instructions which are perhaps twice as powerful as the single address instructions of most minicomputers. The internal efficiency of the IOP in performing its function is enhanced by the use of a 3-deep instruction pipeline (i.e. 3 instructions are in different stages of execution at one time). Instruction pipelining is a form of functionally specialized parallelism because the registers and data paths associated with each stage of the pipeline are

designed to do only the operations required at that stage and are not used for logically distinct functions--e.g. the index adder is distinct from the data adder. The speed of the IOP is further increased by the use of separate, integrated circuit memories for programs and data instead of the usual all-purpose core memory.

The second major unit of the signal processor--the Arithmetic Processor--has roughly 6 times (for the SPS-41) as many parts as a minicomputer but is very specialized architecturally so that it can perform common signal processing calculations about 100 times faster than a minicomputer. The speed of the Arithmetic processor results from extensive parallelism and its efficiency results from extreme functional specialization. For example, four real multiplications and 6 additions as well as reading and writing 4 real numbers can be performed simultaneously.

The importance of rapid execution of such arithmetic operations in signal processing is widely recognized, but there is a second class of operations, namely indexing and control operations which often receive less attention. For example in describing an FFT butterfly operation

$$X'(j) = X(j) + W(n)*X(k)$$
$$X'(k) = X(j) - W(n)*X(k)$$

the arithmetic operations on the data values $X(p)$ are usually emphasized while the complexity of generating the sequence of indices k, j, n and the associated memory addresses is often ignored even though in conventional computers with a reasonably fast hardware multiply, index manipulation can take almost as much time as data manipulation. In the Arithmetic Processor of the SPS-41 and SPS-81 an autonomous subprocessor--the Index Section--is devoted to index calculations. This separation of indexing and data manipulations permits a high degree of further functional specializations because the operations which are commonly used in indexing, e.g. incrementing, decrementing, bit reversing and logical operations are almost never used on data; conversely arithmetic on complex numbers which dominate the data manipulations are rarely used in indexing.

With this general conceptual understanding, processor structure can now be considered in greater detail.

III Processor Structure

The signal processor (SPS-41 or SPS-

81) has two major subunits operating in parallel for higher speed. These separate, asynchronous subunits perform signal processing arithmetic operations (the Arithmetic Processor) and input/output operations (the Input Output Processor) respectively (see Figure 1).

Input Output Processor

The IOP is by itself a small 16 bit, stored program processor which uses a hardware multiprogramming technique for controlling a multiplicity of independent data transfers on a priority basis. Thus, data transfers between peripheral memory (bulk memory and/or host computer memory) and the Arithmetic Processor might be time-shared with, for example, transfers from an analog-to-digital converter to the peripheral memory and with other transfers from the peripheral memory to a digital-to-analog converter and display or other real time output device. To transfer a word the IOP calculates the address of the source and destination and then moves the data along the IOP bus from one peripheral device to the other. It must also increment indices, test for completion of the transfer sequence and perform any other necessary operations. These operations are done using 3 address instructions which can specify two operand source locations, the operation (e.g. add) to be performed and the destinations. One source is in the B memory and the other is in the A memory which is essentially a general purpose register file. Typical bus transfer rates are one to three million words per second.

The multiprogramming hardware of the IOP contains a multiplicity of program counters--one for each independent transfer path or separate program sequence. This hardware divides the IOP into a set of virtual processors (called channels) each of which is normally assigned to handle a separate asynchronous function.

The instruction sequences of the different virtual processors are interleaved on a priority basis from instruction to instruction. The sequence of interlacing instructions between channels is determined by a small associative memory which inspects the status of I/O devices, determines which channel programs could be executed, and continuously selects the channel among these having the highest priority.

The virtual processors or channels of the IOP are similar to priority interrupt levels in a conventional computer except that a) switching between channels is on an instruction to instruction basis and happens with zero overhead, b) lower priority channels can run if a higher pri-

ority channel is held-up, even for a fraction of a microsecond, c) the priority of service of any device is determined by the priority of the virtual processor programmed to handle it and is not hardwired.

Arithmetic Processor

The Arithmetic Processor (AP) performs the digital signal processing functions specified by the IOP. The AP is divided into two sections: the Arithmetic Section which performs the real and complex addition, multiplications and other operations on digitized signals, and the Index Section which calculates the addresses of data and coefficients within the Arithmetic Section to be used in the signal processing operations.

Index Section

Structurally, the Index Section is similar to the IOP but is simpler because only one program is executed at a time.

Functionally the job of the Index Section is quite specialized. The Index Section is the controller of Arithmetic Section. It keeps track of the sequence of signal processing operations to be performed and delegates the actual manipulation of data to the Arithmetic Section (AS) by loading a set of interface registers with the equivalent of a subroutine calling sequence for the function to be performed by the AS. The calling sequence contains a pointer (FCN) to the AS function or instruction together with the operand address in coefficient (COEF) and the data (RDAT) memories of the operands to be used as well as the destination address (WDAT).

Arithmetic Section

The Arithmetic Section serves as a complex arithmetic attachment to the Index Section. It contains the adders and multipliers for performing signal processing operations. It also contains scratch pad data memory for holding intermediate results (e.g. partial sums in direct convolution or the state variables in a recursive filter) and a read-only table of complex exponentials. These computational and storage resources are interconnected by many selectable data paths to provide programming flexibility. The selectable data paths must also be recognized as resources; in fact typically more integrated circuit packages are used for data multiplexing than for registers and adders. To economize on this resource data transfers and arithmetic operations in the AS are performed in a byte serial fashion. The SPS-41 uses 8 bit complex bytes (4 bits real and 4 bits imaginary) and completes

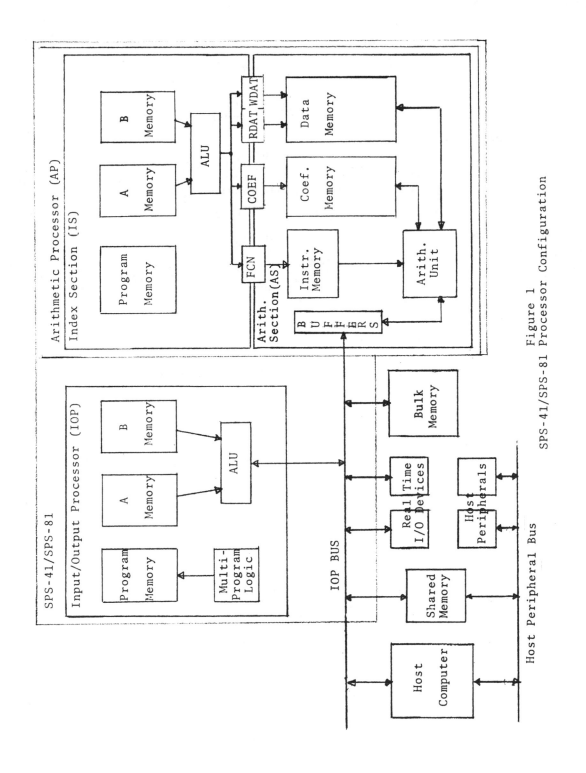

Figure 1
SPS-41/SPS-81 Processor Configuration

107

an instruction (using the addresses supplied by the Index Section) in five cycles of 200 nanoseconds each. The SPS-81 transfers 8 real and 8 imaginary bits at one time and completes an instruction in 3 cycles of 167 nanoseconds each. The byte-serial operation is unseen by the programmer, to whom it appears that Arithmetic Section instructions use parallel transfers which take either one-half or one microsecond.

The instruction set of the AS is stored in a microprogrammed instruction memory in which each word represents one AS function or instruction and contains microcoded bit patterns which control the data paths selected during that instruction. The AS microprogram memory is a read/write memory so that the instruction set can be tailored to the application. One such instruction is the butterfly instruction for the FFT which performs the entire calculation

$$X'(J) = X(J)+[COS\emptyset(N)+jSIN\emptyset(N)]\cdot X(K)$$
$$X'(K) = X(J)-[COS\emptyset(N)+jSIN\emptyset(N)]\cdot X(K)$$

where $X(J)$ and $X(K)$ complex numbers from the Data Memory of the Arithmetic Section, the cosine and sine are from the coefficient memory and the addresses K, J, N are supplied by the Index Section. Other instructions which can be microprogrammed are the second order digital filter instruction:

$$X(K) = X(J)+[A\cdot X(K)+B\cdot Y(K)]$$
$$X(J) = X(J)+[C\cdot X(K)+D\cdot Y(K)]$$
$$Y(K) = X(K),$$

and also complex multiplication, addition of one or two pairs of complex numbers, absolute value (of up to four real numbers) and hundreds of other operations

involving additions, subtractions, multiplications, sorting, inputting/outputting and reading and writing memories.

IV   Processor Operation

The signal processor is free-standing in operation but is interfaced to a host minicomputer to provide hardcopy support. Initialization and initial loading of signal processor programs is done by the host computer. In operation the signal processor either can work independently of the host computer or they can work cooperatively. When working cooperatively, the signal processor performs the signal processing portions of the overall program as a sequence of subroutines called by the host computer. Alternatively the signal processor can operate continuously under its own control with or without synchronization with the host computer program. To facilitate program checkout the host computer can, at any time, stop the processor, inspect its memory and registers and reinitialize its operation. This capability has provided the means to develop a comprehensive operating and debugging system operating under control of the host computer.

V   Conclusion

Architectural considerations in the development of a high speed programmable digital signal processor have been discussed and an approach based on the use of a functionally specialized multiprocessor has been presented. The efficiency of this approach has been illustrated by two commercially available processors which are roughly two orders of magnitude faster and one order of magnitude more efficient than a typical minicomputer when performing signal processing operations.

Computer Architecture for Signal Processing

JONATHAN ALLEN, MEMBER, IEEE

Invited Paper

Abstract—There is an increasing trend to use digital signal-processing techniques to solve real-time problems. This leads to a need for processors which can perform complicated signal-processing algorithms on large amounts of data at high speeds. Computer architectures for this purpose are shown to arise from a consideration of several structural factors, including technology, the algorithms to be performed, data structures, and the programming language. When these factors are complementary, efficient yet economical designs result. The structural factors are described, and then several computer designs are discussed in light of this conceptual framework.

I. INTRODUCTION

DIGITAL SIGNAL PROCESSING was originally developed in order to simulate analog signal-processing systems, such as vocoders, on general-purpose digital computers. In order to experiment with the many design parameters of these systems, it was not feasible to build multiple variations of the system in hardware, so that simulation on a general-purpose computer became attractive, even though the run time of the resulting programs was very long. In recent years, however, many studies have revealed structural aspects of digital signal-processing tasks which could be exploited in hardware design. As a result, there have been a number of hard-wired and programmable machines constructed which provide large speedup over general-purpose processors, and which often also reduce the cost of the calculations. Even though hard-wired devices can usually be made to operate faster than programmable computers, recent advances in microprogramming have led to highly complex but systematically controlled processors which give very high execution rates. The programmable machines, of course, offer flexibility as to algorithms used, data formats, and communications interface, and can thus amortize the design and construction cost over many applications. There is also a strong desire for standardization in many institutions, and this has led to efforts to develop modular basic processors which can be structured to satisfy a wide variety of task specifications. For these reasons, programmable signal-processing machines have grown in popularity and capability, and it is important to understand the factors that have led to this success.

In this paper, we introduce a set of five structural factors which interact to determine the signal-processing machine design. Each of these is discussed in some detail, and their implications for signal processing are noted. This analysis then provides the basis for a number of architectural techniques, which together define the "space" of possible machines. There is no one ideal machine for all applications, but instead

Manuscript received October 10, 1974; revised November 11, 1974. This work was supported in part by the Joint Services Electronics Program under Contract DAAB07-74-C-0630, and in part by the Advanced Research Projects Agency of the Department of Defense, monitored by ONR under Contract N00014-67-A-0204-0064.

The author is with the Research Laboratory of Electronics and Department of Electrical Engineering, Massachusetts Institute of Technology, Cambridge, Mass. 02139.

each computer is a sample point in the space which satisfies the particular speed, cost, size, power, and other constraints of a given application. We discuss several of these "sample points" in some detail, to provide concrete examples of complete designs.

It is important to note that our intent is *not* to catalog the available signal-processing machines. Rather, we hope to reveal those design techniques which have been found to be useful, and to provide the reader with a conceptual basis for the appraisal of any given machine. No survey of machines is intended, and the selection of specific computers for discussion is, of necessity, based on the author's personal experience, the available documentation, and convenience for illustrative purposes. Clearly, no slight is intended toward those designs which have not been discussed or referenced, since we believe that the paper does provide a thorough coverage of the basic principles.

II. STRUCTURAL FACTORS IN SIGNAL-PROCESSING MACHINES

In this section, we introduce five kinds of structure which influence the design of signal-processing computers. The basic task of all of these machines is the efficient execution (in time and cost) of signal-processing tasks. It is not surprising to find 100-to-1 speedups between signal-processing machines, and implementations on general-purpose machines, and there is often also a reduction in cost. We will see that when the structural factors are properly matched, optimal results are obtained. That is, the principle of *structural match* leads to designs where these factors complement one another in a natural way, leading to cost-effective designs.

The five structural factors are:

1) technology,
2) algorithm,
3) data,
4) programming language, and
5) architectural units.

We will now discuss each of these factors in detail.

A. Technology

It has often been claimed that technology completely dominates machine design, and it is certainly the most important factor to be considered. Technology will always determine the basic speed and functional blocks available to the designer, which will inevitably condition the feasibility of any design. This factor is especially important today because of the rapidly changing improvements in technology. The main technological considerations are the following.

a) Logic Family: TTL (and Schottky TTL) has been preferred in small machines where low cost is important. Emitter-coupled logic (ECL) particularly, 10K ECL, has an improved speed-power product, and is used in the largest and fastest

Reprinted from *Proc. IEEE*, vol. 63, pp. 624–633, Apr. 1975.

109

machines since it is the fastest logic family available. It should be remembered, however, that speed is expensive in logic cost, power dissipation, need for special printed circuit boards, special wiring rules, and decreased noise immunity; thus it is always wiser to use the lowest speed logic that will meet the speed requirements. In addition to TTL and ECL, MOS is frequently used for RAM storage, although bipolar memories are used for increased speed.

b) MSI and LSI: 4-bit function modules, such as the popular arithmetic logic units (ALU's), have a strong influence on design. Also, MSI and LSI memories are now fast enough to be used for large register files. TTL has the largest number of MSI structures, but ECL is improving in this regard. Although LSI lends itself to microprocessor design, these units have not as yet been used as structural units because of considerations of speed. With the recent availability of Schottky TTL microprocessors, however, they may find some applications.

c) System Interconnection: The desire for high speed has led to special requirements for circuit boards, backplane wiring, and cabling. The advent of large multiplexors, and of three-state logic, has also favored bussed structures. Since many designs have utilized multiple processors, there has been a need for asynchronous control between processors, and priority arbitration networks to solve the problem of contention for resources.

d) Use of Modules for Multiple Functions: Given the utility of currently available MSI components, it is no wonder that designers have used multiplexors for shifting as well as data selection, ROM's for Boolean function generation in addition to memory storage, and RAM chips to build register files. Increasingly, random logic is replaced by programmed logic-arrays (PLA's) which save a great deal of wiring and space, and also enhance the speed of operation.

e) Multiplier Structures: As we shall see, the need for multipliers is a dominant factor in signal-processing computer design. Several modular chips are available, and high-speed ECL LSI multipliers are under development. No "best" structure has yet emerged, however, and most current machines build their multipliers from ALU's or adders in order to get the desired speed.

B. Algorithm Structure

The existence of highly structured algorithms in signal-processing tasks is undoubtedly the major factor which drives the design of specialized signal-processing machines. It is certainly true that a wide variety of signal-processing algorithms exist, but there is a basic need for two fundamental structures: the second-order section and the fast Fourier transform (FFT), which together suggest many architectural features.

a) Second-Order Section: It is well known that arbitrary recursive filters may be described in terms of an interconnection of second-order sections:

$$y_n = Ay_{n-1} + By_{n-2} + Cx_{n-2} + Dx_{n-1} + x_n \qquad (1)$$

where the coefficients of x and y are real. This modular calculation thus gives rise to the need for four multiplies and four adds. There are numerous ways to calculate the value y_n, but Fig. 1 shows a data flow structure which is maximally parallel and utilizes four distinct multipliers. It is immediately clear that in order to exploit the parallelism, it must be possible to access the operands quickly and in parallel, and that several adders are needed to sum the products. Fig. 2

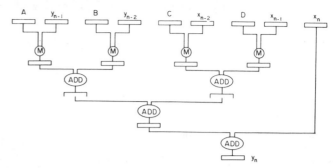

Fig. 1. Maximally parallel recursive second-order section. M ≡ multiply, circles are operators, and rectangles are memory cells.

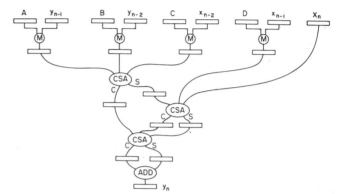

Fig. 2. Second-order section, using carry-save adders. M ≡ multiply, CSA ≡ carry-save adder, circles are operators, and rectangles are memory cells.

shows how the addition process can be speeded up using faster carry-save adders (CSA's) [1] which save, rather than propagate, the carry, followed by one carry-propagate adder which yields the final answer. This diagram reveals the basic *sum-of-products* task which is needed, but it implies a maximum amount of hardware. It is a "maximal space" design in the sense that it achieves high speed at the cost of a lot of hardware, and hence is at one end of the space/time trade-off spectrum. Almost all processors will not choose to implement the second-order section as shown, but many have provided four multipliers and the ability to do parallel adds. The interconnections between these calculations, however, have usually been made under program control, rather than hard-wired as suggested by Figs. 1 and 2.

The arrangement shown in Figs. 1 and 2 is ideally suited for *pipelining.* (In pipelining, a process is split up into several sequential tasks, and execution proceeds assembly-line style, so that many process instantiations can be in progress at any given time.) Consider Fig. 1. There are five levels of registers shown, and as each level of registers is loaded the preceding registers can be reused for a new set of values. In this situation, however, the multipliers will take the longest time, and hence limit the throughput rate of the circuit. This problem can be avoided by pipelining the multiplier itself (as we show in a later section), leading to very high speeds *if* the pipeline can be kept full. This points out again the need to balance storage accesses with processor speed, and also the careful program control needed to exploit the pipeline speed.

It is also important to note that nonrecursive filters are also expressed as the sum of products, so that in most processors, the same facilities are useful for both recursive and nonrecursive filtering.

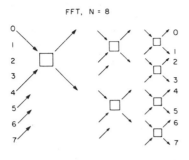

FFT, N = 8

$\frac{N}{2} \log_2 N$ BUTTERFLIES

Fig. 3. 8-point FFT, illustrating decomposition into 12 butterflies.

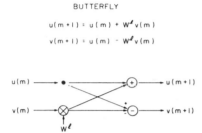

BUTTERFLY

$u(m+1) = u(m) + W^{\ell} v(m)$

$v(m+1) = u(m) - W^{\ell} v(m)$

Fig. 4. Definition of butterfly calculation.

b) The FFT: The FFT [2] is well known to be a fast implementation of the discrete Fourier transform (DFT) calculation;

$$X_k = \sum_{n=0}^{N-1} x_n W^{nk}, \quad 0 \leqslant k \leqslant N-1 \qquad (2)$$

is the DFT of N input values, $0 \leqslant n \leqslant N-1$, expressed as N complex numbers, X_k. From (2), each X_k is clearly the sum of $(N-1)$ complex products ($x_n W^{nk}$, where $W = \exp(j2\pi/N)$) each of which is in turn composed of four real multiplies and two adds. Straightforward calculation of the DFT as a sum of complex products, however, misses much of the inherent structure of the algorithm, which is captured by the FFT. There are several versions of the FFT, but we shall choose the common decimation-in-time for illustrative purposes. Fig. 3 shows a schematic representation of an 8-point FFT, decomposed into 3 (= $\log_2 8$) vertical arrays, each of which involves the calculation of 4 (= 8/2) "butterflies," which are the modular "heart" of the algorithm.

In the first array, the inputs to each butterfly are separated by $N/2$ points; in the second array the input separation is $N/4$ points, and finally the separation in the last array is just $N/8 = 1$ point, for the $N = 8$ example shown here. The expression for each butterfly is

$$u(m+1) = u(m) + W^l v(m)$$

$$v(m,+1) = u(m) - W^l v(m)$$

where $u(m)$ and $v(m)$ are the two input values, and $u(m+1)$ and $v(m+1)$ are the outputs. The butterfly is shown diagrammatically in Fig. 4. We now have the important result that an N-point FFT requires $(N/2) \log_2 N$ butterflies (from Fig. 3), and that clearly each butterfly requires one complex multiply (four real multiplies), and two complex adds, as seen from Fig. 4. The main calculation problems for FFT's are thus similar to those needed for second-order sections. The major differences are in the address arithmetic needed to access operands and store results. In the case of the second-order

section, previous values of x and y ($x_{n-1}, x_{n-2}, y_{n-1}, y_{n-2}$) can be stored in a high-speed buffer within the processor, thus avoiding many main memory accesses. For the FFT, the major saving is provided by the fact that it is an *in-place* algorithm, so that the butterfly outputs can be stored in the same locations as the butterfly inputs. This results in minimal storage, and it is common to calculate an FFT by breaking up the data points, and using a higher radix FFT algorithm. For the present discussion, however, the basic principles can be appreciated from the radix-2 formulation.

Given that an N-point FFT requires $(N/2) \log_2 N$ butterflies, not only can the calculations *within* the butterfly be done in parallel, but there are several options for exploiting parallelism among the separate butterflies.

1) The simplest solution is to perform all $(N/2) \log_2 N$ butterflies sequentially, but allowing for parallelism within the butterfly. A typical execution time for a butterfly on a modern small-to-medium-sized signal-processing machine is approximately 1 μs, and with the addition of address and I/O overhead, a 1024-point FFT takes between 3 ms and 8 ms.

2) If $\log_2 N$ butterfly processors are available, the algorithm can be pipelined horizontally across the array, each processor computing $(N/2)$ butterflies before advancing the data through the pipe. Thus only $(N/2)$ butterfly times, plus overhead, are required.

3) If $(N/2)$ butterflies are available, each vertical array can be done in one butterfly time, and the array can then be processed in a $\log_2 N$-stage pipeline. This leads to a total time of $\log_2 N$ butterfly times plus overhead.

4) Finally, if $(N/2) \log_2 N$ butterflies are available, the entire array can be pipelined, yielding one FFT per butterfly time, plus overhead.

It is clear from this discussion that there is a great deal of opportunity for concurrent computation in FFT execution. For $N = 1024$, a comparison of the butterfly-time multiples is instructive:

$\log_2 N$	$(N/2)$	$(N/2) \log_2 N$
10	512	5120.

Thus improvements in operating speed of nearly 5000 to 1 might be expected from these figures but, in practice, emphasis has been placed on the structure of a single fast butterfly unit, rather than on multiple butterfly units, simply because acceptable performance can be obtained by this means. And the key to a fast butterfly unit is a fast multiplier.

c) Multiplier Structures: Multiplication can be described as the conditional addition of shifted versions of the multiplicand, where each add is conditioned by one of the multiplier bits. Thus, multiplication of two positive binary integers can be displayed as

```
    1 0 1 1 : 11₁₀
    0 1 0 1 :  5₁₀
    1 0 1 1 : 1
  0 0 0 0   : 0
1 0 1 1     : 1
0 0 0 0     : 0
0 1 1 0 1 1 1 : 55₁₀
```

where the multiplier bits are shown to the right of each term to be added. While this model might seem to suggest the desired implementation, in fact there are many ways to perform multiplication, which we discuss here. First, we examine the parallel word-at-a-time methods.

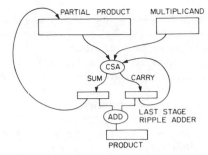

Fig. 5. Shift-and-add multiplier using carry-save adder.

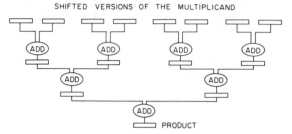

Fig. 6. Tree-add multiplier (8 X 8). All adds on the top level are conditioned by the multiplier bits.

1) Synchronously clocked shift and add: This technique is a direct implementation of the definition given above, and appears in many machines using the AC and MQ registers. It is slow, but can use the processor adder and shift capability, so it is not too costly. Some speed can be added by using a carry-save adder, rather than a ripple adder on all but the last add. Fig. 5 shows how this can be done.

2) Clocked tree adders: Rather than perform the addition sequentially, a tree adder can be used, so that an $N \times N$ multiply only requires $\log_2 N$ add times, as suggested by Fig. 6. Again, carry-save adders may be used to good advantage, particularly, for long word lengths.

3) Pipelined tree adders: The basic tree adder is easily pipelined by introducing registers between the adders. In the high-performance IBM 360/91 computer [3], the double-precision floating-point fraction is 56 bits long. The 56 multiplier bits are recoded to specify a set of 30 adds, which are then realized by a carry-save adder tree followed by one ripple add to propagate the carry. This technique gives very high speed, and while expensive, is the preferred implementation for long-word-length high-speed multiplies.

4) Combinational array: From the pipelined tree adder, it is but one step to remove the registers and clock signals, and yield a combinational array, limited only by logic signal propagation speed [4]. This is the maximally parallel multiplier, and is capable of very high performance. For example, in ECL 10K, a full 2's complement 12 X 12 multiplier has operated in 35 ns, and a 24 X 24 version in 120 ns. There is, of course, the need for many adders, but use of the 10181 ALU has provided the best speed in nonpipelined applications.

In these four examples we have not intended to cover all possible multiplier designs, but only to indicate the space/time trades involved. The spectrum of design goes from clocked synchronous designs, which are relatively slow, require a lot of sequential control, but relatively little hardware, to the strictly combinational designs which are very fast, require no internal sequential control, but result in a great deal of hardware "area." As hardware becomes cheaper, and appropriate MSI and LSI chips become available, we can expect greater use of combinational designs, since the cost for high speed

$$y_n = a_0 x_n + a_1 x_{n-1} + a_2 x_{n-2} - b_1 y_{n-1} - b_2 y_{n-2}$$

$$-1 \le x, y \le +1 \, , \quad B \text{ bits including sign}$$

$$x_n = -x_n^\circ + \sum_{j=1}^{B-1} x_k^j 2^{-j} \qquad x_k^j = 0 \text{ or } 1$$

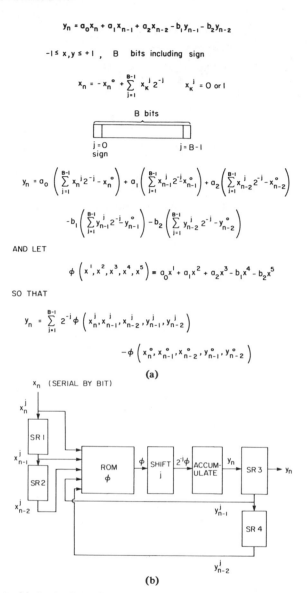

$$y_n = a_0 \left(\sum_{j=1}^{B-1} x_n^j 2^{-j} - x_n^\circ \right) + a_1 \left(\sum_{j=1}^{B-1} x_{n-1}^j 2^{-j} x_{n-1}^\circ \right) + a_2 \left(\sum_{j=1}^{B-1} x_{n-2}^j 2^{-j} - x_{n-2}^\circ \right)$$

$$-b_1 \left(\sum_{j=1}^{B-1} y_{n-1}^j 2^{-j} - y_{n-1}^\circ \right) - b_2 \left(\sum_{j=1}^{B-1} y_{n-2}^j 2^{-j} - y_{n-2}^\circ \right)$$

AND LET

$$\phi \left(x^1, x^2, x^3, x^4, x^5 \right) \equiv a_0 x^1 + a_1 x^2 + a_2 x^3 - b_1 x^4 - b_2 x^5$$

SO THAT

$$y_n = \sum_{j=1}^{B-1} 2^{-j} \phi \left(x_n^j, x_{n-1}^j, x_{n-2}^j, y_{n-1}^j, y_{n-2}^j \right)$$

$$-\phi \left(x_n^\circ, x_{n-1}^\circ, x_{n-2}^\circ, y_{n-1}^\circ, y_{n-2}^\circ \right)$$

(a)

(b)

Fig. 7. (a) Derivation of second-order section calculation by bit-slice techniques. (b) Implementation of second-order section by bit-slice technique. All shift registers (SR) are B bits long.

will become more reasonable. Pipelined designs are slower than combinational arrays *per multiply,* but in situations where the pipeline can be kept full, the effective time per multiply becomes very small. In many signal-processing machines, very substantial software efforts are made to exploit pipeline streaming, but such procedures are usually very difficult to devise.

In addition to word-at-a-time parallel techniques, there is much interest in serial implementations where moderate speed, low power, low "area," and minimal wiring are the dominant constraints.

i) Serial/parallel binary multiplier: An $N \times M$ ($N < M$) bit serial/parallel multiplier can be built using N stages of single-bit carry-save adders. M can be arbitrarily long, but will determine the overall multiply time. The timing control is complicated, and the design is inherently pipelined, but the cost can be very low.

ii) Bit-slice techniques: Fig. 7 shows how a recursive filter may be realized using a ROM and bit-slice additions [5]. Effectively, the bit-wise multiplications of the filter coefficients are done ahead of time and stored in the ROM. This is a clever idea which gives high speed, with fairly low power and chip count, but it is interesting that the technique is used not just to implement one multiplier, but to perform an entire recursive second-order section. It is a good example of the way in which functional specialization can often lead to highly efficient solutions.

C. Data Structures

In this section, we consider the effect of data structures on signal-processing computer design. We list several factors which may be exploited depending on the design constraints.

a) Partitioned Memories: Real and imaginary parts of complex numbers can be separated, as can the two source operands in general three-address instructions. FFT radix size may also dictate the amount of fast buffer registers needed in the arithmetic unit.

b) Structured Access: In FFT's, bit-reversed indexing may be convenient, or "smart" direct memory access (DMA) which stores incoming data in bit-reversed addresses may be provided. For vector calculations, special provision may be made to store and access sparse vectors, many components of which are 0.

c) Word Length: This factor is clearly related to application area (e.g., 12 bits for radar, 16 or 18 bits for speech) and directly affects basic speed, need for scaling, frequency of overflow, memory size, multiplier time, use of rounding and truncation, and overall system cost.

d) Number Representation: For fixed-point calculations, 2's complement is often used, but special systems, such as the CORDIC [6] representation, may result in less hardware for some applications. Large signal-processing machines inevitably provide floating-point capability, with its attendant high cost, but ease of retention of numerical significance. The floating-point units are always pipelined, in part because these machines are specialized for vector operations.

e) Separate Instruction Memory: There is often no need to constrain the instruction word length to the data word length, particularly, in microprogrammed design. This leads to specialized memories, for which accesses can be profitably overlapped in time.

D. Programming Language

Since there is so much emphasis on speed and efficiency, it is not surprising that there has been very little done to develop a suitable high-level language for signal processing. All the big machines are constrained to provide Fortran, but most of the smaller machines have only been coded in assembly language. Perhaps in time, an acceptable set of semantic primitives for signal-processing algorithms will be developed, and these can form the basis for a useful language. In addition to the usual benefits of higher level source coding, such a language would facilitate documentation and the sharing of code, and expand the user community for signal-processing machines. At present, highly optimized routines for frequently used algorithms are being developed (e.g., FFT's, weighting functions, autocorrelation), and these are then coordinated by a higher level user command language which provides linked overlays of these programs. This approach provides much of the efficiency of expert hand coding (a particularly scarce resource on microcoded machines) while providing the user with the ability to map his problem structurally onto these programs.

Higher level languages are also useful where the speed to "get going" is more important than the speed to run. This is essentially the distinction between the research investigation and production runs. It should also be noted that optimizing Fortran compilers have been designed to detect parallelism and (in the case of pipeline machines) reveal possible vector calculations. Frequently, the compiler can efficiently detect exploitable structure at a level near that of the expert hand coder.

E. Hardware Architecture

The above four structural factors have all been examined in order to reveal those architectural features that are likely to be useful in signal-processing computers. Here we summarize these factors.

a) Parallelism: This occurs in many forms. Four parallel multipliers are clearly useful for recursive filtering and complex multiplies. Pipelining is another form of parallelism, and is seen in arithmetic units as well as the overall machine execution cycle. Thus the instruction fetch can be overlapped with data reads and stores and instruction execution. There may also be several independent arithmetic elements, and duplicated memories to facilitate high-speed access.

b) Specialized Memories: The instruction memory may be separate from the data memory, and in the smaller machines the instructions are generally longer than the data word, as befits their microprogrammed design. Since most arithmetic instructions require two operands, two data memories are often provided. It is also common to provide registers which can be manipulated by external conditions (e.g., external device status) but which are also directly addressable within the machine's memory space. This eliminates the need for specialized I/O instructions, and allows for flexible monitoring of I/O status.

c) Specialized Arithmetic Units: We have already mentioned the need for multiple high-speed multipliers. A functional module which computes $(X \cdot Y) + Z$ is also very useful, since it is ideal for sums-of-products calculations, and in tree multiplier implementations, the extra add of Z may be easily accommodated as another branch in the tree. In the large machines, which specialize in vector operations, high-speed floating-point units are used, and these are pipelined into segments which are of appropriate size for the overall data streaming rate. Of particular interest, are arithmetic units that can be dynamically reconfigured (from multipliers, summers, and buffer memories, using multiplexors) under microprogram control so as to provide the programmer with the means to fashion an arithmetic unit structure of his choosing.

d) Multiple Processors: We have already mentioned the use of multiple functional units, but these are controlled by a single instruction stream. In multiprocessing, there can be multiple processors, each of which has its own program, and is specialized to one particular task. Thus we may encounter I/O processors, arithmetic processors, and address processors. The presence of multiple processors raises synchronization problems, and the possibility of conflict in contention for shared resources. Also, it is necessary to balance processor rates in order to remove bottlenecks in the overall data-processing flow. Any or all of these processors can be microprogrammed, or pipelined. While both of these techniques lead to high speed, they also imply difficulty of coding, and the best performance can only be obtained by very careful hand coding.

e) Combinational Versus Sequential Logic: The discussion of multiplier structures considered combinational and sequential logic in terms of the space/time tradeoff. There is a general tendency toward increased use of high-speed combinational circuits, such as array multipliers and multiplexors for shifting, except, of course, in pipelined systems that require careful sequential control.

f) Ability to Check Conditions: Many signal-processing machines provide automatic trapping on data calculation conditions, such as overflow, so that explicit test instructions do not have to be used. These traps can easily be coordinated with the appropriate recovery procedures, so that there is minimal disruption to the main program.

g) Stand-Alone Versus Connect-to-Host: Small signal-processing machines are often connected to a larger host, which provides larger bulk memory, system-programming support, and connection to standard I/O devices such as disks, printers, and tapes. In these situations, the signal-processing machine can be made to look like a special-function box from the host, but, of course, a box that can be altered under program control. The large pipelined machines may be expected to provide all of their own system support. Compilation for signal-processing machine code, however, is often best done on a more conventional processor which is not so specialized to arithmetic tasks.

This list of architectural features which we have enumerated is believed to contain the basic set of factors that constitute the machine designer's options. They provide a framework against which we can describe and compare machines. In the following section we shall use this background to place our description of specific machines in perspective. First we consider small-to-medium-size single-program sequence computers, and then we turn to multiple processor machines and the large pipelined computers.

III. Representative Machines

A. Small-Signal Processor

To start our discussion of small machines, we describe a simple processor constructed by the author at M.I.T. The technology is 10K ECL, including the memories, and the design is highly combinational. Fig. 8 shows the block diagram. The two data memories X and Y are each 1K 24-bit words. The bottom locations of the Y memory, however, contain the index registers, direct memory access control, interval clocks, and processor status bits, all of which can be accessed by the program, as well as by connections from outside the memory. There are no special I/O instructions. The control memory is 1K by 52 bits, which provides two- and three-address instructions. There is no program counter, since each instruction carries a jump address to the next instruction, thus facilitating efficient use of the available instructions. Note also that there are no accumulators; the results of instructions are always returned to the data memories, which can be thought of as large register files.

The processor functions are split into three parts. A large 24 X 24 multiplier is provided, and the Z input to the $X \cdot Y + Z$ array tree is provided from a fixed location in lower Y memory, which is always cleared before the result of a multiply is stored. The ALU is a conventional MSI implementation, providing add, subtract, logic, and bit manipulation operations. The multiplexor performs all shifts and rotates, as well as selecting the desired output from the multiplier.

The basic operation of the machine is thus built on a very simple timing cycle, as befits the large use of combinational circuits. There is no pipelining, since this would provide little gain in this design, but memory accesses are overlapped. While the instructions are long, the design simplicity leads to

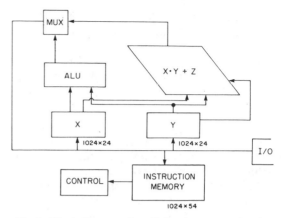

Fig. 8. Block diagram of small-signal processor (SSP).

straightforward coding. The host interface provides generalized alignment capability to provide for connection to machines of arbitrary word length.

This is not an expensive design in hardware, but one that provides a great deal of easily programmable speed in a small package, appropriate to the needs of a research environment. The emphasis is on a straight clean design, which is easy to learn and use.

B. Lincoln Laboratory's Digital Voice Terminal (DVT)

The DVT [7], [8] is a small processor designed to perform real-time speech processing tasks. There is relatively little emphasis on parallelism, speed being achieved largely through the use of small memories and ECL 10K technology. A block diagram for the machine is shown in Fig. 9. It is organized as a two-bus structure with four major registers (A, X, P, B), two memories, and an arithmetic logic unit. The separate program memory has 1024 16-bit words, while the data memory contains 512 16-bit words. X is the index register, P the program counter, A the accumulator, and B (split into two parts) is the I/O buffer register.

As shown in Fig. 9, the DVT has been designed to provide instruction overlap in order to minimize the cycle time. Instruction decoding and operand read time overlaps fetch of the next instruction, and the ALU execution time, as well as the write of the instruction result into the data memory is similarly overlapped with parts of succeeding instructions. Because of this pipelining, it has been possible to utilize a basic cycle time of 53 ns, which is the major factor contributing to high performance.

While most instructions execute in accordance with the timing shown in Fig. 9, the multiply instruction requires 4 cycles, but this is the only exception to the basic instruction timing. The computer proper requires only three circuit boards, while a fourth board is used for interface requirements. Thus a small amount of fast logic has been used to achieve very high-speed performance over a simple instruction set.

C. Lincoln Laboratory's Fast Digital Processor (FDP)

The FDP [9] (Fig. 10) uses four identical arithmetic elements (AE's) rather than the single ALU of the DVT. It has two data memories, M^a and M^b, and a separate program memory M^c, in which each location contains two instructions. All addressing of the data memories is through base registers (located in M^a and M^b) specified by the instruction, which can be indexed. The paths from the data memories to the AE's are ideally suited for setting up a complex multiply, and the inter-AE paths allow the needed shuffling in recursive

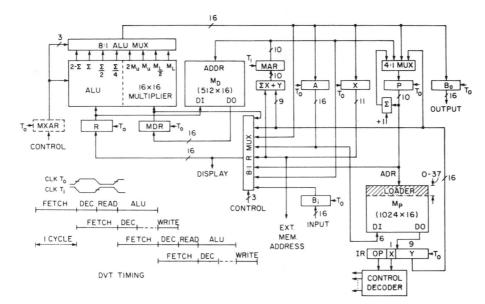

Fig. 9. Block diagram of digital voice terminal (DVT).

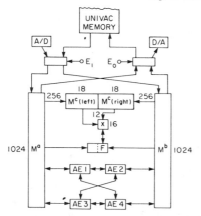

Fig. 10. Block diagram of the fast digital processor (FDP).

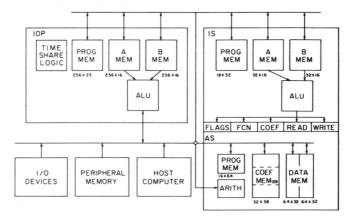

Fig. 11. Block diagram of the SPS-41 computer.

filtering and FFT's to take place without the need for memory accesses.

Each AE contains an adder and 18 X 18 multiplier, and can be controlled independently by the instructions. The instruction repertoire is carefully selected so that nonconflicting operations can be executed simultaneously. Effective use of this feature calls for skilled coding, as does the pipelined instruction fetch, operand access, and instruction decode and execution. Thus while it is a demanding machine to code, the structure exploits many forms of parallelism which can lead to very fast performance.

The machine is designed to be attached to a host and a large core memory. Dedicated A/D and D/A facilities are also provided. All I/O is status-driven by the use of ready flags, which provide the necessary synchronization.

The FDP has been operating successfully for several years, and illustrates that high-performance ECL processors can be built following sound engineering practice. It has also demonstrated the great value of real-time on-line signal processing capability for the design and simulation of radar and speech-processing systems.

D. Signal-Processing Systems 41 (SPS 41)

The SPS 41 [10] represents a successful attempt to achieve high performance by the use of specialized processors, rather than specialized functional units. It is a low-cost TTL tech-

nology machine, designed to be attached to a host which provides all system software support. Three processors are used, each of which has a different structure according to its function.

Fig. 11 shows the system configuration. First, we consider the I/O processor (IOP). The IOP is actually 16 virtual I/O processors, where the entire processor state (accumulators, index registers, program counter) for each processor is stored in the high-speed A memory. The A memory is constructed so that these locations can be used directly and in parallel, just as though they were always in the processor. As a result, context switching between the virtual processes incurs no overhead, and a different I/O processor can be instantiated every 200 ns. The choice of which virtual IOP is to run is made by an associative match against expected I/O conditions. There is an external 16-bit register, each of whose bits can be set by some event, such as "A/D complete" or "memory module free." The program for each virtual I/O processor sets up a mask word which specifies the bit configuration of the external register which should invoke that process. Thus one process might contain the code to read a converted word from the A/D buffer, once the conversion is complete. An associative memory constantly compares each of the 16 process match words with the external register, and provides a signal every clock cycle which indicates these matches. A fixed priority encoder then picks one of the processes which

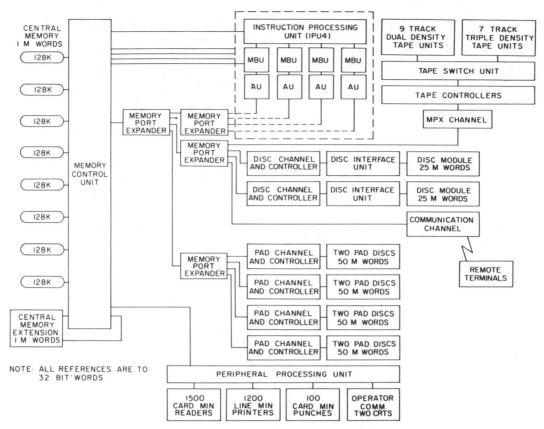

Fig. 12. Block diagram of the Advanced Scientific Computer.

has matched, and transfers control of the IOP to that process. In this way, the IOP is able to provide a set of I/O routines which can be automatically invoked with no overhead, in accordance with the overall I/O status of the moment. The processor structure is a small, but sufficient three-address configuration, which does not require extensive arithmetic capability for I/O operations. Dedicated communication registers are provided to pass data between the IOP and the other two processors, and of course interprocessor synchronization ("handshake") logic is provided.

The second processor is the index section (IS) which furnishes the main control for arithmetic calculations. It is a three-address machine, similar to the IOP, but provides extensive trap facilities and condition tests that are used for loop indexing and control as well as determination of error-recovery sequences and the overall flow of control in the arithmetic section. The IS must perform all address generation, and performs bit reversal and other array sequencing tasks. By functionally removing it from the arithmetic section, program control and operand selection can go on in parallel with arithmetic tasks, which results in a large saving of time.

The arithmetic section (AS) is a slave processor to the IS. As shown in the diagram, the IS specifies the AS functions, coefficients to be used, and read and write addresses. The function code specifies one of 16 64-bit registers in the program memory, which in turn specifies the data-flow configuration of the AS. In this way, the processor is dynamically reconfigurable every cycle time. The AS contains four multipliers, six adders, three data memories, and a read-only sine/cosine table. By the use of extensive multiplexing, the AS may be configured to perform a complex multiply, or the four multipliers can be used for the calculation of a recursive filter iteration. The AS structure is a good example of the

use of microprogramming to achieve specialized arithmetic units usually only found in hard-wired processors, yet retaining cycle-to-cycle flexibility in the determination of the structure.

When all three of the SPS-41 processors are properly coordinated, the machine gives very good performance, considering the use of TTL technology. The need for careful interprocess control, and the detailed level of control afforded by the microcode, however, tend to make such machines hard to code. Some relief from this situation is provided by a set of highly optimized modular routines, such as the FFT, coupled with a high-level language which assembles a complete program through use of linked overlayed program segments. This technique provides much of the speed of high-quality hand code, but allows the user flexibility to assemble the modular processing components needed by his problem.

E. Texas Instruments' Advanced Scientific Computer (TI/ASC)

We now turn to the large vector-oriented machines. The ASC [11], like all vector machines, relies on pipelining for its speed, and up to four independent pipelines can be implemented in a single configuration. There is, however, only one stream of arithmetic instructions, which is designed to utilize the high-memory bandwidth (400 million words/s). Fig. 12 shows a typical system configuration. Eight memory modules are asynchronously switched (and interleaved) onto the peripheral processors, the I/O channels, and the central arithmetic processor.

The central processor contains one instruction-processing unit which controls the memory buffer units which must smooth the data flow into and out of memory to the pipeline rate. The buffer units present operands to the pipelined arithmetic units, which return results to the buffers, and

TABLE I
PARAMETER SUMMARY OF COMPUTERS DISCUSSED IN THE TEXT

	SSP (SECTION 3.1)	DVT (SECTION 3.2)	FDP (SECTION 3.3)	SPS-41 (SECTION 3.4)	TI/ASC (SECTION 3.5)
1. LOGIC FAMILY	ECL	ECL	ECL	TTL	ECL
2. CIRCUIT BOARDS	3-layer wire wrap	3-layer wire wrap	2-plane wire wrap	2-plane wire wrap	17 or 19 layer printed circuit
3. NUMBER OF INTEGRATED CIRCUITS	500	470	10,000	1400	>500,000 equivalent gates
4. MULTIPLY TIME	150 ns	212 ns	450 ns	1 μs	75 ns (single precision floating point, streaming)
5. BASIC CYCLE TIME	100 ns	53 ns	150 ns	200 ns	75 ns
6. WORD LENGTH	24 bits	16 bits	18 bits	16 bits	32 bits
7. MEMORY SIZE	2-1024 word data 1-1024 word program	512 word data 1024 word program	2-4096 word data 2-512 word program	(see Fig. 11)	1 million words
8. FFT TIME, 1024 POINT COMPLEX	5.5 ms	5.0 ms	5.5 ms	8.3 ms	8.0 ms

thence to memory, unless they are needed by neighboring instructions. There is a Fortran compiler for the central processor which searches for vectorizable source code in an effort to maximize pipeline use. In pipeline mode, a new arithmetic result is available every 60 ns, but if the machine must revert to scalar mode, there is appreciable slowdown.

The peripheral processor is actually eight virtual processors time-shared on one physical processor. Conceptually, the operation is much like the SPS 41, except that the virtual processors get fixed time slices set by program control. The virtual processors have access to a set of communication registers, which contain the I/O and central processor status indicators. Since these indicators are directly addressable from the peripheral processor, they can be easily used by the operating system to control overall program flow in the system.

Physically, the ASC is a very large machine based on ECL technology. The power level is very high and cold plates fed from a large refrigeration plant are required. The amount of development engineering required for machines of this size is very large, but for applications like seismic data processing and weather forecasting, the extensive size and throughput speed are needed.

IV. TABULATION OF FEATURES

Table I shows many of the relevant parameters for the machines which have been discussed. While much useful insight can be gained from these figures, the reader is cautioned that direct comparison between machines is very difficult. As we have discussed, each machine has its special strengths, and is designed for a particular set of tasks. For example, the smaller machines generally use fixed-point arithmetic, while

the large vector-oriented computers use pipelined floating-point functional units. There is also a great deal of difference in memory size where the small machines may have less than 1024 words of local memory, but the big machines can have one million words of highly interleaved memory.

Most of the computers can do a 1024-point complex FFT in between 5 and 10 ms, which is a useful number to keep in mind. But these figures are often memory-limited, so that comparisons are not always possible. Thus depending on the configuration, the computer might be using relatively slow core memory, medium speed MOS memory, or high-speed bipolar elements. The reader must be careful to understand what the limiting factors are in each application, so as to obtain a true appraisal of the machine.

V. SUMMARY

In this paper we have attempted to establish a set of requirements for digital signal-processing computers, and to discuss the many factors that influence machine design and performance. We have not tried to give an extensive discussion of the particular machines described, but instead, we have shown how each machine design has exploited the available techniques to meet its design requirements. It will be apparent that there is a great deal of variation in these designs, in part due to the data rates implied by the intended applications. There has certainly been no reluctance to utilize the best technology available, even though architectural features can often reduce the need for brute force speed substantially.

Perhaps the most interesting aspect of these designs is that the best examples are the result of very careful analysis of the algorithmic needs of signal processing, often involving extensive measurement of algorithmic execution on general-purpose machines. This procedure is reminiscent of the kind of design study made for the original "von Neumann" computer at the Princeton Institute for Advanced Study [12]. The features of this machine were dictated almost exclusively by an examination of the computational needs imposed by the solution of linear differential equations. Similarly, the success of current signal-processing machines is strongly determined by the study of the intended task domains. This has led to the use of digital signal processing in on-line real-time applications, so that algorithms which were once developed only for simulation are now introduced for direct use in practical systems. We strongly believe that the fruits of computer architecture study for digital signal processing have largely been responsible for much of the current growth and excitement in this field.

REFERENCES

[1] I. Flores, *The Logic of Computer Arithmetic*. Englewood Cliffs, N.J.: Prentice-Hall, 1963.
[2] W. T. Cochran *et al.*, "What is the fast Fourier transform," *Proc. IEEE*, vol. 55, pp. 1664–1674, Oct. 1967.
[3] S. F. Anderson *et al.*, "The IBM System/360 Model 91; floating point execution unit," *IBM J.*, vol. 11, no. 1, Jan. 1967.
[4] J. Allen and E. R. Jensen, "A new high-speed multiplier design," Res. Lab. Electron., M.I.T., Quart. Progress Rep. 105, Apr. 15, 1972.
[5] A. Peled and B. Liu, "A new approach to the realization of non-recursive digital filters," *IEEE Trans. Audio Electroacoust.*, vol. AU-21, pp. 477–484, Dec. 1973.
[6] J. S. Walther, "A unified algorithm for elementary functions," in *1971 Spring Joint Computer Conf., AFIPS Conf. Proc.* Washington, D.C.: Spartan Press.
[7] P. E. Blankenship, B. Gold, P. G. McHugh, and C. J. Weinstein, "Design study of the advanced signal processor," M.I.T. Lincoln Lab., Lexington, Mass., Lincoln Lab. Tech. Note 1972-17, Apr. 27, 1972.
[8] G. D. Hornbuckle and E. I. Ancona, "The LX-1 microprocessor and its application to real-time signal processing," *IEEE Trans. Comput.*, vol. C-19, pp. 710–720, Aug. 1970.
[9] B. Gold, I. L. Lebow, P. G. McHugh, and C. M. Rader, "The FDP, a fast programmable signal processor," *IEEE Trans. Comput.*, vol. C-20, pp. 33–38, Jan. 1971.
[10] *SPS-41 User's Manual*. Waltham, Mass.: Signal Processing Systems, 1974.
[11] Texas Instruments, "A description of the advanced scientific computer system," Texas Instruments, Austin, Tex., Apr. 1973.
[12] A. W. Burks, H. H. Goldstine, and J. von Neumann, "Preliminary discussion of the logical design of an electronic computing instrument," in *Computer Structures*, C. G. Bell and A. Newell. New York: McGraw-Hill, 1971.

Part II
Additional Reading

R. W. Cook and M. J. Flynn (Bell Lab., Naperville, IL; Elec. Eng. Dep., Northwestern Univ., Evanston, IL), "System design of a dynamic microprocessor," *IEEE Trans. Comput.*, vol. C-19, pp. 213–222, 1970.

P. E. Blankenship, B. Gold, P. G. McHugh, and C. J. Weinstein (M.I.T. Lincoln Lab., Lexington, MA), "Design study of the advanced signal processor," Lincoln Lab Group 24 Note, ESD-TR-72-101, 1972.

J. P. Ihnat, T. G. Rauscher, B. P. Shay, H. H. Smith and W. R. Smith (Naval Research Lab., Washington, DC 20375), "Use of two levels of parallelism to implement an efficient programmable signal processing computer," in *Proc. Sagamore Comput Conf. on Parallel Processing*, 1973, pp. 113–119.

G. Kratz, W. Sproul, and E. Walendziewicz (Federal Systems Div., IBM Corp., Manassas, VA 22110; IBM Corp., Burlington, MA 01803), "A microprogrammed approach to signal processing," *IEEE Trans. Comput.*, vol. C-23, pp. 808–816, 1974.

Part III
Elements of a Digital Signal Processor

Section III-A
Computing Units for Digital Filters

United States Patent [19]

Croisier et al.

[11] **3,777,130**

[45] **Dec. 4, 1973**

[54] **DIGITAL FILTER FOR PCM ENCODED SIGNALS**

[75] Inventors: **Alain Croisier**, Cagnes; **Daniel J. Esteban**, La Gaude; **Marc E. Levilion; Vladimir Riso**, both of Nice, all of France

[73] Assignee: **International Business Machines Corporation**, Armonk, N.Y.

[22] Filed: **Dec. 15, 1971**

[21] Appl. No.: **208,345**

[30] **Foreign Application Priority Data**

Dec. 17, 1970   France 7047123

[52] **U.S. Cl.**................................. **235/152, 235/156**
[51] **Int. Cl.**........................... G06f 1/02, G06f 15/34
[58] **Field of Search**.................... 235/152, 156, 164; 328/162; 333/18; 325/41, 42

[56] **References Cited**

UNITED STATES PATENTS

3,579,102	5/1971	Hatley	325/42
3,619,586	11/1971	Hoff et al.........................	235/152 X
3,543,012	11/1970	Courtney	235/152 UX
3,521,042	7/1970	Blerkom et al.	235/156
3,521,041	7/1970	Blerkom et al.	235/156
3,446,949	5/1969	Trimble	235/156 X

Primary Examiner—Malcolm A. Morrison
Assistant Examiner—James F. Gottman
Attorney—Robert B. Brodie et al.

[57] **ABSTRACT**

A digital filter either of a recursive or transversal type responsive to successive digitally encoded analog signal samples of m bits each. The filter comprises an accumulator for multiplying and summing a weighted hybrid value obtained from a memory medium addressed by a selected one of the m bits of each of N digitally encoded signal samples. If the bits of the N samples used for addressing the memory are derived from successive input signals only, then the filter is of the transversal type. If V of the N signals whose bits are used for addressing are from the input samples and R of the N signals whose bits also are used for addressing are obtained from filter output signals, then the filter is recursive. By addressing the memory with the binary value of like bit positions of the signal samples, then a hybrid value may be stored, which hybrid value need only be multiplied and combined by the accumulator. This permits the use of a substantially smaller memory than that required if the digits of the signals looked up the completed weighted function.

4 Claims, 9 Drawing Figures

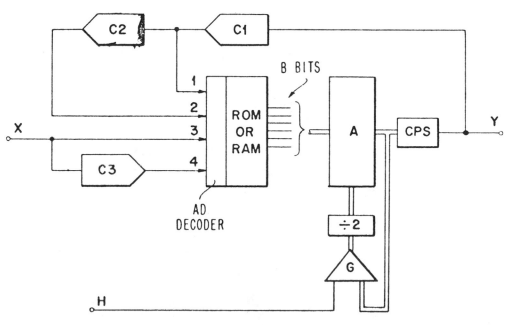

Reprinted from U.S. Patent 3,777,130, Dec. 4, 1973.

FIG. 1

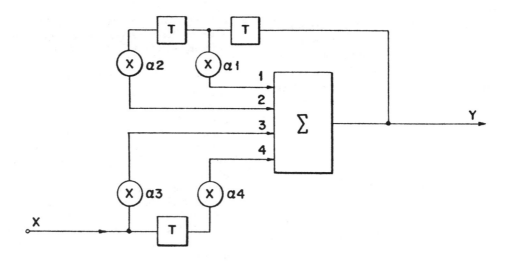

FIG. 2

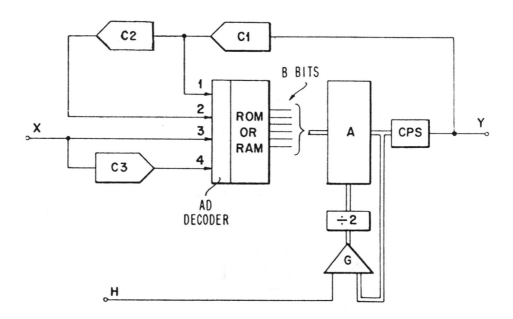

FIG. 3

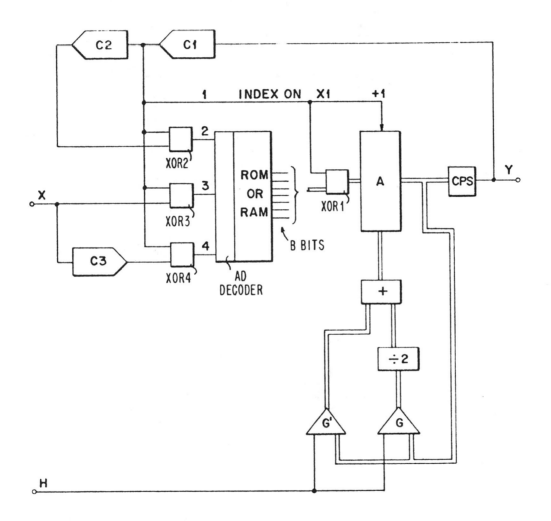

FIG. 4

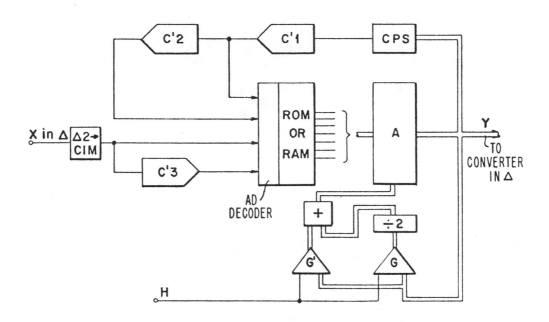

FIG. 5

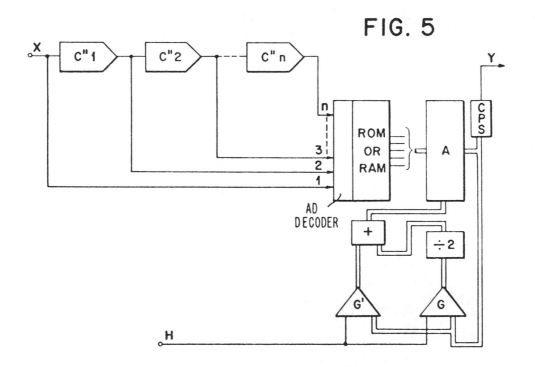

FIG. 6

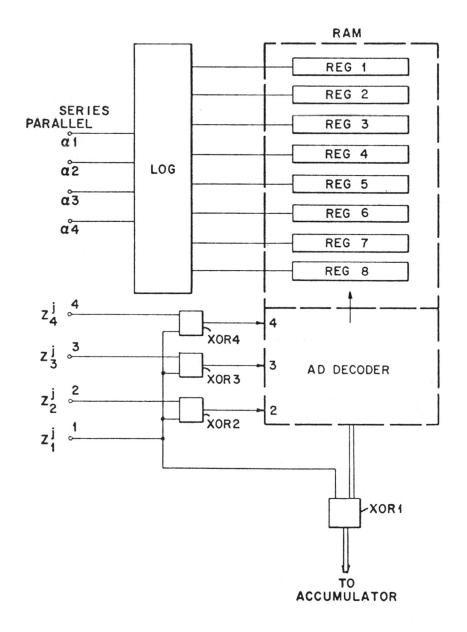

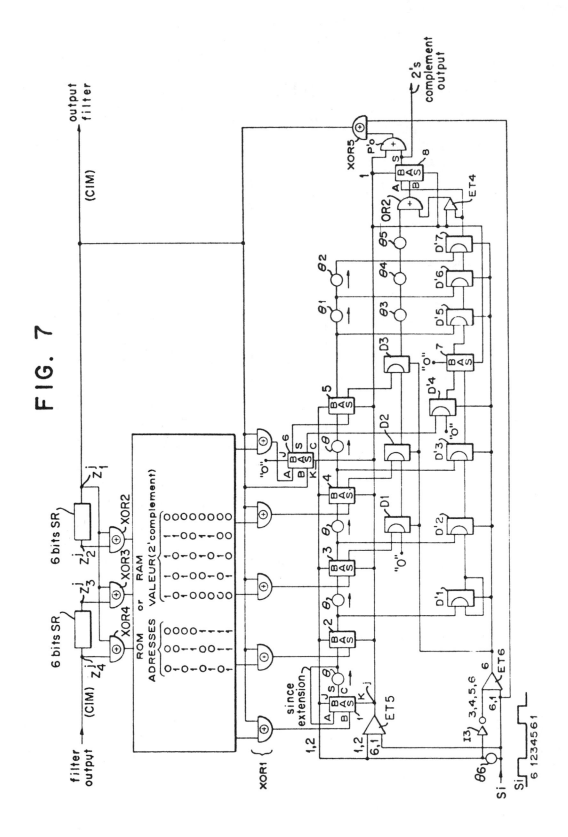

FIG. 7

FIG. 7a

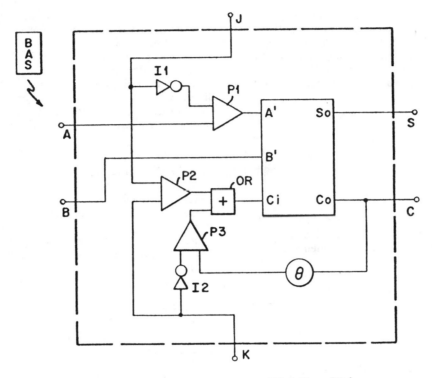

FIG. 7b

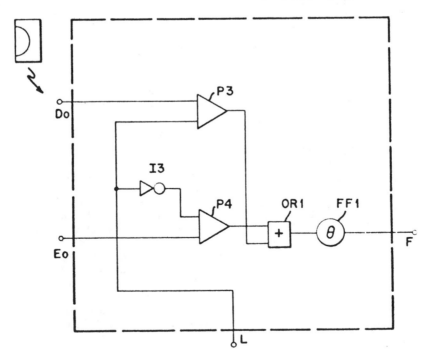

127

DIGITAL FILTER FOR PCM ENCODED SIGNALS

BACKGROUND OF THE INVENTION

This invention relates to a digital filter, the responses of which is computed digitally through readings of binary words recorded in a memory medium, said filter accumulating the words read out of said memory.

In the prior art bulk memory was used in conjunction with digital filtering as a technique for simplifying or eliminating the multiplier portions of such filters. A typical filter transfer function would relate the filter output Y to a series of input signals X(NT), X(NT-T) and/or prior output signals Y(NT-T) according to the relation :

$$Y(NT) = a_1 \, X \, (NT) + a_2 \, X \, (NT-T) + a_2 \, Y \, (NT-T).$$

If the coefficients could be read out from a bulk memory and applied to arm multiplier elements only when used then the customary elaborate resistive weighting networks might be simplified or eliminated. L. B. Jackson in U.S. Pat. No. 3,522,546 filed Feb. 29, 1968 shows such an approach for a transversal digital filter. In a related development, A. J. Deerfield in U.S. Pat. No. 3,370,292 issued on Feb. 20, 1968 taught that a reference table addressable by an intermediate value in a digital filtering sequence could be used to provide values that could be logically combined with input signals in a feedforward path and in a feedback path. However, the Deerfield arrangement was concerned neither with optimum memory capacity, multiplier elimination, and the use of the input signal elements to directly access the stored values of interest.

Study of digital filters shows that they can be built by using digital circuits processing multiplication on successive samples of the analog signal to be filtered, and adding the weightings so obtained. The use of these processes has been reserved for a long time, for the laboratories carrying out simulations to test the characteristics of the designed device. In these cases, the weighting factors chosen from an analysis of the transfer function of the desired filter, are stored and used by the computer under program control.

SUMMARY OF THE INVENTION

It is accordingly an object of this invention to devise a digital filter responsive to successive ordinary binary coded signal samples such as PCM of the type in which a bulk memory is used to obtain intermediate values, which values are subsequently accumulated. It is a related object that the filter be utilizable in either a transversal or recursive configuration and further that the memory be accessed in such a manner that its capacity can be minimized.

The foregoing objects are satisfied by an embodiment in successive binary coded signal samples Z_i are considered as numbers of the form $2^{m-1} Z_i^m + \cdots 2^{j-1}Z_i^j + +2^0 Z_i^1$. Relatedly, the output of the filter Y is taken as a weighted function of Z_i, i.e.,

$$Y = \sum_{i=1}^{N} a_i Z_i$$

If $Z_i = \sum_{j=1}^{m} 2^{j-1} Z_i^j$, then

$$Y = \sum a_i Z_i = \sum_{i=1}^{N} a_i \sum_{j=1}^{m} 2^{j-1}Z_i^j = \sum_{j=1}^{m} 2^{j-1} \sum_{i=1}^{N} a_i Z_i^j$$

$$Y = \sum_{j=1}^{m} 2^{j-1} \, Sj; \; Sj = \sum_{j=1}^{N} a_i z_i^j.$$

The invention contemplates utilizing the jth bit of each of the N input signal samples of M bits each in order to address the memory medium. Restated, Z_1^j, $Z_2^j \cdots Z_N^j$ is applied directly to the memory medium to obtain a corresponding hybrid value, Sj. This is in turn applied to an accumulator where it is appropriately multipled $2^{j-1} Sj$ and combined to form the sum$\Sigma 2^{j-1} Sj$.

Because only N bits address the memory, its capacity can be limited to 2^N different locations. This is in contrast with the prior art. Also, direct addressing by the filter input or output signals thus eliminating the costly serial processing logic found in the feedforward or feedback channels of some prior art systems.

BRIEF DESCRIPTION OF THE DRAWING

FIG. 1 shows the functional diagram of a recursive filter according to the prior art.

FIG. 2 shows the functional diagram of a recursive filter in accordance with this invention, for PCM coded data.

FIG. 3 shows the functional diagram of a recursive filter in accordance with this invention.

FIG. 4 shows the functional diagram of a recursive filter in accordance with this invention, for Δ coded data.

FIG. 5 shows the functional diagram of a transversal filter according to this invention.

FIG. 6 shows the functional diagram of a filter made in accordance with this invention and using a RAM.

FIGS. 7, 7a and 7b show a diagram of a recursive filter in accordance with this invention.

DESCRIPTION OF THE PREFERRED EMBODIMENT

It is noted that a read only memory ROM is considered to be a device which holds permanent data not alterable by signal processing. In contrast, a random access memory RAM is a storage element designed to give a constant access time for any location addressed irrespective of the location previously addressed. In practice ROM usually has a constant access time, the difference between the ROM and RAM being that the information contents of the RAM may be alterable.

A transfer function of any filter, sampled at a frequency FS, can be synthetized by using a device carrying out the operations diagramatically shown on FIG. 1. The successive samples of the signal to be filtered X are transmitted through a delay line composed of cells with an elementary delay T equal to the sampling period. The signal, taken from the terminals of each T delayed call is multiplied by a given factor deduced, in accordance with the selected method, either from the pulse response or from the desired frequency transfer function. The section of the device carrying out these operations defines a section called "direct section". Then the results of these weightings are added in a Σ stage. The filtered output signal Y is re-injected into stage Σ after passing through a second delay line and after weighting operations performed with some other values of said factors α, thus defining a section called "feedback section."

Thus, such a device involves multiplying and adding operations and it seems to be particularly interesting to carry out these operations by using personalized computers after conversion of the samples to be filtered in digital mode. In this case, each sample supplies a logic word, the bits of which, after passing through the various stages of a shift register, providing pure delays, processed in order to carry out the mathematical operations indicated above. In fact, the signal has often be already converted in digital mode, through modulation processes called PCM or Δ, for other processing needs and a device enabling direct filtering of these coded signals is particularly attractive. However, an essential difference should exist between the devices as they process Δ or PCM signals since in the last case, said devices would have to deal with the weight to be assigned to each bit of the PCM word, and with its sign, when in Δ modulation, these constraints do not exist except when the signal (Δ) is converted in (Δ) coded in PCM mode. These problems are particularly critical when building filters of the recursive type where the signals through the direct and feedback sections of the filter should necessarily be in the same code.

The assignee of this invention has already disclosed, in patent application No. PV 7040291 filed in France on Oct. 29, 1970 and now French Pat. No. 2,116,224 entitled "Filtre digital d'une information en code delta" ("Digital filter of a delta coded information"), a fully digital recursive filter. In this device, a ROM is used to store any combination corresponding to the results of the addition of the weighted values. Then, the memory is directly addressed by using a word supplied on the various taps of the delay line. The process used in this device may be applied to the filtering of a signal in PCM mode provided that the constituting elements have been adapted to take into account the particular PCM characteristics.

For example, a filter for PCM with five bit words may be synthetized by using a shifting register, the respective stages of which contain five bit positions. The outputs of every said stages being applied to a ROM adress decoder, said memory supplying as an output, the contribution of the bits affected with the same weight to the sum to be provided. To take into account the weights of the various binary bits, it is possible to use an accumulator composed of a binary adder followed by a shifting register and provided with a feedback loop.

In fact, the time relationships for a low pass or band pass filter similar to the one described referring to FIG. 1, at a sampling time t equal to NT, where T is the sampling period can be written as follows:

$$Y(NT) = \alpha_1\, Y(NT\text{-}T). + \alpha_2\, Y(NT\text{-}2T) + \alpha_3\, X(NT) +$$
$\alpha_4\, X(NT\text{-}T)$ where $\alpha_1, \alpha_2, \alpha_3, \alpha_4$ and the variables X and Y are supposed to be positive. (This system given as an example to introduce the sign necessity can be only an example).

The difference equation can be written in a compact form:

$$Y = \sum_{i=1}^{n} \alpha_i \cdot Z_i$$

where $= n$ is the number of weighting taps on the delay line or shift register.

α_i are the various weighting factors or coefficients such as $\alpha_1, \alpha_2, \alpha_3, \alpha_4$ ... deduced from a sampling of the pulse response or from the filter transfer function.

Z_t is the value of samples Y and X of the second member of the above difference equation

By calling Z_t^j, the j^{st} bit of sample Z_t, in PCM with M bits, we obtain:

$$Z_i = \sum_{j=1}^{M} 2^{(j-1)} \cdot Z_i^j$$

in which $Z_i^j = 0$ or 1 according to the value of the corresponding bit of sample Z_t, and M is equal to the number of bits of a sample word. It should be understood that the number M is defined with the same accuracy as the anticipated results.

Then, the above equation can be written:

$$Y = \sum_{i=1}^{n} \alpha_i \cdot \sum_{j=1}^{M} 2^{(j-1)} \cdot Z_i^j$$

$$= \sum_{j=1}^{M} 2^{(j-1)} \cdot \sum_{i=1}^{n} \alpha_i \cdot Z_i^j = \sum_{j=1}^{M} 2^{(j-1)} \cdot S_j$$

where $2^{(j-1)}$ is equal to the weight of the j^{st} bit, when calling

$$S_j = \sum_{i=1}^{n} \alpha_i \cdot Z_i^j.$$

S_j is the partial result corresponding to the i^{st} bit. In other words S_j is a partial contribution to the final result.

Thus, it appears that, if one knows the pulse response of the desired filter, the weighting factors α_i can be determined, then all the values of S_j can be stored in a memory, taking into account the accuracy of the calculations. Then, the combination of the bits of the various taps of the shifting registers is used as an address to said memory. Then, the operation $\Sigma\, 2^{(j-1)\,\cdot\,j} \cdot S_j$ can be simply carried out by using an accumulator formed with a shifting register associated to a binary adder, or by using any other accumulator able to carry out this operation.

Therefore, it is possible to provide a PCM recursive filter in a simple way. In this case, the required ROM should have a capacity of 2^n words; the number of bits per word B determines the calculation error bound up with the difference equation.

An embodiment of the PCM filtering device as described above is shown on FIG. 2. A ROM or a RAM addressed by four bits and therefore, containing $2^4 = 16$ words corresponding to said partial results S_j, constitutes the central element of the filter. The address decoder of the ROM (AD Decoder) receives at its input, the bits affected with the same weight belonging to the elements of the difference equation defined above, and addresses a memory position supplying the result in parallel on the ROM output. The B bits coming from the ROM are transmitted to an adder A. The B bits coming from the adder and containing the output information Y(NT) are applied back to A through a stage carrying out a division by two or a shift to the right through a gate G controlled by a clock H.

After round off to M-bits, the output of stage A is serialized through CPS before being fedback to the shift registers C1 and C2. Each of the two elements C1 and C2 is formed itself with a shifting register with M bit positions. Thus, the output bit of register C1 constitutes, at any time, the bit of Y(NT-T) applied to input 1 of the ROM address decoder, while the one coming from C2 constitutes the bit of Y(NT-2T) applied to input 2 of said decoder. Inputs 3 and 4 of the decoder are re-

129

spectively supplied with the bits of the PCM sample X(NT) which are sequentially transmitted, and with the ones coming from a shifting register C3 identical to C1 and C2. The bits are applied to input X at a rate of MxFs where Fs is the sampling frequency. Clock H resets accumulator A at sampling rate Fs.

This device ia *number of addressing inputs $n=4$* corresponding to 16 ROM addresses. Therefore, at any time t, if j is the order of the processed bit of sample Z_t, Y can be written as follows:

$$Y = \sum_{j=1}^{M} 2^{(j-1)} x [\alpha_1 Z_1^j + \alpha_2 Z_2^j + \alpha_3 Z_3^j + \alpha_4 Z_4^j].$$

where Z_1^j, Z_2^j, Z_3^j and Z_4^j respectively, represent the bits with weight $2^{(j-1)}$ presents on time t at inputs 1, 2, 3 and 4 defined above. These bits can only be zero or one. For each configuration of the word $Z_1^j Z_2^j Z_3^j Z_4^j$, will correspond a single configuration of the sum S_j, partial contribution, according to the following table:

Z_1^j	Z_2^j	Z_3^j	Z_4^j	S_j
0	0	0	0	0
0	0	0	1	α_4
0	0	1	0	α_3
0	0	1	1	$\alpha_3 + \alpha_4$
0	1	0	0	α_2
0	1	0	1	$\alpha_2 + \alpha_4$
0	1	1	0	$\alpha_2 + \alpha_3$
0	1	1	1	$\alpha_2 + \alpha_3 + \alpha_4$
1	0	0	0	α_1
1	0	0	1	$\alpha_1 + \alpha_4$
1	0	1	0	$\alpha_1 + \alpha_3$
1	0	1	1	$\alpha_1 + \alpha_3 + \alpha_4$
1	1	0	0	$\alpha_1 + \alpha_2$
1	1	0	1	$\alpha_1 + \alpha_2 + \alpha_4$
1	1	1	0	$\alpha_1 + \alpha_2 + \alpha_3$
1	1	1	1	$\alpha_1 + \alpha_2 + \alpha_3 + \alpha_4$

Thus, this shows that the ROM should contain 16 words which will be addressed by the word $Z_1^j Z_2^j Z_3^j Z_4^j$. Then, the words fetched out from the ROM should be added taking into account weight $2^{(j-1)}$. Now, the weighting operations can be obtained by simply shifting the corresponding word, after the result of the previous operations has been obtained, 1 bit position towards the lower orders, before adding the j^{it} word fetched out during the previous operations. In fact, the system described with reference to FIG. 2 proceeding by iterations, performs successive storages and the above operation is carried out by shifting the previous result one position to the right and by adding the result of this operation to the new word S_j fetched out from the ROM. These operations are carried out by the adder A looped through the dividing by-two stage providing the right hand shift. In addition, truncating will be performed by taking the M more significative bits of the overall result taking into account the standardization adopted for the maximum value obtained on the partial sum which determines the point position, rounding will be performed by adding 0.5 to the M. bit word so obtained.

The device described above for filtering PCM data can, in fact, be applied to Δ signals, provided some modifications of details which will be indicated later.

However, the PCM or Δ signals can be positive or negative and the system just described did not show, up to now, any provision for this fact. In fact, if the signals are in binary code called "Two's complement," the bit of S_j occupying order M, therefore, the highest order, is the only one indicating the signal: if it is equal to "1," this means that its contribution to the calculation to be carried out in the accumulator should be subtracted. This requires the use of a ROM not only containing the values S_j, but also the values $-S_j$. The required ROM capacity is then twice the one provided above. It is possible to overcome these constraints and to, keep only 2^n words memorized in several ways; some of these methods use the specific properties of the two's complement code, the other ones use a different code.

Several solutions exist in the first case, two of which have been use here. The first one uses the property by which the value of a number written in two's complement remains unvarying for all extension of the word towards high weights (extension to the left), by repeating the last written bit. In fact, in said code, the contribution of the bit affected with the highest weight is negative while the one of the other bits are positive. Then, it should be easily understood that the value of the number written in two's complement does not vary by extension to the left since this means only applying the property:

$$-a_M \times 2^{M+1} + a_M \times 2^M = -a_M \times 2^M$$

applicable what M and bit a_M may be.

In another way, it is proved that if the sign bit of the multiplier factor of a multiplication of two two's complement numbers is repeated as many times as the number of bits B of the multiplicand, the multiplication can be carried out independently of the sign bit. Consequently, the problem indicated above can be resolved in this case by extending the length of word Z_t to $M+B$ bits by repeating the sign bit. In fact, the accumulator capacity may be unmodified provided that the value scale is choosen so that, after round off operations, the loss of B bits with the lower weights is not significant since it comes to omit the fractional values. However, this processing mode is slow since it requires B elementary times more than expected by the device described above.

The second device using the two's complement code properties, uses the possibility of obtaining the correct result at the end of accumulation process by substracting the bit, sign contribution S_j, ($J=M$), if this bit corresponds to a binary "1" and therefore indicates a negative sign. It is obvious that the immediate solution enabling the application of this process, consists in doubling the ROM capacity by adding to the 2^n values of S_j previously recorded, the corresponding negative values and by distinguishing the presence of signs at M^{st} weight by adding a $n+1$ address bit to the ROM. In fact, this memory extension is avoided by using an index detecting the presence of the sign bits. Then partial contribution S_j for $j=M$ fetched out from the ROM corresponding to the value contained in address $Z_1^M Z_2^M ... Z_n^M$ should be made negative before accumulation. For that purpose the B bits of the content of address $Z_1^M Z_2^M .. Z_n^M$ are complemented and binary "1" is added to the result. This last solution is very advantageous since it requires a much more short processing time than the previous one, while using a ROM of equivalent capacity, i.e. a capacity of 16 words for the given example.

This capacity may be reduced once more by combining the use of a Modified two's-complement Internal Code (CIM) with the indexing techniques already used as it will be explained below. The value of any two's complement coded number (Z) can be given as follows (to make the explanation more simple, only integers are considered; in fact, the argument may be as well applied to the fractional numbers):

$$\{Z\} = -z_M x 2^{(M-1)} + \sum_{k=1}^{M-1} 2^{(k-1)} \cdot z_k$$

where M is the number of bits of word (Z) and z_k or z_M, the binary value of the bit according to its rank. In CIM Code, this same word would be written, taking into account the logic identity $1 = Z_k = Z_k$ and by substituting Z_M for Z_M:

$$\{Z\} = \sum_{k=1}^{M} 2^{(k-2)} (z_k - \bar{z}_k) + 2^{-1} (z_o - \bar{z}_o)$$

where $z_o = 0$.

These two equations show that the CIM coded word can be easily deduced from the two's complement coded word by assigning a bit $z_o=0$ to the rank of order zero and weight 2^{-1} therefore representing an extra bit EB; by reproducing all the M two's complement bits without modification except for the one of the highest order Z_M which is complemented and by reducing the weights of these M bits by one. Therefore, the CIM coded words have one bit more than the ones written in two's complement code.

by calling

$$S_j = \sum_{i=1}^{n} \alpha_i x' (Z_i^j - \bar{Z}_i^j)$$

and

$$S_o = -(\alpha_i + \alpha_2 + \ldots \alpha_n)$$

the partial result corresponding to the j^{st} bit

$$Y = \sum_{j=1}^{M} 2^{(j-2)} x S_j + 2^{-1} x S_o$$

Therefore, it is sufficient to dispose of the values of S_j and S_o.

The above expression shows that once Z_i has been CIM coded, the memory will have to contain all the combinations $\Sigma \pm \alpha_i$. In this case, the memory words written in two's complement code at addresses (0) and (15) of the table are fetched out under control of the Z address words and successively accumulated after shifting whatever the corresponding weight may be. Then, the accumulator has not to detect when $j=M$, but any word fetched out from the memory may be either positive or negative whatever j may be, as shown below.

Non-modified address	Z_1^j	Z_2^j	Z_3^j	Z_4^j	S_j	
(0)	0	0	0	0	$-(\alpha_1 + \alpha_2 + \alpha_3 + \alpha_4)$	
(1)	0	0	0	1	$-(\alpha_1 + \alpha_2 + \alpha_3 - \alpha_4)$	
(2)	0	0	1	0	$-(\alpha_1 + \alpha_2 - \alpha_3 + \alpha_4)$	
(3)	0	0	1	1	$-(\alpha_1 + \alpha_2 - \alpha_3 - \alpha_4)$	
(4)	0	1	0	0	$-(\alpha_1 - \alpha_2 + \alpha_3 + \alpha_4)$	
(5)	0	1	0	1	$-(\alpha_1 - \alpha_2 + \alpha_3 + \alpha_4)$	
(6)	0	1	1	0	$-(\alpha_1 - \alpha_2 - \alpha_3 + \alpha_4)$	
(7)	0	1	1	1	$-(\alpha_1 - \alpha_2 - \alpha_3 - \alpha_4)$	
(8)	1	0	0	0	$+(\alpha_1 - \alpha_2 - \alpha_3 - \alpha_4)$	
(9)	1	0	0	1	$+(\alpha_1 - \alpha_2 - \alpha_3 + \alpha_4)$	
(10)	1	0	1	0	$+(\alpha_1 - \alpha_2 + \alpha_3 - \alpha_4)$	
(11)	1	0	1	1	$+(\alpha_1 - \alpha_2 + \alpha_3 + \alpha_4)$	
(12)	1	1	0	0	$+(\alpha_1 + \alpha_2 - \alpha_3 - \alpha_4)$	
(13)	1	1	1	1	$+(\alpha_1 + \alpha_2 - \alpha_3 + \alpha_4)$	
(14)	1	1	1	0	$+(\alpha_1 + \alpha_2 + \alpha_3 - \alpha_5)$	
(15)	1	1	1	1	$+(\alpha_1 + \alpha_2 + \alpha_3 + \alpha_4)$	

same address; the index on m

By applying this code for Z_i in the calculation of Y, we obtain:

$$Y = \sum_{i=1}^{n} \alpha_i Z_i$$

$$Z_i = \sum_{j=1}^{M} 2^{(j-2)} x (Z_i^j - \bar{z}_i^j) - 2^{-1}$$

$$Y = \sum_{i=1}^{n} \sum_{j=1}^{M} \alpha_i \cdot 2^{(j-2)} x (Z_i^j - \bar{Z}_i^j) - 2^{-1} \alpha_i.$$

$$Y = \sum_{j=1}^{M} 2^{(j-2)} x \sum_{i=1}^{n} \alpha_i x (Z_i^j - \bar{Z}_i^j) - 2^{-1} \alpha_i$$

The symmetry appearing on the above table shows that it is enough to store eight words instead of 16 to have all possible combinations. The bit Z_1^j may be used as an index to complement the address supplied by the word $Z_2^j Z_3^j Z_4^j$ on the one hand, and change the signal of S_j on the other hand, whatever j may be, whenever $Z_1^j = 1$. These operations may be carried out by using XOR circuits.

In fact, this table shows that indexing may be as well performed by using any one of bits Z_1^j, Z_2^j, Z_3^j or Z_4^j, the other ones being used as an address.

The diagram of FIG. 2 should be modified to be adapted to the CIM code. For this purpose, it is enough to increase the capacity of register C1 to C3 by one bit and to equip the serializer CPS with a converter of two's complement code into CIM code, (the bit with the lowest weight, being at round off time replaced by 0; the sign bit being complemented), to inhibit the division by two (shifting operation) for the bit of the lowest order by using a gate G' controlled by clock H every M+1 bits. It should be clearly understood that X(NT) should be previously coded CIM.

Thus, the circuit of FIG. 2 has been modified to perform these operations, which permits to obtain the diagram of FIG. 3. On this figure, the bits Z_2^j, Z_3^j and Z_4^j, before being used to address the memory, go through circuits XOR2, XOR3 and XOR4 respectively, the second output of which is supplied by index Z_1^j, which complements them when this last bit is a binary "1."

In addition, the sign of the word written in two's complement using B bits, fetched out from the memory should also be modified if $Z_1^j = 1$ since the memory contains only one half of the partial contributions. For this purpose, said B bits and the index are submitted to a XOR logic operation by using XOR1 circuit, then a binary "1" is added to the result through the accumulator.

The design of the digital filter described above is not only applicable to the PCM modulation, but also to the Δ modulation transcoded in PCM. In this case the patent application indicated above has shown that the information delivered by the ROM are in multilevel Δ modulation and that they should be re-coded before being re-injected into the feedback section of the filter. This explains a presence of the Δ to CIM converter in the device of FIG. 4, included in the CPS circuit. In the same way, the ROM addressing bits should all be in the same code and the Δ information coded in PCM, is converted into CIM code by Δ2 → CIM.

Although the description of the invention has been carried out with reference to the recursive type filters, the above calculations can also apply to a transversal filter. This filter is even more simple than the recursive filter since it comprises only the "direct" section.

Thus, starting from the device of FIG. 2, one attains easily the device of FIG. 5. The PCM coded signal is aplied to the input of delay line $C''1$, $C''2$, ... $C''n$. The bits appearing at the input of the ROM decoder are used to address the ROM. The process for fetching out words from ROM and accumulating them is identical to the one described above.

In certain applications, it is useful to dispose of a device, the weighting factors of which can be modified while enabling an operation in real time. For example, it is the case of the equalizing devices to be placed on transmission lines. Then, the use of a ROM is no longer possible but the advantages provided by the availability of the partial contributions should be kept. Then, a solution consisting in the use of a RAM enables to resolve the problem. The RAM registers are used to store the partial contributions which can be modified if required, before any use of the device, due to the presence of a logic circuit. FIG. 6 shows the functional diagram of an embodiment of the filter of such a design. Factors α_1, α_2, α_3 and α_4 are transmitted to a LOG stage equipped with computing stages supplying the values of the partial contributions S_j figuring on the above table and previously recorded in the device of FIG. 3 at addresses (0) to (8). These words are stored in registers Reg 1 to Reg 8 of the RAM. Everything being equal everywhere else, the operation of the device of FIG. 6 is similar to the one of FIG. 3 in all points.

Each device of this invention uses an accumulator in which shifting operations are carried out. It is obvious that the fact of intending to operate in real time considerably restricts the choice of this accumulator. In fact,

the overall mathematical operation to be carried out by the memory and accumulator assembly corresponding to a series-parallel multiplication of two facteurs α_n αn^{-1}... α_1 and Z_n $Z_n^{-}{}_1$ ... Z_1, the factor in α appearing in parallel and the one in Z appearing in series, being understood that each figure α_i and Z_i (i varying from 1 to n) is written in binary code. In particular, this operation may be carried out by using a parallel-series accumulator (parallel input-series output) described by Mr. Richards in its book "Arithmetic operations in digital computers" (1955), serial-parallel multiplication, p. 155, provided that some adaptations are applied to this circuit.

The diagram of FIG. 7 shows a filter similar in all points to the one of FIG. 3 in which register C1 has been removed since the accumulator introduces already a delay equivalent to a word duration, but shows the accumulator structure. First, it should be recalled that the words of said registers are in CIM code with M+1 bits, (6 in this case), the ones contained in the memory are in two's comlement with B bits (5 in this case). Thus, the accumulation operations corresponding to the mathematical operation indicated above are performed in two's complement code and the result should be converted in CIM code before being introduced in register C2.

The basic element of this accumulator is a module (BAS) shown on FIG. 7a. It comprises a full adder having two data inputs A', B', a carry input Ci and two outputs So and Co, these two outputs corresponding respectively to the sum and carry outputs of said adder. The module BAS is equipped with two data inputs A and B, two control inputs J and K and two outputs S and C. Outputs S and C are connected respectively to the sum and carry outputs of said adder. Input B is connected directly to B'; input A is connected to A' through a gate P1 controlled by the signal applied to J after complementation by I1. The signals on J and K are transmitted to input Ci througha gate P2 and an OR circuit with two inputs. The carry signal of the adder appearing in Co, is delayed of a bit time 8 by using a delay element and re-applied to input Ci through the second input of the OR circuit and a gate P3 controlled by the signal introduced in K and complemented by I2.

The accumulator device is obtained by connecting several BAS stages in cascade, the output S of one stage being connected to input A of the following stage through a delay element 8, and by introducing in parallel on the inputs B, the results of said partial contributions fetched out from the memory.

Thus, the outputs of the various stages of XOR1 are connected respectively and directly to input B of a stage BAS1 to BAS4. The output of the stage carrying the bit with the lowest weight of the word issued from XOR 1 is connected to input B of BAS5 through BAS6 receiving on the one hand said bit affected with the lowest weight on its input A and, on the other hand, bit Z_1^j on its input B. The intermediate stage BAS6, the input J of which is at "0" and the input K of which is connected to inputs K of BAS1 to BAS5, is ussed to add the binary "1" corresponding to the change of sign indicated above in the description of FIG. 3, when $Z_1^j = 1$. Thus, the XOR1 and BAS6 assembly changes the sign of the partial contribution fetched out from the memory, when necessary.

At each bit time, the bit affected with the lowest weight of the result of the accumulation is ejected by shifting the sum information to the right, which corresponds to the division by two indicated on FIG. 3. In the same time, the sum information of each stage BAS is transferred on input A of the following stage after a bit time delay. Then, the accumulator is ready to receive the next partial contribution on the inputs B and to repeat the previous operation until all bits of word Z_i are used.

Several observations enable an improvement of this accumulator while providing a letter adaptation to the particular needs of this invention.

First of all, one should recall the above observations concerning the processing of the sign of the words written in two's complement code: it has been indicated above that it is sufficient, for carrying this processing, to extend the word to the left by performing M repetitions of the bit affected with the highest weight (sign bit). In fact, the operations being carried out in the successive accumulation steps, it is sufficient to extend this sign bit of one position only on each accumulation. Then, the left hand extension does not require any additional BAS stage; for simulating this extension, it is sufficient to feed the delayed output S of BAS1 directly back to its input A as shown on FIG. 7.

Secondly, a rational use of the device in general, and of the memory in particular, involves the choice of a memory location reserved to the partial contribution.

$$\sum_{i=1}^{n} |\alpha i|$$

which does not exceed the one which would require the number corresponding to the two's power immediately above said contribution. This operation constitutes a "standardization" which determines the position of the point in the accumulation result, and determines a rank p equal to the base-two logarithm of said power (p can be positive or negative). In the case of FIG. 7, $p=2$ and $B=5$, therefore, the maximum partial contribution is equal to three-point-seventy five, which requires, to standardize the result, to neglect the contents of BAS1 and BAS2 at the end of the accumulating process since then, they cannot contain any significant figure for the result. Taking into account the two's complement code properties, these stages can only contain an extension of the sign bit of said partial contribution and therefore may be delated.

The Z word in CIM code containing $M+1$ bits, corresponds to a two's complement word with M bits, i.e. five bits for the example shown on FIG. 7. This explains the presence of 81. In addition, the final result is rounded off and the calculation which leads to this result, again requires an additional bit and this explains the presence of 82.

Thirdly, after $M+1$ bit times, the processing of a Z word is terminated for the memory but the accumulator is not empty= $B-p$ bits remain to be used. The filter slowing down which could result, is avoided by providing two registers R1 and R2 and two stages BAS7 and BAS8 which will terminate the operation and enable the release of BAS1 to BAS6.

Registers R1 and R2 consist of stages D similar to the one shown on FIG. 7b and including two data inputs Do and Eo, a check input L and an output F. Each stage includes a latch FF1 operating as a bit time 8 memory element the output of which is connected to point F and the input of which i is connected to the output of an OR logic circuit (OR1) with two inputs. Inputs Do and Eo feed a gate P3 and P4 respectively, controlled by the signal at L or its complement supplied by I3. The outputs of P3 and P4 feed OR1.

Register R1 consists of stages D1, D2, D3 and of latches — 83, 84, 85 connected in cascade. Its output is taken from the output of 85.

Register R2 includes stages D'1 through D'7 and stage BAS7. Its input is taken from the output of D'7.

The inputs Do of stages D1 to D3 are connected to the outputs C of BAS3 through BAS5. Input Eo of D1 is at "0", the ones of D2 and D3 are connected to output F of the previous stage D belonging to the same register. The output of R1 is obtained by connecting — 83, 84, 85 in cascade to the output of D3.

The inputs Do of stages D'1 through D'3 are connected to outputs S of BAS 2 through BAS4 respectively. The inputs Eo of D'2 and D'3 are connected to outputs F of the previous stage D of R2, respectively. Points F and Eo of D'1 are interconnected. Output C of BAS6 is connected to Do of D'4 the outpu EO of which is at zero level. Outputs F of D'4 and D'3 are connected to inputs A and B of BAS7 respectively, input J of which is at zero and input K of which is common to inputs K of BAS1 through BAS6. The rest of register R2 is constituted of D'5, D'6, D'7, inputs Do of which are connected to output S of BAS5 and to outputs F of D'5 and D'7 respectively. The output of 85 is connected to input B of BAS8 through logic circuit OR2, the second input of which, is connected to the output of D'7 through a logic AND circuit ET 4, inputs K and J of BAS8 are common with K of BAS1 to BAS7. The output of D'7 is applied to input A of BAS8. Output S of BAS8 is connected to an input of an OR logic circuit Po', the output of which is connected to an input of a XOR5 feeding the input of register C2. The synchronisation of the device is obtained by using a binary signal Si equal to "1" at the moments corresponding to the processing of extra bits E/B and Z_M (in the case shown on the figure, words in CIM code arrive in synchronous mode and comprise six bits, therefore $Si=1$ at bit times 1 and 6) and equals zero for the other bit times of each word Z. Signal Si is transmitted directly on the second input of XOR5. It is also transmitted after a delay of one bit time, through 86 (therefore the output of 86 is equal to 1 at times 1 and 2), to input J of stages BAS1 through BAS5. The coincidence information of signals Si and its delayed counterpart, goes through a logic AND circuit ET 5 (therefore, the output of ET5 is equal to 1 on time 1), and drives inputs K of stages BAS1 through BAS8 as well as input J of the latter. Signal Si, delayed of a bit time and complemented by I3 is placed in coincidence with Si in ET6 (therefore the output of ET6 is equal to 1 at time 6 which corresponds to Z_M); the result drives inputs L of stages D1 through D3 and D'1 through D'7. The output of ET5 drives the second input of ET4.

At the moment corresponding to an operation of $M+1$ order (therefore at time 6), the data being transmitted in a synchronous mode, stages BAS1 through BAS7 should be released to be able to begin the calculation of the next Y value. The control logic signal transfers the sum and carry information of the accumulator stages in registers R1 and R2; on the following time (time 1) the partial contribution fetched from the memory which corresponds to the all zero address is multiplied by 2 to take into account the weight assigned to the first bit in CIM code by forcing the carry inputs of BAS1 through BAS5 at 1 (presence of J and K) which transfers this contribution into the corresponding carry outputs. The sum obtained at S is neglected at the next time slot (presence of J).

Therefore, the operation of the device may be summed up as follows: during each bit time, a partial contribution is fetched out of the memory under control of word $Z_2^j Z_3^j Z_4^j$ and its sign is modified if $Z_1^j = 1$, using XOR1 and BAS6. The bits of the fetched out memory word, are introduced in parallel into accumulator section BAS1 through BAS5 (via BAS6, for BAS5). During each bit time, the sum content of each stage BAS1 through BAS5 is shifted to the right, but at the first bit time, the partial contribution is multiplied by 2, the sum of stage BAS1 being fedback to the input of the same stage after a delay of one bit time. After $M+1$ bit times, the sum and carry contents of stages BAS2 through BAS6 are transfered into the stages of registers R1 and R2 and stages BAS may be reloaded for a next accumulation. During this time, the contents of R1 and R2 are added in series in BAS8, and the result converted in CIM code by Po and XOR5 is reinjected into C2. In fact, the words in CIM code having one bit more than those in two's complement code, i.e. $EB=0$, a round off is carried out through BAS8 on the time corresponding to EB by forcing the carry input of BAS8 to 1 (simultaneous presence of J and K) and by systematically replacing the bit of XOR5 by zero before its reinjection into C2.

The filter output may be fetched out either from output S of BAS8, therefore in two's complement code, or from the output of XOR5, therefore in CIM code.

Thus, the device described above enables to carry out — in real time —the accumulation, code conversion and standardization operations required by the filter of this invention, but it should be understood that this invention is not restricted to this embodiment.

In addition, it will be understood by those skilled in the art that the foregoing and other changes in form and details may be made therein without departing from the spirit and the scope of the invention. In particular, more complex filter transfer functions may be provided by setting devices such as the ones described above, in cascade or in parallel.

What is claimed is:

1. A digital apparatus for filtering successive binary coded signal samples Z_i, Z_i being of the form

$$2^{m-1} Z_i^m + 2^{m-2} z_i^{m-1} + \ldots + 2^{2-1} Z_i^j$$

$$+ \ldots 2^0 Z_i^1 = \sum_{i=1}^{m} 2^{j-1} Z_i^j;$$

wherein the output value Y of the filter apparatus is related to Z_i by the function:

$$Y = \sum_{i=1}^{N} a_i Z_i = \sum_{i=1}^{N} a_i \sum_{j=1}^{M} 2^{j-1} Z_i^j$$

$$= \sum_{j=1}^{M} 2^{j-1} \sum_{i=1}^{N} a_i Z_i^j = \sum_{j=1}^{M} 2^{j-1} S_j.$$

each a_i constituting a weighting coefficient and

$$S_j = \sum_{i=1}^{N} a_i Z_i^j;$$

the apparatus comprising:

means adapted to receive N successive signal samples Z_i;

a memory medium having 2^N locations addressable by the signal subset $Z_1^j Z_2^j \ldots Z_N^j = Z_1^{j+1} Z_2^{j+1} - Z_N^{j+1} = Z_1^m Z_2^m - Z_N^m$ for storing corresponding values Sj;

an accumulator for forming the product $2^{j-1} Sj$ and combining the product to form the sum

$$\sum_{j=1}^{m} 2^{j-1} Sj;$$

and

means coupling the receiving means and sequentially responsive to each signal subset $Z_1^j Z_2^j \ldots Z_N^j$ over the range $1 \leq j \leq m$ for extracting the value Sj from the memory medium at the address defined by the subset, and for applying said value Sj to the accumulator.

2. A digital apparatus according to claim 1, wherein each of the signal samples are generated at a rate of $1/T$ samples per second, and further wherein the N binary coded signals Z_i consist of V input signals X(NT), X(NT-T),---, X[NT-(V-1)T] and R output signals Y(NT-T), Y(NT-2T), ---, Y[NT-(R-1)T];

the receiving means including means for applying a corresponding bit from each of the input signals X_i^j (NT), X_i^j (NT-T), ----X_i^j [NT-(V-1)T] and from each of the output signals Y_i^j(NT-T), Y_i^j(NT-2T),---Y_i^j [NT-(R-1)T] to the extracting means over the range $1 \leq j \leq m$.

3. A digital apparatus according to claim 1, wherein each of the signal samples are generated at a rate of I/T samples per second, and further wherein the N binary coded signals Z_i consist of N input signals (X(NT), X(NT-T)--- X[NT-(NT-1)];

the receiving means including means for applying a corresponding bit from each of the input signals X_i^j (NT), X_i^j(NT-T), ---X_i^j [NT-(NT-1)] to the extracting over the range $1 \leq j \leq m$.

4. A transversal digital filter comprising:

means adapted to receive N successive binary coded input digits X(NT), X(NT-T),---X[NT-(NT-1)] of m bits each at a rate of $1/T$ digits per second;

said filter output Y(NT) being related to the input digits by the function:

$$Y(NT) = a_1 X(NT) + a_2 X(NT-T)---a_N X[NT-(NT-1)]$$

$$= \sum_{i=1}^{N} a_i X_i; \text{ each digit } X_i = 2^{m-1} X_i^m + 2^{m-2} X_i^{m-1} + \ldots$$

$$+ 2^{j-1} X_i^j + \ldots + 2^0 X_i^1 = \sum_{j=1}^{m} 2^{j-1} X_i^j; \text{ such that}$$

$$Y(NT) = \sum_{i=1}^{N} a_i X_i = \sum_{i=1}^{N} a_i \sum_{j=1}^{m} 2^{j-1} X_i^j = \sum_{j=1}^{m} 2^{j-1} \sum_{i=1}^{N} a_i X_i^j$$

$$= \sum_{j=1}^{m} 2^{j-1} Sj.$$

$$Sj = \sum_{i=1}^{N} a_i X_i^j, \ a_i \text{ being a weighting coefficient;}$$

said filter

further comprising:

a memory medium having 2^N locations for storing values of Sj addressable by signal subsets $X_1^j X_2^j$ ---X_N^j over the range $1 \le j \le m$;

an accumulator for forming the product $2^{j-1}Sj$ and combining the product to form the sum

$$\sum_{j=1}^{m} 2^{j-1} Sj;$$

and

means responsive to successive signal subsets $X_1^j X_2^j$ --- X_N^j from the receiving means over the range $1 \le j \le m$ for extracting the corresponding value Sj from the memory medium at the address defined by the signal subset and for applying said extracted value to the accumulator.

* * * * *

135

Transversal Filtering Using Charge-Transfer Devices

DENNIS D. BUSS, DEAN R. COLLINS, WALTER H. BAILEY, AND C. RICHARD REEVES

Abstract—Techniques are presented for making transversal filters using charge-coupled devices (CCD's) and bucket-brigade devices (BBD's). In a CCD transversal filter, the delayed signals are sampled by measuring the current flowing in the clock lines during transfer, and the sampled signals are weighted by a split electrode technique. In a BBD transversal filter, the delayed signals are "tapped" with a source follower whose load determines the weighting coefficient. Examples are given of CCD and BBD filters that are "matched" to particular signaling waveforms, and the limitations of charge-transfer devices (CTD's) in matched filtering applications are discussed. Finally, the application of CTD transversal filters to other signal processing functions is discussed.

I. INTRODUCTION

CHARGE-TRANSFER devices (CTD's), which include both charge-coupled devices (CCD's) [1]-[3] and bucket-brigade devices (BBD's) [4], [5], are uniquely applicable to many analog signal processing functions because they are capable of operating directly with analog signals. One of the most important signal processing functions for which CTD's can be used is the time delay of analog signals [6]. When CTD's are used in this application, the signal to be delayed is first sampled at a rate greater than twice the highest frequency in the signal. The analog samples are then clocked down the CTD shift register and appear at the output a delay time T_d later. The delayed signal is finally reconstructed by passing the samples through an appropriate bandpass filter.

The alternatives to CTD's for analog time delay are acoustic delay lines for short time delay, or digital delay preceded by analog/digital conversion and followed by digital/analog conversion. Since CTD's can achieve hundreds of milliseconds of delay, they look very attractive for a large number of signal delay functions. However, the characteristics of CTD delay lines have been analyzed in great detail elsewhere in the literature [6]-[8], and therefore this paper will deal exclusively with the application of tapped CTD delay lines to transversal filtering [9].

A block diagram of a transversal filter is shown in Fig. 1. It consists of a sampling stage S followed by M delay stages D, each of which delays the signal by a time equal to an integral number (one in this paper) of clock periods T_c. The signal is nondestructively sampled at each delay stage, multiplied by the appropriate weighting coefficient h_k $(k = 1, M)$, and the weighted signals are summed together to give the filter output. As can be seen from Fig. 1, the h_k determine the impulse response, or Green's function, of the filter, i.e., the output that results when a single sample of unit amplitude is applied to the input. Moreover, when an arbitrary signal $v_{in}(t)$ is applied to the filter, the filter output is

$$v_{out}(nT_c) = \sum_{k=1}^{M} h_k v_{in}[(n - k + 1)T_c] T_c - kT_c) \quad (1)$$

$$\approx \int_0^{T_d} h(\tau) v_{in}(nT_c - \tau) \, d\tau \quad (2)$$

where $v_{in}(kT_c)$ represents the sampled input signal, and $T_d(=MT_c)$ is the total time delay of the filter. This output is approximately equal to the convolution of the input signal with the impulse response of the filter.

Operationally, CTD transversal filters can perform the same functions as surface wave device (SWD) transversal filters [10], except that SWD filters are limited in the time duration of the impulse response to a few tens of microseconds, whereas CTD filters can process signals having hundreds of milliseconds time duration. CTD filters, on the other hand, are limited in bandwidth to a few tens of megahertz.

The first CTD transversal filter utilized BBD's for

Manuscript received October 19, 1972. This work was supported in part by the Electronic Systems Division of the U. S. Air Force.
D. D. Buss, D. R. Collins, and W. H. Bailey are with Texas Instruments, Inc., Dallas, Tex. 75222.
C. R. Reeves was with Texas Instruments, Inc., Dallas, Tex. 75222. He is now with the Applied Research Laboratories, University of Texas at Austin, Austin, Tex.

Reprinted from *IEEE J. Solid-State Circuits*, vol. SC-8, pp. 138–146, Apr. 1973.

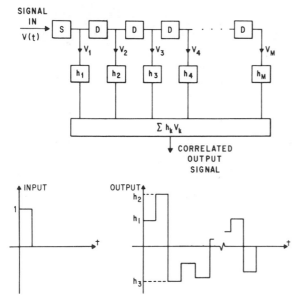

Fig. 1. Block diagram of a transversal filter. This consists of a sampling stage S, delay stages D, and taps with coefficients h_k, $k = 1$, M. The h_k determine the response to a unit input as shown.

the delay element, and was designed to have a bandpass characteristic [11], [12] (see Section IV). A transversal filter, however, can have an arbitrary impulse response of finite time duration and therefore can be used to implement any linear filter. (Any system whose output is linearly related to the input is a linear filter.) In this sense, a transversal filter can be thought of as the fundamental building block of linear systems of which even the analog time delay is a special case.

Filters of the type described above are called sampled data filters [13] because a continuous input signal is sampled in time. Such filters have a wide range of applicability. However, before the advent of CTD's, many such filters required digital implementation. CTD's have the potential of revolutionizing certain sampled data filtering applications because they deal with the analog signals themselves. The potential advantages of performing sampled data filtering functions on a single CTD chip are overwhelming.

More complex sampled data filtering operations can be achieved by feeding the output of a delay line back to the input to achieve what is called a recursive filter. This type of filter is useful in generating an impulse response that is unbounded in time, and has been implemented using BBD's to achieve bandpass filtering [14].

In constructing a transversal filter, it is necessary to have, in addition to an analog time delay, a circuit for sampling, weighting, and summing the outputs, as shown in Fig. 1 and (1). This is accomplished in different ways, depending on whether CCD's or BBD's are used for the delay. Methods of sampling, weighting, and summing are described in Section II.

Since the impulse response of a CTD transversal filter can be selected arbitrarily, these filters can be "matched" to any desired signal waveform, in which

case the filter is called a matched filter [15]–[18]. Matched filters are used to detect a given waveform in the presence of noise with optimum detection probability. CTD matched filters are useful, for example, in low data rate, spread spectrum communication systems. The design and operational characteristics of CTD matched filters are discussed in Section III.

CTD transversal filters also can be designed to achieve a particular spectral characteristic [19]. In order to obtain, for example, a bandpass filter, the impulse response of the filter is chosen to be the Fourier transform of the desired bandpass characteristic. Therefore, design of such bandpass filters is extremely flexible and relatively simple. Filters of this type are discussed in Section IV, together with other possible applications for transversal filters.

II. Design of CTD Transversal Filters

In order to make a CTD transversal filter, it is necessary to nondestructively sample the delay line and to perform the weighted summation indicated in Fig. 1. This is achieved in different ways, depending on whether CCD's or BBD's are used, as is discussed in this section.

A. CCD's

The principle used to nondestructively measure the charge under a CCD electrode is to integrate the current that flows in the clock line during charge transfer [15], [16]. This is illustrated in Fig. 2 for a three-phase (3-ϕ) CCD. When a transferred charge Q_k^t flows from under the kth ϕ_2 electrode to under the kth ϕ_3 electrode, the current that flows in the kth ϕ_3 clock line can be separated into two portions: a portion that would flow if Q_k^t were zero, plus a portion that is approximately proportional to Q_k^t.

If the CCD electrode is modeled by the oxide capacitance C_{ox} in series with a voltage-independent depletion layer capacitance C_d, the charge Q_k^c equal to the integral of the clock line current can be expressed by

$$Q_k{}^c = V_c \frac{C_{ox}C_d}{C_{ox} + C_d} + Q_k{}^t \frac{C_{ox}}{C_{ox} + C_d} \qquad (3)$$

where V_c is the voltage amplitude of the clock driver. When $C_{ox} \gg C_d$, as is the case for high-resistivity substrate material,

$$Q_k{}^c \simeq V_c C_d + Q_k{}^t. \qquad (4)$$

In order to weight each sampled charge with an arbitrary coefficient ($-1 < h_k < +1$), each ϕ_3 electrode is split, as shown in Fig. 2. The upper portions of each ϕ_3 electrode are connected together in a common clock line ($\phi_3{}^{(+)}$), and the lower portions are connected together in a common clock line ($\phi_3{}^{(-)}$). Identical voltage waveforms are applied to $\phi_3{}^{(+)}$ and $\phi_3{}^{(-)}$, but the currents in the two lines are measured separately, and the difference is applied to a differential amplifier external

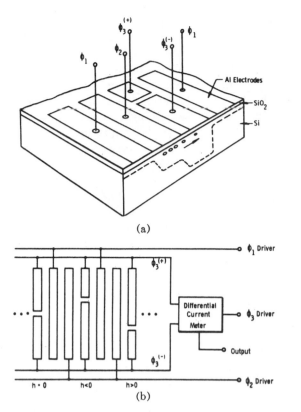

(a)

(b)

Fig. 2. Schematic of the electrode weighting technique for achieving the sampling, weighting, and summing operation indicated in Fig. 1. This technique is used with CCD filters.

to the chip. If the kth electrode is split so that a fraction $\frac{1}{2}(1 + h_k)$ is connected to $\phi_3^{(+)}$ (the h_k are assumed normalized to unity) and a fraction $\frac{1}{2}(1 - h_k)$ is connected to $\phi_3^{(-)}$, then the output of the differential amplifier is

$$v_{out} \propto \sum_{k=1}^{M} \frac{1}{2}(1 + h_k)Q_k^c - \sum_{k=1}^{M} \frac{1}{2}(1 - h_k)Q_k^c = \sum_{k=1}^{M} h_k Q_k^c. \quad (5)$$

The device is operated such that zero signal corresponds to a charge midway between the maximum charge Q_{max} and the "fat zero" charge Q_{fz}. On this basis, the signal charge Q_k^s can be either positive or negative, and is related to Q_k^t by

$$Q_k^s = Q_k^t - \frac{1}{2}(Q_{max} - Q_{fz}). \quad (6)$$

Inserting (4) and (6) into (5) shows that v_{out} consists of a dc component plus a signal component.

$$v_{out} \propto [V_c C_d + \frac{1}{2}(Q_{max} - Q_{fz})] \sum_{k=1}^{M} h_k + \sum_{k=1}^{M} h_k Q_k^s. \quad (7)$$

The dc component can be eliminated by capacitive coupling, leaving only the portion of v_{out} which depends upon the $Q_k^s(t)$. The connection with (1) is established by relating the signal charge under the kth electrode to the input voltage $k - 1$ clock periods earlier:

$$Q_k^s(t) = (C_{ox} + C_d)v_{in}[t - (k - 1)T_c] \quad (8)$$

Equations (3)–(8) ignore the dependence of C_d upon surface potential, which can introduce nonlinearity into

the sampling, weighting, and summing operation unless care is taken to avoid it. Two things can be done to insure linearity: 1) C_d can be made small by utilizing a lightly doped substrate, and 2) by designing the input properly, the nonlinear relationship between $Q_k^s(t)$ and $v_{in}[t - (k - 1)]T_c$ can be made to exactly cancel the nonlinear relationship between v_{out} and the Q_k^s.

The technique described above is called electrode weighting, and a CCD filter made using this technique is shown in Fig. 3. The gaps in the ϕ_3 electrodes are clearly visible. A gap midway across the electrode corresponds to a weighting coefficient of zero, whereas a gap in the upper (lower) half of the electrode corresponds to a negative (positive) coefficient. The impulse response of this filter is an oscillatory function that increases in frequency from zero to half the clock frequency. The operation of filters of this type is discussed in Section III.

B. BBD's

BBD transversal filters can be made using the electrode weighting technique discussed in Section II-A, as was first demonstrated by Sangster [11], [12]. However, because the signal charge in a BBD is stored on a diffused node, this node voltage can be tapped by applying it to the gate of the active transistor of a source follower, as is illustrated in Fig. 4 [17], [18]. BBD filters have been made using both the electrode weighting technique and the gate tapping technique, and the choice of the latter is one of convenience: it is easier to implement the peripheral electronics for the gate tapping technique.

In the circuit of Fig. 4, the current i_k that flows in the kth source follower is proportional to the node voltage v_k and to the conductance G_k of the load transistor. The nodes for which $h_k > 0$ are connected to a common line $\Sigma^{(+)}$, and the nodes for which $h_k < 0$ are connected to a common line $\Sigma^{(-)}$. The current in $\Sigma^{(-)}$ is then subtracted from the current in $\Sigma^{(+)}$ in an external low-impedance differential amplifier to give the correlation output. This particular filter is matched to a 13-bit Barker-coded [20] p-n sequence (see Section III-A). Consequently, $|h_k| = 1$, and the G_k are identical.

This technique is not limited, however, to filters having $|h_k| = 1$, since the conductance G_k of the load transistor can be varied to obtain arbitrary h_k. BBD chirp filters having 100 stages have been fabricated and are discussed in Section III-A.

A further advantage of the gate tapping method is that programmable filters are more easily implemented. A 20-stage filter having unity weighting coefficients ($|h_k| = 1$) has been fabricated. This filter is programmed by switching each source follower to Σ^+ or Σ^-, depending upon the state of MOS switches into which the code has been read. Programmability is very important for many system applications, but will not be discussed further.

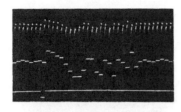

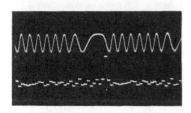

Fig. 3. CCD matched to a chirp signal, i.e., a sinusoid whose frequency decreases linearly with time. The impulse response is clearly visible in the electrode gaps shown in the photomicrograph. Top: CCD chirp filter; middle: impulse response of a 21-chip code; bottom: FM waveform and matched filter output.

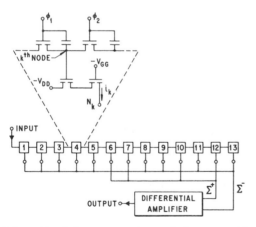

Fig. 4. Schematic of the gate tapping technique for achieving the sampling, weighting, and summing operation. The implementation of this filter is shown in Fig. 5.

III. MATCHED FILTERS

The matched filtering theorem [9] states that in order to detect a signal in the presence of white additive noise with the optimum detection probability, a matched filter should be used, i.e., a filter whose impulse response is the time inverse of the signal to be received.

The principle of matched filtering is important in many applications, but one of the most apparent is in low data rate, spread spectrum communication systems, where it is desired to transmit a peak-power-limited

signal over a noisy channel. The peak power limitation is overcome by spreading the energy in a low-power signal over a long time interval (up to several hundred milliseconds in some applications). The receiver in such a system must be capable of coherently integrating the received signal power for the time duration of the signal, and it requires a matched filter.

This section gives results on testing CTD matched filters and discusses their limitations.

A. Results

As an example of a matched filter, consider a signaling scheme that utilizes a 13-bit Barker-coded [20] p-n sequence. A p-n sequence takes on one of two values, +1 or −1, and a Barker code is a particular sequence that has desirable autocorrelation properties. The 13-bit Barker code is

$$h_k = (-,-,-,-,-,+,+,-,-,+,-,+,-) \quad (9)$$

and the BBD filter shown in Fig. 4 is matched to this code.

The response of the filter to a negative impulse is shown in Fig. 5(a). From this figure it can be seen that the response to a positive impulse is the time inverse of the signal specified by (9), and when the signal itself is applied to the input, the correlation output results in a large peak, shown in Fig. 5(b). This correlation peak results from the constructive addition of signal voltages from the entire signal waveform, and therefore utilizes the energy of the waveform in the optimum way to overcome noise. The output from an ideal filter is shown in Fig. 5(c). The correlation peak is 13 times the input voltage level, and results in a signal-to-noise ratio (S/N) improvement of 13 to 1 (11.1 dB) over a single pulse signal scheme.

The devices whose results are shown here were fabricated on low-resistivity (1–2 $\Omega \cdot$cm) $\langle 111 \rangle$ n-type silicon using an oxide–nitride gate for low threshold voltage. The charge transfer efficiency (CTE) was found to be 99.5 percent per transfer, and a calculation of the output using this CTE is shown in Fig. 5(d). The height of the correlation peak is degraded by CTE from 13 to 11.87, so that the peak output power is only $(11.87)^2 = 140.9$ times the input power. However, imperfect CTE also introduces correlation between the noise voltages on the different nodes, and calculations of this effect [18] indicate that the output noise power is decreased from 13 times the input noise power to 10.95 times the input noise power. The overall S/N improvement is therefore 12.87, which represents a loss in sensitivity of only 0.04 dB.

In order to verify that the predicted sensitivity is in fact achieved, an experiment was performed in which a controlled amount of noise was added to the signal at the filter input. The filter output was fed to a thresholding device whose threshold was set to achieve a

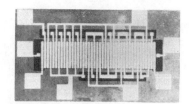

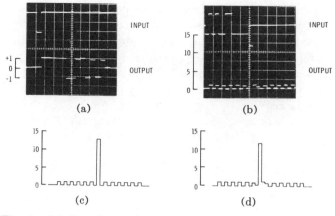

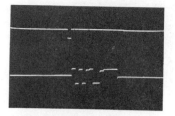

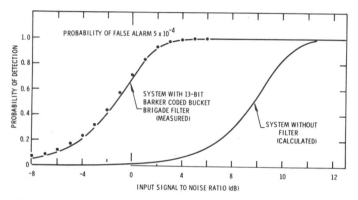

Fig. 5. (a) Impulse response of the filter shown in Fig. 4. (b) Correlation response of this filter. Note the correlation peak near the center of the photograph. (c) Ideal correlation response. (d) Calculated response assuming 99.5 percent CTE.

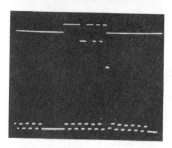

Fig. 7. CCD implementation of the 13-bit Barker-coded p-n filter. No interelectrode gaps are visible because $|h_k| = 1$. Top: 13-bit Barker code device; middle: impulse response; bottom: correlation response.

Fig. 6. Probability of detection versus input S/N ratio achieved using the filter of Fig. 5. The detection threshold is set to give a false alarm probability of 5×10^{-4}. The solid line is calculated assuming Gaussian noise, and the points are measured.

given probability of false alarm (P_{FA}), i.e., the probability of the threshold being exceeded by noise alone in the absence of signal. The probability of detection (P_D), i.e., the probability of a threshold crossing when the signal is added, was then measured, and typical results are shown in Fig. 6. The solid lines represent calculations of P_D versus input S/N with and without the filter, and show that the 11.1-dB S/N improvement is in fact achieved.

The CCD implementation of the 13-bit Barker-coded p-n filter is shown in Fig. 7. The electrode gaps are not present in the photomicrograph of the circuit because, since the weighting coefficients all have unit magnitude, the electrodes are connected entirely to either $\phi_3^{(+)}$ or $\phi_3^{(-)}$. The devices pictured here were processed on 20 $\Omega\cdot$cm $\langle 111\rangle$ n-type silicon using a single-level three-phase CCD design. They had a CTE of 99.9 percent at 1 MHz, and were operated with essentially ideal performance from 10 kHz to 5 MHz.

In order to demonstrate the applicability of CTD matched filters to practical communication systems, two 100-stage BBD filters were designed to be matched to a chirp waveform. They are for use in a system that utilizes a signal of the form

$$v(t) \propto \cos\left[2\pi\left(f_1 t + \tfrac{1}{2}\frac{\Delta f}{T} t^2\right) + \phi\right], \quad 0 < t < T. \quad (10)$$

This waveform "chirps" from frequency f_1 to frequency $f_1 + \Delta f$ in a time T, and the time–bandwidth product, which is a measure of pulse compression ratio or processing gain, is $T\Delta f = 50$. The receiver that was built to detect this waveform is shown in Fig. 8(a). The signal of (10) is mixed to baseband by multiplying by in-phase and quadrature sinusoids of frequency $f_0 = f_1 + \Delta f/2$. The baseband signal that "chirps" from $-(\Delta f/2)$ to $+(\Delta f/2)$ is then detected using the in-phase and quadrature matched filters whose respective impulse responses are given by the weighting coefficients.

$$h_k = \cos\left[\frac{2\pi}{25}(k-50.5)^2\right]\exp\left[-2.648\left(\frac{k-50.5}{49.5}\right)^2\right]$$

$$h_k = \sin\left[\frac{2\pi}{25}(k-50.5)^2\right]\exp\left[-2.648\left(\frac{k-50.5}{49.5}\right)^2\right],$$

$$k = 1,100 \quad (11)$$

and are shown in Fig. 8(b). The receiver was tested by adding a controlled amount of noise to the signal, and by measuring the detection probability as a function of input S/N and probability of false alarm. Fig. 8(c) shows the filter operating with 0-dB input S/N. The correlation peaks shown in the output are used to trigger a thresholding device. The filter has a theoretical improvement in S/N of 18.7 dB down 1.3 dB from the

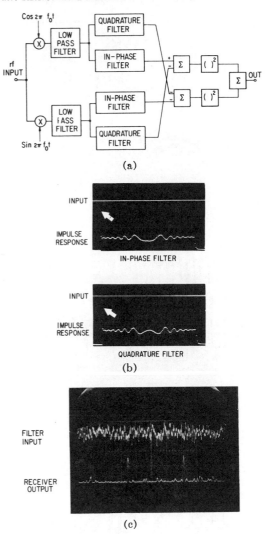

Fig. 8. (a) Block diagram of a receiver for chirp signals (T_dW =50) that utilizes BBD matched filters. (b) Impulse responses of the two BBD filters used in the receiver. (c) Operation of the receiver at 0-dB input S/N. The top trace shows signal plus noise at baseband frequency at the input of one of the filters. The bottom trace shows the filter output in which two correlation peaks corresponding to two received signals rise unambiguously above the output noise.

ideal processing gain of 20 dB. This is because of the Gaussian weighting on the filter impulse responses, which introduces a mismatch between the signal and the filter. The Gaussian weighting results in lower processing gain, but significantly suppresses the sidelobes that are present at times different from the correlation peak. The measured processing gain was within 1.5 dB of the theoretical optimum in all cases tested.

B. Limitations

The time duration (T_d) of signals that can be processed using CTD matched filters is ultimately limited by the storage time [3] of the devices (i.e., the time it takes a stored charge to be lost due to leakage). The storage time depends upon junction leakage in BBD's and upon inversion layer equilibration in CCD's, and it is typically on the order of 1 s for both devices.

The filter length (i.e., the number of delay stages M)

is ultimately limited by CTE. The precise amount of loss due to imperfect CTE that can be tolerated depends upon the application. However, for matched filtering, imperfect CTE degrades the output noise power as well as the output signal power, so that the processing gain is only weakly affected. Calculations indicate that

$$M\epsilon < 2 \qquad (12)$$

is acceptable for many matched filtering applications where ϵ is the loss per stage (i.e., three times the loss per transfer for a three-phase CCD, etc.).

The Nyquist sampling theorem requires that a signal having bandwidth W be sampled at a frequency greater than $2W$, and combining this requirement with (12) gives the following limitation on the T_dW product of signals that can be processed using CTD filters:

$$T_dW < 1/\epsilon. \qquad (13)$$

To the extent that CTE can be predicted, the limitation imposed by (13) can be circumvented by selecting the weighting coefficients to invert the dispersion due to imperfect CTE. The dependence of CTE on signal amplitude makes it impossible to exactly invert this dispersion at all signal levels. However, the effectiveness of the technique is illustrated in Fig. 9, where a 13-bit filter with externally adjustable weighting coefficients is matched to an 11-bit Barker code. The device shown had singularly poor CTE (98 percent), and the degradation of circuit performance is shown in Fig. 9(a) and (b). In Fig. 9(c) and (d), however, the weighting coefficients have been adjusted to effectively invert the dispersion before adding.

When the CTE of a given design and process can be predicted, compensation can be designed into the filter. The required weighting coefficients are obtained by calculating the matrix of weighting coefficients that would be required to invert the dispersion at each node, and by multiplying this matrix by the desired weighting coefficients.

In addition to the limitation stated by (13), the signal bandwidth is limited to less than half the maximum clock frequency of the filter. For CCD's this limitation is currently approximately 20 MHz, whereas BBD's are limited to a few megahertz.

Another limitation on CTD transversal filters is the accuracy with which the weighting coefficients can be determined. Weighting coefficient error poses a severe limitation on many applications for transversal filters, but matched filters are usually operated in a high-noise environment, and the additional "noise" introduced by weighting coefficient error is usually inconsequential. To demonstrate this, an analysis of weighting coefficient error on p-n sequence filters has been performed, based on the assumptions that: 1) errors are uncorrelated, and 2) they contribute to the S/N in the same way as other sources of noise. The result is

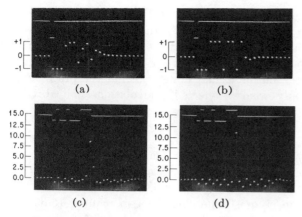

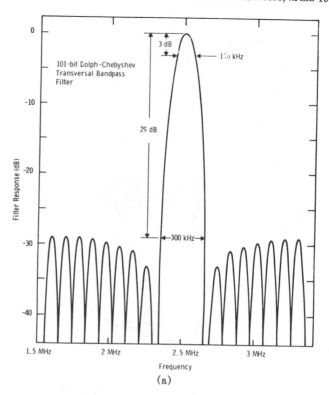

Fig. 9. Charge loss compensation in a BBD filter having poor CTE. The weighting coefficients are chosen to invert the dispersion due to loss. These results are measured on an 11-bit Barker-coded p-n filter. (a) Impulse response without charge compensation. (b) Correlation response without charge compensation. (c) Impulse response with charge compensation. (d) Correlation response with charge compensation.

$$\frac{S}{N}(\text{out}) = M \frac{\frac{S}{N}(\text{in})}{1 + \sigma_{\text{rms}}^2 \left[1 + \frac{S}{N}(\text{in})\right]} \qquad (14)$$

where σ_{rms} is the fractional rms weighting coefficient error and is on the order of a few percent. This expression shows that the ideal processing gain (equal to the number of bits M in the code) is achieved, unless $S/N(\text{in})$ is on the order of σ_{rms}^{-2}, which normally would not be the case.

IV. OTHER APPLICATIONS OF TRANSVERSAL FILTERING

The use of a CTD transversal filter to achieve a desired spectral characteristic has been demonstrated using BBD's [11], [12], [19]. For this application, the impulse response of the filter is chosen to be the Fourier transform of the desired frequency characteristic, in much the same way that SWD spectral filters are designed [10]. The type of spectral characteristic that can be achieved is therefore limited by the finite time duration of the impulse response.

An example of a narrow-band filter characteristic is shown in Fig. 10(a). This is an example of a Dolph–Chebyshev filter, and is achieved using a 101-stage CCD whose impulse response is shown in Fig. 10(b). This class of filter is designed to optimize the tradeoff between the width of the passband and the rejection outside the passband. It has 29-dB out-of-band rejection and a 3-dB bandwidth of $4\frac{1}{2}$ percent of the center frequency. The center frequency is designed to be $\frac{1}{4}$ of the clock frequency f_c and can be varied by varying f_c [=10 MHz in Fig. 10(a)]. Filters of this type are not particularly sensitive to charge transfer loss. In this example, a loss per stage (ϵ) of 10^{-3} reduces the minimum out-of-band rejection by less than 0.5 dB.

Filters of this type are potentially useful for a number of reasons. 1) The frequency of the passband of such

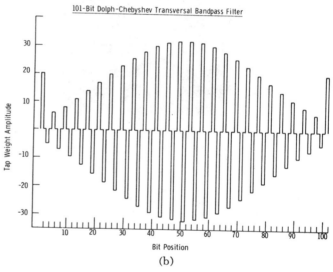

Fig. 10. (a) Frequency characteristic achievable using a 101-stage CCD filter clocked at 10 MHz. (b) Impulse response that gives this frequency characteristic. (The weighting coefficients are unnormalized.)

a filter can be tuned as described above. 2) The frequency characteristic of such a filter is extremely versatile. For example, the phase of the frequency characteristic can be specified in addition to the amplitude, and filters having linear phase across the passband can be constructed simply by making $h_k = h_{M-k+1}$. 3) CTD filters are potentially very-low-noise devices, and it may be possible to utilize them at low signal levels.

A transversal bandpass filter of the type described above is conceptually different from a recursive bandpass filter, which also can be effectively implemented using CTD's [6], [14]. The latter has an impulse response of infinite duration, and therefore filters can be designed having simultaneously a narrow passband and good out-of-band rejection. They are particularly useful in realizing high Q filters, and out-of-band rejection is not limited by weighting coefficient error, as it is in transversal filters. On the other hand, a general frequency characteristic is not easily realizable, and filters of this type are not readily integrated because they require amplifiers having precisely determined gain.

Another potentially important application for CTD transversal filters is in performing Hilbert transforms for use, for example, in single-sideband modulation. Here the impulse response of the filter is determined by the following weighting coefficients (unnormalized):

$$h_k = \frac{1}{k - \frac{(M+1)}{2}}, \qquad k = 1, M; \quad M \text{ even.} \quad (15)$$

The output of the filter is

$$v_{\text{out}}(nT_c) = \sum_k v_{\text{in}}[(n-k+1) + T_c]\left(k - \frac{M+1}{2}\right)^{-1} \quad (16)$$

which approximates the integral

$$v_{\text{out}}(t) = \int_0^{T_d} v_{\text{in}}(t-\tau)\left(\tau - \frac{T'_d}{2}\right)^{-1} d\tau. \quad (17)$$

The ideal Hilbert transform is given in the time domain by

$$v_{HT}(t) = \frac{1}{\pi} \int_{-\infty}^{\infty} v(t-\tau)\frac{1}{\tau} d\tau \quad (18)$$

and differs from the CTD approximation in several ways. For one thing, (16) gives a signal that is the Hilbert transform of the input delayed by $T_d/2$. This is a necessary result of causality, and it requires that other signals that are to be processed together with the transformed signal must be delayed by a similar amount. In addition to being delayed, the CTD Hilbert transform is inexact because of two limitations. 1) The impulse response is not infinite in time duration, as is required by (18). This truncation introduces error, which is most severe when v_{in} has frequency on the order of or less than $1/T_d$. 2) The integral is approximated by a summation that limits the frequency of v_{in} to be less than $1/2T_c$.

The calculated spectral response of a 100-stage CTD Hilbert transformer is given in Fig. 11, ignoring the associated time delay. The real part is zero because of the symmetry of the impulse response about $t = T_d/2$. The imaginary part shows deviations from the ideal at low frequency, as expected.

V. CONCLUSIONS

This paper has explored the potential of charge-transfer devices as transversal, sampled data filters. The mathematical description of such filters and their potential applications in signal processing have been studied extensively in the literature, and this paper has

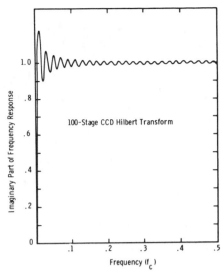

Fig. 11. Calculated response from a 100-stage CCD Hilbert transformer.

discussed the advantages and difficulties of implementing such a filter using CTD's.

Both CCD's and BBD's can be used for transversal filtering, and the sampling, weighting, and summing can be performed without adversely affecting charge transfer. Two techniques for performing sampling, weighting, and summing have been described: the electrode weighting method, for use primarily with CCD's, and the gate tapping method, for use primarily with BBD's.

CTD matched filters have been tested in spread spectrum receivers over a wide temperature range ($-60°C$ to $+80°C$) and operate as predicted. In communication systems utilizing signals that are too long to be processed using SWD's ($T_d > 20$ μs), CTD's are the only alternative to a digital computer. When CTD's can be used, their advantages in cost, power, size, and weight are overwhelming.

The principle advantages of CTD transversal filters in spectral filtering are tunability and flexibility in selecting the spectral characteristic. Weighting coefficient error and finite time duration of the impulse response make it difficult to achieve high Q filters having high out-of-band rejection.

CTD filters have many other unique linear signal processing capabilities, of which the Hilbert transform is an example. Fully utilizing the wide range of these capabilities is a challenge to device designers and to system engineers.

ACKNOWLEDGMENT

The authors are indebted to Dr. J. Holmes and Dr. A. McBride of Texas Instruments, Inc., Dallas, for consultation on matched filters for spread spectrum receivers, and to Dr. E. Hafner of the U. S. Army Electronics Command for pointing out the potential of CTD bandpass filters. They are also grateful to L. Hite, D. Splawn, and D. Awtrey for assistance in fabricating and testing the devices.

REFERENCES

[1] W. S. Boyle and G. E. Smith, "Charge coupled semi-conductor devices," *Bell. Syst. Tech. J.,* vol. 49, pp. 587–593, Apr. 1970.

[2] G. F. Amelio, M. F. Tompsett, and G. E. Smith, "Experimental verification of the charge coupled device concept," *Bell Syst. Tech. J.,* vol. 49, pp. 593–600, Apr. 1970.

[3] For a recent review of CCD's, see M. F. Tompsett, "Charge transfer devices," *J. Vac. Sci. Technol.,* vol. 9, pp. 1166–1181, July/Aug. 1972.

[4] F. L. J. Sangster, "Integrated MOS and bipolar analog delay lines using bucket-brigade capacitor storage," in *1970 IEEE Solid-State Circuits Conf., Dig. Tech. Papers,* pp. 74–75, 185.

[5] For a recent review of BBD's, see L. Boonstra and F. L. J. Sangster, "Progress on bucket-brigade charge-transfer devices," in *1972 IEEE Solid-State Circuits Conf., Dig. Tech. Papers,* pp. 140–141, 228.

[6] W. J. Butler, C. M. Puckette, M. B. Barron, and B. Kurz, "Analog operating characteristics of bucket-brigade delay lines," in *1972 IEEE Solid-State Circuits Conf., Dig. Tech. Papers,* pp. 138–139, 226–227.

[7] C. N. Berglund, "Analog performance limitations of charge-transfer dynamic shift registers," *IEEE J. Solid-State Circuits,* vol. SC-6, pp. 391–394, Dec. 1971.

[8] W. J. Butler, M. B. Barron, and C. M. Puckette, "Practical considerations for analog operation of bucket-brigade circuits," this issue, pp. 157–168.

[9] G. L. Turin, "An introduction to matched filters," *IRE Trans. Inform. Theory,* vol. IT-6, pp. 311–329, June 1960.

[10] C. S. Hartmann, D. T. Bell, and R. C. Rosenfeld, "Impulse model design of acoustic surface-wave filters," *IEEE Trans. Microwave Theory Tech.* (Invited Paper), vol. MTT-21, pp. 162–175, Apr. 1973.

[11] F. L. J. Sangster," The bucket-brigade delay line, A shift register for analog signals," *Philips Tech. Rev.,* vol. 31, pp. 92–110, 1970.

[12] ——, "MOS integrated bucket-brigade transversal filters," presented at Eurocon 71, Lausanne, Switzerland, Oct. 18–22, 1971.

[13] B. Gold and C. M. Rader, *Digital Processing of Signals.* New York: McGraw-Hill, 1969.

[14] D. A. Smith, C. M. Puckette, and W. J. Butler, "Active bandpass filtering with bucket-brigade delay lines," *IEEE J. Solid-State Circuits,* vol. SC-7, pp. 421–425, Oct. 1972.

[15] D. R. Collins, W. H. Bailey, W. M. Gosney, and D. D. Buss, "Charge-coupled-device analogue matched filters," *Electron. Lett.,* vol. 8, pp. 328–329, June 29, 1972.

[16] ——, "Evaluation of the convolution integral using charge coupled devices," presented at the Device Res. Conf., Edmonton, Alta., Canada, June 21–23, 1972.

[17] D. D. Buss, W. H. Bailey, and D. R. Collins, "Matched filtering using tapped bucket-brigade delay lines," *Electron. Lett.,* vol. 8, pp. 106–107, Feb. 24, 1972.

[18] ——, "Bucket-brigade analog matched filters," in *1972 IEEE Solid-State Circuits Conf., Dig. Tech. Papers,* pp. 250–251.

[19] D. D. Buss, C. R. Reeves, W. H. Bailey, and D. R. Collins, "Charge transfer devices in frequency filtering," in *Proc. 26th Ann. Frequency Control Symp.,* June 6–8, 1972.

[20] R. H. Barker, "Group synchronizing of binary digital systems," in *Communication Theory,* W. Jackson, Ed. London: Butterworths, 1953, pp. 273–287.

A MOS LSI Double Second Order Digital Filter Circuit*

Gwyn P. Edwards, Peter J. Jennings and Thomas Preston

Pye TMC, Ltd.

Malmesbury, England

DIGITAL SIGNAL PROCESSING has received much attention in the last 15 years, and computers have found applications in signal processing from process control using mini or micro computers to the two dimensional processing of picture signals from deep space probes, using very large computers.

Despite the numerous advantages of digital processing, no suitable hardware has been available for volume use because of the lack of a suitable technology.

To be described is a programmable digital filter circuit** containing two complete second-order filter sections, packaged in a 12 lead TO-8 can. In terms of analog filter components this replaces two inductors and six capacitors in L-C technology, or as many as six operational amplifiers, 12 resistors and 4 capacitors in active R-C technology. Stable Q factors up to 1024 may be obtained, and the chip is processed in standard low threshold P-MOS technology, giving good yields.

Although the circuit was designed for a specific application, further applications were considered at all stages of the design. Consequently the result is a very useful general purpose circuit. Some of the criteria used in the design were: sampling rate for incoming data — 8 kHz (minimum), word length of arithmetic — 15 bits, for good dynamic range, clock rate — 1 MHz maximum (for 8 kHz sampling rate), low power consumption, for high packing density, and pin count preferably not greater than 12, so that a cheap but reliable metal pack could be used (TO-8).

The first two criteria were set by the requirements of the system for which the chip was designed, the others being logical constraints for a successful design.

For complete flexibility, so that non-minimum phase filters could be designed, a 4 multiplier second order section was needed; Figure 1. This does not allow full control of the magnitude of the transfer function, but a 3-bit scaling factor is included at the output, and this is considered adequate. Consequently the obtainable transfer functions are given by:

$$H(Z) = G \left\{ \frac{1 + I_1 Z^{-1} + I_2 Z^{-2}}{1 + K_1 Z^{-1} + K_2 Z^{-2}} \right\}$$

Where $G = 1$, $1/2$, $1/4$ or $1/8$, and the coefficients I_1, I_2, K_1 and K_2 lie in the range $-(2 - 2^{-10})$ to $+(2 - 2^{-10})$.

---

*The work in this paper was performed under DCVD contract K/LT31b/1043 for the Royal Aircraft Establishment, Farnborough.

**TMC539

[1]Ebert, P.M., Mazo, J.E., and Taylor, M.G., *Bell System Technical Journal*, Vol. 9/No. 9; Nov., 1969.

System simulation had shown that 15-bit arithmetic and 12-bit coefficients (including sign) would satisfy the requirements for dynamic range and coefficient accuracy. Two's complement arithmetic was chosen, because of its tolerance of overflow of the partial sums in an accumulator, as long as the final sum does not overflow. This increases the effective word-length of the accumulator by 2 bits, a valuable feature. To prevent the overflow oscillation that is possible in recursive filters using this form of arithmetic[1], the output of the accumulator is hard limited in the event of overflow.

The multiplier design chosen was the so-called pipeline multiplier, a design which not only fits in well with the system design, but is also eminently suitable for realization in dynamic MOS. The principle is shown in Figure 2. The M-bit data (signal) enters from the left in serial form, LSB first. The N-bit coefficient is stored in a serial-in parallel-out register, and is gated into the adders by the data. The adders, when realized in dynamic MOS, take one complete clock period to complete an addition, so that the carry output is fed back to the carry input where it automatically has the correct significance. The product appears at the right, the LSB appearing just one clock after the input LSB enters the multiplier. The total multiplication time is M + N clock cycles, which in this case is 25 cycles. This figure then determines the total system architecture, since the multiplier is the largest single component in the system, and should therefore be multiplexed, if possible. The ratio of the clock frequency to the sampling frequency gives the number of cycles available for processing each sample. With a clock frequency of 1 MHz and a sampling rate of 8 kHz this figure is 125, and this indicates that it should be possible to use a single multiplier to perform all 4 multiplications in this case. The resultant system then looks as shown in Figure 3. The complete data cycle is 120 clock cycles.

To achieve complete programmability the coefficients and scaling factors are stored externally, and fed in as a single serial word for both filter sections. It was decided that the simplest way to enter this data was to repeat it every data cycle, and so it is padded to make it 120 bits long. Although it is possible to use any 1 μs RCM or PROM to store this data, a special ROM

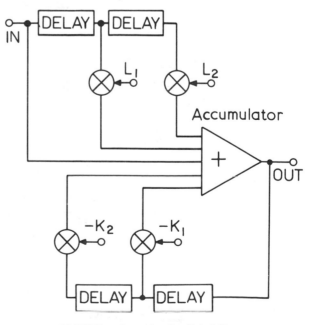

FIGURE 1—Second order digital filter.

Reprinted from *1975 IEEE Int. Solid-State Circuits Conf., Dig. Tech. Papers*, Feb. 1975, pp. 20–21.

was designed for optimum storage. This ROM is self-scanning and generates the timing and sync pulses necessary to control a sample and hold circuit and A/D converter and the filter chip itself. The ROM is programmed by the computer, the only input needed being the coefficients and scaling factors themselves.

With reference to Figure 3, the new data sample $X(n)$ is fed into the input, as data $X(n-2)$ shifts into the multiplier. The data $X(n-1)$ shifts into the $X(n-2)$ store and $X(n)$ shifts into the $X(n-1)$ store. $X(n)$ also shifts into the previously cleared accumulator. The first coefficient, I_2, multiplies $X(n-2)$ and the product is added to the contents of the accumulator. The data $Y(n-2)$ then shifts into the multiplier, where it is multiplied by K_2, and added to the contents of the accumulator. Simultaneously, data $Y(n-1)$ shifts into the $Y(n-2)$ store, and store $Y(n-1)$ is left empty. The procedure is repeated with the new contents of the $X(n-2)$ and $Y(n-2)$ stores, but this time the data are also recirculated back into the stores, as they are needed in the next cycle. The accumulator now contains the total sum

$$X(n) + I_2 \ldots X(n-2) + K_2 \ldots Y(n-2) + I_1 \ldots X(n-1)$$

$$+ K_1 \ldots Y(n-1)$$

Note that the signs of K_1 and K_2 are the reverse of those used in the transfer function. The sum in the accumulator is checked for overflow and fed into the $Y(n-1)$ store. After scaling it is fed out, exactly one cycle after the input was fed in. The cycle then repeats.

The circuit was designed for realization in P-channel MOS, using 4 phase dynamic techniques for the following reasons: only 4 phase gives the necessary low power consumption, only in 4 phase can the necessary complex gate structures be easily realized, 4 phase gives the highest speed capability in MOS circuits — this in turn eliminates the need to design specially for high speed operation all but a few of the gates in the circuit, and in one model some 30 gates do not use minimum geometry transistors, 4 phase is *highly designable*, yielding a circuit with a very high probability of first-time working using extensive CAD, 4 phase

affords a process independent design, essential for multiple sourcing.

The final circuit contains 960 gates which range in complexity from simple single input half shift bits to 5 input mixed logic gates. The gate design was deliberately kept simple for clock speed reasons. The circuit was designed using CAD at all stages, and the system in use yields a 93% probability of a chip working completely to specification. The chip is 205 x 209 mils (approx. 5 x 5 mm) and is packaged in a 12 lead TO-8 can.

In practice it has been found that the performance exceeds the minimum design requirements in all ways. In particular, the chip will work at clock rates of over 2 MHz, giving sampling rates approaching 20 kHz. The power consumption is approximately 60 mW at 1 MHz. The chip has been programmed to give a wide range of filter characteristics.

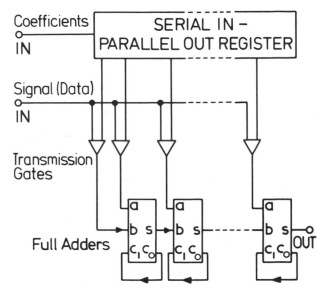

FIGURE 2—Pipeline multiplier.

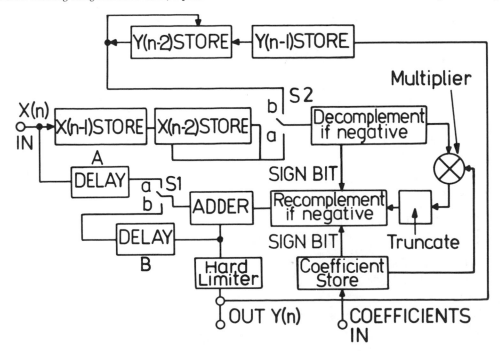

FIGURE 3— Digital filter with single multiplexed multiplier.

The Design and Operation of Practical Charge-Transfer Transversal Filters

RICHARD D. BAERTSCH, MEMBER, IEEE, WILLIAM E. ENGELER, SENIOR MEMBER, IEEE, HOWARD S. GOLDBERG, MEMBER, IEEE, CHARLES M. PUCKETTE, IV, MEMBER, IEEE, AND JEROME J. TIEMANN, SENIOR MEMBER, IEEE

Abstract—Some of the design considerations for charge-transfer split-electrode transversal filters are discussed. Clock frequency, filter length, and chip area are important design parameters. The relationship of these parameters to filter performance and accuracy is described. Both random and tap weight quantization errors are considered, and the optimum filter length is related to tap weight error.

A parallel charge-transfer channel, which balances both capacitance and background charge, and a coupling diffusion between split electrodes greatly improves accuracy. A one-phase clock is used to simplify the readout circuitry. Two off-chip readout circuits are described, and the performance of two low-pass filters using these readout circuits is given. Signal to noise ratios of 90 dB/kHz and an overall linearity of 60 dB have been achieved with this readout circuitry.

I. INTRODUCTION

CHARGE-TRANSFER devices (CTD's) offer a number of very attractive advantages for signal processing [1].

Applications in frequency filtering and time-domain matched filtering appear highly suited to one of these new devices—the split-electrode transversal filter [2], [3]. Very powerful design techniques exist for designing the tap weights for finite impulse response (FIR) transversal filters [4], and the split-capacitor CTD structure can implement these with high accuracy and low cost.

Manuscript received August 4, 1975; revised September 15, 1975.
The authors are with the Corporate Research and Development Center, General Electric Company, Schenectady, NY 12301.

Work is now being done at many locations to develop practical devices and circuits using charge-transfer transversal filters [5]–[9]. It is the purpose of this paper to discuss the properties of these devices in the context of some selected system applications and to present some specific examples where practical solutions could be obtained. The next section of the paper describes some of the design considerations that apply to the CTD transversal filter structure in the context of low-pass response. Section III is devoted to a discussion of tap weight tolerance aspects. In Section IV, clocking and output circuitry are considered. Some experimental data are presented in Section V, and Section VI summarizes the key points discussed in the paper.

II. PRACTICAL DESIGN CONSIDERATIONS

There are a number of tradeoffs to be made when designing a filter chip. To illustrate these tradeoffs, consider the design of low-pass filters and the problem of selecting the number of taps and clock frequency. Rabiner *et al.* [10] give an approximate empirical expression for the relationship between the parameters of optimum finite impulse response low-pass filters:

$$N = \frac{-10 \log_{10}(\delta_1 \delta_2) - 15}{14 (F_s - F_p)/F_c} + 1 \tag{1}$$

where N is the number of taps, F_p, F_s, and F_c are the passband edge, stopband edge, and clock (sampling) frequencies, respec-

Reprinted from *IEEE Trans. Electron Devices*, vol. ED-23, pp. 133–141, Feb. 1976.

147

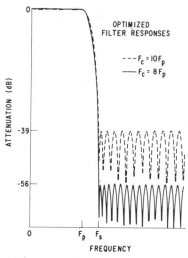

Fig. 1. Calculated filter response for two optimized filters. Passband and transition band specifications are identical, but ratio of clock frequencies is 5/4.

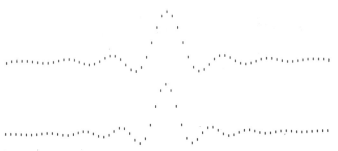

Fig. 2. Calculated impulse response (tap weights) of two low-pass filters of Fig. 4. Upper response corresponds to $F_c = 10 \, F_p$; lower to $F_c = 8 \, F_p$.

tively, and δ_1 and δ_2 are the amplitudes of the passband and stopband ripples, respectively. Typically, system requirements will fix F_s and F_p. Thus N and F_c must be appropriately chosen in order to obtain the desired levels of passband ripple and stopband attenuation. Some of the practical considerations involved in selecting a value for each of these parameters and for one related to these, namely the area of the CTD chip, are discussed below.

A. Choice of Clock Frequency

Consider the frequency response characteristics of the two designs shown in Fig. 1. The passband and transition band characteristics of these two low-pass filter designs are nearly identical, but the stop band attenuations differ by about 17 dB. They are both optimal designs [11] and they both have the same number of taps, but the sampling rates (clock frequencies) required to produce the same passband frequencies differ in the ratio of 5/4. Thus when the band edges are matched in frequency, the actual time duration of the impulse responses of these two filters differ as shown in Fig. 2, and the one with the longer duration (lowest clock frequency) has the better performance. Thus generally speaking, one should use the lowest possible clock frequency consistent with alias response considerations. The choice of clock frequency is usually determined by the permissible

complexity of the anti-alias analog filter which, in some form or other, must precede the sampled data CTD filter. This analog filter is necessary to prevent aliasing of signals near the clock frequency into the passband of the CTD filter. If one uses a sharp cutoff prefilter, one can use a lower clock frequency for the CTD filter and, therefore, obtain a longer time duration for the impulse response and have better CTD filter performance. However, this entails either a great number of components or tighter tolerances (or both), for the prefilter and, therefore, implies greater expense.

As a practical guideline, one can normally assume that if a 3-pole prefilter is used (requiring 1 op amp or resonator), the usable frequency region extends to about $\frac{1}{6}$ of the clock frequency. If a 5-pole filter is employed (requires 2 op amps or resonators), the usable fraction increases to about $\frac{1}{3}$.

B. Number of Taps

One might hope to increase the duration of the impulse response and hence improve performance by increasing the length of the filter (number of taps), but this approach also has limitations.

In general, the tap weights of frequency selective filters tend to zero at both ends of the filter. For example, an idealized low-pass transversal filter has tap weights given by

$$W_n = \frac{\sin 2\pi n F_p / F_c}{2\pi n F_p / F_c}, \quad -\infty < n < \infty.$$

In practice, two aspects of the device fabrication process limit the smallest tap weight which can be realized and hence the length of the filter. First, since computerized pattern generators are used in the photolithographic mask-making process, tap weights must be rounded off to integral multiples of a minimum coordinate spacing. Thus for any tap weight less than $\frac{1}{2}$ this minimum will be rounded to zero. Second, device process variations, such as nonuniform etching etc., will result in random tap weight errors and will put an effective lower limit on tap weight size. The effects of tap weight quantization and random errors are considered in more detail in Section III.

In addition to these fabrication limitations, insertion loss impacts the acceptable length of a filter. As one adds more taps to the general frequency selective filter, one is merely adding more and more small values at the ends. Thus the summed signal charge gets negligibly larger while the total electrode capacity continues to increase, resulting in a net decrease of signal voltage and a loss in signal-to-noise ratio.

C. Chip Area

Both types of tap weight error discussed above must be reduced to a level consistent with the desired filter length. In principle, this can be accomplished by making the chip suitably wide. However, increasing the chip area will reduce device yield and, therefore, increase the cost, and, since the capacitance of the electrodes is proportional to width, driver requirements also become more difficult.

There is another problem associated with the width of the transfer channel which has not yet been mentioned. If the

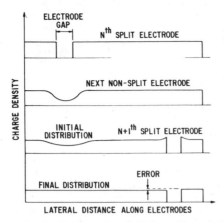

Fig. 3. Charge density is plotted as function of lateral distance along electrode for structure in which no charge is stored under electrode split. Error associated with this structure is illustrated.

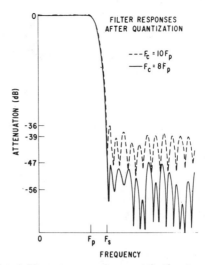

Fig. 4. Calculated filter response after quantization to one part in 600 of two filters of Fig. 1.

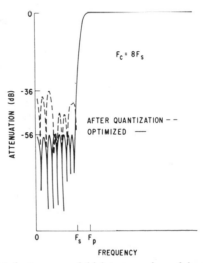

Fig. 5. Calculated response of high-pass analog of low-pass filter of Figs. 1 and 4 with $F_c = 8 F_p$. Both quantized and nonquantized responses are shown.

channel is wide, the time constant for equilibration of surface potential across the width of a particular reservoir can become quite long. If the gap cut in a split electrode produces a non-uniformity in the charge density and if this density fluctuation does not have time to equilibrate while the charge packet is within the adjacent nonsplit electrode, the charge will not be split into the correct proportions when it is transferred to the succeeding stage. Transversal filter designs which use a channel stop or thick oxide at the electrode split will be limited by this error. This error is particularly severe when the impulse response varies rapidly from stage to stage or when high frequency operation is contemplated.

Consider the charge distribution across the width of the signal channel within the Nth stage as shown in Fig. 3. As soon as the charge is transferred to the adjacent nonsplit stage, it starts to equilibrate the hole in the charge density caused by the gap cut, but unless this density fluctuation has a chance to fully equilibrate before the packet is transferred to the next stage, an error will result as shown. This error appears at much lower frequencies than those for which transfer losses become important, because the channel width is much larger than the length of a stage in the transfer direction. The time constant for lateral equilibration [12] is given by

$$T = W^2 / \mu (V_{app} - V_t) \qquad (2)$$

where μ is the mobility, V_{app} is the electrode voltage, V_t is the threshold voltage, and W is the longest distance over which lateral equilibration occurs.

If W is 10 mils, the lateral equilibration time constant is about 3×10^{-7} s for p channel and 1×10^{-7} s for n channel. One solution to this problem is to eliminate the hole in the charge density profile completely by bridging the gap cut with a coupling diffusion. This diffused region will assure that the surface potential is continuous across the gap, and when the charge packet is transferred to the adjacent nonsplit electrode, a uniform charge density will be transferred.

III. Tap Weight Tolerance Studies

As was noted in the preceding section, tap weight quantization and device processing variables limit the precision of tap

weights. These two factors are discussed in more detail in this section.

Tap weight quantization, in general, presents the designer with an interesting challenge. Typically one designs a filter with a given set of parameters, scales the tap weight vector so that the maximum tap weight equals the largest value permitted by the details of the mask construction, and then rounds off all remaining tap weights to the nearest integral multiple of the minimum coordinate spacing mentioned above. When this process is completed, the resulting response may or may not meet the stopband specifications even though the ideal design far exceeded them. It is usually possible to gain a few decibels improvement in the stopband characteristics of the quantized tap weight response by making minor variations in the design parameters, e.g., cutoff frequency, and picking the one that has the best quantized response characteristics.

The "dynamic range" of a set of tap weights varies quite differently with different types of filters and, therefore, places varying requirements on the tap weight accuracy

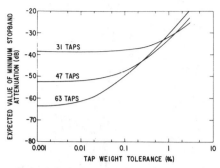

Fig. 6. Monte Carlo calculation of expected value of minimum stopband attenuation versus tap weight tolerance for three optimized low-pass filter designs. See text for details of calculation.

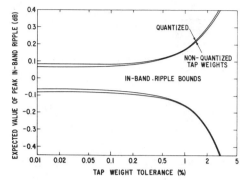

Fig. 7. Monte Carlo calculation of expected value of peak in-band ripple versus tap weight tolerance for 63-tap low-pass filter of Fig. 6. In one case, tap weights were quantized to 1 part in 600.

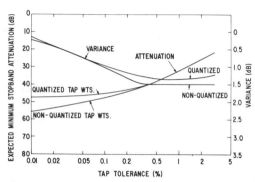

Fig. 8. Monte Carlo calculation of expected value and variance of minimum stopband attenuation versus tap weight tolerance for 63-tap low-pass filter of Fig. 6. Quantization was to 1 part in 600.

needed to realize them. A high-pass filter, for example, can be modeled as a low-pass filter in parallel with a unity gain path with the outputs of the two parallel paths being subtracted to yield the high-pass filter output. As a result, the tap weights of a high-pass filter may be viewed as a single large central tap weight superimposed on a low-pass filter tap weight vector of opposite sign and equal total weight. Since the large tap weight sets the maximum scale and thereby the absolute value of the quantization step for a given resolution, fewer levels of quantization are available for the tap weights of the high-pass function than would be if the scaling was controlled by the low-pass function alone. Fig. 4 shows the effect of quantization to 1 part in 600 of the two optimum low-pass filters shown in Fig. 1. Fig. 5 shows the effect of quantization on the high-pass "analog" to the low-pass filter with $F_c = 8 F_p$. While the stopband attenuation of the low-pass filter is degraded from 56 to 47 dB, the same quantization reduces the stopband rejection of the high-pass filter to 36 dB.

The effects of random tap weight errors have been analyzed using Monte Carlo [13] techniques, and Fig. 6 shows a typical result. To generate the data of this figure, a family of low-pass filters was designed using the Parks–McClellan algorithm [11] to achieve optimum equiripple response characteristics. Filter lengths of 31, 47, and 63 taps were selected with the normalized passband cutoff set equal to 0.125. The stopband cutoff was set equal to 0.175 and the ratio of the passband to stopband ripple was set at 5. An ensemble of frequency responses was then calculated for each filter using tap weights that were calculated by adding an independent random error to each of the optimum values. The equation for the random error is

$$\Delta_n = T * \max \{W_n\} * RN$$

where

$\max \{W_n\}$ = maximum tap weight

T = tolerance

RN = random number uniformly distributed between +1 and −1.

The response ensemble was scanned in the stopband to find the minimum stopband attenuation; these values were then averaged and the data thus derived were plotted. Similar data have been generated for other designs. The general conclusion is that longer filters require increased tap weight accuracy,

i.e., smaller random errors, if they are to perform better than shorter filters.

The combined effects of quantization and random errors are illustrated in Figs. 7 and 8. Fig. 7 shows how the average value of the peak positive and negative passband ripples varies as a function of the random tap weight error tolerance, with and without tap weight quantization. Note that tap weight quantization to 600 levels has very little effect on the in-band characteristics. In Fig. 8, the average amplitude of the minimum stopband ripple, expressed as decibels of attenuation, is plotted together with its variance. Here the effect of quantization is more apparent. This is not surprising because the attenuation is due to a delicate vector cancellation between all of the taps. These results indicate that random tap weight errors in the range of 0.1 to 0.3 percent can be tolerated for this 63-tap design.

IV. CLOCKING AND SIGNAL RECOVERY

A. General

A wide variety of techniques have been suggested for clocking, charge insertion, and signal recovery in CTD's, and their advantages and disadvantages have been discussed elsewhere [14]–[16]. The primary considerations, apart from complexity, are signal to noise ratio and linearity. Recovery of the output signal from transversal filters raises some new problems beyond those encountered in other CTD's, such as simple delay lines. First, the desired output signal voltage is smaller. It is derived by subtracting the output signals from the two split-electrode

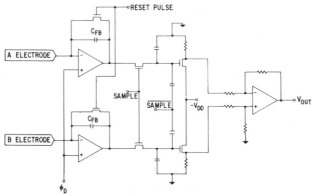

Fig. 9. Circuit which keeps split-electrode segments clamped at fixed voltage.

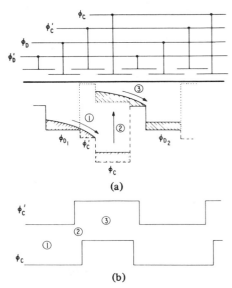

Fig. 10. Surface potentials and clock waveforms for p-channel overlapping gate structure using one-phase clock. Electrodes labeled ϕ_D and ϕ'_D are connected to dc voltages.

portions, and each of these is usually much larger than the difference. Thus even though the sense electrode output voltages are large, the dynamic range available for the actual output signal is usually reduced. Signal-to-noise and dynamic range considerations are, therefore, more important in transversal filters than in simple delay lines. Second, an uncorrectable error is introduced if the depletion capacitances of the reservoirs depend on the electrode output voltages. This error arises because the depletion capacitance is a function of both the charge in the individual packet and the potential of the overlying sense electrode. Although the dependence on the signal charge itself can be overcome by compensation at the input, the change due to the electrode potential depends on the total charge in all of the reservoirs and, therefore, cannot be compensated. This error will be called "crosstalk." One solution to this problem is to clamp the electrode potentials with operational amplifiers as shown in Fig. 9. This strategy forces the electrode voltages to remain fixed and eliminates the "crosstalk" between the charge samples, but it imposes severe requirements on the amplifiers. First, since uncorrelated amplifier noise is introduced before subtraction takes place, the amplifier must have low noise, and second, even if the sense electrodes are not clocked, the amplifier must handle the dynamic range of the full electrode signal rather than that of the difference signal. In practice, these problems are worse than the "crosstalk" problem, and we have found it preferable to permit the electrode potentials to change. In this case, a single differential op amp can be used, and the common mode signal can be eliminated with the common mode rejection of the amplifier. Two circuits using this technique will be described later.

A problem common to all data recovery schemes is the presence of large clock transients, and any useful scheme must have some method of suppressing them. This suppression can be greatly aided if a differential output is used and the transients can be made to balance. In the transversal filter, a differential output is required in any case, but the transients induced on the *A* and *B* portions of the split electrodes will not be equal unless the tap weights sum exactly to zero. Since a filter cannot have a response down to dc unless the tap weight sum differs from zero, balanced transient pick-up will not be obtained in the general case. To solve this problem, a

parallel charge-transfer channel has been incorporated in the experimental structures whose area is exactly equal to the difference in the total areas of the split electrode portions. Since all overlap capacitances are the same in the parallel channel as in the signal channel, transients from all sources are balanced. No signal charge is sent down this channel, but only a background charge which is equal in density to the background charge of the main channel. The background charge transferred under the two halves of the split electrodes is thus identical, and, when the difference is taken, the output signal is independent of background charge. Thus the filter will respond to a change in dc signal but not to a change in dc background. The parallel channel is *necessary* for any filter which requires a frequency response which is flat to dc and in which the output dc devel is to be independent of background charge.

B. One-Phase Clock Scheme

A schematic cross section of the charge transfer structure is shown together with a surface potential plot at two different times in the cycle in Fig. 10(a), and the corresponding clock voltage waveforms are shown in Fig. 10(b). The split electrodes, on which the output signal appears, are labeled ϕ_D, and these are interleaved by the ϕ_C electrodes which are not split. The primed electrodes are transfer gates, whose function is simply to prevent the flow of charge in the reverse direction. The voltage waveforms on the transfer gates are essentially identical to those for the corresponding reservoirs, but their potentials are always lower (closer to ground). Although the circuit operates correctly with the same timing on both clock waveforms, the actual waveforms shown have been used for many of the experiments. Three points in time within one cycle are shown on the waveforms, and the corresponding potentials are also indicated. Potentials at time 1 are shown dashed, while those at time 3 are shown dotted.

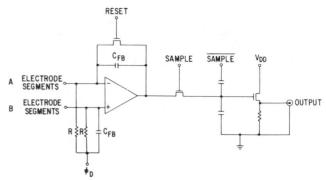

Fig. 12. Charge-sensitive amplifier circuit using resistors to reset voltage on electrodes.

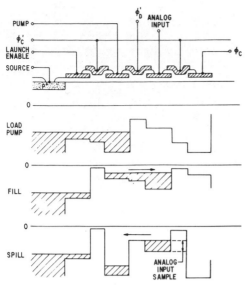

Fig. 11. Surface potentials at three different times illustrating "fill and spill" input method. Charge launched is proportional to difference between ϕ'_D and analog input.

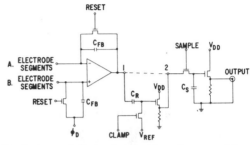

Fig. 13. Precharge and float circuit using charge-sensitive amplifier.

Note that the split electrodes ϕ_D are held at relatively constant potential throughout the cycle, and that charge transfer is accomplished by driving the intervening ϕ_C electrodes alternately higher and lower. There were two reasons for choosing this one-phase clocking method. First, the signal recovery is easier, since the signal does not ride on top of a high-amplitude clock, and second, the number of drivers required is reduced.

C. Fill and Spill Input

A linearized input scheme [14], [15] is shown schematically in Fig. 11. Here an excess quantity of charge is loaded under an electrode-called pump when the ϕ'_C electrode voltage drops. This excess charge is transferred under the analog input electrode when ϕ'_C and the pump electrode move toward ground. A quantity of charge proportional to the difference between the voltage applied to the analog input and the ϕ'_D electrode remains under the analog input electrode after the pump electrode voltage has dropped and the excess charge spilled.

Note that this input scheme requires that only a dc voltage be applied to the input diffusion, so that the possibility of charge injection is minimized. The charge launched is linear with the input analog voltage when a dc voltage is applied to the ϕ'_D electrode. It is invariant to the threshold to the extent that the upper and lower electrode thresholds track, which will depend on the details of the particular fabrication process employed.

D. Output Circuitry

The signal recovery circuit is shown schematically in Fig. 12. It is basically a current integrator or "charge-sensitive" amplifier followed by a sample and hold. In operation, the reset FET is first closed, thereby discharging the integration capacitor C_{FB} and then opened again. After the reset transistor is opened, the split electrodes are essentially floating, so that when the signal charge packets are moved under them, their potentials

change. The operational amplifier tries to keep both input terminals at the same potential by driving charge through the feedback capacitor. It can be seen from the symmetry of the input terminals that the charge supplied must be equal to the difference between the charges induced on the split-electrode portions. The output voltage is, therefore, proportional to this difference. The electrodes are reset to the "constant" potential ϕ_D by the resistors labeled R. The function of these resistors is to reset the split electrodes to the voltage ϕ_D by the end of the clock cycle. The resistor should be chosen such that RC_T is approximately $\frac{1}{10}$ the clock period, where C_T is the total capacitance to ground at either of the amplifier inputs including that of the transversal filter. This circuit operates best with an amplifier with sufficient slew rate to integrate the charge difference before the split electrode voltages have decayed appreciably. In addition, the resistors and on-chip and off-chip capacitance must be accurately matched so that the RC time constant of both halves is the same. Under these conditions the circuit shown in Fig. 12 will give accurate results. It should be pointed out that the output voltage of the charge sensitive amplifier will correctly reflect the difference in charge transferred to the two halves of the split electrode *even after* the voltages on the split electrodes have decayed to their initial value. Because the split electrodes return to the same voltage each clock cycle, this circuit does not have the crosstalk error described previously.

An alternate circuit is shown in Fig. 13. In this case, the two halves of the split electrode are reset to the ϕ_D voltage by turning on two FET's. Just prior to transfer of charge, both FET's are turned off and the difference in charge transferred is integrated on the feedback capacitor. This circuit, which will be referred to as precharge and float, suffers from the

TABLE I
TRADEOFF BETWEEN LINEARITY AND rms-SIGNAL-TO-rms-NOISE RATIO
FOR THE PRECHARGE AND FLOAT CIRCUIT OF FIG. 13

| Linearity | Signal-to-Noise Ratio | |
	Single Sampling	Double Sampling
40 dB	62 dB	68 dB
50 dB	59 dB	65 dB
60 dB	54 dB	60 dB

crosstalk error mentioned previously since the voltage which the two split halves finally reach depends on the total charge in the filter. It should be noted that an operational amplifier with a relatively slow slew rate can be used in this circuit.

An essential feature of both circuits described above is that feedback around the operational amplifier maintains the two portions of the electrodes at the same potential. If this were not done, charge that was initially transferred into one of the two portions of the split electrodes could transfer through the coupling diffusion to the other portion.

The precharge and float circuit of Fig. 13 can be operated with points 1 and 2 connected as shown by the dotted line, or by using an FET to clamp one end of the capacitor C_R to a reference voltage while the electrodes are being reset. If the clamp FET is turned off after the reset FET but before the charge has transferred, the noise associated with resetting the electrodes will be eliminated. This technique is referred to as correlated double sampling [17]. Both circuits, implemented with external components, have been used to obtain the results which will be described in the following sections.

E. Linearity and Noise

Measurements of the overall linearity and signal to noise ratio obtained with the CTD filter have been made. The linearity is obtained by measuring the harmonic content at the output when a sinusoidal input voltage is applied. The linearity is observed to depend on the signal level. This implies that a measurement of signal-to-noise ratio is meaningful only if the linearity of the output signal is specified.

A linearity of 50 dB is obtained with an input signal corresponding to $\frac{1}{2}$ the maximum input signal for the precharge and float circuit (see Fig. 13), while a linearity of 57 dB is obtained for the circuit of Fig. 12 under the same condition. As discussed above, the improved linearity in the latter case is obtained because the output electrodes return to the same voltage every clock period after the charge transfer. However, the resistors are an additional noise source and the signal-to-noise ratio of this circuit is reduced. Note that the linearity of either circuit can be improved by loading the electrodes with additional capacitance, but this also decreases the signal-to-noise ratio.

The tradeoff between linearity and signal-to-noise ratio is illustrated in Table I. The data in Table I show the ratio of the rms signal to rms noise integrated over a 50-kHz bandwidth for three different signal levels corresponding to an output linearity of 40, 50 and 60 dB for the precharge and float circuit of Fig. 13 with correlated double sampling and without

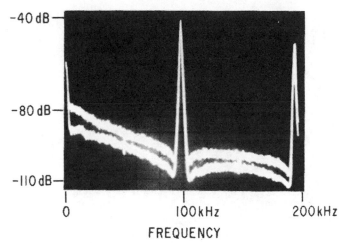

Fig. 14. Noise spectra at output of CTD low-pass filter with (lower trace) and without (upper trace) correlated double sampling for 100-kHz clock frequency. Analyzer bandwidth was 1 kHz.

(i.e., "single" sampling). The signal and noise at the sampled and held output were measured with a wide-band rms voltmeter after filtering with an *L–C* low-pass filter with a 50-kHz cutoff. For these measurements, the CTD low-pass transversal filter cutoff and clock frequencies were 10 and 80 kHz, respectively. While the results given in Table I refer specifically to the precharge and float circuit, virtually identical signal to noise ratios are obtained for the circuit of Fig. 12 when 10-kΩ resistors are used to reset the electrodes. Thus although the noise levels of the two circuits differ, the signal-to-noise ratio obtainable for a specified linearity is roughly the same because the circuit with the higher noise level has a higher degree of linearity. Correlated double sampling will eliminate reset noise and reduce $1/f$ noise associated with the amplifier. This technique reduced the integrated noise over a 50-kHz bandwidth by approximately 6 dB as shown in Table I.

The noise spectra obtained at the sample and hold output with (lower trace) and without (upper trace) correlated double sampling are shown in Fig. 14. The analyzer bandwidth was 1 kHz. Since 0 dB corresponds to an output signal with a linearity of 40 dB, the rms signal-to-noise ratio is observed to be about 90 dB/kHz in the passband of the CTD low-pass filter. A noise power of −90 dB/kHz is equivalent to a noise voltage at the amplifier output of 1 μV/$\sqrt{\text{Hz}}$. The two peaks observed in Fig. 14 are the fundamental and second harmonic of the clock. Although a sample-and-hold circuit was used to obtain these spectra, there is some clock feedthrough due to the finite sampling time.

V. EXPERIMENTAL RESULTS

The two low-pass filters whose computed frequency responses are shown in Fig. 4 have been fabricated. They are both 63-tap p-channel overlapping gate structures fabricated on 4 Ω·cm material. The filter parameters are: filter *A*: $F_p/F_c = 0.1$, $F_s/F_c = 0.131$, $\delta_1/\delta_2 = 1$, and filter *B*: $F_p/F_c = 0.1238$, $F_s/F_c = 0.165$, $\delta_1/\delta_2 = 5$. The optimum taps were quantized to 600 levels. Since the coordinate quantization of the available artwork generator was 0.00005 in, this quantization results in a channel width of 0.030 in. The total elec-

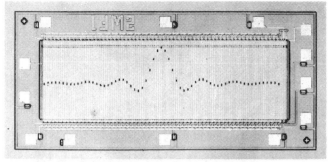

Fig. 15. Photomicrograph of 63-tap low-pass filter which will be referred to as filter A. Parallel channel is shown near top of charge-transfer channel.

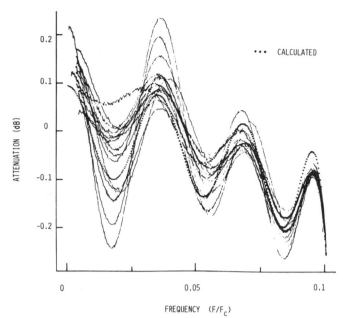

Fig. 18. Comparison of calculated and observed passband response for several different samples of filter A.

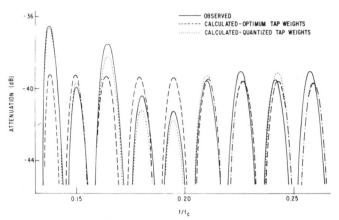

Fig. 16. Comparison of calculated and observed stopband attenuation of filter A.

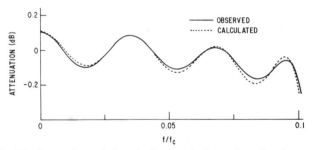

Fig. 17. Comparison of the calculated and observed passband response of selected sample of filter A.

trode capacitances are of the order of 100 pF per phase, which is within the acceptable range for simple drivers. A photomicrograph of filter A is shown in Fig. 15. Note that the parallel channel which was discussed in Section IV may be seen immediately above the upper halves of the split electrodes.

Figs. 16–18 show details of the correspondence between the computed and observed frequency responses in the stopband and passband regions of filter A. The performance in the stopband of a typical device is shown in Fig. 16. Here, both the theoretical optimum response as well as that of the rounded off taps are shown. In this region, the relative importance of errors is greatly magnified, since the entire response is at -40 dB. From the fact that the experimental curve lies closer to the rounded off curve than to the opti-

mum, it can be seen that the round-off error of 1/600 of full scale is larger than the random tap weight error for this device.

The expected and the observed responses within the passband are shown in Fig. 17 for another device. The agreement, which was within 0.02 dB, also indicates a tap weight accuracy of about 0.1 percent. The slight droop in both response curves was due to the sample and hold circuit used at the output which was included in the calculated response. Unfortunately, the passband response of Fig. 17 was not typical. Fig. 18 shows an ensemble of passband response curves superimposed on the calculated response. The deviations are seen to be of order of 0.1 dB. Referring to Fig. 7 which shows passband ripple dependence on tap weight tolerance, it may be seen that a random error of about 1 percent would be required to account for this level of deviation. This amount of error is inconsistent with the stopband results. Therefore, this excess passband deviation cannot be caused by random error but could be some form of correlated error. While random errors contribute to the frequency response inaccuracies as $\sqrt{N}$, correlated errors can be expected to contribute as N, i.e., correlated errors will be about 8 times more serious for a 63-tap filter.

The simplest forms of correlated error are mask translation and rotation. Even relatively large mask rotations will result in negligible changes in the passband response of low-pass filters. On the other hand, mask translations will cause significant perturbations of the passband response [7]. However, a calculation of the effects of a simple mask translation does not agree with the responses shown in Fig. 18. The excess passband deviation may be the result of a more complex correlated tap weight error, or it may be unrelated to tap weight error but rather may relate to errors in the method of charge detection.

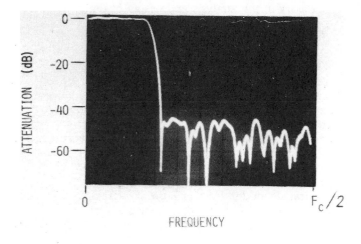

LOW PASS FILTER RESPONSE

$$F_P = 1/8\, F_C$$

Fig. 19. Performance of filter *B*. Stopband attenuation appears to be limited by random tap weight errors.

Preliminary measurements of the frequency response of filters of type *B* have been taken, and a sample is shown in Fig. 19. Typical minimum stopband attenuation appears to fall in the range −42 to −45 dB. Reference to Fig. 8 indicates that these devices also have a tap weight tolerance in the range of 0.1 to 0.3 percent which is then consistent with the measurements taken on the type *A* filters.

VI. SUMMARY

This paper discusses some of the considerations involved in designing CTD split electrode transversal filters. Much of the discussion on tap weight error and all of the experimental data relate specifically to low-pass filters. However, most of the observations made apply to a broader range of frequency selective filters.

Generally, the "best" transversal filter performance for a fixed number of taps is obtained when the filter frequency response occupies a large fraction of the Nyquist bandwidth. However, this increases the requirements on any anti-aliasing filters.

If the clock frequency is fixed, the performance is theoretically improved by increasing the filter length (i.e., number of taps). In practice, however, the filter length is limited by tap weight inaccuracy (charge-transfer inefficiency also becomes a problem when N gets large). For the low-pass filter described above, 63 taps give adequate performance for a tap weight accuracy of 0.1 percent, and a further increase in length would not improve performance.

The major sources of tap weight inaccuracy are random processing variations and tap weight quantization. Increasing the chip width will minimize these tap weight inaccuracies, but this tactic is limited by yield and peripheral circuit con-

siderations. The results above indicate that a random tap weight accuracy of 0.1 percent can be achieved with moderate chip area. When, for example, 50 dB out-of-band rejection in a low-pass filter is desired, this level of accuracy is required.

Accurate signal recovery circuitry is required for good transversal filter performance. A one-phase clock simplifies the output circuitry since the split electrodes can be operated at a dc voltage. A parallel channel which balances capacitance and background charge and a coupling diffusion between the split electrodes greatly improve accuracy. The experimental results attest to the accuracy that has been achieved with these techniques. Signal to noise ratios of 90 dB/kHz and an overall linearity of 60 dB have been achieved with this signal recovery circuitry.

REFERENCES

[1] R. D. Baertsch, W. E. Engeler, H. S. Goldberg, C. M. Puckette, and J. J. Tiemann, "Two classes of charge-transfer devices for signal processing," in *CCD 74 Int. Conf. Proc.*, Sept. 1974, pp. 229–236.

[2] F. L. J. Sangster, "The bucket brigade delay line, a shift register for analog signals," *Philips Tech. Rev.*, vol. 31, pp. 97–110, 1970.

[3] D. R. Collins, W. H. Bailey, W. M. Gosney, and D. D. Buss, "Charge-coupled-device analogue matched filters," *Electron. Lett.*, vol. 8, no. 13, pp. 328–329, 1972.

[4] L. R. Rabiner and B. Gold, *Theory and Application of Digital Signal Processing*. Englewood Cliffs, NJ: Prentice-Hall, 1975.

[5] D. D. Buss, D. R. Collins, W. H. Bailey and C. R. Reeves, "Transversal filtering using charge-transfer devices," *IEEE J. Solid-State Circuits*, vol. SC-8, pp. 134–146, Apr. 1973.

[6] D. A. Sealer, C. H. Séquin, A. M. Mohsen, and M. F. Tompsett, "Design and characterization of charge-coupled devices for analog signal processing," in *1975 Int. Conf. Communications Rec.*, vol. 1, June 1975, pp. 2–10.

[7] H. S. Goldberg *et al.*, "Design and performance of CTD split-electrode filter structures," in *1975 Int. Conf. Communications Rec.*, vol. 1, June 1975, pp. 2–10.

[8] A. Ibrahim, L. Sellars, T. Foxall, and W. Steenaart, "CCD's for transversal filter applications," in *Tech. Dig., Int. Electron Devices Meeting*, Dec. 1974, pp. 240–243.

[9] J. A. Sekula, P. R. Prince, and C. S. Wang, "Nonrecursive matched filters using charge-coupled devices," in *Tech. Dig., Int. Electron Devices Meeting*, Dec. 1974, pp. 244–247.

[10] L. R. Rabiner, J. F. Kaiser, O. Herrmann, and M. T. Dolan, "Some comparisons between FIR and IIR digital filters," *Bell Syst. Tech. J.*, vol. 53, pp. 305–331, Feb. 1974.

[11] J. H. McClellan, T. W. Parks, and L. R. Rabiner, "A computer program for designing optimum FIR linear phase digital filters," *IEEE Trans. Audio Electroacoust.*, vol. AU-21, pp. 506–526, Dec. 1973.

[12] W. E. Engeler, J. J. Tiemann, and R. D. Baertsch, "Surface-charge transport in a multielement charge-transfer structure," *J. Suppl. Phys.*, vol. 43, pp. 2277–2285, May 1972.

[13] C. M. Puckette, W. J. Butler, and D. A. Smith, "Bucket brigade transversal filters," *IEEE Trans. Commun. Technol.*, vol. COM-22, pp. 926–934, July 1974.

[14] M. F. Tompsett, "Surface potential equilibration method of setting charge in charge-coupled devices," *IEEE Trans. Electron Devices*, vol. ED-22, pp. 305–309, June 1975.

[15] S. P. Emmons and D. D. Buss, "Noise measurements on the floating diffusion input for charge-coupled devices," *J. Appl. Phys.*, vol. 45, pp. 5305–5306, 1974.

[16] C. H. Séquin and A. M. Mohsen, "Linearity of electrical charge injection into charge-coupled devices," *IEEE J. Solid-State Circuits*, vol. SC-10, pp. 81–92, Apr. 1975.

[17] M. H. White, D. R. Lampe, F. C. Blaha, and I. A. Mack, "Characterization of surface channel CCD image arrays at low-light levels," *IEEE J. Solid-State Circuits*, vol. SC-9, pp. 1–13, Feb. 1974.

A modular approach to the hardware implementation of digital filters

M. A. BIN NUN, B.Sc., M.Sc.*

and

M. E. WOODWARD, B.Sc., Ph.D.*

SUMMARY

Recent advances in the technology of medium and large scale integrated circuits (m.s.i. and l.s.i.) have made possible economical hardware implementations for real-time digital filtering. A flexible design approach for such implementations is presented. The processing mode can be varied to give any hybrid structure between the purely serial and parallel realizations. This leads to a design approach which can be adjusted to suit hardware availability. The resulting structures are modular and are in line with current trends in m.s.i. and l.s.i. technology in that they lend themselves readily to implementations using semiconductor read-only or random access memories.

Department of Electronic and Electrical Engineering, University of Technology, Loughborough, Leicestershire LE11 3TU.

Reprinted with permission from *The Radio and Electron. Engineer*, vol. 46, pp. 393–400, Aug./Sept. 1976.

The theory in the analysis and design of digital filters is well established, and their advantages over conventional analogue filters, made up of resistors, capacitors, inductors and crystals, have been widely discussed.[1,2] Until quite recently, the implementation of digital filtering has been confined mainly to simulation on general-purpose computers. The rapid development in the technology of medium and large-scale integrated circuits (m.s.i. and l.s.i.) however, is making possible the construction of special-purpose hardware for real-time digital filtering. Conventional implementations reported in the literature invariably compute the filter algorithm in the familiar binary arithmetic, either in the serial[3] or in the parallel[4] mode. Furthermore, the actual hardware synthesis is usually at the discrete gate level, and the structures proposed are mainly for specific configurations.

In this paper, a modular approach to the hardware implementation of digital filters is proposed. This approach is general, flexible and is at the system and sub-system level, and is thus very suited to m.s.i. and l.s.i. devices. In this approach, a basic second-order digital filter section may be constructed as a regular inter-connection of simple identical 'sub-filter modules'. The structure of a typical module and the processing mode of the overall section are flexible and may be adjusted to suit specific requirements. As there is a very wide range of logic families (t.t.l., e.c.l., m.o.s., etc.) and of m.s.i. and l.s.i. devices currently on the market, only a general guide as to the trade-off between circuit complexity and operating speed will be described.

The hardware implementation of the proposed approach using semiconductor memories is also discussed.

2 Digital Filtering

In general, the term 'digital filter' refers to any device which operates on an input number sequence to produce a second sequence of numbers by means of a computational algorithm. If the digital filter is part of a signal processing system, like that shown in Fig. 1, the input number sequence is usually the digital version of an analogue signal. The output sequence may be converted to the analogue form if required.

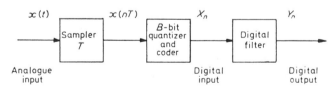

Fig. 1. Block representation of a digital signal processing system.

High-order digital filters are normally realized as either a cascade or a parallel network of basic second-order sections,[1,2] which, in the former case, are ordered for minimum round-off noise and have outputs suitably scaled.[5,6]

A typical second-order section is shown in Fig. 2. The input and output sequences, (X_n) and (Y_n) respectively, are related by the following difference equation:

$$Y_n = \sum_{i=0}^{2} A_i X_{n-i} - \sum_{i=1}^{2} B_i Y_{n-i} \qquad (1)$$

where A_i and B_i are the filter coefficients obtainable from its transfer function.

The filter network in Fig. 2 consists of a non-recursive and a recursive part. Both are essentially the same in both structure and operation in that each may be represented by an expression of the form

$$V_n = \sum_{i=0}^{2} C_i U_{n-i} \qquad (2)$$

where, for the recursive part, $C_0 = B_0 = 0$.

In the subsequent discussion of the proposed design approach, it is therefore only necessary to consider the more general non-recursive part, which has the input-output relationship

$$Z_n = \sum_{i=0}^{2} A_i X_{n-i} \qquad (3)$$

3 Design Approach

The proposed design approach is based on computing the filtering algorithm given by equation (3), not only in the conventional binary system, but in the general radix R arithmetic, where R is an integer power of 2, i.e.

$$R = 2^p, \quad p = 1, 2, 3, \ldots \text{ etc} \qquad (4)$$

It is assumed that fixed-point arithmetic is used, and that, in order to process equation (3) to a specified accuracy, B' and B'' binary digits (bits) are required to represent each of the data and coefficient words respectively. Also, to simplify the discussion on the design approach, the data and coefficient words are assumed to be non-negative integers, i.e.

$$0 \leqslant X_{n-i} \leqslant 2^{B'} - 1$$

and

$$0 \leqslant A_i \quad \leqslant 2^{B''} - 1$$

In practice, the data and coefficients are represented as binary fractions and the two's complement[5, 6, 8] notation is most commonly used to handle negative numbers.

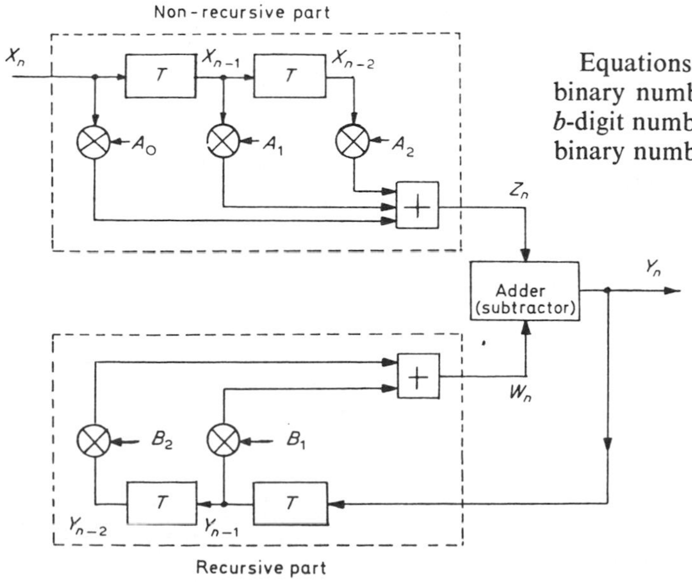

Since any B-bit binary number M can be represented in the form

$$M = \sum_{r=0}^{B-1} m_r 2^r, \quad m_r = 0 \text{ or } 1 \qquad (5)$$

the binary forms of the data and coefficients will be

$$X_{n-i} = \sum_{k=0}^{B'-1} x_{n-i,k} 2^k \qquad (6)$$

and

$$A_i = \sum_{j=0}^{B''-1} a_{i,j} 2^j \qquad (7)$$

where

$$i = 0, 1, 2, \quad x_{n-i,k}, a_{i,j} = 0 \text{ or } 1$$

Conventionally, equations (6) and (7) are substituted directly into equation (3) for the subsequent computation of the filter output Z_n. A comprehensive discussion on the possible hardware organizations and processing modes for implementations based on binary arithmetic is given by Freeny in his tutorial paper.[7]

In the proposed modular approach, a B-bit binary number M is first partitioned into b blocks, each of p bits, where

$$B = b \times p, \quad b \text{ and } p \text{ being integers} \qquad (8)$$

($p = 3$, and $p = 4$ result in the familiar octal and hexadecimal systems respectively).

Thus equation (5) may now be represented as

$$M = (m_{B-1} 2^{p-1} + \ldots + m_{B-p+1} 2^1 + m_{B-p} 2^0)(2^p)^{b-1}$$
$$+ \ldots + (m_{p(k+1)-1} 2^{p-1} + \ldots + m_{pk+1} 2^1$$
$$+ m_{pk} 2^0)(2^p)^k + \ldots + (m_{p-1} 2^{p-1}$$
$$+ \ldots + m_1 2^1 + m_0 2^0)(2^p)^0$$

or

$$M = \sum_{k=0}^{b-1} M_k (2^p)^k \qquad (9)$$

where

$$M_k = \sum_{h=0}^{p-1} m_{pk+h} 2^h \qquad (10)$$

and

$$0 \leqslant M_k \leqslant 2^p - 1$$

Equations (9) and (10) simply mean that the B-bit binary number in equation (4) is now represented as a b-digit number in the radix 2^p, where each digit is a p-bit binary number.

Non-recursive part

Fig. 2.
Second-order digital filter section with sample period T.

Recursive part

3.1 Example

Let M be the 6-bit ($B = 6$) binary number, 1 0 1 1 0 1. Expressing this in terms of equation (5), then,

$$M = 1 \times 2^5 + 0 \times 2^4 + 1 \times 2^3 + 1 \times 2^2 + 0 \times 2^1 + 1 \times 2^0.$$

If M is partitioned into three blocks, each of two bits ($b = 3$, $p = 2$), then M can be expressed as

$$M = (1 \times 2^5 + 0 \times 2^4) + (1 \times 2^3 + 1 \times 2^2) + (0 \times 2^1 + 1 \times 2^0)$$

or, in terms of equation (9)

$$M = (1 \times 2^1 + 0 \times 2^0)(2^2)^2 + (1 \times 2^1 + 1 \times 2^0)(2^2)^1 \\ + (0 \times 2^1 + 1 \times 2^0)(2^2)^0$$

Thus, M is now represented as a 3-digit number in the radix 2^2, where the digits, M_k of equation (9), are 2-bit binary words, and, using equation (10) are given by

$$M_0 = 01, \quad M_1 = 11 \quad \text{and} \quad M_2 = 10$$

3.2 Computing in the Radix 2^p

In general, each data word may be partitioned into b' blocks each of p' bits, and each coefficient word into b'' blocks of p'' bits.

Using equation (9), equation (3) can be rewritten, in which Z_n, the output of the non-recursive filter section, is expressed as a triple sum,

$$Z_n = \sum_{i=0}^{2} \left[\sum_{k''=0}^{b''-1} A_{i,k''}(2^{p''})^{k''} \right] \left[\sum_{k'=0}^{b'-1} X_{n-i,k'}(2^{p'})^{k'} \right] \quad (11)$$

where

$$A_{i,k''} = \sum_{h''=0}^{p''-1} a_{i,p''k''+h''} 2^{h''} \quad (12)$$

and

$$X_{n-i,k'} = \sum_{h'=0}^{p'-1} x_{n-i,p'k'+h'} 2^{h'} \quad (13)$$

for $i = 0, 1, 2$, and

$$(b'')(p'') = B'', \quad (b')(p') = B'$$

The order of summation in equation (11) is then changed, resulting in

$$Z_n = \sum_{k'=0}^{b'-1} (2^{p'})^{k'} \sum_{k''=0}^{b''-1} (2^{p''})^{k''} \sum_{i=0}^{2} (A_{i,k''})(X_{n-i,k'}) \quad (14)$$

Equation (14) forms the basis of the proposed modular approach to the hardware implementation of digital filters.

3.2.1. *Example*

Consider a second-order non-recursive filter having the coefficients

$$A_0 = 6_{10}, \quad A_1 = 13_{10} \quad \text{and} \quad A_2 = 9_{10}$$

Also, suppose that at a particular sampling instant the data consists of

$$X_n = 12_{10}, \quad X_{n-1} = 5_{10} \quad \text{and} \quad X_{n-2} = 7_{10}.$$

If both data and coefficients are represented by 4-bit binary numbers, ($B' = B'' = 4$), then

$$A_0 = 0110, \quad A_1 = 1101, \quad A_2 = 1001$$

and

$$X_n = 1100, \quad X_{n-1} = 0101 \quad \text{and} \quad X_{n-2} = 0111$$

Each of these words is now split into two blocks ($b' = b''$

$= 2$), each of two bits ($p' = p'' = 2$), say. The filter output Z_n at this particular sample instant may then be computed by the substitution of the actual values of the data and coefficients, now represented in the radix 2^2, into equation (3). This computation is illustrated by Table 1.

Table 1

	$R^3 R^2 R^1 R^0$		$R^3 R^2 R^1 R^0$		$R^3 R^2 R^1 R^0$	Sum of partial products in like rows
Coefficient	A_0 01 10	A_1	11 01	A_2	10 01	
	$\times$		$\times$		$\times$	
Data	X_n 11 00	X_{n-1}	01 01	X_{n-2}	01 11	
	00 00		00 01		00 11	01 00
	00 00		00 11		01 10	10 01
	01 10		00 01		00 01	10 00
	00 11		00 11		00 10	10 00

Each 4-bit partial product is the result of a 2-bit by 2-bit parallel multiplication, i.e. the data and coefficient blocks are multiplied in radix $R = 2^2$ arithmetic. The partial products in like rows are now added. This corresponds to the first summation of equation (14). The remaining stages of summation, as specified by equation (14) for the computation of the section output Z_n, are shown in Table 2.

Table 2

Second, final summation according to equation (14)								Filter output Z_n			
R^3	R^2	R^1	R^0		R^3	R^2	R^1	R^0			
		01	00								
+						10	10	00			
	10	01							11 00 10 00		
	10	00				+					
+						10	10	00			
10	00										

As a result, the original filter, whose data and coefficients are represented by 4-bit binary words, is now regarded as being made up of four simpler units whose data and coefficients consist of only 2-bit binary words.

4 Possible Realizations

Two possible realizations for the computation of equation (14) are shown in Figs. 3 and 4. They differ both in hardware complexity and operating speed.

4.1 Parallel Processing

In the direct realization illustrated in Fig. 3, the second-order non-recursive section consists of a parallel interconnection of, what will be termed, sub-filter modules.

These modules, enclosed by the broken lines in Fig. 3, are organized into b' groups each group containing b'' modules, where b' and b'' are the number of partition blocks as described by equation (11). For the overall section, $b' \times b''$ modules would be required in all.

A typical module has the same general structure and computing algorithm as that of the overall section. Each of the data and coefficients of a module, however, are now only p' bit and p'' bit words respectively.

In operation, these sub-filter modules implement the first summation in equation (14). The output of each group is obtained by adding the weighted outputs of all the modules in that particular group. Similarly, the section output Z_n is obtained by summing the weighted outputs of all the groups, as specified by the outer summation of equation (14).

In this direct realization, the output weightings are done by hard-wired shifts.

4.2 Sequential Processing

In contrast to the realization shown in Fig. 3, where $b' \times b''$ modules operate concurrently, a single module, performing $b' \times b''$ module computations in time succession, may be used.

This sequential mode of processing is illustrated in Fig. 4, in which a basic sub-filter module is time-shared among the data and coefficient blocks. The accumulator

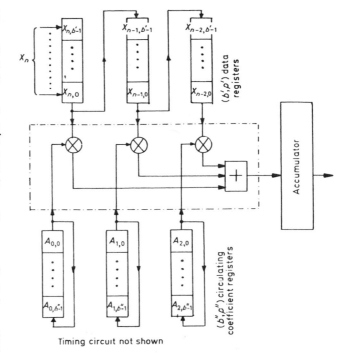

Timing circuit not shown

Fig. 4. Time-sharing of a single sub-filter module.

keeps a running sum of successive module outputs and also incorporates the required weightings to them.

The blocks of each of the data words are accommodated in a (b', p') register store while those of each of the co-efficients are stored in a (b'', p'') circulating register store, where a typical (b, p) register is one having b stages, each stage accommodating a p-bit word, as shown in Fig. 5(a).

For every clock shift of the data registers these circulating coefficient stores go through a complete cycle of b'' shifts. Since the data registers have to be clocked b' times, the required section output, Z_n, will be obtained in $b' \times b''$ register clock periods after the arrival of the section input, X_n, at a particular sampling instant.

The data and coefficient blocks are so arranged as to be in increasing order of significance at the start of every sampling instant.

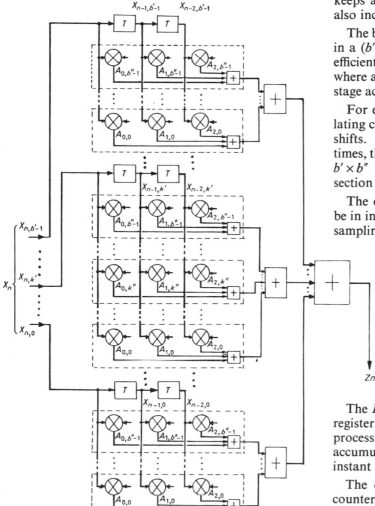

Fig. 3. Modular circuit configuration of a non-recursive digital filter section.

The B'-bit input, X_n, is loaded in parallel into an input register of the form shown in Fig. 5(b). In the subsequent processing, the blocks of X_n are accessed sequentially, the accumulator being reset to zero prior to every sampling instant nT.

The control of the overall section can consist of a counter and simple logic circuitry to account for the different clock rates of the data and coefficient registers.

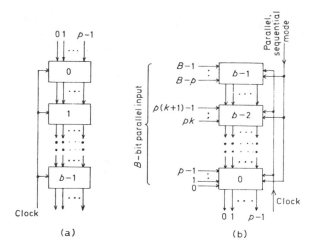

Fig. 5. Store and input registers.

4.3 Features

In the direct realization, as shown in Fig. 3, the circuit configuration of the overall filter section is highly modular. All the component units have an identical structure, and the interconnection between them is very regular. In consequence, the hardware implementation of the section is systematic and straightforward. Furthermore, testing and fault diagnosis are greatly simplified.

Since a typical module has the same computing algorithm as that of the original section, the 'feel' for the overall filtering operation is retained when interconnecting modules. Also, the hardware requirement of a module is determined only by the manner in which the original data and coefficient words have been partitioned. The structure is therefore easily adjusted to suit particular requirements and available hardware components. To illustrate this, consider a non-recursive section, whose data and coefficients are represented by 6-bit and 4-bit binary words respectively. Then Table 3 shows the possible ways in which these words may be partitioned into blocks, according to equation (8).

Table 3

	Data			Coefficient		
Number of blocks	6	3	2	1	4	2	1
Number of bits/block	1	2	3	6	1	2	4

The structure of the basic module depends very much on the size of its component multipliers. For this particular filter section there are, altogether, $4 \times 3 = 12$ different multiplier sizes, which range from a 1-bit $\times$ 1-bit to a 6-bit $\times$ 4-bit configuration, with one convenient size being the 2-bit $\times$ 2-bit one. An interesting size is the 1-bit (data) $\times$ 4-bit, as it is of the type used in the familiar shift-and-add technique for multiplication.[3, 7, 8, 9]

A final feature of the proposed approach is that, after the structure of the basic module has been decided upon, the actual mode of processing the filter algorithm is flexible. The parallel and sequential realizations, dis-

cussed previously and shown in Figs. 3 and 4, are just two extremes, hybrid forms being possible. For example, one hybrid realization might consist of a set of basic modules, operating concurrently, this being regarded as a basic time-shared unit for subsequent sequential processing. Another hybrid form might be one in which sets of data blocks are processed in parallel by a number of time-shared basic modules each operating sequentially.

In general, in between the parallel and the completely sequential realizations there is a spectrum of hardware structures and processing modes, the final choice being left to the system designer.

4.3.1. *Example*

Consider a non-recursive section having 8-bit data and coefficient words, (i.e. $B' = B'' = 8$). If each of these words are partitioned into four blocks, each of two bits ($b' = b'' = 4$, $p' = p'' = 2$), the resulting basic module has a word length of 2 bits. The direct realization of this section, as in Fig. 3, would require $b' \times b'' = 16$ of these basic modules. The completely sequential mode is shown in Fig. 6(a), while Figs. 6(b) and (c) illustrate two possible hybrid realizations. In the former, two basic modules make up the time-shared unit, while in the latter the input X_n is split into two parallel halves, each of which are then processed sequentially. It is seen that when both examples of hybrid processing are compared with the completely sequential one, two basic modules are required. Their computing time, however, is reduced by half. The parallel mode, of course, has an even shorter computing time which, in this example, is sixteen times as fast as that of the completely sequential mode.

5 Practical Considerations

The performance of the overall filter section depends primarily on the structure of the basic module and the manner in which the computing algorithm is processed. The hardware requirement and implementation of a typical sub-filter module are described below, and the computation time for the section output is derived for the two extreme modes of processing. The trade-off between circuit complexity and operating speed is also discussed.

5.1 Hardware Implementation of Sub-Filter Module

The hardware organization of a typical module is shown in Fig. 7. The required arithmetic operations are three p' bit $\times p''$ bit multiplications and two $(p'+p'')$ bit additions. These operations may be implemented by any suitable m.s.i. multiplier and adder chips currently on the market. An attractive alternative, however, is to implement the module using semiconductor memories, (either read-only (r.o.m.) or random access (r.a.m.)), acting as stored look-up arithmetic tables.[12]

One way of using these memory chips is to replace each p' bit $\times p''$ bit multiplier, shown in Fig. 7, by a r.o.m. or r.a.m. of suitable storage. Variable and fixed coefficient multiplications using r.o.m.s are illustrated in Fig. 8(a) and (b). The former offers versatile operation at the expense of large memory storage when the word lengths of the data and coefficient blocks are large. The fixed coefficient multiplication requires less memory storage but is less versatile.

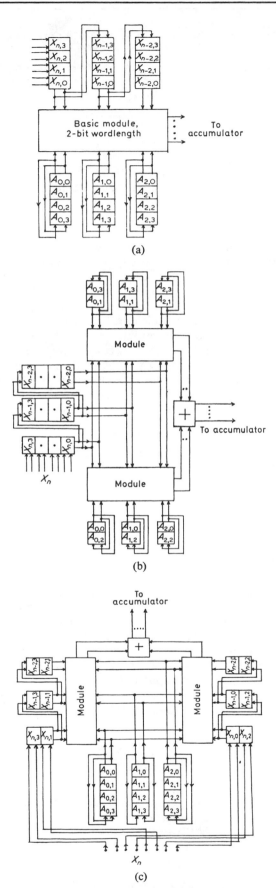

Fig. 6. Processing modes using 2-bit basic modules.
(a) Completely sequential
(b), (c) Two possible hybrid forms

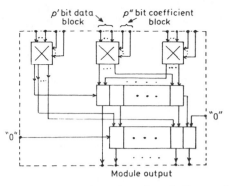

Fig. 7. Hardware configuration of a sub-filter module.

The configuration in Fig. 8(c), however, combines partially-variable coefficient capability with reasonable memory storage requirements. A total of 2^q different coefficients can be stored in the r.o.m.

For data and coefficient blocks of short lengths, i.e. p' and p'' small, even the complete sub-filter modules may be implemented as a look-up store using a r.o.m. of sufficiently large memory storage, as shown in Fig. 9. There is thus no necessity for the two P-bit ($P = p'+p''$) adders previously required.

In general, the implementation of digital filters using l.s.i. semiconductor memories is simple, straightforward and incorporates programmability. It also offers the possibility of volume production of digital filter i.c. chips using existing manufacturing facilities. As digital filters are still not being used extensively enough, there is obviously a reluctance to custom-design and manufacture special i.c.s apart from very simple filter configurations.[10] The market demand for semiconductor memories, however, is great enough to support its own technology.

5.2 Operating Speed of Filter Section

The minimum value of the sampling period T for the basic nonrecursive section depends on the time it takes to compute the output Z_n after the arrival of a particular input X_n.

If t_M is the time to compute the output of a typical sub-filter module, then

$$t_M = t_a + t_s \qquad (15)$$

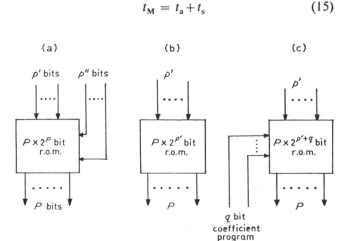

Fig. 8. R.o.m. realizations of p' bit $\times p''$ bit multipliers.

where t_a = time to perform a p' bit $\times p''$ bit multiplication, and

t_s = time to sum three $(p'+p'')$ bit words.

For the realizations shown in Figs. 8(a) to (c), t_a will be the access time of any particular r.o.m. used. Similarly, for the realization shown in Fig. 9, t_M corresponds to the access time of the r.o.m. implementing the complete sub-filter module.

For the direct realization shown in Fig. 3, the total time, T_p, required to compute Z_n is given by

$$T_p = t_M + t_g + t_y \qquad (16)$$

where t_g = time to sum the outputs of all the modules in any particular group

and t_y = time to sum the outputs of all the groups.

Details on the propagation delay during the process of addition can be found in any standard text on digital arithmetic (e.g. Ref. 8).

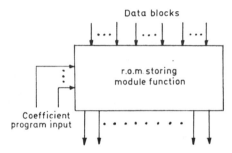

Fig. 9. R.o.m. realization of a sub-filter module.

If equation (14) is processed sequentially (see Section 4.2, Fig. 4), the computing time, T_q, is given by

$$T_q = (t_M + t_r) \times (b') \times (b'') \qquad (17)$$

where t_r = time to add the module output at time $k\Delta_t$ to the accumulator output Δ_t previously, Δ_t being the period of the register clock (see Fig. 4).

In equation (17), it is assumed that the time taken to

clock the accumulator output is much less than the computation time for the module output.

If f_p, f_q are the maximum possible sampling frequencies for the section in the parallel and sequential realizations respectively, then

$$f_p \leqslant \frac{1}{T_p} \quad \text{and} \quad f_q \leqslant \frac{1}{T_q}$$

The computation time for hybrid realizations may be determined using the general principles discussed.

5.3 Trade-off Between Circuit Complexity and Operating Speed

The relative advantages of the various processing modes depend on their respective circuit complexity, module count and operating speeds. The parallel mode has the fastest processing speed and requires virtually no control circuitry. The number of sub-filter modules needed, however, is a maximum (being $b' \times b''$ modules in total). At the other extreme, the sequential mode requires only one module and an accumulator, but operates $b' \times b''$ times slower than the parallel realization. Also, some control logic is necessary for the proper accumulation and weighting of the module output. The hybrid mode offers a compromise by enabling the designer to select the most suitable combination of module count and processing speed to match his specific requirement.

6 General Second-order Section

As the recursive and non-recursive parts of the general second-order digital filter section (Fig. 2) have basically the same structure, the modular approach already discussed can be directly applied to realize this general section.

The resulting basic module then consists of two modules, each similar to that shown in Fig. 7. The block diagram of the direct modular realization of the general second-order section is shown in Fig. 10.

Since Y_n, the section output, is now in a feedback loop, it has to be truncated or rounded off to prevent the number of bits required for its representation from increasing indefinitely. Also Y_n has to be scaled, usually by simple powers of two.[4, 11] Other general practical considerations such as overflow detection, limit cycle oscillations, and manipulation of negative numbers using the two's complement code, have been adequately discussed by previous authors.[5, 6, 7]

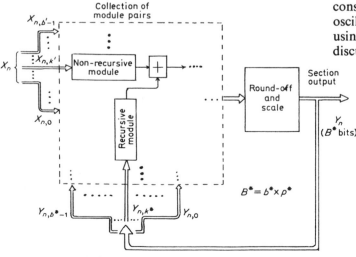

Fig. 10.
Modular organization of a general second-order filter section.

7 Conclusions

A method has been presented for the hardware design of general second-order digital filter sections. The procedure is systematic, flexible, and is in accordance with current hardware trends in that it makes use of m.s.i. or l.s.i. technology. The resulting hardware structures are modular, have uniform interconnection patterns, and variable processing modes.

The versatility and flexibility of the proposed technique should make possible the economical design of special-purpose digital filter hardware for any applications requiring real-time processing.

8 References

1. Gold, B. and Rader, C. M., 'Digital Processing of Signals' (McGraw-Hill, New York, 1969).
2. Rabiner, L. R. and Rader, C. M. (eds.), 'Digital Signal Processing' (IEEE Press, New York, 1972).
3. Jackson, L. B., Kaiser, J. F. and McDonald, H. S., 'An approach to the implementation of digital filters', *IEEE Trans. on Audio and Electroacoustics*, **AU-16**, No. 3, pp. 413–21, September 1968.
4. Gabel, R. A., 'A parallel arithmetic hardware structure for recursive digital filtering', *IEEE Trans. on Acoustics, Speech and Signal Processing*, **ASSP-22**, No. 4, pp. 255–8, August 1974.
5. Liu, B., 'Effect of finite word length on the accuracy of digital filters—a review', *IEEE Trans. on Circuit Theory*, **CT-18**, No. 6, pp. 670–7, November 1971.
6. Oppenheim, A. V. and Weinstein, C. J., 'Effects of finite register length in digital filtering and the fast Fourier transform', *Proc. IEEE*, **60**, No. 8, pp. 957–76, August 1972.
7. Freeny, S. L., 'Special-purpose hardware for digital filtering', *Proc. IEEE*, **63**, No. 4, pp. 633–48, April, 1975.
8. Lewin, D., 'Theory and Design of Digital Computers' (Wiley, New York, 1972).
9. Peled, A. and Liu, B., 'A new hardware realization of digital filters', *IEEE Trans. on Acoustics, Speech and Signal Processing*, **ASSP-22**, No. 6. pp. 456–62, December 1974.
10. Pye TMC, Ltd., London, 'Monolithic Modular Digital Filters', IEEE International Solid-State Circuits Conference, February 1973.
11. Croisier, A., Esteban, D. J., Levilion, M. E. and Riso, V., U.S. Patent 3,777,130, December 1973.
12. McDowell, J., 'Large Bipolar ROMS and PROMS Revolutionize Conventional Logic and System Design', Monolithic Memories Inc., Applications Seminar, April 19th, 1973.

Manuscript first received by the Institution on 9th June 1975 and in final form on 4th December 1975. (Paper No. 1730/CC 261.)

Section III-A
Additional Reading

L. Jackson, J. Kaiser, and H. McDonald (Bell Lab., Murray Hill, NJ), "An approach to the implementation of digital filters," *IEEE Trans. Audio Electroacoust.*, vol. AU-16, pp. 413–421, 1968.

J. Heath and C. Carroll (Elec. Eng. Dep., Auburn Univ., Auburn, AL 36830), "Special-purpose computer organization for double-precision realization of digital filters," *IEEE Trans. Comput.*, vol. C-19, pp. 1146–1152, 1970.

S. Zohar (JPL, California Inst. Technol., Pasadena, CA 91103), "New hardware realizations of nonrecursive digital filters," *IEEE Trans. Comput.*, vol. C-22, pp. 328–338, 1973.

S. Zohar (JPL, California Inst. Technol., Pasadena, CA 91103), "The counting recursive digital filter," *IEEE Trans. Comput.*, vol. C-22, pp. 338–346, 1973.

W. Little (Elec. Eng. Dep., Univ, Waterloo, Waterloo, Ont., Canada), "An algorithm for high speed digital filters," *IEEE Trans. Comput.*, vol. C-23, pp. 466–469, 1974.

A. Peled and B. Liu (Elec. Eng. Dep., Princeton Univ., Princeton, NJ 08540), "A new hardware realization of digital filters," *IEEE Trans. Acoust., Speech, Signal Processing*, vol. ASSP-22, pp. 456–462, 1974.

J. Rattner, J. C. Cornet, and M. Hoff (INTEL Corp., Santa Clara, CA) "Bipolar LSI computing elements usher in new era of digital design," *Electronics*, pp. 89–96, Sept. 5, 1974.

J. Tiemann, W. Engeler, R. Baertsch, and D. Brown (General Elec. Corp. Res and Dev., Schenectady, NY 12301), "Intracell charge-transfer structures for signal processing," *IEEE Trans. Electron Devices*, vol. ED-21, pp. 300–308, 1974.

A. Peled, B. Liu, and K. Steiglitz (Elec. Eng. Dep., Princeton Univ., Princeton, NJ 08540), "A note on implementation of digital filters," *IEEE Trans. Acoust., Speech, Signal Processing*, vol. ASSP-23, pp. 387–389, 1975.

J. Mick (Advanced Micro Devices, Sunnyvale, CA), "AMD 2900 bipolar microprocessor family," in *Proc. 8th Annu. IEEE Workshop on Microprogramming*, 1975, pp. 56–63.

P. Thompson and A. Belanger (Dep. Elec. Eng., Univ. Ottawa, Ottawa, Ont. K1N 6N5, Canada), "Digital arithmetic units for a high data rate," *The Radio and Electron. Engineer*, vol. 45, pp. 116–120, 1975.

R. Brodersen R. Hewes, and D. Buss (Texas Instruments, Inc., Dallas, TX 75222), "A 500-stage CCD transversal filter for spectral analysis," *IEEE Trans. Electron Devices*, vol. ED-23, pp. 143–152, 1976.

S. Lau (Signetics, 881 E. Arques Ave, Sunnyvale, CA 94086), "Design high performance processors," *Electron. Des.*, pp. 86–95, Mar. 29, 1977.

J. Nemec, G. Sim, and B. Willis (Signetics, 811 E. Arques Ave, Sunnyvale, CA 95050), "A primer on bit slice processors," *Electron. Des.*, pp. 52–60, Feb. 1, 1977.

J. Buie and T. Zimmerman (TRW Syst., Redondo Beach, CA) "Very large scale integrated circuits for digital signal processing: Part I," *IEEE Circuits and Syst. Newsletter*, pp. 2–8, Feb. 1977.

J. Buie and T. Zimmerman (TRW Syst., Redondo Beach, CA), "Very large scale integrated circuits for digital signal processing: Part II," *IEEE Circuits and Syst. Newsletter*, pp. 2–7, Apr. 1977.

T. Zimmerman and D. Barbe (TRW Syst., Redondo Beach, CA; Naval Res. Lab., Washington, DC), "A new role for charge-coupled devices: Digital signal processing," *Electronics*, pp. 97–103, Mar. 31, 1977.

A Digital Processor to Generate Spectra in Real Time

RICHARD R. SHIVELY, MEMBER, IEEE

Abstract—A digital processor capable of computing the discrete Fourier transform for a range of audio signals in real time has been built as part of a facility to conduct research in signal processing. The digitized sample values can be complex. The arithmetic unit is configured to perform complex connectives, and automatic array scaling is used to make numerical accuracy independent of signal level. The Cooley–Tukey "fast Fourier transform" is the algorithm used.

Index Terms—Complex number arithmetic, Cooley–Tukey algorithm, digital communication, digital filtering, fast Fourier transform, real-time signal processing.

INTRODUCTION

EVALUATING the complex Fourier coefficients of sampled data is a fundamental task in signal processing. The range of practical applications was substantially increased with the derivation by Cooley and Tukey[1] of the "fast Fourier transform"

(FFT), which reduces the number of multiplications and additions required in computing all Fourier coefficients for a function sampled at N points from order of N^2 to order of $N \log N$. Forming spectra is perhaps the most familiar application, but efficiency in numerical operations other than explicit spectrum analysis has been improved, including: 1) the solution of partial differential equations[2] and 2) convolution by transforming, multiplying transforms, then inverse transforming.[3],[4] Examples of signal processing which might be performed digitally in real time with the use of the FFT include seismographic analysis, vocoding (voice transmission in terms of spectral content), adaptive digital filtering and gain-phase measurement, as in servomechanisms or transmission line equalization,[5] and, in general, forming periodograms of random processes.

The Fast Fourier Transform Processor (FFTP) is a small special-purpose computer designed to perform the discrete Fourier transform for variable-length sample records. It is integrated into a general-purpose (GP) computer system (IBM 1800) to provide a facility for

Manuscript received September 21, 1967. This paper was presented at the First Annual IEEE Computer Conference, Chicago, Ill., September 6–8, 1967. The work reported here was supported by the U. S. Naval Electronic Systems Command.

The author is with Bell Telephone Laboratories, Inc., Whippany, N. J.

Reprinted from *IEEE Trans. Comput.*, vol. C-17, pp. 485–491, May 1968.

166

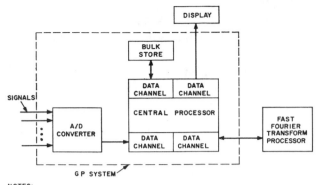

NOTES:
1. ALL DATA CHANNELS CAN OPERATE CONCURRENTLY WITH COMPUTATION.
2. PERIPHERAL DEVICES NOT INVOLVED IN CONTINUOUS, REAL-TIME OPERATION ARE NOT SHOWN.

Fig. 1. System for signal processing in real time.

research in signal processing techniques. The advantage of a specialized device is apparent when comparing the performance desired with the capability of a current large-scale scientific computer. A signal processing experiment which was used as a benchmark calls for executing a particular iterative operation in the FFT at a 6.5-μs rate. Execution times of only the arithmetic instructions required for the same operation total 39.8 μs on the GE 635, for example. (The fastest complete subroutine to date averages 120 μs for the task on that computer.) The speed desired would therefore not be available even with sole possession of the central processor of one of the larger computers. Consequences of the faster operation with the FFTP are real-time operation for many signal processing experiments, and at reduced cost.

The combined system is capable of processing a number of signals in real time. The GP computer, which has process-control capabilities, provides 1) multiplex A/D conversion for the signals, 2) accumulation of sample records, using bulk store when necessary, 3) buffered data channel transmission to/from the FFTP, and 4) the arithmetic capacity for signal processing other than Fourier analysis. The elements of the complete system are shown in Fig. 1. Before the FFTP organization is described, a brief derivation of the algorithm will be included.

Derivation of the Base-2 Form of FFT

The algorithm may be heuristically explained for sample records which are powers of 2 in length (a more general derivation appears in the Appendix) by observing how the Fourier coefficients for two sets of samples which are interleaved and equidistant can be algebraically combined to yield the Fourier coefficients for the composite sample record. The algorithm in fact consists of a recursive application of this operation. (A step where an r-way collation of interleaved records is involved corresponds to a factor of r in N.) For example, given the set of equidistant samples of a function, viz.,

$f(0), f(1), \cdots, f(N-1)$, the complex Fourier coefficients are given by[1]

$$D(n) = \frac{1}{N} \sum_{s=0}^{N-1} f(s) W^{ns}, \qquad n = 0, 1, \cdots, N-1 \quad (1)$$

where

$$W = \exp\left(-j\frac{2\pi}{N}\right) \quad \text{and} \quad j = \sqrt{-1}.$$

If the even- and odd-numbered sample values are regarded as two *distinct* sample records, the two sets of Fourier coefficients, respectively, are

$$D^0(n) = \frac{2}{N} \sum_{s=0}^{(N/2)-1} f(2s) W^{2sn}, \qquad (2)$$

$$D^1(n) = \frac{2}{N} \sum_{s=0}^{(N/2)-1} f(2s+1) W^{2sn}, \qquad (3)$$

$$n = 0, 1, \cdots, \frac{N}{2} - 1.$$

For any $n \leq (N/2)-1$, all products in (1) for which f has an even argument appear identically in (2); products in (1) for which f has odd arguments appear in (3) to within the phase shift W^n. This yields the desired relation for $N/2$ of the coefficients:

$$D(n) = \tfrac{1}{2}[D^0(n) + D^1(n)W^n],$$

$$n = 0, 1, \cdots, \frac{N}{2} - 1. \quad (4)$$

Equation (4) may be interpreted as applying the shifting theorem to reference the D^1 to the same origin used for the D^0, then expressing the nth coefficient of the composite record as the average of those of the two interleaved records. The remaining half of the complex coefficients for the composite record are obtained using

$$\exp -j\left(\frac{2\pi}{N} s\left(n + \frac{N}{2}\right)\right)$$

$$= \begin{cases} \exp\left(-j\frac{2\pi}{N}\right) sn, & s \text{ even} \\ -\exp\left(-j\frac{2\pi}{N}\right) sn, & s \text{ odd} \end{cases} \quad (5)$$

which, when applied to (1), (2), and (3) yields

$$D\left(n + \frac{N}{2}\right) = \frac{1}{2}\left[D^0(n) - D^1(n)W^n\right]$$

$$n = 0, 1, \cdots, \frac{N}{2} - 1. \quad (6)$$

[1] Samples may be complex, e.g., signal and quadrature, or complex spectral values for the inverse transform. Simultaneous transformation of two real records, with corresponding sample values as the real and imaginary parts, respectively, is possible, but numerical accuracy is reduced.

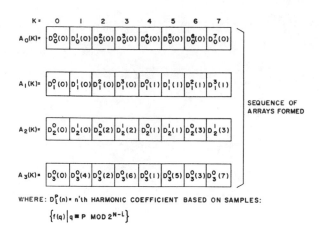

WHERE: $D_i^p(n) =$ n'th HARMONIC COEFFICIENT BASED ON SAMPLES:

$$\{f(q)\,|\,q \equiv P \text{ MOD } 2^{N-i}\}$$

Fig. 2.   Example of reversed-digit ordering of harmonics due to computing "in place."

By induction, the $D^0(n)$ and $D^1(n)$ may each be expressed individually in terms of the Fourier coefficients computed for interleaved subsets of the even and odd samples, i.e., for each of four $N/4$-length sample records. If N is a power of 2, recursive dissection can apply a total of $\log_2 N$ times. Hence, starting with N samples, which are N series each with only a zeroth order term, equations of the form of (4) and (6) are iteratively applied, with each iteration halving the number of series and doubling the range of n. Using superscript to denumerate series and subscript to indicate iteration, the procedure may be described as follows:

$$D_i^p(n) = \frac{1}{2}\left[D_{i-1}^p(n) + D_{i-1}^r(n) \exp\left(-j\frac{2\pi}{2^i}n\right)\right] \qquad n = 0, 1, \cdots, 2^{i-1}-1 \qquad (7)$$

$$D_i^p(n + 2^{i-1}) = \frac{1}{2}\left[D_{i-1}^p(n) - D_{i-1}^r(n) \exp\left(-j\frac{2\pi}{2^i}n\right)\right] \qquad p = 0, 1, \cdots, 2^{-i}N-1 \qquad (8)$$

where

$$r = p + 2^{-i}N$$

$D_i^p(n)$ = nth harmonic coefficient based on the samples

$$\{f(q): q \equiv p \bmod 2^{-i}N\},$$

and D_0^p is identically the sample record. After each iteration, $i=1, 2, \cdots, \log_2 N$, there are $N/2^i$ distinct series, each with 2^i coefficients, so the total number of coefficients remains a constant N. Only one complex multiplication is required per result pair during each iteration since the products in (7) and (8) differ only in sign. Therefore, using the binary form of the FFT, the total number of (in general, complex) multiplications to find N Fourier coefficients is

$$\tfrac{1}{2} N \log_2 N$$

compared with order of N^2 by direct evaluation of (1).[2]

[2] In the base-4 organization of the FFT, symmetry in weights reduces the number of complex multiplications to 3/8 $\log_2$ N.

As an adjunct to computational efficiency, the memory space used during the FFT process can be limited to those locations which hold the N complex sample values, because the results of (4) and (6) may overwrite the pair of operands in forming them. To formalize this procedure, denote the array of memory locations as $A_i(K)$, $K=0$, 1, $\cdots$, $N-1$, where $A_0(K)(=f(K))$ represents the sample record, and A_i is the array after the ith iteration. Then the operation of equations (7) and (8) can be expressed as

$$A_i(k_{m-1}, \cdots, k_{m-i}, \cdots, k_0)$$
$$= \tfrac{1}{2}\big[A_{i-1}(k_{m-1}, \cdots, k_{m-i+1}, 0, k_{m-i-1}, \cdots, k_0)$$
$$+ (-1)^{k_{m-i}} \cdot A_{i-1}(k_{m-1}, \cdots, k_{m-i+1}, 1, k_{m-i-1}, \cdots, k_0)$$
$$\cdot \exp(-j\theta(K, i))\big] \qquad (9)$$

where

$k_l = 2^l$ weight digit in the binary representation of K

$i = 1, 2, \cdots, m$

$m = \log_2 N$

$\theta(K, i) = 2^{-i+1}\pi(2^{i-2}k_{m-i+1}2^{i-3}k_{m-i+2} + \cdots + 2^0 k_{m-1}).$

Expressing the array index K in binary provides an expedient way of describing the pattern in which the intermediate and final coefficients appear due to overwriting operands with results. In fact, as demonstrated in the Appendix, the harmonic represented by any $A_i(K)$ is identified by reversing the field to the left of k_{m-i} in K. This digit reversal is also evident in the expression for θ above, which is identically $2^{-(i+1)}\pi n$ in (7) and (8). The reversed digit sequence of Fourier coefficients in successive A_i arrays is illustrated in Fig. 2. The final array A_m is

$$D(n) = A_m(n_R) \qquad (10)$$

where

n_R = the number obtained by a digit-wise reversal of n, i.e., using the most significant digit of n as the least significant digit of n_R, etc.

ORGANIZATION OF THE FAST FOURIER TRANSFORM PROCESSOR

The elements of the FFTP are illustrated in Fig. 3. The table memory (TM) holds the pre-computed complex weights, i.e., the $\exp j\theta(K, i)$ of (9). Electronically alterable, the TM will be instrumental in experiments

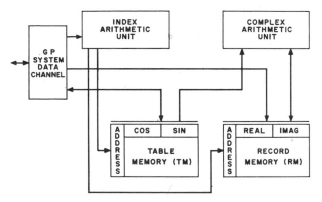

Fig. 3.   Elements of FFTP.

which call for varying numerical precision, and will enable choosing between the regular transform and the inverse via programmed negation of the imaginary part of the weights. Eventually, it will be replaced by a more economical read-only memory. The 8192 word, 1-μs-cycle-time record memory (RM) holds the A_i arrays during computation. System configurations in which both the FFTP and the GP computer shared direct access to memory space were considered, since an alternating assignment of memory modules to the two computers would remove the need for memory-to-memory transfers. Such an arrangement was not used, however, because 1) the FFTP has a duty cycle of over 2/3 on a 1-μs memory, 2) only a very limited number of commercially available computer systems in the class desired have provision for simultaneous (versus interleaved) access to separate modules of memory shared by a customer device and the computer, and 3) the data channel transfer affords an opportunity for the FFTP to perform routine format conversions and to rectify the reversed digit ordering of results [see (10)], tasks which otherwise would consume significant amounts of the GP computer time. The index arithmetic unit generates required sequences of addresses to the TM and RM, both during transfers to/from the GP computer and during FFTP operation. Programmable options in the index arithmetic unit permit 1) variable (complex) record length, viz., 2^6, 2^7, $\cdots$, 2^{13}, 2) variable formats which enable packing limited precision sample values in the GP memory, and 3) loading (unloading) data blocks of arbitrary length and starting points into (from) either the TM or RM. The complex arithmetic unit will now be described in detail.

COMPLEX ARITHMETIC UNIT

Attributes which enhance the speed of the complex arithmetic unit are:

1) complex operands;
2) array scaling to avoid floating point addition; and
3) complex multiplication using a configuration which is "isomorphic" with the arithmetic required, carry-save addition, and base-4 recoding of the multiplier.

Complex operands, i.e., real and imaginary parts stored in the same word, simply effect a halving of the number of memory references otherwise necessary. Conversion to the single-number-per-word format of the general-purpose computer is an integral part of the data channel transfers.

Array scaling is used in place of floating-point arithmetic to make numerical accuracy independent of the signal level. Floating-point arithmetic, with exponents in each of the real and imaginary numbers, would add significantly to execution time and memory capacity, and would require a final denormalization since arithmetic in the IBM 1800 (as well as other computers in its class) is fixed point. The alternative used is to maintain a common exponent for all elements in the array. As the operation defined by (9) is executed, the coefficient of 1/2 is included only when the range of elements in array $i-1$ could otherwise lead to results in the ith array which exceed the range representable in memory. If the count of the iterations where the factor of 1/2 was required is denoted EX, and A_i' denotes the scaled ith array, then

$$A_i(K) = A_i'(K) \cdot 2^{\text{EX}-i}. \qquad (11)$$

The criterion for deciding whether to rescale the elements of array A_i is the observation of whether any element of array A_{i-1} is outside a particular region on the complex plane. Interpretation of the real and imaginary parts of numbers as signed fractions leads to a range of representation delineated by the square in Fig. 4. The region with which to compare the elements of A_i is therefore the circle of radius 1/2, since if complex numbers x, y satisfy $|x| < 1/2$, $|y| < 1/2$, then the sum of the form in (9),

$$x + y \exp (j\phi), \qquad 0 \le \phi < 2\pi,$$

is bounded by the unit circle. This demonstrates that $|A'_{i-1}(K)| < 1/2$, for all K, is a *sufficient* condition for omitting the factor of 1/2 on the ith iteration in (9). Consideration of multiple iterations is required to demonstrate that such a bound is *necessary*, i.e., that overflow can eventually occur if any points outside the circle of radius 1/2 are within the region defined by any alternative scaling threshold.

The test of whether $|A'_{i-1}(K)| < 1/2$ is true is approximated by jointly observing the leading digits of the real and imaginary parts of each result, after it has been conditionally rescaled. The rectilinear bound chosen is indicated in Fig. 5.

The *complex arithmetic* is performed using a parallel, carry-save, two's-complement arithmetic loop equipped to perform a left-directed base-4 recoding of the "-ier" during multiplication, and comprising separate accumulators for concurrent formation of real and imaginary parts of results (see Fig. 6). Two carry-save adders are concatenated on each accumulator to allow adding "-cand" multiples of equal significance during complex

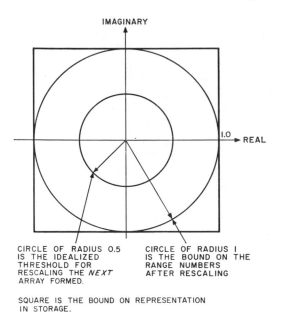

Fig. 4.   Range of complex operands.

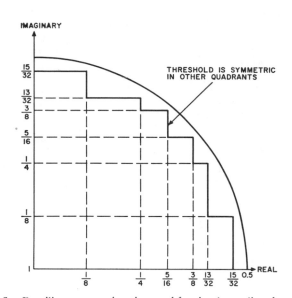

Fig. 5.   Rectilinear approximation used for circular scaling threshold.

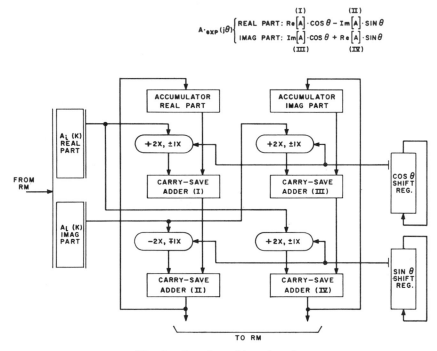

Fig. 6.   Complex arithmetic unit.

multiplication. The four adders are in one-to-one correspondence with the four real products required during complex multiplication, as indicated in Fig. 6. Other than the obvious advantage of a diminished percentage of time consumed by register delay, the cascaded adders serve to:

1) eliminate the need for intermediate storage (time or registers) to hold one real product while the other is formed;

2) improve numerical accuracy relative to adding separately formed rounded products because contributions from the sum of the truncated portions

of the two products are naturally propagated prior to the right shift at each step (viz., maximum round-off error is halved); and

3) simplify assimilating from stored carry form prior to storage in memory.

The well-known *carry-save addition*[6] refers to using both the sum and carry digits as outputs of the adder to reduce the time/addition to the delay of a single digit position in the adder. Flip-flops are thus required for both a sum and carry bit in each position. Results remain unassimilated until both the complex multiplication and addition are completed in (9).

Binary digits of the multiplier are paired as base-4 digits and a *recoding*[7] is used to re-express the base-4 numbers in terms of digit values -1, 0, 1, and 2 instead of the conventional 0, 1, 2, and 3. Providing adder input options of $+M$, $-M$, and $+2M$ for a binary multiplicand M costs only one 2-input gate per option, while forming $+3M$ would involve use of an adder; hence the advantage of having the multiplier in recoded form is that only one adder pass is required per base-4 digit of the multiplier. Therefore one step in the arithmetic loop in Fig. 6 accounts for the equivalent of 8 multiplier bits: 2 bits of 2 multipliers, each of which is acting in 2 real multiplications. To express the recoding of a (real) fraction, let y_i denote the base-4 digit of weight 4^{-i}, representing the pair of binary digits $x_{2i-1}x_{2i}$. Let m_i denote a Boolean variable associated with each y_i and defined as

$$m_i = x_{2i-1}x_{2i} \vee x_{2i-1}m_{i+1}, \qquad (12)$$

where "$\vee$" denotes logical OR.

The recoded y_i, denoted y_i', has the value

$$y_i' = y_i + m_{i+1} - 4m_i. \qquad (13)$$

Further recoding to maximize the probability of zero digits (and therefore effecting variable shift distances) would be unprofitable because the adder network of Fig. 6 requires that digits of equal significance in the real and imaginary parts of the complex multiplier be processed simultaneously.

A by-product of the recoding is evident if (9) is rewritten as follows:

$$A_i(K) = A_{i-1}(K) + A_{i-1}(K + 2^{-i}N) \\ \cdot \exp(j\theta), \qquad (14a)$$

$$A_i(K + 2^{-i}N) = A_{i-1}(K) - A_{i-1}(K + 2^{-i}N) \\ \cdot \exp(j\theta) \qquad (14b) \\ = 2A_{i-1}(K) - A_i(K).$$

The $2x$ multiple used for recoding is thus also applicable to forming the second of each result pair in a way which avoids retaining the first product as an intermediate result.

Real-Time Capabilities of the FFTP

A measure of the capability of the FFTP is the range of signal bandwidths and frequency resolutions for which the machine can generate discrete Fourier transforms in real time. Denote:

$N =$ record length in number of samples,
$T =$ time length of sample record in seconds,
$a =$ FFTP speed factor relative to real time, i.e., computation time per record $\leq T/a$, and
$k =$ time (in seconds) required to form each $A_i(K)$.

The parameter a is equivalently defined as the product of 1) the number of signals being processed, and 2) the redundancy, or overlap, of successive finite time

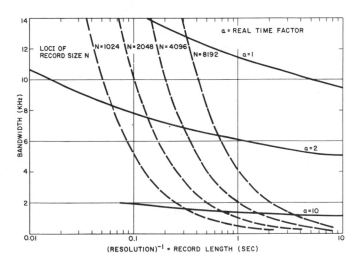

Fig. 7. Bandwidth/resolution capability of FFTP in real time.

records into which a signal is segmented. Redundancy can be defined as N/N_{new}, where N_{new} is the subset of the N samples not also included in the preceding record. If sample values are real, the Nyquist frequency f_n is

$$f_n = N/2T. \qquad (15)$$

Real-time processing equates available elapsed time to computation time:

$$T/a = kN \log_2 N. \qquad (16)$$

Combining (15) and (16),

$$T = \log_2^{-1}\left[\frac{1}{2akf_n} - \log_2 2f_n\right] \qquad (17)$$

For the FFTP, $k = 3$ μs, using 30-ns/node logic and a 1-μs memory. The solid lines in Fig. 7 indicate the limits of FFTP performance for various values of a. These limits are modified to the extent that exchange of data and results between the GP and FFTP is not concurrent with FFTP computation. In practice, data transfers have been measured to add the equivalent of roughly one iteration time to the $\log_2 N$ iterations required in computation. A potential bandwidth factor of two exists beyond that indicated in Fig. 7, since complex sample values may be used. The memory capacity required for various combinations of bandwidth and resolution is indicated by the dashed lines representing loci of constant $f_n \cdot T$ in Fig. 7. These lines correspond to a subset of the programmable record lengths available.

Concluding Remarks

The Fast Fourier Transform Processor provides an expansion of program-controlled digital real-time signal-processing capability with a modest size device. The organization for efficient execution of complex arithmetic is amenable to more general operations (e.g., complex vector inner products, convolutions) with only a generalization in the indexing. High bandwidth channels could be accommodated by iterative copies of the complex arithmetic unit working in parallel, due to the parallel nature in which successive arrays are formed. Formation of the power spectrum as the product of each transform value and its conjugate would consume less than half the time for one of the $\log_2 N$ iterations.

Appendix

An Alternative Derivation

This form of derivation of the FFT, for N a power of any integer, demonstrates how the reversed digit ordering of transform values is a consequence of overwriting operands with results. Assume record length N is expressible as r^3 for arbitrary r; the nested procedure developed extends naturally to higher powers of r. If indices s and n of (1) are expressed as

$$s = a_2 r^2 + a_1 r + a_0$$

$$n = b_2 r^2 + b_1 r + b_0,$$

then W^{sn} may be expanded as follows:

$$W^{sn} = W^{a_2 b_0 r^2 + a_1(b_1 r^2 + b_0 r + a_0 b_2 r^2 + b_1 r + b_0)};$$

i.e., since $W^{r^3} = W^{r^4} = 1$, only the products involving terms of order r^2 or less (r^{k-1} or less for $N = r^k$) need be retained in the exponent. If the sample record $\{f(s)\}$ is held in an array A_0, then the successive arrays formed evaluating (1) may be indicated by nested summations, using W^{sn} in the form indicated above:

$$\frac{1}{N} \sum_{a_0=0}^{r-1} \sum_{a_1=0}^{r-1} \sum_{a_2=0}^{r-1} A_0(a_2, a_1, a_0) W^{a_2(b_0,0,0)} W^{a_1(b_1,b_0,0)} W^{a_0(b_2,b_1,b_0)}$$

$$\underbrace{\qquad\qquad\qquad}$$
$$A_1(b_0, a_1, a_0)$$

$$\underbrace{\qquad\qquad\qquad\qquad}$$
$$A_2(b_0, b_1, a_0)$$

$$\underbrace{\qquad\qquad\qquad\qquad\qquad}$$
$$A_3(b_0, b_1, b_2) = D(b_2, b_1, b_0)$$

where 3-tuple (x, y, z) denotes the number $xr^2 + yr + z$. For each given a_1 and a_0 in the inner summation, r elements of A_0 (the range of a_2) are involved in the generation of r different results (corresponding to the range of b_0). If these r results systematically overwrite the r operands, then the index of array A_1 thereby formed has b_0 in place of a_2. The indices of A_2 and A_3 are similarly explained. The intermediate results are Fourier series on reduced, interleaved sample records, and by comparison of the order of b_j digits in the array index to that in the exponent, it may be observed that the number of the harmonic is identified by reversing the b_j digit field in the array index.

Acknowledgment

The cooperation and advice of B. P. Bogert and R. Klahn in planning the system, and the assistance of M. J. Gilmartin and E. Gomez in the logical design of the FFTP, have been most appreciated. Discussions with W. T. Hartwell were also helpful.

References

[1] J. W. Cooley and J. W. Tukey, "An algorithm for the machine calculation of complex Fourier series," *Mathematics of Computation*, vol. 19, pp. 297–301, April 1965.
For precedents also note J. W. Cooley, P. A. W. Lewis, and P. D. Welch, "Historical notes on the fast Fourier transform," *IEEE Trans. Audio and Electroacoustics*, vol. 15, pp. 76–79, June 1967.
[2] R. W. Hockney, "A fast direct solution of Poisson's equation using Fourier analysis," *J. Assoc. Computing Machinery*, vol. 12, no. 1, pp. 95–113, 1965.
[3] W. M. Gentleman, "Fast Fourier transform—for fun and profit," *1966 Fall Joint Computer Conf., AFIPS Proc.*, vol. 29. Washington, D. C.: Spartan Books, 1966, pp. 563–578.
[4] H. D. Helms, "Fast Fourier transform method of computing difference equations and simulating filters," *IEEE Trans. Audio and Electroacoustics*, vol. 15, pp. 85–90, June 1967.
[5] R. W. Luckey, "Theoretical ideals and their practical attainment for digital communication on telephone channels," *1967 IEEE Internat'l Conv. Rec.*, pt. 2, vol. 15, pp. 114–121.
[6] F. S. Beckman, F. D. Brooks, Jr., and W. J. Lawless, Jr., "Developments in the logical organization of computer arithmetic and control units," *Proc. IRE*, vol. 49, pp. 53–66, January 1961.
[7] J. E. Robertson, "Theory of computer arithmetic employed in the design of the new computer at the University of Illinois," in *Theory of Computing Machine Design* (Notes for the University of Michigan Engineering Summer Conf., Ann Arbor, Mich., June 13–17, 1960).

Fast Fourier Transform Hardware Implementations—An Overview

GLENN D. BERGLAND, Member, IEEE

Bell Telephone Laboratories, Inc.
Whippany, N. J. 07981

Abstract

This discussion served as an introduction to the Hardware Implementations Session of the IEEE Workshop on Fast Fourier Transform Processing. It introduces the problems associated with implementing the FFT algorithm in hardware and provides a frame of reference for characterizing specific implementations. Many of the design options applicable to an FFT processor are described, and a brief comparison of several machine organizations is given.

Manuscript received February 14, 1969.

Introduction

Software implementations of the Cooley–Tukey fast Fourier transform (FFT) algorithm [1] have in many cases reduced the time required to perform Fourier analysis by nearly two orders of magnitude. Even greater gains can be realized through special-purpose hardware designed specifically for performing the FFT algorithm. In order to design this hardware one should examine:

1) The reasons for building special-purpose hardware;
2) The options that should be considered;
3) The tradeoffs that must be made;
4) Other considerations.

Special-Purpose Hardware

Most applications for special-purpose FFT processors result from signal processing problems which have an inherent real-time constraint. Examples include digital vocoding, synthetic-aperture radar mapping, sonar signal processing, radar signal processing, and digital filtering. In these examples, a processing rate slower than real-time would overload the system with input data or lead to worthless results.

Other applications involve off-line processing where the volume of data makes processing impractical unless a dedicated machine is used. Studies in radio astronomy and crystallography have involved Fourier analysis taking nearly a month to perform on a general-purpose computer. In several cases, the use of special-purpose hardware could reduce this time to less than a day and make a corresponding reduction in cost.

Experience with the FFT processor built by Bell Telephone Laboratories [2] indicates that the cost reduction resulting from special-purpose hardware is nearly as great as the reduction which came with the Cooley–Tukey algorithm. The FFT signal processing system costs 5 times less per hour than a large general-purpose computer while performing the fast Fourier transform algorithm 20 times faster. Thus, on the FFT part of the processing, a 100 to 1 cost saving is possible. As a result of this reduction in cost, people who had not even heard of the fast Fourier transform three years ago are now finding that they cannot get along without it.

Options

The many and varied forms of the FFT algorithm have been described at length in the literature [3]–[11]. The execution times and memory requirements of software implementations of these algorithms can be evaluated rather conveniently. The criteria which apply to evaluating hardware implementations, however, are not as easily specified.

Reprinted from *IEEE Trans. Audio Electroacoust.*, vol. AU-17, pp. 104–108, June 1969.

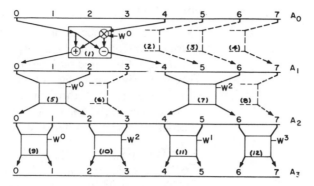

Fig. 1. Fast Fourier transform flow diagram for $N = 8$.

The first design choice often made concerns constraining the number of data points to be analyzed to being a power of 2 (i.e., $N = 2^m$ for $m = 0, 1, 2, \cdots$). This represents a tradeoff of versatility for cost and performance. This choice is not as limiting as it was previously. The convolutional form of the FFT [11] can be used to find the discrete Fourier transform for any value of N even though the FFT processor performing the convolutions requires that N be a power of 2.

If the input time series consists of real numbers, the second option which should be considered involves the use of a real-input algorithm [10] or a modified complex-input algorithm [12]. By exercising this option, a two-to-one improvement in performance and a two-to-one reduction in storage can be achieved.

While a radix-8 algorithm may be near optimum for a software implementation, the simplicity of the radix-4 and radix-2 algorithms is a considerable advantage when dealing with hardware. Since the cost is proportional to the number of options included, the use of only one basic operation in the radix-2 algorithm in many cases offsets the additional computation required.

The organization of an FFT processor is usually dictated by the performance and cost requirements and the technology assumed. Four families of machine organizations, which have appeared in some form in the literature, will be described and characterized.

The Sequential Processor

The first hardware implementation considered involves implementing the basic operation shown in Fig. 1, in hardware [13]. This basic operation (i.e., one complex multiplication followed by an addition and a subtraction) can be applied sequentially to the 12 sets of data shown in the diagram. The same memory can be used to store the input data, the intermediate results, and the resulting Fourier coefficients. Since only one basic operation is involved and the accessing pattern is very regular, the amount of hardware involved can be relatively small. A

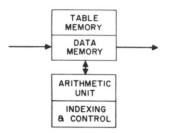

Fig. 2. The functional block diagram of a sequential fast Fourier transform processor.

simplified block diagram of the resulting processor is shown in Fig. 2.

This organization is similar to that of a small general-purpose computer except that the table memory, data memory, arithmetic unit, and control unit can usually all operate concurrently. Since the processor operates on batches of data, a real-time environment would usually dictate that some buffering precede or be incorporated into the data memory.

For this discussion, the sequential processor will be characterized as having: 1) one arithmetic unit, 2) $(N/2) \log_2 N$ operations performed sequentially, and 3) an execution time of $B(N/2) \log_2 N$ μs where B is the time required for performing one basic operation. The reordering of the Fourier coefficients can be done either in place or during I/O.

The Cascade Processor

To improve the performance of the processor, parallelism can be introduced into the flow diagram shown in Fig. 1 [14], [15]. By using a separate arithmetic unit for each iteration, the throughput can be increased by a factor of $\log_2 N$. In the diagram of Fig. 1 this means that the first arithmetic unit performs the operations labeled 1 through 4, the second performs operations 5 through 8,

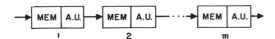

Fig. 3. The functional block diagram of a cascade processor.

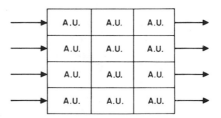

Fig. 5. The functional block diagram of an array processor.

Fig. 4. The functional block diagram of a parallel-iterative processor.

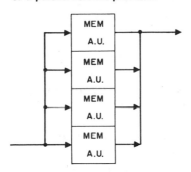

and the third performs operations 9 through 12. A simplified block diagram of the resulting processor is shown in Fig. 3.

In this processor, the buffering required for processing a continuous stream of data is incorporated directly into the organization and takes the form of a delay line.

For this discussion, the cascade processor will be characterized as having: 1) m arithmetic units, 2) m iterations performed in parallel, 3) $N/2$ operations performed sequentially, 4) an execution time of $(B \cdot N)$ μs per record, and 5) buffering incorporated within the processor in the form of time delays.

Although this discussion is directed toward radix-2 algorithms, versions of this processor for radix-4 algorithms, real-valued algorithms, and arbitrary-radix algorithms should be apparent. It should also be apparent that this organization lends itself well to multichannel operation where sets of samples are interleaved. Although this adds to the amount of buffering within the processor, in many applications it allows one to realize this buffering via relatively inexpensive drum or disk storage used in the form of time delays. As recently shown by Sande [16], this same magnetic drum can also be used to perform the reordering.

The Parallel Iterative Processor

A third alternative for improving performance involves introducing parallelism within each iteration. By using four arithmetic units, the operations labeled 1 through 4 can be performed in parallel before performing operations 5 through 8 in parallel, etc. The processor performs the iterations sequentially, but performs all of the operations

within each iteration in parallel. A simplified block diagram of the resulting processor is shown in Fig. 4.

In practice, this organization would often be combined with the sequential processor so that only the degree of parallelism actually needed is implemented. Without the use of large-scale integration, the cost of $N/2$ arithmetic units (as shown in Fig. 4) would usually be prohibitive.

The problem areas associated with this organization involve the communication between the arithmetic units and the generation of the required sine and cosine functions. Both of these problems, however, have been dealt with successfully [17], [18].

For this discussion, the parallel iterative processor will be characterized as having 1) $N/2$ arithmetic units, 2) $N/2$ operations performed in parallel, 3) m iterations performed sequentially, and 4) an execution time of $B(\log_2 N)$ μs.

The Array Analyzer

For completeness, a processor can be considered in which all 12 of the operations of Fig. 1 are performed in parallel [19]. By pipelining three different sets of data through this processor simultaneously, the effective execution time is simply the time required for performing one basic operation. A simplified block diagram is shown in Fig. 5 for the example of $N = 8$.

For this discussion, the array analyzer will be characterized as having: 1) $(N/2)(\log_2 N)$ arithmetic units, 2) $(N/2)(\log_2 N)$ operations performed in parallel, and 3) an execution time of B μs. At this point in time, the cost of this approach severely limits its application.

Summary

By assuming the relatively fast processing rate of one μs per basic operation, the approximate processing rates of the different families of analyzers can be compared in Table I. The time saving of special-purpose hardware is apparent when these times are compared to the typical 500 000 μs execution time of a large general-purpose computer. Note that you can introduce as much parallelism into the fast Fourier transform algorithm as your problem demands.

TABLE I

Ambitious Processing Rates for $N = 1024$ With $B = 1 \mu s$

Machine Organization	Arith. Units	Execution Time (μs)	Processing Rate (samples/s)
Sequential	1	5000	200 000
Cascade	10	1000	1 000 000*
Parallel Iterative	512	10	100 000 000
Array	5120	1	1 000 000 000

* Capable of doing two channels at this rate simultaneously.

Tradeoffs

In designing a special-purpose fast Fourier transform processor, there are many possible tradeoffs which can be made in terms of cost, speed, and accuracy. These tradeoffs are related specifically to the arithmetic unit, the memory, the control unit, and the algorithm being implemented.

As described previously, there is usually a cost penalty associated with allowing N to be other than a power of 2. If enough options are added, the control unit can rapidly overtake the arithmetic unit in complexity.

When versatility is more important than speed, it may be worth changing from a hard-wired control unit to a software or microprogrammed control unit.

The choice of a core memory, a semiconductor memory, or some combination of the two in a sequential processor will generally be dictated by the performance and cost requirements placed on the system. In the cascade processor, a plot of cost versus speed can be very erratic since the internal storage could be anything from magnetic drum storage to semiconductor shift registers.

The arithmetic units for each type of processor can vary considerably. The cost ratio between building five inexpensive arithmetic units and building one very expensive one can dictate the organization of the processor. One also has the option of building one fast real-input arithmetic unit, or four slower arithmetic units tied together to form a complex-input arithmetic unit. In some cases a combinatorial (or static) multiplier is required. In other cases the less expensive iterative multiplier is fast enough. The speed is also highly dependent on whether the numbers are represented in fixed point, floating point, or "poor man's floating point" (i.e., with an exponent common to the whole array).

A more complete list of design options is given in the FFT processor survey [20].

Other Considerations

In many cases, people tend to focus on only the FFT hardware since it is the best defined part of the system. Those parts of the problem which should not be over-looked are preprocessing, postprocessing, data reduction, and diagnostics.

The preprocessing function often involves applying an appropriate data window, forming redundant records, and buffering. Postprocessing frequently involves smoothing, interpolating, automatic gain controlling, convolving, and correlating.

Since every set of N numbers put into an FFT processor results in N Fourier coefficients coming out, any data reduction functions which can be defined are usually worth building into the hardware.

The problem of designing a set of diagnostic checks for the FFT processor is helped considerably when the processor is a computer attachment. Even then, however, the testing function should be given at least as much thought as the FFT algorithm.

Conclusions

Four families of FFT machine organizations have been defined which represent increasing degrees of parallelism, performance, and cost. Within each family, however, the cost and performance of two processors can still differ widely due to choices of arithmetic unit, memory, and control. It is clear that, given enough parallelism and enough money, FFT processing can be done digitally at rates less than one sample per second or as high as a billion samples per second.

References

[1] J. W. Cooley and J. W. Tukey, "An algorithm for the machine calculation of complex Fourier series," *Math. Comp.*, vol. 19, pp. 297–301, April 1965.
[2] R. Klahn, R. R. Shively, E. Gomez, and M. J. Gilmartin, "The time-saver: FFT hardware," *Electronics*, pp. 92–97, June 24, 1968.
[3] J. W. Cooley, "Complex finite Fourier transform subroutine," SHARE Doc. 3465, September 8, 1966.
[4] W. M. Gentleman and G. Sande, "Fast Fourier transforms for fun and profit," *1966 Fall Joint Computer Conf., AFIPS Proc.*, vol. 29. Washington, D. C.: Spartan, 1966, pp. 563–578.
[5] G. D. Bergland, "The fast Fourier transform recursive equations for arbitrary length records," *Math. Comp.*, vol. 21, pp. 236–238, April 1967.

[6] N. M. Brenner, "Three FORTRAN programs that perform the Cooley–Tukey Fourier transform," M.I.T. Lincoln Lab., Lexington, Mass., Tech. Note 1967-2, July 1967.

[7] R. C. Singleton, "On computing the fast Fourier transform," *Commun. ACM*, vol. 10, pp. 647–654, October 1967.

[8] G. D. Bergland, "A fast Fourier transform algorithm using base 8 iterations," *Math. Comp.*, vol. 22, pp. 275–279, April 1968.

[9] M. C. Pease, "An adaption of the fast Fourier transform for parallel processing," *J. ACM*, vol. 15, pp. 252–264, April 1968.

[10] G. D. Bergland, "A fast Fourier transform algorithm for real-valued series," *Commun. ACM*, vol. 11, pp. 703–710, October 1968.

[11] L. I. Bluestein, "A linear filtering approach to the computation of the discrete Fourier transform," *1968 NEREM Rec.*, pp. 218–219.

[12] J. W. Cooley, P. A. W. Lewis, and P. D. Welch, "The fast Fourier transform algorithm and its applications," IBM Research Paper RC-1743, February 1967.

[13] R. R. Shively, "A digital processor to generate spectra in real time," *IEEE Trans. Computers*, vol. C-17, pp. 485–491, May 1968.

[14] G. D. Bergland and H. W. Hale, "Digital real-time spectral analysis," *IEEE Trans. Electronic Computers*, vol. EC-16, pp. 180–185, April 1967.

[15] R. A. Smith, "A fast Fourier transform processor," Bell Telephone Labs., Inc., Whippany, N. J., 1967.

[16] G. Sande, University of Chicago, Chicago, Ill., private communication.

[17] M. C. Pease, III, and J. Goldberg, "Feasibility study of a special-purpose digital computer for on-line Fourier analysis," Advanced Research Projects Agency, Order 989, May 1967.

[18] G. D. Bergland and D. E. Wilson, "An FFT algorithm for a global, highly-parallel processor," this issue, pp. 125–127.

[19] R. B. McCullough, "A real-time digital spectrum analyzer," Stanford Electronics Labs., Stanford, Calif., Sci. Rept. 23, November 1967.

[20] G. D. Bergland, "Fast Fourier transform hardware implementations—a survey," this issue, pp. 109–119.

A Fast Fourier Transform Algorithm for a Global, Highly Parallel Processor

G. D. BERGLAND, Member, IEEE

D. E. WILSON

Bell Telephone Laboratories, Inc.
Whippany, N. J. 07981

Abstract

A fast Fourier transform (FFT) algorithm is presented for an unstructured, parallel ensemble of computing elements with global control. The procedure makes efficient use of a fixed-size memory and minimizes data transmission between computing elements. Included are some practical considerations of the trade-offs between element utilization and gain of computing speed via parallelism.

Introduction

Recent advances in electronic device technology have great significance for the future of computing. The availability, for example, of large-scale integrated circuits already is being widely exploited to implement novel machine organizations. Some of these new computer architectures differ so radically from conventional machines that many computational procedures and algorithms will have to be restructured to take advantage of these developments.

This paper presents a version of the fast Fourier transform appropriate for a highly parallel computer. The suggested algorithm should be of general interest since many new machines, such as the ILLIAC IV, attain very high average instruction execution rates by means of some form of parallelism. The machine considered here, the Parallel Processing Ensemble, is particularly appropriate since its structure requires consideration of several features characteristic of advanced computer architectures. Specifically, the design of the algorithm requires consideration of how the parallelism is to be introduced and executed in modest-sized data memories.

Hardware Organization of the Parallel Processing Ensemble

Consider a computing machine organized as an array of processing elements, each element consisting of data memory and an arithmetic unit capable of performing a complete repertoire of arithmetic operations. Let this ensemble be driven by a common control unit so that the elements execute each instruction simultaneously in parallel. Let each element contain a programmable activity register such that an instruction to the processing ensemble is executed by an individual element if and only if its activity register contents match a programmable state register in the control unit. Thus subsets of processing elements can be specified to participate in an operation.

The input to the ensemble shall be connected to each element through logic allowing additions and multiplications. The machine is assumed unstructured in the sense that there are no direct data paths establishing neighbor-type connections between the computing elements.

This Parallel Processing Ensemble, summarized in Fig. 1, has evolved from work by Githens and Crane [1] on distributed logic memories. It is particularly configured to exploit the advantages of device replication and dense packing gained through large-scale integrated circuit technologies. Bell Telephone Laboratories currently is developing an ensemble of elements containing 1024 words of 32 bits each. Since the ensemble is unstructured, the number of elements is arbitrary. The computation speed of each element need be only modest since the average instruction execution rate is enhanced by parallel computation.

The computation of Fourier transforms on such a machine, and in particular the application of the fast Fourier transform (FFT), requires an algorithm struc-

Manuscript received February 14, 1969; revised April 1, 1969.

Reprinted from *IEEE Trans. Audio Electroacoust.*, vol. AU-17, pp. 125–127, June 1969.

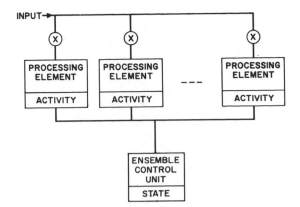

Fig. 1. Parallel processing ensemble.

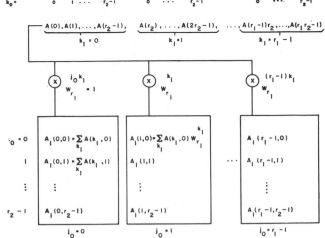

Fig. 2. Computation of $A_1(j_0, k_0)$.

tured to handle the case where the number of sample points is greater than the element memory size, and to circumvent inefficient communication between the computing elements. In addition, assuming there is some choice in the number of computing elements to be used, it should be possible to determine just how much parallelism can be advantageously introduced.

FFT Algorithm for Parallel Processing

Consider transforming the N data points $A(0)$, $A(1)$, $\cdots$, $A(N-1)$ by

$$X(j) = \sum_{k=0}^{N-1} A(k)W^{jk}, \qquad j = 0, 1, \cdots, N - 1. \quad (1)$$

As usual, assume that N can be factored, $N=r_1r_2$, but with the added constraint that each element contains data storage sufficient to perform at least an r_2-point transform. As in the standard FFT procedure, substitute

$$j = j_1r_1 + j_0$$

and

$$k = k_1r_2 + k_0$$

where

$$j_1, k_0 = 0, 1, \cdots, r_2 - 1$$
$$j_0, k_1 = 0, 1, \cdots, r_1 - 1$$

to obtain the first stage of the FFT:

$$X(j_1, j_0) = \sum_{k_0=0}^{r_2-1} \hat{A}_1(j_0, k_0)W_{r_2}^{j_1k_0} \quad (2)$$

where

$$\hat{A}_1(j_0, k_0) = A_1(j_0, k_0)W_{r_1r_2}^{j_0k_0} \quad (3)$$

$$A_1(j_0, k_0) = \sum_{k_1=0}^{r_1-1} A(k_1, k_0)W_{r_1}^{j_0k_1} \quad (4)$$

and

$$W_s = e^{2\pi i/s}.$$

The procedure proposed here first operates on the input data to form the $A_1(j_0, k_0)$ in registers $k_0=0, 1, \cdots, r_2-1$ of elements $j_0=0, 1, \cdots, r_1-1$. As shown in Fig. 2, the input stream is considered as r_1 sets (for $k_1=0, 1, \cdots, r_1-1$) of r_2 points each. As k_1 varies, the contents of the input multipliers are adjusted, and their output is added to registers appropriate to form the desired $A_1(j_0, k_0)$. The $\hat{A}_1(j_0,k_0)$ are then formed by parallel multiplications by the "twiddle factors," $W_{r_1r_2}^{j_0k_0}$.

The final step of the algorithm is the computation of the r_2-point transforms of (2). This computation can be executed simultaneously in parallel using the standard FFT, for the suggested procedure has segmented the data structure so that no interelement transfers are needed. The roots of unity used here and in the preceding steps can be generated in the processing elements by multiplicative iteration such as the marching technique described by Sande [2].

Computation Required

For the case $N=r_1 \cdot r_2=2^p2^q$, computation of (2), (3), and (4) requires a total of

$$q2^{q-1} + 2^q + 2^{p+q} \quad (5)$$

global complex multiplications. We can consider choosing 2^p (the number of parallel computing elements) to minimize expression (5) subject to the constraint that a 2^q-point transform can be performed in each element. As shown in Fig. 3, increasing the number of elements and hence the amount of parallelism indeed does reduce the required number of multiplications. However, the gain decreases sharply as p increases, so that equipment utilization probably becomes the controlling factor.

In the special cases $p=1$ and $p=2$, the $W_{r_1}^{j_0k_1}$ in (4) become ± 1 and $\pm\sqrt{-1}$, so only additions and conjugations but no multiplications are required on the input. Expression (5) then reduces to

$$q2^{q-1} + 2^q. \quad (6)$$

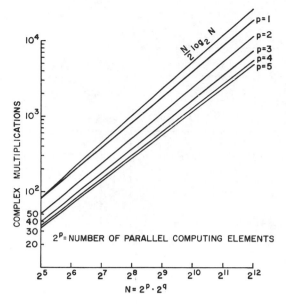

Fig. 3. Complex multiplications required for various degrees of parallelism.

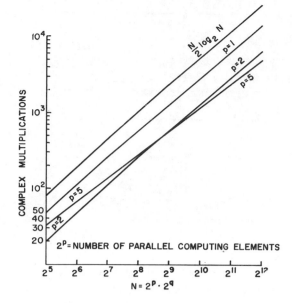

Fig. 4. Complex multiplications required considering the special case $p=1, 2$.

This result, plotted as Fig. 4, shows that $p=2$ using four computing elements is a good choice which actually gives better results than $p=5$ for up to 2^9 data points.

Conclusions

The proposed FFT algorithm allows an unstructured, global, highly parallel computer to be applied to transforms with more sample points than the fixed-size processing element memories can individually handle. The technique uses parallelism to gain computational speed, but it is shown that this gain becomes progressively smaller as the number of elements is increased. Thus the real utility of the algorithm is in providing an efficient method for sharing the computation of a Fourier transform among two or four elements. This reduces the execution time and expands the size of the FFT which can be performed. The algorithm appears most useful for applications in which a large number of data sets are to be processed simultaneously.

References

[1] B. A. Crane and J. A. Githens, "Bulk processing in distributed logic memory," *IEEE Trans. Electronic Computers*, vol. EC-14, pp. 186–196, April 1965.
[2] G. Sande, "Fast Fourier transforms—A pragmatic programmers viewpoint," presented at the IEEE Workshop on FFT Processing, October 1968.

On Generating Multipliers for a Cellular Fast Fourier Transform Processor

W. R. CYRE, STUDENT MEMBER, IEEE, AND
G. J. LIPOVSKI, MEMBER, IEEE

Abstract—One possible hardware implementation for the fast Fourier transform (FFT) of 2^m samples is to have 2^{m-1} cells, each of which performs two of the necessary computations during each of the m passes through the processor. But in each of these m passes, each of the 2^{m-1} cells may require a different multiplier coefficient for its computations. The two most obvious solutions are costly. The multipliers could be stored in a central memory and sent to each cell when needed; however, it takes time to transmit them and uses many pins, or interconnections between cells. Alternatively, the multipliers could be stored in a ROM in each cell. This makes each cell bigger, and the cells are no longer identical copies of one another. We consider a third possibility in this note. In each pass the multipliers are generated from the values of the multipliers used in the previous pass. This technique requires no increase in the number of pins per cell and little increase in the time required to perform the Fourier transformation.

Index Terms—Cellular processor, Cooley–Turkey algorithm, fast Fourier transform, fast Fourier transform hardware, parallel processing, special-purpose processor.

INTRODUCTION

A number of interesting implementations for the fast Fourier transform (FFT) have been suggested. These systems may be roughly classified as programs or algorithms for use on conventional uniprocessors [1]–[3]; special arithmetic units for use with conventional uniprocessors [4], [5]; pipeline processors [6]; and special-purpose parallel or cellular processors [7], [8]. The purpose of this note is to examine the problem of obtaining the multipliers required by the FFT in cell structured processors.

The applicability of parallel computing techniques to the fast Fourier transform was noted by Cooley and Tukey in their original publication [1] of the algorithm. The structure of a special-purpose processor for the FFT was considered by Pease [7], who found an adaptation of the FFT solving a formidable problem regarding the interconnection of an array of computing cells that simultaneously perform the computations required in a stage of the FFT. Such a machine would have 2^m cells and could compute a stage of the FFT in a single pass. During each pass, each cell would have to be provided with the appropriate multiplier for the computation. The purpose of this note is to present a method of obtaining these multipliers in an economical way, requiring little storage, one complex location per cell, and exploiting the inherent arithmetic powers of the cell without burdening it with lengthy computations.

The multiplier generation scheme is presented mathematically in the following section and is incorporated with a modified form of the FFT yielding a general algorithm. While this algorithm serves as a basis for a special-purpose parallel processor, it is sufficiently general to be applicable as the procedure for a general-purpose uniprocessor program.

Manuscript received February 11, 1971; revised July 16, 1971. This work was supported in part by NSF Grant GK-2786.

The authors are with the Center for Informatics Research and the Department of Electrical Engineering, University of Florida, Gainesville, Fla.

Following the mathematical presentation, an example of a parallel structured processor consisting of an array of identical cells having a fixed system of interconnections and implementing the algorithm is given. In a final section, the advantages of this multiplier generation scheme over other acquisition techniques are considered.

DEVELOPMENT OF THE ALGORITHM

The modified FFT that permits the method of obtaining multiplier values presented here consists of the application of Pease's adaptation [7] to a form of the FFT derived by decimation in frequency [2], and is based on the following definition of the discrete Fourier transform:

$$A(r) = \frac{1}{N} \sum_{k=0}^{N-1} X(k) W^{rk}, \qquad r = 0, 1, \cdots, N-1 \quad (1)$$

where N is the number of data in the data set $\{X(k)\}$, $\{A(r)\}$ is the transform set, and

$$W = \exp(-2\pi j/N). \quad (2)$$

The existence of the modified FFT requires the following restriction on the data set:

$$N = 2^m \quad (3)$$

where m is some natural number. Although Pease presented his adaptation in matrix notation, the use of notation employed by Cooley and Tukey [1] is preferred here. This notation is essentially that used in (1), but with the indices k and r expressed as binary numbers as in (4). An additional index ν is also defined here for use later.

$$k = k_{m-1}2^{m-1} + \cdots + k_1 2 + k_0 = (k_{m-1}, \cdots, k_1, k_0)$$
$$r = r_{m-1}2^{m-1} + \cdots + r_1 2 + r_0 = (r_{m-1}, \cdots, r_1, r_0)$$
$$\nu = \nu_{m-1}2^{m-1} + \cdots + \nu_1 2 + \nu_0 = (\nu_{m-1}, \cdots, \nu_1, \nu_0) \quad (4)$$

where

$$k_i = 0, 1$$
$$r_i = 0, 1$$
$$\nu_i = 0, 1$$
$$i = 0, 1, \cdots, m-1. \quad (5)$$

In this notation, the FFT derived by decimation in frequency can be stated as in Algorithm 1 below. (The derivation appears in Cyre and Lipovski [10].)

Algorithm 1: The discrete Fourier transform $\{A(r)\}$ of a data set $\{X(k)\}$ of size 2^m can be computed in m stages by iterated application of (6),

$$X_{p+1}(r_0, \cdots, r_{p-1}, r_p, k_{m-p-2}, \cdots, k_0)$$
$$= \tfrac{1}{2}[X_p(r_0, \cdots, r_{p-1}, 0, k_{m-p-2}, \cdots, k_0)$$
$$+ (-1)^{r_p} X_p(r_0, \cdots, r_{p-1}, 1, k_{m-p-2}, \cdots, k_0)]$$
$$\cdot W^{r_p(k_{m-p-2}2^{m-p-2} + \cdots + k_0)2^p} \quad (6)$$

Reprinted from *IEEE Trans. Comput.*, vol. C-21, pp. 83–87, Jan. 1972.

181

where

$$p = 0, 1, \cdots, m - 1$$

$$X_0(k) = X(k)$$

$$A(r_{m-1}, \cdots, r_1, r_0) = X_m(r_0, r_1, \cdots, r_{m-1}). \quad (7)$$

The adaptation presented by Pease [7] is based on an FFT derived decimation in time, but applies with equal validity to Algorithm 1. Pease's adaptation consists of permuting the set of partial results $\{X_p(\nu)\}$ before each stage of the FFT including the first. This permutation is the same for all stages and may be expressed by the following isomorphism:

$$Y_p(r_p, k_{m-p-2}, \cdots, k_0, r_0, \cdots, r_{p-1})$$
$$= X_p(r_0, \cdots, r_{p-1}, r_p, k_{m-p-2}, \cdots, k_0). \quad (8)$$

The results of the $p+1$th stage of the FFT are then mapped onto $\{Y_{p+1}(\nu)\}$ as expressed in (9). (Note the left circular shift to the index of Y_{p+1}.)

$$Y_{p+1}(k_{m-p-2}, \cdots, k_0, r_0, \cdots, r_{p-1}, r_p)$$
$$= X_p(r_0, \cdots, r_{p-1}, r_p, k_{m-p-2}, \cdots, k_0). \quad (9)$$

By making the substitutions indicated in (8) and (9) into Algorithm 1, and renaming the index variables as in (10), Algorithm 2 is obtained.

$$\nu_{m-1} = k_{m-p-2}$$
$$\vdots$$
$$\nu_{p+1} = k_0$$
$$\nu_p = r_0$$
$$\vdots$$
$$\nu_0 = r_p. \quad (10)$$

Algorithm 2: The discrete Fourier transform $\{A(\nu)\}$ of a data set $\{X(\nu)\}$ of size 2^m can be computed in m stages by iterated application of (11),

$$Y_{p+1}(\nu_{m-1}, \cdots, \nu_1, \nu_0)$$
$$= \tfrac{1}{2}[Y_p(0, \nu_{m-1}, \cdots, \nu_1)$$
$$+ (-1)^{\nu_0} Y_p(1, \nu_{m-1}, \cdots, \nu_1)]$$
$$\cdot W^{\nu_0(\nu_{m-1}2^{m-1} + \cdots + \nu_{p+1}2^{p+1})2^{-1}} \quad (11)$$

where

$$P = 0, 1, \cdots, m - 1$$

$$Y_0(\nu) = X(\nu)$$

$$A(\nu_{m-1}, \cdots, \nu_0) = Y_m(\nu_0, \cdots, \nu_{m-1}). \quad (12)$$

It is now appropriate to present the theorem central to this discussion, namely, the procedure for generating the multiplier values used in Algorithm 2 (and in Algorithm 1). The set of multiplier values $\{M_p(\nu)\}$, is defined by the following:

$$M_p(\nu_{m-1}, \cdots, \nu_1) = W^{(\nu_{m-1}2^{m-1} + \cdots + \nu_p 2^p)2^{-1}},$$

$$p = 1, 2, \cdots, m - 1. \quad (13)$$

The method of obtaining the multiplier set is stated as Theorem 1.

Theorem 1: The multiplier values $\{M_{p+1}(\nu)\}$ used in the $p+1$th stage of the FFT described in Algorithm 2 can be generated using the following:

$$M_{p+1}(\nu_{m-1}, \cdots, \nu_2, \nu_1)$$
$$= (-1)^{\nu_1}[M_p(\nu_1, \nu_{m-1}, \cdots, \nu_2)]^2. \quad (14)$$

Proof:

$$M_{p+1}(\nu_{m-1}, \cdots, \nu_2, \nu_1)$$
$$= W^{(\nu_{m-1}2^{m-1} + \cdots + \nu_{p+1}2^{p+1})2^{-1}}$$
$$= W^{(\nu_{m-1}2^{m-2} + \cdots + \nu_{p+1}2^p)}W^{\nu_1 2^{m-1}}W^{\nu_1 2^{m-1}}$$
$$= (-1)^{\nu_1}W^{(\nu_1 2^{m-1} + \nu_{m-1}2^{m-2} + \cdots + \nu_{p+1}2^p)}$$
$$= (-1)^{\nu_1}[W^{(\nu_1 2^{m-1} + \nu_{m-1}2^{m-2} + \cdots + \nu_{p+1}2^p)2^{-1}}]^2$$
$$= (-1)^{\nu_1}[M_p(\nu_1, \nu_{m-1}, \cdots, \nu_2)]^2. \quad (15)$$

The results of Theorem 1 can be combined with Algorithm 2 to produce Algorithm 3.

Algorithm 3: The discrete Fourier transform $\{A(\nu)\}$ of a data set $\{X(\nu)\}$ of 2^m points can be computed in m stages by iterated application of the following formulas:

$$Y_{p+1}(\nu_{m-1}, \cdots, \nu_1, 0)$$
$$= \tfrac{1}{2}[Y_p(0, \nu_{m-1}, \cdots, \nu_1) + Y_p(1, \nu_{m-1}, \cdots, \nu_1)] \quad (16)$$
$$Y_{p+1}(\nu_{m-1}, \cdots, \nu_1, 1)$$
$$= \tfrac{1}{2}[Y_p(0, \nu_{m-1}, \cdots, \nu_1) - Y_p(1, \nu_{m-1}, \cdots, \nu_1)]$$
$$\cdot M_{p+1}(\nu_{m-1}, \cdots, \nu_1) \quad (17)$$
$$M_{p+1}(\nu_{m-1}, \cdots, \nu_2, \nu_1)$$
$$= (-1)^{\nu_1}[M_p(\nu_1, \nu_{m-1}, \cdots, \nu_2)]^2 \quad (18)$$

where

$$p = 0, 1, \cdots, m - 1$$

$$M_0(\nu_{m-1}, \cdots, \nu_2, \nu_1)$$
$$= W^{(\nu_{m-1}2^{m-1} + \cdots + \nu_2 2^2 + \nu_1 2^1 + \nu_{m-1})2^{-1}}$$

$$A(\nu_{m-1}, \cdots, \nu_0) = Y_m(\nu_0, \cdots, \nu_{m-1}). \quad (19)$$

Equations (16) and (17) have been obtained from (11) by evaluating ν_0.

An Example

A processor structure which follows from Algorithm 2 is a set of 2^{m-1} computing cells. Each is to be capable of performing the operations indicated in (11) for both $\nu_0=0$ and $\nu_0=1$. That is, cell $(\nu_{m-1}, \cdots, \nu_2, \nu_1)$ computes $Y_{p+1}(\nu_{m-1}, \cdots, \nu_1, 0)$ and $Y_{p+1}(\nu_{m-1}, \cdots, \nu_1, 1)$ for any value of p as illustrated in Fig. 1. A processor of this structure processing an FFT is shown in Fig. 2 for the case $m=4$. This system is essentially that of Pease's [7] except that the multiplier values shown in the cells differ from his since an alternate algorithm was chosen here.

Now, incorporating the multiplier generation scheme of

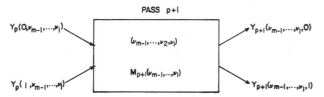

Fig. 1. Cell for Algorithm 2.

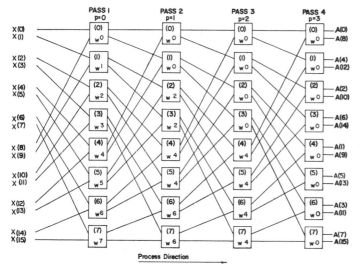

Fig. 2. FFT process with Algorithm 2, $m=4$.

Fig. 3. Cell for Algorithm 3.

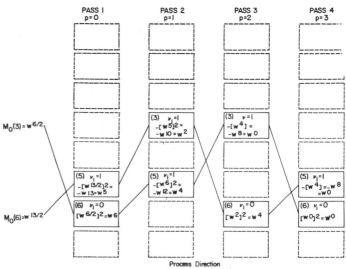

Fig. 4. Numerical example showing the multipler generation process, $m=4$.

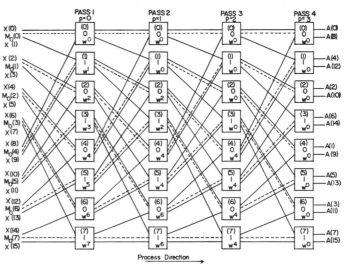

Fig. 5. FFT process with Algorithm 3, $m=4$.

Theorem 1 requires no need for more powerful arithmetic facilities since the cell of Fig. 1 is capable of negating and multiplying (for squaring the multipliers). Hence, only the interchange of multiplier values between cells must be provided for as suggested in Fig. 3. A numerical example showing the generation of some of the multipliers appears in Fig. 4. As a result of this inclusion, an implementation for Algorithm 3 would appear as shown in Fig. 5. The important point of this illustration is that every interconnection required for a multiplier (broken lines in Fig. 5) is precisely parallel to an existing interconnection used for one of the Y_p.

The generalization of this is that cell $(\nu_{m-1}, \cdots, \nu_2, \nu_1)$ must be interconnected to receive inputs from cells $(\nu_1, \nu_{m-1}, \cdots, \nu_2)$ and $(\nu_1, \nu_{m-1}, \cdots, \nu_2)$, and that this condition is independent of which pass the process is in.

IMPLICATIONS

In order to discuss the merits of the multiplier generation scheme proposed in Theorem 1 and used in Algorithm 3, it is necessary to mention other techniques for obtaining the multipliers. One method would be to store the values in a table. Storing such a table in each cell would produce a monumental waste of memory, since only one cell requires all the entries of the table, with many cells requiring fewer than half the entries during the processing of a transform. Opposed to this, the multiplier scheme presented here requires but one complex memory location per cell. While the storage of a multiplier value table centrally would decrease the cell storage requirements, the interconnections between the central storage and the cells would be a problem, not to mention the problem of arranging that each cell receive the proper multiplier value at the proper time.

Another technique that could be used to obtain the multiplier values would be to generate them as needed by raising the value W of (2) to the appropriate power. This method would require considerably greater computational effort than the simple squaring process described by Theorem 1. A consideration in using any generation scheme, including that of Theorem 1, as opposed to a table storage technique is the time added to the processing of a transform for the multiplier values' generation. With careful scheduling, the time added by the technique of Theorem 1 can be made much less than the apparent time of one multiplication per stage. By scheduling the transmission of operands $Y_p(0, \nu_{m-1}, \cdots, \nu_1)$ and $Y_p(1, \nu_{m-1}, \cdots, \nu_1)$ to the cell during the squaring of the multiplier value, the impact of the squaring can be reduced and the arithmetic facilities of the cell can be kept busy throughout the processing.

Another consideration in the generation scheme is the growth of errors due to the inaccuracies of representing the values in a limited length binary format. It is felt, however, that this growth of errors may be satisfactorily limited by choice of a scheme for rounding off values during arithmetic operations, since the process is well defined.

Before closing, it is appropriate to make a few comments on the structure of the processor suggested earlier. While the number of computing cells and the pattern of their interconnections is fixed, the number 2^n of data in the data set is not restricted to the number 2^m for which the processor is designed. The case where $n > m$ is considered by Pease [9], and the technique for $n < m$ can be found elsewhere [8]. In fact, where $n \cdot i = m$, the structure can compute the transforms of i independent data sets, each of 2^n entries simultaneously, and in less time than that required for a data set of 2^m entries. In addition, it is possible to compute inverse transforms on the structure merely by deleting the scaling (division by one-half) in (16) and (17) and changing the values of the initial multiplier value set $\{M_0(\nu)\}$.

CONCLUSIONS

It is believed that the modified FFT algorithm employing a simple scheme for producing the multiplier values presented here could lead to an economically feasible structure for a special-purpose parallel processor for the FFT.

REFERENCES

[1] J. W. Cooley and J. W. Tukey, "An algorithm for the machine calculation of complex Fourier series," *Math. Comput.*, vol. 19, p. 297, Apr. 1965.
[2] W. T. Cochran *et al.*, "What is the fast Fourier transform?" *IEEE Trans. Audio Electroacoust.*, vol. AU-15, pp. 45–55, June 1967.
[3] R. C. Singleton, "A method for computing the fast Fourier transform with auxiliary memory and limited high-speed storage," *IEEE Trans. Audio Electroacoust.*, vol. AU-15, pp. 91–98, June 1967.
[4] W. Y. Dere and D. J. Sakrison, "Berkeley array processor," *IEEE Trans. Comput.* (Short Notes), vol. C-19, pp. 444–447, May 1970.
[5] R. Klahn *et al.*, "The time saver: FFT hardware," *Electronics*, vol. 41, p. 92, June 24, 1968.
[6] H. L. Groginsky and G. A. Works, "A pipeline fast Fourier transform," *IEEE Trans. Comput.*, vol. C-19, pp. 1015–1019, Nov. 1970.
[7] M. C. Pease, "An adaptation of the fast Fourier transform for parallel processing," *Ass. Comput. Mach. J.*, vol. 15, p. 252, Apr. 1968.
[8] W. R. Cyre, "A cellular computer for the computation of the discrete Fourier transform," M.S. thesis, Univ. Florida, Gainesville, Dec. 1970.
[9] M. C. Pease, "Organization of large scale Fourier processors," *Ass. Comput. Mach. J.*, vol. 16, p. 474, July 1969.
[10] W. R. Cyre and G. J. Lipovski, "A fully recursive fast Fourier transform algorithm for a cellular processor," Cen. Informatics Res., Univ. Florida, Gainesville, Tech. Rep. 71-101, 1971.

A Parallel Radix-4 Fast Fourier Transform Computer

MICHAEL J. CORINTHIOS, MEMBER, IEEE, KENNETH C. SMITH, MEMBER, IEEE,

AND JUI L. YEN, MEMBER, IEEE

Abstract—The organization and functional design of a parallel radix-4 fast Fourier transform (FFT) computer for real-time signal processing of wide-band signals is introduced.

Several machine oriented FFT algorithms obtained by factoring the discrete Fourier transform (DFT) to an arbitrary radix and which are well suited for the organization of parallel wired-in processers are considered. This class of machine oriented algorithms is distinguished by the fact that it yields machine implementations ranging from fully hard-wired serial sequential processors to partially wired-in cascade processors with no feedback and with a level of parallelism that is proportional to the radix of implementation. Moreover, this class of algorithms can yield the computed Fourier coefficients in a properly ascending order without the need for pre- or postordering of data.

The organization of a system for digital-spectral and time-series analysis implementing a high-speed algorithm is then outlined. It is shown that doubling the processing speed by simultaneous processing of two real-valued time series in such parallel wired-in computers is possible. System considerations for reducing roundoff errors and for performing other processes based on the Fourier transform are discussed.

The organization and design of a radix-4 256-word synchronous sequential FFT signal processor which has been constructed and which performs real-time processing of signals sampled at a rate of up to 1.6 million samples/s is described. Outlined are the basic concepts which have been developed and used to minimize logic circuitry in the different units of the machine. Oscilloscope displays showing the whole sequence of computations involved in real-time Fourier transformation at a sampling frequency of 1.6 MHz are included. The FFT of 256 complex samples is computed in 160 μs.

Finally, configurations of systems for signal processing using other linear transforms of generalized spectral analysis are described.

Index Terms—Computer architecture, convolution, correlation, digital filtering, digital processing of signals, fast Fourier transform (FFT), special-purpose computer, spectral analysis, time-series analysis.

I. INTRODUCTION

THIS PAPER outlines the basic concepts which have been developed and employed in the organization and construction of a high-speed fast Fourier transform (FFT) signal processing computer.

Manuscript received December 15, 1972; revised November 15, 1973. This work was supported in part by the National Research Council of Canada under Grants A3148, A3951, and A8448.

M. J. Corinthios is with the Department of Electrical Engineering, Ecole Polytechnique, Université de Montréal, Montreal, P.Q., Canada.

K. C. Smith and J. L. Yen are with the Department of Electrical Engineering, University of Toronto, Toronto, Ont., Canada.

FFT algorithm is an efficient way of computing the finite Fourier transform of a time series [2]. The computational saving introduced by the FFT algorithm has rendered digital real-time signal processing potentially feasible in many areas of research including vibration analysis [3], the detection and analysis of radio spectral lines [4], speech processing and communication [5], seismic exploration [6] and electroencephalogram and electrocardiogram analysis [7]. In addition, the technique of factoring the discrete Fourier transform (DFT) to obtain a "fast" algorithm has been shown to be applicable to generalized spectral analysis [8], and to a more general and abstract class of problems, as to finite Abelian groups [9].

The objective of the research reported in this paper has been the organization of a processor for the spectral analysis of wide-band signals (in the MHz range) in real time. The high-processing speed thus called for necessitated the search for algorithms which would be well adapted for parallel machine architecture and wired-in organization of a special purpose computer. The problem is then one of computer architecture in which a proper match is sought between the implemented algorithm and the building blocks of the machine.

Several considerations have guided the search for FFT algorithms suitable for implementation by a special purpose machine. Among these considerations were the emphasis on elimination or reduction of addressing of data, the storage of data in long sequentially accessed queues, the possibility of partitioning the memory into a number of submemories, the words of which to be simultaneously accessed for parallel processing, and the advantage of incorporating a properly ordered set of weighting coefficients and obtaining properly ordered Fourier coefficients without preordering the input. In addition, a sequential rather than cascade processor was believed to be of more feasible cost, since the latter would incorporate a number of arithmetic units (AU's) that is proportional to the number of iterations of the algorithms, i.e., proportional to $\log_r N$, where N is the number of samples in the input record. Moreover, it was considered important to employ algorithms that can be easily implemented by a cascade processor when higher speeds of processing are essential enough to justify the cost. With these considerations in mind several algorithms have been suggested by Corinthios [10]–[12].

Reprinted from *IEEE Trans. Comput.*, vol. C-24, pp. 80–92, Jan. 1975.

The processor described in this paper is a high-speed radix-4 machine implementing one of a class of algorithms that allows full-time utilization of the AU. A member of this class of algorithms, which will be referred to as the "high-speed algorithms" has been introduced in [12]. This class of algorithms is described in Section II. The organization of a system for on-line digital spectral analysis is then outlined. System considerations for reducing round off errors and for performing other processes based on Fourier transform are discussed.

The organization of the different units of the radix-4 256-word synchronous sequential FFT processor which has been constructed and which performs real-time processing of signals sampled at a rate of up to 1.6 million samples/s is then described. Machine configuration and test results are then outlined. Oscilloscope displays showing the whole sequence of computations involved in real-time Fourier transformation at a sampling frequency of 1.6 MHz are included.

II. HIGH-SPEED FFT ALGORITHMS

In the following, two high-speed algorithms are described. The first is an "asymmetric algorithm" which yields an asymmetric machine where a complex multiplier is included in each but one of its parallel channels [11]. The second is a symmetric one which yields a higher processing speed, but requires one more complex multiplier than the asymmetric one.

Let f_s denote the sth sample of the time series obtained by sampling a generally complex time function $f(t)$ for a duration T. For N such samples the DFT is defined by

$$F_r = \frac{1}{N} \sum_{s=0}^{N-1} (\exp 2\pi j r s / N) f_s \qquad (1)$$

where F_r is the rth Fourier coefficient and $j = (-1)^{1/2}$. Both the time increment (s) and frequency increment (r) range between 0 and $N - 1$.

If we denote the sets f_s and F_r, respectively, by the column vectors

$$f = \text{col} (f_0, f_1, \cdots, f_{N-1}), \qquad (2)$$

and

$$F = \text{col} (F_0, F_1, \cdots, F_{N-1}); \qquad (3)$$

and if we define a matrix T_N of coefficients given by

$$(T_N)_{rs} = \exp (2\pi j r s / N) \qquad (4)$$

$$= w^{rs} \qquad (5)$$

where

$$w = \exp (2\pi j / N) \qquad (6)$$

then (1) can be written in the form

$$F = (1/N) T_N f. \qquad (7)$$

To simplify the notation, as in the papers [10]–[12], we preserve only the exponent of w. That is, we write k in

place of w^k. Then T_N can be written as

$$T_N = \begin{bmatrix} 0 & 0 & 0 & 0 & \cdots & 0 \\ 0 & 1 & 2 & 3 & \cdots & N-1 \\ 0 & 2 & 4 & 6 & \cdots & 2(N-1) \\ 0 & 3 & 6 & 9 & \cdots & 3(N-1) \\ \cdot & \cdot & \cdot & \cdot & \cdots & \cdots \\ 0 & N-1 & 2(N-1) & 3(N-1) & \cdots & (N-1)^2 \end{bmatrix}$$

$$(8)$$

In this notation, multiplication of entries becomes addition.

In the following the number of samples N is restricted to values that are multiples of an integer, referred to in the following as the radix r, i.e., $N = r^n$. Let $P_K^{(r)}$ be the ideal-shuffle-base-r permutation matrix of dimension K. The finite Fourier transformation matrix T_N can be partitioned and factored yielding the high-speed ordered-input ordered-output (OIOO) asymmetric algorithm [12]

$$T_N = \prod_{m=1}^{n} (\mu_m^{(r)} S_m^{(r)}). \qquad (9)$$

The pertinent definitions of matrices as derived in [12] are stated in the following, where the symbol x stands for the Kronecker product of matrices and $p_m^{(r)}$ is a permutation defined by

$$p_i^{(r)} = I_{r^{n-i}} \times P_r i^{(r)} \qquad (10)$$

and

$$p_1 = \mu_1 = I_N \qquad (11)$$

where the notation I_K denotes the identity matrix of dimension K. $\mu_m^{(r)}$ is the weighting or twiddle operator and is given by

$$\mu_i^{(r)} = I_{r^{n-i}} \times D_r i^{(r)} \qquad (12)$$

where

$$D_{N/k}^{(r)} = \text{quasidiag} (I_{N/rk}, K_k, K_{2k}, K_{3k}, \cdots, K_{(r-1)k}) \qquad (13)$$

and

$$K_m = \text{diag} \left\{ 0, m, 2m, 3m, \cdots, \left(\frac{N}{rk} - 1\right) m \right\}; \qquad (14)$$

in general

$$S_{m-1}^{(r)} = S^{(r)} p_m^{(r)}; \qquad m = 2, 3, \cdots, n \qquad (15)$$

with

$$S_1^{(r)} = S^{(r)} = (I_{N/r} \times T_r) \qquad (16)$$

and

$$T_r = \begin{bmatrix} 0 & 0 & 0 & 0 & 0 & 0 \\ 0 & N/r & 2N/r & 3N/r & \cdots & (r-1)N/r \\ 0 & 2N/r & 4N/r & 6N/r & \cdots & 2(r-1)N/r \\ \cdot & \cdot & \cdot & \cdot & \cdots & \cdot \\ 0 & (r-1)N/r & \cdot & \cdot & \cdots & (r-1)^2N/r \end{bmatrix}$$
$$(17)$$

An example of the high-speed OIOO asymmetric algorithm for $N = 8$, $r = 2$ is shown in graph form in Fig. 1.

In a way similar to that which has been utilized in [12] for obtaining the high-speed asymmetric algorithm we can arrive at the high-speed OIOO symmetric algorithm which yields higher speed at the expense of an additional multiplier

$$T_N = \prod_{m=1}^{n} (\sigma_m U_m) \qquad (18)$$

where

$$U_i = I_r{}^{i-1} \times D_{N/r}{}^{i-1} \qquad (19)$$

$$\sigma_m = R_{m-1}S, \qquad (20)$$

and

$$R_m = I_r{}^{m-1} \times P'_{N/r}{}^{m-1}; \qquad (21)$$

where

$$P_K' = P_K{}^{-1}. \qquad (22)$$

III. SYSTEM ORGANIZATION OF A DIGITAL SPECTRUM ANALYZER

Fig. 2 shows in block form a possible configuration of a global system for digital spectral analysis. The system incorporates a high-speed processor as its basic central processing unit. In addition, the system comprises an A/D converter, an input buffer memory and means for simultaneous processing of two real records [1], for obtaining averaged power spectra and performing other processes of time-series analysis. Means for automatic array scaling is incorporated in the control unit.

The input function is fed to the system at the input terminal marked IN in the figure. It is sampled and quantized using the A/D converter the output of which is stored sequentially into the input buffer memory marked IB in the figure. IB thus accumulates the elements of the input vector f to be transformed. When N samples have been accumulated, IB contains the N-word input record ready for processing.

The contents of IB are then unloaded into memory MEM1 of the central processor. The central processor performs a high-speed FFT algorithm and yields the output Fourier coefficients at the terminal marked OUT in the figure.

A. Automatic Array Scaling

Truncation or roundoff errors may occur as a result of performing cumulative fixed-point arithmetic in a machine of limited word length. Array scaling, a compromise between fixed-point and floating-point computation, employs a feature that is similar to normalization in floating-point arithmetic. By shifting the bits of a word to the left until all leading zeros are eliminated when the word is positive, and all one's eliminated when the word is negative and two's complement representation is employed, normalization helps preserve least significant bits resulting from arithmetic operations followed by a truncation operation.

As shown in Fig. 2, the control unit includes two boxes for detecting the number of leading zeros at the input to IB and the output of the AU. The first detects the size of data in the input time series, such that when the Nth point has been observed the number of leading zeros in the word of maximum size is determined. The second detector performs a similar function throughout the processing iterations. Thus at any iteration, other than the last, the words of the array at the output of the arithmetic unit are monitored and the leading zeros in the maximum word recorded. The control unit, moreover, includes an accumulator for summing the number of left shifts performed at each iteration and presenting it at the end of processing as a scale factor associated with the output array.

B. Machine Organization for Performing Other Processes Based on Fourier Transforms

As shown in Fig. 2, the Fourier coefficients at the output marked OUT of the central processing unit are fed into an auxiliary memory. In order to perform operations which call for the multiplication of two transforms in real time such auxiliary memory would be added to the central processing unit. Operations such as cross correlation and convolution can thus be performed in real time using the auxiliary memory for temporarily storing the first transform until the second is computed.

The remaining part of Fig. 2 shows a method for simultaneous processing of two real-valued time series and obtaining averaged power spectra. The algorithm for processing two real-valued functions simultaneously and obtaining their transforms separately is developed in [1]. This algorithm calls for simultaneous accessing of pairs of words in the F array that are symmetrically located around its middle point. The auxiliary memory is thus divided into two halves, into the first of which the Fourier coefficients $F_0, F_1, \cdots, F_{N/2-1}$ are stored; the second stores $F_{N/2}, F_{N/2+1}, \cdots, F_{N-1}$. The decoder in the figure includes simply two adders and two subtractors, each of which is followed by a division by 2 in the form of one-bit shift-right operation. Separation of the components of the two transforms is accomplished by successively performing the addition, subtraction, and division operations on the real and imaginary components of each pair of words of the

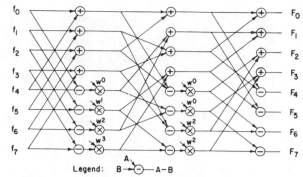

Fig. 1. High-speed OIOO asymmetric algorithm for $N = 8$, $r = 2$.

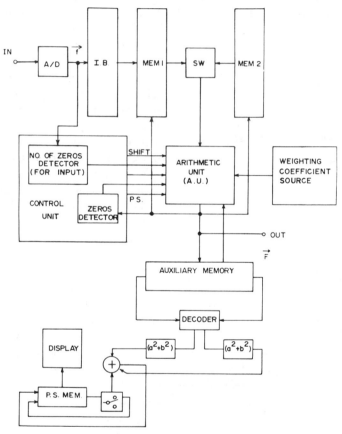

Fig. 2. System for digital spectrum analysis.

array F. Simultaneous accessing of the proper pairs of words is achieved by right-shift signals applied to the first half of the auxiliary memory simultaneously with left-shift signals applied to the second half. The second half of the auxiliary memory should allow such left-shift operation in addition to the right-shift operation utilized in storing the second half of the array F. Right-shift left-shift registers or random access memories can be used in constructing the second half of the auxiliary memory.

Fig. 2 shows interconnections for computing averaged power spectra. The real and imaginary components a and b, respectively, of each of the decoder outputs are squared and added and the resulting power spectra accumulated into an $N/2$-word memory, P.S. MEM in the figure, which

may be in the form of recirculating shift registers. The accumulated power spectrum may then be divided by the number of accumulated power spectra to yield the averaged power spectrum, or this number may be associated with the assumulated power spectrum as a scale factor.

Finally, we should observe that the scale factor associated with the output array F has to be accounted for in all the operations described in this section.

IV. FUNCTIONAL DESIGN OF A RADIX-4 HIGH-SPEED FOURIER PROCESSOR

The organization and functional design of a radix-4 real-time high-speed Fourier processor which has been

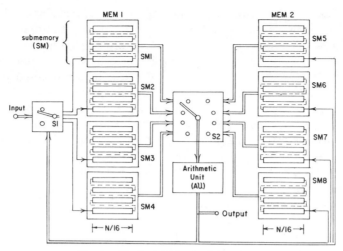

Fig. 3.   Radix-4 high-speed processor.

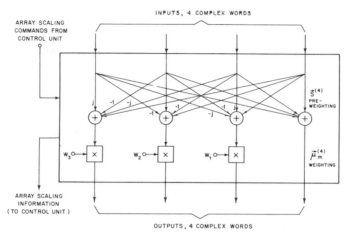

Fig. 4.   Schematic of an arithmetic unit for an asymmetric radix-4 processor. Circles including plus sign indicate 4-word adders; squares with X sign indicate complex multipliers.

constructed will now be described. The processor is an asymmetric type machine designed to compute Fourier transforms of 256-word input records in real time.

A. Basic Organization of High-Speed Processors

The Appendix shows the speed of machines implementing the high-speed algorithm relative to those implementing the fully wired-in algorithms described in [11]. Since the difference in implementation cost is minor, a high-speed algorithm was chosen for implementation. The sequential operation of a basic processor will now be described. Reference is made to Fig. 3 which shows a block diagram of an example of a radix-4 machine, even though the description applies to a general-radix machine. As shown in Fig. 3 the machine includes two memories MEM1 and MEM2, each storing N words, an AU and two switches. The AU includes preweighters and weighters as is shown schematically in Fig. 4. Both MEM1 and MEM2 are divided into r submemories (SM), each of which is again divided into r equal length

queues. Switch $S2$ gates r words at each clock pulse to the AU. In all but the first iteration these words constitute the data at the topes of the r queues of a selected SM. In the first iteration, the queues of each SM are connected to form a long queue, and the r words at the tops of the thus formed queues are fed to AU through $S2$. When the input data to the AU are selected from MEM1, designated then as a "source," the output r words of the AU are stored in MEM2, designated "sink," and vice versa. When either MEM1 or MEM2 is in the "sink" mode, the r queues in each of its SM's are connected to form one long queue, to the "rear" of which data is fed.

The nth iteration calls for preweighting only. Thus the data at the output of the preweighter are gated out of the processor during the nth iteration, and the Fourier coefficients are in proper order. We also note that, since the last iteration includes no multiplication the power spectrum can be evaluated during the nth iteration by making use of the otherwise idle multipliers. Power spectra can thus be computed in the same time as that required to perform the Fourier transformation. The power spectrum is also obtained in proper order which eliminates the need of reordering that may be otherwise be necessary.

B. The AU

The AU shown in Fig. 4 performs the preweighting and weighting operations which involve mainly complex addition, complex subtraction and complex multiplication. In addition, the AU comprises means for performing right- and left-shifts, for avoiding overflow and for array scaling. Each complex number, coded in two's complement is 24-bits long and comprises a real and an imaginary component of 11 bits plus a sign bit each.

In the following we assume the MEM1 contains the input record, the machine is ready to perform the first iteration of the algorithm and the input buffer memory IB is accumulating the samples of the subsequent record. The processor implements the OIOO asymmetric algorithm given by (9) above with $r = 4$. We note that for this value of the radix the operator T_r has the value

$$T_4 = \begin{bmatrix} 1 & 1 & 1 & 1 \\ 1 & j & -1 & -j \\ 1 & -1 & 1 & -1 \\ 1 & -j & -1 & j \end{bmatrix} \qquad (23)$$

The Preweighting Unit: The preweighting unit accepts four input complex words, 24 bits each, and yields at its output four complex words of the same length. It applies the preweighting operator S_m of (15) and (16), to the input operands. The preweighting unit includes eight four-word adders/subtractors the inputs to which are the inputs to the arithmetic unit after being weighted by the values $\pm j$.

We adopt a binary fraction representation of numbers. Array scaling decisions are based in the first iteration upon scanning of the array words upon entry into MEM1. In any of the subsequent iterations the decision is based upon the result of scanning the array words during the preceding iteration.

Let us denote the four selected and properly ordered input words by

$$z_k = z_{kr} + jz_{ki}; \qquad k = 0,1,2,3 \qquad (24)$$

where the subscripts r and i stand for real and imaginary components, respectively. Let us further denote the outputs of the preweighters by

$$v_k = v_{kr} + jv_{ki}; \qquad k = 0,1,2,3. \qquad (25)$$

The input–output transformation performed by the preweighting unit can be written in the matrix form

$$v = T_4 z \qquad (26)$$

where z and v are vectors whose elements are z_k and v_k,

respectively, for $k = 0,1,2,3$ and T_4 is given by (23).

It is possible to implement the transformation given by (26) directly. However, a more efficient implementation can be achieved by a factorization of the matrix T_4 that is identical to the original factorization that has been performed on the matrix T_N. This is a further application of the FFT algorithm to the computation of the preweighting transformation matrix. It can be shown that the result of factorization of T_4 may be written in the form

$$T_4 = C_4 E_2 (I_2 \times T_2) \qquad (27)$$

$$= \begin{bmatrix} 1 & 1 & & \\ & & 1 & 1 \\ 1 & -1 & & \\ & & 1 & -1 \end{bmatrix} \begin{bmatrix} 1 & & & \\ & 1 & & \\ & & 1 & \\ & & & j \end{bmatrix} \begin{bmatrix} 1 & 1 & & \\ & & 1 & 1 \\ 1 & -1 & & \\ & & 1 & -1 \end{bmatrix} \qquad (28)$$

It can be shown that through such factorization only four two-word adders/subtractors are needed to compute outputs such as v_{2r} and v_{4r}, as compared to six such units had straightforward evaluation without the factorization of T_4 been performed. This applies for the real and imaginary components of each of the four channels.

The Weighting Unit: The weighting unit comprises three complex multipliers for multiplying the input complex words v_1, v_2, and v_3 by the input weighting coefficients w_1, w_2, and w_3, respectively. Each of these complex multipliers calls for four multipliers for real numbers, an adder and a subtractor.

The word lengths in the different units of the machine is selected to yield an absolute output error relative to full-scale input amplitude of less than 1 percent. Results of an error analysis using a computer simulation program of the machine with a set of different word lengths were compared to floating point computation of the transform on the 360/65 IBM machine for different input functions such as the random, sine, square, and ramp functions. It was found that with a quantization to 8 bits of the input function, with the particular array scaling mechanism utilized, the error criterion was satisfied when the memory of the machine has a word length of 12 bits for each of the real and imaginary components. Hardware and feasibility considerations have shown that a word length of 11 bits (10 bits + sign) for the operands to the multiplier were a convenient choice. With such constraints, and with the 20-bit plus sign output of the multipliers kept at that double precision length until after the addition and subtraction operations were performed to yield the complex outputs of the weighting unit, the error criterion was found to be still satisfied. These word lengths were therefore utilized in the construction of the machine.

A Multiplier for Real Numbers: The real-numbers multiplier has a three-dimensional form in the form of parallel planes, as has already been described in [11]. Its structure is that of a binary tree each node of which contains a parallel n-bit adder, where n is the word length. Higher speeds could be achieved by synchronizing the arrival of sums and carries to each 4-bit parallel adder, through propagation of carries between planes.

It is noted that the multiplier organization lends itself well to pipelining. Thus by the incorporation of latches between the multiplier's planes we can obtain speeds of multiplication approaching the speed of addition within a plane.

The Real-To-Complex (RTC) Unit: The inputs to the RTC unit are the outputs of the four multipliers, namely $v_r w_r$, $v_i w_i$, $v_r w_i$, $v_i w_r$. The inputs are thus four words, each represented by 20 bits plus a sign bit and a control signal for conditional left shift, constitute the inputs to the RTC unit. The outputs of the RTC unit are monitored for the detection of the number of leading zeros as a means for forming the array sdaling decisions of the subsequent iteration. The RTC unit completes the complex multiplication operation by adding and subtracting the outputs of the real-numbers multipliers.

C. The Storage and Switching Units

The storage and switching units contain memories MEM1 and MEM2 used for the storage of data, and the switching units incorporated in the processor, namely, units S1 and S2 in Fig. 2 above. The storage unit receives the arithmetic unit outputs AU01 to AU04. Its output is fed to the switching unit S2. The storage units queues were implemented as long-shift registers. Multiplexers were used for implementing the switching unit.

D. The Weighting Coefficients Storage Unit

The weighting coefficients W_1, W_2, and W_3 are stored in three read-only memories. Each of the real and imaginary component is quantized to 10 bits plus a sign bit. One extra bit is added to some component, to act as a flag that commands bypassing the multiplier.

E. The Input Buffer Memory

The input buffer memory IB is divided into four submemories in the form of long queues, each of which is in turn divided into four shorter queues. It accepts input data quantized to 11 bits plus a sign bit.

The four outputs of IB, denoted IB1, IB2, IB3, and IB4, are connected to the switching unit S1.

F. Sequencing and Control Signals

The sequencing operations called for by the implemented algorithm and the scaling of data throughout processing are performed by signals generated by the control unit. In [1] a concise description of the different events that occur sequentially in the processor and the control signals employed for achieving them is outlined.

In addition to generating signals for moving data between the memories, the arithmetic unit generates signals for writing and reading data into and out of the input buffer memory, for generating the addressing signals of the ROM's and for array scaling.

The addressing for the ROM's is obtained through the utilization of the six least significant bits of the machine's master counter, to the input of which the main clock is connected. These least significant bits are gated into a weighting-coefficients-address latch at intervals during processing, as specified by the operator μ_m of the high-speed asymmetric algorithm. An accumulator incorporated in the control unit adds the number of shifts performed during one transform and stores the result as a scale factor associated with the output array.

V. MACHINE CONFIGURATION AND PERFORMANCE

A. Machine Configuration

Except for memories MEM1 and MEM2 the circuits of the machine employ SSI and MSI TTL integrated circuits. Bipolar random access memories are used in implementing the input buffer memory circuitry, and bipolar programmable read only memories (PROM's) are used as the storage medium for the weighting coefficients. MEM1 and MEM2 utilize MOSFET shift registers.

Fig. 5 shows a photograph of the different circuits of the machine before final assembly. These include 12 real-number multipliers, memories MEM1, MEM2, switches S1 and S2 and the preweighting unit. In addition, the figure shows the weighting coefficients unit, the control unit, the input buffer memory, and three RTC units. The processor employs a total number of 1800 integrated circuit packages. Figs. 6 and 7 show different views of the assembled processor.

B. Performance of the Assembled Fourier Processos

In this section the performance of the assembled processor when performing Fourier transformation in real time is described. A periodic ramp function the samples of which have the values $0,1,2,\cdots,255$ is the input testing function. The outputs of the AU were observed throughout the four iterations and compared bit-by-bit with the results of a computer simulation program. The test was carried at different sampling frequencies ranging from static conditions to the frequency 1.6 MHz which was observed to be nearly the maximum sampling frequency for correct operation. The shift registers employed in the machine are specified to have a maximum cutoff frequency of 2 MHz. Their response to a shifting clock is delayed by 120 to 160 ns, but delays as large as 200 ns were observed. It is the belief of the authors that this varying amount of delay between registers is the main reason for the cutoff frequency of the machine not being closer to 2 MHz. The total computation time per clock pulse is estimated not to exceed 350 ns. Thus the arithmetic unit would allow a sampling frequency that is near to 3 MHz.

Fig. 5. Top view of all the panels in the machine before final assembly.

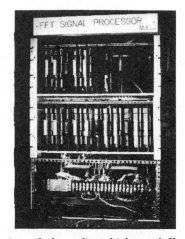

Fig. 6. Front view of the radix-4 high-speed Fourier processor.

Fig. 7. Side view of the high-speed Fourier processor.

Figs. 8 and 9 show the sequence of rotations and attenuations undergone by the two AU outputs AU01 and AU04 in the complex plane during each of the 256 clocks of real-time operations. These displays have been obtained by attaching D/A converters to the real and imaginary component of each AU output and feeding these two components to the X and Y deflections, respectively, of the oscilloscope. Fig. 8(a) shows the fourth iteration of AU01, while Fig. 8(b) is a simultaneous display of all iterations of AU01. Similarly, Fig. 9(a) and (b) show respectively the fourth iteration and a superposition of all iterations of AU04.

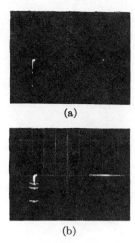

(b)

Fig. 8.   (a) Iteration 4 of AU01. (b) All iterations of AU01.

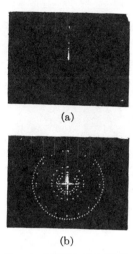

(b)

Fig. 9.   (a) Iteration 4 of AU04. (b) All iterations of AU04.

To verify these results the outputs of a radix-4 FFT computer program employing floating point arithmetic were plotted in the complex plane and proved identical with the oscilloscope photographs. Figs. 10 and 11 show two of these computer outputs for AU01 and AU04 and are seen to be identical to the oscilloscope displays of these outputs [Figs. 8(b) and 9(b)].

VI. CONCLUSION

By choosing a value of four for the radix of factorization of the DFT, and by implementing a high-speed machine oriented algorithm, we were able to combine parallel machine architecture with wired-in design. Algorithms obtained by factorization to higher radices call for a fewer number of multiplications. Moreover, the reduction of truncation or roundoff errors associated with them, due to the reduction in the number of iterations or stages of precessing, constitutes an additional advantage which is significant in determining the word length and hence the size of the machine.

The time of computing the Fourier transform of 256

generally complex samples in real time has been shown to equal 160 μs reducible to 128 μs and to even less time if fast memory is used. For 1024 samples the corresponding time equals 640 μs.

A. The Class of Machines as General Signal Processors

The class of algorithms and implementing machines outlined above has been discussed in relation to Fourier transforms and power spectrum computation of signals. Such a limitation needs not be imposed on the scope of applications of these processors, however. In fact, these processors should be able to perform the general task of applying a highly symmetric transformation matrix to an input vector. The machines are thus array processors in which the input is a vector in the form of an array which has to be transformed into a new vector through the application of some particular transformation, such as the Walsh, Hadamard, or other transforms of generalized spectral analysis. This transformation matrix is highly symmetric and can be factored into a series of matrix Kronecker products, in a similar way to that applied in factoring the DFT to obtain FFT algorithms. The fac-

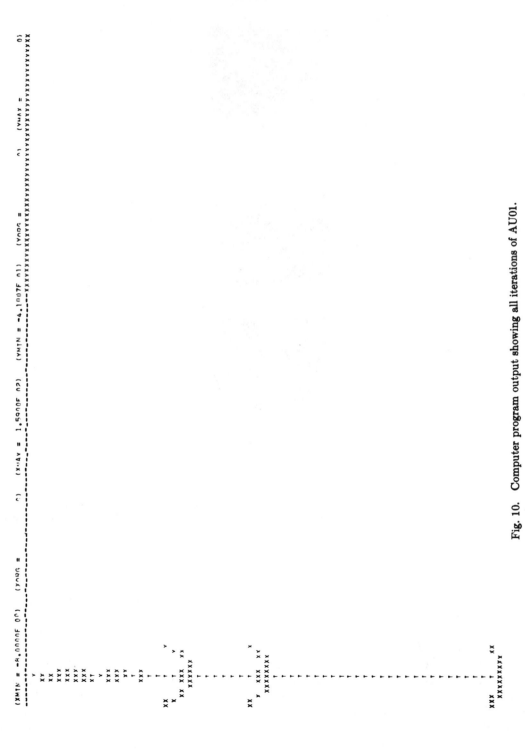

Fig. 10. Computer program output showing all iterations of AU01.

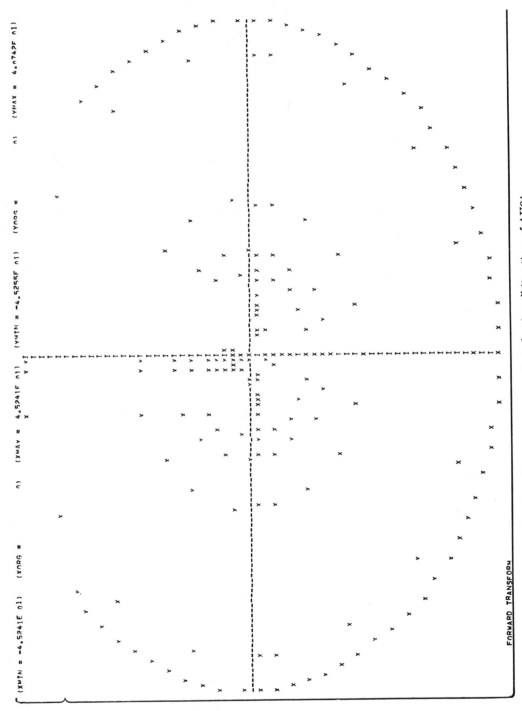

Fig. 11. Computer program output showing all iterations of AU04.

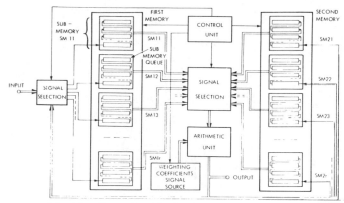

Fig. 12. Generalized high-speed signal processor.

TABLE I
COMPUTATION TIME t_c AND MAXIMUM SAMPLING FREQUENCY f_{max} FOR REAL-TIME FOURIER TRANSFORMATION OF $N = 4096$ SAMPLES

Radix r	Fully Wired-In Machines				High-Speed Asymmetric Machines	
	Asymmetric Machines		Symmetric Machines			
	t_c (ms)	t_{max} (samples/s)	t_c (ms)	f_{max} (samples/s)	t_F (ms)	f_{max} (samples/s)
2	15.32	265 000	12.84	316 000	6.43	637 000
4	5.63	714 000	5.37	748 000	1.64	2 500 000
8	3.04	1 303 000	3.01	1 317 000	0.69	5 970 000

The assumptions made in this table are as follows.
Assumption 1: $t_{sh} = 0.20$ µs.
Assumption 2: For $r = 2$, $t_p = 0.06$ µs, $t_m = 0.28$ µs.
Assumption 3: For $r = 4$, $t_p = 0.10$ µs, $t_m = 0.30$ µs.
Assumption 4: For $r = 8$, $t_p = 0.20$ µs, $t_m = 0.38$ µs.

torization produces an iterative computation algorithm in the form of a product of matrices. The weighting coefficients involved in the computation are related to the original transformation matrix before factorization, and need be generated according to the implemented algorithm and fed to the arithmetic unit of the processor. Fig. 12 shows the organization of the high-speed signal processor for general spectral analysis. Design and sequencing of operations of these machines should be similar to the ones described in here in relation to the particular application of Fourier transformation.

APPENDIX

Comparison of Maximum Sampling Frequency for Different Machine Organizations

We summarize here the results of a comparison that has been made [1] to evaluate the relative speed between the fully wired-in machines and the high-speed machines. Table I lists the results of this comparison for a record length of 4096 samples. Equations defining the maximum speed for each machine organization can be found in [1]. The assumptions made in Table I involve the following symbols: the time t_{sh} indicates the reciprocal of the maximum frequency of shifting data in memory; the time t_p

indicates the preweighting time; t_m indicates the total arithmetic time, i.e., the time of preweighting followed by weighting.

Table I shows the higher processing speeds possessed by machines of higher radices. The table also shows the higher sampling frequencies associated with high-speed machines as compared to the fully wired-in machines, for the same radix of factorization of the DFT. The high-speed *symmetric* machines are not included in the table. Their speed of processing is higher than the asymmetric ones, and this difference in processing speed reduces for higher radices; as is the case for fully wired-in machines.

REFERENCES

[1] M. J. Corinthios, "A class of fast Fourier transform computers for high speed signal processing," Ph.D. dissertation, Dep. Elec. Eng., Univ. Toronto, Toronto, Ont., Canada, Dec. 1971.
[2] W. T. Cochran *et al.*, "What is the fast Fourier transform?," *Proc. IEEE*, vol. 55, pp. 1664–1674, Oct. 1967.
[3] C. A. Glew, "The octave band vibration analyzer as a machinery defect indicator," presented at the Amer. Soc. Mechanical Engineers Int. Conf. Vibrations and Design Automation, Toronto, Ont., Canada, Sept. 8–10, 1970, Paper 71.
[4] J. L. Yen, "A variable resolution radio frequency spectrometer employing time scaling," *Proc. IEEE* (Lett.), vol. 58, pp. 1373–1374, Sept. 1970.
[5] J. F. Kaiser, "The digital filter and speech communication," *IEEE Trans. Audio Electroacoust. (Special Issue on Speech Communication and Processing—Part I)*, vol. AU-16, pp. 180–183, June 1968.
[6] D. Silverman, "The digital processing of seismic data," *Geophysics*, vol. XXXII, pp. 998–1002, Dec. 1967.

[7] G. Dumermuth and H. Fluhler, "Some modern aspects numerical spectral analysis of multi channel electroencephalographic data," *Med. Elec. Biol. Eng.*, vol. 15, pp. 319–331, 1967.

[8] H. C. Andrews and K. L. Caspari, "A generalized technique for spectral analysis," *IEEE Trans. Comput.*, vol. C-19, pp. 16–25, Jan. 1970.

[9] T. W. Cairns, "On the fast Fourier transform on finite Abelian groups," *IEEE Trans. Comput.* (Short Notes), vol. C-20, pp. 559–571, May 1971.

[10] M. J. Corinthios, "A time-series analyzer," in *Proc. Symp. Computer Processing in Communication*, MRI Symp. Ser., vol. 19. New York: Polytechnic Press, 1969.

[11] ——, "The design of a class of fast Fourier transform computers," *IEEE Trans. Comput.*, vol. C-20, pp. 617–623, June 1971.

[12] ——, "A fast Fourier transform for high speed signal processing," *IEEE Trans. Comput.*, vol. C-20, pp. 843–846, Aug. 1971.

[13] R. R. Shively, "A digital processor to generate spectra in real time," *IEEE Trans. Comput.*, vol. C-17, pp. 485–491, May 1968.

On The Design of a Real Time Modular FFT Processor

A. POMERLEAU, M. FOURNIER, AND H. L. BUIJS

Abstract—This article describes the implementation of a modular fast Fourier transform (FFT) processor for real-input applications. The nature of the signal has been exploited to reduce to a minimum the number of multiplications and the calculations are performed in an ordered sequence in order to evaluate only the nonredundant terms at each pass. The number of components required for transforming N points is given as a unction of the number of passes. A processing rate of one point per clock cycle at frequencies up to 10 MHz is realizable making the processor ideally suited for a number of real time computations.

I. INTRODUCTION

The introduction of the Cooley–Tukey algorithm [1] which has brought the number of complex operations[1] in the evaluation of the discrete Fourier transform from N^2 to $n \times N/r \times r^2$ in the case of an N complex point transform where $N = r^n$ has made possible a large quantity of applications. However, when the speed obtained from a strictly serial machine does not meet the specifications for real time applications or when in-place treatment is required, special purpose computers [2]–[6] must be implemented.

Speed, efficiency, and precision are the predominant factors in the implementation of a fast Fourier processor. The options offered to the designer for a higher processing rate are a reduction in the number of operations and a computation of many operations in parallel. The recent development in digital circuitry has not only made the latter well suited for the present but more likely to be the form of treatment to be used in the future. The efficiency can be achieved by an evaluation of only the nonredundant terms which is more likely to be useful in real input applications, a full-time utilization of the arithmetic units (AU) and the development of a modular system which can make a processor scalable without having to modify the existing parts. Higher precision can be obtained when the Fourier transform is computed with a fixed point arithmetic by the minimization of the number of rescaling operations and by representing the critical terms with more bits. The algorithm described in this paper has been adapted in view of its implementation. It enables one to choose the proper configuration when a tradeoff has to be made between complexity, speed, and precision. It is mostly useful for real time applications (treatment of one real point per clock cycle) and specially adapted for real input data. It also finds applications in image processing where the input is real and where one-dimensional transforms must be performed in a very short time.

Manuscript received November 14, 1975.

The authors are with the Department of Electrical Engineering, Laval University, Quebec, Canada.

[1]Complex operation: it is defined here as a complex multiplication followed by a complex addition.

II. THEORY

Consider

$$F(j) = \sum_{n=0}^{N-1} f(n) \exp -\frac{2\pi i}{N} nj \qquad (1)$$

where $j = 0, 1 \cdots N-1$.

Let $N = r^{n-1} \cdot r$, then n and j can be uniquely defined by

$$j = r^{n-1} j_{11} + j_{01}$$

where

$$0 \leqslant j_{01} \leqslant r^{n-1} - 1$$
$$0 \leqslant j_{11} \leqslant r - 1$$
$$n = r n_{11} + n_{01}$$

where

$$0 \leqslant n_{01} \leqslant r - 1$$
$$0 \leqslant n_{11} \leqslant r^{n-1} - 1.$$

Expanding the indices of the complex exponential, simplifying and decomposing the equation into successive partial results give

$$F'(j_{01}, n_{01}) = \sum_{n_{11}=0}^{r^{n-1}-1} f(r n_{11} + n_{01}) \exp \frac{-2\pi i}{r^{n-1}} n_{11} j_{01} \qquad (2)$$

$$F''(j_{01}, n_{01}) = F'(j_{01}, n_{01}) \exp \frac{-2\pi i}{r^n} n_{01} j_{01} \qquad (3)$$

$$F(r^{n-1} j_{11} + j_{01}) = \sum_{n_{01}=0}^{r-1} F''(j_{01}, n_{01}) \exp \frac{-2\pi i}{r} n_{01} j_{11}. \qquad (4)$$

In the above derivation the input function, its transform and the intermediate results are complex. Equations (2) and (4) constitute, respectively, sets of r^{n-1}-and r-point Fourier transforms and (3) represents a complex multiplication which will be referred to as the twiddle. For a two-pass FFT, the authors [6] have demonstrated that when the input is real and when $F'(j_{01}, n_{01})$, $F''(j_{01}, n_{01})$, and $F(r^{n-1} j_{11} + j_0)$ are decomposed in real and imaginary parts, one obtains the following symmetry relations:

$$F'_R(r^{n-1} - j_{01}, n_{01}) = F'_R(j_{01}, n_{01}) \qquad (5)$$

$$F'_I(r^{n-1} - j_{01}, n_{01}) = -F'_I(j_{01}, n_{01}) \qquad (6)$$

$$F''_R(r^{n-1} - j_{01}, n_{01}) = F''_R(j_{01}, n_{01}) \cos \frac{2\pi}{r} n_{01}$$
$$\qquad\qquad - F''_I(j_{01}, n_{01}) \sin \frac{2\pi}{r} n_{01} \qquad (7)$$

$$F''_I(r^{n-1} - j_{01}, n_{01}) = -F''_R(j_{01}, n_{01}) \sin \frac{2\pi}{r} n_{01}$$
$$\qquad\qquad - F''_I(j_{01}, n_{01}) \cos \frac{2\pi}{r} n_{01} \qquad (8)$$

Reprinted from *IEEE Trans. Circuits and Syst.*, vol. CAS-23, pp. 630–633, Oct. 1976.

$$F_R\left(r^{n-1}j_{11}+r^{n-1}-j_{01}\right)=\sum_{n_{01}=0}^{r-1}F_R''(j_{01},n_{01})\cos\frac{2\pi}{r}\cdot n_{01}(j_{11}+1)$$

$$-F_I''(j_{01},n_{01})\sin\frac{2\pi}{r}n_{01}(j_{11}+1)\quad(9)$$

$$F_I\left(r^{n-1}j_{11}+r^{n-1}-j_{01}\right)=\sum_{n_{01}=0}^{r-1}-F_R''(j_{01},n_{01})\sin\frac{2\pi}{r}\cdot n_{01}(j_{11}+1)$$

$$-F_I''(j_{01},n_{01})\cos\frac{2\pi}{r}n_{01}(j_{11}+1).\quad(10)$$

These symmetries imply that one may develop the entire final result using only 50 percent of the possible intermediate results. In order to avoid evaluating redondant terms, one may store the following:

$$F_{RC}\left(j_{11},j_{01}\right)=\sum_{n_{01}=0}^{r-1}F_R''(j_{01},n_{01})\cos\frac{2\pi}{r}n_{01}j_{11}\quad(11)$$

$$F_{RS}\left(j_{11},j_{01}\right)=\sum_{n_{01}=0}^{r-1}F_R''(j_{01},n_{01})\sin\frac{2\pi}{r}n_{01}j_{11}\quad(12)$$

$$F_{IC}\left(j_{11},j_{01}\right)=\sum_{n_{01}=0}^{r-1}F_I''(j_{01},n_{01})\cos\frac{2\pi}{r}n_{01}j_{11}\quad(13)$$

$$F_{IS}\left(j_{11},j_{01}\right)=\sum_{n_{01}=0}^{r-1}F_I''(j_{01},n_{01})\sin\frac{2\pi}{r}n_{01}j_{11}\quad(14)$$

and obtain the final result

$$F_R\left(r^{n-1}j_{11}+j_{01}\right)=F_{RC}\left(j_{11},j_{01}\right)+F_{IS}\left(j_{11},j_{01}\right)\quad(15)$$

$$F_R\left(r^{n-1}j_{11}+r^{n-1}-j_{01}\right)=F_{RC}\left(j_{11}+1,j_{01}\right)-F_{IS}\left(j_{11}+1,j_{01}\right)\quad(16)$$

$$F_I\left(r^{n-1}j_{11}+j_{01}\right)=-F_{SR}\left(j_{11},j_{01}\right)+F_{CI}\left(j_{11},j_{01}\right)\quad(17)$$

$$F_I\left(r^{n-1}j_{11}+r^{n-1}-j_{01}\right)=-F_{SR}\left(j_{11}+1,j_{01}\right)-F_{CI}\left(j_{11}+1,j_{01}\right).\quad(18)$$

Such a procedure implies a reduction by a factor of two of both indices j_{11} and j_{01} in the evaluation of the transform. However it requires a read-out section at the output of the second pass to make sums and differences of pairs of terms to obtain the final results.

Equation (2) is a r^{n-1}-point DFT with a real input. Applying the procedure described above iteratively, one finally obtains a n radix-r pass FFT.

This procedure has the advantage of requiring a total of $rnN+2(n-1)N$ real multiplications and $rnN+(n-1)N+(n-1)N$ additions including the n passes and the $n-1$ twiddle operations and read-out sections. This is advantageous compared to the case of processing two real data vectors of N terms as a complex one which requires $4rnN+4(n-1)N$ multiplications and $2rnN+2(n-1)N+2N$ additions.

III. System Implementation

The features of the implementation of an n-pass FFT in a hardware circuit according to the above formalism with a processing rate of one real point per clock cycle are as follows.

$1°$—n identical modules operating simultaneously and evaluating r-point transforms via a serial-input parallel-output circuit.

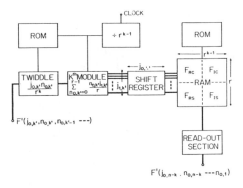

Fig. 1. Diagram of kth pass.

$2°$—n groups of r circulating memories having a capacity ranging from 1 word to r^{n-1} words. These execute the iterative additions.

$3°$—$n-1$ complex multipliers to compute the twiddle operations.

$4°$—n buffer memories having a capacity ranging from r words to r^n words. These permit the pipelining of the passes as well as being the source of the read-out section to allow the evaluation of only the nonredundant terms in the preceeding r-point transform.

$5°$—$n-2$ adders to make sums and differences of pairs of terms.

The scalability of the system is achieved by cascading identical r-point Fourier transform modules preceeded by a complex multiplier for the twiddle operation and followed by the appropriate circulating memory, buffer memory and read-out section. The capacity of the circulating memory must be equal to $B+\log_2 r$ bits when the input words and the coefficients are represented by B bits. This quantity of bits representing the intermediate results is required to reduce the number of rescaling operations.

Fig. 1 shows the diagram of the kth pass, it includes a r-point transform module, a complex multiplier with its associated ROM, a circulating memory, a buffer memory, and an accumulator. It is evident that the first pass does not require the complex multiplier for the twiddle operation. One notes also that the clock must be divided by a factor r as one proceeds from the $k-1$th pass to the kth pass.

The r-point Fourier transform module described here is a serial-input parallel-output circuit where all the bits forming a word are propagated in parallel. When r is a multiple of 4 and when the input data is real and treated in magnitude and the sign is taken into account in the adders, the module requires the following components.

a) r real adders with their associate memories.

b) $(r-4)/4$ multipliers operating in parallel on real numbers. This quantity is required since there are only $(r-4)/4$ absolute different values in the r roots of 1, neglecting 0 and 1, if r is a multiple of 4.

c) A relatively small quantity of multiplexers since some of the adders have always access to the same weighted values.

d) Control units having three main functions:

i) to direct the weighted data toward the proper accumulator;

ii) to add or subtract the weighted data;

iii) to apply the inhibit function (multiplication by zero).

Fig. 2 shows the implementation of a radix-8 point Fourier transform. The control functions are stored in ROM's having a capacity of $r\times r$ bits.

199

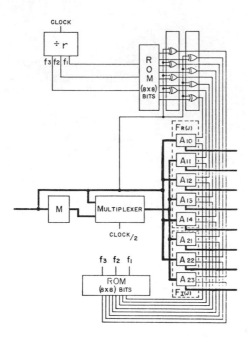

Fig. 2. Implementation of radix-8 point Fourier transform.

TABLE I
COMPONENTS REQUIRED FOR A $N = r^n$ FFT

NUMBER OF PASSES	1 (N)	2 ($N = r^2$)	3 ($N = r^3$)	n ($N = r^n$)
MULTIPLIERS	$\frac{N-4}{4}$	$\frac{2(N^{1/2}-4)+2}{4}$	$\frac{3(N^{1/3}-4)+4}{4}$	$\frac{n(N^{1/n}-4)2n-2}{4}$
ADDERS	N	$2N^{1/2}+2$	$3N^{1/3}+4$	$nN^{1/n}+2n-2$
MULTIPLEXERS		depends on r		
MEMORIES (WORDS)	$2N$	$3N+2N^{1/2}$	$3N+2(N^{2/3}+N^{1/3})$	$3N+2(N^{\frac{n-1}{n}}+...N^{\frac{1}{n}})$
ROM MEM (TWIDDLE)	—	r^2	r^3+r^2	$r^n+r^{n-1}+...r^2$

TABLE II
COMPONENTS REQUIRED FOR A $N = 4096$ FFT

NUMBER OF PASSES	1 $r=4096$	2 $r=64$	3 $r=16$	4 $r=8$	6 $r=4$
MULTIPLIERS	1023	32	13	10	10
ADDERS	4096	130	52	32	34
MULTIPLEXERS (quantity-entries)	$N/8-N/4$ $N/16-N/8$ $1-2$	$N/4-N/4$ $N/8-N/8$ $2-2$	$6-4$ $3-2$	$4-2$	—
MEMORIES (WORDS)	8192	12,416	12,832	13,456	15,016

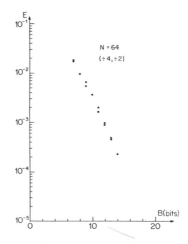

Fig. 3. Variation of error as function of number of bits B representing input words and trigonometric coefficients.

have a processing speed of one point per clock cycle continuously. For this reason the increase in memory capacity with n is not very important. Table II gives the quantity of components for $N = 4096$.

From Tables I and II it appears that radix 4 or radix 8 are the best choices for hardware implementations.

IV. SYSTEM EVALUATION

In this section, an evaluation of the number of components required as function of the number of passes is given. Table I shows the various quantities of multipliers, adders, and memories required for the general case of a radix-r FFT processor with a throughput rate of one point per clock cycle. As seen from the table, the number of multipliers and adders decreases to a minimum as n increases. This point is achieved when the number of components required for the twiddle factors becomes an important part of the total hardware. Concurrently, the number of memories increases with n but less rapidly than the reduction in the number of multipliers and adders. In the efficient design of a system it is very important to minimize the number of multipliers required while the number of memories is far less critical due the recent developments in this domain. One notes that except for the one-pass case every implementation requires an input memory of N words and for all cases it requires one buffer and one output memory at the output to

V. SIMULATION

A fixed point FFT circuit based on the algorithm described previously was simulated on a general purpose computer. The identical mathematical operations were programmed in fixed point and in floating point arithmetic. The error generated by the fixed point computation was evaluated by assuming a precise result with the floating point arithmetic. This was done to analyze the effect of truncation errors. Fig. 3 shows the variation of the error as function of the number of bits representing the input words and coefficients "B" for different sequences of random input numbers. The number of points is 64 and the rescaling factors at the output of the first and second pass are, respectively, 4 and 2.

A detailed study is presently under way to develop a general formulation for the error propagation of an n pass radix r FFT algorithm using fixed point arithmetic. The study will include the variation of the error as function of the number of passes for a fixed N, the variation of the error as function of N for a fixed

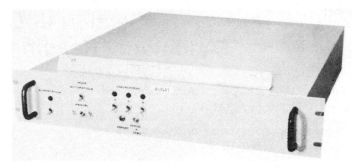

Fig. 4.   General view of Fourier processor.

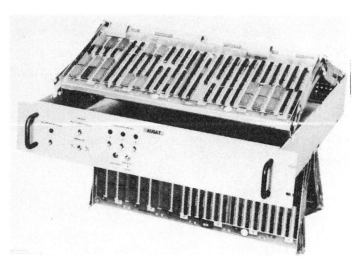

Fig. 5.   Fourier processor showing circuit boards.

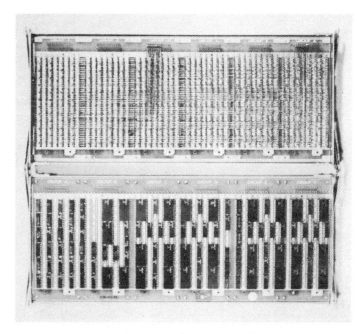

Fig. 6.   Top and bottom view of circuit boards.

number of passes and the variation of the error as function of the number of bits representing the trigonometric coefficients.

VI.   REALIZATION

A prototype has been realized to prove the feasibility of the system. It consists of a two-pass radix-8 processor capable of treating data sampled at a rate up to 3.7 MHz. In the system, the multiplications are done in magnitude and sign and the accumulators use 2's complement. TTL logic has been used throughout. Figs. 4–6 show the system. It consists of three boards having each roughly 100 IC's. The power required is approximately 75 W. The input words and the trigonometric coefficients are represented by 7 bits plus sign while the accumulators at the output of each small Fourier transform unit have a capacity of 12 bits in order to accumulate groups of 8 points without having the necessity of rescaling in case of overflows. For subsequent processing the most useful 8 bits are propagated only. Different rescaling factors at the output of each pass have been tried in order to reduce the error propagation and, with the arithmetic logic units used as accumulators, overflows have been allowed but replaced by the maximum value for further processing.

VII.   CONCLUSION

An implementation for a FFT processor whereby n radix-r passes are carried out in parallel and in which each radix-r point transform is computed via a serial-input parallel output circuit has been described. The processing rate obtained is one point per clock cycle. A modular structure has also been obtained by separating the kth pass from its associated twiddle. The development of symmetry relations have permitted to reduce considerably the number of operations for real input applications. It has reduced the number of multiplications to $rn - 2(n-1)$ and the number of additions to $rN - 2(n-1)$ per real point compared to the case of processing two real data vectors in a complex transform which requires $4rn + 4(n-1)$ multiplications and $2rn + 2(n-1) + 2$ additions per complex point.

A derivation of the number of components required for a fixed N as a function of the number of passes has shown that radix 4 and radix 8 are the most appropriate values for hardware implementations. They permit 16, 64, 256, 1024, 4096 $\cdots$ and 64, 512, 4096 $\cdots$ point transforms, respectively.

REFERENCES

[1] J. W. Cooley and J. W. Tukey, "An algorithm for the machine computation of complex Fourier series," *Math. Comput.*, vol. 19, pp. 297–301, Apr. 1965.
[2] R. L. Veenkant, "A serial-minded FFT," *IEEE Trans. Audio Electroacoust.*, vol. AU-20, pp. 180–185, Aug. 1972.
[3] M. J. Corinthios, "The design of a class of fast Fourier transform computers," *IEEE Trans. Comput.*, vol. C-20, pp. 617–623, June 1971.
[4] ——, "A fast Fourier transform for high-speed signal processing," *IEEE Trans. Comput.*, vol. C-20, pp. 843–846, Aug. 1971.
[5] B. Gold and T. Bially, "Parallelism in fast Fourier transform hardware," *IEEE Trans. Audio Electroacoust.*, vol. AU-21, pp. 5–16, Feb. 1973.
[6] H. L. Buijs, A. Pomerleau, M. Fournier, and W. G. Tam, "Implementation of a fast Fourier transform (FFT) for image processing applications," *IEEE Trans. on Acoustics, Speech, and Signal Processing*, vol. ASSP-22, no. 6, Dec. 1974.
[7] P. D. Welch, "A fixed point fast Fourier transform error analysis," *IEEE Trans. Audio Electroacoust.*, vol. AU-17, pp. 151–157, June 1969.

M. Corinthios (Elec. Eng. Dep., Univ. Toronto, Toronto, Ont., Canada), "The design of a class of fast Fourier computers," *IEEE Trans. Comput.*, vol. C-20, pp. 617–623, 1971.

G. Bergland (Bell Lab., Whippany, NJ 07981), "A parallel implementation of the fast Fourier transform algorithm," *IEEE Trans. Comput.*, vol. C-21, pp. 366–370, 1972.

M. Corinthios (Elec. Eng. Dep., Univ. Toronto, Toronto, Ont., Canada), "A fast Fourier transform for high speed signal processing," *IEEE Trans. Comput.*, vol. C-20, pp. 843–846, 1971.

S. Zohar (JPL, California Inst. Technol., Pasadena, CA 91103), "Fast hardware Fourier transformation through counting," *IEEE Trans. Comput.*, vol. C-22, pp. 433–441, 1973.

A Suggestion for a Fast Multiplier*

C. S. WALLACE†

Summary—It is suggested that the economics of present large-scale scientific computers could benefit from a greater investment in hardware to mechanize multiplication and division than is now common. As a move in this direction, a design is developed for a multiplier which generates the product of two numbers using purely combinational logic, *i.e.*, in one gating step. Using straightforward diode-transistor logic, it appears presently possible to obtain products in under 1 μsec, and quotients in 3 μsec. A rapid square-root process is also outlined. Approximate component counts are given for the proposed design, and it is found that the cost of the unit would be about 10 per cent of the cost of a modern large-scale computer.

INTRODUCTION

A CONTEMPORARY computer spends a large percentage of its time executing multiplication, and to a lesser extent, division. The recent advent in very large machines of "bookkeeping" controls (operating in advance of the arithmetic unit to execute memory fetches, stores and address modification, etc.) has tended to increase this percentage by relieving the arithmetic unit of many trivial burdens. The arithmetic unit of such a machine, when used for scientific computations, will spend nearly half its time multiplying or dividing. Paradoxically, the amount of hardware built into large machines specifically for these operations is rarely very great. Thus the situation has arisen, viewed in the context of a very large machine involving a heavy investment in memory, peripheral equipment and controls, that it may be advantageous to the economy of the machine as a whole to increase the hardware investment in the operations of multiplication and division, even beyond the point where an increment of this investment yields an equal incremental increase in multiplication-division speeds. This paper will describe a type of multiplication-division unit designed primarily for high speed, and will discuss its economics.

LINES OF APPROACH

Multiplication of binary fractions is normally implemented as the addition of a number of summands, each some simple multiple of the multiplicand, chosen from a limited set of available multiples on the basis of one or more multiplier digits. The author can see no good reason to depart from this general scheme. Acceleration of the process must then be based on one or more of the following expedients:

1) Reduction in the number of summands;

2) Acceleration of the formation of summands;
3) Acceleration of the addition of summands.

The last will be discussed first.

ADDITION

The basic addition processes usually employed in computers add two numbers together. The possibility exists of adding together more than two numbers in a single adder to produce a single sum. However, the logical complexity of the adder required appears to grow quite disproportionately to the resulting increase in speed, and there appears to be no advantage in trying to sum even three numbers at a time into a single sum.

An expedient now quite commonly used [3]–[5] is to employ a pseudoadder which adds together three numbers, but rather than producing a single sum, produces two numbers whose sum equals that of the original three. In the context of the basic problem of adding together many summands, one pass through such an adder reduces the number of summands left to be summed by one, as does a pass through a conventional adder. The advantage of the pseudoadder is that it can operate without carry propagation along its digital stages and hence is much faster than the conventional adder. A simple form for such an adder is a string of full adder circuits of the normal sort, where the carry inputs are used for the third input number, and the carry outputs for the second output number. This and other possible forms are discussed by Robertson [3]. In multiplication, one pseudoadder is usually used, and storage is provided for two numbers. On each pass through the adder, the two stored numbers and one multiple of the multiplicand are added, and the resulting two numbers returned to storage.

Thus, the time required varies linearly with the number of summands. In any scheme employing pseudo-adders, the number of adder passes occurring in a multiplication before the product is reduced to the sum of two numbers, will be two less than the number of summands, since each pass through an adder converts three numbers to two, reducing the count of numbers by one. To improve the speed of the multiplication, one must arrange many of these passes to occur simultaneously by providing several pseudoadders.

Assuming that all summands are generated simultaneously, the best possible first step is to group the summands into threes, and introduce each group into its own pseudoadder, thus reducing the count of numbers by a factor of 1.5 (or a little less, if the number of summands is not a multiple of three). The best possible second step is to group the numbers resulting from the

* Received June 18, 1963. This work was supported in part by the Atomic Energy Commission under Contract No. AT (11-1)-415, and was done while the author was temporarily on the staff of the University of Illinois, Urbana.

† Basser Computing Department, School of Physics, University of Sydney, Sydney, N.S.W., Australia.

Reprinted from *IEEE Trans. Electron. Comput.*, vol. EC-13, pp. 14-17, Feb. 1964.

204

first step into threes and again add each group in its own pseudoadder. By continuing such steps until only two numbers remain, the addition is completed in a time proportional to the logarithm of the number of summands.

Successive steps may use the same set of pseudo-adders (using progressively fewer of the set in each step) by using temporary storage registers for the outputs of the pseudoadders. However, for current transistor-diode circuitry, there are strong arguments for using separate pseudoadders for each step, without storage for intermediate resuts. The equipment cost is little if at all increased, since the additional pseudoadders required will not need many more components than the flip-flop registers eliminated, and the control circuitry is greatly simplified. Although a quite simple three-transistor pseudoadder stage can be designed with present components to give a delay time of about 60 nsec, problems of distribution of gating signals and flip-flop recovery time would make it very difficult to make successive passes through the same pseudoadders more often than about once per 150 nsec. Thus the purely combinational adder would have a considerable speed advantage. As an example of the arrangement resulting from these considerations, Fig. 1 shows a set of 18 pseudoadders connected to take 20 summands

$(W_1$ to $W_{39})$ and express their sum as the sum of two numbers. These are shown added in a conventional carry-propagating adder to produce the final product. The design of this adder will not be discussed, as several excellent designs having carry-propagation times of the order of 100 nsec have been devised [1], [5].

GENERATION OF SUMMANDS

In the simplest form of multiplication, there are as many summands as multiplier digits, each either 0 or 1 times the multiplicand. A wide range of schemes involving recoding the multiplier into a new (possibly redundant) form using some negative digits have been developed to reduce the number of summands [3]. Since all summands are to be generated simultaneously, and then summed very quickly, it is desirable that the recoding scheme used should 1) require only multiples of the multiplicand obtainable by shifting and complementing, and 2) be a local recoding in which each recoded digit depends only on a small group of original multiplier digits. The best system found gives base-four recoded multiplier digits which can be $+2$, $+1$, 0, -1 or -2, and each is determined entirely by three adjacent original binary multiplier digits. Considering the process as a base-four recoding, digits 0, 1, 2, 3 are recoded into digits 0, 1, -2, -1, respectively, if the next less significant original base-four digit is 0 or 1, and into 1, 2, -1, 0 if the next less significant original digit is 2 or 3. The number of summands is half the number of binary multiplier digits. Attempts to reduce the number further appear to require multiples not obtainable by shifting. Some complications arise in the pseudoadder structure because of the negative multiplier digits, which, in a two's complement system, require correction digits to be added in. However, detailed examination shows that these problems are superable without loss of speed or undue circuit cost.

DIVISION

Most normal division processes are essentially serial, and hence, not well suited to employ efficiently the highly parallel multiplier. The best approach seems to be to generate reciprocals by an iterative process of multiplications. The following algorithm is a version of one first described by Wheeler [2]. Given a positive normalized fraction x, and some approximation p to $1/x$, set $a_1 = px$ and $b_1 = p$ and iterate

$$a_{n+1} = a_n(2 - a_n), \qquad b_{n+1} = b_n(2 - a_n).$$

This process converges quadratically, a_n to 1, and b_n to $1/x$. Simple logic which inspects the first six digits of x can be used to generate a p of the form $1 \cdot q\ r\ s\ t$ such that $|1-px| \leq 1/32$, *i.e.*, a_1 has the form $\bar{d} \cdot ddddefghjk$, etc. p can be recoded to give three summands. The first iterative step should increase to 10 the number of similar digits immediately after the binary point. It can be shown that an a_2 of this form is obtainable by use of a

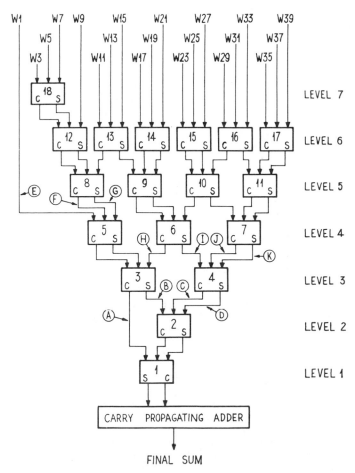

Fig. 1—The adder tree.

multiplier which is not exactly $2 - a_1$, but rather

$$1 - 2^{-5}(\bar{d} \cdot efghj),$$

where the number in brackets is regarded as a signed two's complement fraction. This multiplier can be obtained directly from a_1, and requires only four summands after recoding. Similarly, an approximate multiplier can be used in the next iterative step requiring seven summands, and one in the third step requiring 12 summands. Only three iterative steps are needed to produce a 40-bit reciprocal. If these approximate multipliers are used in both multiplications of the iterative step, the correct answer is produced. The advantage of using the approximate multipliers is twofold. Firstly, the smaller number of recoded multiplier digits allows the multiplication to be done by only part of the pseudo-adder tree, and the multiplication time, especially in the earlier steps, is thereby reduced. (In Fig. 1, summands for px and the first iterative step can be introduced at points A, B, C and D, and those for the second step at points E to K.) Secondly, the number of digits in b_n is small in the early steps. This fact, together with the fact that the more significant digits of the a's need not be formed, means that, for a 40-bit word length, both multiplications in each of the first and second iterative steps can be performed simultaneously by splitting the pseudoadders into two shorter-word-length sections. Depending on the word length, some extension of some of the pseudoadders may be necessary. The a-multiplication in the last iterative step need not be done. Thus, a 40-bit reciprocal can be generated with only four passes through the multiplier, and at least the first three of these can be quicker than a full multiplication.

Square Root

A variant of the reciprocal iteration can be made to yield reciprocal roots. Given x positive and normalized, and p an approximation to root $1/x$, set $a_1 = p^2 x$, $b_1 = p$ and iterate

$$a_{n+1} = a_n(1\tfrac{1}{2} - a_n)^2; \qquad b_{n+1} = b_n(1\tfrac{1}{2} - a_n),$$

where b_n converges quadratically to root $1/x$. Once again, approximate multipliers can be used. The possibility of doing two multiplications simultaneously has not been investigated in detail. However, even if this is not feasible, the process would appear to be quicker than the customary Newton method using repeated divisions.

Speed and Cost

A detailed examination has been made of a design for a multiplication-division unit for 40-bit numbers. The design is based on saturating complementary diode-transistor AND-OR-NOT circuits. Each pseudoadder stage requires three transistors and 18 diodes, and involves two stages of logic. Multiplier recoding requires one stage. A pnp adder is shown in Fig. 2.

To estimate speeds, it is assumed that:

1) Each stage of logic introduces a propagation delay of 30 nsec.

2) The delay of high-current drivers for fanout of multiplicand and recoded multiplier digits is 100 nsec.

3) The settling time of the carry-propagating adder is 100 nsec.

4) The result will be gated into a register with a settling time of 100 nsec.

On these assumptions, which are believed to be realistic for the present fairly cheap components in good packaging, the multiplication time becomes 750 nsec.

The reciprocal-generating time, excluding prenormalization, is 2220 nsec. The time for a complete division is therefore about 3 μsec. The time for generating a reciprocal root, assuming that no multiplications are done simultaneously, is 6 μsec.

The tree of pseudoadders requires 750 full-adder circuits. Generation of summands requires 840 single-transistor logic stages for multiplication, and a further

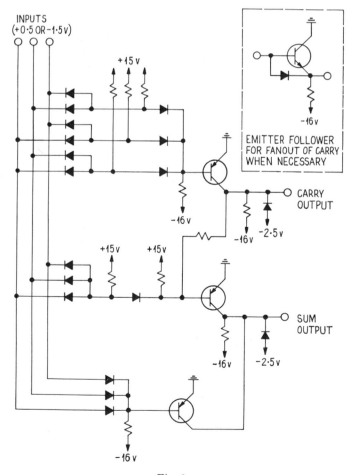

Fig. 2.

561 stages for division if division summands are introduced in later stages of the adder tree to save time. A total of 140 high-current drivers are needed. The total semiconductor cost, excluding the carry-propagating adder and operand and result registers, which would be present in a conventional arithmetic unit, is 4591 transistors, and 33,083 diodes.

DISCUSSION

The multiplier unit requires a great deal of equipment, amounting perhaps to 10 per cent of the total semiconductor complement of a very large modern computer, but probably, because of its simplicity, costing rather less than 10 per cent of the cost of the computer. In a sense, this equipment is used inefficiently. It is useful for only some arithmetic operations, and even in these, circuits with delay times of 30 nsec are used only about once per microsecond. However, some mismatch between propagation delay and repetition rate is apparently inherent in the type of circuit postulated, and equally bad mismatches could probably be found in many present computers. If the word length is increased, the equipment cost rises as the square of the word length, and the times as the logarithm of the word length. The inefficiency, or ratio between propagation rate and repetition rate, rises logarithmically. However, for 40-bit words, the inefficiency is not intolerable.

The speeds achievable appear to be greater by a factor of at least four than those obtained in conventional units. Multiplication and division times would be reduced to approximate parity with the time required for, *e.g.*, floating point addition. Parity in the times for all arithmetic operations would be of considerable benefit to machines employing advanced controls, as at present these advanced controls tend to run out of work when long arithmetic operations are performed, unless many levels of look-ahead buffering are provided, in which case the control organization, especially in the treatment of jumps, becomes very complicated and difficult to design. Machines without look-ahead buffering between memory and arithmetic units should benefit even more. At present, such machines tend to be designed with memories and controls which can keep up with the faster arithmetic operations, and which therefore lie idle during multiplications and divisions. If one can assume that, *e.g.*, a third of all arithmetic operations in scientific computers are multiplications, and that these at present take about four times as long as additions, etc., the use of the fast unit would approximately double the speed of computation.

A simpler unit might be preferable in some cases, in which half as many adders are used to perform a multiplication in two steps. The equipment cost would be almost halved, and the multiplication time almost doubled. Reciprocal times would not be affected, as the half-sized adder tree would still be large enough to do in one step the largest multiplications required in the iteration.

REFERENCES

[1] D. B. G. Edwards, "A parallel arithmetic unit using a saturated transistor fast carry circuit," *Proc. IEE*, vol. 107, pt. B, p. 673; November, 1960
[2] M. V. Wilkes, D. J. Wheeler, and S. Gill, "Preparation of Programs for an Electronic Digital Computer," Addison-Wesley, Cambridge, Mass.; 1951.
[3] J. E. Robertson, "Theory of Computer Arithmetic Employed in the Design of the New Computer at the University of Illinois," presented at Conf. on Theory of Computing Machine Design, University of Michigan, Ann Arbor, June, 1960.
[4] "Whirlwind I Computer Block Diagrams," Project Whirlwind, Rept. No. R-127-1, September, 1947.
[5] J. Lucking and J. O'Neil, English Electric KDF 9 Logic Diagrams, private communication; January, 1963.

SOME SCHEMES FOR PARALLEL MULTIPLIERS [*]

L. DADDA [**]

The possibility of combinational switching networks obtaining the product of two binary numbers is investigated. Some schemes are proposed, all based on the use of parallel counters, i.e. combinational switching networks which produce at the outputs in codified binary form the number of « ones » present at the inputs.

The proposed schemes obtain the product in two steps: the first obtains two numbers whose sum equals the product, without carry propagation; the second step obtains the product in a carry propagating adder.

The practical implementation of parallel counters is also considered.

1. – INTRODUCTION.

The realization of a parallel multiplier for digital computers has been considered in a recent paper by C. S. Wallace [1] who proposed a tree of pseudo-adders (i.e., adders without carry propagation) producing two numbers, whose sum equals the product. This sum can be obtained by applying the two numbers to a carry-propagating adder.

The purpose of this note is to present some schemes for parallel multipliers, based on a different principle and having some advantages over the one by Wallace. Also some of the proposed schemes will obtain two numbers whose sum equals the product.

2. – THE MULTIPLIER SCHEME, BASED ON PARALLEL COUNTERS.

The new schemes are based on the use of logical blocks that we will call « parallel (n, m) counters »: these are combinational networks with m outputs and n ($\leq 2^m$) inputs. The m outputs, considered as a binary number, codify the number of « ones » present at the inputs. In a subsequent paragraph some implementations of such parallel counters will be illustrated.

Consider now the process of multiplication of two binary numbers, each composed of n bit, as been based on obtaining the sum of ν summands.

These summands are obtained, in the simplest schemes, by shifting left the multiplicand by 1, 2, 3, $(n-1)$ places, and multiplying it by the corresponding bits of the multiplier. In this case, $\nu = n$.

As it is well known, the number of summands can be made less than n by using some simple multiples of the multiplicand, on the basis of two or more multiplier digits [1].

The reduction of the number of summands will not be considered here. The case ($\nu = n$) will be therefore assumed, as the scheme proposed will work also for a reduced number of summands.

Consider now the case of two positive factors. To obtain the product, first represent the summands by the usual matrix as indicated in upper portion fig. 1; (in the figure, $n = 12$). In the same figure, the significant bits are

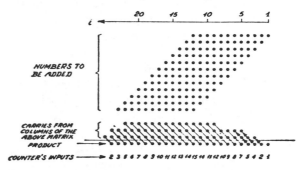

Fig. 1. — Multiplication (12×12 bit) through addition, in a single stage, using a parallel counter for each column. Carries are propagated through the counters.

represented by dots: moreover, bits at the left and at the right of the significant ones are supposed to be zeros.

The process of multiplication is as follows. The single bit in column $i = 1$ represents the least significant bit of the product, so it does not require any transformation. The two bits in column $i = 2$ are applied to a (2,2) counter: the least significant of the two outputs represents the second least significant bit of the product, and is recorded in fig. 1 on the last line, $i = 2$; the most significant output represents a carry, and is therefore recorded in column $i = 3$.

In column 3 we have 4 bit: three of them belong to the original matrix, the fourth is the carry just mentioned. This four bits will be applied to a (4.3) counter, whose three outputs will be recorded: in column 3 (the least significant, representing the third least significant bit of the product) in column 4 and in column 5 (the most significant), respectively.

The following columns are treated in a similar way, using suitable counters.

The inputs of each counter are in part the bits of the corresponding column of the summands matrix, in part carry bits produced by the counters of the preceeding columns. In fig. 1, carries produced by a given counter are connected by a diagonal segment.

The set of the least significant bits produced by all counters represents the result.

The above scheme is the most elementary one that can be devised. However, it suffers of a serious disadvantage, namely that of carry propagation delay through the counters.

(*) This paper has been presented at the « Colloque sur l'Algèbre de Boole », Grenoble, 11-17 january 1965.

(**) L. DADDA, Istituto di Elettrotecnica ed Elettronica del Politecnico di Milano.

(1) C. S. WALLACE: *A suggestion for a fast multiplier.* - « IEEE Trans. on Electronic Computers », vol. EC-13, pp. 14÷17, february 1964.

In fact, counters with a large number of inputs are in general implemented by complicated circuits, having therefore a substantial inherent delay.

If one wishes to minimize the effects of such delay, a different scheme should be adopted. This scheme is based on the following remark. Consider the problem of obtaining the product as divided in two steps. In the first step, obtain from the original set of addends a set of two numbers, whose sum equals the product. The second step obtains the product in a carry-propagating adder.

Carry propagation cannot be avoided: it is simply confined to this second step, where it can be accomplished by special, fast circuits.

Let us now describe the above process with reference to fig. 2, that represents a 12×12 product.

The first step of the process consists of cascaded stages (in the example, 3 stages): the first stage trans-

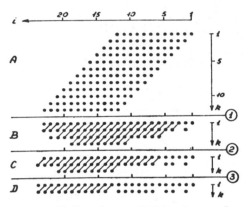

Fig. 2. — A multiplier scheme, obtaining two numbers, whose sum equals the product of 12×12 bit, through three stages, using a parallel counter for each stage and for each column. Carries are not propagated.

forms the matrix A into the matrix B; the second stage matrix B into C, and so on, until a matrix, composed of two rows only, is obtained: these two rows represent the numbers that, summed in a carry propagating adder, produce the result.

In the first stage, we begin by transcribing the single significant bit in column $i = 1$ (in the right upper corner) from matrix A into matrix B. The same is done for column $i = 2$, composed of two significant bits only.

The three bits of column $i = 3$, are applied to a $(3,2)$ counter: the least significant, of the two output bits, is recorded in B, $i = 3$; the most significant bit is recorded in B, $i = 4$, in the second row. Which row is chosen for this second bit is inessential, provided it is recorded in column $i = 4$; the rule followed in Fig. 2 is convenient because it produces a compact matrix B.

The $i = 4$ column has 4 bit, and correspondingly, the parallel counter must have $m = 3$ outputs: the least significant bit will be recorded in B, $(i, k) = (3,1)$; the next bit in B, $(i, k) = (4,2)$; the third, most significant bit in B, $(i, k) = (5,3)$.

Note that in fig. 2 matrix B, the diagonal segment, joining together the above three bits, signifies that these bits are the outputs of the parallel counter fed by the column just above the least significant bit ($k = 1$). The rule is followed in all similar cases.

The process described above for column $i = 3$ and

$i = 4$ is repeated for the subsequent columns, using each time an appropriate parallel counter.

The matrix B, thus obtained from A, has four rows: it is then transformed into matrix C by the same process.

Matrix C has 3 rows, so it is transformed into matrix D, a two-row matrix: the two rows represent the result of the process.

The above process can be justified as follows. With reference to the original matrix A, it can be said that the product is equivalent to the sum of all the bits $b_{i,k}$ in the same matrix, each multiplied by a weight, 2^{i-1}:

$$P = \sum_{1}^{n}{}_k \sum_{1}^{2n-1}{}_i b_{i,k} 2^{i-1}$$

The contribution to P of each column i, is:

$$P_i = \sum_{1}^{n}{}_k b_{i,k} 2^{i-1} = 2^{i-1} \sum_{1}^{n}{}_k b_{i,k}$$

This same contribution is represented in matrix B by the output of the counter, $\overset{k}{\underset{1}{\sum}}_k b_{i,k}$, whose least significant bit is in column i, and therefore has weight 2^{i-1}.

The matrix B, therefore, is equivalent to matrix A as far as the evaluation of the product is concerned.

Matrices C and D are also equivalent to A, having been obtained from B and C respectively by the same transformation.

The procedure described can be applied to factors with arbitrary value of n, on the assumption that parallel counters having a suitable number of inputs are available.

The number of stages required is easily determined, and appears as in table I.

TABLE I. – *Number of stages required for a parallel multiplier (vs. number of bits the multiplier) using parallel counters without limitation on the number of inputs.*

Number of bits in the multiplier	Number of stages
3	1
$3 < n \leq 7$	2
$7 < n \leq 15$	3
$15 < n \leq 32$	4
$32 < n \leq 64$	5

3. – THE USE OF COUNTERS WITH A LIMITED NUMBER OF INPUTS: $(2,2)$ AND $(3,2)$ COUNTERS.

Counters with a large number of inputs are difficult to realize. It is therefore important to see how the method could be applied using counters with a limited number of inputs, n_1.

It is apparent that the method can be modified as follows. If the number of significant bits in a column of the matrix to be transformed (initially matrix A) is greater than the number n_1 of inputs to the available counters, divide the bits in groups, each having at most n_1 bits. Each group can then be applied to the counter's inputs, each counter providing thus for each group the number of ones coded in binary.

Such counts are placed in the B matrix, all with the

least significant bit in column i, and using as many rows as necessary.

The same holds for the subsequent transformations, until a 2-row matrix is obtained.

The most important remark on the above procedure is that the number of stages necessary will in general be greater than that required with unrestricted counter inputs.

One might, in this connection, look for the minimum number of inputs, that can still be used for the implementation of the method.

This minimum number is of course *two*; (2,2) counters can be used as shown in the examples in Fig. 3, and Fig. 4, representing the cases $n = 3$ and $n = 4$ respectively.

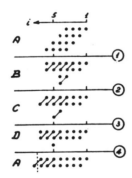

Fig. 3. — A multiplier structure, obtaining two numbers, whose sum equals the product of 3×3 bit, through the use of 2 input/2 output parallel counters.

The example $n = 3$ works as follows. Columns $i = 1$ and $i = 2$ are reproduced in B. Column $i = 3$ is composed of 3 bit: therefore 2 of them are applied to a (2,2) counter, whose outputs are reproduced in B, columns $i = 3$ and $i = 4$ respectively (in the figure, they are connected together by a segment); the 3rd bit is simply reproduced in B, $i = 3$.

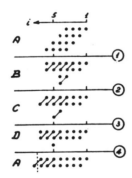

Fig. 4. — Same as fig. 3, for the product of 4×4 bit.

Columns 4 has 2 bit, as column 2: nevertheless it is transformed by a (2,2) counter, to produce the bits in columns 4 and 5 of B, because in B, column $i = 4$ there is already the carry from column 3. The single bit in column 5 is simply reproduced.

The case $n = 4$ is completely analogous. Considering cases with larger n, it can be found that the number of necessary stages, when using (2,2) counters, is 2^{n-2}. This means that, for pratical values of n (e.g., $n = 30$), the number of stages would become very large and consequently the total delay would become too great.

As we will see in the following, the number of stages is drastically reduced if counters with $n = 3$ or more are used. On the other hand, it must be noted that counters with n larger than 2 are not difficult to implement. This is certainly the case for $n = 3$, that is a full adder network.

Fig. 5 represents the multiplication process for the case $n = 12$ (like fig. 2), using (3,2) counters and, when necessary, also some (2,2) counters. It can be seen that the total number of stages required is 5 (instead of 3,

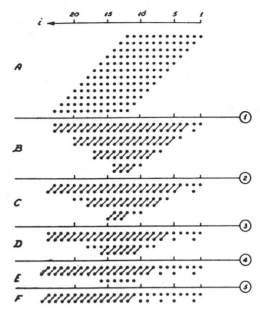

Fig. 5. — Same as fig. 2, through the use of 3 or 2-input/2 outputs parallel counters.

which represents the absolute minimum; see fig. 2). The process is carried out in fig. 5, with the following rules.

Columns 1 and 2, are simply reproduced in B (and in all following matrices).

Column 3, having 3 bit, is transformed in B into 2 bit: the least significant in column 3, the most significant in column 4 (second row). (They are connected by a diagonal segment, as used previously).

Column 4 has 4 bit: three of them are transformed by a (3,2) counter, the fourth is simply reproduced in B, (4,3).

Column 5 has 5 bit: three of them are transformed by a (3,2) counter, the last two by a (2,2) counter: the latter's outputs (in B, (5,3) and B, (6,4), respectively) are joined by a diagonal segment crossed by a bar to signify that they are outputs of a (2,2) counter.

Similar rules are applied to all the following columns, through the last column (23rd) which has a single bit.

The matrix B obtained by the application of the process, can be shown to be equivalent to A, as far as the evaluation of the product is concerned.

The same process can be used to obtain C from B, D from C, E from D and F from E. F has two rows, whose sum represents the product.

Some remarks can be made about the described process, which was based on (3,2) counters.

a) the number s of stages can be determined as follows.

It can be seen that the last 2-row matrix can be derived by a 3-row matrix. This is true regardless of the type of counters used.

A 3-row matrix can be derived from a 4-row matrix: in fact, three of the bits of each column can be reduced to two, by a (3,2) counter; the fourth bit is simply reproduced. This is obtained in the $(s-1)th$ stage.

A 4-row matrix can be derived from a 6-row matrix, as can be easily verified. This is the $(s-2)th$ stage.

A 6-row matrix can be derived from a 9-row matrix: $(s-3)th$ stage.

A 9-row matrix can be derived from a 13-row matrix: $(2+2+2+2+1 \rightarrow 3+3+3+3+1)$. This is the $(s-4)th$ stage.

In the example of fig. 4, $n = 12$, so that the number of stages is given by: $s-4 = 1$; $s = 5$, as obtained.

Proceeding with the same rules, table II, valid for (3,2) counters, can be drawn up.

TABLE II. – *Number of stages required for a parallel multiplier (vs. number of bits of the multiplier) using (3,2) counters only.*

Number of bits in the multiplier	Number of stages
3	1
4	2
$4 < n \leq 6$	3
$6 < n \leq 9$	4
$9 < n \leq 13$	5
$13 < n \leq 19$	6
$19 < n \leq 28$	7
$28 < n \leq 42$	8
$42 < n \leq 63$	9

b) The scheme of fig. 5 is not the only one possible with (3,2) counters.

Fig. 6 represents a process, sligtly different from that in fig. 5 and leading to a considerable saving in components. In fact, the scheme in fig. 5 requires a total of

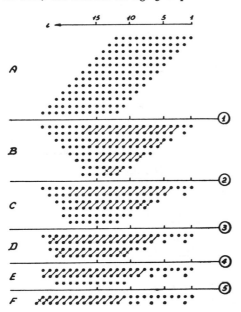

Fig. 6. — Same as fig. 5, with a different scheme using less counters.

136 counters (101 are (3,2) counters, 35 are (2,2)); the scheme of fig. 6 requires 116 counters (104 are (3,2), 12 are (2,2)).

The rules applied in fig. 6 are the following.

In the first stage, columns 1 to 13 are treated in the same way as in fig. 5.

Columns 14, 15, 16 and 17 (having 10, 9, 8, 7 bit

respectively in matrix A, are only partially reduced, so that in matrix B they are composed of 8 bit (taking into account the carries from the preceeding columns).

All remaining columns are reproduced in matrix B without any reduction.

The reason of doing so is essentially the following. It is not convenient to try reduction of the number of bits in a given column, when it is preceeded by columns having a larger number of bits, because carries from the latters tend to increase the number of bits.

It should be remarked that in passing from matrix B to matrix C the last two rows of matrix B are reproduced in C without any transformation.

c) A sligtly different criterion is applied in fig. 7,

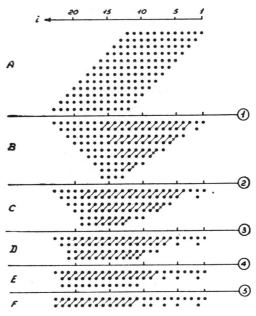

Fig. 7. — Same as fig. 6, with a different scheme, using less counters.

where a further reduction in the number of counters is achieved (113 instead of 116).

The scheme in fig. 7 is the same as in fig. 6 for columns 1 to 12.

Column 13 and the followings, are only partially reduced so that in matrix B they have no more than 9 bit (while in Fig. 6, 8 is the maximum number of rows in matrix B.

Although nothing can be said in general about the effect of such a rule, it can however be noted that both 9-bit columns and 8-bit columns are reduced successively to 6, 4, 3, and 2 bit in the succeeding matrices. The reduction of such columns from matrix A to matrix B requires less counters for 9 column than for 8. Moreover, although in the succeeding stages more counters are required for a 9-row than for an 8-row B matrix, there is a net saving in the total number of counters.

d) Another reduction scheme can finally be described, as the example in fig. 8 shows. It requires the least number of component of all schemes considered: 110 counters (96 of (3,2) type; 14 of (2,2) type).

The rules applied in Fig. 8 can be described as follows. First, notice that in the original matrix A the middle column (12th) has 12 bit, and that proceeding from that columns to the right and to the left, columns have a decreasing number of bits.

In passing from matrix A to matrix B, columns are only partially reduced, so that no more than 9 rows are obtained. For example, column 10 (10 bit) is trans-

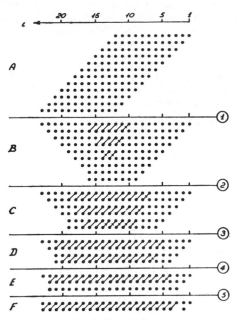

Fig. 8.   Same as fig. 7, with a different scheme, using less counters.

formed in a 9-bit column in B, by reproducing 8 bit without transformation and transforming only 2 bit, by a (2,2) counter.

Consequently, only some columns in the central portion of matrix A are actually transformed.

In passing from matrix B to C, columns having no more than 6 bit are obtained. In succeeding transformations, columns with no more than 4, 3 and 2 bit respectively are obtained.

The above rules can be generalized for $n \times n$ bits multiplications as follows.

Consider first the following series:

$$2; 3; 6; 9; 13; 19; 28; 42; 63; \dots$$

(where each term is obtained from the preceeding, by multiplying it by 3/2 and taking the integral part). The terms of this series correspond to the number of those matrices obtained from the final, 2-row matrix, and applying the reverse of the transformation described in the preceeding examples.

Given then the original A matrix for a $n \times n$ bits multiplication, obtain through the first transformation a matrix B having a number of rows coinciding with the nearest term of the above serie which is less than n.

All the following matrices will have a number of rows coincident with the terms of the series (in decreasing order of magnitude).

From the above examples it appears that the best rule is the last one described.

Although no proof is given here of the optimality of such rule, nevertheless all examples worked out for different values of n are in accordance with the results obtained for $n = 12$.

e) It is interesting to compare the described schemes with the Wallace scheme. This can be considered as a parallel multiplier composed of (3,2) counters.

The Wallace multiplier is based on a tree of pseudo-adders, as shown in the block-diagram of fig. 9 (Wallace notation). Each pseudo-adder is effectively composed of a set of (3,2) counters, as appears in fig. 10, where the notation used in the preceeding figures of this paper is used.

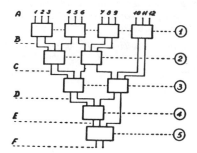

Fig. 9. — Block diagram for a parallel (12 × 12) multiplier structure, according to Wallace.

Fig. 10, concerning the case $n = 12$, requires a total of 136 counters (102 are (3,2), 34 are (2,2)), that is the same number of counters required in the fig. 5 scheme. This coincidence is not valid in general. It can be shown that, for $n > 12$ the Wallace scheme requires less counters than the fig. 5 scheme.

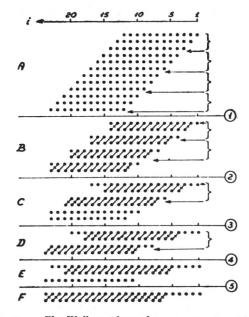

Fig. 10. — The Wallace scheme for a (12 × 12) multiplier.

However, the schemes based on the rules illustrated in the preceeding paragraph *d* (see fig. 8) requires less counters than Wallace scheme.

For instance, for the case $n = 24$ one obtain:

— Wallace scheme: 575 counters
— fig. 8   scheme: 506 counters
— fig. 5   scheme: 606 counters.

f) The following remarks can be made about the described schemes. In all the examples (fig. 5, 6, 7, 8) it can be seen that the bits in the least significant portion of the result are produced through a number of stages smaller than the total.

Examining, for instance, fig. 5, it can be verified that:

— the least significant bit ($i = 1$) and the two bit in column $i = 2$ are produced without any stage.

— the bit in column $i = 3$ is produced through the first stage;

— the bit $i = 4$ is produced through the second stage; etc. etc.

This is very important if the speed of the circuit is considered, as each stage introduces a certain delay.

In fact, the above remark means that the least significant portion of the two final numbers is produced with a delay that increases progressively from the least significant bit (no delay) on.

Because the two final numbers must be added together, to obtain the product, in a carry-propagating adder, this means in turn that the carry propagation delay in the least significant half of the adder is overlapped by the progressively increasing delay through the multiplier structure. Whether the carry delay in the adder is greater than the multiplier delay or not, depends of course from the type of circuit used and also from the operands.

It can be seen also in the examples given (see e.g. fig. 5) that the second final summand (second row in matrix F) has some zeros, regardless of the bits of the original operands. Such situation can be accounted for in the construction of the adder, using half adders in the stages corresponding to the zeros of the second summand, thus simplifying the final adder.

4 – THE USE OF HIGHER ORDER COUNTERS: (7,3) AND (15,4) COUNTERS.

The (3,2) counter, i.e. the full adder, is the commonest form of implementation of the parallel counters concept, and the use of such counters in parallel multipliers has been discussed in the preceeding point.

Higher order counters, i.e. counters having a larger number of inputs and outputs, although not currently used, are nevertheless entirely feasible with today's technology, as will be shown in the next paragraph. This is certainly the case for (7,3) counters. Moreover, high order counters compare very favorably with (3,2) counters as far as the number of components is concerned. It is therefore interesting to investigate briefly on the problem of multiplier's implementation using such counters.

It can be shown that most of the considerations illustrated in the preceeding paragraph are valid for higher order counters. In particular, the scheme illustrated in paragraph d) proves to be the best, as far as the total number of counters is concerned.

The most important point to be illustrated is the number of stages required, as a function of the counters order.

Suppose that, beside (3,2) counters, (7,3) counters are available. Starting now from the final 2-row matrix, observe that it can be obtained from a set of 2-output counters, i.e. (2,2) or (3,2) counters. This means that the next matrix must have only 3 rows.

A 3-row matrix can be obtained from a set of 3-output counters, i.e. from counters having 7 inputs, at most. The next matrix must therefore have 7 rows at most.

A 7 row matrix can be decomposed in two 3-row matrix and a 1-row matrix. This means in turn that it can be derived, through (7,3) counters, from a matrix having $7 + 7 + 1 = 15$ rows.

Proceeeding with such rules, the following series can be obtained:

$$2; 3; 7; 15; 35; 79; \cdots$$

that can be used as the series of the preceeding paragraph (valid for (3,2) counters).

For example, if a multiplier is to be designed for numbers having 48 bit, it can be seen that 5 stages are required. The first stage will obtain a 35-row matrix, the second a 15-row matrix, etc.

If now we suppose that (15,4) counters are available, beside (3,2) and (7,3) counters, the following series can be obtained, using rules similar to those applied for the preceeding case:

$$2; 3; 7; 21; 61; 226; \cdots$$

It can be seen therefore, that for a 48 bits multiplice, 4 stages will be required.

As was announced previously, high order counters can afford an important saving in components. For example, if counters based on threshold devices are used (see next paragraph), the total numbers of transistors, required by the multiplier structure for 24 bit (excluding the carry propagating adder and the network generating matrix A) is as follows:

(3,2) counters:	Wallace scheme:	1150 transistors
	scheme d):	1012 transistors
(7,3) counters:	scheme d):	490 transistors

5. – REMARKS ON PARALLEL COUNTERS.

The schemes discussed in the preceeding paragraphs are all based on the use of parallel counters. It is therefore worthwhile to discuss briefly on their practical implementation.

Before describing some counters, let us discuss on some characteristics that prove useful in the peculiar application considered.

Among the different type of full adders, the most suitable for the application in parallel multipliers, from the point of view of economy and speed, are those which require input variables of one form only (natural or complemented), so that output variables of the same form only must be generated. If such condition is satisfied, outputs of one stage can be used directly as inputs to the next stages, without the need of inverters, leading in general to a considerable saving in components and to a reduction of stage delay.

It must be noted that the above restriction can be partially released by allowing the use of counters producing outputs of only one form but different from the input's form (« inverting counters »). We will examine later some simple circuits, of this type.

The use of inverting counters does not modify substantially the described schemes. Consider the use of such counters in the scheme of fig. 5 and suppose that all the bits of the final matrix F are to be obtained in true form. Assume then the preceeding matrix E to be in complemented form, the preceeding matrix D in true form, etc.: i.e., matrices are alternatively in true or complemented form. This situation can be obtained if, when transforming from one matrix to the next, one use inverting counters or, when bits were simply to be reproduced, inverters.

All inverters can nevertheless be avoided, if single bits in the original matrix A are produced in a suitable form. Consider for example, columns 1 and 2: according to the previous rule they should be in complemented form in matrix A: but they can be simply transfered from A to F if they are produced in A in true form. On the contrary, column 3 must be produced in A in complemented form, so that the single bit produced in matrix B, column 3) in true form, can be directly transfered to F, and so on.

It can thus be said that inverting counters can be used, provided that bits in the original matrix A are produced in a suitable form.

An interesting feature of all schemes of parallel multipliers is that each counter output is loaded by a single input of a counter of the next stage. This feature can be conveniently accounted for in the electrical design.

Some considerations will now be made on the implementation of parallel counters, with reference to some of the available logic circuitry and taking into account the above remarks.

a) « And-or-not » logic. A full-adder, satisfying the above requirement, can be based on the following equations:

$$R = A B + A C + B C$$
$$S = R (A + B + C) + A B C$$

where:

A, B, C, are the input variables

R, S are the outputs.

A full adder of this type has been reported by Wal-

been investigated. Nevertheless it can be said that the number of components will increase rapidly along with n.

Similar conclusions can be accepted for « nor » (or « nand ») logic, although cheaper circuits will be obtained.

b) Threshold gates. Counters using threshold gates can be of the non-inverting type or of the inverting type

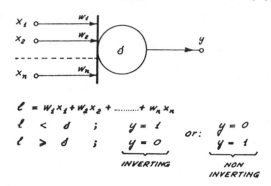

Fig. 11. — The logical definition of threshold gates.

according to the type of threshold gate used (see fig. 11). An interesting scheme for inverting counters, is reported in Fig. 12 (for a (3,2) counter), and Fig. 13 (for (7,3) counter.

A simple realization of an inverting (3.2) counter using resistor-transistor gates, is represented in fig. 12,b.

It is probably the simplest circuit that can be devised for a full-adder, as it uses only 2 transistors (one for each output) and some resistors. Using available components, a delay of less than 100 ns can be obtained.

An investigation has been undertaken in our laboratory in order to explore the possibilities of threshold counters for parallel multipliers.

c) Current switching. Current switching circuits offer a mean for implementing parallel counters. Current swit-

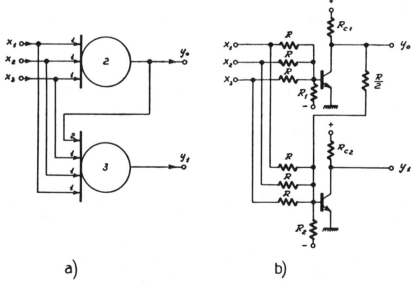

a)   b)

Fig. 12. — a) = (3,2) parallel counter, using inverting threshold gates. b) = a realization of an inverting (3,2) counter, using resistor-transistor threshold circuits.

lace [1]. It is an inverting counter, requiring 18 diodes and 3 transistors, and having a total delay of 60 ns.

It does not seem that the realization of counters of higher order, and satisfying the above requirement, has

ching can be realized using transistors or criotrons. Transistor current switching circuits are the fastest logical circuits realizable with a given transistor type [2].

Using available transistors, it should be possible to

realize (3,2) counters having a delay of 10÷20 ns. They are, however less economical than all other circuits.

It should be noted that special circuits (i.e. not suitable

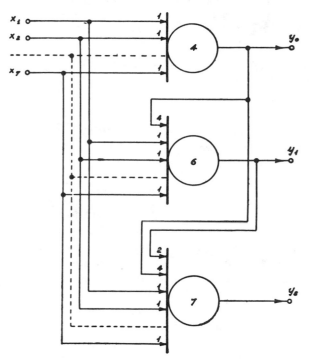

Fig. 13. --- a (7,3) parallel counter, using inverting threshold gates.

for general purpose logic) could probably be devised in order to obtain fast and cheap counters. A similar situation is afforded by parallel adders, that can be realized using expecially designed circuits (see: [2]).

6. – Conclusions.

Having established the possibility of a parallel digital multiplier, some considerations can now be made about the important aspects of speed and cost than can be encountered in a practical design.

It is worthwhile first to recall that if one assumes [1] that a third of all arithmetic operations in scientific

[2] D. B. Jarvis, L. P. Morgan, J. A. Wearer: *Transistor current switching and routing techniques.* - « IRE Trans. on Electronic Computers », vol. EC-9, n. 3 pag. 302, september 1960.

computers are multiplications and that these at present take about four times as long as additions, the use of a fast multiplier allowing a multiplication in a memory cycle time, would approximately double the speed of computation.

There is therefore a chance that a parallel multiplier could become a convenient mean to improve the value of a computer, owing to the fact that it cost can be shown to be only a few percent of the total computer cost.

The following is an estimate about the type of multiplier circuits, based on actual memory cycle times.

Let us first note that the total multiplication time is composed of two parts: the first is the time elapsed from the application of the signals representing the two factors to the inputs of the multiplier, to the availability of the inputs to the carry-propagating adder; the second part is the delay proper of the adder, mainly consisting in the carry propagation delay.

In the design of a practical multiplier, one can assume as a goal to obtain a total delay equal or less that to the cycle time of the high-speed memory, so that the computer can work at its maximum speed, limited only by the memory speed. The choice of the type of circuits depends therefore from the memory cycle time.

If a core memory having a cycle of 4 μs or more is considered, threshold gates allow a very convenient solution. The fastest core memories have cycle time in the order of 1 μs. In this cases, probably threshold gates could again be used, provided (3,2) counters having delays of the order of 50 ns are designed and carry propagating adders with less than 100 ns delay are employed.

In cases where fastest memories are considered (for instance, magnetic film memories, or tunnel diodes memories) having cycle times of 200 ns or less, fastest counters should be designed, for instance of the current switching type.

Although the problem is beyond the scope of this paper, it must also be noted that the realization of parallel multipliers should also influence computer organization. It is well known, indeed, that some important features of fast computers depend on the fact that during operations, that last longer than one memory cycle (typically, during multiplication or division), memory can be made available for other operations (e.g. input-output).

It appears therefore necessary to review the computer structure, as far as it depends from the duration of multiplications.

The paper was first received 29th *Avril* 1965.

Generation of Products and Quotients Using Approximate Binary Logarithms for Digital Filtering Applications

ERNEST L. HALL, MEMBER, IEEE, DAVID D. LYNCH, MEMBER, IEEE, AND
SAMUEL J. DWYER, III, MEMBER, IEEE

Abstract—An approximate method for rapid multiplication or division with relatively simple digital circuitry is described. The algorithm consists of computing approximate binary logarithms, adding or subtracting the logarithms, and computing the approximate antilogarithm of the resultant. Using a criteria of minimum mean square error, coefficients for the approximations are developed. An error analysis is given for three cases in which the algorithm is useful. Finally, applications to digital filtering computations are considered which illustrate that log-antilog multiplication is not simpler than an array multiplier for computing single products, but is useful for parallel digital filter banks and multiplicative digital filters.

Index Terms—Antilogarithm converter, binary-to-binary logarithm converter, computer multiplication, digital filter realization.

INTRODUCTION

AN ALGORITHM for computer multiplication by binary logarithms was described by Mitchell [1] and expanded by Combet, Van Zonneveld, and Verbeek [2]. This method has only modest accuracy and limited application for general purpose computation. However, there is a class of digital filtering problems in which the speed, nature of the signals, and component count, offset accuracy considerations. Real-time digital filtering of radar video for moving target detection, synthetic aperture processing, and pulse compression are in this class. Because of the statistical nature of the sampled signals, the large amount of signal integration required, and the characterization of detection performance on a probabilistic basis, the accuracy of a single computation has less importance than the mean and variance of the operation on the signal ensemble. Radar video is characterized by broad bandwidth and corresponding high data flow rates which make real time multiplication with readily available logic very difficult. Furthermore, multiple filters are usually required because the noise is colored and the filter bandpass is but a small fraction of the actual signal bandwidth.

In Section I the binary-to-binary logarithm conversion is reviewed. In Section II the antilogarithm conversion is developed. In Section III a detailed error

Manuscript received May 1, 1968; revised July 14, 1969.
E. L. Hall is with the Department of Electrical Engineering, University of Missouri, Columbia, and Emerson Electric Company, St. Louis, Mo.
D. D. Lynch is with the Emerson Electric Company, Electronics and Space Division, St. Louis, Mo.
S. J. Dwyer, III, is with the Department of Electrical Engineering, University of Missouri, Columbia, Mo.

analysis is given. Finally, Section IV contains examples of the use of the log-antilog technique for digital filter applications.

I. BINARY-TO-BINARY LOGARITHM CONVERSION

A simple method for the computation of the base two logarithm of a binary number was developed by Mitchell [1]. The method consists of encoding the binary number into a form from which the characteristic is easily determined and the mantissa is easily approximated.

Let N be a nonzero finite length binary number and let m and j represent the binary power of the most and least significant bits of N, respectively. The case of $N=0$ is easily handled separately. N may be written as

$$N = Z_m Z_{m-1} \cdots Z_{j+1} Z_j$$

with

$$Z_m = 0, 1; \quad m, j = 0, \pm 1, \cdots; \quad m \geq j.$$

Clearly,

$$2^{m+1} > N \geq 2^j.$$

N is also given by

$$N = \sum_{i=j}^{m} Z_i 2^i.$$

Now let Z_k be the most significant nonzero bit of N, $m \geq k \geq j$. Then,

$$N = 2^k + \sum_{i=j}^{k-1} Z_i 2^i.$$

Factoring out 2^k results in

$$N = 2^k \left\{ 1 + \sum_{i=j}^{k-1} Z_i 2^{i-k} \right\} = 2^k(1 + x)$$

where

$$x = \sum_{i=j}^{k-1} Z_i 2^{i-k} \quad \text{and} \quad 1 > x \geq 0 \text{ since } k \geq j.$$

Thus, N has been encoded into the form $N = 2^k(1+x)$. The base two logarithm of N is

$$\log_2 N = k + \log_2 (1 + x).$$

Reprinted from *IEEE Trans. Comput.*, vol. C-19, pp. 97–105, Feb. 1970.

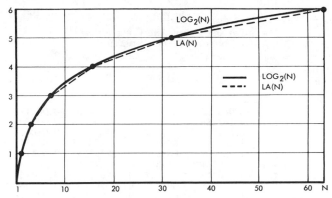

Fig. 1.   Piecewise linear approximation to binary logarithm.

Since $1 > x \geq 0$, the logarithm characteristic is k and the mantissa is only a function of x.

A linear approximation of $\log_2 N$ is of the form

$$LA(N) = k + ax + b.$$

The geometrical interpretation of this approximation is shown in Fig. 1 and consists of a piecewise linear approximation between the points where $\log_2 N$ attains integral values.

The linear coefficients a and b may be selected to maximize some return function. If simplicity is the desired return function, then $a=1$ and $b=0$ are the best coefficients. As shown by Mitchell, the maximum error

$$E = \log_2 N - LA(N)$$

with $a=1$, $b=0$, is 0.086.

If an easily computed set of coefficients is desired, then one may use the linear terms of a Taylor series expansion of $\log_2 (1+x)$ about the point $x = x_0$, $1 > x_0 \geq 0$ to obtain

$$a = \log_2 \epsilon /(1 + x_0)$$
$$b = \log_2 (1 + x_0) - x_0 \log_2 \epsilon /(1 + x_0).$$

The error in this approximation is

$$E = - x_0 \log_2 \epsilon - (1 + x_0) \log_2 (1 + x_0).$$

Combet *et al.* [2] described another method for selecting the coefficients. This method consists of partitioning the range of x into four parts and again making a piecewise linear approximation. The linear equations given in [2] were reportedly found by trial and error using a criteria of minimum error, and constraining the coefficients to be easily implemented with binary circuitry. That is, the coefficients were chosen to be fractions with integer numerators and power of two denominators. With a four subinterval partition, the single division error was reduced by a factor of six.

The authors propose that for many applications, including digital filtering, mean-square error is a desirable error criteria, although maximum error and easy implementation must also be considered. The coefficients for a linear least squares fit to $\log_2 (1+x)$ over, $1 > x_2 \geq x \geq x_1 \geq 0$, will now be developed.

The mean-squared error is defined as

$$\overline{E}^2 = \frac{1}{x_2 - x_1} \int_{x_1}^{x_2} \{\log_2 (1 + x) - (ax + b)\}^2 dx.$$

To minimize $\overline{E}^2$ with respect to a and b it is necessary that

$$\frac{\partial \overline{E}^2}{\partial a} = 0 = \int_{x_1}^{x_2} -2x\{\log_2 (1 + x) - (ax + b)\} dx$$

$$\frac{\partial \overline{E}^2}{\partial b} = 0 = \int_{x_1}^{x_2} -2\{\log_2 (1 + x) - (ax + b)\} dx.$$

Let

$$I_1 = \int_{x_1}^{x_2} \log_2 (1 + x) dx$$

$$= \log_2 \epsilon \{ Y \log_\epsilon Y - Y \} \Big|_{1+x_1}^{1+x_2}$$

$$I_2 = \int_{x_1}^{x_2} x \log_2 (1 + x) dx$$

$$= \log_2 \epsilon \left\{ \frac{Y^2}{2} \log_\epsilon Y - Y^2/4 \right\} \Big|_{1+x_1}^{1+x_2} - I_1,$$

then

$$a = \left\{ I_2 - (x_2 + x_1) I_1/2 \right\}$$

$$\Bigg/ \left\{ \frac{x_2^3 - x_1^3}{3} - \frac{(x_2^2 - x_1^2)(x_2 + x_1)}{4} \right\}$$

$$b = I_1/(x_2 - x_1) - a(x_1 + x_2)/2.$$

Thus, for any partition of the interval $[0, 1]$, the best linear mean-square coefficients can be determined and $\overline{E}^2$ evaluated. Also, the maximum error for any subinterval is easily determined. The coefficients, the mean-square error, and the maximum absolute error are given in Table I for 1, 2, 4, and 8 equispaced subinterval partitions.

For a particular realization, it is convenient to work with the linear equations in the form:

$$x + cx + d \quad \text{if } a \geq 1$$
$$x + c\bar{x} + d \quad \text{if } a < 1$$

TABLE I

MEAN-SQUARE ERROR AND COEFFICIENTS
FOR LOGARITHM APPROXIMATION

Number of Subintervals	Subinterval	a	b	$\overline{E}^2$	$|E_{\max}|$
1	1	0.984255	0.065176	0.641074E-3	0.065176
2	1	1.163555	0.021303	0.192903E-4	0.021303
	2	0.827788	0.181567	0.581653E-5	0.010518
4	1	1.285610	0.006243	0.278225E-6	0.006243
	2	1.050957	0.063330	0.387113E-6	0.004141
	3	0.888761	0.143537	0.642476E-6	0.002186
	4	0.770244	0.231857	0.289856E-7	0.002186
8	1	1.359165	0.001681	0.173267E-7	0.001681
	2	1.215426	0.019368	0.550871E-7	0.001371
	3	1.099427	0.048200	0.814192E-7	0.001129
	4	1.003868	0.083914	0.297152E-7	0.000933
	5	0.923414	0.124049	0.130118E-6	0.000794
	6	0.854749	0.166916	0.128720E-6	0.000695
	7	0.806959	0.202033	0.186847E-6	0.001232
	8	0.734065	0.265769	0.150003E-6	0.001186

TABLE II

LOGARITHM EQUATIONS

Range	Mantissa
$0 \leq x < 1/4$	$x^* = x + 37x/128 + 1/128$
$1/4 \leq x < 1/2$	$x^* = x + 3x/64 + 1/16$
$1/2 \leq x < 3/4$	$x^* = x + 7\bar{x}/64 + 1/32$
$3/4 \leq x < 1$	$x^* = x + 29\bar{x}/128$

where

$$\bar{x} = 1 - x.$$

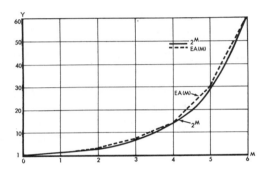

Fig. 2. Piecewise linear approximation to binary exponent.

Also, for simple binary circuitry, it is necessary to obtain c and d as sums of binary fractions. In general the number of bits necessary for an input N as previously defined is $m-j-1$. However, for a given application one may be able to use a smaller number of bits with only a slightly larger maximum or mean-square error.

The linear logarithm equations for a four subdivision realization are given in Table II. The coefficients are the minimum mean-square coefficients quantitized to seven bits. The maximum error, which was computed at the critical values and extrema, ranges over $-0.00782 < E_{\max} < 0.00994$. The realized maximum mean-squared error is $\overline{E}^2{}_{\max} = 3.33 \times 10^{-6}$.

II. ANTILOGARITHM CONVERSION

The following method of computing the antilogarithm is used by Mitchell [1].

Let

$$M = LA(N) = k + x$$

$$0 \leqq x < 1, \quad k \text{ an integer.}$$

Then

$$2^M = 2^k \cdot 2^x.$$

Since k is an integer, multiplication by 2^k is simply a shift operation. An approximation to 2^M is given by $EA(M) = 2^k(1+x)$. This approximation is shown in

Fig. 2 and consists of a piecewise linear approximation to 2^M between the points where M takes on integral values.

The authors propose an improved approximation to the antilogarithm conversion which allows the error to be reduced to any desired level at the cost of increased complexity. The method is similar to the logarithm conversion and consists of partitioning the interval, $0 \leq x < 1$, into subintervals and making linear approximations over these subintervals. Mean-square error is again used as the error criteria. Maximum error is also computed.

The linear least squares fit to 2^x over the interval, $0 \leq x_1 \leq x \leq x_2 < 1$, will now be developed. The linear mean-squared error is defined as

$$\overline{E}^2 = \frac{1}{x_2 - x_1} \int_{x_1}^{x_2} \{2^x - (ax + b)\}^2 dx.$$

To minimize $\overline{E}^2$ with respect to a and b it is necessary that

$$\frac{\partial \overline{E}^2}{\partial a} = 0 = \int_{x_1}^{x_2} -2x\{2^x - (ax + b)\} dx$$

and

$$\frac{\partial \overline{E}^2}{\partial b} = 0 = \int_{x_1}^{x_2} -2\{2^x - (ax + b)\} dx.$$

218

TABLE III

MEAN-SQUARE ERROR AND COEFFICIENTS
FOR ANTILOGARITHM APPROXIMATION

Number of Subintervals	Subintervals	a	b	E^{-2}	$\lvert E_{\max} \rvert$
1	1	0.992089	0.946650	0.656127E-3	0.061261
2	1	0.826852	0.988453	0.813603E-5	0.012333
	2	1.169200	0.813322	0.143051E-4	0.017487
4	1	0.756609	0.997295	0.894069E-7	0.002759
	2	0.900147	0.960905	0.283122E-6	0.003275
	3	1.068757	0.876172	0.23818E-6	0.004054
	4	1.273014	0.722413	0.730156E-6	0.004519
8	1	0.726814	0.999170	0.223517E-7	0.000839
	2	0.787594	0.991472	0.223517E-7	0.000846
	3	0.859510	0.973650	0.372529E-7	0.000872
	4	0.945204	0.941145	0.149011E-7	0.001242
	5	1.021377	0.902764	0.134110E-6	0.001095
	6	1.110733	0.847371	0.208616E-6	0.001372
	7	1.221244	0.764536	0.819563E-7	0.001323
	8	1.331134	0.667864	0.163912E-6	0.001400

TABLE IV

ANTILOGARITHM EQUATIONS

$0 \leq x < 1/4$	$Y = x + 1/4\bar{x} + 3/4$
$1/4 \leq x < 1/2$	$Y = x + 13/128\bar{x} + 55/64$
$1/2 \leq x < 3/4$	$Y = x + 9/128x + 7/8$
$3/4 \leq x < 1$	$Y = x + 35/128x + 23/32$

Let

$$I_1 = \int_{x_1}^{x_2} 2^x dx = \log_2 \epsilon \{2^{x_2} - 2^{x_1}\}$$

$$I_2 = \int_{x_1}^{x_2} x 2^x dx = 2^x \left[\frac{x \log_\epsilon 2 - 1}{(\log_\epsilon 2)^2} \right]\Big|_{x_1}^{x_2}.$$

Then

$$a = \left\{ I_2 - \frac{(x_2 + x_1)}{2} I_1 \right\} \Big/ \left\{ \frac{(x_2^3 - x_1^3)}{3} - \frac{(x_2^2 - x_1^2)(x_1 + x_2)}{4} \right\}$$

$$b = \left\{ I_1 - a \frac{(x_2^2 - x_1^2)}{2} \right\} / (x_2 - x_1).$$

Thus, for any partition of $[0, 1]$, the linear mean-square error coefficients a and b may be determined and $\bar{E}^2$ evaluated. The absolute maximum error may also be determined over each subinterval. These values are given in Table III for 1, 2, 4, and 8 subinterval partitions.

The linear antilogarithm equations for a four subdivision realization are given in Table IV. The coefficients are the mean-square coefficients quantized to seven bits. The maximum error ranges over

$$-0.00327 < E_{\max} < 0.00796;$$

the realized maximum mean-squared error is $\bar{E}^2_{\max} = 1.475 \times 10^{-6}$.

III. ERROR ANALYSIS

In this section, an error analysis is given for several cases in which a log-antilog conversion would be desirable. The first case considered will be the product of two variables. Next, a special case of a product of a constant and a variable is considered. This special case arises in many digital filter applications. Finally, the error for a quotient of two variables is considered.

This analysis is mainly concerned with errors due to the approximation. Quantization error, truncation error, and coefficient error have been dealt with in other papers and would depend on the actual hardware used to implement the conversions. For one of the authors' applications [3] an exact digital simulation was made to study these effects.

A. Product Error

Suppose that the log-antilog conversion was used to approximate the product of two numbers. How much error would be incurred? Let M_1 and M_2 represent two binary numbers which are encoded into the form:

$$M_1 = 2^{k_1}(1 + x_1) \quad \text{where } 0 \leq x_1 < 1, \, k_1 \text{ an integer}$$

$$M_2 = 2^{k_2}(1 + x_2) \quad \text{where } 0 \leq x_2 < 1, \, k_2 \text{ an integer.}$$

The approximate binary logarithms, denoted by LA, are given by

$$LA(M_1) = k_1 + x_1 + y_1$$

$$LA(M_2) = k_2 + x_2 + y_2$$

where y_1 and y_2 are the linear correction terms, i.e.,

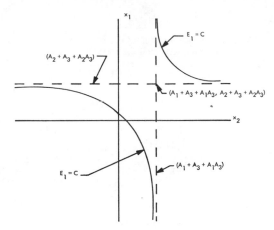

Fig. 3.   Curve of constant error $E_1 = C$.

$$y_1 = a_1 x_1 + b_1$$

$$y_2 = a_2 x_2 + b_2.$$

The values of a_i and b_i, $i = 1, 2$, are constants over a certain interval of x_i and are given in Table II. No carry can occur in the sum $x_i + y_i$ with the coefficients given in Table II so that

$$0 \leq' x_1 + y_1 < 1$$

$$0 \leq x_2 + y_2 < 1.$$

Adding the approximate logarithms of M_1 and M_2 gives the approximate logarithm LP of the product $P = M_1 M_2$. Thus,

$$LP = k_1 + k_2 + x_1 + y_1 + x_2 + y_2.$$

Since a carry from the mantissa to the characteristic can occur, there are two cases to consider.

For Case 1, no carry: $x_1 + y_1 + x_2 + y_2 < 1$.
For Case 2, carry: $x_1 + y_1 + x_2 + y_2 \geq 1$.

Case 1: The approximate binary exponent $EA(P)$ is given by

$$EA(P) = 2^{k_1 + k_2}(1 + x_1 + x_2 + y_1 + y_2 + z_{12})$$

where z_{12} is the linear correction term, i.e.,

$$z_{12} = a_3(x_1 + x_2 + y_1 + y_2) + b_3.$$

Case 2:

$$EA(P) = 2^{k_1 + k_2 + 1}(x_1 + x_2 + y_1 + y_2 + z_{12})$$

where z_{12} is the linear correction term, i.e.,

$$z_{12} = a_3(x_1 + y_1 + x_2 + y_2 - 1) + b_3.$$

The coefficients a_3 and b_3 are constants over certain regions and are given in Table IV. The error in using the approximate product is given by

$$E = P - EA(P) = M_1 M_2 - EA(P).$$

Case 1:

$$E = 2^{k_1 + k_2}\{(1 + x_1)(1 + x_2)$$
$$- (1 + x_1 + y_1 + x_2 + y_2 + z_{12})\}$$

$$E = 2^{k_1 + k_2 + 1}\{x_1 \cdot x_2 - (y_1 + y_2 + z_{12})\}.$$

Let the normalized error be defined as

$$E_1 = E/2^{k_1 + k_2}.$$

Case 2:

$$E = 2^{k_1 + k_2 + 1}\{(1 + x_2)(1 + x_1)$$
$$- 2(x_1 + x_2 + y_1 + y_2 + z_{12})\}$$

$$E = 2^{k_1 + k_2}\{(1 - x_1)(1 - x_2)/2 - (y_1 + y_2 + z_{12})\}.$$

For this case, let the normalized error be defined as

$$E_2 = E/2^{\{k_1 + k_2 + 1\}}$$

A direct attempt at finding the critical points of E_1 and E_2 would involve setting the partial derivatives equal to zero. For Case 1,

$$\frac{\partial E_1}{\partial x_1} = x_2 - a_1 - a_3 - a_1 a_3$$

$$\frac{\partial E_1}{\partial x_2} = x_1 - a_2 - a_3 - a_2 a_3$$

which would indicate that the critical point is

$$(x_1, x_2) = (a_2 + a_3 + a_2 a_3, a_1 + a_3 + a_1 a_3).$$

However, this point never falls in the interval of interest for the given coefficients. This fact is clearly indicated by the $E_1 = $ constant curves shown in Fig. 3. A similar result holds for E_2. If

$$E_1 = C = x_1 x_2 - (a_1 + a_3 + a_1 a_3)x_1 - (a_2 + a_3 + a_2 a_3)x_2$$
$$- (b_1 + b_2)(1 + a_3) - b_3,$$

then

$$x_1 = \frac{(a_2 + a_3 + a_2 a_3)\left\{x_2 + \dfrac{C + (b_1 + b_2)(1 + a_3) + b_3}{a_2 + a_3 + a_2 a_3}\right\}}{x_2 - (a_1 + a_3 + a_1 a_3)}.$$

A graph of this equation is shown in Fig. 3.

In fact, E is a hyperbolic paraboloid and is a monotonic function over the regions of interest, and therefore, it attains its maximum and minimum values at the boundary of the region.

The maximum absolute values of the normalized error E over the 16 regions of x_1 and x_2 are given in Table V. The maximum error is 0.01907 and occurs at $x_1 = x_2 = \frac{1}{4}$. The values in Table V were arrived at by computing E at 4096 equispaced points in the (x_1, x_2) plane. The maximum product error is only $\frac{1}{4}$ as large as the product error computed by Mitchell [1] for single interval approximations to the logarithm and exponential function.

B. Product Error—Special Case

The special case of the product of a variable and a constant will now be considered. This case arises in all linear constant coefficient digital filter applications. It is assumed that the logarithm of the constant is exact. As one would expect, the resulting product error is smaller.

Let N and C represent two binary numbers encoded into the form

$$N = 2^{k_1}(1 + x_1)$$
$$C = 2^{k_2}(1 + x_2).$$

The approximate logarithm of N is given by

$$LA(N) = k_1 + x_1 + y_1 \quad \text{where } y_1 = a_1 x_1 + b_2.$$

The binary logarithm of C is given by

$$\log_2 (C) = k_2 + \log_2 (1 + x_2).$$

The approximate logarithm of the product $P = CN$ is given by

$$LP = k_1 + k_2 + x_1 + y_1 + \log_2 (1 + x_2).$$

Two cases must again be considered.

For Case 1, no carry: $x_1 + y_1 + \log_2 (1 + x_2) < 1$.
For Case 2, carry: $x_1 + y_1 + \log_2 (1 + x_2) \geq 1$.

The approximate binary exponent of P is given by:

Case 1:

$$EA(P) = 2^{k_1 + k_2}\{1 + x_1 + y_1 + \log_2 (1 + x_2) + z_{12}\}$$

where

$$z_{12} = a_3\{x_1 + y_1 + \log_2 (1 + x_2)\} + b_3.$$

Case 2:

$$EA(P) = 2^{k_1 + k_2}\{x_1 + y_1 + \log_2 (1 + x_2) + z_{12}\}$$

where

$$z_{12} = a_3\{x_1 + y_1 + \log_2 (1 + x_2) - 1\} + b_3.$$

The product error is defined as

$$E = P - EA(P).$$

Case 1:

$$E = 2^{k_1 + k_2}\{(1 + x_1)(1 + x_2)$$
$$- (1 + x_1 + y_1 + \log_2 (1 + x_2) + z_{12})\}.$$

Let the normalized error be defined as

$$E = E/(2^{k_1 + k_2}).$$

Case 2:

$$E = 2^{k_1 + k_2 + 1}\{(1 + x_1)(1 + x_2)/2$$
$$- (x_1 + y_1 + \log_2 (1 + x_2) + z_{12})\}.$$

Let the normalized error be defined by

$$E_2 = E/[2^{k_1 + k_2 + 1}].$$

The normalized error is again a monotonic function over certain regions and attains its maximum and minimum values at the boundaries of these regions. The maximum absolute values of the error are shown in Table VI. The largest error is 0.01321 which occurs at $x_1 = 25/64$, $x_2 = 14/32$ and is substantially smaller than the product error for the general case. Although this point (x_1, x_2) is not on the boundary of one of the 16 main regions, it is on a product boundary since a_3 changes inside the region.

C. Quotient Error

The error incurred in a division operation will now be considered. Let the dividend D_1 and the divisor D_2 be binary numbers encoded into the form

$$D_1 = 2^{k_1}(1 + x_1), \quad 0 \leq x_1 < 1$$
$$D_2 = 2^{k_1}(1 + x_2), \quad 0 \leq x_2 < 1.$$

The approximate logarithms of D_1 and D_2 are given by

$$LA(D_1) = k_1 + x_1 + y_1, \quad y_1 = a_1 x_1 + b_1$$
$$LA(D_2) = k_2 + x_2 + y_2, \quad y_2 = a_2 x_2 + b_2.$$

Subtracting these logarithms gives the approximate logarithm LQ of the quotient $Q = D_1/D_2$:

$$LQ = k_1 - k_2 + x_1 - x_2 + y_1 - y_2.$$

TABLE V
MODULUS VALUES OF PRODUCT ERROR

X_2 \ X_1	$0 \leq X_1 < \frac{1}{4}$	$\frac{1}{4} \leq X_1 < \frac{1}{2}$	$\frac{1}{2} \leq X_1 < \frac{3}{4}$	$\frac{3}{4} \leq X_1 < 1$
$0 \leq X_2 < \frac{1}{4}$	0.01907	0.01280	0.01059	0.01270
$\frac{1}{4} \leq X_2 < \frac{1}{2}$	0.01280	0.01758	0.01163	0.00838
$\frac{1}{2} \leq X_2 < \frac{3}{4}$	0.01059	0.01163	0.00773	0.00994
$\frac{3}{4} \leq X_2 < 1$	0.01277	0.00838	0.00994	0.01531

TABLE VI
MODULUS VALUES OF PRODUCT ERROR SPECIAL CASE

X_2 \ X_1	$0 \leq X_1 < \frac{1}{4}$	$\frac{1}{4} \leq X_1 < \frac{1}{2}$	$\frac{1}{2} \leq X_1 < \frac{3}{4}$	$\frac{3}{4} \leq X_1 < 1$
$0 \leq X_2 < \frac{1}{4}$	0.01046	0.01035	0.01010	0.00932
$\frac{1}{4} \leq X_2 < \frac{1}{2}$	0.01229	0.01321	0.01150	0.00728
$\frac{1}{2} \leq X_2 < \frac{3}{4}$	0.01168	0.01103	0.00677	0.00994
$\frac{3}{4} \leq X_2 < 1$	0.01276	0.00742	0.01000	0.01100

TABLE VII
MODULUS VALUES OF QUOTIENT ERROR

X_2 \ X_1	$0 \leq X_1 < \frac{1}{4}$	$\frac{1}{4} \leq X_1 < \frac{1}{2}$	$\frac{1}{2} \leq X_1 < \frac{3}{4}$	$\frac{3}{4} \leq X_1 < 1$
$0 \leq X_2 < \frac{1}{4}$	0.00985	0.00741	0.00692	0.00590
$\frac{1}{4} \leq X_2 < \frac{1}{2}$	0.01500	0.00724	0.00490	0.00364
$\frac{1}{2} \leq X_2 < \frac{3}{4}$	0.01779	0.00724	0.00657	0.00497
$\frac{3}{4} \leq X_2 < 1$	0.01776	0.00779	0.00612	0.00594

Again, two cases must be considered depending on the occurrence of a borrow from the characteristic to the mantissa.

Case 1, no borrow: $x_1 + y_1 \geq x_2 + y_2$.

Case 2, borrow occurs: $x_1 + y_1 < x_2 + y_2$.

Case 1:

$$EA(Q) = 2^{k_1 - k_2}\{1 + x_1 + y_1 - x_2 - y_2 + z_{12}\}$$

where

$$z_{12} = a_3\{x_1 + y_1 - x_2 - y_2\} + b_3.$$

Case 2:

$$EA(Q) = 2^{k_1 - k_2 - 1}\{2 + x_1 + y_1 - x_2 - y_2 + z_{12}\}$$

where

$$z_{12} = a_3\{1 + x_1 + y_1 - x_2 - y_2\} + b_3.$$

The actual quotient is given by

$$Q = D_1/D_2 = 2^{k_1 - k_2}\left\{\frac{(1 + x_1)}{(1 + x_2)}\right\}.$$

The error is defined as

$$E = Q - EA(Q)$$

which for the two cases is the following.

Case 1:

$$E = 2^{k_1 - k_2}\left\{\frac{(1 + x_1)}{(1 + x_2)} - (1 + x_1 + y_1 - x_2 - y_2 + z_{12})\right\}.$$

Let the normalized error be defined by

$$E_1 = E/2^{k_1 - k_2}.$$

Case 2:

$$E = 2^{k_1 - k_2}\left\{\frac{(1 + x_1)}{(1 + x_2)} - 1/2(1 + x_1 + y_1 - x_2 - y_2 + z_{12})\right\}.$$

Again let the normalized error be defined by

$$E_2 = E/(2^{k_1 - k_2}).$$

The maximum value of E for the 16 regions of the x_1, x_2 plane is listed in Table VII. This error is five times smaller than the quotient error computed by Mitchell.

IV. APPLICATIONS TO DIGITAL FILTERING

To illustrate the applications in which the log-antilog conversion would be advantageous, three examples are given. The first example shows that for a single multiplication a cobweb array is simpler. The second example illustrates how the log-antilog conversion can be used advantageously for a parallel filter bank. The last example of a multiplicative filter illustrates a situation in which a log-antilog conversion is necessary.

Example 1—Nonrecursive Digital Filter: The difference equation of a nonrecursive digital filter [4] may be written as

$$Y_n = \sum_{i=0}^{N-1} a_i x_{n-i}.$$

Using the log-antilog conversion the computation may be performed by

$$Y_n = \sum_{i=0}^{N-1} \exp\{\log|a_i| + \log|x_{n-i}|\}.$$

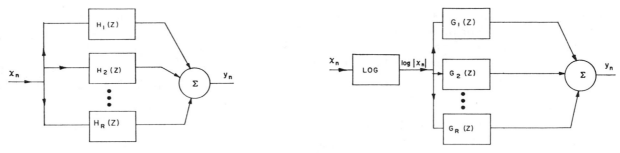

Fig. 4.   Parallel filter bank.

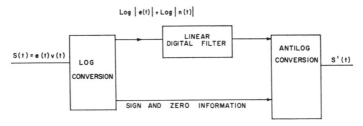

Fig. 5.   Multiplicative digital filter.

The special cases of $a_i \leq 0$ or $x_{n-i} \leq 0$ are easily handled by either complementing or clearing the antilogarithm result. Also, the computation of $\log |a_i|$ may be done a priori.

The tradeoff between the two computations is: a direct multiplication versus a log conversion, an addition, and an exponentiation. A comparison of hardware complexity and computation time can be made for the particular example of multiplying two six-bit numbers. An indicator of hardware complexity is the number of full adder circuits required. For a cobweb array multiplier, 30 adders are required if all product bits are retained; however, only 21 adders are required if the product is truncated to six bits. For the log conversion, twelve adders are required, for the log addition eight are used, and for the antilog conversion ten are needed, or a total of 30 adders are required to obtain 6-bit accuracy. Thus, for a multiplication the cobweb array is less complex and simpler than the log-antilog conversion.

Example 2—Parallel Digital Filter Bank: A particular digital filter configuration which often arises is the parallel filter bank which may be described by a z-transfer function of the form

$$H(z) = H_1(z) + H_2(z) + \cdots + H_r(z).$$

The block diagram of this filter is shown in Fig. 4(a). If each of the H_i are of the nonrecursive type, then the log conversion of x_i may be performed first as shown in Fig. 4(b). The resulting filters, G_i, would then require only an addition and an exponentiation for each multiplication. If any of the H_i are of the recursive [5] type

described by a difference equation of the form

$$Y_n = \sum_{i=1}^{N-1} a_i x_{n-i} - \sum_{i=1}^{M} b_i Y_{n-i},$$

then, again the computation of $\log x_i$ may be moved ahead of the remaining filters.

Once more assuming 6-bit numbers, the cobweb array truncated to 6 bits would require 21 adders for each multiplication. An addition and exponentiation require 18 adders. Thus, if the number of filters R is four or more, the log-antilog conversion would require less hardware.

Example 3—A Multiplicative Digital Filter: Recently, Oppenheim *et al.* [6] presented a general method for nonlinear filtering of multiplied and convolved signals. The multiplicative techniques were applied to audio dynamic range compression and expansion and image enhancement. The block diagram of a multiplicative filter is shown in Fig. 5. If the input signal $S(t)$ consists of the product of two components $e(t)$ and $b(t)$, then the logarithm conversion reduces the process to the familiar additive process which may be filtered using linear techniques. The antilogarithm conversion reconstitutes the filtered signals.

The log and antilog conversions developed in this paper could be used for any digital realization of the multiplicative filter.

V. Summary

Algorithms for approximate binary logarithms and exponents and some applications of these algorithms to digital filtering have been described. Since the maximum product and division errors occur as percentages of the operands, these algorithms are suited for high-speed hardware rather than GP computer applications.

One such application is real time digital filtering. The computations involved are usually sums of products of a variable and constant coefficients. Using the log-antilog algorithms gives complete freedom of coefficient selection. For single multiplications a cobweb array multiplier is simpler. However, for other configurations, such as a parallel digital filter bank, the log-antilog technique is less complex. Also, there are applications, such as multiplicative digital filters, where log and exponent conversions are necessary.

REFERENCES

[1] J. N. Mitchell, Jr., "Computer multiplication and division using binary logarithms," *IRE Trans. Electronic Computers*, vol. EC-11, pp. 512–517, August 1962.
[2] M. Combet, H. Van Zonneveld, and L. Verbeek, "Computation of the base two logarithm of binary numbers," *IEEE Trans. Electronic Computers*, vol. EC-14, pp. 863–867, December 1965.
[3] E. L. Hall, D. D. Lynch, and R. E. Young, "A digital modified discrete Fourier transform Doppler radar processor," *1968 EASCON Rec.*, pp. 150–159.
[4] J. F. Kaiser and F. Kuo, *System Analysis by Digital Computer*. New York: Wiley, 1966, pp. 218–277.
[5] C. M. Rader and B. Gold, "Digital filter design techniques in the frequency domain," *Proc. IEEE*, vol. 55, pp. 149–171, February 1967.
[6] A. V. Oppenheim, R. W. Schafer, and T. G. Stockham, Jr., "Nonlinear filtering of multiplied and convolved signals," *Proc. IEEE*, vol. 56, pp. 1264–1291, August 1968.

A 40-ns 17-Bit by 17-Bit Array Multiplier

STYLIANOS D. PEZARIS, MEMBER, IEEE

Abstract—A high-speed array multiplier generating the full 34-bit product of two 17-bit signed (2's complement) numbers in 40 ns is described. The multiplier uses a special 2-bit gated adder circuit with anticipated carry. Negative numbers are handled by considering their highest order bit as negative, all other bits as positive, and adding negative partial products directly through appropriate circuits. The propagation of sum and carry signals is such that sum delays do not significantly contribute to the overall multiplier delay.

Index Terms—Array multiplier, Dadda's multiplier, digital multiplier, fast multiplier, parallel multiplier, Wallace's multiplier.

I. INTRODUCTION

High-speed multipliers are useful for many digital filtering applications. To obtain highest possible speed, array multipliers, rather than conventional sequential add-and-shift multipliers, must be used. The Lincoln Laboratory array multiplier described in this paper was designed with emphasis on speed, with the restriction, however, that speed should not be pushed so far that state of the art problems are encountered. Thus, the circuits used are current-steering MECL-like with speed intermediate between the MECL II and MECL III lines. They are packaged in conventional dual-in-line 14-pin packages. Power dissipation per package is a reasonable 350 mW. Interconnections between packages are made through a conventional 4-layer printed circuit board.

In spite of these restrictions, the multiplier tested yields the full 34-bit product of two 17-bit positive or negative numbers in just 40 ns. This high performance was achieved primarily by the following means.

1) A special 2-bit gated adder circuit with 2-bit anticipated carry is used.

2) Negative (2's complement) numbers are handled by treating their highest order bit as negative, all other bits as positive, and adding negative partial products directly by two variants of the basic 2-bit gated adder circuit.

3) The propagation paths for sum and carry signals between adders are such that sum delays do not significantly contribute to the overall multiplier delay.

These three main characteristics of the design are discussed in the following sections.

II. THE L101, A 2-BIT GATED ADDER WITH ANTICIPATED CARRY

The L101 is a Lincoln Laboratory designed circuit that forms the heart of the multiplier. It is a 2-bit adder with gated inputs and 2-bit anticipated carry. The gated inputs are used for forming partial products. Carry delay is 1.6 ns. Sum delay is 2.8 ns. The circuitry used is ECL, similar to the Motorola MECL line.

Manuscript received June 9, 1970. This work was sponsored by the Department of the Air Force.

The author is with the M.I.T. Lincoln Laboratory, Lexington, Mass. 02173.

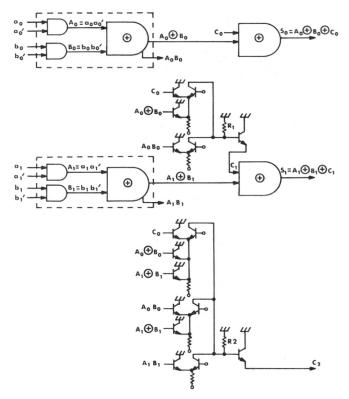

Fig. 1. Basic characteristics of the L101 2-bit adder.

The basic characteristics of the L101 are shown in Fig. 1. It consists of four EXCLUSIVE-OR gates and two carry circuits. The EXCLUSIVE-OR gates use two-level series gating (they are similar to the MECL MC1030 gates). The partial products, designated as A_0, B_0, A_1, and B_1 in the figure, are generated by duplicate transistors at the inputs of the corresponding EXCLUSIVE-OR gates. This simple way of generating partial products requires *negative* logic (logical ONE = -1.6 V, logical ZERO = -0.8 V); except for this input gating the adder would of course operate equally well with either negative or positive logic.

The two carry circuits generate the carry C_1 into the second stage, and the output carry C_2, according to the equations (C_0 is the input carry):

$$C_1 = C_0(A_0 \oplus B_0) + A_0B_0$$
$$C_2 = C_0(A_0 \oplus B_0)(A_1 \oplus B_1) + A_0B_0(A_1 \oplus B_1) + A_1B_1.$$

The signals $A_0 \oplus B_0$, $A_1 \oplus B_1$, A_0B_0, and A_1B_1 are generated by the two input EXCLUSIVE-OR gates. To evaluate C_1 and C_2 in terms of C_0 and the $A_0 \oplus B_0$, $A_1 \oplus B_1$, A_0B_0, A_1B_1 we must evaluate the above AND-OR functions. In general, evaluation of an AND-OR function requires two gate delays. In this case, however, the terms to be ORed are mutually exclusive, and therefore the OR function can be evaluated by simply adding the output currents of the AND

Reprinted from *IEEE Trans. Comput.*, vol. C-20, pp. 442–447, Apr. 1971.

225

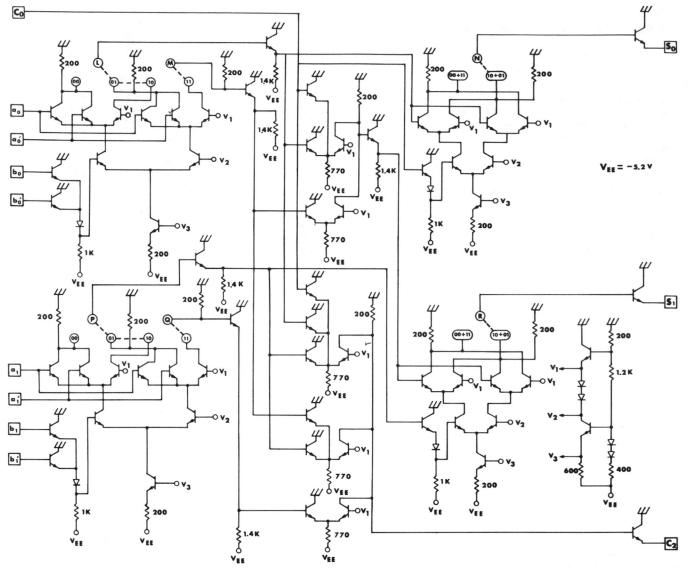

Fig. 2. Schematic of the L101 2-bit adder. (Dotted lines are second-level metal interconnections, see Fig. 5.)

stages by a resistor (R_1, R_2 in Fig. 1), thus obtaining C_1 and C_2 with (almost) a *single* gate delay.

In addition to the L101, two variants of it, the L102 and L103, that add negative partial products are also used in the multiplier. With a view towards facilitating the discussion of these circuits in the next section, we introduce here the following notation.

L101 has five input variables A_1, B_1, A_0, B_0, C_0, and three output variables C_2, S_1, S_0. If we think of these variables as binary *arithmetic*, rather than binary *logical* variables, then, given any inputs A_1, B_1, A_0, B_0, C_0, the L101 produces outputs C_2, S_1, S_0 satisfying

$$A_1 + B_1 + A_0 + B_0 + C_0 = C_2 + S_1 + S_0.$$

In this equation, of course, A_1 can have any one of two allowable values, B_1 similarly, A_0 similarly, etc. To indicate that a binary arithmetic variable P has the possible values u and v, where, in general, $u \gtreqless 0$ and $v \gtreqless 0$, we use the notation

$$P = (u, v)$$

with the first value u corresponding to the logical ZERO state (-0.8V), and the second value v to the logical ONE state (-1.6V). A choice of values for the L101 variables is

$$A_1 = (0, 2), B_1 = (0, 2), A_0 = (0, 1), B_0 = (0, 1),$$
$$C_0 = (0, 1), C_2 = (0, 4), S_1 = (0, 2), S_0 = (0, 1).$$

This is clearly not the only possible choice. For example, since the circuit performs a linear arithmetic operation, multiplication of all these values by the same arbitrary constant would give us another possible choice. Multiplying by -1 we obtain the useful choice

$$(0, -2), (0, -2), (0, -1), (0, -1), (0, -1),$$
$$(0, -4), (0, -2), (0, -1).$$

To indicate the arithmetic operation that the adder can perform, and a particular choice of values for its variables we use the notation

$$(0, 2) + (0, 2) + (0, 1) + (0, 1) + (0, 1)$$
$$= (0, 4) + (0, 2) + (0, 1).$$

This notation proves to be very convenient for discussing adders such as the L102 and L103, whose input values are not all of the same sign.

The L101 circuit schematic is shown in Fig. 2. Typical output pull-down resistors used are 1K. The dotted lines connecting the points L to 01 and 10, M to 11, N to $10+01$, P to 01 and 10, Q to 11, and R to $10+01$ are second-level metal connections that make the circuit be an L101 rather than an L102 or L103. The connections required for the L102 and L103 are described in the next section.

Fig. 3 shows the circuit chip. The chip's size is 35-by 45-mil. Two levels of metallization are used. The masks for the circuit were designed at Lincoln Laboratory and the circuits were produced by the Microelectronics Division of Philco-Ford, Blue Bell, Pa.

III. ARRAY MULTIPLICATION OF 2's COMPLEMENT NUMBERS

Given $N+1$ binary arithmetic variables $X_0, X_1, \cdots, X_N$, with $X_0, \cdots, X_{N-1}$ having the possible values $(0, 1)$ and X_N the possible values $(0, -1)$, any integer X within the range

$$-2^N \leq X \leq 2^N - 1$$

has a unique expansion

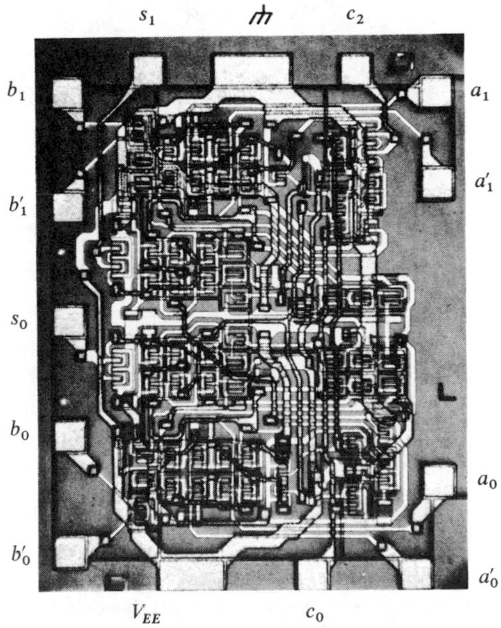

Fig. 3. The L101 2-bit adder chip.

$$X = \sum_{n=0}^{N} X_n 2^n$$

in terms of the $X_0, \cdots, X_N$. This expansion is known as the 2's complement representation of X and numbers given by this representation are called 2's complement numbers.

The product of two 2's complement numbers X, Y

$$X = \sum_{n=0}^{N} X_n 2^n, \quad X_0, X_1, \cdots, X_{N-1} = 0, 1, \quad X_N = 0, -1$$

$$Y = \sum_{n=0}^{N} Y_n 2^n, \quad Y_0, Y_1, \cdots, Y_{N-1} = 0, 1, \quad Y_N = 0, -1$$

can of course be found by first converting them to positive numbers, then multiplying these positive numbers, and finally converting the product to a negative number if $X \cdot Y < 0$. This, however, is not the fastest method, especially so if the numbers X and Y are being calculated by adders, so that their highest order bits become available last. In the

Fig. 4 illustrates this method by showing a 5-bit by 5-bit carry-save multiplier using single-bit adders. In the figure, adders are represented by circles. Signals representing num-

Type I (all positive inputs), performing	$(0, 1) + (0, 2) + (0, 1)$	$= (0, 2) + (0, 1)$	
Type II (one negative input), performing	$(0, -1) + (0, 1) + (0, 1)$	$= (0, 2) + (0, -1)$	
Type II' (two negative inputs), performing	$(0, 1) + (0, -1) + (0, -1)$	$= (0, -2) + (0, 1)$	
Type I' (all negative inputs), performing	$(0, -1) + (0, -1) + (0, -1)$	$= (0, -2) + (0, -1)$	

bers ≥ 0 are identified by black arrows, signals representing numbers ≤ 0 by hollow arrows. All $X_i Y_k$ are ≥ 0 except the $X_0 Y_4$, $X_1 Y_4$, $X_2 Y_4$, $X_3 Y_4$, $X_4 Y_0$, $X_4 Y_1$, $X_4 Y_2$, $X_4 Y_3$ that are ≤ 0. The figure makes evident that we need the following types of adders.

Types I and I' correspond to identical truth tables (because if $x + y + z = u + v$, then $-x - y - z = -u - v$) and therefore to identical circuits. Similarly, Types II and II' correspond to identical circuits. Thus, *two* types of circuits are required for this multiplier. (Note, however, that we might require more than one type of "Type II" circuits if the electrical characteristics of the three inputs are not identical. For example, if the last input is the fastest, we might require a $(0, -1) + (0, 1) + (0, 1)$ *and* a $(0, 1) + (0, 1) + (0, -1)$ circuit.)

For implementing this method with 2-bit adders *three* types of circuits (the L101, L102, L103) are required, as seen in the next section. The arithmetic operations performed by these three types are given below, in the notation introduced in Section II.

	A_1	B_1	A_0	B_0	C_0	C_2	S_1	S_0
L101:	$(0, 2) + (0,$	$2) + (0, 1) + (0,$		$1) + (0, 1)$	$= (0, 4) + (0,$		$2) + (0,$	$1)$
L102:	$(0, 2) + (0,$	$-2) + (0, 1) + (0,$		$1) + (0, 1)$	$= (0, 4) + (0,$		$-2) + (0,$	$1)$
L103:	$(0, 2) + (0,$	$-2) + (0, 1) + (0,$		$-1) + (0, 1)$	$= (0, 4) + (0,$		$-2) + (0,$	$-1)$

Lincoln multiplier the numbers X and Y are multiplied directly, by adding the partial products $X_i Y_k$ *with their signs* through appropriate circuits.

Thus, L102 evaluates

$$0 - 2 + 1 + 1 + 1 \quad \text{as} \quad 0 + 0 + 1,$$

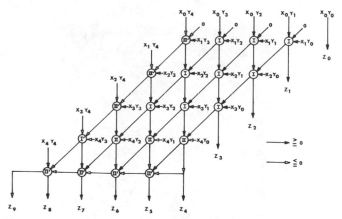

Fig. 4. A 5-bit array multiplier that multiplies signed (2's complement) numbers by adding negative partial products directly.

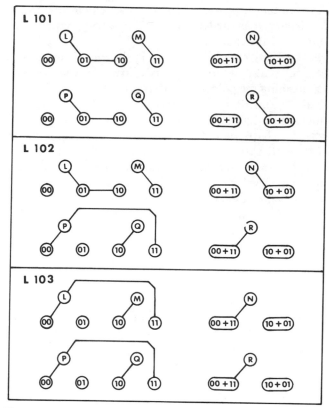

Fig. 5. Second-level metal interconnections that cause the basic 2-bit adder chip to become an L101, L102, or L103 adder.

$$2 + 0 + 0 + 0 + 0 \quad \text{as} \quad 4 - 2 + 0, \quad \text{etc.}$$

and L103 evaluates

$$2 - 2 + 1 - 1 + 1 \quad \text{as} \quad 4 - 2 - 1, \quad \text{etc.}$$

By writing out the truth table for the L102 we can verify that the logic performed by it is correctly expressed by the equations

$$S_0 = A_0 \oplus B_0 \oplus C_0$$
$$C_1 = C_0(A_0 \oplus B_0) + A_0 B_0$$
$$S_1 = C_1(\bar{A}_1 \bar{B}_1 + A_1 B_1) + \bar{C}_1(\bar{A}_1 B_1 + A_1 \bar{B}_1)$$
$$C_2 = C_0(A_0 \oplus B_0)(\bar{A}_1 \bar{B}_1 + A_1 B_1)$$
$$\quad + A_0 B_0(\bar{A}_1 \bar{B}_1 + A_1 B_1) + A_1 \bar{B}_1$$

and for the L103 by the equations

$$S_0 = C_0(\bar{A}_0 \bar{B}_0 + A_0 B_0) + \bar{C}_0(\bar{A}_0 B_0 + A_0 \bar{B}_0)$$
$$C_1 = C_0(\bar{A}_0 \bar{B}_0 + A_0 B_0) + A_0 \bar{B}_0$$
$$S_1 = C_1(\bar{A}_1 \bar{B}_1 + A_1 B_1) + \bar{C}_1(\bar{A}_1 B_1 + A_1 \bar{B}_1)$$
$$C_2 = C_0(\bar{A}_0 \bar{B}_0 + A_0 B_0)(\bar{A}_1 \bar{B}_1 + A_1 B_1)$$
$$\quad + A_0 \bar{B}_0(\bar{A}_1 \bar{B}_1 + A_1 B_1) + A_1 \bar{B}_1.$$

These logic functions[1] can be evaluated with a basic L101 chip by modifying some second level metal interconnections that select outputs from the EXCLUSIVE-OR gates. The interconnections required are shown in Fig. 5.[2]

---

[1] The sum functions are identical for all three (L101, L102, L103) circuits; they are written above in different forms to indicate the way in which each circuit evaluates them.

[2] One might ask if the same variation of second-level metal technique can be used to produce, from an L101, adders such as

| A_1 | B_1 | A_0 | B_0 | C_0 | C_2 | S_1 | S_0 |

$$(0, 2) + (0, 2) + (0, 1) + (0, 1) + (0, -1) = (0, 4) + (0, 2) + (0, -1).$$

The answer to this question is no. If the input carry is of opposite sign to both other first stage inputs, or if the carry to the second stage is of opposite sign to both other second stage inputs, the scheme does not work. Fortunately, the design of the multiplier does not require such adders.

IV. THE OVERALL LOGICAL ORGANIZATION OF THE 40-ns MULTIPLIER

Fig. 6 shows a 9-bit multiplier of identical overall logical organization to the 17-bit by 17-bit multiplier built at the Lincoln Laboratory. The multiplier of Fig. 6 multiplies two 9-bit 2's complement numbers

$$X = \sum_{n=0}^{8} X_n 2^n, \qquad X_0, X_1, \cdots, X_7 = 0, 1, \qquad X_8 = 0, -1$$

and

$$Y = \sum_{n=0}^{8} Y_n 2^n, \qquad Y_0, Y_1, \cdots, Y_7 = 0, 1, \qquad Y_8 = 0, -1$$

and forms an 18-bit 2's complement product

$$Z = \sum_{n=0}^{17} Z_n 2^n, \qquad Z_0, Z_1, \cdots, Z_{16} = 0, 1, \qquad Z_{17} = 0, -1.$$

In Fig. 6, adders are represented by circles. With the exception of the last row adders, carry outputs feed carry inputs and propagate *diagonally*. Throughout the multiplier, sum outputs feed sum inputs and propagate *vertically*. In the last row of adders, carries originating within the row feed carry inputs and propagate horizontally, and carries from the previous row feed sum inputs and propagate diagonally.

The logical organization is basically of the carry-save

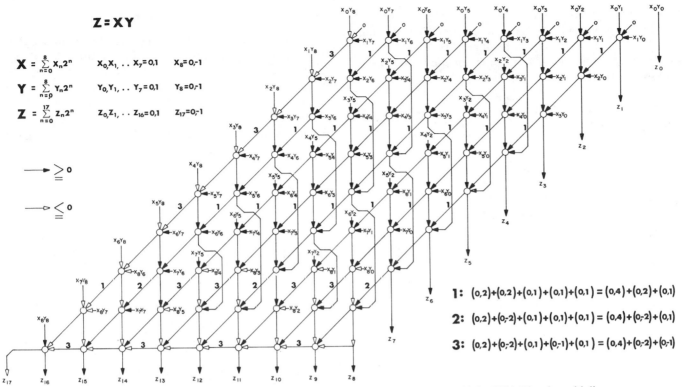

Fig. 6. A 9-bit by 9-bit multiplier of identical overall logical organization to the 17-bit by 17-bit Lincoln multiplier.

Fig. 7. The 17-bit by 17-bit Lincoln multiplier.

type,[3] modified by a "sum-skip" arrangement to speed-up vertical propagation of signals. Sum signals jump after every three adders (every four adders in the 17-bit multiplier). The longest path using as many carries as possible is the path along the diagonal from $X_1 Y_0$ to Z_9 and then along the horizontal from Z_9 to Z_{16}. The longest path using as many sums as possible is the path along the vertical from $X_0 Y_8$ to Z_8 and then along the horizontal from Z_8 to Z_{16}.

In the 17-bit by 17-bit multiplier these paths are 4 sum + 12 carry delays long, or about 30 ns, and 9 sum + 6 carry delays long, or about 35 ns. Thus, these two extreme paths have reasonably equal delays.

In Fig. 6, signals representing arithmetic values $\geqq 0$ are identified by black arrows, signals representing arithmetic values $\leqq 0$ by hollow arrows. The numbers 1, 2, or 3, drawn next to carry lines joining two adders, identify these two adders as parts of an L101, L102, or L103, respectively. The figure also shows the basic arithmetic operations performed by each of these circuits, in the notation of Section II. As

[3] A. Habibi and P. A. Wintz, "Fast multipliers," *IEEE Trans. Computers* (Short Notes), vol. C-19, Feb. 1970, pp. 153–157.

mentioned previously, each adder can also perform the operations resulting from these basic operations by changing the signs of all terms; for example the L101 and L103 adders in the lower left-hand corner of the multiplier are used in this fashion.

A point of interest is that Z_8 comes out of an adder as a negative bit; since we want Z_8 to be positive we need a circuit capable of performing the operation

$$(0, -1) = (0, 1) + (0, -2).$$

As easily seen, the circuit required is nothing more than a wired connection, feeding a $(0, -2)$ carry to the next higher bit position.

Fig. 7 is a photograph of the 17-bit by 17-bit multiplier The card's size is 9- by 7-in. Four-layer interconnections are used (one ground plane, one voltage plane, and two signal planes).

V. CONCLUSION

The main design characteristics of the Lincoln Laboratory multiplier were discussed. The multiplier's speed, although rather high, can certainly be significantly improved by using state of the art methods in the fabrication of the circuits and in the interconnections between the circuits. Even further speed improvements are probably possible by extending the anticipated carry to 3 bits and providing more elaborate sum propagation paths.

ACKNOWLEDGMENT

The author would like to thank S. A. Idsik of Philco-Ford, Blue Bell, Pa., for his efforts, which were instrumental for the successful fabrication of the adder circuits.

A Monolithic 16 x 16 Digital Multiplier

George W. McIver, Ralph W. Miller and Timothy G. O'Shaughnessy

TRW Systems Group

Redondo Beach, Cal.

THE DESIGN, FABRICATION and testing of a 16 x 16 multiplier fabricated on a single monolithic chip will be described.

The chip was designed for use in a small, fast, multipurpose processor being built for avionics applications. The multiplier is set up for a two's complement number system to be compatible with that processor. The chip also features tri-state buffers for the output signals and holding registers for the input signals. This feature not only allows the external leads in the system to be time shared, but also allows the chip signal leads to be time shared, reducing the total number of leads to 32 data lines, 4 control signals, plus several leads for power supply and ground.

Figure 1 shows a schematic for the most commonly repeated cell. One important difference in the design of this circuit from most previous circuits can be determined by studying this schematic; the logic levels are not restored at the output of each block. The reasons for this is that risetimes do not add linearly but approximately as root sum of squares. Thus, if one stage has τ risetime to some circuit threshold, N stages between thresholds have $N^{1/2}\tau$ delay rather than $N\tau$ as one would get with thresholding at each stage. This makes an important difference in the delay times for large asynchronous circuits. The reason one can afford to do this for an LSI chip is that the on-chip environment is much less subject to switching transients, ground noise, etc.

This technique of using many stages of logic before restoration of logic levels is particularly appropriate for a *double-railed* logic system, where a signal and its complement are separately synthesized and both are sent to the next logic elements; eliminating intermediate inverters which would have threshold effects leading to linearly accumulating delay times.

Figure 2 is a photograph of a completed chip, showing that portion of the circuit which corresponds to Figure 1. Corresponding circuit elements occupy about the same realtive positions in both Figure 1 and Figure 2. Figure 3 is a block layout showing how the individual cells are assembled to form the complete circuit. The circuit is exceedingly repetitive; this was used to good advantage, as mask generation was accomplished via layout on automated layout equipment*. The layout of *cell* A was optimized for minimum dimensions, and the other cells were made to fit.

This circuit was fabricated by the triple diffusion process[1] starting with homogenous P-type wafers of 3 Ω-cm resistivity. In this process, the collector, base and emitter are formed by successive diffusion steps. This process is actually very old in the history of integrated circuits, but was abandoned in favor of buried layer epitaxial construction for most applications. There were two major reasons: (1)—the lightly doped collector diffusion was very difficult to control; (2)—the lower r_c' of the buried layer. This second objection is still present, but is not an important item in the design of emitter follower logic circuits.

With the present technology it is easy to control the collector doping sufficiently well to make LSI circuits. Using ion implantation for the collector deposition, the collector sheet can be held to ±5 per cent with relative ease. Most resistors are made using the collector under a base diffusion, however, and the accuracy of these resistors is only ±20 per cent because of diffusion variability, Figure 4 is a cross section of triple diffused devices, showing a coalesced NPN, PNP and load resistor.

Counting each emitter or resistor as a device, the device count for this chip is about 16,700. The chip size is 301 x 279 mils, giving a figure about 5 mil^2/device. This device density is somewhat higher than for standard epitaxial construction due to the fact that all devices are self-isolated and may be closely packed.

Yield of functional devices at wafer probe test has been excellent, averaging about 3 good die per wafer — out of only 19 possible. This good yield is due to the combination of the triple diffusion process — which gives very few defects, albeit poorer transistors than epitaxial construction — with emitter follower logic, which does not require exceptional device performance.

The wafer probe test is performed in the following way. A read-only memory is programmed to have a sequence of input data in one block and the corresponding correct answers in another block; the input words are fed to the chip and the output of the chip compared bit-by-bit to the correct answer. The results of the comparison are displayed on an oscilloscope to give the operator instant visibility as to which bits are in error and in which word position. The display is a plot with X-position corresponding to input word number and Y-position corresponding to output bit number. The Z-axis is modulated in such a way that one gets a spot at each position where a bit did not compare. In this way systematic errors can be detected and the mask set corrected.

Tests have been performed on packaged units. The results of these tests indicate a fixed delay of about 200 ns for all data outputs, plus a delay proportional to $N^{1/2}$ where N is the number of logic delay stages in the matrix associated with the output. This last term is about 130 ns for 31 stages (the maximum) giving a total multiply time of 330 ns.

---

*Applicon 762

[1] Buie, J. L., and Breuer, D. R., "A Large-Scale Integrated Correlator," *The Journal of Solid-State Circuits*", p. 357-363; Oct., 1972.

Reprinted from *1974 IEEE Int. Solid-State Circuits Conf., Dig. Tech. Papers*, vol. XVII, Feb. 1974, pp. 54–55, 228.

Operation of the Circuit

To load data into the holding registers, the tri-state buffers for that register are disabled by applying 2.5 V to the READ terminal, the data lines are energized, and the appropriate LOAD terminal is toggled high. After about 330 ns, the data may be taken from the multiplier by enabling the READ commands. Data may be loaded into both registers simultaneously if desired, and output of the most significant half product may be taken at the same time as the least significant half product. Alterna-tively, the load may be accomplished one word at a time and either the most significant half or least significant half product may be read out first.

Figure 5 shows a set of typical waveforms for this circuit.

Acknowledgments

The authors would like to express their appreciation to K. Morishige for an excellent layout, and to G. Graves for assist-ance in the design and testing of these circuits.

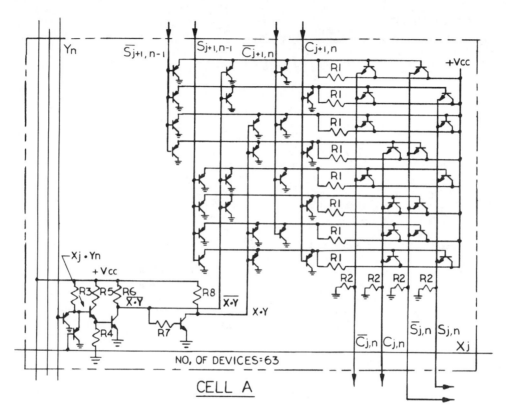

FIGURE 1—Schematic diagram for most commonly repeated cell.

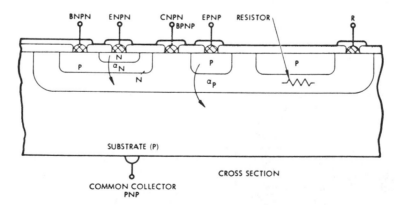

FIGURE 4—Cross-section of NPN and resistor. This figure illustrates how these devices may be coalesced to save space.

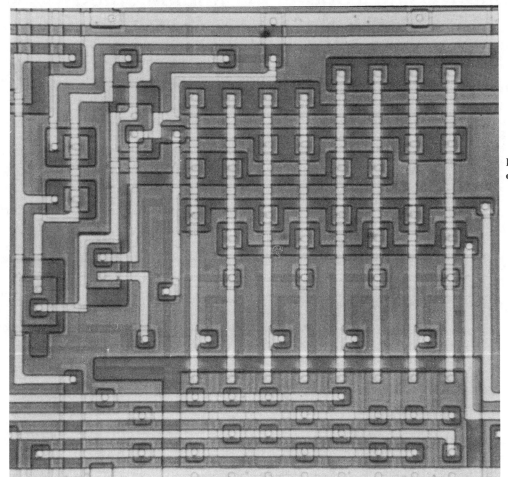

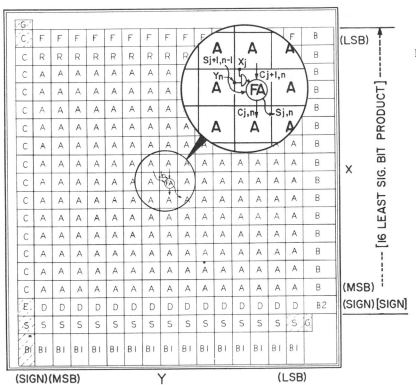

(LSB)

[16 LEAST SIG. BIT PRODUCT]

X

(MSB)
(SIGN) [SIGN]

(SIGN) (MSB)   Y   (LSB)
[SIGN] [MSB] -------- [16 MSB PRODUCT] ----------

[Left]

FIGURE 3—Block layout showing how individual cells are assembled to make a multiplier.

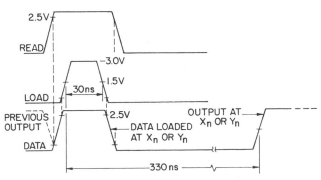

FIGURE 5—Timing illustration showing the relationship between READ, LOAD and DATA signals.

Multiplication Using Logarithms Implemented with Read-Only Memory

THOMAS A. BRUBAKER, MEMBER, IEEE, AND JOHN C. BECKER, MEMBER, IEEE

Abstract—A method for designing the read-only memories (ROM's) needed for multiplication using logarithms is developed. By defining the word length of the multiplicand, multiplier, and product as n bits and the word length of the rounded logarithms as m bits, design curves are given that allow various values of n and m to be selected for a given multiplier accuracy. Then a table is used to determine which combination results in an implementation with the least number of bits.

Index Terms—Antilogarithms, logarithms, multiplication, read-only memory.

INTRODUCTION

IN most computer systems the multiply operation is done via an instruction if a hardware multiplier is included or via a subroutine call if a software multiplication program is used. In either case multiply operations are done sequentially. However, in certain applications, such as digital filtering, it is often desirable to implement a number of multiply operations simultaneously to increase the data rate. While this can be done using conventional hardware multipliers, the cost and complexity of the resulting system is not acceptable to many potential users. As a result there is a need to develop new methods for implementing digital multipliers.

Currently, most hardware multiplication algorithms consist of add and shift operations. This method of multiplication along with a variety of refinements is discussed by a number of authors, with a well-known reference being Flores [1]. Direct multiplication can also be done using table look up implemented using read-only memory (ROM). The primary difficulty is the number of bits that are required in the ROM.

Another procedure that has been used extensively for multiplication in mechanical devices such as the slide rule utilizes logarithms. In digital computation, Mitchell [2] developed a method of computing the logarithm of a number to base 2. Hall *et al.* [3] further investigated the method in terms of its application for the implementation of digital filters. The primary limitation appears to be the hardware requirements. Bell *et al.* [4] and Kingsburg and

Rayner [5] suggested using ROM's to implement the necessary logarithms and antilogarithms via table look up. However, little mention is given to the number of bits needed in the ROM's.

In this paper design curves are developed for ROM's needed to generate the logarithm and antilogarithm transformations needed for multiplication. For an acceptable value of worst case error due to truncation, the word lengths needed for the two transformations can be chosen. Several examples are included that show the word length requirements for a given error. Also, the number of bits for a given accuracy is shown to be less than the number of bits using a direct multiply.

MULTIPLICATION USING ROM

Direct Multiplication

For direct multiplication, the combined multiplicand and multiplier define a unique address in the memory. The contents of this address forms the product. If the multiplicand is represented by n bits and sign and the multiplier by m bits and sign the complete product contains $m + n$ bits and sign. Since the sign bit is usually treated separately the total number of bits required for direct multiplication using a ROM is

$$N = (2^{n+m})(n + m). \qquad (1)$$

However, in many applications, the product is rounded to p bits plus sign and if this is done as part of the ROM design the number of bits required is

$$N_1 = (2^{n+m})(p). \qquad (2)$$

The error when rounding is employed is bounded by

$$-\frac{q}{2} < e < \frac{q}{2}, \qquad (3)$$

where q represents the value of the least significant bit in the rounded product. The number of bits needed in a ROM for various values of q,p and for $n = m$ of 8 and 10 bits is shown in Table I. Here the product is scaled by 2^n. In terms of error, if the multiplicand, multiplier, and product are represented by n bits, the least significant n bits are rounded. The maximum error given as a percentage of the range of the input quantities is given by

$$e_{max} \text{ in percent} = \frac{0.5}{2^n - 1} 100. \qquad (4)$$

Manuscript received August 29, 1974; revised December 9, 1974. This work was supported by the Lawrence Livermore Laboratory under Contract 2439905 and by the Wright-Patterson Air Force Base under Contract F33615-73-C-1253.

T. A. Brubaker is with the Department of Electrical Engineering, Colorado State University, Fort Collins, Colo. 80523.

J. C. Becker is with Hewlett-Packard Company, Loveland, Colo. 80537.

Reprinted from *IEEE Trans. Comput.*, vol. C-24, pp. 761–765, Aug. 1975.

TABLE I
WORD LENGTH REQUIREMENTS FOR DIRECT MULTIPLICATION USING ROM

n	q	p	N_1
8	0	16	1048576
8	2^{-6}	14	917504
8	2^{-4}	12	786432
8	2^0	8	524288
10	0	20	20971520
10	2^{-6}	16	16777216
10	2^{-4}	14	14680064
10	2^0	10	10485759

The product is scaled by 2^n.

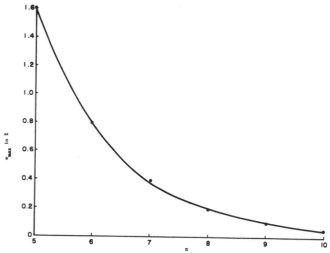

Fig. 1. Error curve for rounded products generated by direct multiplication.

A plot of (4) is shown in Fig. 1 as a function of n.

Multiplication Using Logarithms

Multiplication using logarithms is based on the relationship

$$AB = \text{antilog} \ (\log A + \log B). \tag{5}$$

Using (4) a multiplication algorithm is now developed and word length requirements are established. Since logarithms are only defined for positive numbers, only the magnitudes of A and B are considered and the correct sign for the product is assumed to be generated externally. In the remainder of the paper multiplication using logarithms is called logarithmic multiplication. Logarithms to the base 2 are obviously used.

The first consideration in the design is that the number of bits needed in the ROM's is dependent on the dynamic range of the logarithmic multiplier. To illustrate this, suppose a dynamic range of one thousand is required. When logarithms to base 2 are used, ten logarithmic cycles are required. This means that the mantissa, which repeats itself over each cycle, is stored ten times which amounts to a high degree of redundancy. To eliminate this, the multiplicand and multiplier are represented in a type of floating point format resulting in

$$A = (x)(2^i) \tag{6}$$

and

$$B = (y)(2^j), \tag{7}$$

where x and y are bounded by $1 \leq x, y < 2$. The logarithm of the product is now given by

$$\log \ (AB) = i + j + \log \ (xy) \tag{8}$$

with the resulting product being

$$AB = 2^{(i+j)} \ \text{antilog} \ (\log x + \log y) = 2^{(i+j)}z. \tag{9}$$

Thus, the generation of the actual product requires a shifting operation along with the table look up.

The design of the ROM's to generate z given x and y is now started by looking at the antilogarithm transforma-

tion. The model for this is shown in Fig. 2 where e_3 represents the error source. This error is defined as

$$e_3 = x_{(n)} - x \tag{10}$$

where $x_{(n)}$ represents the output rounded to n bits. The error due to rounding is plotted as a function of x in Fig. 3. This curve has been verified experimentally.

Since the logarithm of x must also be quantized a more complete model is shown in Fig. 4. Here

$$e_2 = \log_{(m)} x - \log x \tag{11}$$

is the error and the subscript m represents the word length of the rounded logarithm. The functions $\log_{(m)} x$ and e_2 are plotted in Fig. 5(a) and (b). The total error at the output is now given by

$$e = \text{antilog} \ (\log x + e_2) + e_3 - x$$
$$= \text{antilog} \ (\log_{(m)} x) + e_3 - x. \tag{12}$$

Fig. 6 shows the effect of e_2 on the output error when e_3 is equal to 0.

The complete model for the logarithmic multiplier is shown in Fig. 7. Here it is assumed that the inputs x and y have been rounded to n bits. Also, the multiplier output is assumed to be rounded to n bits so that the word length of the multiplicand, multiplier, and product are equal. The error at the output is now bounded by

$$e \leq e_{\max} = \text{antilog} \left(\log x_{(n)} + \log y_{(n)} + \frac{q_1}{2} + \frac{q_2}{2} \right)$$
$$+ \frac{q_3}{2} - x_{(n)}y_{(n)} \tag{13}$$

where $x_{(n)}$ is the multiplicand, $y_{(n)}$ the multiplier, and $q_1/2$, $q_2/2$, and $q_3/2$ are the upper bounds on the three errors e_1, e_2, and e_3. To obtain (13) in terms of n and m, the values of q_1 and q_2 are first made equal to q where q is defined as

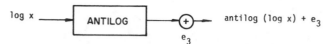

Fig. 2. Representation of an antilog operation including a quantization error source.

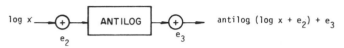

Fig. 3. Rounding error for the antilogarithm.

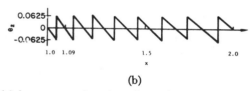

Fig. 4. Representation of the antilog operation including two sources of quantization errors.

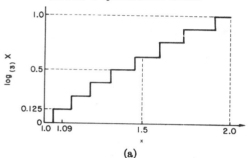

(a)

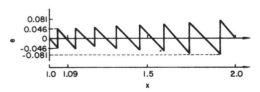

(b)

Fig. 5. (a) $\log_{(m)} x$ as a function of x with $m = 3$. (b) Rounding error of the logarithm as a function of X with $M = 3$.

Fig. 6. Error in the function antilog X due to quantizing $\log X$ with $m = 3$.

$$q = \frac{1}{2^m}. \qquad (14)$$

Since the actual product has a maximum value less than 4, the value of q_3 is

$$q_3 = \frac{\text{product upper bound}}{2^n} = \frac{4}{2^n} = \frac{1}{2^{n-2}}. \qquad (15)$$

Defining $p = \log x_{(n)} + \log y_{(n)}$, (13) can be rewritten as

$$e \le e_{\max} = \text{antilog}\left(p + \frac{1}{2^m}\right) + \frac{1}{2^{n-1}} - x_{(n)}y_{(n)}. \qquad (16)$$

The maximum error $e_{\max}$ as a percentage of the maximum scaled product of two or the input range of two is shown in Fig. 8 as a function of m for various values of n. Looking at (16), as the word length of the logarithm increases significantly beyond the product word length the point of diminishing returns is soon reached. This is seen from (16) where as $m \to \infty$

$$\lim_{m \to \infty} e_{\max} = \frac{1}{2^{n-1}} \qquad (17)$$

If the product is scaled to the range of the input operands as m approaches infinity $q_3/2$ becomes

$$= \lim_{m \to \infty} e_{\max} = 2^{-n}$$

and the range is

$$R = 2^{-n+1}(2^n - 1). \qquad (18)$$

This allows (17) to be rewritten as

$$\lim_{m \to \infty} (e_{\max} \text{ as a percent of } R) = \frac{(0.5)(100)}{2^n - 1} \qquad (19)$$

which is exactly the same as (4). Therefore, in the limit as m becomes large, the logarithmic multiplier exhibits the same error as a conventional multiplier. This explains the asymptotic nature of the curves shown in Fig. 8.

Given an acceptable value of error the number of bits needed to implement the ROM's can now be determined. The number of bits needed for each logarithmic ROM is $(m)(2^n)$ while the number needed for the antilogarithm is $(n)2^m$. Thus, the number of bits NB is

$$NB = (2m)2^n + (n)2^m. \qquad (20)$$

Table II shows the number of bits required for various combinations of product and logarithm word lengths. By using Fig. 8 and Table II the optimal size ROM's can be determined.

EXAMPLE

For an error of 1 percent there are a variety of combinations of m and n that will work. However, in terms of bits, $m = 7$ and $n = 7$ gives a bit requirement of 2688 bits. Using direct multiplication with 7-bit inputs and outputs requires 24 576 bits. For an error of 0.5 percent $m = 8$ $n = 8$ gives 6144 bits compared to 114 688 using conventional multiplication. For an error of 0.1 percent $m = 11$ and $n = 10$ requires 43 008 bits. Using conventional multiplication a ROM with 2 359 256 bits is required.

MULTIPLICATION TIME

A direct multiplication using ROM requires one memory access while logarithmic multiplication requires two memory access times plus an addition. Thus the speed for logarithmic multiplication is about one-third the speed of direct multiplication. In either case the speed is dependent on memory technology. Currently it appears that a multiplication using logarithms can be done in about 100 ns.

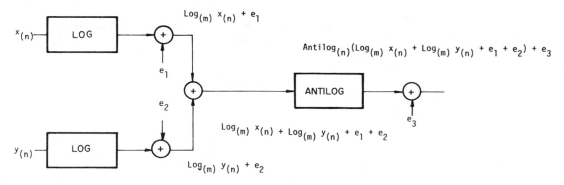

Fig. 7. Model for logarithmic multiplication showing all error sources.

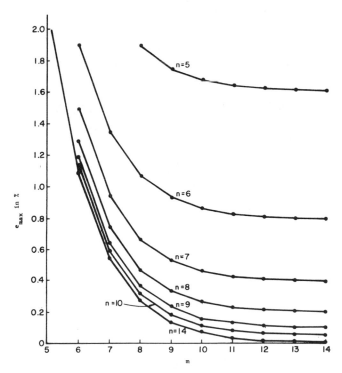

Fig. 8. e_{max} as a percentage of half range plotted as a function m
for various values of n.

TABLE II
TOTAL NUMBER OF ROM BITS REQUIRED FOR LOGARITHMIC
MULTIPLICATION AS A FUNCTION OF LOGARITHMIC AND
PRODUCT WORD LENGTHS

		NUMBER OF PRODUCT BITS (n)							
		6	7	8	9	10	11	12	13	14
	5	832	1,504							
	6	1,152	1,984	3,584						
	7	1,664	2,688	4,608	8,320					
NUMBER OF LOG BITS (m)	8	2,560	3,840	6,144	10,496	18,944				
	9	4,224	5,888	8,704	13,824	23,552	42,496			
	10		9,728	13,312	19,456	30,720	52,224	94,208		
	11			22,016	29,696	43,008	67,584	114,688	206,848	
	12				49,152	65,536	94,208	147,456	249,856	450,560
	13					108,544	143,360	204,800	319,488	540,672
	14						237,568	311,296	442,368	688,128

For a multiplier implemented using an add-shift algorithm the speed depends on the form of the algorithm and the type of circuitry. Furthermore, in most add-shift algorithms the complete product is generated, and it is necessary to utilize additional time to form a rounded product. Current speeds appear to be in the order of 150 ns for a multiplier with 10-bit operands.

CONCLUSIONS

A design method for multiplication using logarithm and antilogarithm transformations implemented in ROM has been developed. For a given error considerably less bits are needed for the three ROM's than for a direct multiplication using an ROM. The hardware appears very well suited for implementing parallel multiplication in applications such as digital filters.

REFERENCES

[1] I. Flores, *The Logic of Computer Arithmetic.* Englewood Cliffs, N. J.: Prentice-Hall, 1963.
[2] J. N. Mitchell, Jr., "Computer multiplication and division using binary logarithms," *IRE Trans. Electron. Comput.*, vol. EC-11, pp. 512–517, Aug. 1962.
[3] E. L. Hall, D. D. Lynch, and S. J. Dwyer, "Generation of products and quotients using approximate binary logarithms for digital filtering applications," *IEEE Trans. Comput.*, vol. C-19, pp. 97–105, Feb. 1970.
[4] C. G. Bell, J. Grason, and A. Newell, *Designing Computers and Digital Systems.* Maynard, Mass.: Digital Equipment Corp., 1972.
[5] N. G. Kingsburg and P. J. W. Rayner, "Digital filtering using logarithmic arithmetic," *Electron. Lett.*, vol. 7, no. 2, pp. 56–58, 1971.

Two's Complement Pipeline Multipliers

R. F. LYON

Abstract—Digital filters and signal processors when realized in hardware often use serial transfer of data. Multipliers which are capable of accepting variable coefficients and data in sign and magnitude notation and producing serial products of the same length as the input data word have been known for some time. This concise paper addresses the design of multipliers capable of accepting data in 2's complement notation, or both data and coefficients in 2's complement notation. It also considers multiplier recoding techniques, such as the Booth algorithm. Specialized (fixed coefficient) multiplier designs are considered briefly. Finally, multiplier rounding and overflow characteristics are discussed, and a rough comparison is made between the complexity of the various designs.

I. INTRODUCTION

Many digital data processing systems, such as digital filters, use serial binary representations of data sequences, or signal samples. Even a few general purpose computers use serial arithmetic. The main problem associated with serial arithmetic has usually been the time or complicated circuitry needed to perform a multiplication.

Paper approved by the Associate Editor for Communication Electronics of the IEEE Communications Society for publication without oral presentation. Manuscript received August 1, 1975; revised December 8, 1975.

The author was with Bell Laboratories, Holmdel, NJ 07733. He is now with Stanford Telecommunications, Inc., Palo Alto, CA 94043.

The need to rapidly perform multiplications on a stream of numbers packed closely in time prompted the development of the pipeline multiplier by Jackson, Kaiser, and McDonald in 1968 [1]. This multiplier accepts positive data words separated by a single extra bit time slot (i.e., a zero sign bit), multiplies each by a positive coefficient, and rounds the products to the same length as the inputs at the same rate.

The delay from data input to product output depends on the number of bits of multiplier, or coefficient, and may be compensated for in other data delays. The resulting multiplier is modular, i.e., for an n-bit coefficient the circuit consists of n identical sections.

But the representation of negative numbers in two's complement form, as is convenient for addition and subtraction, poses problems for multiplication.

Freeny *et al.* [2] have used two's complement to sign and magnitude converters with sign strippers to form positive words with one bit of separation in time. The exclusive-OR of the saved data sign and the coefficient sign controlled a complementer at the output to convert back to the correct two's complement product. The main disadvantage of this method is the inconvenience of the nonmodular design and separate sign handling.

This inconvenience is great enough that Spinks [3] decided to build a serial pipeline multiplier (for a special application) which used two's complement data directly. His circuit uses an ordinary pipeline multiplier, followed by an adder which adds a correction term depending on the coefficient (which is fixed in this case) and the sign of the data word.

Most implementations of pipeline multipliers have had a group of parallel connections for the coefficient bits and control signals. The circuit can, however, be partitioned so that the only parallel connections are power, ground, and clock, and all other connections are serial (see Section II).

Reprinted from *IEEE Trans. Commun.*, vol. COM-24, pp. 418–425, Apr. 1976.

A simple modification of the modular pipeline multiplier allows it to do correct two's complement additions of partial products (Section III), so that two's complement data words can be multiplied by positive coefficients without using a correction term.

From there the circuit can be slightly modified by the addition of a last stage, unlike the other modules, to handle either sign-and-magnitude (Section IV) or two's complement (Section V) coefficients.

Alternatively, full modularity can be retained by using multiplier recoding as in Booth's algorithm [4], [5] (Section VI). More extensive recoding results in more complicated modules (Section VII), but only half as many modules are needed for a net hardware savings.

In the case of multipliers with fixed coefficients, even simpler modules and delays may be connected to implement a minimized, custom-recoded design (Section VIII).

The rounding and overflow properties are not alike for all four of the new multiplier designs, and the differences deserve careful consideration (Section IX), as do the relative complexities (Section X). Custom designs may be similarly evaluated.

The basic designs may be further adapted to do complex multiplications or multiplications in other number systems, such as BCD, balanced ternary, odd halves binary, and base $\sqrt{-2}$.

II. THE BASIC PIPELINE MULTIPLIER

A serial-parallel multiplier [5] takes at least $N + K$ bit times (clock counts) to form the $N + K$ bit product of an N-bit multiplicand (data word) and a K-bit multiplier (coefficient); this restricts the operation rate to one multiplication every $N + K$ bit times, even if the result is rounded or truncated to the N high order bits. The pipeline multiplier also requires at least $N + K$ bit times per operation, but can do one operation every N bit times by starting one operation before finishing the previous operation, without additional hardware. The term "pipeline" describes a system which has operation period less than its operation delay, without parallel processing.

In order to achieve one multiplication per N bit times, the use of any single part (say gate, or flip-flop) of the circuit must be restricted to no more than N (consecutive) bit times per multiplication. Since all data are serial, this means every partial product (data word times one bit of coefficient) and every partial product sum must be restricted to N bits. This is not possible when the first partial product to enter the sum is the most significant one, as in the serial-parallel multiplier (Fig. 1), unless the low order parts of all partial products are discarded, resulting in large errors.

The pipeline multiplier accumulates partial product sums starting with the least significant partial product. After each addition, the result is an N-bit number which is truncated to $N - 1$ bits before the next partial product (twice as significant) is added. Of course, overflow is possible if the data word is not restricted to $N - 1$ bits, instead of the possible N. Hence one extra bit time separation of words may be required. This separation is normally provided by removing the sign of an N-bit word.

The implementation of the pipeline multiplier is illustrated in Fig. 2. It consists of K modules, with serial interconnections for the data word and the partial product sum. The coefficient bits are applied by parallel connections, with the least significant bit corresponding to the first (leftmost) module. Timing signals to control the truncation are also applied in parallel. Notice that the first module has an unused partial product sum input—this may be used to add a small offset so that the internal truncation effects an actual rounding [6].

Several minor additions to the circuit improve its practi-

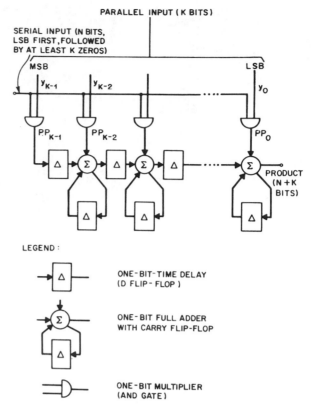

Fig. 1.   Serial-parallel multiplier.

cality. First, notice that there is a path of combinatorial logic from the PPS_{-1} input through all the adders to the output. The propagation delay along this path limits the allowable bit rate. By inserting clocked delays on all the serial interconnections, we allow an increased bit rate, and hence an increased operation rate, though we double the delay through the multiplier.

Second, rather than applying control signals r_i in parallel, we can incorporate another serial register in the module to propagate the control signal through the modules in turn.

Finally, we can include yet another serial register along with latches so that the coefficient Y may be entered serially at the same time as X and the control signal. The resulting module circuitry is shown in Fig. 3.

III. MODIFICATION TO ALLOW TWO's COMPLEMENT DATA WORDS

If data words are represented in two's complement notation, the circuit described will not work when the data are negative, i.e. when sign bit (SB) = 1. But the algorithm of adding partial products to the partial product sum should still work if the additions are done properly. The key is that two's complement numbers implicitly have sign bits extended infinitely to the left.

Notice in Fig. 2(c) that each addition involved the insertion of a zero bit at the left end of the partial product sum. This is done by the AND gate and control signal, which equivalently truncates the low order bit of the partial product sum in the next multiplication. For proper addition, a sign extension, not a zero, should be inserted.

Fig. 4 shows the circuitry for inserting zeros and sign extensions.

One other modification required is a provision for clearing the carry flip-flop after each multiplication; previously, with positive numbers and no overflow, the clearing was automatic.

The resulting module is diagrammed in Fig. 5.

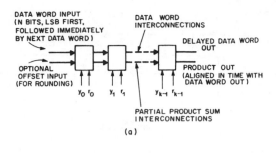

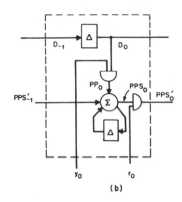

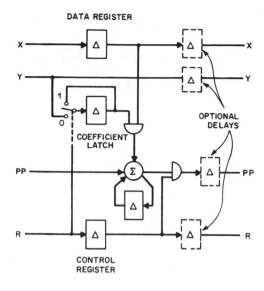

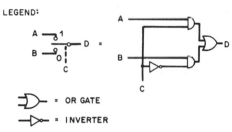

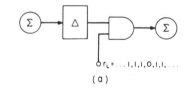

Fig. 3. Extended basic module.

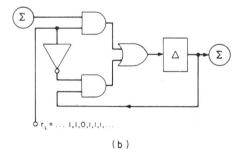

Fig. 2. Serial pipeline multiplier. (a) Block diagram. (b) Detailed diagram of blocks. (c) Numeric interpretation of logic.

Fig. 4. (a) Truncation (zero-insertion) logic; (b) Sign-extension logic.

IV. SIGN AND MAGNITUDE COEFFICIENTS

If the K-bit coefficient is represented as $y_K y_{K-1} \cdots y_2 y_1$ where y_K is the sign bit and $y_{K-1} \cdots y_2 y_1$ is the magnitude, then we can easily build a multiplier that uses $y_{K-1} \cdots y_2 y_1$ as coefficient, and follow this by a true/complement circuit controlled by y_K. That is, implement

$$P = X \cdot (y_{K-1} \cdots y_1 y_0) \cdot (-1)^{y_K}. \tag{1}$$

Fig. 6 shows a possible complementer circuit and the multiplier block diagram. Notice the connections to the control shift register and the coefficient shift register as well as the product output.

V. FULLY TWO'S COMPLEMENT MULTIPLIER

The coefficient $y_K y_{K-1} \cdots y_2 y_1$ in two's complement notation has the value

$$Y = \sum_{i=1}^{K-1} y_i 2^{i-n} - y_K 2^{K-n} \tag{2}$$

if the radix point is placed to the right of bit y_n. For the pipeline multiplier we generally use $n = K - 1$ so that $-2 \le Y < 2$. The point is that the bit y_K differs from the others only in sign, so that the partial product $y_K X$ should be subtracted from the partial product sum, not added to it. The result will

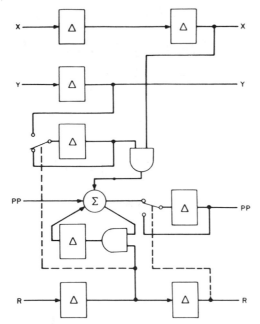

Fig. 5.   Two's complement module.

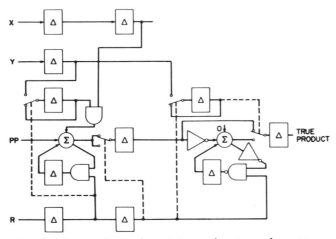

Fig. 6.   Last two's complement stage and post-complementer.

be the correct product. Notice that in going from the last adding module to the subtracting module, the partial product sum should not be truncated, and zero should be subtracted from the least significant bit (if one wished to use $n = K$ and $-1 \leqslant y \leqslant 1$, then this statement should be ignored).

Fig. 7 shows an implementation of this multiplier.

VI. MULTIPLIER RECODING–BOOTH'S ALGORITHM

Booth's algorithm can be used to build a two's complement multiplier in which all coefficient bits are treated alike. The method is equivalent to recoding the coefficient as a sequence of ternary digits $(-1,0,+1)$ with binary weighting.

The original coefficient

$$Y = \sum_{i=1}^{K-1} y_i 2^{i-K+1} - 2 y_K \tag{3}$$

can be rewritten as follows [4], [5]:

$$Y = \sum_{i=1}^{K} y_i' 2^{i-K+1} \tag{4}$$

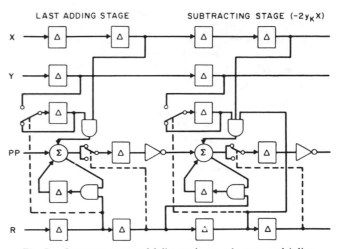

Fig. 7.   Last two stages of fully two's complement multiplier.

where

$$y_i' = y_{i-1} - y_i \; \epsilon \{-1, 0, +1\}$$

(y_0 is taken to be zero). Multiplication proceeds by adding the negative, zero, or positive partial products formed by multiplying each y_i' by the data word. Table I enumerates the possibilities. The additions must, of course, be done in two's complement arithmetic, using sign extensions when needed. The table suggests using y_i to determine whether to add or subtract, while $y_i \oplus y_{i-1}$ gates the data word.

There are several approaches to controlled adder/subtracters, all involving the "controlled one's complementer," which is simply an exclusive-OR gate. The approaches to implementing $A - B$ serially are: 1) controlled complementer on B input to adder, along with controlled carry clear/preset; 2) controlled complementers on both A input and sum output, no modification of carry logic; 3) when adder has separate sum and carry logic networks, controlled complementer on A input to carry logic only; 4) reductions depending on the logic for determining whether to add or subtract, or logic gating B input.

For example, using method 1), we preset the carry to the value of y_i, and add $y_i \oplus ((y_i \oplus y_{i-1}) \cdot X)$ to add a partial product. This reduces to adding simply $X \cdot y_{i-1} + \bar{X} \cdot y_i$ (carry present to y_i still), which is implemented by a data selector, or switch.

Fig. 8 shows the resulting module. Note the extra delay elements needed to prevent the early arrival of y_{i-1}.

A multiplier using this module has been built and operated, using only $3\frac{1}{2}$ TTL chips per section.

VII. FURTHER MULTIPLIER RECODING

The coefficient may be further recoded as follows:

$$Y = \sum_{\substack{i=1 \\ i \; \text{odd}}}^{K} y_i'' 2^{i-K+1}$$

where $y_i'' \in \{-2, -1, 0, +1, +2\}$ as shown in Table II. Multiplying by this mixed base representation requires only $\lceil K/2 \rceil$ adder/subtracters and circuits to select X, $2X$, or zero.

Each pipeline multiplier module [7] as shown in Fig. 9 has a few more bit delay elements and other logic than previous designs, but only one module is needed for every two bits of coefficient length. It may sometimes be advantageous to put the recoding logic in a block before the modules, and

TABLE I
BOOTH'S ALGORITHM

Original Multiplier		Recoded Multiplier	Gating	Action	
y_i	y_{i-1}	y_i'	$y_i \oplus y_{i-1}$		
0	0	0	0	add	zero
0	1	+1	1	add	data word
1	0	−1	1	subtract	data word
1	1	0	0	subtract	zero

TABLE II
FIVE-LEVEL MULTIPLIER RECODING

Original Multiplier			Recoded Multiplier	Action	
y_{i+1}	y_i	y_{i-1}	y_i''		
0	0	0	0	add	0
0	0	1	+1	add	X
0	1	0	+1	add	X
0	1	1	+2	add	2X
1	0	0	−2	subtract	2X
1	0	1	−1	subtract	X
1	1	0	−1	subtract	X
1	1	1	0	subtract	0

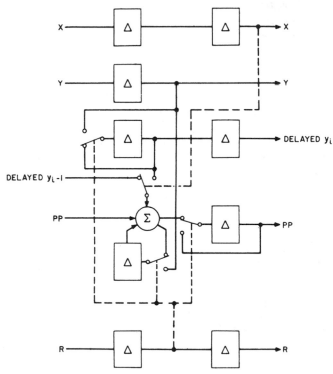

Fig. 8. Booth's algorithm module.

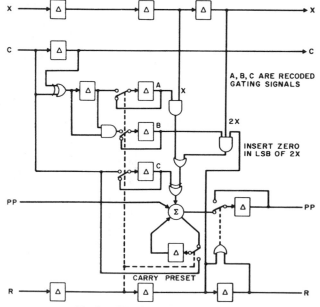

Fig. 9. Five-level recoded module.

send three bits to each stage via two registers instead of the single coefficient register. This saves logic, but destroys modularity.

Multiplier recoding to a larger set of digit values will not help, in general, because $\pm 3 \cdot X$ is not available without using another adder.

VIII. CUSTOM RECODING FOR HARDWARE MINIMIZATION

In many digital signal processing applications, multipliers are dedicated to multiplying a data sequence by a fixed coefficient. In many cases the number of adders and subtracters needed to implement multiplication by a constant is fewer than half the number of bits in the constant; and no shift register or latches are needed for the coefficient if it is represented by a hardwired configuration.

Techniques exist [8] for reducing a coefficient to a minimum number of +1 and −1 digits, the other digits being zero. As an example, an 8-pole low-pass digital filter that required 8-bit coefficients to meet the design specifications was redesigned with only three nonzero digits per coefficient [9]; thus each multiplier requires only two adders if no rounding is required.

IX. ROUNDING AND OVERFLOW PROPERTIES

We will restrict our discussion to the case of coefficients in the range $-2 \leqslant Y < 2$, so that the range of possible products is greater than the range of possible data inputs. This does not necessarily mean that such overrange products cannot be correctly represented at the output, but only that they cannot be used as future data inputs. The allowable data inputs will be represented by $N - 1$ of the N bits that enter the multiplier for each operation, with the Nth bit being a sign extension, or in the case of the Booth's algorithm design, being ignored. The output may use all N bits.

First, suppose no offset is added to the true product, so the output is a truncation. Truncation of two's complement partial product sums is a "floor" function, i.e., the greatest integer less than or equal to the argument. In the first design (two's complement data, sign and magnitude coefficient) the result is not a function of the product alone, since truncation is followed by a true/complement operation. Thus, for example, $\frac{1}{2} \times 3$ yields $\lfloor \frac{3}{2} \rfloor = 1$, while $-\frac{1}{2} \times (-3)$ yields $-\lfloor -\frac{3}{2} \rfloor = 2$.

In any of the designs using two's complement coefficients, truncation effects a uniform floor function.

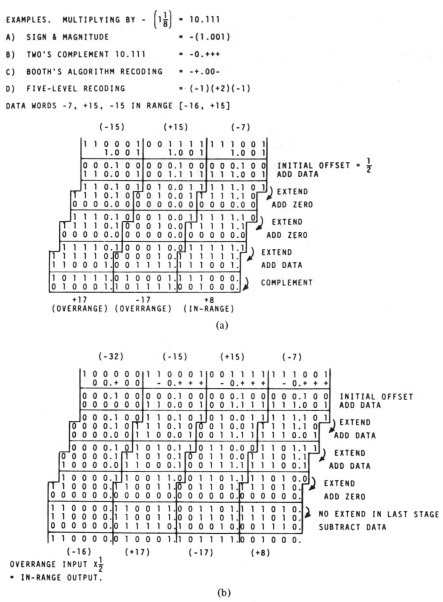

EXAMPLES. MULTIPLYING BY - $\left(1\frac{1}{8}\right)$ = 10.111

A) SIGN & MAGNITUDE = -(1.001)

B) TWO'S COMPLEMENT 10.111 = -0.+++

C) BOOTH'S ALGORITHM RECODING = -+.00-

D) FIVE-LEVEL RECODING = (-1)(+2)(-1)

DATA WORDS -7, +15, -15 IN RANGE [-16, +15]

Fig. 10.   Multiplication examples for two's complement data. (a) Sign and magnitude coefficient. (b) Two's complement coefficient. (Figure continued on next page.)

Now suppose we use the unused partial product sum input to add a single bit with a significance of $\frac{1}{2}$ LSB (referred to the product or data word, not to internal partial products). Then the truncation of the product of value $P + \frac{1}{2}$ may be represented as $\lfloor P + \frac{1}{2} \rfloor$, which is a rounding, or nearest integer operation. Again, in the sign and magnitude coefficient design, there is a possible complement operation after this rounding, so that the half integers may be rounded either up or down. In the two's complement designs, half integers round up. Alternatively, half integers may be rounded down by adding ones in all bits of significance $\frac{1}{4}$ LSB and lower, but zero at the $\frac{1}{2}$ LSB significance.

In the case of the Booth's algorithm (ternary recoded) design, the addition of an offset at the unused input can cause internal overflows, depending on the values of the data word and coefficient word. For example, if the data word is the 5 bit number 10001 (-15_{10}), and the first recoded multiplier digit is -1, and any positive offset is added, then the first adder output will exceed the value 01111 ($+15_{10}$), and hence will have MSB = 1, which will be incorrectly extended to give a negative sign (SB = 1). See Fig. 10. This problem is avoided

if the first stage is modified to *not* do a sign extension, and a correct sign extension is supplied in the data word.

There is another case in which the Booth's algorithm design will make an error; if the input is the one-all-zeros code (e.g., 10 000 = -16_{10}), then its negative is not representable in $N - 1$ (=5) bits, and again internal overflow will result. The modification suggested above cures this problem also.

The five-level recoded design does not have similar problems since the least significant nonzero recoded digit cannot be either $+2$ or -2, as the reader may verify.

The allowable input range of the three designs other than Booth's algorithm is actually the full N bits if only certain special coefficients are used (e.g., $+\frac{1}{2}$). In general, each coefficient has a range of inputs for which the product will be correct. See Fig. 10 for examples. Recall, however, that not all *correct* outputs are *in-range*.

X. COMPARATIVE COMPLEXITY

Fig. 11 shows block diagrams for five multiplier designs, the sign magnitude design, and four new designs. Each block

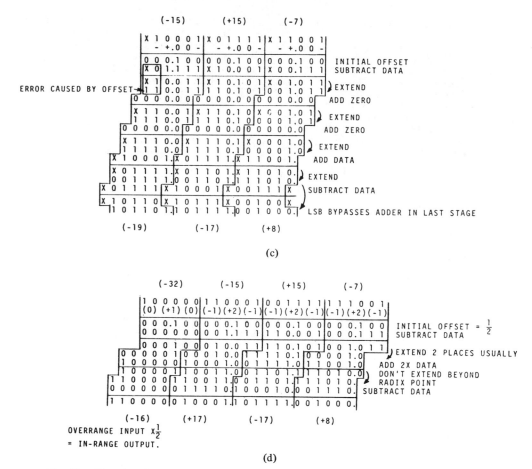

Fig. 10. (Continued). (c) Booth's algorithm coefficient. (d) Five-level recoded coefficient.

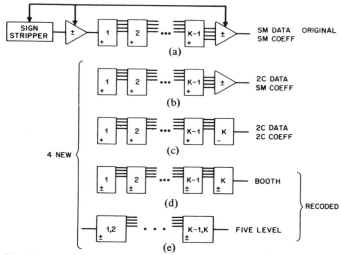

Fig. 11. Comparison of original and four new multipliers. (a) Original sign magnitude. (b) Two's complement data, sign magnitude coefficient. (c) Fully two's complement. (d) Two's complement with Booth's algorithm. (e) Two's complement with 5-level coding.

represents one multipler section with one adder or adder/subtracter. The triangles are true/complement units for sign correction. The numbers in each stage are the indices of the coefficient bits controlling that stage.

Thus we see that the sign magnitude unit requires $K - 1$ stages, two true/complement units, and an external sign stripping circuit involving one word delay. With modification for two's complement data, but keeping sign magnitude coefficients the requirement is $K - 1$ stages plus one true/comple-

ment unit. Each stage is more complicated by only a few gates. Changing to two's complement coefficients requires $K - 1$ stages just as above, followed by a Kth stage which subtracts instead of adding. Implementing Booth's algorithm in a K-stage adder/subtracts design requires a little more circuitry for multiplier recoding unless coefficients are entered in an already recoded format. Finally, further recoding to five levels requires more complicated recoding logic, but requires only $K/2$ adder–subtracter stages; each stage also has one extra delay flip-flop in the data and control lines.

The detailed comparison at the gate level will depend more on the constraints of the technology used than on the general design.

XI. CONCLUSIONS

We have described a multiplier that has the desirable characteristics which will make it useful in a variety of signal processing applications. Its capability to handle two's complement positive and negative numbers makes it compatible with standard hardware and standard data formats. Its modular design lends itself to medium scale integration, thus allowing all multiplier sizes to be assembled from standard units. The serial interconnection scheme allows the use of a simple control signal and prevents the clutter of parallel wiring. The data throughput rate is approximately the same as the throughput rate of the serial adders from which it is constructed.

ACKNOWLEDGMENT

Neither the work on multipliers nor the publication of this concise paper would have been possible without the continuing help and encouragement of R. B. Kieburtz. Numerous other co-workers at Bell Laboratories also provided help that was greatly appreciated.

REFERENCES

[1] L. B. Jackson, S. F. Kaiser, and H. S. McDonald, "An approach to the implementation of digital filters," *IEEE Trans. Audio and Electroacoust.*, vol. AU-16, pp. 413-421, Sept. 1968.

[2] S. L. Freeny, R. B. Kieburtz, D. V. Mina, and S. K. Tewksbury, "Design of digital filters for an all digital TDM-FDM translator," *IEEE Trans. Circuit Theory*, vol. CT-18, pp. 702-711, Nov. 1971.

[3] A. H. Spinks, "2 kHz modulator of the digital *A*-channel bank," unpublished work, July 1970.

[4] A. D. Booth and K. H. V. Booth, *Automatic Digital Calculators*, 2nd ed. New York: Academic, 1956.

[5] Y. Chu, *Digital Computer Design Fundamentals.* New York: McGraw-Hill, 1962.

[6] R. B. Kieburtz, "Modular pipeline multiplier," unpublished work, June 5, 1972.

[7] E. K. Cheng, unpublished multiplier design, California Inst. Technol., Pasadena, July 1974.

[8] H. L. Garner, "Number systems and arithmetic," *Advances in Computers*, vol. 6. New York: Academic, 1965, pp. 163-164.

[9] R. F. Lyon, "Multiplier hardware minimization in digital filters," unpublished work, Aug. 1973.

A Low-Power, Bipolar, Two's Complement Serial Pipeline Multiplier Chip

JACK KANE, MEMBER, IEEE

Abstract—A 4-bit, general-purpose, two's complement serial pipeline multiplier chip has been designed and fabricated in the bipolar GIMIC-O process. The chip can provide the following functions in 24-pin dual-in-line packages:

1) two's complement/two's complement 4-bit serial pipeline multiplier with programmable coefficients,
2) sign magnitude/two's complement 4-bit serial pipeline multiplier with programmable coefficients,
3) 5-bit dynamically programmable adder/subtractor,
4) 2^{-K} scaler,
5) overflow corrector.

Packages can be cascaded to provide functions of length greater than 4 bits.

Nonsaturating circuit techniques, emitter function logic combined with current-steering trees, are effectively utilized to make high-performance, low-power circuits using a simple bipolar technology. The multiplier circuitry is compatible at inputs and outputs with standard emitter coupled logic and uses a standard -5.2 ± 10 percent power supply. Fully programmable multiplication at clock rates greater than 20 MHz is achieved with a power consumption of 37.5 mW/bit.

INTRODUCTION

A SERIAL pipeline multiplier, serving as the basis of a digital filter, was first described by Jackson, Kaiser, and McDonald [1] in 1968. The multiplier was based on an algorithm for multiplying positive numbers represented in sign-magnitude form; the implementation was described in terms of small-scale and medium-scale digital functions with the realization that higher integration levels would be necessary to bring power, cost, size, and reliability to levels that would make digital filtering techniques competitive with their analog counterparts. Until recently, such components were unavailable.

Because of the popularity of two's complement number representation in digital processing, use of sign-magnitude multipliers as described above requires additional circuitry to translate between two's complement and sign-magnitude forms. In 1973 Lyon [2] developed algorithms for serial pipeline multiplication which directly utilized two's complement data and two's complement coefficients or a mixed representation of two's complement data and sign-magnitude coefficients.

Prior to the start of the multiplier design effort, a study was undertaken to evaluate and define logic for a general-purpose multiplier chip which would be applicable to the specific Bell System application and also be of greatest use to other digital filter designers. It was decided that a slight modification of Lyon's two's complement/two's complement multiplier be implemented despite its additional complexity and that, with the addition of a few external leads, a number of additional

functions required for digital filter implementation could be provided by the same chip with only ceramic modification. The proposed generalized multiplier chip would provide the following functions:

1) two's complement/two's complement 4-bit serial pipeline multiplier with programmable coefficients,
2) sign-magnitude/two's complement 4-bit serial pipeline multiplier with programmable coefficients,
3) 5-bit dynamically programmable adder/subtractor,
4) 2^{-K} scaler,
5) overflow corrector.

The 4-bit multiplier chips could be cascaded for longer multipliers.

The multiplier chip designed is the realization of the generalized multiplier logic referred to above. In comparison to other recent multiplier implementations, this approach offers versatility regarding data format and a good throughput rate fc/N where N is the data word length and fc is the clock frequency. The former is achieved by somewhat more complex logic. The latter is a consequence of rounding partial sums at each multiplier bit and continuously maintaining them at the same number of significant bits as the input data. The cost is a somewhat greater hardware complexity in terms of registers. The multiplier utilizes a mix of emitter function logic (EFL) [3] and current-steering logic to provide an emitter coupled logic (ECL) compatible chip operating at clock frequencies greater than 20 MHz in a fully programmable coefficient mode. Total chip power for 4 bits at -5.2 V is nominally 150 mW. The chip represents 225 equivalent gates and is fabricated in the GIMIC-O [4] bipolar process with single layer metallization.

MULTIPLIER LOGIC

The digital multiplier chip is a realization of two's complement/two's complement (TC/TC) multiplication logic proposed by Lyon and modified slightly, as described by Tewksbury [5], to provide a more generalized functional capability. Fig. 1 shows a block diagram of a typical bit of the multiplier. Two coefficients (C_0 and C_{-1}) are needed per bit of TC/TC multiplication, the C_{-1} input being provided by the C_0 output of the previous bit. Coefficient loading occurs under the control of "rounding signal" $R1$ through data selectors $DS1$ and $DS2$. Data bits (D) select C_0 or C_{-1} through data selector $DS3$, as prescribed by Booth's algorithm [6], to form gated data (D^*).

A 1-bit full adder combines gated data D^*, a previous partial sum P_{-1}, and the saved carry (C_S) from the previous addition. The resulting sum is saved in a partial sum flip-flop and the resulting carry in a carry-save flip-flop. A data selector, $DS4$, pre-

Manuscript received May 10, 1976, revised June 25, 1976.
The author is with Bell Laboratories, Allentown, PA, 18103.

Reprinted from *IEEE J. Solid-State Circuits*, vol. SC-11, pp. 669–678, Oct. 1976.

247

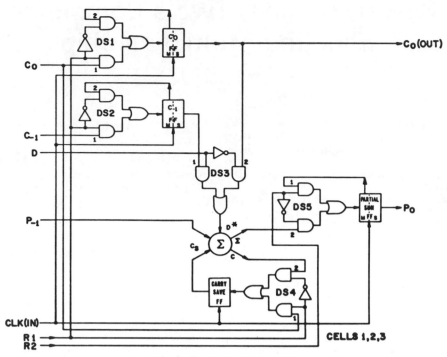

Fig. 1. Typical multiplier bit.

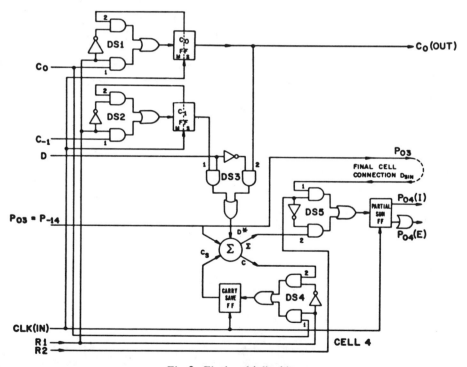

Fig. 2. Final multiplier bit.

ceding the carry-save flip-flop, allows the presetting of the carry to a logical "1" or "0" under the control of $R1$. A data selector, $DS5$, preceding the partial sum flip-flop, allows sign extensions to be performed under the control of $R2$.

In the Lyon TC/TC multiplication algorithm, the final section of the multiplier requires a change from the others which is realized by bringing the previous cell output into the partial sum data selector. The implementation of this is shown in the cell 4 logic diagram of Fig. 2. To allow for a single chip design, the required data selector input is brought out as an external lead, $DSIN$. On adjacent leads are brought out the partial sum outputs of the fourth cell, $P04(I)$, and the previous one, $P03$. The connection, on a ceramic, of $P04(I)$ to the data selector input makes cell 4 similar to the other cells and allows

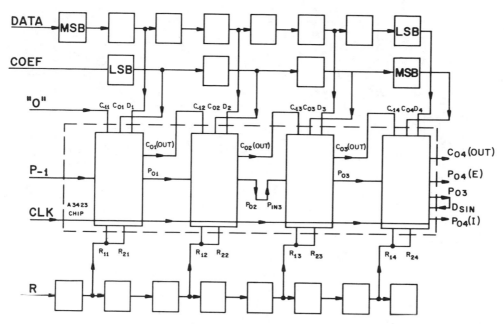

Fig. 3. 4-bit TC/TC multiplier.

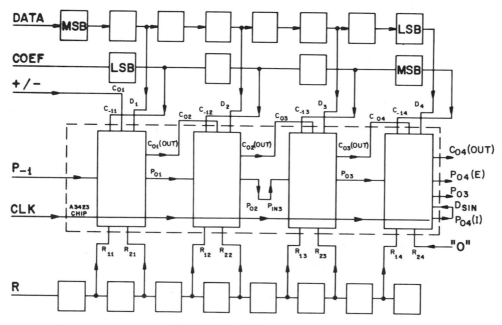

Fig. 4. 4-bit TC/SM multiplier.

direct cascading to make longer multipliers. The connection of $P03$ to the data selector input makes that cell the final one of the TC/TC multiplier.

Figs. 3 and 4 show the register connection to the multiplier chip for implementation of 4-bit TC/TC and TC/SM multipliers, respectively.

MULTIPLIER CIRCUITRY

To aid in the description of the circuitry in the multiplier chip, a basic EFL gate will first be reviewed. Such a gate is shown in Fig. 5. The gate is comprised of transistors $Q1$ and $Q2$, diode $D1$, and resistors $R1$, $R2$, and $R3$. $QD1$ and $QD2$ represent open emitter outputs from another gate. With $V_{ref} = -0.5\ V_{BE}$, input levels at $IN1$ and $IN2$ are $-2\ V_{BE}$ (clamped by the input transistor at $-1.5\ V_{BE}$) for logic "0" and $-1\ V_{BE}$ for logic "1."

If either input to the EFL gate is low, the corresponding base–emitter junction of $Q1$ turns on. The voltage at that input is clamped at $V_{ref} - V_{BE} = -1.5\ V_{BE}$ and input current I_1 is provided by $Q1$. Resistor $R3$ is selected such that $I_1 R3 = 1\ V_{BE}$. If both inputs are low, $2I_1$ flows through $Q1$; to avoid saturation, diode $D1$ clamps the voltage at the col-

249

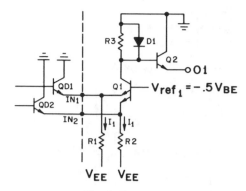

Fig. 5. EFL gate.

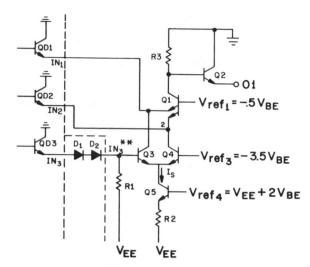

Fig. 6. Data selector.

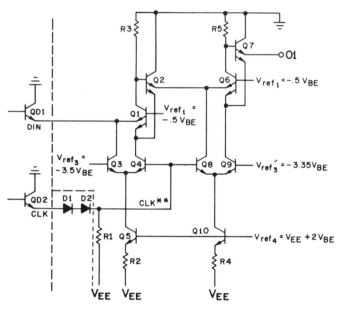

Fig. 7. Edge-triggered D flip-flop.

lector of $Q1$ to -1 V_{BE}. Thus, output voltage 01 for any low input is seen to be $-V_{BE} - V_{BE(Q2)} = -2$ V_{BE}, a logical "0" level.

If $QD1$ and $QD2$ both place high levels of -1 V_{BE} on the inputs of $Q1$, $Q1$ will be off and input currents I_1 will be supplied by the driving gates. Since no current flows through $R3$, the collector of $Q1$ is at 0 volts and the output voltage 01 is at $0 - 1$ $V_{BE(Q2)} = -1$ V_{BE}, a logical "1." Thus, an AND function of inputs is available at the output of the gate with voltage levels properly restored for driving subsequent gates. Note that a wired OR capability additionally exists at the output.

The EFL gate as described is nonsaturating and noninverting. The common base input followed by the common collector output provides a fast logic circuit. Additionally, the clamping action of $Q1$ on the input voltage creates a 0.5 V_{BE} voltage swing on gate interconnections, reducing charging time of circuit parasitics. The gate speed is primarily limited by the capacitive parasitics at the collector of $Q1$.

It has been shown that the EFL gate is driven by an open emitter output at -1 V_{BE} and -2 V_{BE} levels and the same logic levels are generated at the output. Note that these levels are compatible with standard ECL circuits and, consequently, a mix of EFL and ECL can be used where advantageous.

COEFFICIENT/DELAYED-COEFFICIENT DATA SELECTOR

A data selector used to select between the coefficient and delayed-coefficient flip-flops is shown in Fig. 6. Note the combination of a basic EFL gate with a current-steering pair—$Q3$, $Q4$—and an active current source—$Q5$.

$QD1$, $QD2$, and $QD3$ represent open emitter output transistors from a driving gate, generating voltage levels of -1 V_{BE} and -2 V_{BE}. If $IN3$ is high (-1 V_{BE}), $IN3^{**}$ is at -3 V_{BE} and transistor $Q3$ is on. Current I_S is steered through this transistor and input $IN1$ is selected. With this condition set up, operation of the data selector is as described for a basic gate. If $IN3$ is low (-2 V_{BE}), $IN3^{**}$ is at -4 V_{BE} and current I_S is steered through $Q4$, selecting $IN2$.

The level shifting network (comprised of $D1$ and $D2$) interfaces between the external input levels of -1 V_{BE} and -2 V_{BE} and the required input levels of -3 V_{BE} and -4 V_{BE}.

Several differences can be noted between this circuit and the basic gate. First, the clamp diode at the collector of $Q1$ is no longer necessary since a single unit of current I_S flows through $R3$. Second, current I_S, as determined by current

source $Q5$, $R2$, and V_{ref3}, is given by $V_{BE}/R2$ and has essentially a diode-type negative temperature coefficient. We will see later that this is significant in helping to keep $Q1$ out of saturation at high temperatures. Third, current I_S is independent of power supply V_{EE}, thus making the entire data selector operation independent of the external supply.

BASIC EDGE-TRIGGERED D FLIP-FLOP

The basic flip-flop used in the multiplier chip is a modification of an EFL edge-triggered master–slave D flip-flop, as described by Skokin [3]. A schematic of this flip-flop is shown in Fig. 7.

Transistors $QD1$ and $QD2$ provide data and clock, respectively, at -1 V_{BE}, -2 V_{BE} ECL levels. Level shifters $D1$ and $D2$ shift the clock to the desired -3 V_{BE}, -4 V_{BE} levels. While the clock is in the low state, $Q3$ is on and the master portion of the flip-flop (comprised of $Q1$, $Q2$, $Q3$, $Q4$, $Q5$)

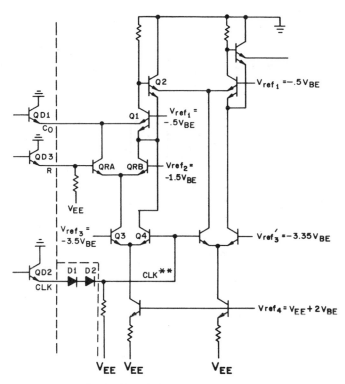

Fig. 8. Coefficient flip-flop with data selector.

is enabled to receive new data, its state being continuously updated. When the clock rises, $Q3$ is turned off and $Q4$ is turned on. The state of the flip-flop is latched up by feedback between $Q1$ and $Q2$. The held state is that which existed at the input terminal within a minimum setup time before the positive clock transition. Thus, for proper operation, the input must be held stationary at the desired level before the clock transition for a minimum setup time. Once $Q3$ turns off, input DIN can no longer accept new data.

Also occurring on the positive clock transition is the transfer of information to the slave flip-flop (comprised of $Q6$, $Q7$, $Q8$, $Q9$, $Q10$). While the clock was low, $Q8$ was held off and the input of the slave was incapable of accepting new information. Its state was held by feedback between $Q6$ and $Q7$; the path for source current was through $Q9$. On the positive clock transition, $Q8$ turns on and the state of the master is loaded into the slave. New information is available at the output $Q1$ after the flip-flop propagation delay. When the clock returns to its low state, the new information is held latched in the slave and the input to $Q6$ is again disabled. Note that the clock reference levels to the master and slave are slightly offset to insure that the slave is latched before the master is again enabled, thereby avoiding a race condition.

As described for the previous circuitry, the current sources in the master and slave provide current with a V_{BE} temperature coefficient and independence of the V_{EE} supply.

Coefficient and Delayed Coefficient Flip-Flop with Data Selector

The schematic of the coefficient flip-flop and data selector is shown in Fig. 8. It differs from the basic flip-flop by the addition of a differential pair—QRA and QRB; QRA is driven

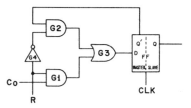

Fig. 9. Coefficient flip-flop with data selector—logical representation.

by a control signal R and QRB is held at a $-1.5\ V_{BE}$ reference. Note that the R input can be driven directly at $-1\ V_{BE}$ and $-2\ V_{BE}$ levels.

The data selector function which is provided by Fig. 8 is shown in Fig. 9. When R is high, gate $G1$ is enabled and the input C_0 is fed to the data input of the flip-flop. When R is low, $G2$ is enabled and the previous state of the master of the D flip-flop is maintained.

Referring back to the schematic of Fig. 8, when R is high, transistor QRA is on and the flip-flop functions exactly as described for the basic flip-flop. When R goes low, QRA turns off, disabling the C_0 input. At the same time, QRB turns on and the data are latched in the master of the flip-flop. Since latching of the coefficient in the master can occur while the clock is low, the coefficient input must be held at the desired level for a minimum setup time before the R downward transition.

Partial Sum Flip-Flop and Sign Extend Data Selector

The partial sum flip-flop and sign extend data selector circuit is identical to Fig. 8 except that the base inputs to

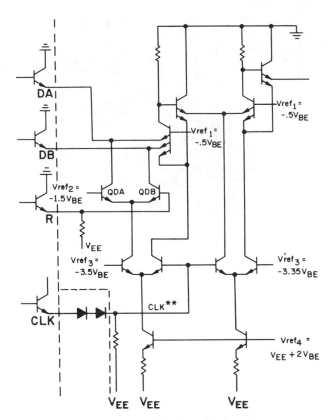

Fig. 10. Carry-save flip-flop with data selector.

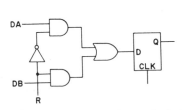

Fig. 11. Carry-save flip-flop with data selector—logical representation.

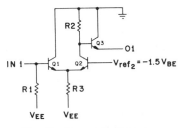

Fig. 12. Output buffer gate.

QRA and QRB are reversed. Now, no new information enters the flip-flop while R is high, the previous state being held. When R is low, new information is accepted by the master. As above, information coming into the flip-flop data input must be stable at the desired level for a minimum setup time before the R upward transition.

CARRY-SAVE FLIP-FLOP AND DATA SELECTOR

A flip-flop with a data selector which must truly select between two arbitrary inputs rather than between an input and the previous flip-flop state is used in the carry-save portion of the multiplier. The circuit is shown in Fig. 10. Three emitters are now provided on the input transistor, one providing feedback for the flip-flop master and two for inputs DA and DB. When R is low, QDA is on and input DA is active. When R is high, QDB is on and input DB is active. Once the input selection has been made, the operation is identical with that of the basic flip-flop.

The logical representation of this flip-flop and data selector is shown in Fig. 11.

FINAL STAGE PARTIAL SUM FLIP-FLOP AND DATA SELECTOR

The data selector for the final stage of a TC/TC implementation must accept an input from the full adder or from either $P03$ or $P04$. The flip-flop is made like the carry-save flip-flop with the adder output going into one input and the other input going to an external beam. $P03$ and $P04$ are brought out to adjacent beams and a connection is made on the ceramic for either $P03$ or $P04$. The data selector connection is such that, when R is low, the adder output is selected.

To drive external logic from the final stage, a buffer OR gate is used. The schematic is shown in Fig. 12. The current source is now resistor $R3$ to eliminate the diode temperature variation of the output voltage swing. Since V_{ref} is $-1.5\ V_{BE}$ in this gate, saturation of $Q2$ is no longer a problem. The output emitter follower is designed to provide 2.5 mA of output current, significantly greater than any of the internal emitter followers. Input levels at $IN1$ are $-1\ V_{BE}$ and $-2\ V_{BE}$, the direct outputs of the internal circuitry. Output levels are

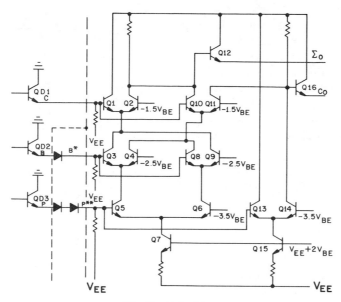

Fig. 13. Full adder.

-1 V_{BE} and $[R2/R3 (-2.5 \, V_{BE} - V_{EE}) - V_{BE(Q3)}]$. $R2/R3$ is selected to provide a V_{BE} drop across $R2$ at 25°C (-0.70 V). The output level at this temperature is then $(-0.70 - V_{BE(Q3)})$. As temperature is increased, a lower level is maintained than if the output low voltage strictly had a $-2 \, V_{BE}$ characteristic.

Full Adder

The full adder used in the multiplier is shown in Fig. 13. It is a three-level current-steering tree as simplified from a fully expanded tree by Baugh and Wooley [7]. Reference levels are $-1.5 \, V_{BE}$, $-2.5 \, V_{BE}$, and $-3.5 \, V_{BE}$ with an active current source of the type described for the data selector and flip-flop. Diode level shifts are provided at the inputs as needed to interface with the $-1 \, V_{BE}$, $-2 \, V_{BE}$ output levels of the other circuitry.

Chip Power Supplies

All reference voltages used in the multiplier circuitry are generated on the multiplier chip from a standard ECL -5.2 V $\pm$ 10 percent supply. Two V_{EE} leads and three ground leads are brought out to chip beams and are connected on the ceramic.

A single $-0.5 \, V_{BE}$ supply located at the center of the chip provides the main reference level. The current source reference level of $V_{EE} + 2 \, V_{BE}$ is independently generated at two sites in the chip. Flip-flop and data selector reference levels of $-1.5 \, V_{BE}$, $-3.5 \, V_{BE}$, and $-3.35 \, V_{BE}$ are generated once in each multiplier cell. Finally, the three adder levels ($-1.5 \, V_{BE}$, $-2.5 \, V_{BE}$, and $-3.5 \, V_{BE}$) are generated at each adder site.

Technology

The GIMIC-O technology was selected for the fabrication of the multiplier chip. Selection was made on the basis of density, cost, and yield projections. GIMIC-O is a bipolar, nonepitaxial technology; in essence, it is a triple-diffused technology with the collector and base regions ion implanted for good parameter control. Fabrication begins on a π substrate, 8–15 $\Omega \cdot$ cm. Phosphorus is then implanted and dif-

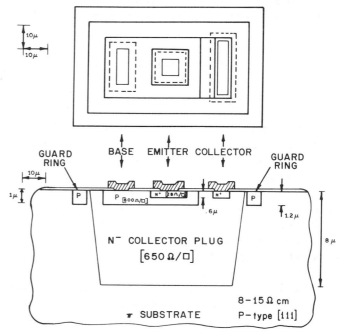

Fig. 14. Minimum GIMIC-O transistor.

fused to an 8 μ depth to give a 650 $\Omega/\square$ n$^-$ collector. A double boron implant gives a 1.2 μ deep base; the low-energy component gives a 600 $\Omega/\square$ surface and the high-energy component provides gain control. Phosphorus is then diffused to a 0.6 μ depth to give a 25 $\Omega/\square$ n$^+$ emitter. The device is completed with contact windows and Ti–Pt–Au metallization.

A minimum transistor in the GIMIC-O process is shown in top view and cross section in Fig. 14. Because of the relatively narrow base of the devices, transistors in the process are inherently fast and are largely limited by a high parasitic collector resistance. The choice of nonsaturating, current-steering circuitry at low power levels is an ideal mate for this technology and allows the fabrication of relatively high-speed, low-power circuits.

The GIMIC-O technology provides well-controlled p-type 600 $\Omega/\square$ resistors with a temperature coefficient of 0.1 percent/°C. Collector resistance is approximately 700 $\Omega/\square$ without base and 1000 $\Omega/\square$ under the base with a temperature coefficient of 0.75 percent/°C. Emitter resistance is less than 27 $\Omega/\square$ and transistor gains range from 50 to 175.

The emitter diffusion is used as a crossunder material. Several types of crossunders are possible, two of which are used in the multiplier:

1) n^+ emitter on π substrate—low capacitance, low density,

2) n^+ emitter on p^+ base on π substrate—high capacitance, high density.

Type 1) crossunders are used for signal leads. Type 2) are used for crossing power supplies and reference supplies.

ANALYSIS AND DESIGN

The previously described multiplier circuitry was analyzed over a wide range of operating conditions. To satisfy system requirements, the multiplier was designed to have a worst case operating frequency of 18 MHz over a 0–85°C temperature range and a ±10 percent power supply range. Circuit power levels were selected to provide this performance.

Computer simulation over a wide range of transit times indicates that the multiplier circuitry is limited by R_c parasitics rather than intrinsic transistor speeds. Consequently, tradeoffs exist between circuit speed and power dissipation. Increases in the power level of the circuitry are limited by the possibility of saturation of the input transistors of the EFL gate. The saturation potential exists because the nominal 0.5 V_{BE} forward bias on the base–collector of the transistor is increased by both the high resistance of GIMIC-O transistors and by their high temperature coefficient. Two things have been done in the multiplier circuitry to prevent saturation of the EFL input transistor over the operating temperature range.

1) The current source for the EFL gates has a V_{BE} temperature coefficient, decreasing the drop across the collector resistance at high temperature.

2) The input transistor has a double collector contact, as shown in Fig. 15. Collector 1 is used to connect the external resistor r_{ext} to the transistor. This is a relatively high current path. Collector 2 is used to supply contact for the base of the following transistor; only a small base current flows through it. Consequently, collector resistance r_{c1} can be used as part of the overall collector resistor required to generate the output voltage swing. No additional drop occurs to the intrinsic collector of the transistor.

Saturation possibility also exists on inputs $R1$, $R2$, D, and P_{-1} when these inputs are high. A nominal forward bias of 0.5 V_{BE} can occur on the base–collector junction of the transistor to which they connect; current flowing through parasitic collector resistance can increase this forward bias further on the intrinsic base–collector junction. Collector resistance on these transistors can be reduced by half-U or U-shaped emitter diffusions in the collectors.

Another speed limiting factor in the present circuit can exist if the EFL FF inputs are loaded with large capacitances. When the clock is high, the current source to the input is off and the

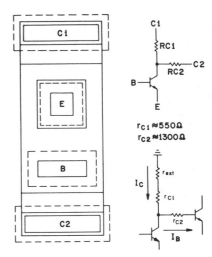

Fig. 15. GIMIC-O transistor with Kelvin contact connection.

voltage on the input leads can float up to ground. When the clock goes low, the current must have time to discharge the input capacitance to as low as $-1.5\ V_{BE}$. The discharge rate is limited by the current source and, consequently, a minimum low time exists between clocks. This is not a severe limitation if these inputs are connected to their associated shift register or multiplier pins on a common ceramic substrate, but can be a limitation in a DIP breadboard.

The computer simulation of the multiplier circuitry did not include the action of the substrate p-n-p which is always present in GIMIC-O transistors. The presence of this p-n-p additionally helps keep the devices in the multiplier circuitry out of saturation by diverting excess drive to the substrate after the collector–base of the transistor is turned on. Since the gain of the p-n-p can go as low as 2, the measures described above had to be taken, but with a typical gain of 20, the p-n-p is generally effective in eliminating a large portion of the storage delay.

All external inputs of the multiplier chip present a threshold of $-1.5\ V_{BE}$, making the inputs compatible directly with other ECL logic. Input signal level shifting within the circuit for connection to various levels in the trees is most often accomplished by diodes. A notable exception is the clock driver circuitry, where a double emitter follower is used to insure good capacitive charging characteristics. Each clock driver supplies one cell.

As described earlier, the active current source for the logic provides a V_{BE} voltage across a resistor, thereby making the source current independent of power supply. The negative temperature characteristic helps prevent saturation by decreasing the collector voltage swing as temperature increases. While this decreases internal noise margins, the temperature tracking of the internal output levels with all of the internal reference levels insures swings which remain properly centered about input thresholds.

The output buffer gate is designed to provide 2.5 mA output current at ECL compatible levels. The additional delay is tolerable since this gate is not in the critical multiplier path. If the output is to provide the P_{-1} input to another chip, an

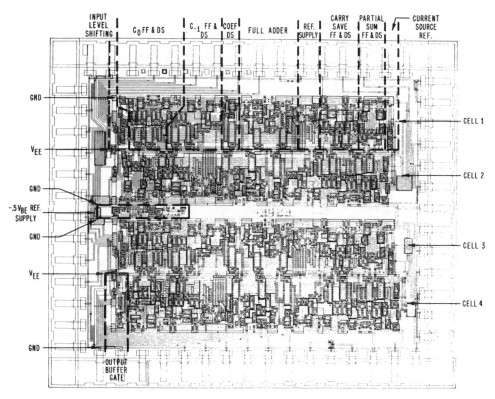

Fig. 16. Multiplier chip composite drawing.

internal output $P04(I)$ can be used. The output buffer utilizes a resistive current source to eliminate the V_{BE} temperature characteristic of the voltage swing and provide a swing similar to standard ECL.

LAYOUT

The multiplier chip organization is shown in the composite drawing in Fig. 16. It can be seen that the chip is organized as four cells with the $-0.5\ V_{BE}$ supply in the center. Cell wiring proceeds in horizontal channels across the cells, utilizing an n^+ diffusion in the collector region of otherwise minimum transistors as crossunder regions. Increases to either the capacitance or resistance of the transistor are small. Additionally, the circuit forms are not greatly sensitive to capacitive loading at collectors of transistors in lower levels of the current trees.

Crossunders are used primarily on reference power supplies. When signal lines must be crossed, the crossunder is placed in a portion of the path that carries only base current. As described earlier, emitter n^+-on-substrate crossunders are used for signal leads. For greater packing density, emitter n^+-on-base p^+-on-substrate crossunders are sometimes used for reference supplies.

Also in Fig. 16, the various logical portions of cell 1 are indicated. In each cell, ground runs across the top of the cell and V_{EE} across the bottom, as shown. Three ground and two V_{EE} lines are brought out and connected on the ceramic.

In the layout of the multiplier chip, minimum geometry transistors with extended collectors are primarily used. Where collector resistance must be lowered because of saturation

potential, a half-U or U-shaped emitter diffusion is placed in the collector to surround the transistor emitter. At the input of EFL-type gates, the double collector transistor described earlier is used.

Resistors used in the design are p-type and greater than $9\ \mu$ wide, except in some noncritical locations where $7\ \mu$ widths have been used. Minimum gold line width is $10\ \mu$; minimum metal spacing is $8\ \mu$ in small regions and $10\ \mu$ for long runs. Minimum contact windows are $50\ \mu^2$. A conservative set of design rules has been used in this design, resulting in a 12 300 mil^2 active area. A layout based on tighter design rules offers a potential for improved speed.

RESULTS

Two lots of multiplier chips have been processed in the Allentown, PA Device Development Laboratory. A photomicrograph of one of the completed chips is shown in Fig. 17. The lots have been tested on a SENTRY 600 test set and very good yields have been observed.

The multiplier chips are given a complete set of parametric and functional tests. All parametric results were close to design values. For functional testing, the chip is exercised in 2-bit sections. A set of 152 test vectors selected with the aid of a logic analysis program detect all but 3 of 451 faults in each half of the chip.

Chips have been packaged in 24-pin DIP's as TC/TC multipliers, TC/SM multipliers, and serial adders, and tested for speed in these configurations. In completely programmable modes (with all inputs varying pseudo randomly), correct operation was obtained at 23–25 MHz. The units were driven

Fig. 17. Photomicrograph of multiplier chip.

by MECL-10K components and outputs were compared to those of a logically equivalent breadboard of MECL-10K components.

CONCLUSIONS

A 4-bit general-purpose serial multiplier chip has been designed and fabricated. The chips are processed in the low cost GIMIC-O process with single layer metallization. Chips can be connected to perform five serial functions necessary for digital filter application with different ceramic patterns:

1) TC/TC multiplication,
2) TC/SM multiplication,
3) serial addition,
4) 2^{-K} scaling,
5) overflow correction.

All of these functions can be provided in 24-pin DIP's.

Nonsaturating circuit techniques, emitter function logic combined with current-steering trees, have been effectively utilized to make a high performance, low power circuit using a simple bipolar technology. The multiplier is ECL compatible at inputs and outputs. Operation at clock frequencies greater than 20 MHz for fully programmable multiplication at 37.5 mW/bit is obtainable. Good yields have been obtained, consistent with the expectations for the GIMIC-O technology.

The multiplier was designed to satisfy a specific system requirement, but has been generalized to maximize exploratory applicability to other users. Customized designs for high volume applications, based on results to this point, offer potentials of yet higher yield, higher operating frequencies, and lower power.

ACKNOWLEDGMENT

The author is grateful to G. L. Baldwin, J. H. Condon, S. K. Freeny, C.-Y. Kao, C. F. Kurth, R. A. Pedersen, and S. K. Tewksbury for helpful suggestions and discussions. The author is also grateful to J. A. Grant and R. W. Hallock for chip and package testing support.

REFERENCES

[1] L. B. Jackson, J. F. Kaiser, and H. S. McDonald, "An approach to the implementation of digital filters," *IEEE Trans. Audio Electroacoust.*, vol. AU-16, pp. 413-421, Sept. 1968.
[2] R. F. Lyon and R. B. Kieburtz, private communication.
[3] Z. E. Skokin, "EFL logic family for LSI," in *Int. Solid-State Circuits Conf., Dig. Tech. Papers*, 1973.
[4] P. T. Panousis and R. L. Pritchett, "GIMIC-O—A low cost, non-epitaxial bipolar LSI technology suitable for application to TTL circuits," presented at the Int. Electron Devices Meeting, 1974.
[5] S. K. Tewksbury, private communication.
[6] A. D. Booth and K. H. V. Booth, *Automatic Digital Calculators*, 2nd ed. New York: Academic, 1956.
[7] C. R. Baugh and B. A. Wooley, private communication.

T. Kilburn, D. Edwards, and D. Aspinall (Univ. Manchester, Manchester, England), "A parallel arithmetic unit using a saturated transistor fast carry circuit," *Inst. Elec. Eng. paper 3302M*, 1960, pp. 573–584.

A. Habibi and P. Wintz (Elec. Eng. Dep., Purdue Univ., Lafayette, IN), "Fast multipliers," *IEEE Trans. Comput.*, vol. C-19, pp. 153–157, 1970.

H. Ling (IBM Res. Lab, San Jose, CA), "High speed computer multiplication using a multiple-bit decoding algorithm," *IEEE Trans. Comput.*, vol. C-19, pp. 706–709, 1970.

T. Hallin and M. Flynn (Bell Lab., Naperville, IL 60540; Dep. Comput. Sci., The Johns Hopkins Univ., Baltimore, MD), "Pipelining of arithmetic functions," *IEEE Trans. Comput.*, vol. C-21, pp. 880–886, 1972.

S. Bandyopadhyay, S. Basu, and A. Choudhury (Dep. Radio Physics and Electron., Univ. Calcutta, Calcutta, India), "An interative array for multiplication of signed binary numbers," *IEEE Trans. Comput.*, vol. C-21, pp. 921–922, 1972.

A. Kamal and M. Ghannam (Elec. Eng. Dept., Cairo Univ., Giza, Cairo, Egypt; EEE Lab Natural Res. Center, Giza, Cairo, Egypt), "High speed multiplication systems," *IEEE Trans. Comput.*, vol. C-21, pp. 1017–1021, 1972.

C. Baugh and B. Wooley (Bell Lab., Holmdel, NJ 07733), "A two's complement parallel array multiplication algorithm," *IEEE Trans. Comput.*, vol. C-22, pp. 1045–1047, 1973.

P. Blankenship (M.I.T. Lincoln Lab., Lexington, MA 02173), "Comments on a two's complement parallel array multiplication algorithm," *IEEE Trans. Comput.*, vol. C-23, p. 1327, 1974.

J. Gibson and R. Gibbard (Elec. Eng. Dep., Univ. Canterbury, Christchurch, New Zealand), "Synthesis and comparison of two's complement parallel multipliers," *IEEE Trans. Comput.*, vol. C-24, pp. 1020–1027, 1975.

L. Rubinfield (Comput. Syst. Lab., Washington Univ., St. Louis, MO 63110) "A proof of the modified Booth's algorithm for multiplication," *IEEE Trans. Comput.*, vol. C-24, pp. 1014–1015, 1975.

C. Toma (Elec. Dep., Traian Vuia Polytechnic Inst. of Timisoara, Timisoara, Romania), "Cellular logic array for high speed signed binary number multiplication," *IEEE Trans. Comput.*, vol. C-24, pp. 932–935, 1975.

A Versatile Multiplying Digital-to-Analog Converter

N. THEDCHANAMOORTHY, MEMBER, IEEE, AND
J. B. PLANT, MEMBER, IEEE

Abstract—A modified binary-weighted resistor multiplying digital-to-analog (MDAC) converter with a full scale (±12 V) analog bandwidth in excess of 500 kHz is described. Its settling time following changes in digital inputs of either polarity is less than 2 μs. The dc resolution is 0.01 percent and the dynamic error increases from 0.01 percent at 50 kHz to 0.1 percent at 250 kHz.

Index Terms—Analog switch, computer output devicer, digital-to-analog converter, electronically variable resistor, interface components.

I. INTRODUCTION

A multiplying digital-to-analog converter (MDAC), being essentially an electronically variable resistor, permits the rapid adjustment of circuit parameter values by means of a digital signal. Whereas a conventional digital-to-analog converter (DAC) uses a fixed reference voltage and a digital signal of fixed sign, the four-quadrant MDAC accepts both digital and analog signals of any polarity as inputs; the output being the product of the two signals.

This paper describes a modified version of the binary-weighted resistor MDAC having improved full-scale (±12 V) analog bandwidth. This and other advantages are discussed in Section II. A very fast (on and off) analog switch of novel design essential to the MDAC is described in Section III. A fast pulse generator used to drive the switch is described in Section IV. A summary of the MDAC performance is given in Section V.

Manuscript received July 27, 1971; revised April 18, 1972. This work was supported by Defense Research Board Grant 4003-06.
N. Thedchanamoorthy is with the Department of Mathematics, Algonquin College, Ottawa, Ont., Canada.
J. B. Plant is with the Department of Electrical Engineering, Royal Military College of Canada, Kingston, Ont., Canada.

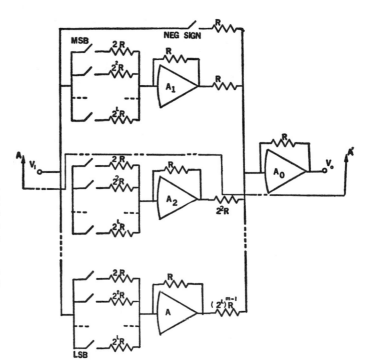

Fig. 1. Basic and modified MDAC.

an upper limit is placed on l by the allowed loading on the input signal V_i, which determines the minimum value of R, and the leakage (or off) resistance R_L of the analog switch, which given R and the required accuracy, implies an upper limit on the LSB resistor (see the Appendix) which has the value $2^l R$.

These difficulties can be overcome by using $R\text{-}2R$ ladder network types in parallel as shown in Fig. 1. The idea is based on the fact that

$$2^n = (2^l)^m, \qquad n = ml. \qquad (1)$$

The number of different resistor sizes is reduced to $l+m-1$ and, more important, the maximum value of a resistor in series with an analog switch is $2^l R$. For example, in the 12-bit unit used by the authors $m=2$ and $l=6$ resulted in a very practical value of $64R$ for the least significant bit resistor in each of the two parallel stages at a cost of one additional operational amplifier.

III. THE ANALOG SWITCH

The kth bit of the MDAC is shown in Fig. 2, where the components shown with suffix 2 are additions used to increase the speed of the more common JFET analog switch which is indicated by the components with suffix 1.

The most elementary JFET switch consists of only the transistor Q_1 with the analog input V_i supplied at the source S, the control V_c supplied at the gate G, and the output taken from the drain D. For $V_{GS} > \epsilon$ ($\epsilon \simeq 0$), the JFET behaves as a semiconductor diode, whereas, for

II. THE MODIFIED MDAC

Two MDAC designs are common: the $R\text{-}2R$ ladder network type and the binary-weighted resistor type [1]. Although the former uses only two sizes of precision resistors R and $2R$, it requires not only twice as many resistors and analog switches per bit as the latter, but also has longer digital settling times due to the stray capacitance of every $R\text{-}2R$ junction. An l-bit binary-weighted resistor type requires $l+1$ precision resistors of values $2^k R$, $k = 0, 1, \cdots, l$ and l analog switches as shown above the line AA' in Fig. 1. For such networks.

Reprinted from *IEEE Trans. Comput.*, vol. C-21, pp. 1113–1116, Oct. 1972.

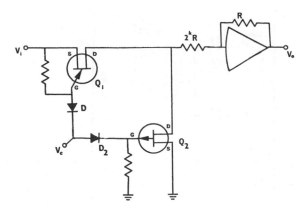

Fig. 2. High-speed switch.

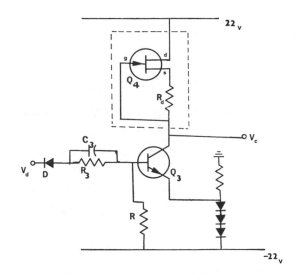

Fig. 3. Control signal generator.

$$V_p < V_{GS} < \epsilon, \qquad (2)$$

its source drain terminal behavior is that of a variable resistor r_{SD}, which is a monotonic function of V_{GS} attaining its smallest value at $V_{GS} \simeq 0$ and such a high value at $V_{GS} \leq V_p$, the "pinchoff" voltage,[1] that the switch is considered OFF. The control must keep the switch OFF for all values of V_i; hence

$$V_{c(\min)} < V_{i(\min)} + V_p. \qquad (3)$$

In the absence of R_1 and D_1 in Fig. 2, (2) implies that

$$V_{c(\max)} - \epsilon < V_i < V_{c(\max)} - V_p \qquad (4)$$

where $V_{c(\max)}$ is the control which keeps the switch ON. Relation (4) seriously limits the useful range of V_i, and worse, from an accuracy point of view, as V_i ranges over the limits of (4) r_{DS} will range from approximately zero to the OFF value. The addition of R_1 and D_1 eliminates these serious limitations. If $V_{c(\max)} > V_{i(\max)}$ for the ON control, D_1 remains back biased and

$$V_{GS} = \frac{(V_{c(\max)} - V_i)}{1 + (R_b/R_1)}, \qquad (5)$$

where R_b is the off resistance of D_1. Since $R_b \gg R_1$, r_{DS} will remain very small for all values of V_i which is no longer constrained by V_p. A control voltage satisfying (3) will forward bias D_1 and Q_1 will be turned off.

The turn-on time of Q_1 is limited by the rise time of V_c which is discussed later. However, to turn Q_1 off the GD capacitance must be discharged through the $2^k R$ resistor; hence the turnoff time increases rapidly with k. This situation could be remedied by placing the switch between the $2^k R$ resistor and the summing junction but then these currents produce large voltage spikes at the output. The addition of the components with suffix 2 achieves the desired result without producing large output voltage spikes. The p-channel JFET Q_2 provides a low-resistance (the r_{DS} of Q_2) discharge path to ground when the n-channel JFET Q_1 is to be turned off.

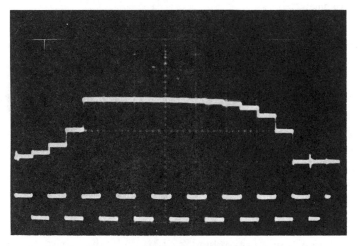

Fig. 4. Response of MDAC to changes in magnitude bits of digital input.

IV. THE CONTROL SIGNAL GENERATOR

The control signal generator is shown in Fig. 3 where the innovation consists of that portion of the diagram enclosed by dotted lines. In the more common circuit, the n-channel JFET Q_4 and resistor R_d are replaced by a collector resistor R_c. In both circuits, the signal V_D is supplied by DTL or TTL and good turn-on times for Q_3 are obtained using the capacitor C_3. The turn-off time for Q_3, however, diminishes with the collector resistance whose lower limit is determined by thermal problems. The components inside the dotted line in Fig. 4 constitute a variable collector resistance which allows a faster turn off at reduced collector currents. The reverse voltage bias V_{GS} developed across the resistor R_d is proportional to the collector current; hence the $r_{DS}(\text{ON})$ of Q_4 increases with the collector current. Once Q_3 is on, its collector current is limited to a small value by a large r_{DS} of Q_3, but as Q_3 begins to turn off, r_{DS} decreases so that the stored charge in Q_3 has a low-resistance discharge path. The slope of the turn-off characteristic of Q_3 in Fig. 4 can be varied by means of R_d to minimize switching spikes.

V. Experimental Results

A four-quadrant 12-bit MDAC was built and tested. The upper trace in Fig. 4 is of the output voltage (scale 5 V/div) when the analog input is held constant at −10 V and the digital input is changed at the rate indicated by the lower trace (time base 10 μs/div). The output, expressed as a fraction of the input, varies from left to right according to the sequence $(\sigma_1-\sigma_5)$, $(\sigma_1-\sigma_4)$, $\cdots$, $(\sigma_1-\sigma_2)$, 0, σ_{12}, σ_{11}, $\cdots$, σ_1, $(\sigma_1-\sigma_{12})$, $(\sigma_1-\sigma_{11})$ $\cdots$ :: where

$$\sigma_k \equiv \sum_{w=k}^{12} \frac{1}{2^w} \qquad (6)$$

The analog input is again −10 V dc in Fig. 5, but now the digital input is alternately $+\sigma_1$ and −1. σ_1 corresponds to all of the magnitude bits being on with the sign bit off and vice versa for −1; this represents the worst case. The time scale in Fig. 5 is 1 μs/div. The settling time is about 2 μs and the slew rate is about 50 V/μs.

The MDAC tested has a 20 V (peak-to-peak) bandwidth in excess of 500 kHz. The principal source of error in the design was found to be due to the interelectrode capacitance of the JFET in its off state. This feedthrough was found to limit the worst case accuracy to 0.01 percent at 50 kHz, 0.1 percent at 250 kHz, and 0.15 percent at 400 kHz.

The performance specifications which are summarized in Table I compare favorably with both recent designs [2] and commercially available MDAC's.

VI. Conclusions

A simple modification of the basic binary weighted resistor type DAC can reduce the number of different values of precision resistors from $ml+1$ to $m+l-1$ at the cost of $m-1$ additional operational amplifiers per DAC. The modification minimizes leakage problems which are serious when using a large number of bits.

Switchoff times have been significantly reduced by means of an analog switch using n-channel and a p-channel JFET. Equalization of the on and off times of the individual channels to reduce switching spikes can be achieved using a JFET with reverse bias proportional to the collector current in the collector circuit of the pulse generator.

The main limitation of the design is the capacitance feedthrough across the off analog switches which should be lessened, at increased cost, with the use of lower capacitance JFET's.

Appendix

When an input is summed through n-resistances 2^kR, $k=1, 2, \cdots, n$ by a single-operational amplifier, leakage problems arise when the off resistance R_L of a channel switch is comparable to the resistance 2^nR of the LSB channel. When only the MSB switch is off, a bound on the value of R_L is

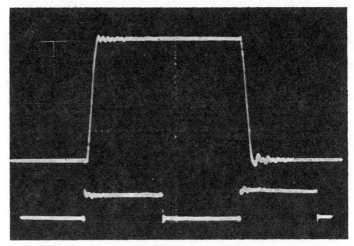

Fig. 5. Response of MDAC to changes in sign bit of digital input.

TABLE I
PERFORMANCE SPECIFICATIONS OF THE FOUR-QUADRANT MDAC

Permissible analog inputs	−12 to +12 V
Output voltage	−12 to +12 V
Number of bits	12 plus sign bit
Resolution	1/2 LSB = 1/8196 of input
Settling time	2 μs (to 0.1 percent), 10 μs (to 0.01 percent)
Slew rate	50 V/μs
Large signal (full power) bandwidth:	>500 kHz
Accuracy	0.1 percent (to 50 kHz), 0.1 percent (250 kHz), 0.15 percent (400 kHz)

$$\frac{1}{R_L + 2R} < \frac{1}{2^{n+1}R}, \qquad (7)$$

i.e., the effect of the leakage at the MSB alone is less than the resolution of the MDAC ($\frac{1}{2}$LSB). In the worst case, with all switches off, we require

$$\sum_{k=1}^{n} \frac{1}{R_L + 2^kR} < \frac{1}{2^{n+1}R}. \qquad (8)$$

For the case of the modified MDAC relation (7) remains the same and (8) becomes

$$\left(\sum_{k=1}^{l} \frac{1}{(R_L + 2^kR)}\right)\left(\sum_{r=0}^{m-1} \frac{1}{2^{lr}}\right) < \frac{1}{2^{n+1}R}. \qquad (9)$$

Now

$$\sum_{k=1}^{n} \frac{1}{R_L + 2^kR} < \frac{n}{R_L + 2R};$$

hence, a conservative design is achieved using the criteria

$$\frac{n}{R_L + 2R} < \frac{1}{2^{n+1}R} \qquad (10)$$

in the case of the unmodified design and

$$\frac{l}{R_L + 2R} < \frac{1}{2^{n+1}R}$$

in the case of the modified design. The former requires $R_L/R > n(2)^{n+1} - 2$ whereas the latter only requires $R_L/R > l(2)^{n+1} - 2$.

REFERENCES

[1] D. F. Hoeschele, Jr., *Analog-to-Digital/Digital-to Analog Conversion Techniques.* New York: Wiley, 1968, ch. 4 and 5.
[2] S. Marjanovic and D. R. Noaks, "A high-speed, high-accuracy, digitally-set potentiometer," *Radio Electron. Eng.,* vol. 38, pp. 345–351, Dec. 1969.

Interpolative Digital-to-Analog Converters

G. R. RITCHIE, MEMBER, IEEE, JAMES C. CANDY, MEMBER, IEEE, AND
WILLIAM H. NINKE, MEMBER, IEEE

Abstract—Interpolative digital-to-analog (D/A) converters produce a final output via a two-step process. First, each digital input word is used to control a circuit whose output oscillates rapidly (i.e., many times faster than new digital input values are provided) between coarsely spaced analog values (i.e., many times coarser than the resolution specified by the input word). Second, the oscillating analog signal is low-pass filtered to give the final output. The oscillation pattern is chosen to produce an average value that corresponds to the fine resolution specified by the input word and to ensure that the power of the error (the difference between the oscillating signal and the desired fine resolution output) occurs predominantly out of band. By this means, high-speed operation reduces the need for many finely spaced analog signal amplitudes, a tradeoff which is especially desirable for integrated circuit implementation.

In this paper, the basic operation of interpolative D/A converters is described. Three alternative means of generating patterns are compared with respect to circuit complexity, and amount of baseband distortion introduced. The relative insensitivity of these converters to circuit value variations is emphasized. Applications of the interpolative technique to decoding digital words in both linear and piecewise linearly companded formats are given.

I. INTRODUCTION

CONVENTIONAL techniques [1]–[5] for digital-to-analog (D/A) conversion often use a network of switches and resistors to generate an output analog signal as the weighted sum of a number of individual signals controlled by the input digital code. In decoding N-bit binary words, for example, the switched network normally contains N switches and must be capable of precisions in excess of 1 in 2^N in order to space the output levels in the correct order. When N is large, e.g., greater than 10, these networks are difficult and expensive to construct, and do not lend themselves well to silicon integration; integrated circuits are better adapted to performing coarse

amplitude operations at high speed than to providing high precision in signal amplitudes.

This paper describes a technique for converting periodically supplied digital input signals to analog form by using finer time resolution than the digital input signal period, but coarser amplitude resolution than eventually desired in the filtered output signal. The requirements for precision in the amplitudes of the outputs of the switched resistor network are thereby relaxed. A tradeoff is made between speed of operation and precision of operation, and such a tradeoff is well suited to implementation in integrated circuit form. Moreover, the technique is especially appropriate for the decoding of digitized speech signals which have been compressed according to piecewise linear laws.

To understand the fundamentals of the proposed technique, consider the input N-bit data word, supplied at sampling period T, to be composed of two subwords, one an M-bit word consisting of the most significant bits of the input word, and the other an L-bit word consisting of the least significant bits. Denote the particular values of these words by m and l, respectively. The M-bit word will be applied to a conventional D/A; rather than providing 2^N levels, however, this D/A will provide only $(2^M + 1)$ output levels. The L-bit word will be used to modulate the D/A output in a way which, when low-pass filtered with a filter of cutoff frequency $1/2T$, provides, effectively, fine resolution between these levels.

In general, as illustrated in Fig. 1, the value n of a particular input code word will be somewhere between the mth and the $(m + 1)$th of the $(2^M + 1)$ available output levels. In a conventional D/A implementation in which the digital value is held fixed during a sample period (or in a shared decoder situation in which a sample and hold is used in each channel), the output signal would assume the value n, as shown, during the total interval T. We can express this desired output value as

Paper approved by the Associate Editor for Data Communication Systems of the IEEE Communications Society for publication without oral presentation. Manuscript received April 8, 1974.

The authors are with Bell Laboratories, Holmdel, N. J. 07733.

Reprinted from *IEEE Trans. Commun.*, vol. COM-22, pp. 1797–1806, Nov. 1974.

263

$$n = l + m2^L, \qquad (1)$$

which can also be written as

$$n = l(m + 1) + (2^L - l)m. \qquad (2)$$

If now the normal sample interval T is subdivided into 2^L timing subintervals and the output is made equal to level m for $(2^L - l)$ subintervals and equal to level $(m + 1)$ for l subintervals (see Fig. 1), the average output level over the sample period will be exactly that level given by (2), i.e., the desired analog output value. Because this procedure of averaging between coarse levels is related to simple linear interpolation, we shall refer to converters of this type as interpolative D/A converters.

It should be stressed that, although an interpolative D/A will generate exactly the desired *average* output, the output waveform does differ from the more usual sampled-and-held waveform; there is a significant mean-square error. In fact, if all of the input codes are equally likely, the mean-square error is given by

$$\overline{E^2} = \frac{1}{2^{2L}} \sum_{l=1}^{2^L} \left[(2^L - l)l^2 + l(2^L - l)^2 \right]$$

$$= \frac{2^{2L} - 1}{6} \qquad (3)$$

where the spacing of the 2^N ideal PCM levels is taken to be unity. The power spectrum of the error is determined by the particular set of oscillatory patterns which is chosen to interpolate between the 2^M allowed output levels. Fortunately, it is possible to choose these patterns in such a way that most of the distortion given by (3) lies at frequencies far outside the baseband. Some sets of patterns give better performance, from the standpoint of baseband distortion, while others are simpler to implement. Three different implementations of the interpolative D/A technique will now be presented. The first uses a modulo-K accumulator, the second a binary rate multiplier, and the third a form of pulse-width modulation. These circuits will be compared with respect to circuit complexity, sensitivity to circuit imperfections, and the amount of baseband distortion introduced. The use of a random number generator to produce an interpolation pattern has recently been advocated in connection with a D/A proposal related to ours [7]. The difficulty of obtaining simply a uniform distribution of random numbers has caused us to ignore this approach in favor of the three mentioned.

II. A CIRCUIT BASED ON MODULO-2^N ACCUMULATION

A. The Circuit

The circuit in Fig. 2 illustrates the basic technique for D/A conversion. It uses an 8-bit input word which is uniformly representative of positive analog amplitudes. The values M and L used in this example are both chosen to be 4. A narrow clock pulse C_2 is in phase with the input

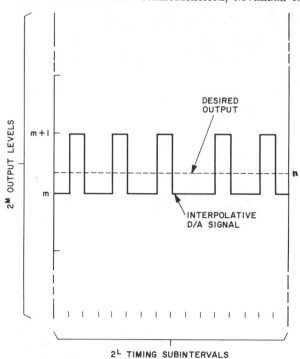

Fig. 1. Illustration of interpolation by time averaging, $L = 4$.

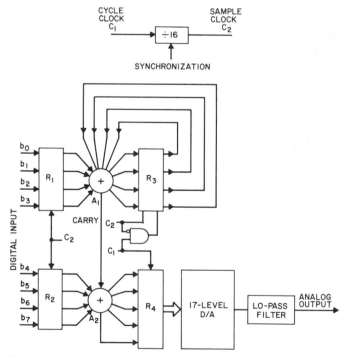

Fig. 2. Interpolative D/A converter that employs digital accumulation.

data and a second clock C_1 provides pulses at a rate that is 16 times (2^L) faster than the first clock. The clock waveforms are illustrated in Fig. 3.

As clock pulse C_2 loads the input data, the least significant 4 bits go to register R_1 and the most significant bits to register R_2. At the same time, the content of the register R_3 is made equal to eight (in general, 2^{L-1}). A binary adder circuit $A1$ generates the sum of the least significant bits of the input and the content of the accumu-

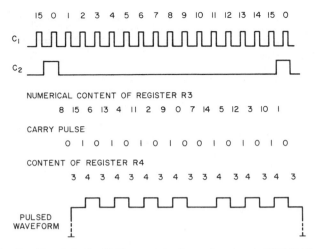

Fig. 3. Signals in the D/A converter for an input code 0011.0111 ∝ 3 7/16.

lator register R_3. The modulo-16 (in general, modulo-2^L) value of this sum is placed back into register R_3 on the leading edge of each pulse of clock C_1.

Every time this sum exceeds fifteen ($2^L - 1$) a carry signal is fed to a second binary adder $A2$ and summed with the value of the most significant bits. The output of adder $A2$ enters the output register R_4 at the leading edge of each C_1 clock pulse. A resistor network, driven by the contents of register R_4, produces the analog output. This output corresponds to the value of the most significant bits if there is no carry signal generated by adder $A1$. When there is a carry, the output corresponds to one more than the most significant bits. If we represent the numerical value of the least significant bits by l and the value of the most significant bits by m, then l is added to the contents of R_3 sixteen times during each cycle. A carry is generated l times and no carry $(16 - l)$ times during each sample period, and the average output voltage is

$$m(16 - l) + (m + 1)l = 16m + l$$

which is the desired analog value.

Table I shows diagramatically the times that carry pulses occur and increase the output voltage. Each row corresponds to a particular value for the least significant bits and each column corresponds to a time interval of clock pulse C_1. Notice that the carry pulses occur at fairly evenly spaced times and are approximately symmetrically positioned in the sample period. This uniformity reduces the inband component of the D/A noise, as will be seen in the next section.

B. Performance of the Circuit

Although the output waveform of an interpolating D/A has the same dc value as a signal ideally reconstructed from the digital sample, there is an appreciable time-varying difference between the two signals, as indicated by (3) and Fig. 1. To provide a reference frame, we will compare the baseband component of this error or D/A noise, to the magnitude of the quantizing noise in the ideally

reconstructed signal. When unit magnitude represents the smallest PCM step size, the quantizing noise has an average baseband power equal to 1/12.

The power spectrum of the noise may be determined by using the technique described in the Appendix. Its form for the accumulator type D/A is shown in Fig. 4. The total D/A noise power, as given by (3) for the $l = 4$ case, is $10 \log (42.5) = 16.3$ dB. The baseband noise, however, is only -18.5 dB, which is small compared to PCM quantizing noise of -10.8 dB. By adding the D/A noise power to the quantizing noise power, we find that the noise penalty for the accumulator type interpolating D/A is less than 0.7 dB. Curve (a) in Fig. 5 is a low-frequency expansion of Fig. 4, and shows the nature of the baseband D/A noise more clearly.

The example described above demonstrates that the D/A noise is small when four bits are assigned to the least significant group; in general, the noise will depend on L, the number of bits so assigned. A large value for L increases the total noise as given by (3), but it simultaneously increases the cycle rate in proportion to 2^L, thus moving the noise to higher frequency. The graph in Fig. 6(a), obtained by simulation, shows how the D/A noise depends on the value L. It is satisfying to see that the D/A noise is always much less than the expected PCM noise. The choice of relative values for M and L can therefore be made from practical considerations; it need not be restricted by considerations of noise.

C. Tolerance of the Circuit to Imprecision

An important factor in evaluating D/A converter circuits is their tolerance to component imprecisions, and there are two major sources of imprecision in the circuit of Fig. 2. Errors can arise from incorrect levels generated by the resistor network and from mistiming which introduces variations into the width of the pulses in the resistor network. In practice there is little difficulty in obtaining clocks having adequately stable frequencies to insure uniform timing intervals over a sample time. Notice that in Fig. 2 the clock C_2 is connected directly to the output register R_4 without interruption, ensuring regular timing of the output waveform.

Amplitude errors can be caused by imprecise circuit components and by switching transients. One method for reducing effects of such imprecision is to avoid use of $(1 + M)$-bit permuted codes in the output register R_4, using instead a 2^M-bit register containing ONES in the m least significant cells. For example, in Fig. 2 if a 5-bit binary code is held in register R_4, and permutation of values for these bits provides the required seventeen $(2^M + 1)$ output states, severe transients and errors can occur at major bit transitions of the code, as when the output changes from level sixteen (01111) to level seventeen (10000) and, consequently, all five bits change simultaneously, four going off and one switching on. Careful matching of circuit values is required in order to avoid error in this step size, which depends on the difference

TABLE I
TIMING OF CARRY PULSES FROM AN ACCUMULATOR FOR VARIOUS VALUES OF THE LEAST SIGNIFICANT BITS, l ($L = 4$)

Amplitude l	Time Intervals															
	1	2	3	4	5	6	7	8	9	10	11	12	13	14	15	16
0	0	0	0	0	0	0	0	0	0	0	0	0	0	0	0	0
1	0	0	0	0	0	0	0	1	0	0	0	0	0	0	0	0
2	0	0	0	1	0	0	0	0	0	0	0	1	0	0	0	0
3	0	0	1	0	0	0	0	1	0	0	0	0	1	0	0	0
4	0	1	0	0	0	1	0	0	0	1	0	0	0	1	0	0
5	0	1	0	0	1	0	0	1	0	0	0	1	0	0	1	0
6	0	1	0	1	0	0	1	0	0	1	0	1	0	0	1	0
7	0	1	0	1	0	1	0	1	0	0	1	0	1	0	1	0
8	1	0	1	0	1	0	1	0	1	0	1	0	1	0	1	0
9	1	0	1	0	1	0	1	1	0	1	0	1	0	1	0	1
10	1	0	1	1	0	1	0	1	1	0	1	1	0	1	0	1
11	1	0	1	1	0	1	1	1	0	1	1	0	1	1	0	1
12	1	1	0	1	1	1	0	1	1	1	0	1	1	1	0	1
13	1	1	0	1	1	1	1	1	0	1	1	1	1	0	1	1
14	1	1	1	1	0	1	1	1	1	1	1	1	0	1	1	1
15	1	1	1	1	1	1	1	1	0	1	1	1	1	1	1	1

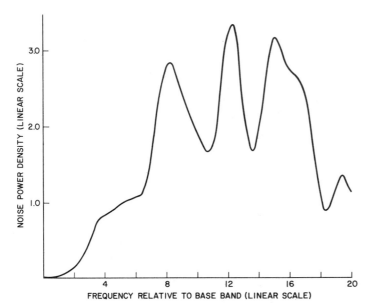

Fig. 4. Spectrum of the modulation noise introduced by the D/A that uses accumulation, $L = 4$.

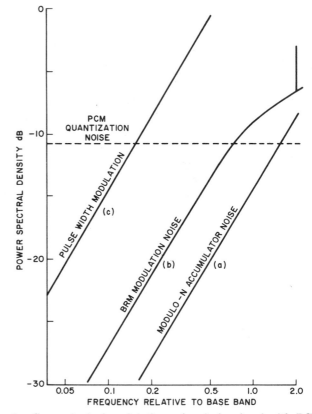

Fig. 5. Comparison of modulation noises in baseband with PCM quantization noise.

of two comparatively large values. Such difficulties are avoided by providing the register R_4 with sixteen (in general, 2^M) stages and the output network with sixteen equally weighted register taps, one for each output level except the first, which corresponds to zero. The register is now loaded such that the lowest m registers are set to ONE while the remaining registers are ZERO. Now increasing the output by one unit requires only that one stage changes state, and the step size is directly proportional to the output generated by that stage; the tolerance of the circuit is improved by the order of 2^M. The additional complexity is not a concern for circuits in which M is less than five. It is one of the advantages of the interpolative D/A technique that the number of bits in the most significant set can be kept relatively small, thus permitting use of the above approach for deriving the output. The fine resolution of the analog output is obtained by interpolating evenly spaced values between the levels defined by the resistor network. Thus there is little practical

difficulty in constructing D/A converters by the method described where the spacing of the fine output values has precision that is directly proportional to the precision of the major circuit components rather than on the small difference of large circuit parameters.

The limitations on the resolutions that can be obtained by this method are twofold. First there is the limit of about five ($2^5 = 32$) on the number of bits that can be conveniently used in the most significant group before the circuit becomes either very complex or fussy, and secondly there is a limit on the number of least significant bits which is set by switching speed. We find in practice

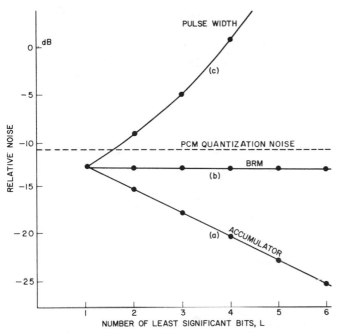

Fig. 6. Dependence of noise on the size of the least significant word.

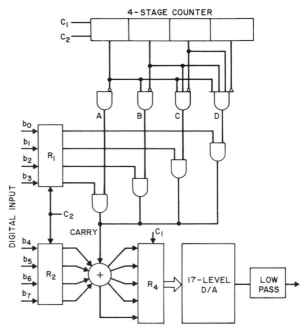

Fig. 7. Interpolative D/A converter that employs a binary rate multiplier (BRM).

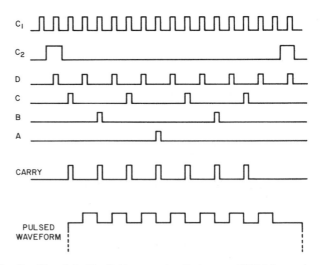

Fig. 8. Signals in the D/A converter that uses a BRM for an input code 0011.0111 ∝ 3 7/16.

that switching transients have a minor effect on the baseband transmission of the circuit; eight-bit resolution has been obtained at a 30-MHz rate for clock pulse C_1 with TTL circuits. The reason that switching transients have only a small effect on resolution can be seen from Table I; notice that while interpolating, each step up of the output voltage is accompanied by a step down in an adjacent cycle. Thus transients tend to cancel out when they are low-pass filtered, especially for high cycle rates.

III. USE OF BINARY RATE MULTIPLIERS

The circuit of Fig. 2 uses an accumulator to generate a sequence of l nearly evenly spaced pulses in response to an input word that has least significant bits representing the value l. An alternative well known technique for generating evenly spaced pulses in response to binary input codes is the binary rate multiplier (BRM). A digital-to-analog converter that uses a BRM is shown in Fig. 7 and its waveforms are illustrated in Fig. 8. It can be seen that the least significant bit of the input word is able to gate one pulse to the adding circuit during a sample time, the next significant bit gates two pulses, and so on, each bit of the least significant group gating the number of pulses appropriate to its order in the binary word. The pulse patterns generated by the BRM for each input value are illustrated in Table II. These patterns differ from those generated by an accumulator (Table I); in fact, the BRM patterns are somewhat inferior because they are not as evenly distributed or as symmetrical with respect to the sample time. Because of this deficiency the baseband D/A noise of the D/A converter in Fig. 7 is 6 dB larger than that of the D/A in Fig. 2, but it is still about 2 dB less than PCM quantizing noise. The overall noise penalty for the BRM circuit is therefore 2.1 dB. Fig. 9 illustrates the spectrum of the modulation noise introduced by the BRM circuit for random inputs, assuming $L = 4$. The

baseband noise is plotted as curve (b) in Fig. 5. The advantage of the BRM over the accumulator is that much of its circuitry may be shared among several D/A converters, whereas the accumulator must be dedicated to one channel at a time; moreover, the BRM is a simpler circuit even for single channels.

IV. USING PULSE-WIDTH MODULATION

The simplest means of utilizing the time domain in D/A converters is pulse-width modulation. We will see, however, that although the circuits for modulating pulse width can be simple, the technique introduces significant modulation noise into the signal unless precautions are taken. Fig. 10 illustrates a method for modulating the width of a pulse in accordance with the value of the least significant group of bits of the input word. Waveforms associated with this circuit are shown in Fig. 11; the output

TABLE II
TIMING OF CARRY PULSES FROM THE BRM FOR VARIOUS VALUES OF THE LEAST SIGNIFICANT BITS, l ($L = 4$)

Amplitude l	Time Intervals															
	1	2	3	4	5	6	7	8	9	10	11	12	13	14	15	16
0	0	0	0	0	0	0	0	0	0	0	0	0	0	0	0	0
1	0	0	0	0	0	0	0	1	0	0	0	0	0	0	0	0
2	0	0	0	1	0	0	0	0	0	0	0	1	0	0	0	0
3	0	0	0	1	0	0	0	1	0	0	0	1	0	0	0	0
4	0	1	0	0	0	1	0	0	0	1	0	0	0	1	0	0
5	0	1	0	0	0	1	0	1	0	1	0	0	0	1	0	0
6	0	1	0	1	0	1	0	0	0	1	0	1	0	1	0	0
7	0	1	0	1	0	1	0	1	0	1	0	1	0	1	0	0
8	1	0	1	0	1	0	1	0	1	0	1	0	1	0	1	0
9	1	0	1	0	1	0	1	1	1	0	1	0	1	0	1	0
10	1	0	1	1	1	0	1	0	1	0	1	1	1	0	1	0
11	1	0	1	1	1	0	1	1	1	0	1	1	1	0	1	0
12	1	1	1	0	1	1	1	0	1	1	1	0	1	1	1	0
13	1	1	1	0	1	1	1	1	1	1	1	0	1	1	1	0
14	1	1	1	1	1	1	1	0	1	1	1	1	1	1	1	0
15	1	1	1	1	1	1	1	1	1	1	1	1	1	1	1	0

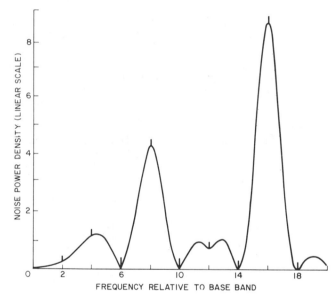

Fig. 9. Spectrum of the modulation noise in the BRM D/A converter ($L = 4$).

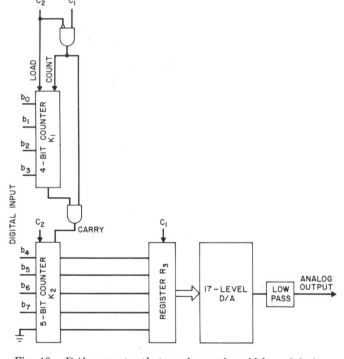

Fig. 10. D/A converter that employs pulse-width modulation.

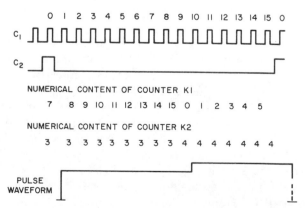

Fig. 11. Signals in the D/A that uses pulse-width modulation for an input 0011.0111 $\propto$ 3 7/16.

of the resistor network equals m for the first $(16 - l)$ cycles and then steps up to $(m + 1)$ for the remaining l cycles.

The spectrum of the D/A noise introduced by the converter is given in Fig. 12. Its baseband components exceed PCM quantization noise by 12 dB, an amount which is intolerable for most applications. An obvious method for reducing this noise is to redesign the circuit so that the time when the output equals $(m + 1)$ is placed centrally with respect to the sample time. This modification reduces the modulation noise by 7.2 dB, but has the disadvantage of using fairly complex circuits that are unattractive when compared with the previously described interpolative D/A circuits.

The pulse-width modulation technique is most useful when the action of the circuit is compressed into a fraction of the sample time, as illustrated in Fig. 13. Comparing this response with that in Fig. 11, we see that the output

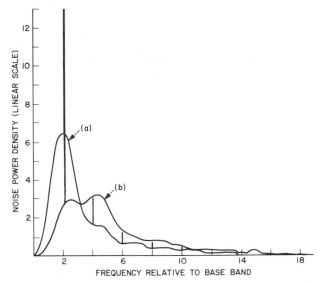

Fig. 12. Spectrum of the modulation noise from pulse-width modulation ($L = 4$). (a) Offset pulses. (b) Centered pulses.

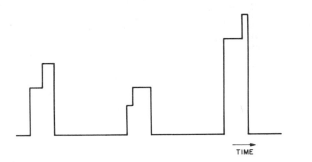

Fig. 13. Example of time compression of the D/A waveform.

occurs in one quarter of the sample time instead of the whole period. Such compression of the signal waveform moves the modulation noise out to high frequencies and reduces the baseband components as illustrated by the graph in Fig. 14, which shows baseband noise plotted against the time compression ratio for a converter having $L = 3$.

Compression of the waveform requires a faster cycle clock, but it has advantages in addition to reducing the baseband D/A noise. The circuit may now be time shared with other channels and moreover, the spectral response of the converter is improved. To appreciate this advantage it must be noted that use of rectangular shaped pulses which span the sample time effectively introduces a filter action having spectral response $[\sin (\omega T/2)]/(\omega T/2)$, that is, a filter response that droops by approximately 4 dB in baseband. When the pulse width is compressed by a factor K the filter response is given by $[\sin (\omega T/2K)]/(\omega T/2K)$, which droops by only 0.3 dB when $K = 4$. Such compression of the signal width can, of course, be used with any interpolative D/A converter, but its ability to improve the noise performance is important only for the pulse-width-modulated converter. Other methods are available for reducing modulation noise; for example, an "integrate-and-dump" filter would average the pulse over the entire sample interval and thus completely remove the

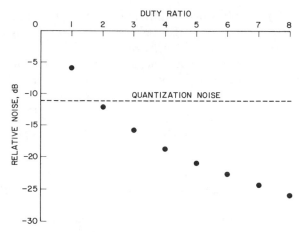

Fig. 14. Reduction of modulation noise by time compression for a converter that employs pulse-width modulation ($L = 3$).

modulation noise. However, this scheme requires a fast acting analog switch, a practical inconvenience.

It is conceivable that the pulse-width-modulation technique could be attractive for application to video signals despite the large amount of additional noise. Video signals demand a very high sampling rate, consequently the simplicity of pulse-width modulation is an advantage. The D/A modulation can be shown to be highly correlated with the rate of change of the signal; the noise is small for constant signal amplitude, but is large for rapidly changing signal. Such noise can be tolerable in video displays because the sensitivity of viewers to noise decreases sharply in regions of a picture where the brightness varies.

V. PROPERTIES OF THE LOW-PASS FILTER

All the D/A converters described in this study need a low-pass filter to remove modulation noise. The specification of this filter depends, of course, on the applications. Circuits that drive an output transducer directly are unlikely to need high-grade filters because the modulation noise is situated mostly far outside the baseband. Carefully designed filters will be required, however, whenever the analog output is fed to a nonlinear process or to a modulating process. In such systems there is a danger of the D/A noise being reflected to baseband frequencies. No great difficulty is experienced in providing adequate filters because the density of the noise is low for frequencies up to twice the baseband.

For illustration, a number of filter functions were used to remove the noise from the output of a D/A converter in which $L = 4$ and the pattern generator was an accumulator. The filtered noise was summed for frequencies up to twenty times the baseband and compared with the *inband* PCM quantization noise. The following results were observed.

1) A single real pole with the 3-dB cutoff at the edge of baseband reduces the total noise to a value which is 7 dB greater than the baseband PCM noise.

2) Two real poles with the combined 3-dB cutoff at the edge of baseband reduce the total noise to a value equal to the baseband PCM noise.

3) A five-pole four-zero filter flat within 0.05 dB up to 0.8 of baseband and 16 dB down at the band edge reduces the noise to 8 dB less than PCM noise.

4) A five-pole filter incorporating compensation for the $\sin \omega/\omega$ filtering covered by the aperture of the D/A converter reduces noise to 7 dB less than the PCM noise.

VI. INTERPOLATIVE D/A CONVERTERS FOR PIECEWISE LINEARLY COMPRESSED SIGNALS

The interpolating technique for D/A converters has been described assuming uniform quantization of signal amplitude. It can also be used for systems where the quantization levels are uniformly spaced only within defined segments of the signal range. Such companding laws have been described by Kaneko [8]. A typical example ($\mu - 255$ law) is shown in Fig. 15; here each segment is twice as large as the next lower segment, and is subdivided in sixteen uniformly spaced quantization levels. A common code format for such companded signals is a first bit signifying polarity of the sample, followed by a group of bits M defining the segment, and a final group L defining the quantization interval within the segment. Notice that the binary code for the magnitude of each segment boundary is a row of ONES.

Fig. 16 shows a circuit for decoding such signals into their analog form. The interval word is held in register L, the segment word in register M, and the polarity bit is held in register S. The pulse generator may be a modulo-2^L accumulator, as described previously, or a BRM; its output increments the segment number at appropriate times in adding circuit A. The sum is decoded so as to load m ONES into a 2^M-bit register as previously described. This code, a row of ZEROS followed by a row of ONES, may be identified with the binary value of the bounds of the segments 1, 3, 7, 15, 31, 63, 127, 255. It is loaded into register R_4 and used to activate a resistive ladder network to provide outputs that correspond with values of the segment boundaries. The circuit action causes the output to oscillate between the lower and upper boundary of the appropriate segment for each input word. The oscillations are affected by changing the value of only one bit of the 2^M-bit register; thus the precision of the segment and its subintervals depends directly on the accuracy of the relevant circuit parameters, rather than on the difference of circuit values.

The polarity bit controls gates that invert the signal. Fig. 17 is an oscilloscope display of the filtered and unfiltered D/A output representing a sine wave at a frequency of one-eighth the digital value sampling rate.

The modulation noise generated by this circuit for input magnitudes that lie in a given segment will have properties which are similar to those described previously for uniform quantization. Of course, the magnitude of the noise will depend on the particular segment which is considered just as the PCM noise itself depends on the segment. But the *ratio* of D/A noise to quantizing noise is the same within each segment, and the D/A noise has the same

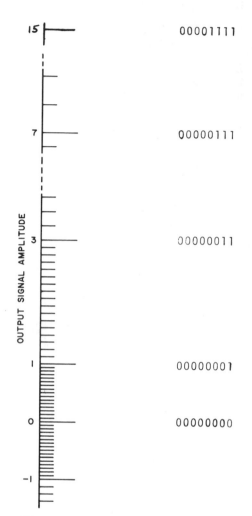

Fig. 15. Example of segmented companding.

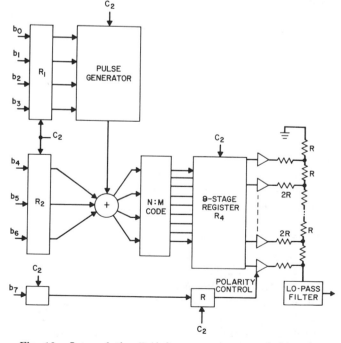

Fig. 16. Interpolative D/A for segment-companded inputs.

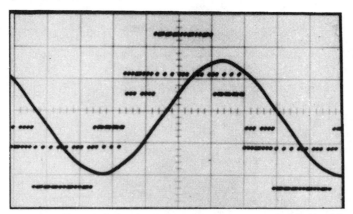

Fig. 17. Filtered and unfiltered outputs of a companded D/A with
1-kHz sine wave signal.

characteristics as in the uniform quantization case. Measurements on an interpolative D/A converter for signals companded in accordance with 15-segment μ-law ($M = 3$) and having sixteen intervals ($L = 4$), have shown that the D/A noise is negligible compared to the PCM noise. It has also been observed that changes of components on the order of 6 percent in the resistor network introduce harmonic distortion which is less than the PCM noise, thus confirming that the converter is very tolerant of imprecision of circuit values. More detailed measurements on this circuit and analyses of the tolerances in this circuit will be published in the future.

VII. CONCLUSION

The interpolative D/A converters make use of both the amplitude and the time domain by enabling the input word to control the height and the effective width of a pulse signal. Baseband components of this signal provide the analog output. High overall resolution can be achieved, yet the converters require comparatively low resolution circuits.

The pulsed signal is permitted only a small number of discrete amplitudes in order that it may be generated by using separate switches for every amplitude increment. Such an arrangement is very tolerant of circuit imperfection. The large noise inherent to such coarsely spaced levels has been restricted mostly to high frequencies by suitable choice of pulse wave shapes.

The most successful means for controlling the baseband D/A noise is a modulo-2^L accumulator but a BRM is also satisfactory. For comparison, the properties of pulse-width modulation are described, although it has limited use. Application of the interpolative technique to piecewise linearly companded signals is very attractive, especially for integrated circuit implementation.

APPENDIX
CALCULATION OF THE POWER SPECTRUM OF D/A NOISE IN THE INTERPOLATIVE D/A

The distortion introduced by interpolative D/A converters has been studied theoretically using spectral analysis techniques. In particular, the power spectrum of the

D/A noise was calculated for each interpolative D/A implementation under consideration. The technique used in these calculations, derived from signal flow graph theory [9], [10], is outlined here.

Consider a discrete time random source which continually generates outputs from a set of N equally likely, independent waveforms. Each of these waveforms is described by its Fourier transform, $G_j(f)$. From signal flow graph theory it may be shown that the continuous portion of the power spectrum of the source output is given by

$$P_C(f) = \frac{p(1-p)}{T} \sum_{j=1}^{N} |G_i(f)|^2 - \frac{p^2}{T} \sum_{j \neq k}^{N} \sum^{N} G_j(f)G_k^*(f)$$

(A1)

and the discrete portion of the power spectrum is given by

$$P_d(f) = \frac{p^2}{T^2} \sum_{n=-\infty}^{N} \left\{ \sum_{j,k}^{N} \sum^{N} G_j(nf_r)G_k^*(nf_r) \right\} \cdot \delta(f - nf_r)$$

(A2)

where $p = 1/N$, T is the repetition interval, $f_r = 1/T$, and $G_j^*(f)$ is the complex conjugate of $G_j(f)$.

This result is directly applicable to the interpolative D/A converters, because in the case of a linear D/A, the error between the output of an interpolative D/A and the ideal PAM level depends only on the value of the least significant bits l. For each code l, the error has a particular waveform, whose transform is $G_l(f)$. If then, we assume the input process is such that all 2^L least significant codes are equally likely, (A1) and (A2) will give the power spectrum of the D/A noise. All that remains is to calculate the Fourier transforms of the individual error waveforms, G_l.

If the analog signal corresponding to code l is $p_l(t)$ (the broken curve in Fig. 1) and the interpolative D/A output is $b_l(t)$ (the solid curve in Fig. 1), then the error signal is just

$$g_l(t) = p_l(t) - b_l(t).$$ (A3)

Furthermore, if we assume a square pulse shape, $p_l(t)$ is given by

$$p_l(t) = l \cdot \mathrm{rect}\left(\frac{t}{T}\right)$$ (A4)

where

$$\mathrm{rect}\left(\frac{t}{T}\right) = \begin{cases} 1, & \text{if } |t/T| \leq 1/2 \\ 0, & \text{if } |t/T| > 1/2. \end{cases}$$

During each of the 2^L timing subintervals of the sample period T, the least significant part of the interpolative D/A output may take on only two values: it is either 0 or 2^L. Therefore we may write

$$b_k(t) = 2^L \sum_{n=1}^{2^L} a(l,n)$$

$$\cdot \text{rect}\left(2^L \frac{\{t - [(2n - 2^L - 1)/2^{L+1}]\cdot T\}}{T}\right) \quad (A5)$$

where the matrix

$$a(l,n) = \begin{cases} 1, & \text{if } l\text{th waveform} = 2^L \text{ in subinterval } n \\ 0, & \text{if } l\text{th waveform} = 0 \text{ in subinterval } n. \end{cases}$$

Substituting (A5) and (A4) into (A3) and transforming gives

$$G_l(f) = lT \,\text{sinc}\,(fT) - T \sum_{n=1}^{2^L} a(l,n)\,\text{sinc}\left(\frac{fT}{2^L}\right)$$

$$\cdot \exp\left[-j2\pi f\left(\frac{2n - 2^L - 1}{2^{L+1}}\right)T\right] \quad (A6)$$

where $\text{sinc}\,(u) = [\sin(\pi\mu)]/\pi\mu$.

A simple computer program has been written to substitute (A6) into (A1) and (A2) and to calculate the D/A noise power spectrum. Investigating the effect of changing the sets of interpolating patterns was performed by changing only the matrix $a(l,n)$.

ACKNOWLEDGMENT

The authors would like to thank S. L. Freeny and B. A. Wooley for their cooperation and helpful advice.

REFERENCES

[1] H. Schmid, *Electronic Analog/Digital Conversions.* New York: Van Nostrand Reinhold, 1970.
[2] D. F. Hoeschele, Jr., *Analog-to-Digital/Digital-to-Analog Conversion Techniques.* New York: Wiley, 1968.
[3] D. H. Sheingold and R. A. Ferrero, "Understanding A/D and D/A converters," *IEEE Spectrum,* vol. 9, pp. 47–56, Sept. 1972.
[4] D. N. Kaye, "Focus on A/D and D/A converters," *Electron. Des.,* vol. 21, pp. 56–65, Jan. 4, 1973.
[5] K. W. Cattermole, *Principles of Pulse Code Modulation.* New York: American Elsevier, 1969.
[6] H. H. Henning and J. W. Pan, "D2 channel bank: System aspects," *Bell Syst. Tech. J.,* vol. 51, pp. 1640–1658, Oct. 1972.
[7] E. Insam, "No-ladder d-a converter works from one 5-V supply," *Electronics,* vol. 46, p. 113, Dec. 1973.
[8] H. Kaneko, "A uniform formulation of segment companding laws and synthesis of codecs and digital compandors," *Bell Syst. Tech. J.,* vol. 7, pp. 1555–1588, Sept. 1970.
[9] W. H. Huggins, "Signal-flow graphs and random signals," *Proc IRE,* vol. 45, pp. 74–86, Jan. 1957.
[10] L. A. Zadeh, "Signal-flow graphs and random signals," *Proc. IRE* (Corresp.), vol. 45, pp. 1413–1414, Oct. 1957.
[11] J. C. Candy, "A use of limit cycle oscillations to obtain robust analog-to-digital converters," *IEEE Trans. Commun.,* vol. COM-22, pp. 298–305, Mar. 1974.

Multiplying D/A Converter

S. MARJANOVIC

Abstract—A multiplying D/A converter (MDAC) based upon the use of bipolar high precision current sources and inverted ladder networks is described. It is shown that if super-gain IC operational amplifiers are used with current sources a converter accuracy of 0.01 percent over the full temperature range can be achieved.

Index Terms—Current generator, D/A converter, Darlington configuration, ladder network, super-gain amplifier.

I. INTRODUCTION

In fast hybrid computing systems where a large number of iterations per second is required, it is necessary to have a system of electronically set coefficient units together with electronically controlled mode amplifiers [1].

The electronic coefficient unit is implemented as a multiplying D/A converter (MDAC), which is basically a D/A converter (DAC) having a reference source replaced by a variable analog input voltage [2], [3]. For MDAC the design problems are therefore more complex than in the case of DAC since additional constraints are imposed upon the switches which must retain the stated accuracy for an input signal of both polarities. For this reason the bipolar switch should have low ON and high OFF resistance and must be capable of producing fast switching action.

The aim of the present correspondence is to describe a new design of the MDAC the accuracy of which is entirely independent of the finite ON resistance of the switches used to implement the circuit.

II. MULTIPLYING D/A CONVERTER

The DAC's based upon switched current sources are, however, free from switching problems since the value of the bit current is not affected by the series resistance inserted in the current output path [4]. This type of converter did not gain much popularity in the past because of the limited accuracy of the current source.

The proposed MDAC employs binary weighted, high precision current sources which are returned to the summing junction of the output amplifier, as shown in Fig. 1. The current source consists of a complementary transistor pair T_1 and T_2 connected in the feedback loop of a high gain amplifier. Such a combination acts as a bipolar current source, since collector currents depend only on the ladder bit current. For this reason the switching is greatly facilitated since no restrictions are imposed upon the switch offset voltage and the ON resistance. In the converter diagram of Fig. 1 the switching action is performed with the diodes D_1 and D_2 for currents of one polarity, and D_3 and D_4 for currents of the opposite polarity. The speed of switching is therefore determined only by the high frequency performance of the diodes used.

Since the current source inputs are at ground potential the transistor collectors have to be appropriately biased for the proper operation. A floating battery, consisting of two high precision constant current sources I_0 and chain of diodes D_0, has to be inserted between the summing junction of the output amplifier and current sources. The details of this arrangement are shown in Fig. 2. The accuracy of the biased current I_0 depends primarily on matching of the resistors R_1 and R_2 ($R_1 = R_2$) connected between the supply rails and noninverting inputs of the amplifiers A_1 and A_2, as well as on matching of the resistors R_3 and R_4 ($R_3 = R_4$) connected between the power supply rails and the inverting inputs of the same amplifiers. The amplifier and transistor imperfections have the same effects as with the bipolar current sources.

Manuscript received June 25, 1973; revised March 21, 1974. This work is part of a project carried out jointly by the Mihailo Pupin Institute, Belgrade, Yugoslavia and the Institute for Automation and Remote Control of the Soviet Academy of Sciences, Moscow, U.S.S.R. Part of this project was sponsored by the Research Council of SR Serbia.

The author is with the Faculty of Electrical Engineering, University of Belgrade, Belgrade, Yugoslavia and the Mihailo Pupin Institute, Belgrade, Yugoslavia.

The complete diagram of the bipolar current generator is shown in Fig. 3. Each transistor is replaced by a Darlington configuration, thus considerably increasing the equivalent transistor alpha. Another modification with respect to the generator of Fig. 2 consists of adding biases to each transistor pair. In this way a significant reduction in the cross-over distortion results, for a much smaller voltage swing at the amplifier output is now required to meet the necessary transistor base-emitter bias when the bit current changes polarity.

III. ERROR ANALYSIS

The overall accuracy of the proposed DAC is affected by the following sources of error: the leakage of the switching diodes, the finite output resistance of the feedback transistors, the spread of the current gain of the feedback transistors, the collector saturation current of the feedback transistors, the bit amplifier input offset voltage, the bit amplifier input bias current, and the ladder resistor tolerances.

In the analysis performed in this section, the error will be computed against 1 mA full scale current corresponding to 10 V full scale input voltage applied to a 10 k/20 k ladder network.

The leakage of the switching diodes can be reduced to a very low level by keeping the voltage across the OFF diodes close to zero. With matched diodes leakage current per bit does not exceed 1 nA (1 ppm) even over the full temperature range ($-55°C$–$125°C$).

The finite output resistance of the feedback transistors introduces an error due to the variations in the switching diode voltages, caused by the large variations of the bit currents. With the single transistor in the feedback loop the output resistance is insufficiently high, being of the order of a few megohms. When a Darlington configuration is substituted for this transistor, as shown in Fig. 3 it is possible to boost the output resistance easily by two orders of magnitude. Thus the maximum total error is a few ppm only.

Since the transistor gain with the Darlington configuration is considerably enhanced and the base current correspondingly reduced, the error due to the base current spread can be kept at the level of only a few ppm. If the transistors T_1 and T_2 have $h_{fe} = 400$ and 100, respectively, the MSB base current contributes 12.5 ppm only, while the error due to the gain spread is reduced by a maximum of a factor of 2.

The effect of the collector saturation current on overall accuracy is negligible since the transistors T_1 and T_2 form a common base pair.

However, the major source of error is the operational amplifier which, together with feedback transistors, acts as a low input to high output impedance transformer. Since the noninverting inputs of the bit amplifiers are connected to a fixed voltage, the amplifier input offset voltage causes discrepancies in the currents of $2R$ branches even if an ideal ladder network is used. Each millivolt of the offset in the MSB branch introduces a 100 ppm error, while the same offset in a lesser significant branch contributes to the error approximately 1 mV/$3R$ or 66 ppm The worst case is when the MSB offset voltage has drifted in one direction and in all other branches in the other direction. The error, measured as a deviation of the converter output voltage from the expected value, is less than 100 ppm even in the worst case when the converter changes the bit states from 0111$\cdots$ to 1000$\cdots$.

The drifting of the offset input voltage may also affect the linearity of the converter. If the input offset voltage is held within the permissible limits over the full temperature range, the effects of the offset drifting can be ignored.

The error due to the input bias current of the bit amplifiers introduces serious problems in the design of this type of MDAC. Since the bias current flows directly into the emitter of the feedback transistor, the bias currents of each bit add up, producing a cumulative error. With an N bit ladder network each nanoampere of bias current will produce an equivalent error of N ppm Thus, with a 14 bit ladder for an overall accuracy of 0.01 percent, the input bias current should not exceed 7 nA.

The stringent requirements imposed upon the magnitude of the bit amplifier input bias current preclude the use of the majority of available integrated amplifiers unless each bit current is trimmed separately. Operational amplifiers with an FET input stage exhibit an extremely low bias current at room temperature, although this current rapidly increases at higher temperatures. The offset voltage,

Reprinted from *IEEE Trans. Comput.*, vol. C-23, pp. 986–988, Sept. 1974.

273

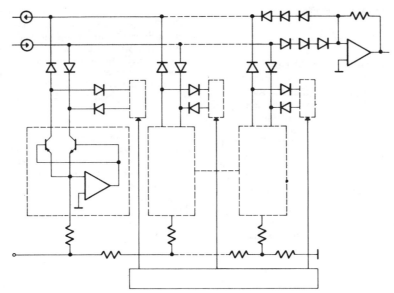

Fig. 1.   MDAC using precision current sources.

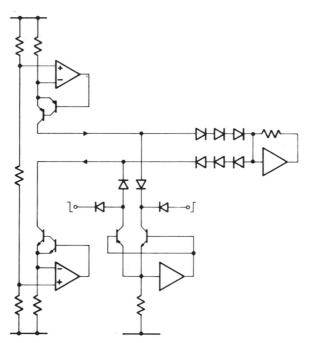

Fig. 2.   MDAC biasing arrangement.

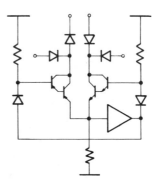

Fig. 3.   Complete diagram of the bipolar current generator.

741 amplifier is also much larger than with super gain amplifiers which as a result, limits the temperature range for the stated accuracy. The measurements carried out on 100 units show that 0.01 percent static accuracy can be maintained over the range from room temperature up to 40°C, which is quite sufficient for computer applications.

The dynamic behavior of the potentiometer has been tested with respect to both varying digital and analogue inputs. The setting time for 0.01 percent accuracy was found not to be larger than 10 μs, while the crossover voltage did not exceed 1 mV for input signal frequencies up to 100 Hz and 10 mV to 1 kHz.

V. CONCLUSION

The problems encountered in the design of MDAC's are primarily concerned with the switch, which should have low resistance and low offset voltage when conducting. The proposed converter is based upon switched, high precision current sources which use high performance super-gain integrated operational amplifiers connected to an inverted ladder network. It has been shown in the error analysis that such a converter, built with "off the shelf components," can operate over the full temperature range without external trimming. The experimental results obtained with the converter made with popular 741 amplifier have proven that an overall static accuracy of 0.01 percent can be achieved, although over the limited temperature range and with external trimming.

ACKNOWLEDGMENT

The author wishes to express his gratitude to Prof. B. Ya. Kogan from the Institute for Automation and Remote Control, Moscow, for his valuable support during the completion of this project.

on the other hand, is usually considerably higher than that of bipolar input stages.

The introduction of super-gain operational amplifiers [5] with low offset voltage and extremely low input bias current has made the design of this DAC feasible. Such an amplifier is, for example, LM 108A whose maximum offset voltage and input bias current do not exceed 1 mV and 2 nA, respectively over the full temperature range.

The remaining source of error is the limited accuracy of the ladder network. This problem can be solved by using low temperature coefficient resistors which have been available on the market for quite a time.

IV. EXPERIMENTAL RESULTS

An MDAC using the popular 741 amplifier as a current generator has been built and tested. Since the offset voltage and bias currents of this amplifier are much larger than is allowed for in 0.01 percent static accuracy, an external trimming potentiometer is added for offset current cancellation. The temperature current drift with a

REFERENCES

[1] S. Marjanovic and D. R. Noaks, "Design criteria for the mode control hybrid computer amplifiers," *Proc. Inst. Elec. Eng.*, vol. 117, Apr. 1970.
[2] R. M. Howe, "Digital coefficient unit: breakthrough in hybrid computation." *Applied Dynamics Publication*, Feb. 25, 1969.
[3] N. Thedchanomoorthy and J. B. Plant, "A versatile multiplying digital-to-analog computer," *IEEE Trans. Comput.* (Corresp.), vol. C-21, pp. 1113–1116, Oct. 1972.
[4] S. Marjanovic, "High accuracy digital analogue converter," *Electron. Lett.*, vol. 9, no. 6.
[5] R. J. Widlar, "Design techniques for monolithic operational amplifiers," *IEEE J. Solid-State Circuits*, vol. SC-4, pp. 184–191, Aug. 1969.

A/D Conversion Using Geometric Feedback AGC

DENNIS R. MORGAN, MEMBER, IEEE

Abstract—A digital signal processing technique is described which utilizes a built-in automatic gain control (AGC) function. A particularly attractive algorithm called "geometric feedback" is developed which has certain desirable properties. A simple analytic solution of the response is derived for the special case of linear geometric feedback.

Index Terms—A/D conversion, automatic gain control (AGC).

I. INTRODUCTION

IN many signal processing applications, the long-term dynamic range of the signal is too large to be accommodated using practical A/D converters. The use of automatic gain control (AGC) prior to A/D conversion is commonly used in this situation to reduce the long-term dynamic range. Short-term signal variations must still, of course, be within the range of the A/D converter.

Minicomputers are now commonly used in many real-time signal processing systems. In this case, it is desirable to use the vast amount of computational power that is available in order to minimize the external hardware required. The present correspondence is concerned with this aspect of design as it applies to AGC.

A readily available component that is particularly useful for digital AGC is the multiplying D/A converter (MDAC). A block diagram of a signal processing system using this component in an AGC loop is shown in Fig. 1. Here a digitally controlled attenuator is formed by using the MDAC in the feedback loop of an op-amp. The attenuation sequence that controls the MDAC is computed from the input samples using some algorithm.

A particularly attractive algorithm called "geometric feedback" will be developed in this correspondence which has certain desirable properties. In particular, the feedback function can be tailored to give the desired large-signal transient response while the small-signal bandwidth remains independent of input level.

Manuscript received May 15, 1974; revised April 15, 1975.
The author is with the Electronics Laboratory, General Electric Company, Syracuse, N. Y. 13201.

Reprinted from *IEEE Trans. Comput.*, vol. C-24, pp. 1074–1078, Nov. 1975.

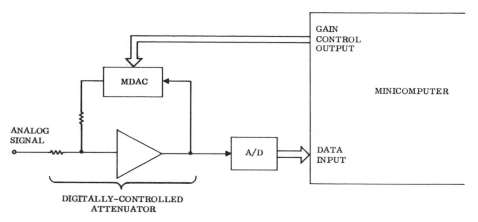

Fig. 1. Block diagram of signal processing system with digital AGC.

II. ANALYSIS

Fig. 2 shows an envelope equivalent block diagram of a discrete-time AGC amplifier where $x(n)$ is the input and $y(n)$ the output. For convenience, the inputs and outputs are assumed to have been scaled to a reference of unity with no other gain factors appearing in the loop. An error sequence $e(n)$ is derived by subtracting the reference from the output and is filtered by an accumulator. The accumulator output $b(n-1)$ controls a nonlinear attenuator which is represented by the function $f(b)$ and a divider. An alternative configuration of Fig. 2 could, of course, be arranged by replacing the divider with a multiplier and replacing f with $1/f$. The function f is assumed to be a continuous, strictly monotonically increasing function.[1]

The system of equations describing the model is given by

$$y(n) = x(n)/a(n-1) \tag{1a}$$

$$a(n) = f[b(n)] \tag{1b}$$

$$b(n) = b(n-1) + e(n) \tag{1c}$$

and

$$e(n) = y(n) - 1. \tag{1d}$$

The time index n for these variables implies discrete samples taken every T seconds.

It can be shown by linearization that for a nominal trajectory $x_n = a_n = \bar{x}$ and $y_n = 1$, the normalized small-signal transfer function of Fig. 2 is given by [1]

$$H(z) = \frac{z-1}{z-\alpha} \cdot \frac{1}{\bar{x}} \tag{2}$$

where

$$\alpha = 1 - K \tag{3}$$

and

$$K = f'[f^{-1}(\bar{x})]/\bar{x} > 0. \tag{4}$$

The "loop gain" K and hence the transfer function are seen to vary according to the average input level $\bar{x}$. A

small-signal time constant is defined as

$$\tau = -T/\ln \alpha, \quad \text{for } 0 < \alpha < 1. \tag{5}$$

As can be seen from the transfer function, the AGC amplifier is stable in a small-signal sense provided that $|\alpha| < 1$, i.e., the incremental loop gain satisfies the condition $0 < K < 2$.

As in the continuous case, it is noted that for exponential feedback $f(b) = \exp(\gamma b)$, the loop gain $K = \gamma$ is constant and hence the small-signal response is independent of input level [1]–[3]. This is a desirable characteristic for many applications. Besides maintaining a level-independent frequency response, exponential feedback also affords an extra measure of protection against conditional instability since the loop gain is constant.

For exponential feedback, (1b) and (1c) can be combined as

$$a(n) = a(n-1) \exp[\gamma e(n)]. \tag{6}$$

This suggests the alternative configuration shown in Fig. 3 which is equivalent to Fig. 2 for $g(e) = f(e) = \exp(\gamma e)$. Since a constant error would give rise to a geometric attenuation sequence, this configuration is deemed "geometric feedback." The function g is required to be strictly positive, monotonically increasing, and in addition $g(0) = 1$.

For steady-state conditions, it is easy to see that the incremental loop gain is given by

$$K = g'[g^{-1}(1)] \tag{7}$$

and the small-signal relationships (2), (3), and (5) all hold with (4) replaced by (7). It is significant that (7) is independent of signal level, a desirable property as previously mentioned. If $g(e) = f(e) = \exp(\gamma e)$, then (4) and (7) are of course equivalent.

The significance of the geometric feedback configuration is that the function g can be tailored to give the desired large-signal transient response while the small-signal response remains independent of input level.

An alternative configuration of Fig. 3 could be arranged by replacing the divider with a multiplier and replacing g with $1/g$. This configuration may be more desirable for implementation in some cases.

---

[1] Alternatively, a monotonically decreasing function can be used if the polarity of the error signal is reversed, i.e., $e(t) = 1 - y(t)$.

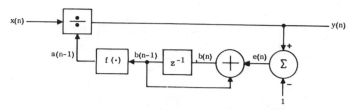

Fig. 2.   Envelope equivalent circuit of discrete AGC amplifier with accumulator filter.

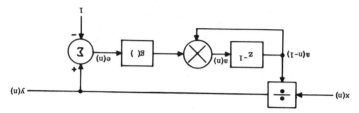

Fig. 3.   Envelope equivalent circuit of discrete geometric feedback AGC amplifier.

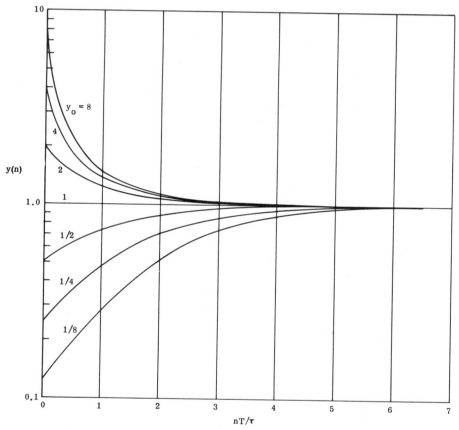

Fig. 4.   Linear geometric feedback AGC amplifier response to step input.

The general system equations are

$$y(n) = x(n)/a(n-1) \qquad (8a)$$

$$a(n) = a(n-1)g[e(n)] \qquad (8b)$$

$$e(n) = y(n) - 1 \qquad (8c)$$

and the difference equation for the attenuation is

$$a(n+1) = a(n)g[x(n+1)/a(n) - 1]. \qquad (9)$$

If g is a linear function of the form $g(e) = 1 + \gamma e$ (the first-order expansion of $\exp(\gamma e)$), then (9) becomes the linear difference equation

$$a(n+1) = a(n) + \gamma[x(n+1) - a(n)] \qquad (10)$$

which is the discrete version of the continuous case with exponential feedback [1].

The z transform of the solution of (10) is

$$A(z) = \frac{\gamma z}{z - \alpha} X(z) \qquad (11)$$

where, as before, $\alpha = 1 - \gamma$ and the same conditions apply regarding the effect of γ on stability.

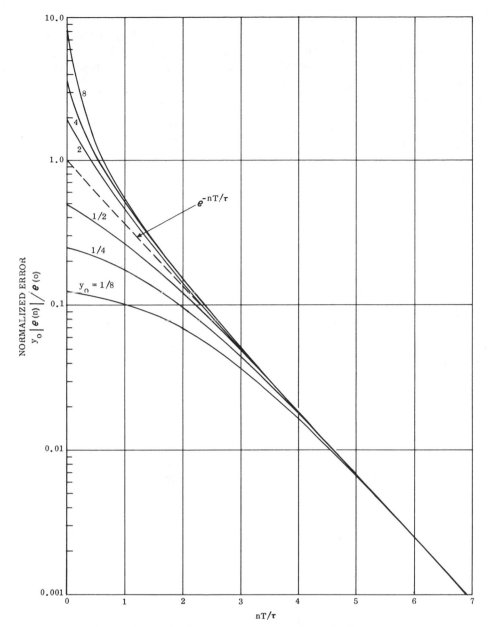

Fig. 5. Normalized error response to step input for linear geometric feedback AGC amplifier.

For a step input

$$x(n) = \begin{cases} x(0), & n \geq 0 \\ x(0)/y_0, & n < 0 \end{cases}$$

the solution of (11) in terms of y is

$$y(n) = \begin{cases} [1 - (1 - 1/y_0)\alpha^n]^{-1}, & n \geq 0 \\ 1, & n < 0 \end{cases} \tag{12}$$

where $y_0 = y(0)$ specifies the initial output level and is equal to the ratio of the input step transition. Equation (12) is plotted in Fig. 4 for various input levels. As can be seen convergence is faster for $y_0 < 1$ but slower for $y_0 > 1$ as would be expected since $\exp(\gamma e) > 1 + \gamma e$.

In practice, it is necessary to limit $1 + \gamma e$ so that $g > g_{\min} > 0$, for all e. A plot of normalized error is shown in Fig. 5 and demonstrates the asymptotic exponential behavior predicted from the small-signal theory.

For other choices of g, the response will generally involve a nonlinear difference equation. Methods for analyzing this situation using the discrete Volterra series are described in [1].

III. CONCLUSIONS

A new digital AGC algorithm has been developed which is called "geometric feedback." This algorithm has the desirable property that the small-signal response is independent of input level. This property holds independent of the particular nonlinearity used. Therefore, the nonlinearity can be tailored to give the desired large-signal

IEEE TRANSACTIONS ON COMPUTERS, VOL. C-24, NO. 11, NOVEMBER 1975

transient response while preserving level invariant small-signal response.

In the simplest form, a linear feedback function results in a linear difference equation which can be solved in terms of an arbitrary input. Level-invariant small-signal response was demonstrated by illustrating the asymptotic convergence of the error to an exponential decay.

Other types of nonlinearities in the geometric feedback algorithm are a subject for future investigations.

REFERENCES

[1] D. R. Morgan, "On discrete-time AGC amplifiers," *IEEE Trans. Circuits Systems*, vol. CAS-22, pp. 135–146, Feb. 1975.
[2] W. K. Victor and M. H. Brockman, "The application of linear servo theory to the design of AGC loops," *Proc. IRE*, vol. 48, pp. 234–238, Feb. 1960.
[3] A. G. Morris, "A constant volume amplifier covering a wide dynamic range," *Electron. Eng.*, vol. 37, pp. 502–507, Aug. 1965.

A Charge-Transfer Multiplying Digital-to-Analog Converter

JOSÉ F. ALBARRÁN, MEMBER, IEEE, AND DAVID A. HODGES, SENIOR MEMBER, IEEE

Abstract—A new charge-transfer multiplying digital-to-analog converter employs an array of binary-weighted MOS capacitors and MOS transistors as its only elements. It can be fabricated on the same chip and by the same process as most charge-coupled devices and bucket-brigade devices, and provides two- or four-quadrant multiplication. An experimental n-channel metal-gate MOS realization demonstrated accuracy to 7 bits plus sign, total harmonic distortion 60 dB below fundamental, 70 dB dynamic range, and 200 kHz bandwidth.

I. INTRODUCTION

BUCKET-brigade and charge-coupled devices provide useful signal processing functions such as time delays and transversal filters in monolithic integrated circuit form [1], [2]. With the addition of variable-coefficient multipliers, complete system functions such as Fourier transformers [1] and programmable filters [3] are realizable. Previously, the desired multiplication functions have been obtained with analog multipliers or multiplying digital-to-analog converters which were not amenable to monolithic realization along with charge-transfer devices [4].

This paper describes a new four-quadrant multiplying digital-to-analog converter which is compatible in technology and performance with bucket-brigade and charge-coupled devices. It employs a binary-weighted MOS capacitor array and MOS transistor analog switches, and can be integrated in single-chip form along with charge-transfer devices.

In the remainder of this paper, Section II describes two- and four-quadrant versions of the charge-transfer multiplying digital-to-analog converter (CTMDAC). Section III discusses the limitations of the circuit. The experimental results are discussed in Section IV. Finally, in Section V, these results are extrapolated to an advanced fabrication process, and further developments of the circuit technique are discussed.

II. THE CTMDAC

A. Description of Operation

The schematic diagram of a four-bit CTMDAC is shown in Fig. 1(a) and (b). The circuit consists of an array of four binary weighted MOS capacitors, with their top plates connected to the first stage of the CTD (in this case an n-channel BBD), and to the precharge and discharge transistors MP and MD. The bottom plate of each capacitor is connected to a SPDT analog switch. Each switch is controlled by the AND of a clock and one bit, B_i, of the digital multiplier coefficient.

Clock timing and important voltages in the circuit are shown in Fig. 1(c). Initially, in the sample-precharge phase ϕ_1 [Fig. 1(a)] the bottom of each capacitor is connected to either ground or a positive voltage V_{in}, as determined by the bit associated with the capacitor. During ϕ_3, the voltage at node x is pulled below $(V_\phi - V_T)$, where V_ϕ is the clock high level and V_T is the threshold of the MOS transistors MP and MT.

Manuscript received June 15, 1976; revised August 12, 1976. This work was supported by the Joint Services Electronics Program under Contract F44620-76-C-0100.

J. F. Albarrán was with the Department of Electrical Engineering and Computer Sciences and the Electronics Research Laboratory, University of California, Berkeley, CA. He is now with the Facultad de Ingenieria, National Autonomous University of Mexico, Mexico City, Mexico.

D. A. Hodges is with the Department of Electrical Engineering and Computer Sciences and the Electronics Research Laboratory, University of California, Berkeley, CA 94720.

Reprinted from *IEEE J. Solid-State Circuits*, vol. SC-11, pp. 772–779, Dec. 1976.

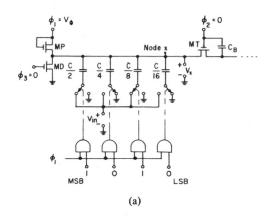

(a)

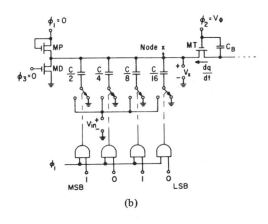

(b)

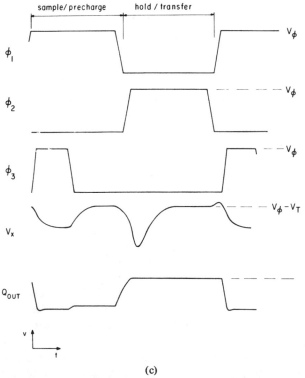

(c)

Fig. 1. Basic operation of the CTMDAC. Total capacitance of the binary weighted array is C_T. (a) The signal is sampled at the bottom plates of the array, while the top plate (node x) is preset to $V_\phi - V_T$. (b) The bottom plates of the capacitors are grounded, and node x is returned to $V_\phi - V_T$, transferring the charge to the BBD. (c) Clock timing, voltage at node x and charge transferred during a complete cycle.

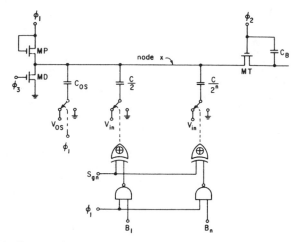

Fig. 2. Four-quadrant multiplication. A bias charge ($V_{os}C_{os}$) allows the switching sequence at the bottom plates to be reversed for negative digital words. The value of the bias charge is not critical, but the operation allows $(n+1)$ bit accuracy with only n-bit matching accuracy required for the capacitor array.

At the end of ϕ_3, V_x is raised to $(V_\phi - V_T)$ by the precharge transistor MP. Hence, at the end of ϕ_1 the charge at node x is

$$Q_{x1} = \sum_{i=1}^{4} \left[B_i \frac{C}{2^i} (V_\phi - V_T - V_{in}) \right.$$
$$\left. + \bar{B}_i \frac{C}{2^i} (V_\phi - V_T) \right] + Q_p (V_\phi - V_T) \qquad (1)$$

where B_i is the bit value associated with the ith capacitor, and $Q_p(V)$ is the charge in the parasitic capacitance at node x, as a function of voltage V. With this operation, the input voltage has been sampled and held with an aperture time equal to the time ϕ_1 is held high. Next, in the hold-transfer phase ϕ_2, [Fig. 1(b)], the bottom plates of all capacitors are returned to ground, while the voltage at node x is being held at $(V_\phi - V_T)$ by transferring the excess charge into the first stage of the BBD. At the end of this cycle, the charge at node x is

$$Q_{x2} = \sum_{i=1}^{4} \frac{C}{2^i} (V_\phi - V_T) + Q_p (V_\phi - V_T). \qquad (2)$$

The net charge transferred to the BBD storage element is the difference between the previous two values of charge

$$Q_{in} = Q_{x2} - Q_{x1} = \sum_{i=1}^{4} B_i \frac{C}{2^i} V_{in}. \qquad (3)$$

Hence, in this example, the charge launched into the BBD is the product of the digital word [1 0 1 0] and the analog voltage V_{in}, (i.e., $\frac{5}{8} V_{in}$). Note that V_{in} would be designated the reference voltage in conventional digital-to-analog converter terminology.

B. Four-Quadrant Operation

Three modifications to the previous circuit transform it into the four-quadrant multiplier shown in Fig. 2. The first modification is the addition of a capacitor C_{os} and a dc supply V_{os}, for the purpose of launching a constant offset or bias charge. Second, the sign bit of the digital word (S) is used to reverse the switching sequence at the bottom plates of the capacitors when the sign is negative. As a result, for a negative digital word (i.e., $S = 1$), the bottom plates of the capacitors are switched from ground to V_{in}, thus reversing the flow of the charge launched to the BBD. Finally, the input signal (V_{in}) should be sampled and held before it is fed to the switches of the converter.

Following the line of reasoning used in Section II-A, it can be derived that the charge launched to the BBD has the form

$$Q_{in} = C_{os}V_{os} + (-1)^s \sum_{i=1}^{n} \frac{B_i}{2^i} CV_{in}. \tag{4}$$

The bias charge ($C_{os}V_{os}$) permits the signal charge to be negative, as long as $Q_{in} > 0$. For normal CTD operation, the value of the bias charge is not critical. Hence, the value of C_{os} is noncritical to the operation of the CTMDAC. Thus, the addition of C_{os} and V_{os} plus some combinational logic allows the CTMDAC to be accurate to $n + 1$ bits (i.e., n bits plus sign), requiring the matching of only n capacitors with n bit accuracy.

III. LIMITING FACTORS

By virtue of its insensitivity to parasitic capacitance, the CTMDAC's accuracy is limited almost solely by the accuracy of the binary capacitor array. Other limitations of the CTMDAC, such as speed and noise are similar to those of other CTD input techniques. The size of the capacitor array is a direct tradeoff between accuracy on one hand, and circuit area, size of the charge packet, and speed on the other.

A. Accuracy

The accuracy with which adjacent MOS capacitors can be matched has been shown to be in the order of 9–10 bits (i.e., 0.1 to 0.05 percent maximum mismatch) [5]-[7]. For instance, split CCD electrodes of 10 μm length and 750 μm width have been shown to match with 9 bit accuracy [5]. Also, a capacitor array similar to the one used in the CTMDAC has exhibited 10 bit accuracy with a high yield, using a total capacitance of 240 pF [6]. Capacitor ratio mismatch due to oxide gradients and undercutting is minimized using a multi-segment common-centroid geometry with dummy metal stripes. In order to launch a charge packet that is compatible with CTD's normal signal range, the capacitor array should have a total value in the order of a few picofarads. Unfortunately the matching accuracy deteriorates as the size of the capacitors is reduced.

The smallest capacitor that can be made in the above process, using an oxide thickness of 1000 Å, is determined by the minimum feature. If this value is 12 μm then the smallest capacitance is 0.05 pF. The largest capacitor in an n-bit array is 2^{n-1} times larger. Therefore, in an 8-bit array, the largest capacitor has a value of 6.4 pF, and the total array capacitance is 12.8 pF. From McCreary's [8] and the author's experimental results, it has been observed that for an n-channel metal-gate process with 12-μm minimum feature, an average match-

ing accuracy of 7 bits for such a capacitor array is easily obtainable.

Since this capacitance is much larger than a standard CTD cell capacitance it is necessary to reduce the charge launched to the CTD. Several techniques to do this can be used. Some of them are process related, like a smaller minimum feature with better controlled etching techniques (e.g., plasma etching), and a thicker oxide for the capacitor array. Others are circuit techniques, such as dumping away a fraction of the charge launched to the CTD, fixed subtraction, and reducing the maximum input voltage swing.

B. Speed

The speed limitations of the CTMDAC are similar to those of a BBD. The input device (MT) and the precharge transistor must charge the complete capacitor array until they are self-turned OFF at a voltage ($V_\phi - V_T$). The transfer of a charge in the worst case condition can be described by expressions derived for BBD operation, which show that a practical limit for the clock frequency in a BBD is [11]

$$f_c \cong \frac{kT}{q} \frac{\beta}{2C_T} \tag{5}$$

where

$$\beta = \frac{W}{L} \mu C_{ox}. \tag{6}$$

In these equations, C_T is the total capacitance of the array, W and L are the width and length of the MOS transistor (i.e., MP and MT), μ is the mobility in the transistor channel, and C_{ox} is the gate oxide capacitance per unit area. As an example, for the n-channel metal-gate MOS process described previously, $\mu C_{ox} \cong 10 \ \mu A/V^2$. Hence, for a 1-MHz clock frequency and $C_T = 12$ pF, the MOS transistors (MP and MT) should have $W/L \cong 100$.

To a lesser extent, the analog switches at the bottom plates limit the maximum operating speed of the CTMDAC. However, their mode of operation is much faster than that of a CTD, and each switch drives a capacitance smaller than C_T. Furthermore, parasitics at the bottom plates of the capacitors do not hurt the performance of the circuit. Hence these switches can be large. Similarly, the function of switch MD is noncritical for the operation speed of the CTMDAC; its size can be considerably smaller than that of MP or MT.

As the size of the capacitors is reduced by improved technology, the operating speed of the device can be proportionally improved. On the other hand, if the CTMDAC described in the previous section is attached to a CTD, the size of $MT(W/L = 100)$ would be compatible with the size of the CTD electrodes.

C. Linearity

The mode of operation of the CTMDAC is based on the return of the voltage at node x to the same value (i.e., $V_\phi - V_T$) at the end of each clock phase. This eliminates the contribution of parasitic capacitances at node x, which effectively have the same voltage across their plates (and hence the same

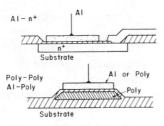

Fig. 3. Silicon dioxide capacitor structures compatible with most standard CTD technologies. (a) Aluminum over n+, used in this work. (b) Polysilicon or metal over polysilicon.

charge) at the end of each cycle. However, mismatches in the threshold voltage of *MP* and *MT*, as well as differences between the highest potential of ϕ_1 and ϕ_2 (i.e., V_{ϕ_1} and V_{ϕ_2}), result in a contribution of the parasitic capacitors to the charge launched to the CTD. These mismatches can be expected to be small, so that the charge contributed by the nonlinear depletion layer capacitance is linearized. The effect of V_ϕ and V_T mismatches can further be reduced by using a tetrode BBD structure [10], in which the input transistor has its gate held at a constant voltage.

The parasitics at the bottom plates of the capacitors do not affect the linearity of the CTMDAC, since they are connected to low impedance nodes during every clock phase. Since the CTMDAC launches a charge to the CTD that is linearly related to the input voltage, the contribution of the nonlinear depletion layer capacitance should be considered when the output technique is chosen. If minimum distortion is desired, an output stage that senses only the mobile charge in the CTD element should be used.

D. Noise

By its similitude to the BBD transfer mechanism, the noise in the CTMDAC can be derived from [9], as

$$V_{nei} = \sqrt{\frac{2kT}{C_T}} \qquad (7)$$

where V_{nei} is the rms noise-equivalent input voltage and C_T is the total capacitance of the array. For $C_T = 12$ pF the noise equivalent input voltage is 2.6 μV/Hz$^{1/2}$ at room temperature.

IV. EXPERIMENTAL RESULTS

An integrated version of the CTMDAC was fabricated using an aluminum gate NMOS process employing a 3 $\Omega \cdot$ cm $\langle 100 \rangle$ oriented p-type substrate. Minimum feature size was 12 μm. Capacitor cross section was as shown in Fig. 3(a). A 1000 Å thermal oxide formed the capacitor and transistor gate dielectrics. Alternative MOS processes are entirely feasible for this application; one possibility is indicated in Fig. 3(b). Both capacitor plates must be highly conductive. Inversion-layer capacitors are not satisfactory.

A. Circuit Design

The complete circuit is shown in Fig. 4. Inside the dotted lines is the portion of the circuit that was integrated. The control logic and the clock circuits were built with MSI CMOS digital circuits. The switches were implemented using PMOS-

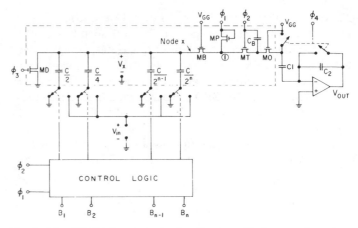

Fig. 4. The CTMDAC experimental realization. The integrated portion is inside the dotted lines. Array capacitance is C_T. The clock and control circuits are CMOS. The switches are MOS and the integrator uses an FET-input operational amplifier. The output of the integrator is sampled and held for some measurements.

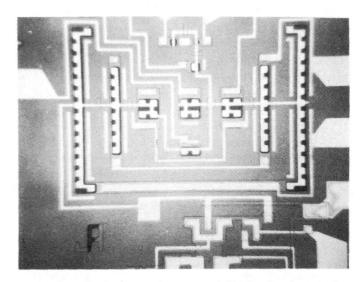

Fig. 5. Photomicrograph of the integrated CTMDAC. The capacitor array uses a multisegmented, common centroid geometry with dummy metal stripes to control undercutting during etch. The minimum feature is 12 μm, and the total area is 0.7 $\times$ 0.8 mm^2.

bipolar SPDT for the bottom plates of the capacitors and CMOS SPST for the output circuit. The clock voltage was +15 V.

The integrated portion of the circuit consisted of an 8-bit binary weighted capacitor array with total capacitance of 12.8 pF, the precharge and discharge transistors (*MP* and *MT*), a single-stage tetrode BBD, and an output transistor *MO*. The capacitor array was designed for minimum size, following the ideas outlined in Section III-A. The resulting array occupies an area of 0.7 $\times$ 0.8 mm^2 and is shown in the photomicrograph of Fig. 5. A multisegment common-centroid geometry is used for optimized capacitor matching. The transistors *MP* and *MT* have a *W/L* of 20, and have a common centroid geometry for improved matching. The storage capacitance of the BBD, CB,

TABLE I
TOTAL NUMBER OF CAPACITOR ARRAYS SURPASSING EACH ACCURACY
LEVEL. THERE WERE 46 SAMPLES OF 56-pF AND 14-pF ARRAYS AND 11
SAMPLES OF 12.8-pF ARRAYS

	Array Capacitance C_T, pF		
1/2 LSB Accuracy	56[a]	14[a]	12.8
4 bits	46	46	11
5	46	45	10
6	46	44	9
7	45	38	6
8	44	33	2
9	38	9	1
10	23	0	0

[a] Data from McCreary [8].

is about 12 pF in order to equalize the voltage swings in the CTMDAC and BBD.

The output circuit is designed to sense the free total charge in the BBD cell. A resetable integrator, using an FET-input operational amplifier and capacitor C_2, is used to integrate the charge contained in the BBD. A large coupling capacitor C_1 is used to maintain the voltage at the drain of MO nearly constant, thus keeping it in saturation and minimizing the effects of nonlinear depletion-layer capacitance. When ϕ_2 and ϕ_4 are high, the BBD receives the charge launched by the CTMDAC, while the integrator and C_1 are set to 0 V and $V_{GG}(=15\text{ V})$, respectively. During the time that ϕ_2 is high, MO is maintained OFF, as long as the voltage at its source is higher than $(V_{GG} - V_T)$. Then, as ϕ_2 goes low, MO is turned ON. Current flows from the integrator to the BBD capacitance C_B through the coupling capacitor C_1. When the source of MO reaches asymptotically $V_{GG} - V_T$, the BBD storage element has returned to its equilibrium state. Hence the charge launched by the CTMDAC to the BBD has been integrated in C_2, and a new cycle can commence. In order to eliminate the reset transition from the output signal, a sample and hold was used after the integrator.

Any mismatch in the threshold voltages of MT and MP causes a dc offset in the overall transfer characteristics. Assuming a threshold mismatch of 0.1 V and capacitance on node 1 of one-tenth the BBD capacitance C_B, this offset is only 0.1 percent of full scale. It can be neglected in most cases.

B. Capacitor Matching

Integrated MOS capacitor arrays in the chips of Fig. 5 (11 arrays) as well as from chips made by McCreary [6] (46 arrays) were evaluated for ratio matching accuracy. Process used was the same for both cases; the capacitor arrays were formed by defining patterns in aluminum metallization. Similar layout precautions were followed in both instances. The results of direct capacitance measurements on these arrays are summarized in Table I.

The data show that ratio accuracy for the 12.8 pF arrays was considerably poorer than for the 14 and 56 pF arrays. This is due to inferior control of lithographic and etching steps during fabrication of the 12.8 pF arrays. McCreary's data suggest that it should be possible to achieve a high yield of 8-bit accurate arrays for 14 pF total capacitance and 10-bit accurate arrays for 56 pF total capacitance, using this metal-gate process. Despite their accuracy limitations, the 12.8 pF arrays were used for tests of the multiplier because the other devices on that chip were required in this application.

C. Operating Results

First, the input-output linearity was measured for a 3 kHz sinusoidal input applied to the largest capacitor at a clock frequency of 50 kHz. The output spectrum, measured after a sample and hold and a 20 kHz pass filter are shown in Fig. 6(a) and (b) for a 10-V and 3-V pp input, respectively. The distortion is primarily of second order, and is more than 60 dB below the fundamental. Later, to illustrate four-quadrant multiplication, the largest capacitor and a dc supply were used to provide the bias charge described in Section II-B. A four-bit digital ramp was fed to the next three largest capacitors and the sign bit. Fig. 7(a) shows the resulting waveform (center) when a sinusoidal analog input is multiplied by the digital ramp. Notice the change of sign of the product when the digital ramp changes sign. In Fig. 7(b) the center waveform displays the product of the digital ramp and an analog triangular input.

The accuracy of the multiplier correlates with the accuracy of the capacitor array. As expected, a multiplier accuracy of half a least significant bit was obtained for 6, 7, and 8 bits using the largest capacitors of the array. The inaccuracies can be directly related to mismatches among the capacitors. A careful elimination of electrostatic feedthrough had to be achieved in order to avoid interaction between the digital control signals and the analog output. This problem should be less severe in a completely monolithic realization.

A noise measurement of the complete system of Fig. 4 shows a dynamic range of 70 dB. Most of the noise is from the output circuit, and it is contributed by the reset noise [11] of the switches, the power supplies and the integrator. A fully-integrated system, carefully engineered, should show substantially improved dynamic range.

According to the discussion in Section III-B, the size of C_T

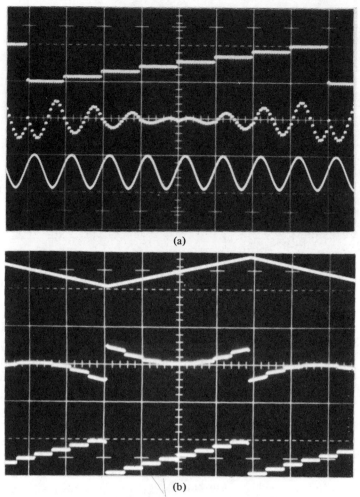

Fig. 6. Spectrum of the output waveform for a 3-kHz sinusoidal analog input, at a clock frequency of 50 kHz. (a) For a 10-V pp input (second harmonic is −60 dB below the fundamental). (b) For a 3-V pp input.

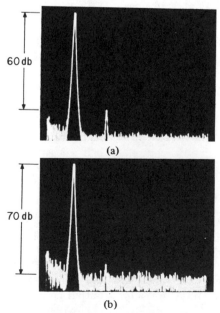

Fig. 7. Four-quadrant operation. (a) Top trace: the output for a dc analog input; bottom: sinusoidal analog input; center: the product. (b) Top trace: a triangular analog input; center: the product; bottom: output for a dc analog input.

TABLE II
CTMDAC Performance Obtained and Extrapolated to an
Improved Technology

Technology	Metal gate BBD	Multilayer Polysilicon CCD
Min-feature	12μ	5μ
Resolution	8 bits (7+sign)	8 bits (1)
Accuracy	1/2 LSB	1/2 LSB
Total array cap.	12pF	3pF
Area of the array	.7×.8 mm^2	.4×.4 mm^2 (2)
max-speed of operation	200KHz	1-5MHz (3)
Linearity (charge vs. voltage) for 1V rms input	.05% (4)	.05% (5)
Dynamic range (1V rms input)	70dB(4)	100db (5)

(1) A maximum of 10 bits plus sign can be expected at the expense of increasing the size of the capacitor array.

(2) Includes the switches at the bottom plates of the capacitors.

(3) The size of the input and precharge transistors is critical.

(4) For the complete system, including the output circuitry.

(5) For the CTMDAC alone.

and the W/L of MP and MT predict a maximum clock frequency of 200 kHz. Experimentally, the system shows frequency degradation for clock frequencies in excess of 200 kHz.

V. Conclusions

The linear CTD input technique demonstrated in this work was used to implement a CTMDAC with the results shown in the first column of Table II. It is believed by the authors that using a better technology, a CTMDAC with better performance should be achieved. As an example, using an overlapping electrode CCD, with three layers of polysilicon and a 5-μm minimum feature, the results shown in the second column of Table II are extrapolated from those of the first column.

Other applications are possible for the input technique described, such as a weighted adder. If two independent signals (V_{S_1} and V_{S_2}) are fed to two capacitors (C_1 and C_2), in the manner described in Sections II-A and B, the charge launched to the BBD would be ($C_1 V_1 + C_2 V_2$). The sign of the coefficients could be chosen, using the technique described in Section II-B. The resulting circuit (a charge-transfer weighted adder) could be used in such circuits as recursive filters and signal generators. With a smaller number of capacitors, their relative values can be better matched (e.g., 0.1 percent mismatch), as has been observed in split electrode CCD systems [5].

Finally, if a voltage output is required, the addition of an integrator would achieve the necessary signal transformation. The common top plate of the capacitor array (node x) and the integrator capacitor would be connected to the inverting input of the amplifier. The precharge and discharge transistors (MP and MD) would be replaced by a single reset switch in parallel with the integrator capacitor. Using a high gain amplifier, the common node of the capacitors remains at a constant voltage, thus eliminating any contribution from parasitic capacitances. The technique described in Section II-B would still provide four-quadrant multiplication. Its speed would be limited by the settling time of the amplifier. The insensitivity of the circuit to parasitic capacitance permits the use of an external amplifier, having all the capacitors and switches in a single integrated circuit. Nevertheless, recent work by Tsividis and Gray [12] shows the feasibility of including the amplifier in the same chip.

Applications for these circuits (i.e., multiplying converters and weighted adders), having either a charge output or a voltage output, are: amplitude modulation, signal generation, programmed weighted adders, precise attenuation, character generators, and so on. The use of MOS technology allows the presence of CTD analog delay lines, analog switches and dense digital circuitry (including ROM's). Hence, complete systems with a considerable degree of sophistication are possible with a minimum number of external components, and in particular the precision elements, which are composed of weighted capacitor arrays.

Acknowledgment

The authors are grateful to J. L. McCreary, R. W. Brodersen, and P. R. Gray for helpful discussions and to D. McDaniel and D. Rogers for their technical support during the fabrication process. The discussions with R. McCharles and Y. Tsividis were also helpful. Constructive comments from several reviewers are much appreciated.

References

[1] R. W. Brodersen et al., "A 500 stage CCD transversal filter for spectral analysis," IEEE J. Solid-State Circuits, vol. SC-11, pp. 75–83, Feb. 1976.

[2] D. A. Sealer and M. F. Tompsett, "A dual differential charge-coupled analog delay device," IEEE J. Solid-State Circuits, vol. SC-11, pp. 105–108, Feb. 1976.

[3] J. Mattern and D. R. Lampe, "A reprogrammable filter bank using charge-coupled device discrete analog signal processing," IEEE J. Solid-State Circuits, vol SC-11, pp. 88–92, Feb. 1976.

[4] J. F. Albarrán and D. A. Hodges, "A charge transfer multiplying digital-to-analog converter," in 1976 Dig. Tech. Papers, Int. Solid-State Circuits Conf., Feb. 1976, pp. 202–203.

[5] R. D. Baertsch et al., "The design and operation of practical

charge-transfer transversal filters," *IEEE J. Solid-State Circuits*, vol. SC-11, pp. 65–74, Feb. 1976.

[6] J. L. McCreary and P. R. Gray, "All MOS charge redistribution analog-to-digital conversion techniques—Part I," *IEEE J. Solid-State Circuits*, vol. SC-10, pp. 371–378, Dec. 1975.

[7] D. M. Brown *et al.*, "High-frequency MOS digital capacitor," *IEEE Trans. Electron Devices*, vol. ED-22, pp. 938–944, Oct. 1975.

[8] J. L. McCreary, private communication.

[9] R. W. Brodersen and S. P. Emmons, "Noise in buried channel charge-coupled devices," *IEEE Trans. Electron Devices*, vol. ED-23, pp. 215–223, Feb. 1976.

[10] F. L. J. Sangster, "Integrated bucket brigade delay time using MOS tetrodes," *Philips Tech. Rev.*, vol. 31, p. 266, 1970.

[11] C. H. Séquin and M. F. Tompsett, *Charge Transfer Devices* (Supplement 8 to Advances in Electronics and Electron Physics). New York: Academic, 1975.

[12] Y. P. Tsividis and P. R. Gray, "An integrated NMOS operational amplifier with internal compensation," *IEEE J. Solid-State Circuits*, this issue, pp. 748–753.

A Single-Chip 8-Bit A/D Converter

Adib R. Hamade* and Eugene Campbell

National Semiconductor Corp.

Santa Clara, CA

A MONOLITHIC 8-BIT A/D converter, fabricated with P-channel metal gate process will be covered in this paper. The D/A portion of the converter affords conversion without missing codes. The circuit is intended to interface with digital control systems in the expanding industrial and automotive markets, but can be used in a wide variety of applications.

Figure 1 shows a block diagram of the A/D converter which uses a successive approximation conversion technique. A D/A converter, a comparator, control logic and tri-state output buffers are all included on one MOS chip. The reference voltage is external to permit ratiometric operation of the system when used with transducers and other units that operate from a reference bus.

The 3-bit D/A converter portion consists of eight resistors, of the values shown in Figure 2, connected in series. The resistor chain acts as a voltage divider, with the voltage at each succeeding junction one LSB higher than the one below it. A switching matrix is connected to the junctions of the resistors in the chain, as shown in the figure, and these switches are operated by the control lines A, B, C, and their complements $\bar{A}$, $\bar{B}$, $\bar{C}$. This matrix can select any location in the resistor network and connect it to one input of the comparator. The voltage at the selected location is compared to the analog voltage which is applied at the other comparator input. As the resistor network is comprised of series resistors, all steps must exhibit a monotonic relationship to each other. Data from the present 8-bit circuit indicates that normal processing control will produce better than 1/4-bit step linearity. This linearity degrades only slightly over the temperature range from −55°C to 125°C. Such a D/A element could also be configured to perform another useful function. The resistor network could be set up to generate an arbitrary monotonic non-linear transfer curve. This permits the A/D converter to linearize nonlinear inputs or the reverse, without resorting to complex digital processing.

For the 8-bit linear converter, the resistor chain consists of 256 resistors, and the switching matrix contains 510 PMOS transistors. Figure 4 illustrates the monolithic realization of the resistor chain and the switching matrix. As can be seen, no ohmic contacts are necessary to connect the resistor junctions to the switches, but instead small protrusions from the resistor diffusion act as the source of the PMOS switch transistor. Similarly, the drains of these transistors act as the sources of the next switch transistors in the matrix, and so no ohmic contacts are necessary. Because a MOS input comparator is used no current flows through the switches, their resistance is not critical, and they can be small geometry transistors.

The on-chip comparator is illustrated in Figure 3. The design is configured as a chopper amplifier with modifications to permit high speed operation and fast recovery times. The comparator is initialized before every sample by switching the input of each stage directly to a bias rail. This sets all stages in the linear region and charges the coupling capacitors. All stage inputs are then disconnected from the bias rail and the comparator input is connected first to V_{in} and then to the output of the resistor network. The resulting pulse is amplified by a high gain ac amplifier and then detected by a polarity sensitive output switch circuit. Use of the initialization circuit allows operation with minimum overdrive on a sample preceded by a sample with heavy overdrive. This comparator provides the stability usually associated with chopper type amplifiers, yet only requires approximately 300 mil^2 die area.

The complete 8-bit A/D converter has been fabricated on a 120 x 123 mil PMOS chip. A photomicrograph of the chip is shown in Figure 5. 8-bit accuracy is obtained without much difficulty and the technique seems quite extendable to 10 bits.

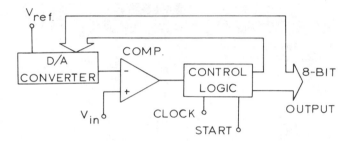

FIGURE 1—System block diagram.

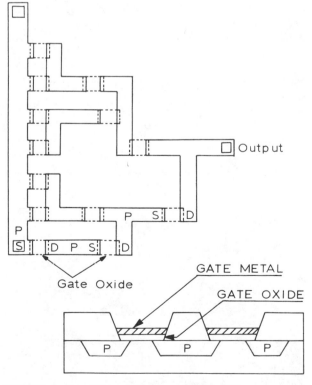

FIGURE 4—Monolithic realization of 3-bit D/A converter portion.

*Currently with APD, Baghdad, Iraq

Reprinted from *IEEE Int. Solid-State Circuits Conf., Dig. Tech. Papers*, Feb. 1976, pp. 154–155.

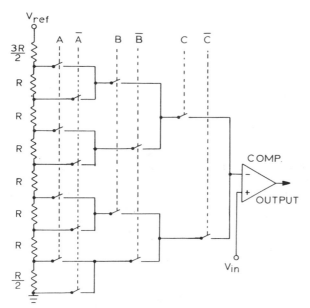

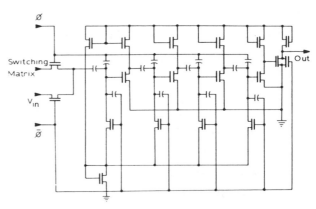

FIGURE 3—Switching conparator.

[Left]

FIGURE 2—The 3-bit converter.

[Below]

FIGURE 5—Chip photo.

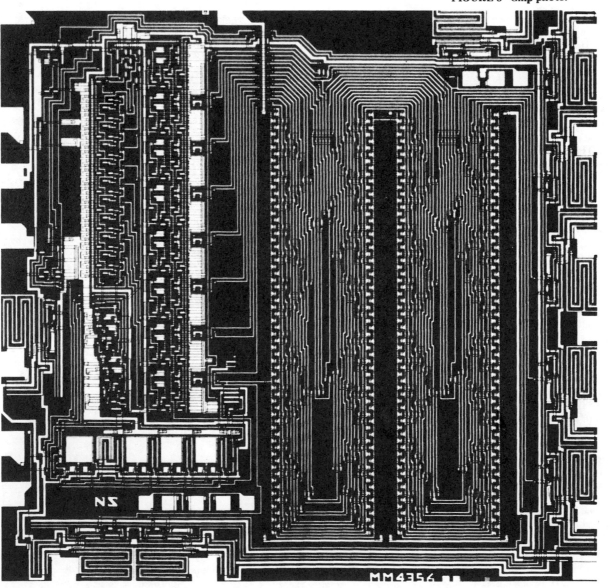

S. Zohar (JPL, California Inst. Technol., Pasadena, CA 91103), "A/D conversion for radix-2," *IEEE Trans. Comput.*, vol. C-22, pp. 698–701, 1973.

J. Candy (Bell Lab., Holmdel, NJ 07733), "A use of limit cycle oscillations to obtain robust analog to digital converter," *IEEE Trans. Commun.*, vol. COM-22, pp. 298–305, 1974.

R. Nordstrom (Tektronix, Beaverton, OR), "High-speed integrated A/D converter," in *IEEE Int. Solid-State Circuits Conf., Dig. Tech. Papers*, 1976, pp. 150–151.

Part IV
Applications

Systems Analysis of a TDM–FDM Translator/Digital A-Type Channel Bank

STANLEY L. FREENY, MEMBER, IEEE, R. BRUCE KIEBURTZ, SENIOR MEMBER, IEEE,
KENT V. MINA, AND STUART K. TEWKSBURY

Abstract—In keeping with the trend to greater use of digital circuits for signal processing, a project was undertaken to realize in an exploratory way an important telecommunication function using as great a proportion of digital hardware as possible. The function chosen is that of the A-channel bank; viz., the frequency division multiplexing (FDM) of 12 voiceband signals onto a single wire. Because of the nature of its operation the device to be described can also perform a translation between FDM analog signals and time division multiplexed (TDM) digital signals. This paper describes the overall system design of the device with particular emphasis on a noise analysis. The principal sources of noise are the A/D conversion points and the roundoff points that occur at the outputs of multipliers. Each noise source is examined in turn and its contribution to the total noise assessed. It is concluded that the A/D conversion points are the most important noise sources and the most costly to deal with.

I. INTRODUCTION

THE introduction of digital integrated circuits and their continual price reduction have made it possible to mechanize digital systems heretofore impractical. However, it is not always simple to digitize functions that have previously been done in an analog fashion. Our group has investigated in depth the problem of digitizing one of the basic building blocks of the FDM telephone plant, the A-type channel bank. Because of the nature of the digital signal processing, the digital

Manuscript received June 15, 1971; revised August 1, 1971.
The authors are with Bell Telephone Laboratories, Inc., Holmdel, N. J. 07733.

version of the channel bank is also capable of translating back and forth between FDM and TDM formats. The purpose of this paper is to first describe the system in general terms, then present a noise analysis of the system in terms that relate noise performance to system complexity, and finally to discuss some important considerations in the analog/digital interfaces. Companion papers [1], [2] published elsewhere give additional details of the design.

II. SYSTEM DESCRIPTION

The A-type channel bank is a basic building block in the FDM hierarchy of long-distance telephony. The transmitter portion of the A bank accepts 12 voiceband signals and, by means of balanced modulators and crystal bandpass filters, single sideband modulates the lower sidebands of each of these signals into an appropriate 4-kHz segment of the 60-to-108-kHz groupband. This function is shown in block diagram form in Fig. 1. Using similar modulators and filters, the receiver portion performs the reverse translation from groupband to voiceband.

The system performance requirements for the A-type channel bank are quite involved, but those that strongly affect a digital design can be stated concisely: in-band amplitude response variation within ±0.5 dB (for each channel, transmitter and receiver in tandem) from 500 to 3000 Hz; at least 55 dB interchannel crosstalk re-

Reprinted from *IEEE Trans. Commun. Technol.*, vol. COM-19, pp. 1050–1059, Dec. 1971.

294

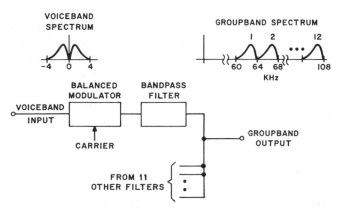

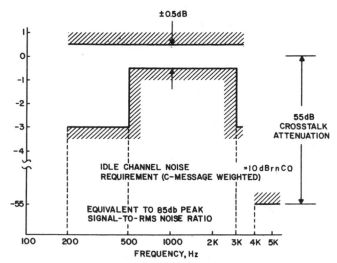

Fig. 1. Block diagram of *A*-type channel bank transmitter.

Fig. 2. Summary of *A*-channel bank specifications.

jection; and rms idle channel noise contribution (*C*-message weighted) no greater than 85 dB below the overload point. These requirements are summarized in Fig. 2.

Since one of the motivations of our study was to utilize digital processing wherever possible and evaluate the results, the processing steps involved digital filters, modulators, attenuators, etc. An initial study [1] eliminated, on the basis of an excessive parts count, an approach in which the modulator and bandpass filter combination of the present *A* bank would be mimicked by digital counterparts. Of several possible alternatives, the one finally selected was a digital version of the Weaver modulator as described by Darlington [3]. The Weaver method falls into that class of methods in which the baseband signal is split into two paths and various steps of modulation and filtering are performed in each path in such a way that when the two paths are again joined, the unwanted sideband cancels out.

Let us first consider a description of the Weaver approach for analog signals and then introduce the modifications introduced by a digital realization. A block diagram of the Weaver transmitter appears in Fig. 3. We assume the voice band signal to have a spectrum confined to the band from about 100 Hz to 4 kHz. The signal is split into two branches and is modulated by midchannel (2 kHz) carriers 90° apart in phase, producing the output spectra shown. (These spectral plots are really pictorial representations of Fourier transforms in which overlapping sidebands are depicted as being distinct. This artifice facilitates visualizing how various sidebands cancel at the appropriate points.) Two identical low-pass filters (LPF) remove all energy above 2 kHz. In the second modulation step, the sideband combinations produced in the two branches so far are translated to the desired channel position in the groupband. If the two modulated signals are now added together the unwanted sideband is cancelled out. The degree to which this cancellation takes place depends, of course, on how closely the rejected sideband underwent identical transmission in the two branches. This is precisely the point that makes this type of single sideband generation difficult with analog processing. Stability and repeatability are fundamental attributes of digital circuits,

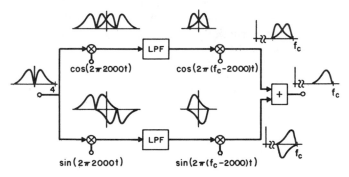

Fig. 3. Weaver SSB generation.

however, and the requisite accuracy can be obtained by an appropriate choice of word length. Hence the rejection of the unwanted sideband can be accomplished to whatever degree is necessary in a digital version of the Weaver modulator without encountering the fundamental limitations of the analog version. It should be pointed out in passing that a strong point of the Weaver method is that cancellation takes place in the same groupband channel, instead of in an adjacent channel as in other methods of this type, thus considerably relaxing the requirements on the degree of cancellation.

Let us now turn to the digital implementation of the circuit in detail. One of the first questions to be faced is one of sampling rate, since it has a first-order effect on amount of hardware. Referring again to Fig. 1 we see that the highest frequency in the groupband is 108 kHz, implying the need for a sampling rate at least twice this for the digital groupband signal. However, it is possible to take advantage of the blank space below 60 kHz, this being accomplished as follows [8]. Converting a digital signal to analog form involves the familiar steps of 1) changing the PCM word stream into a stream of amplitude-modulated pulses whose spectrum contains the desired analog signal as well as images or sidebands of it spaced symmetrically about multiples of the sampling frequency; 2) application of the PAM stream to a low-pass filter that yields the desired signal, as shown in

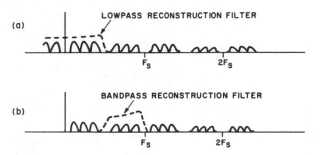

Fig. 4. Low-pass and bandpass D/A reconstruction.

Fig. 4(a). The presence of the images suggests that, in our case, one can first create in the region from 0 to 60 kHz the mirror image of what is desired and then use a bandpass filter to select the correct signal, as depicted in Fig. 4(b). Since the PAM pulses cannot be true impulses, the repeated signal images will be attenuated by the squared magnitude of the Fourier transform of the actual pulse shape. To compensate for this both the lowpass and bandpass reconstruction filters have a rising frequency characteristic, the effect being more pronounced for the bandpass case. Theoretically any sampling rate between 108 and 120 kHz will suffice, but choosing one near the extremes places an excessive burden on the bandpass filter. If ease of design of this filter were the sole criterion then a rate of 115.9 kHz is optimum (this is for the normal bandpass design with geometric symmetry). It turns out to be very advantageous to make the sampling rate an integer multiple of the standard 8-kHz PCM rate, and the choice is rapidly narrowed to 112 kHz. In the transmitter it is thus a 4-to-52-kHz groupband that is produced digitally. Similarly, the A/D converter in the receiver operates at a 112-kHz sampling rate and produces a 4-to-52-kHz band with no overlap or ambiguity of spectral components.

The key to a substantial reduction in hardware parts count was suggested by Darlington and involves making the filter a two-step operation. How this is done is illustrated in Figs. 5 and 6. The encoding of the baseband analog signal, the first modulation step, and the lowpass filtering step are done at a 16-kHz sampling rate, since it is desirable to operate the complex high-performance low-pass filter at as low a rate as possible. The rate is then increased by factor of 7-to-112-kHz and a transversal (nonrecursive) filter is used to remove the resulting signal images [Figs. 6(d) and 6(e)] that occur at multiples of the 16-kHz rate. A transversal filter is used to remove the unwanted images for the simple reason that it requires fewer multipliers than a recursive filter to perform the same task. This is true because in the transmitter six of every seven input samples to the filter are zero and this fact can be used to reduce by a factor of 7 the actual number of hardware multipliers required by a transversal filter, whereas this cannot be done with a recursive type. In the receiver, only one out of seven output samples need actually be generated, which leads to the same result.

For simplicity we have thus far considered in detail only the transmitter portion of the Weaver approach. In this case, however, let us consider the receiver as well. This is illustrated in Figs. 7 and 8. An encoder converts the analog groupband signal to a 112-kword/s PCM signal, which is then split into 24 branches, two per channel. In each branch-pair the channel to be demodulated is brought to baseband [Figs. 8(b) and 8(c)] by midchannel carriers spaced 90° apart in phase. Again the necessary filtering is done in two steps. First, in anticipation of a 7:1 reduction in sampling rate, energy is removed from those portions of the high-rate spectrum from which it would otherwise be aliased into the baseband. This can be accomplished with exactly the same transversal filter as is used in the transmitter. (However each output sample is formed from a sum of 7 times more terms than in the send direction.) Second, recursive filters identical to those used in the transmitter remove all energy above 2 kHz in the lower-rate spectrum. Finally, another 2-kHz modulation step is performed and the two branches added together to cancel the remaining unwanted energy [Figs. 8(f) and 8(g)] and produce the desired output signal.

The philosophy behind this approach is to do the sharp cutoff filtering operations at the lowest feasible sampling rate. A rate lower than 16 kHz is actually possible but 16 was chosen primarily because of a practical difficulty. While the voiceband signal is nominally limited to 4 kHz, this is not necessarily true in practice and when the device functions as an A-type channel bank (and must, therefore, provide its own encoding) some provision must be made for removing extraneous energy above 4 kHz. Scrutiny of Figs. 5 and 6 will convince one that the 16-kHz rate allows for removel of all extraneous components from 4 to 12 kHz, which turns out to be a good compromise. Note also when the terminal functions as a TDM–FDM translator by removing the A/D interface and replacing it with a T-carrier interface (Figs. 6 and 8), unwanted signal images that result from the 8-to-16-kHz sampling rate translation are automatically removed by the recursive filters as well.

The remaining sections of this paper discuss 1) a noise calculation for the system, and 2) some important considerations in the analog/digital interfaces.

III. Noise Performance

In the previous section it was stated that one of the three primary requirements of the A-type channel bank was an 85-dB ratio between the peak overload point and the rms idle channel noise. This idle channel noise is commonly measured by applying zero input signal to the transmitter and then measuring the outputs of the receiver. The behavior of our digital terminal under similar circumstances is not well understood as yet and is therefore difficult to predict. This comes about because of the complicated interaction between the idle channel behavior of the delta modulator encoders (to be described

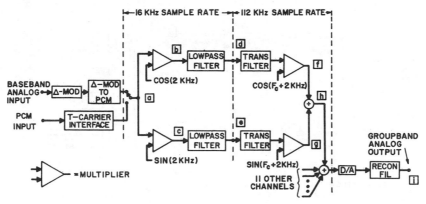

Fig. 5. Digital Weaver modulator.

in the next section) and the natural limit-cycle behavior [4], [5] of the recursive digital filters.

However, it is not necessary to face this difficulty in order to get a meaningful assessment of the noise performance of this system. Because an *A*-channel bank (or an FDM–TDM translator) is invariably but one of a great many active devices that appear in series to complete a long-distance telephone connection, what is in fact of most importance is the amount of excess or incremental noise that the device adds to the signal passing through it. Put another way, an *A*-channel bank is never the sole contributor of noise but is merely required to add no more than its alloted share of extra noise to the signal it is handling. Hence, there is almost always some signal present at the input to the channel bank. Although this signal is often quite small, it is nevertheless big enough to successfully break up the limit-cycle behavior referred to above and allow the more familiar assumptions about quantizing noise to be made.

Specifically, the sources of noise internal to the digital system are the various points where a long digital word must be rounded to a shorter one (at the output of a multiplier with noninteger coefficient, for example), and we will assume that each such operation is equivalent to a requantization of the signal and thus introduces noise of power

$$\delta^2/12, \qquad (1)$$

where δ is the amplitude represented by the least significant bit of the rounded word. This noise is further assumed to be uncorrelated with the signal and to have a flat spectral density over the Nyquist bandwidth. Jackson [6] found these assumptions to be quite successful in predicting the noise performance of recursive digital filters and our experience is that they can be used for more complex digital systems as well.

In addition to the noise produced by these roundoff points, there is of course the quantizing noise produced at the A/D interfaces. This is identical in character to the noise described above, since it arises in essentially the same way.

Under the assumptions just made, the digital system is effectively "linearized" in that each roundoff point is

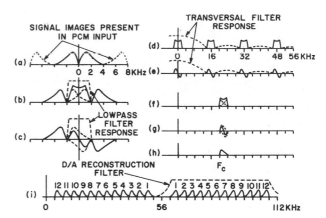

Fig. 6. Spectra for digital Weaver modulator.

conceptually removed and replaced with an additive noise source that introduces noise of power given by (1). We will thus assess the noise performance of the entire system by examining each source in turn. This job is facilitated by choosing some common reference point to which all quantizing and roundoff noise is referred. We choose as this point the peak power of a full-load in-band sine-wave signal, since the system has been designed so that it will just accommodate any such sine wave throughout without overload. From the existing specifications, this power, measured at a standard level point, turns out to be approximately 7 dBm = 5×10^{-3} W.

Referring again to Figs. 5 and 7 and the associated spectral plots of Figs. 6 and 8, we evaluate each source in order.

A. Baseband A/D Converter

If the digital word length produced by this converter is B_Q bits, and if it operates in a reasonably efficient manner, then it produces noise of power given by (1). There are 2^{B_Q} quantization steps in the peak-to-peak signal range, hence

$$\delta = 2 \times 2^{-B_Q} \text{ peak signal range.}$$

Substituting this fact into (1) gives

$$\frac{2^{-2B_Q}}{3} (5 \times 10^{-3}) \text{ W} \qquad (2)$$

as the actual quantizing noise power. This formula will

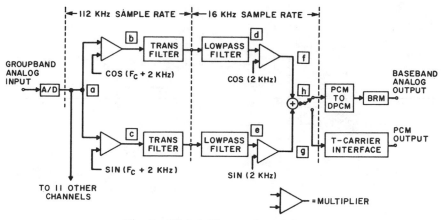

Fig. 7.   Digital Weaver demodulator.

be used as a model for most subsequent calculations in this section.

Since we deal with more than one sampling rate, it is less confusing if we convert all noises with flat spectra into spectral densities. The noise of (2) occupies an 8-kHz bandwidth (corresponding to a sampling rate of 16 kHz), and so the (one-sided) spectral density is

$$\frac{2^{-2B_Q}}{24}(5 \times 10^{-3}) \text{ W/kHz.} \tag{3}$$

B. 2-kHz Modulators

If the outputs of these modulators (multipliers) were rounded to the same length as the word produced by the baseband A/D converters, noise of the order of (3) would be produced; however, in anticipation of an increase in word length in the recursive digital filters, a word longer than B_Q bits is retained at this point making the contribution of these modulators negligible.

C. Recursive Low-Pass Filters

This filter, which is of 9th order, contains a large number of roundoff noise sources. The total noise produced by all these sources was computed by Jackson's procedure. Since this procedure is well documented elsewhere [6], we will omit details of the calculations here and simply present the results, which are summarized in Fig. 9. Here the output noise spectral density is plotted in decibels above the basic quantizing noise of the signal, i.e., the flat density of (3). Hence, this is the spectrum that would result if the word length used in the recursive filter were B_Q bits. Each additional bit used reduces the noise power by a factor of 4 and lowers the curve by 6 dB. The noise of Fig. 9 is of course not flat because the noise produced by roundoff points which occur early in the filter are modified by the frequency response of later sections. Therefore, the output noise spectrum must be a function of the ordering of the filter sections and the plot of Fig. 9 represents the minimum amount of noise corresponding to the optimum ordering of the sections.

From this point the noise produced by the recursive filters is modified by the frequency response of the transversal filter [Figs. 6(d) and 6(e)], then the noises from the two branches of each channel are combined and finally all 12 channels are added together. In this latter step, noise that is out of band for a given channel will cause in-band interference in an adjacent channel; however, this effect is mitigated by the attenuation of the transversal filter.

When all these various factors are taken into account and the C-message weighting curve[1] (Fig. 10) applied to the resulting spectrum, the average noise, measured at the standard reference point, works out to be

$$35 - 6B_R \text{ dBm} \tag{4}$$

where B_R is the word length used in the filter.

D. Transversal Filters

These filters are 20th order (21 taps). However, because six of seven input samples are 0, each transmitter filter has only three of its 21 multipliers active in any one channel at a given time. Thus each filter has in effect three roundoff points, which together produce a white noise across the 56-kHz band of total power

$$(5 \times 10^{-3})\frac{2^{-2B_X}}{3} \cdot 3 = (5 \times 10^{-3})2^{-2B_X} \text{ W}$$

where B_X is the number of bits retained at the output of the transversal filter. This corresponds to a density of

$$(5 \times 10^{-3})\frac{2^{-2B_X}}{56} \text{ W/kHz.}$$

In the final summing point of the transmitter the noises of 24 such contributors are combined to produce a density of

$$(5 \times 10^{-3})\tfrac{3}{7} \cdot 2^{-2B_X} \text{ W/kHz.} \tag{5}$$

[1] This noise-weighting curve takes account of the response of the model 500 telephone set as well as subjective properties of the hearing mechanism.

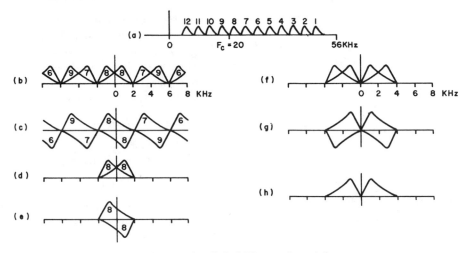

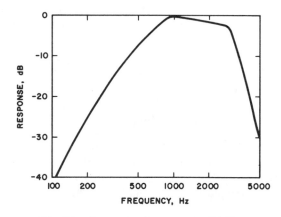

Fig. 8. Spectra for digital Weaver demodulator.

E. High-Speed Modulators

Like the 2-kHz modulators, these sources are each single roundoff contributors and their noise is made negligible because of the excess bits being retained at this point.

F. Groupband D/A Conversion

At the summing point for the 12 channels, there is an increase of the total signal power that must be accompanied by an increase in the peak overload point. This must be done taking into account the statistical properties of the individual signals, the statistical properties of the way the channels are utilized during the busy hour and the effects, subjective and otherwise, of various amounts of overload distortion. A good discussion of this subject appears in [6, ch. 9]. From this reference the following formula is given for the required peak overload power, measured at the standard level, for typical channel signal statistics and activity factors

$$P_p = -13 + 10 \log M + \Delta_c \text{ dBm}$$

where

P_p peak overload point in dBm,
M number of channels,
Δ_c multichannel load factor.

The quantity Δ_c is a function of M and is plotted in Fig. 11. From Fig. 11 the Δ_c corresponding to $M = 12$ is about 22.5. Thus

$$P_p = -13 + 10.8 + 22.5 = 20.3 \text{ dBm.}$$

Since the single-channel overload point is 7 dBm, this is an increase of about 13 dB. Counting 6 dB/bit, we must increase the most significant end of the digital word at the summing point by 2 bits.

Whatever excess bits have been carried to this point must now be discarded and the signal word rounded to B_S, the number of bits to be retained in the D/A con-

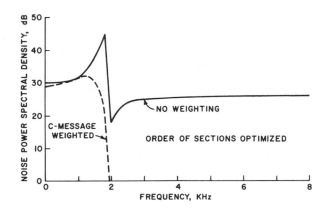

Fig. 9. Roundoff noise in recursive low-pass filter.

Fig. 10. *C*-message frequency weighting.

version process. With respect to the original normalization this introduces a quantizing noise power equal to

$$(5 \times 10^{-3})16 \cdot \frac{2^{-2B_S}}{3} \text{ W}$$

over the 56-kHz band, or a density of

$$(5 \times 10^{-3})\tfrac{2}{21} \cdot 2^{-2B_S} \text{ W/kHz.} \tag{6}$$

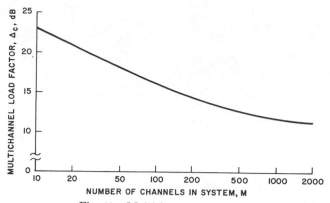

Fig. 11. Multichannel load factor.

The factor of 16 enters above, because two of the B_S bits lie to the left of the normalization point.

G. Groupband A/D Conversion

If this operation is done to an accuracy of B_A bits, then, by exactly the same reasoning used in Section III-F, the noise density produced is

$$(5 \times 10^{-3}) \tfrac{2}{21} \cdot 2^{-2B_A} \text{ W/kHz.} \qquad (7)$$

H. High-Speed Modulators

As before, these modulators use words of increased length and therefore produce negligible noise.

I. Transversal Filters

In contrast to the transversal filter in the transmitter, the one in the receiver has 21 active multipliers per channel, although it must produce output words at only 1/7 the rate. Moreover, it must handle a larger amplitude signal than the transmitter filter. In effect the full group band appears at the input to the receiver transversal filter; however, it performs enough filtering so that only one extra dynamic range bit is necessary in the output. The 21 roundoff sources produce a total power of

$$(5 \times 10^{-3}) 28 \cdot 2^{-2B_Y} \text{ W}$$

where B_Y is the number of bits retained, including the extra dynamic range bit. Two such filters contribute independently to the final output and the noise is spread over an 8-kHz band; hence, the density is

$$(5 \times 10^{-3}) \tfrac{2}{8} \cdot 28 \cdot 2^{-2B_Y} = (5 \times 10^{-3}) 7 \cdot 2^{-2B_Y} \text{ W/kHz.} \qquad (8)$$

J. Recursive Low-Pass Filters

These filters operate the same in the receiver as in the transmitter except that in the receiver only the in-band noise is important. When the spectrum of Fig. 9 is translated by the 2-kHz modulators, the two-channel branches combined and the C-message weighting curve applied, the result is about 3 dB less than that for the transmitter filters

$$32 - 6B_R \text{ dBm.} \qquad (9)$$

It is assumed that in the case of the recursive filters the transmitter and receiver filters use a common word length B_R. This greatly simplifies the multiplexing of the hardware for these two functions. Also, because of the filtering operation performed here, it is not necessary to retain excess dynamic range bits any further.

K. 2-kHz Modulators

Again, excess bits are retained through this function and its noise contribution is negligible.

L. Baseband D/A Conversion

After the two branches of each channel are combined, the word is terminated to B_P, the number of significant bits to be used in the baseband D/A converter. This introduces a noise power

$$(5 \times 10^{-3}) \frac{2^{-2B_P}}{3} , \text{ W}$$

which is distributed over an 8-kHz band. The density is thus

$$(5 \times 10^{-3}) \frac{2^{-2B_P}}{24} \text{ W/kHz.} \qquad (10)$$

M. Summary

We summarize the various noise contributions by first converting all the spectral densities to actual powers by applying the C-message weighting curve and integrating the result, and then expressing the answer in decibels referred to 1 mW. The following is the result.

Source	Power in dBm
Baseband A/D converter	$-4 - 6B_Q$
Transmitter recursive filter	$35 - 6B_R$
Transmitter transversal filter	$6 - 6B_X$
Groupband D/A converter	$- 6B_S$
Groupband A/D converter	$- 6B_A$
Receiver transversal filter	$18 - 6B_Y$
Receiver recursive filter	$32 - 6B_R$
Baseband D/A converter	$-4 - 6B_P.$

From a practical standpoint, the bits in the system which cost the most are those in the groupband A/D and D/A conversion processes. This is because of the combination of speed and accuracy required in these operations. A reasonable estimate of the present state of the art is $B_S = B_A = 15$. Substituting this into the above table yields -87 dBm for the sum of these two contributors. Recalling that the stated requirement is $7 - 85 = -78$ dBm, it would seem that this requirement should be easily met since 9 dB of margin is left for the various other sources. However, all the calculations in this section have been based on ideal operation of the various components. When practical circuit imperfections are taken into account, particularly those associated with the groupband A/D and D/A interfaces, it is felt that much of this margin will be used up and that the nominal 15-bit accuracy is necessary.

In the feasibility model of the system that we have built, the intent was to study certain less well-understood phenomena, such as the limit cycle behavior referred to previously, and to investigate the present limits to the state of the art. For this reason many of the word lengths were chosen larger than what would be called for by this analysis. In particular, the values chosen were $B_Q = B_S = B_A = B_P = 15$, $B_R = 22$, $B_X = 18$, and $B_Y = 20$. When these values are substituted into the formulas, the total noise is found to be about -85 dBm, leaving a margin of 7 dBm for circuit imperfections. Although the experimental investigation of the system is not yet complete, all measurements made thus far are in agreement with the calculations presented in this section.

IV. ANALOG–DIGITAL INTERFACES

When used to perform the A-band function, the terminal also provides the baseband encoding and decoding operations. Perchannel delta-modulation codecs are used, rather than conventional shared converters. This approach reduces problems (such as adjacent-channel crosstalk) which are characteristic of shared encoders but it requires simple converter circuitry since each codec is duplicated 12 times in the terminal.

A particularly simple digital encoder is the delta modulator (ΔM) shown in Fig. 12. This method of encoding was chosen, together with means similar to those studied by Goodman [12], for converting the high-rate ΔM signal to a 16-kword/s PCM signal.

The relevant parameters in a delta modulator are the size of the quantizing step and the clock or sampling rate. The relationship between these parameters and the signal/noise performance of the device has been well studied [13]. A given step size produces a given amount of quantizing noise; thus a stated noise requirement fixes the step size. The sampling rate must then be chosen high enough to allow the delta modulator to follow rapid signal changes when they occur, otherwise the granular noise will be swamped out by slope overload noise. For our system the required step size and sampling rate, with no subsequent processing, are about 100 μV and 200 MHz, respectively. Both these figures are beyond the present state of the art. However, because of its high sampling rate, most of the granular noise of a delta modulator lies outside the signal band. Hence, in the conversion to PCM it is possible to filter out much of this noise with a digital filter, as Goodman observed. This is the function performed by the digital transversal filter of Fig. 12. This filter is designed, moreover, to take advantage of the particular spectral shape of the idle channel and small signal noise produced by a practical delta modulator [14]. The use of this filter allows 15-bit PCM to be produced with step size and sampling rate values of 2 mV and 12 MHz, respectively, these values being much more reasonable than those above.

For the baseband PCM to analog conversions, per-

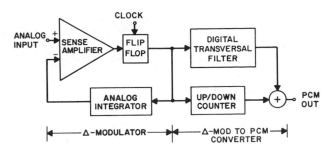

Fig. 12. Delta modulator and delta mod-to-PCM converter.

channel ΔM decoders (similar to the feedback integrator of the ΔM encoder) are attractive largely because of their simplicity and a particularly simple PCM-to-ΔM conversion algorithm. The desired ΔM sample sequence corresponds to a linear interpolation between adjacent PCM levels. First, the PCM signal is converted to N-bit differential PCM (DPCM). The PCM sample interval is then divided into 2^N equispaced ΔM sampling instants at which a total of N_+ positive ΔM samples and N_- negative ΔM samples are defined. N_+ and N_- are chosen such that $N_+ - N_-$ equals twice the DPCM sample value and $N_+ + N_- = 2^N$. It can easily be shown that, if the DPCM sample is expressed in 2's complement binary format with the sign bit equal to 1 for positive sample values,

$$N_+ = \sum_{i=0}^{N-1} n_i 2^i \tag{11}$$

where n_i is the ith bit of the DPCM sample and N_{N-1} is its sign bit.

This relationship between N_+ and n_i suggests that the positive ΔM samples may be obtained using N data generators, labeled with an index i ranging from 0 to $N - 1$, with the following characteristics.

1) The ith generator produces 2^i positive ΔM samples which are gated by n_i.

2) The positive ΔM samples from different generators are mutually exclusive such that the gated samples can be combined without interference.

3) The 2^i positive ΔM samples from each generator are uniformly distributed over the PCM sample interval to give the linear interpolation between PCM levels. All these requirements are satisfied by defining the positive ΔM samples of the ith generator to be the $0 \rightarrow 1$ transition, of the ith stage of an N-bit binary counter being clocked at a rate $2^N f_{PCM}$, where f_{PCM} is the PCM word rate. This device, indicated in Fig. 13 is called a binary rate multiplier (BRM) [10]. The counter may be shared over the 12 channels and only the gating is implemented on a per-channel basis.

The groupband D/A and A/D conversions are difficult for several reasons. First, the rate is higher; even taking advantage of the null spectrum below 60 kHz, the sampling rate must be 112 ksamples/s. Futhermore, a full 15-bit accuracy is needed at all signal levels. The distinction

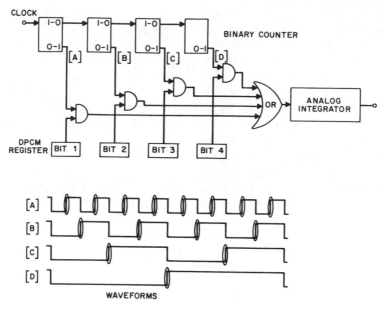

Fig. 13. Binary rate multiplier.

is that the voiceband encoding can tolerate a relatively constant signal-to-noise ratio as signal level increases, whereas the groupband encoding requires a constant minimum value of noise power at all signal amplitudes. These converters represent a formidable difficulty at this point and further work in this area is needed.

V. Physical Realization

A feasibility model of essential parts of the system has been built using commercially available ICs in dual in-line packages. Based on experience gained in building this model, an estimate was made of the number of custom silicon IC chips necessary for all parts of a complete system except the groupband A/D and D/A converters. The total number of chips required is 320, these being made up with something less than 20 chip codes, and the total estimated power dissipation is 135 W. These estimates are based on the following assumptions.

1) A high-speed bipolar technology using beam leads and ceramic substrates.

2) 32 bits/chip elastic memory.

3) 256 bits/chip bulk memory.

4) 4 bits/chip pipeline multipliers [9].

5) A power dissipation of approximately 1/2 W/chip.

VI. Conclusions

We have presented a system description of an all-digital device that can function either as a TDM–FDM translator or as an A-type channel bank. Particular emphasis has been placed on the noise analysis of the system when functioning as an A-type channel bank. A companion paper [1] published elsewhere presents details of the digital filter design for the system.

Insofar as noise performance is concerned, it was pointed out that the relevant factor is the amount of excess noise the device adds to signals passing through it. Formulas were developed for predicting the amount

of noise added at each point in the system in terms of word length. It was concluded that the rather stringent requirement of an excess of added noise no greater than -85 dB with respect to the peak signal value can be met with the present state of the art. However, high-speed groupband A/D and D/A converters which operate at present practical limits are required. Nevertheless, many are presently working on the analog–digital interface problem and the likelihood of cheaper and better solutions to it in the near future is quite high.

References

[1] S. L. Freeny, R. B. Kieburtz, K. V. Mina, and S. K. Tewksbury, "Design of digital filters for an all digital frequency division multiplex–time division multiplex translator," *IEEE Trans. Circuit Theory*, vol. CT-18, pp. 702–711, Nov. 1971.

[2] ——, "An exploratory terminal for translating between analog frequency division and digital time division signals," *Proc. Int. Communications Conf.*, Montreal, Canada, pp. 22-31–22-36.

[3] S. Darlington, "On digital single-sideband modulators," *Proc. 1969 IEEE Int. Symp. Circuit Theory*, San Francisco, Calif., pp. 14–15.

[4] I. W. Sandberg, "A theorem concerning limit cycles in digital filters," *Proc. 7th Annu. Allerton Conf. Circuit and System Theory*, pp. 63–68.

[5] P. M. Ebert, J. E. Mazo, and M. G. Taylor, "Overflow oscillations in digital filters," *Bell Syst. Tech. J.*, vol. 48, pp. 2999–3020, Nov. 1969.

[6] L. B. Jackson, "On the interaction of roundoff noise and dynamic range in digital filters," *Bell Syst. Tech. J.*, vol. 49, pp. 159–184, Feb. 1970.

[7] BTL staff, *Transmission Systems for Communications*, 4th ed., Western Electric Co., pp. 220–236, 1970.

[8] J. S. Whyte, "Pulse code modulation, Part I," *The Post Office Elec. Eng. J.*, vol. 54, pp. 86–91, July 1961.

[9] L. B. Jackson, J. F. Kaiser, and H. S. McDonald, "An approach to the implementation of digital filters," *IEEE Trans. Audio Electroacoust.*, vol. AU-16, pp. 413–421, Sept. 1968.

[10] H. S. McDonald, "Impact of large-scale integrated circuits on communication equipment," *Proc. 1968 Nat. Electronics Conf.*, vol. 24, pp. 569–572.

[11] C. F. Kurth, "SSB-frequency division multiplexing utilizing TDM digital filters," *IEEE Trans. Commun. Technol.*, vol. COM-19, pp. 63–71, Feb. 1971.

[12] D. J. Goodman, "The application of delta modulation to analog-to-PCM encoding," *Bell Syst. Tech. J.*, vol. 48, pp. 321–343, Feb. 1969.

IEEE TRANSACTIONS ON COMMUNICATION TECHNOLOGY, VOL. COM-19, NO. 6, DECEMBER 1971

[13] J. B. O'Neal, "Delta modulation quantizing noise analytical and computer simulation results for Gaussian and television input signals, *Bell Syst. Tech. J.,* vol. 45, pp. 117–141, Jan. 1966.

[14] J. E. Iwersen, "Calculated quantizing noise of single integration delta modulation coders," *Bell Syst. Tech. J.,* vol. 48, pp. 2359–2389, Sept. 1969.

GEOPROCESSEUR: A COMPUTER FOR GEOPHYSICAL RESEARCH

F. ANCEAU, Ph. DROUET

ENSIMAG – B.P. 53
38041 Grenoble-Cedex, France

C. BEAUDUCEL – P. COURBOULET – J. CRETIN

IFP – 1 et 4 Avenue de Bois-Preau
92502 Rueil-Malmaison, France

This paper presents the GEOPROCESSEUR, a computer oriented towards geophysical research. The hardware structure of this computer is oriented towards fast computation and execution of special operations (array operations, Fast Fourrier Transform, Convolution). This computer is organized as a set of specialized virtual processors, each of which schedules its own software processes. This processor structure is built as a microprogram hypervisor.

1. INTRODUCTION

Traditionally computations used for Geophysical and Seismic research are carried out in two steps :
- Collecting data on the site,
- Analysing of these data in a Computing center.

The possibility of performing certain computations during data collection permit the quality of the measurements to be tested and the geophysical research strategy to be modified.

This requires having a powerful computing station on a vehicle or in a boat. A medium size fast computer, oriented towards this kind of computation, (array operations, Fast Fourier Transform) has been designed by 2 research teams from the "Institut Français du Pétrole" and from the "Ecole Nationale d'Ingénieurs Mathématiciens de Grenoble". Presently a prototype is running at this Institut. This computer has been called the "GEOPROCESSEUR".

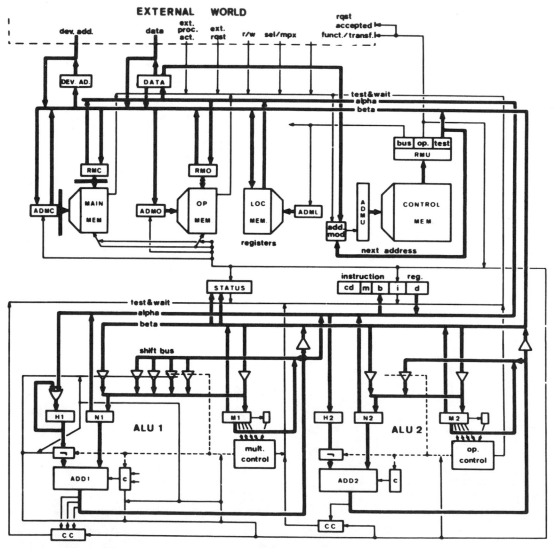

Fig. 1. HARDWARE STRUCTURE

Reprinted with permission from *Inform. Processing 74, Proc. IFIP Congr. 74*, Aug. 5–10, 1974, pp. 55–59.

Using a special purpose computer seemed more economical than the use of a classic computer associated with an array processor. The measurements from collecting devices are given in 19 bit floating point format. It is this format has determined the size of the computer word (20 bits).

Instead of designing a classical computer structure we tried to implement the primitives used at the user program level, directly using hardware and microprograms.

This computer may be connected with other Geoprocesseurs in a multiprocessor configuration.

This conception greatly reduces the system overhead.

2. HARDWARE STRUCTURE

The hardware structure of the computer (fig. 1) is organized around four buses : two buses for data, one bus for test and one bus for internal and external events. The microprogram may connect external or internal flags to the test bus and it may use the information on this bus for branching on condition.

The microprogram connects to the event bus idle indicators of certain parts of the machine and for an idle indicator connected it can wait by action on the clocks.

The hardware resources of the machine are decomposed into :

- two arithmetic units running in parallel. This arithmetic power is used for special operations (FFT, Convolution).
  (i) one of them is a classical arithmetic and logic unit being also capable of carrying out self controlled multiplication using the Both algorithm (which tests three bits of the multiplier cyclicly).

  (ii) The other ALU is able to perform many self controlled functions :
    - fixed and floating point multiplication and addition
    - floating point normalisation
    - fixed to floating point conversion and vice versa
    - shift by 1, 2, 4 bits in parallel.
- four memories :
- a main memory
- an operator memory to store
  - the second operand of a convolution operation,
  - the trigonometric tables for a Fast Fourrier Transform
  - the descriptors of the multiplexed subchannels.

This organization allows the two operands of an operation to be fetched in the same cycle.
- a local memory (16 fast registers) containing the value of users' registers and the information used by the microprogramed hypervisor
- a control memory of 2 K words of 48 bits containing the microprogram.

3. SYSTEM ORGANIZATION

This computer, as seen by the programmer, is organised as five virtual specialized processors
- a fast channel,
- a real time processor,
- a special processor,
- a multiplexed channel having 62 sub-channels,
- a processing unit.

Principal characterics of each processor are the following :

- the fast channel processor is able to execute simple I/O operations on fast peripheral devices (i.e. Disks).
- the real time processor and processing unit can only execute classical operations
- the special processor is able to perform some special operations (FFT, Convolution)
- the multiplexed channel executes I/O transfers on classical peripheral devices such as card reader, magnetic tape, etc... Operative I/O instructions are possible. For example : transfer with arithmetical operations between words coming from external devices and on array stored in main memory. This transfer may start on the occurrence of a given word from a peripheral device.

A common set of instructions is also available for each processor : arithmetic and logical operations, array and synchronisation instructions. The processors are not physically realized, but correspond to different processes of the microprogram. Programs written for this computer are organized as processes. Each process consists of a process descriptor, a program and a data area. A process can be executed only by a processor of a given type. The process descripter contains this type, initial value for registers, a save area for registers and further information needed by the hypervisor.

The hypervisor allocates hardware to a virtual processor ; local memory beeing initialized with either initial or saved values of the registers of the first process to be activated. The current instructions set is defined by some bits of the status register, representing the name of the virtual processor during execution.

3.1 - Functions of the microprogram

The microprogram of the Geoprocesseur executes the following functions :
- interpretation of instructions : decoding and execution of instructions according to the type of active processor.
- Scheduling of users' procecesses : allocation and deallocation of processor to processes.
- Dispatching of processors : Allocation and deallocation of hardware resources to a processor.
- Dialogue with peripheral devices : Transfer of information after testing of I/O indicators.
- Simulation of front panel functions : Visualisation and modification of memories, control of execution, initial program loading.
- Detection of errors : Tests of hardware indicators, control of instructions execution.

3.2 - Structure of the system

This computer is organized in a hierarchical manner [2] with four main levels (fig.3).
- Level 1. Software processes: processing of data,
- Level 2. Virtual processors: microprogrammed processing of processes,
- Level 3. Functional resources: global instruction execution and global I/O functions,
- Level 4. Hardware: processing of microinstructions.

This structure is realized by the implementation of the microprogrammed hypervisor which contains system functions permitting emulation and management of levels 2 and 3.

3.3 - Synchronisation primitives

Each level uses its own synchronisation mechanism

- Level 1: P and v operations for job synchronisation
- Level 2: μp and μv operations used for allocating a virtual processor to a process.
- Level 3: np and nv operations used for global resource allocation to the processors.

The same formalism has been adopted for each level as a hierarchical organization implies that a synchronisation operation at a given level may induce an operation of the same type at lower levels [13].

All synchronisation operations are executed under the control of microprogram. The indivisibility of these operations is not a problem because there is only one executing hardware and critical sections of microprogram are not interruptible.

3.4 – User Processes Synchronisation

Each process has two private semaphores called respectively :
- "a resource semaphore" indicating when the process requested for executing a given job considered as a resource.
- "a waiting semaphore" indicating when the process is waiting for the completion of another process.

A circular buffer associated with each resource semaphore contains parameters associated to tasks to be executed.
Let us rename the synchronisation operations as follows :

v (resource j,q) – "activation of resource j with
                    parameter q"
p (resource j)   – "end of process j"
v (wait j,q')   – "release process j with the reply
                    q' "
p (wait j,n)   – "wait for n releases"

The activation of resource j is achieved by incrementing the resource semaphore by 1 and putting the parameter into the circular buffer. The "end of resource" operation decrements the resource semaphore by 1 and fetches a parameter from its buffer.

The activability of a process is characterized by its resource semaphore. A process is "executable" only if its resource semaphore is positive, the process being a candidate for execution on its processor.
The execution of a program associated to a process co rresponds to one activation. The order of execution for different activations if FIFO.

The resource buffer has both an user function and a system function. Each function needs a word in the buffer. The activation parameter is a pointer into a data list, the activated process will use this list for executing the job. This parameter corresponds to the user function, the first word of the data list receiving the reply from the activated process.
The hypervisor inserts the address of the process which executed the activation instruction into a second word of the buffer. This address will be used by the hypervisor to execute the release instruction, this word corresponds to the system function.

A release operation corresponds always to an "activation of resource" operation on current process. A process can release only one process during one execution of its program.

A process may activate several processes. An event co rresponds to the complete execution of a process.

Simplified operations are available as a means of communication with the external world. Hardware connections allow direct activation of processes from the external world ; in such a case the activated process requires neither a list of parameters nor a reply from the activated process. Real time processes are activated in this manner. The address of an external devi ce wishing to activate a process is used as an index into a table which provides the address of the process to be activated.

This feature is used instead of an interrupt mecha nism.
To allow the structure to be extendable at the software level, we have added two instructions which permit a global semaphore called "solo" to be manipulated.
- P(solo) – "begin critical section"
- v(solo) – "end of critical section".

The instructions allow indivisible sequences to be created and allow the creation of synchronisation op erations. These new operations use the synchronisa tion instructions for transmitting their activity to the machine level. To obtain indivisibility the sema phore "solo" controls external calls of processes.

3.5 – Processor Synchronisation

Each of the five main processors has a private commu nicating semaphore Δ restricted to its parameter buffer : this the list of linded descriptors of candidat processes, the head and queue of this list are in dicated by two pointers stored in main memory at fixed addresses (fig.2).

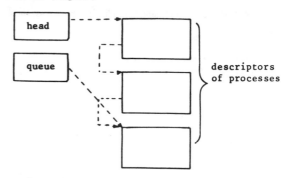

Figure 2. Processes queue

Each new process which is a candidate for execution will be added to the end of the list. These manipulations represent the second level of synchronisation (μv and μp operations). The scheduling policy of pro cesses if FIFO.

The global state of the list is represented by a bit in the hardware status register which is scanned by the processor dispatcher. These manipulations represent the third level of synchronisation (nv and np operations).

The activability of a processor is characterised by its status bit in the status register. The states of a processor are :
- Free : Δ = 0 processor not candidate to use hardware
- Activable Δ > 0 status bit is one, processor candidate to use the hardware
- Wait state Δ > 0 status bit is zero, the processor
              is waiting for an external event
- Active : the hardware is used by the processor,
              the first process of the list processor is
              executed by this processor.

Hardware is allocated to activable processors depending on their priorities. Decreeasing priorities are respectively given to : Fast channel, real time, special processor, multiplexed channel, processing unit.

3.6 – Switching of active Processors

An active processor may be interrupted in two ways :
- the active process is terminated and the list of processes which are candidate for execution is emp ty. The processor returns to the free state and then the processor dispatcher scans the status re gister to find an activable processor.

- a processor with a higher priority than the active processor becomes activable either because it was in wait state and the event has occurred, or because it was free and a process context is put in its buffer. In this case the active processor is stopped, the current process context is saved and the new activable processor is activated.

4. MULTIPROCESSOR CONFIGURATION

Several of these computers may be connected into a multiprocessor configuration with a common main me mory, without any changes to the microprogramed hypervisor. In such a case a process is characteri zed by its type and, if the process does not run on the processing unit, it must be also characterized by the address of the hardware processor which must execute it.

Communication between processes running on different computers is possible, but we must change the nv ope- ration since it is essential to warn that computer whose lists have been modified by another computer.

For this purpose, we have a hardware mechanism which asks for the microprogramed hypervisor of a given computer to read information into the main memory. The information is represented by a word at a fixed location containing a copy of the status register with the modified status bits.

The list of processing unit is unique and may read or modified by any microprogram.
A computer can extract the first process of this list in order to execute it. When this process is stopped, it returns to the list of processing unit processes.

The modification of this list makes use of the solo semaphore. The solo semaphores of different computers are electronically linked together to extend their internal exclusion to the entire system.

5. CHANNELS

5.1 - Fast Channel

The fast channel processor is represented by two processors :
- a channel instruction processor. It is able to exe- cute all channel program instructions, but it is only able to decode the transfet instruction
- an I/O processor. It is only able to transfer data or function words to and from the external world.

When executing an I/O instruction the channel proces- sor disactivates itself (Waitstate). The transfer is initialized and then the I/O processor will be acti-

vated at each elementary transfer. This activation takes place after testing the hardware I/O indica- tors between each instruction executed.

The I/O processor and the active processor run in quasi-parallelism. The end of transfer releases the channel processor.
Synchronisation between these two sub-processors is achieved via two private semaphores S1 and S2. Sema phore S1 releases the I/O processor in order to make a transfer and S2 is used to put the channel instruc- tion processor in the wait state.

Semaphore S1 is represented by the channel word count. It has a 0 value when the word count has a 0 value and 1 otherwise. It is convenient to implement S2 with the status bit associated with the channel in or der to simplify the dispatches. When S2 has 0 value (Status bit to 0) the processor is in the wait stage, it cannot then be actived by the dispatcher proces- sor. An I/O error or end of transfer releases the channel processor and sets the status bit to 1. Then the channel processor again becomes activable.

5.2 - Special processor and the multiplexed channel processor

The multiplexed channel is a pool of many equivalent sub-channels. Each of them is linked to a simple peripheral device identified by its external address (2 to 63). From a hierarchical point of view, we in troduce an intermediate level of processors having sub-channels as processes [2].

All sub-channels look alike, but each sub-channel has its own context (Δ) containing the pointers to the list of processes waiting for service, the word count and the current location of a initiated block trans- fer, if any. Each sub-channel is divided, like the fast channel processor, into two sub-processors. For technological reasons, the contexts of these sub-chan nels are stored in the same fast memory (operator me mory) used by the special processor already mention ned.

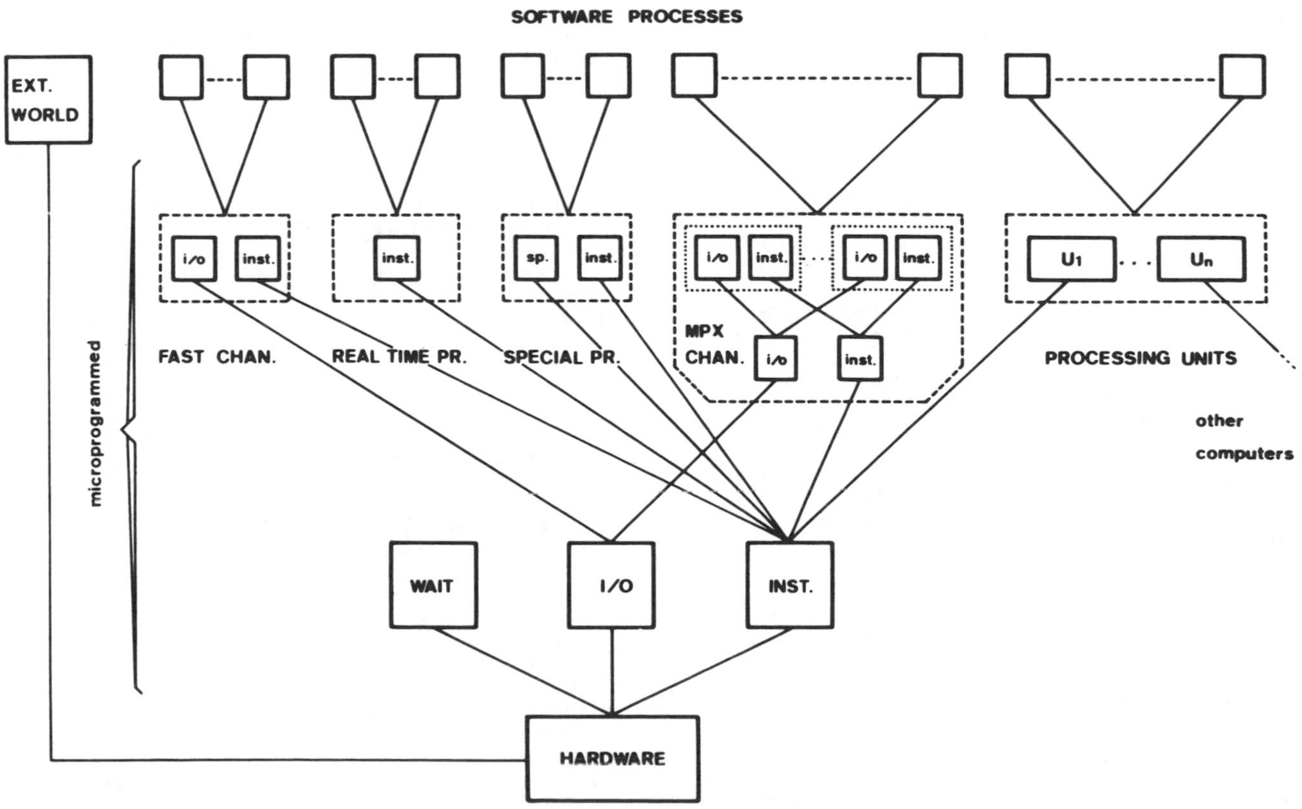

Fig. 3. HIERARCHICAL STRUCTURE

COMPUTING STEPS	Table 1	Execution time (msec.)	
		CDC 6600	Geoprocesseur
CONVERSION		30	70
STATIC AND DYNAMIC CORRECTIONS		2	36
DETERMINATION OF CONVOLUTIONS' OPERATOR		73	23
CONVOLUTION 1500 x 100...............................		165	150
FILTERING 1500 x 50		82	75
NORMALISATION		3	15
		355 msec	369 msec

The status bits of each sub-channel are also stored in this memory. The status bit of the multiplexed channel is represented by the union of all status bits

In order to obtain exclusive use of this memory we impose the following restrictions :
- Each process activated for the multiplexer channel is first added to the list of the special processor
- Special instructions must be preceded by a request for a special operation (Reserved instruction for special processor).
- An instruction "End of special operation" must be executed at end of use of memory.
- Transfer instructions from a multiplexes sub-channel process must be preceded by an instruction called "Open Call" [1], which transfers the process context from the special processor to the sub-channel.

The special processor will be put in the wait state, using the same mechanism as the fast channel, when the operator memory is used by the sub-channels processors. Its status bit in the state register is set to zero. At the end of all sub-channel processes this status bit is set to one and the special processor can execute its special instruction.

6. ERROR RECOVERY

Many faults can be detected by a periodic microprogrammed test of hardware indicators and by testing of the validity of instructions.
- I/O Errors
- machine malfunction
- user program error.

The microprogram will always attempt to save its own state in order to allow a restart.

- For I/O error recovery we can use an instruction which stops a block transfer and reinitializes the channel from another sub-channel.
- When a machine malfunction occurs, either at the hardware level (internal parity, electric voltage), or within logical tests in the microprogram, we save the current process and pass control to the microprogram which interprets the front pannel.
- When a user program fault occurs, two routes are possible :
  - the user has not foreseen the error, in which case the process is stopped and a system process is activated directly by the microprogram. The system process examines the fault process and sends a message to the operator.
  - the user has foreseen the possibility of errors, in which case the microprogram branches to and address in the user program, the process is not interrupted.
- The microprogram examines the status of the process and replaces it in order to execute following tasks, thus failure propagation is avoided.

7. MACHINE PERFORMANCE

The hardware central processor unit uses about 2000 ECL integrated circuits. The internal cycle time of

the microprograms is 100 ns. The central memory which uses MOS components has an access time of 350 ns and the operator memory has an access time of 200 ns.

The mean execution times of the following instructions are :
- conditional branch $-0,8\mu s$
- integer addition between accumulator and memory $-1,2\mu s$
- integer multiplication between accumulator and memory $-2,2\mu s$
- short floating point multiplication between accumulator and memory $-3\ \mu s$

The switching time between two processes (call of re source instruction) is about 14 μs.

The microprogrammed convolution lasts n.m. 800 ns where n is the size of the operator array (<1 K words) and m the size of the signal array.

The microprogrammed Fast Fourier Transform takes 30 ms to processing a table of 1 K complex values.

Table 1 shows a comparison of the performances of a CDC machine (6600) and the GEOPROCESSEUR for executing the same geophysical job.

8. CONCLUSION

We consider that this project has opened some theoretical perspectives pertaining to new notions of computer architecture.

REFERENCES

[1] J.R. Abrial, Description d'un modèle synthérique de fonctionnement d'un système moderne. Séminaire IRIA March 1971 (French)

[2] F. Anceau, Microprogrammed system for tasks management. NATO Advanced Summer Institute on programming. August 1971 - Hermann, 2.

[3] R. Daley, J.B. Dennis, Virtual memory, processes and sharing in multics. Communications of the AMC, vol. 11, no.5, May 1968, 306.

[4] E.W. Dijkstra, A constructive approach to the problem of program correctness, December 1968

[5] E.W. Dijkstra, The structure of the "THE" multiprogramming system, Communications of the ACM vol. 11, no.5,May 1968, 341.

[6] E.W. Dijkstra, Hierarchical ordering of sequential processes, The Eindhoven EWD 310-0.

[7] P. Brinch Hansen, The nucleus of a multiprogramming system. Communications of the ACM,vol. 13, no.4, April 1970, 238.

[8] P. Brinch Hansen, A comparison of two synchronizing concepts, Acta informatica 1, 1972.

[9] P. Brinch Hansen, Multiprogramming with monotors, Carnegie Mellon University. November 1971.

[10] B. Lampson, A scheduling philosophy for multiprocessing systems, Communications of the ACM, vol. 11, no 5, May 1968, 347.

[11] J. Rohmer, Hierarchical systems, Simulation and design, IERE Joint Conf. on Computers, London, November 1972, 375.

[12] H.J. Sall, W.E. Riddle, Communicating semaphores, Stanford University, CCTM 117, December, 1971.

[13] P. Ullmann, Coopération entre tâches et dispatching, EMP Fontainebleau, janvier 1971 (French).

[14] L. Van Horn, Tree criteria for designing computing systems to facilitate debugging. Communications of the ACM,vol. 11, no. 5, May 1968, 360.

[15] N. Wirth, On multiprogramming, machine coding and computer organization, Communications of the ACM, vol. 12, no. 9, September 1969, 489.

[16] B.J. Huberman, Principles of operation of the Venus Microprogram, MITRE Corporation contract n F 19 (628) - 68 - C - 0365, May 1970.

The Radar Arithmetic Processing Element
As an MTI Filter

Barry P. Shay

Communications Sciences Division
Naval Research Laboratory

ABSTRACT

The Radar Arithmetic Processing Element (RAPE) was designed, developed, and built at the Naval Research Laboratory to demonstrate the feasibility of performing a subset of radar pre-detection signal processing algorithms in real time via a program controlled processor. The organization of the machine reflects the similarity of the kernels of various signal processing tasks. Multiple functional units, including memories, multipliers, and adders are simultaneously controlled and sequenced by a micro-program stored in a programmable read only control memory. High speed operation is obtained by both functional or horizontal concurrency and pipelining or vertical concurrency. In addition instruction fetch, execution, and next instruction generation are overlapped to allow for continuous processing.

The RAPE has been successfully utilized as an MTI processor in an acutal radar environment. The radar environment consisted of a modified TPS-47 L-band radar system located at the ITT Gilfillan plant in Van Nuys, California. The RAPE was programmed to perform various 2nd order filter configurations over 512 range gates (approximately 40 miles). This allowed stationary clutter within a 40 mile range to be cancelled, while moving targets within this range were passed. The influence of particular filter characteristics upon the processed video was recorded by photographing the PPI scope for each filter configuration. The dependence of the clutter residue on the width of the filter notch was evident.

PART I — MACHINE DESCRIPTION

I. INTRODUCTION

A programmable signal processor is considered to be a collection of machine resources, such as adders, multipliers, memories, and registers, which are configured and sequenced by a micro-program stored in a distinct control memory. The control allows data paths between these resources to be formed, on an instruction to instruction basis, so that the kernels of various signal processing algorithms may be easily realized. This concept is the basis of the design of the Signal Processing Arithmetic Unit (SPAU) of the Navy's AN/UYK-17 signal processing computer (1,2,3). In the Radar Arithmetic Processing Element (RAPE), a prototype of the SPAU, the configuration of multipliers and adders have been constrained to efficiently realize the fast Fourier Transform (FFT) butterfly and the second order digital filter. Memory accessing, bus utilization, instruction sequencing, and input/output are, however, all under direct micro-program control. Facility has been provided to accomodate external resources such as an address generator and a coefficient store. These resources may also be provided by a single external controller, e.g. a Mini, in which case the RAPE may be considered a high speed peripheral device.

II. GENERAL DESCRIPTION

The Radar Arithmetic Processing Element (RAPE) is a programmable module capable of performing a subset of digital signal processing tasks either as a stand alone device or as an element of array of such modules. As a stand alone device the RAPE can be dedicated to particular tasks by controlling it with a read only memory. As an element of an array it may be controlled from an external source (e.g. a Mini) and serve as a high speed peripheral device.

The RAPE consists of four distinct functional units: (1) the arithmetic unit (AU), (2) the memory unit (MU), (3) the sequence unit (SU), and (4) the control unit (CU). The CU acts as the master controller of the whole system. It contains the control memory (CM), which stores the microprograms, two command registers for broadcasting the control, and associated address registers and logic. An overall view of the RAPE appears in Fig. 1.

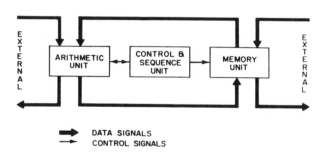

DATA SIGNALS
CONTROL SIGNALS

Fig. 1 — General Machine organization

The control word is segmented into four control sections one of which controls the AU, another the MU, and a third the SU. The fourth section, called the LITERAL, supplies parameters to various registers throughout the system. The control sections are further segmented to provide individual control of various subunits of the main functional units. This permits a large number of resources within the machine to be controlled concurrently.

III. FUNCTIONAL DESCRIPTION

ARITHMETIC UNIT

The arithmetic unit (AU) of the RAPE consists of multiple functional units along with associated registers. Four multipliers and two adder/subtractors are interconnected to perform the arithmetic which is common to the FFT butterfly and the second order digital filter in canonic form. Four additional adder/subtractors are used to provide the required arithmetic which is not common to both calculations. The configuration of the multipliers and adders and their associated registers is shown in Figure 2, (a), (b), (c).

Reprinted from *Nat. Telecommun. Conf. Rec.*, Dec. 2-4, 1974, pp. 507–514.

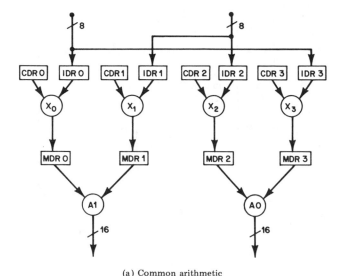

(a) Common arithmetic

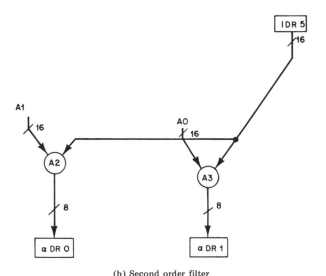

(b) Second order filter

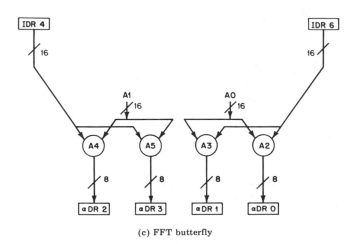

(c) FFT butterfly

Fig. 2 — Arithmetic Unit

The registers labeled IDR0, IDR1, IDR2, and IDR3 are used to hold operands read from the memory unit. These registers can be loaded simultaneously at the instruction cycle rate. The registers CDR0, CDR1, CDR2 and CDR3 serve to hold coefficients or parameters required for various signal processing algorithms. Each of these registers may be loaded from the LITERAL field of the control word at the instruction rate, or from an external source such as a read only memory.

The completed products are simultaneously loaded into the registers labeled MDR0, MDR1, MDR2 and MDR3 at the instruction execution rate. Thus four new products may be formed during the execution of a single instruction. These products represent input operands of the adders labeled ADD0 and ADD1. The outputs of these adders are directed to the remaining adders via data selectors. These selectors are controlled from the maintenance panel to provide the data paths required to effect the remainder of the second order filter or the FFT butterfly.

The registers labeled IDR4 and IDR6 provide data inputs from the memory unit directly to ADD4 and ADD2, respectively. These inputs are used for FFT calculations. The register IDR5 provides a data input from an external source to the adder ADD3. This input provides the data stream for digital filter calculations. Data may be simultaneously loaded into the input registers at the instruction execution rate.

The registers labeled αDR0, αDR1, αDR2 and αDR3 represent the output registers of the arithmetic unit. Each register is associated with an adder output. These registers provide data to be written into the memory unit or to be output to an external device. For FFT calculations, the four registers hold the real and imaginary parts of two complex data words. For filter calculations two of the registers hold the filter output and the feedback term. As with all the other local registers, the output registers may be loaded at the instruction cycle rate.

MEMORY UNIT

The memory unit can be considered a data source and sink for the arithmetic unit. Data, originating in the memory unit, is read and processed by the arithmetic section. The processed data is then written into the memory unit to await further processing by the arithmetic unit. The reading, processing, and writing all proceed concurrently, at the instruction cycle rate, in a pipelined fashion.

Input and output data paths between the AU and the MU are provided by four sixteen bit channels — two input and two output — as shown in Figure 3. Utilization of these channels is controlled by the microprogram. During the execution of a microinstruction, data may be accessed from the MU over both input channels, written into the MU from both output channels, or both. Thus, data may circulate through the MU — AU at a maximum rate of sixty-four bits per instruction cycle. The sixty-four bits represent four complex data words.

Two sixteen bit input channels to the MU from the external world are also provided. Each of these channels provides an input source to any one or more of the data memories. When the machine is operating in an external mode, the utilization of these channels is also under microprogram control.

Each input channel to the AU may receive data from any one of the four data memories. Similarly, data from either output channel of the AU may be written into any one or more of the data memories.

NTC 74

311

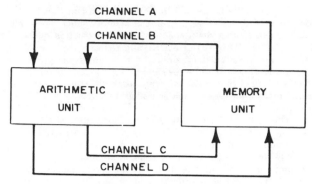

Fig. 3 — Data channels

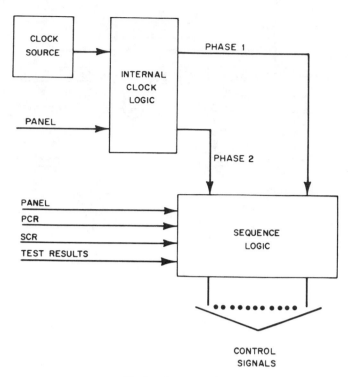

Fig. 4 — Sequence unit

Associated with the MU are four address register/counters. Each of these registers may address any one or more of the data memories. Data may be read from one or more memories and written into one or more memories in a single machine instruction cycle at the same or different addresses. Address changes occur by either incrementing the registers in pairs or by loading them individually from the LITERAL field of the control word. Provision is also made for an external data path into each address register. These addresses could, for example, originate from an external address generator or some other device, e.g. a Mini.

SEQUENCE UNIT

The sequence unit (SU) generates and distributes a two phase clock throughout the system and provides the required decision logic for testing various branch conditions. Three counter/registers are used for indexing and can be loaded, incremented, and/or tested during a single instruction cycle. The result of a test determines the location of the next microinstruction to be executed.

A simplified diagram of the sequence unit appears in Figure 4. The activation of the control signals depend upon the contents of the two command registers, PCR and SCR, the test results, and the phase of the clock. Each instruction begins execution on the occurrence of clock phase P1. The instruction is actually fetched on clock phase P2 of the previous instruction cycle. During P1 of the current cycle the next address is set. This address may be the same as the current address (REPEAT), one plus the current address (STEP), or the value stored in the LITERAL field of the current instruction (JUMP TO LITERAL). These address changes may be unconditionally set or determined conditionally by testing any one of the three index register/counters.

All data registers are loaded on the occurrence of clock phase P1, with the exception of the output registers of the four multipliers. These registers are loaded on P2. This allows data, read from the data memories, to propagate through the AU in a single clock cycle. Facility is provided, however, to load these registers on P1 if need be. This would allow data to pipeline through the AU at the multiply rate, effectively doubling the execution rate of the machine.

The data memories are read on P1 by simply loading the input registers to the AU. Since data memory address changes also occur on P1, the location of data read during the current cycle must be set during the previous cycle. However, writing into the data memories occurs during P2 so that write addresses set during the current cycle are effective during the same cycle.

The control memory is read on clock phase P2 by loading the primary command register PCR. The contents of various fields of this register determine the operation of the machine during clock phase P1 of the next cycle. On the occurrence of P1 execution begins and, simultaneously, the contents of PCR are transferred to the secondary command register, SCR. The contents of certain fields of this register determine the operation of the machine during phase P2 of the current cycle; simultaneously, the next instruction is loaded into PCR. In this manner the machine continually sets up the next address while executing part of the current instruction during P1, and completes executing the current instruction, while fetching the next instruction during P2.

CONTROL UNIT

The control unit (CU) consists of a programmable read only memory called the control memory (CM), an address register/counter (CMAR) and two command or instruction registers. The sequence of control words read from the CM, as discussed in the previous section, determine the operation of the machine. The contents of a single control word represents an encoding of the set of microoperations which are executed in a single machine instruction cycle. The set of concurrently executable operations constitute a single microinstruction.

The rate at which microinstructions may be executed is limited by the slowest controllable resource in the system. In this particular implementation (TTL non-pipeline mode) this rate is determined by the multiply-add time of approximately 200 ns (8-bit array multiply followed by 16 bit add). The rate at which instructions are actually executed, however, is determined by the real time constraints of the application, as will be seen in PART II.

The control word of the RAPE is forty-eight bits long, and is divided into sections as shown in Figure 5. Each section

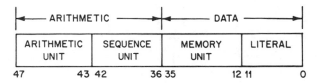

Fig. 5 — Control word format

of the control word determines the operation of the corresponding functional unit. These sections are further segmented into fields, each of which is associated with a subsection of a major functional unit. The actual machine resources comprising each hardware section are correspondingly controlled by encoded subfields.

The four control sections consist of five control fields comprised of twenty-three encoded subfields. The five control fields are summarized below:

1. LITERAL CONTROL — this control field is represented by the first twelve bits of the control word. The first eight bits contain the LITERAL whose destination is determined by the contents of the next four bits. There are twelve possible destinations for the LITERAL: three index registers, four data memory address registers, four coefficient data registers, and the control memory address register. The LITERAL may also represent the branch address if a conditional test is specified.

2. ADDRESS BUS CONTROL — this field determines the allocation of address registers to data memories. Each address register may be allocated to any one or more data memories. Whether the address registers will be incremented by ones or twos is also controlled by this field.

3. DATA BUS CONTROL — this field controls the usage of both input and output data channels to the arithmetic unit. Data may be read from any memory over either or both input channels. Likewise data may be written into any one or more memories from either output channel. In conjunction with a switch on the maintenance panel, this field also controls the usage of the two external input channels to the memory unit.

4. BRANCH CONTROL — this field determines the utilization of the three index registers and the control memory address register. Each of the index registers may be tested for zero;* the result determines the next control memory address. One of the counters may also be tested and reset if zero; the control memory address register is then incremented. If the test result is false, the counter is incremented and the same instruction repeated.

5. ARITHMETIC CONTROL — this field controls the operation of four of the six adders and, in conjunction with a switch on the panel, whether or not the arithmetic unit will be operating in a pipelined manner. Each adder may either add or subtract depending upon the state of the corresponding bit in this field.

PART 2 — RADAR APPLICATION

I. INTRODUCTION

The application of the RAPE as an in line real time radar processor was demonstrated by utilizing it as an MTI filter in actual radar environment. The configuration of the system appears in Fig. 6. The RAPE was programmed to compute various two and three pulse cancellers over 512 range gates of one microsecond each. The RAPE was clocked from the radar

*The counters are actually tested for the 1's complement of 0.

system at a 4 MHz rate. This clock was split into two phases by the internal clock logic (see Figure 4), resulting in a 2 MHz instruction execution rate. The encode command to the A/D converter was activated on every other instruction and coincided with the loading of the input registers. In this manner the incoming signal was sampled once every microsecond. Since the pulse period of the radar was about one millisecond, filter notches were produced at D.C. and multiples of 1 KHz. The width of the notches directly affect the MTI performance, and so various filters were implemented by simply altering the coefficients of the canonic second order realization.

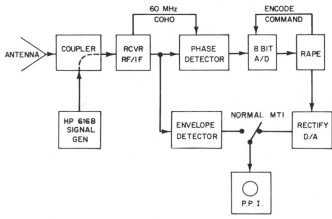

Fig. 6 — Radar/Rape test configuration

II. SECOND ORDER FILTER

The canonic realization of a second order filter is shown in Fig. 7. The difference equations representing such a filter are expressed in equations (1) and (2) below. The symbol $X(k)$ represents the input sample at time k, and $Y(k)$ represents the corresponding

$$(1) \quad Y(k) = X(k) + \alpha_1 W_1(k) + \alpha_2 W_2(k)$$

$$(2) \quad Wo(k) = X(k) + \beta_1 W_1(k) + \beta_2 W_2(k)$$

output point. The symbols $Wo(k)$, $W_1(k)$, and $W_2(k)$ represent intermediate variables at time k. The coefficients which determine the filter response are represented by α_1 and α_2 for the feedforward terms and by β_1 and β_2 for the feedback terms. The intermediate variables during the $k+1^{th}$ sampling interval may be determined recursively from $W_0(k)$, as shown in equations 3 and 4.

$$(3) \quad W_1(k+1) = W_0(k)$$

$$(4) \quad W_2(k+1) = W_1(k) = W_0(k-1)$$

The RAPE may be programmed to realize the second order filter by associating the input channels A and B to the arithmetic section with the intermediate variables $W_1(k)$ and $W_2(k)$ respectively. The output channels of the AU, C and D, are associated with $W_0(k)$ and $Y(k)$ respectively. The four input registers to the multipliers, labeled CDR0, CDR1, CDR2, and CDR3 are used to hold the coefficients α_1, α_2, β_1, and β_2 respectively.

Two of the data memories, say DM0 and DM1, are chosen to hold the intermediate variables W_1 and W_2. During the kth sampling interval channel A will be used to access DM0 and channel B to access DM1. From equation 4 it is seen that

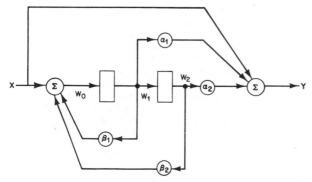

Fig. 7 — Second order filter

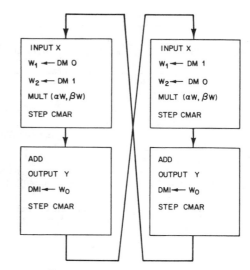

Fig. 8 — Second order filter flowchart

during the $k+1^{th}$ sampling interval W_2 is the value that W_1 was during the kth interval. This data transfer is simulated by reading DM0 over channel B during the $k+1^{st}$ interval. Thus DM0 holds $W_2(k+1)$. The intermediate variable $W_0(k)$ is formed during the kth interval and is written into DM1 from channel C during that interval. Since $W_1(k+1) = W_0(k)$, DM1 now holds $W_1(k+1)$. Thus, during the $k+1^{st}$ interval DM1 is read over channel A.

During the $k+2^{nd}$ sampling interval the roles of the data memories are as they were during the kth interval. For the $k+3^{rd}$, they are the same as for the $k+1^{st}$. Thus the second order filter may be realized by the repeated application of two distinct memory associations with data channels. In the first $W1\leftarrow DM0$, $W2\leftarrow DM1$, $DM1\leftarrow Wo$, and in the second $W1\leftarrow DM1$, $W2\leftarrow DM0$, $DM0\leftarrow Wo$.

Each sampling interval spans two instruction cycles. In the first cycle, data is read over channels A and B and deposited into the appropriate registers of the AU. Also in this cycle the encode command to the A/D converter is given for the next sample, while the current sample is gated into the AU. During the next instruction cycle the filtered data is formed and output, while the intermediate feedback term $Wo(k)$ is formed and written into the proper data memory from channel C. Thus, equations (1) and (2) are computed in two instruction cycles with the intermediate variable W_0 written into memory to be used as W1 during the next cycle. Two more instruction cycles, with the roles of the memories reversed, completes the filter computation. In this manner a steady stream of data is filtered by being operated upon by a continuous loop of four micro instructions.

The four instructions are summarized by the flowchart in Fig. 8. The statements in each box represent the set of events which occur in a single micro-instruction. The statement MULT $(\alpha W, \beta W)$ represents the computation of the four products $\alpha_1 W_1$, $\alpha_2 W_2$, $\beta_1 W_1$, and $\beta_2 W_2$. The ADD statement represents the sums formed in equations (1) and (2) (actually the partial sums represented by the matrix product $[(\alpha_1 \alpha_2 / \beta_1 \beta_2)]$ $[(W_1/W_2)]$ are formed during the first instruction, but are not "captured" in a register until the second instruction.) When the four instructions are stored consecutively in the control memory, three of them contain the statement STEP CMAR. The fourth instruction contains the address of the first instruction in the LITERAL subfield, along with the encoded destination of the CMAR.

The photographs in Fig. 9, represent the frequency responses of various filters realized by the RAPE executing the program represented in Fig. 8. The test setup used to generate these responses is shown in Fig. 10. Different filters were realized by simply entering coefficients from the maintenance panel.

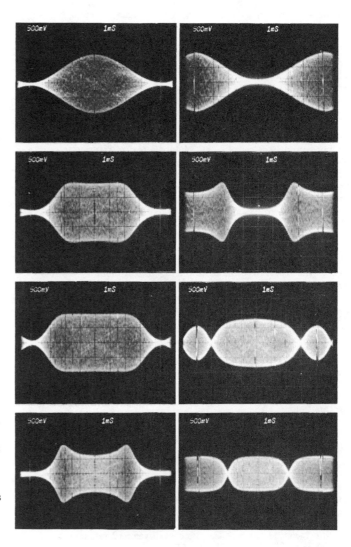

Fig. 9 — Filter responses

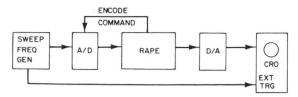

Fig. 10 — Filter response test configuration

III. MTI APPLICATION

The preceeding filters all require only a single memory location in each data memory to store the intermediate variables represented by W_1 and W_2. When processing radar returns, however, one memory address must be associated with each range cell. The returns associated with each cell must be filtered so that moving targets within that range cell may be distinguished from stationary clutter returns at the same range. The number of range cells depends upon the PRF of the radar and the associated pulse width. Presuming a 1 μs pulse width and 1 kHz PRF results in one thousand 1 μs range gates covering a range of about 80 miles; each cell corresponds to about 200 feet resolution. Complete filtering on all range cells requires storage capacity of 1,000 locations for W_1 and 1,000 locations for W_2. The storage capacity of the RAPE permits coverage of up to about 40 miles represented by 512 range gates, or 1,024 memory locations.

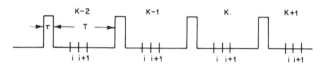

Fig. 11 — Transmitted pulsed waveform

The waveform in Fig. 11 represents the transmitted radar pulse train. Each pulse period is presumed to be divided into T/τ range cells, indexed by i. The MTI cancellation is performed by essentially multiplexing the second order digital filter over 512 range cells. By incorporating the index i into equations (1), (2), (3) and (4) we have

(5) $\quad Y_i(k) = X_i(k) + \alpha_1 W_1(k,i) + \alpha_2 W_2(k,i)$

(6) $\quad W_{oi}(k) = X_i(k) + \beta_1 W_1(k,i) + \beta_2 W_2(k,i)$

(7) $W_1(k+1,i) = W_{oi}(k)$

(8) $W_2(k+1,i) = W_1(k,i) = W_{0i}(k-1),$

The filter output for any range gate during the kth pulse period represents a weighted sum of values computed during the previous two pulse periods for the same range gate.

The RAPE may be programmed to perform the caluclations represented by equations (5), (6), (7) and (8) by modifying the flowchart of Fig. 8 so that provision is made for the range index. This is done by associating with each range gate i an address in a particular data memory. Two data memories are associated with each $W_1(k,i)$ and $W_2(k,i)$ so that all the memory capacity of the RAPE is used. Address register/counters are used to store the range index so that the proper address may be accessed. The basic filter instruction of Fig. 8 is repeated 512 times for each pulse period. Two index registers, BCTR and SCTR, are used to keep track of the number of instructions executed within

each program loop. A flowchart of the program appears in Fig. 12.

Instructions 1 through 6 and 12 through 17 serve to initialize the various counters and registers listed. Each initialization instruction is of the type REG←LIT. Instructions 7 and 18 represent WAIT instructions in which the RAPE waits for a signal from the radar to start processing. The signal is synchronized with both the radar PRF and the clock source and is generated once per pulse period. Its reception causes the CMAR of the RAPE to be loaded with the number stored in the LIT subfield representing the start address for the next instruction. The remaining instructions are similar to those of Figure 8 except that the data memory address registers, labelled DMAR (·), are incremented so that the proper range cell is processed. The roles of the various data memories as they relate to different pulse periods are summarized in Figure 13.

IV. MTI PERFORMANCE

The RAPE was used as an MTI processor in a modified TPS-47 L-band radar system at the ITT plant in Van Nuys, California. The PPI scope photograph in Fig. 14 represents the normal video return (see Fig. 6) within a twenty mile radius of the ITT plant. The returns from stationary clutter (mainly mountains) are seen as the large white mass covering most of

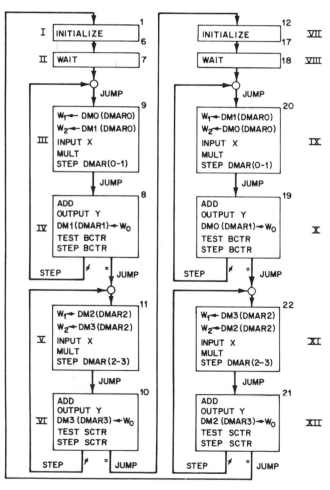

Fig. 12 — MTI flowchart

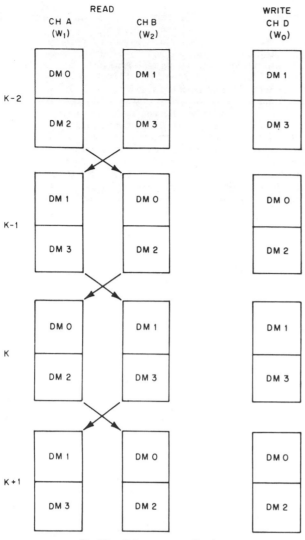

Fig. 13 — Data memory utilization

V. CONCLUSIONS

It has been demonstrated that real time radar processing can be achieved by a processor operating under program control, with no loss in performance over more traditional hardwired devices. The flexibility of such a machine precludes the need to develop a new device for each application and radar system. A single machine may be used in a variety of applications by simply providing a new program for each application. For example, it is known that for some applications narrowband filtering using FFT's is superior to MTI canceller techniques, while in other applications the reverse is true. In fact, in some applications a cascade of both types of filters may be desirable. This emphasizes the need for a processor that can realize both techniques.

ACKNOWLEDGMENT

The author wishes to thank Robert Burns of ITT Gilfillan for his invaluable assistance during the course of the radar test.

REFERENCES

1. B.P. Shay, "Design Considerations of a Programmable Pre-Detection Digital Signal Processor for Radar Applications," NRL Report 7455, Dec. 1972.

2. J.P. Ihnat, et. al., "The Use of Two Levels of Parallelism to Implement an Efficient Programmable Signal Processing Computer," 1973 Sagamore Computer Conference on Parallel Processing.

3. W.R. Smith, et. al., "AN/UYK-17 Signal Processing Element Architecture," NRL Report 7668, July, 1974.

illuminated area. The most prominent clutter peaks have been measured to be approximately 70 db. The filtered returns are pictured in Fig. 15(a-d). These photographs represent six sweeps of the radar scope so that the paths of moving targets are easily seen. A staggered pulse period was used, for all the photographs displayed, to eliminate blind speeds at multiples of the PRF of the radar.

The photograph in the upper left hand corner of the figures represents the frequency response of the corresponding MTI canceller used. It can be seen that the strength of the clutter residue is certainly a function of the filter response. The effect of scaling the input data by a factor of four can be seen by comparing Figures 15(a) and (b). In Fig. 15(b) some clutter peaks, north-northeast of center, are more pronounced than in Fig. 15(a). It is difficult to conclude anything about the strength of the target returns since the environment changed between photographs.

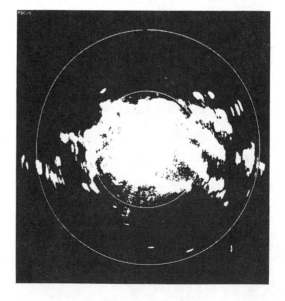

Fig. 14 — Normal video

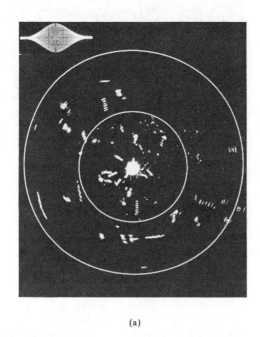

(a)

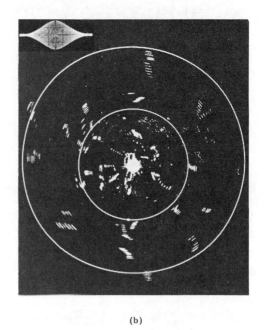

(b)

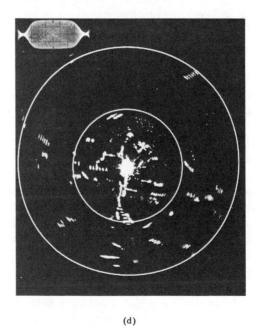

(c)

(d)

Fig. 15 — Filtered video

NTC 74

A Special-Purpose Computer for Digital Signal Processing

RENATO DE MORI, SILVANO RIVOIRA, AND ANGELO SERRA

Abstract—This paper describes a special-purpose processor for use in performing various operations on sampled signals. The system is fast, flexible, and programmable for performing, in real time, operations such as fast Fourier transformation (FFT) and digital filtering of acoustically derived signals.

The main components of interest are a microprogrammed control unit (MCU) and a fully parallel arithmetic unit (AU) implemented with emitter-coupled logic (ECL) microcircuits. A memory unit (MU) and an input–output unit (IOU) are also included.

Index Terms—Arithmetic units (AU's), digital filters, microprogramming, parallel multipliers, special-purpose computers (SPC's).

INTRODUCTION

IN SPITE of the great level of sophistication reached in the design of general-purpose minicomputers recently available on the market, special-purpose machines are still needed for some digital operations on sampled signals in real-time. Particularly, the most common works for the acoustic researcher, such as Fourier transformations, digital filtering and synthesis of speech waveforms can be done in real-time only with special-purpose machines. Some recent examples of such special-purpose machines are the fast digital processor produced at the Massachusetts Institute of Technology Lincoln Laboratory [1] and the special-purpose computer (SPC) designed by White and Nagle at Auburn University [2].

The machine that will be described in this paper is in the middle ground established by the two above-mentioned computers and is of the same generation since construction was started in 1969, using the first emitter-coupled logic (ECL) microcircuits available on the European market. In fact the arithmetic unit (AU), consisting of a parallel multiplier and a carry–lookahead adder connected through auxiliary registers, has been implemented with ECL chips in order to achieve maximum speed.

The multiplier is a reduced one in the sense that about 15 percent of the chips devoted to the processing of the least significant weight bits have been removed, and the error due to this truncation has been partially compensated by the introduction of a correcting bias. The details of this reduction will be treated later on; however it is worth

Manuscript received June 15, 1973; revised February 15, 1974. This work was performed at the Centro di Elaborazione Numerale dei Segnali, Istituto di Elettrotecnica del Politecnico di Torino and was supported by Consiglio Nazionale della Ricerche of Italy.

R. de Mori and S. Rivoira are with the Istituto di Elettrotecnica del Politecnico di Torino and the Istituto Elettrotecnico Nazionale Galileo Ferraris, Turin, Italy.

A. Serra is with the Centro di Elaborazione Numerale dei Segnali (Consiglio Nazionale delle Ricerche), Istituto di Elettrotecnica del Politecnico di Torino, Turin, Italy.

mentioning that the reduction error is negligble with respect to the error in the result of a multiplication caused by the roundoff of the multiplier and the multiplicand.

Another original property of the multiplier is that it performs a multiplication and two double-precision additions simultaneously by a carry-save network which provides, through few logic levels, two addends whose sum is the result of the multiplication and the addition. These addends can be added together in a carry-lookahead adder or stored in two separate registers for subsequent addition to the partial product bits of the successive multiplication; thus, when an operation such as a convolution is to be performed, the AU performs a sequence of pseudomultiplications and pseudoadditions, but only one complete addition at the end of the sequence.

The control unit has a collection of microprograms that can be selected by a keyboard or other external commands, to perform a fast Fourier transformation (FFT) over a variable number of samples, to implement digital filters of various orders in various forms and to perform other operations.

The microprograms are designed to obtain the highest possible speed. Each microinstruction is executed in 100 ns and pseudomultiplication and pseudoaddition require only 100 ns.

Digital filters are implemented using a second-order block (SOB) as a basic unit. An SOB may be defined in terms of its z-domain transfer function [8] as follows:

$$H(z) = \frac{A + Fz^{-1} + Hz^{-2}}{1 + Dz^{-1} + Ez^{-2}}.$$

By combining such blocks in various ways, higher order filters can be obtained. Furthermore, an SOB may be implemented by different programming forms. The jth SOB is implemented in the actual system by the canonic form corresponding to the following difference equation:

$$W_j(nT) = X_j(nT) - D_jW_j(nT - T) - E_jW_j(nT - 2T)$$

$$Y_j(nT) = A_jW_j(nT) + F_jW_j(nT - T)$$

$$+ H_jW_j(nT - 2T) \qquad j = 1,2,\cdots,7, \quad (1)$$

where T is the sampling period and $X_j(nT)$ and $Y_j(nT)$ are the nth samples, respectively, of the input and output of the jth SOB. These parameters are both represented by 10-bit words.

Each SOB has a state variable, $W_j(nT)$, represented by a 14-bit word. The characteristics of the jth SOB are specified by the 14-bit coefficients A_j,D_j,E_j,F_j,H_j.

The SPC described in this paper has been implemented

Reprinted from *IEEE Trans. Comput.*, vol. C-24, pp. 1202–1211, Dec. 1975.

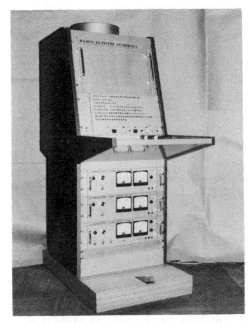

Fig. 1.   Special-purpose computer.

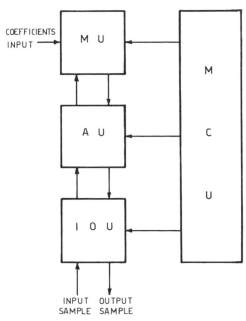

Fig. 2.   General block diagram of the processor.

in the hardware configuration shown in Fig. 1. The equipment shown is capable of implementing several digital filters with a maximum of 14 poles and a computation time of 5 μs for each filter.

STRUCTURE OF THE SPECIAL-PURPOSE PROCESSOR

The processor design follows some ideas previously presented in [3]. It consists of an AU, a microprogrammed control unit (MCU), a memory unit (MU) and an input–output unit (IOU). The block diagram is presented in Fig. 2.

The operands are represented in two forms, namely sign-and-magnitude and two's complement. As a result of a compromise between speed and cost, the former representation is used for multiplications while the latter is used for additions. The sign-and-magnitude representation allowed a considerable hardware saving in the parallel multiplier implemented with ECL chips, while the conversion between the two representations is time expensive. Fortunately, in the application described herein, conversion is performed on numbers which contain errors (input quantization, partial results roundoff or truncation) such that it is practical to perform such conversions with a one's complementation and avoid carry propagation delays without introducing any significant additional error in the output data.

Processor input and output word length is ten bits representing magnitude and sign, while the inputs to the AU are two 14-bit numbers in sign-and-magnitude format. The AU inputs are always a constant and an input variable or a state variable resulting from previous computations.

The calculation of an output sample or a state variable is always a sequence of multiplications and additions; the latter are always performed on the number of bits cor-

responding to the maximum result which can be obtained by adding together the maximum number of double-precision products allowed by the machine control unit.

All processing and transfers between units are by means of parallel data handling.

The type and the form of the linear system to be implemented are entered into a buffer register from a keyboard. These data specify the operations of the MCU. Specifications can vary over a wide range and can command, for example, the simultaneous implementation of various different digital filters with several poles and zeros in either the cascade or the parallel form. The coefficients of the filters can be entered from the keyboard and can be modified by an external device such as a digital computer. In the latter case an interface stores a coefficient and its address and sends it to the memory under the permission of the MCU. The interface also sends out the processor device busy and data delivered signals. This feature has been found to be particularly useful when using the special purpose processor for speech synthesis in real time.

ARITHMETIC UNIT

The block diagram of the AU is shown in Fig. 3(a). Here double arrows indicate parallel transfer of data bits. A state-variable V and a coefficient C, represented in sign-and-magnitude, are stored, respectively, in the two registers RV and RC. While the signs of the two factors are sent to the sign network SN, the magnitudes enter the multiplier network $M1$. This network generates the partial product bits (PPB's) and performs a partial addition of them. Fig. 3(b) provides clarification of the principles of operation of $M1$. The set ① of Fig. 3(b) contains the matrix of PPB's; some of the PPB's are grouped into triplets and added by the full adders which are represented by rectangles on the figure. The full adders have two out-

319

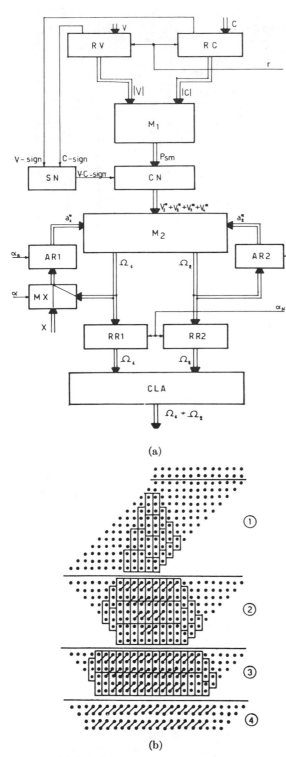

(a)

(b)

Fig. 3. (a) AU. (b) Organization of multiplier array $M1$.

puts, namely sum and carry, that must be added with the ungrouped PPB's. The bits of the set ② of Fig. 3(b) are the ones that remain to be added after the first level of full adders.

Similar considerations can be made for sets ③ and ④. The set ④ contains four rows of bits that have to be added to form the product and these rows are obtained from the original matrix of PPB's after a delay corresponding to a cascade of three full adders. These four rows can

be seen as four numbers that will be indicated by v_1, v_2, v_3, v_4. If P_{sm} is the magnitude of the product CV, one gets

$$P_{sm} = v_1 + v_2 + v_3 + v_4.$$

The technique used in the design of the multiplier is a generalization of the carry-save addition concept proposed in [4].

The network $M2$ in Fig. 3(a) adds the outputs of $M1$ with the results of previous operations stored into the auxiliary registers $AR1$ and $AR2$. In order to perform this operation correctly and rapidly, the outputs of $M1$ are one's complemented by the network CN if the product CV is negative. It is well known that additions and subtractions in the one's complement notation require corrections; in this application these corrections are not required because errors due to using the one's complement are negligible compared to the errors resulting from other sources such as quantization, roundoff, and truncation of the operands [5], [6]. This fact will be used in the next sections for justifying a further reduction in the circuitry.

Let $v_1^*, v_2^*, v_3^*, v_4^*$ be the outputs of the network CN, a_1^* and a_2^* be the outputs of the auxiliary registers $AR1$ and $AR2$. A multiplexer MX allows us to store an input sample into the register $AR1$. All these numbers enter $M2$ as double-precision one's complement words; their bits are added by the network $M2$ with a procedure similar to that performed by the network $M1$, leading to two rows of bits. These two rows that can be considered as two numbers Ω_1 and Ω_2 are related to $v_1^*, v_2^*, v_3^*, v_4^*, a_1^*, a_2^*$ as follows:

$$\Omega_1 + \Omega_2 = v_1^* + v_2^* + v_3^* + v_4^* + a_1^* + a_2^*. \quad (2)$$

The addends Ω_1 and Ω_2 are stored into the auxiliary registers $AR1$ and $AR2$ and become a_1^* and a_2^* for the next-cycle computation. Thus, if a sequence of multiplications and additions is to be performed, once the two addends Ω_1 and Ω_2 have been obtained and stored into the auxiliary registers, a new simultaneous operation of multiplication and addition can take place in a fast sequence until the last multiplication is performed. Only at this time the two final addends Ω_1 and Ω_2 are stored into the results registers $RR1$ and $RR2$ and, while a new fast sequence of multiplications and additions can start, the result of the previous sequence is obtained adding the contents of $RR1$ and $RR2$ in a fast carry-lookahead adder.

The delay introduced by the network $M2$ is that of a cascade of four full adders.

All the AU is implemented using ECL (MECL II) microcircuits; the networks $M1$ and $M2$ are implemented with full adders having a typical delay of 5 ns, thus a typical delay introduced by the cascade of $M1$, CN and $M2$ is 40 ns. The duration of the machine cycle can thus be limited to a value such as 100 ns.

No special noise problems have been encountered on ECL circuit boards, since most of the ECL portion of the processor is a combinational network and the clock rate is a relatively slow 10 MHz.

The printed circuit boards are double sided with diffuse

grounds. The random-access memory (RAM) unit has been isolated from the processor by a screen and connections between boards are by means of twisted pairs of the shortest possible length.

REDUCED PARALLEL MULTIPLIER

It has been mentioned in the previous section that constants and variables are handled in the SPC as fixed-point numbers. For this fact the constants and the variables are rounded or truncated when they enter the AU. The multipliers and multiplicands are therefore affected by a truncation or a roundoff error, and a state variable, once computed, is truncated before storage in the memory. The statistical result of these errors has been previously investigated and some interesting conclusions that can be found in the literature [8], [9] will be recalled in the following.

Because of the error that always affects both the multiplicand and the multiplier, a subset of PPB's will be affected by an error. Processing these bits with a parallel subnetwork of full adders will therefore lead to a set of bits that are always subject to error. Moreover, the PPB's affected by this input errors are those of lowest weight; if some of them are disregarded, a new source of error is introduced, but a saving in components is obtained. This error and the corresponding saving increases as the weight of the disregarded PPB's increases and can be tolerated as long as it does not markedly increase the total error in the result, the total error is the combination of errors due to roundoff truncation, and disregarded PPB's.

The multiplier implemented in the SPC is a reduced one in the sense that PPB's of least significant weights are disregarded and not processed. A quantitative analysis of the errors introduced by this reduction and its comparison with the other sources of errors is provided below.

A. Roundoff of the Factors

The standard deviation σ_F of the error contribution to the product is

$$\sigma_F = E_1 E_2 \frac{H}{4} \qquad (3)$$

where E_1 and E_2 are the amplitude of the elementary quantization steps of the first and the second factor. H is the range of the two factors.

This means that if the magnitudes of the two factors are represented with M ($= \log_2 H$) bits, then, on the average, the error magnitude is of the order of the last $M - 2$ bits of the $2M$ bit product.

B. Roundoff of the Result

Accepting the hypothesis that the probability density of the product values is constant, the standard deviation σ_P of product roundoff is given by

$$\sigma_P = \frac{E_0}{(12)^{1/2}} \qquad (4)$$

where E_0 is the product quantization step. Proof and discussion of the hypothesis can be found in [10], [11].

C. Reduction of Parallel Multipliers

Let the partial product bits be ordered in a matrix where each column corresponds to a weight and the least weight is on the right side as shown in Fig. 4. If N columns corresponding to the N least significant weights are eliminated, a reduction error affecting the product is introduced. The standard deviation σ_R of this error can be computed under the hypothesis that any bit a_i of the multiplicand or b_j of the multiplier is independent of any other and their probabilities are

$$P\{a_i = 0\} = P\{a_i = 1\} = P\{b_j = 0\} = P\{b_j = 1\} = \tfrac{1}{2}. \qquad (5)$$

The detailed calculations of σ_R as function of N are reported in [9].

The reduction error can be partially compensated by adding a binary number (the bias of Fig. 4) to the remaining columns of the partial product bit matrix.

If the reduction error is negligible with respect to the total roundoff error of the product, the elimination of N columns of the partial product bit matrix will not significantly reduce the accuracy of the processor output.

Let

$$\sigma_T = (\sigma_F{}^2 + \sigma_P{}^2)^{1/2} \qquad (6)$$

be the standard deviation of the total roundoff error and assuming

$$E_0 = E_1 E_2 H,$$

one gets [9]

$$\sigma_T = E_1 E_2 H (\tfrac{5}{6})^{1/2}. \qquad (7)$$

In the case of a multiplier with factors of 13 bits each and assuming $E_1 = E_2 = 1$, (7) becomes

$$\sigma_T = (2^{13} - 1)(\tfrac{5}{6})^{1/2} \simeq 2^{13}.$$

The reduction error can be computed starting from the relation

$$\sigma_R = \left(\epsilon \left[\left\{ \sum_{i=1}^{N} \sum_{j=1}^{N-i+1} \alpha_{ij} \right\}^2 \right] \right)^{1/2} \qquad (8)$$

where ϵ represents expected value and

$$\alpha_{ij} = a_i b_j 2^{i+j-2}.$$

The values of σ_R have been computed as function of N [9]; particularly, if $N = 8$ and $E_1 = E_2 = 1$, a value $\sigma_R = 448$ can be found; adding a bias $b = 512$, a final standard deviation of the reduction error $\sigma_R = 238$ is obtained. By suppressing the partial product bits of the eight least significant columns a saving of about 15 percent in the components has been achieved.

If a reduction error $\sigma_R \simeq 10^3$ was allowed, 10 columns could be eliminated to obtain a 20 percent saving in component count.

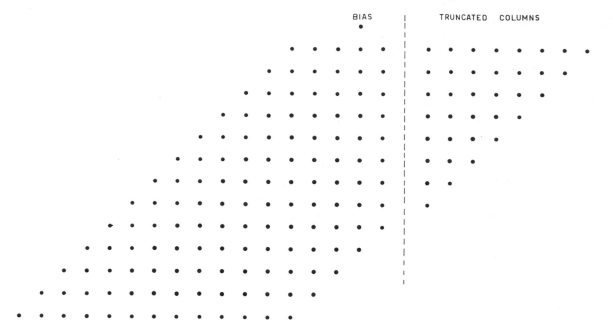

Fig. 4. Product bit matrix.

MEMORY UNIT AND INPUT–OUTPUT UNIT

The MU contains two subunits namely the state-variable memory (SVM) and the coefficients memory (CM); each of these units has a storage capacity of 1024 14-bit words and is implemented with fast-access TTL RAM's. The data from the SVM and the CM are read in parallel and transmitted through TTL/ECL voltage level translators to the input registers of the AU (see Fig. 5). The input to the SVM comes from the AU through an ECL/TTL voltage level translator, whereas the input to the CM can come from the keyboard or an external device.

The SVM and the CM are addressed by separate counters which can be preset or reset by control signals. The use of separate counters provides a high-speed capability during the execution of a sequence of multiplications and additions; the count enable of these counters and the write enable of the memories are commands issued by the control unit.

The input to the processor can come from an A/D converter or from an external digital device. The control unit sends a request for data by a conversion start signal and is informed that a new input is available by receiving a conversion complete signal.

The input data, which are 10-bit words in two's complement fractional format, are read into a TTL input buffer (see Fig. 5) and are sent either to input memory (IM) or to the AU through a TTL/ECL voltage level translator; they can be entered as addends into an auxiliary register or as factors into an input register; in the latter case they are converted, by a two's complementer, to sign-and-magnitude representation.

The output words at the output of the carry-lookahead adder in the arithmetic unit are sent, through an ECL/TTL voltage level translator, to a TTL output register. The output of this register is converted into an

analog signal by a 10-bit D/A converter or is sent to another external digital device.

Even though the multiplier is reduced, the output of the carry-lookahead adder is a 24-bit number. Some bits have been eliminated by the $M1$ network as mentioned earlier, but some most significant weights have been added in the $M2$ network in order to avoid overflows during additions.

As the state variables must be represented by 14-bit numbers and the outputs must be of 10 bits, the problem of making the best selection of the 24 bits available arises. This problem has been treated in [6] with regard to the state variables of a linear block. For the output variables it is possible to perform shifts of variable lengths under the control of the MCU.

CONTROL UNIT

The CU, whose block diagram is shown in Fig. 6, is microprogrammed and was designed in accordance with a general approach proposed by Gerace [12]. The microprograms are stored into read-only memories consisting of interchangeable diode matrices.[1]

The microprograms perform various operations useful in digital signal processing. Some microprograms are implementing various combinations of digital filters in the parallel or in the cascade form. Programs are made of microinstructions characterized by two words, namely the control word and the jump word.

The *control word* is composed by a set of control variables which must be excited to make perform a desired operation by the machine. The most important of these control variables are shown in Fig. 5 and have the following functions.

[1] Some efforts to store microprograms in RAM's connected with a general-purpose computer (GPC) are presently in progress.

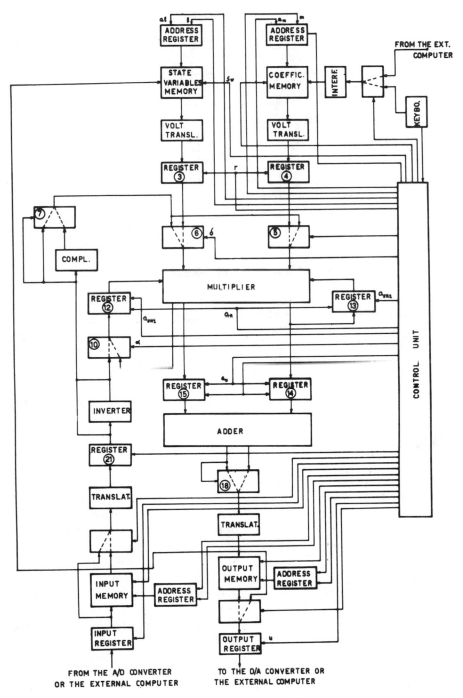

Fig. 5.   Detailed block diagram of the processor.

a_l, a_m clear the address counters of the CM and the SVM;

l, m count enable signals of the address counters;

S_k, S_w write enable signals for CM and SVM;

r write enable for the input registers of the AU;

δ address selector for the multiplexer of the input register of the AU;

a_r write enable for the auxiliary registers;

$a_{zR1}; a_{zR2}$ clear of the auxiliary registers;

a_N write enable for the input register of the carry-lookahead adder;

a_{zR} clear of the above register;

α address selector for the multiplexer of the auxiliary register;

d write enable for the register ㉑ in Fig. 5;

u write enable for the output register; and

c conversion start.

These variables are indicated in Fig. 6 by $\{\alpha_i\}$.

The *jump word* is indicated by variables $\{\beta_i\}$ in Fig. 6 and indicates the next microinstruction to be executed. The $\{\beta_i\}$ are stored in the instruction register 0 and define the actual microinstruction after the rising edge of the next clock interval; this instruction is represented by the variables $\{\gamma_i\}$.

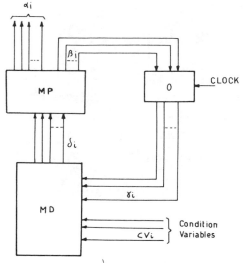

Fig. 6. Structure of the control unit.

The sets $\{\beta_i\}$ and $\{\alpha_i\}$ are not only dependent on $\{\gamma_i\}$; they are also functions of some *conditional expressions* $\{\delta_i\}$; these functions are specified by the content of the read-only memory indicated by MP in Fig. 6. The conditional expressions are obtained via a decoder indicated by MD in Fig. 6 and are functions of $\{\gamma_i\}$ and of a set of *condition variables* $\{CV_i\}$.

The condition variables represent the status of the computation during a sampling interval or a request for interrupt to update the coefficients. The most important of these variables are the following.

d_p A/D conversion complete;

H request for updating a coefficient; and

$Q_0 - Q_{10}$ status of the computation with respect to the number of filters to implement and their order.

The structure of the MCU allows overlapping of the operations to obtain a very high speed.

Appendix A relates the operations sequence required to compute a fourth-order parallel form filtered sample.

APPLICATIONS

The SPC has been designed for processing speech signals. Using a sampling rate of 10 kHz it allows us to obtain a bank of 40 sixth-order filters implemented in the parallel form.

Table I shows the number of clock intervals required for performing filters of different orders in the parallel form. The clock rate is 10 MHz.

The computer has also been used as a real-time speech synthesizer controlled by a DDP 516 Honeywell computer [13]. In this case a single digital filter with poles and zeros is implemented; its inputs can be either a signal representing the glottal waveform or a frication noise. These inputs as well as the filter coefficients, which are slowly varied as a function of time, are provided by the general-purpose computer (GPC). As the special processor requires about 5 μs to compute an output sample, there are

TABLE I

Filter Order	2nd	4th	6th	8th	10th	14th
Number of Clock Pulses	12	19	25	31	37	49

95 μs allowed for sending a new input sample and for updating the coefficients. The update rate is not limited by the special processor, but by the GPC. The maximum update rate capability is well above that required for speech synthesis purposes.

The special-purpose processor can also compute the FFT of the speech signal in real time. The FFT computation starts by considering N input samples as $N/2$ samples of a complex signal. These samples are processed through $N_s = \log_2 N/2$ steps in which N_s sets of $N/2$ variables are successively computed to achieve a complex Fourier transform. The computations are based on recursively performing the butterfly block operations shown in Fig. 7(a), $N_s \cdot N/4$ times. The microinstructions used for performing the butterfly block are listed in Fig. 7(b). A butterfly block is computed in $\tau_B = 20$ clock intervals.

Once the complex Fourier transform has been obtained in a time

$$T_1 = (N/4) \log_2 (N/2)\tau_B$$

the real FFT is computed after $8N$ clock intervals. Assuming a clock interval of 100 ns, the time for computing an FFT is, respectively, 500 μs for $N = 128$, 1100 μs for $N = 256$, and 2400 μs for $N = 512$. A real-time computation capability of an FFT of a signal sampled at 20 kHz is thus achieved.

The input samples are stored in the input memory while the output data are stored in the output memory (see Fig. 5) and all the intermediate variables are stored in the state-variable memory.

The input samples are stored in the input memory under a command issued by the MCU after receiving an interrupt; as the sampling rate is considerably slower than the rate at which the samples are processed, the new

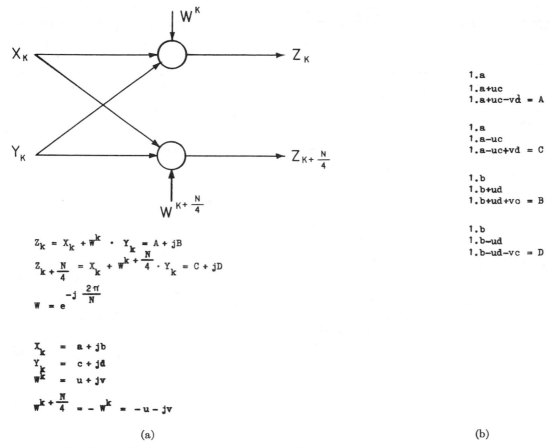

$$Z_k = X_k + W^k \cdot Y_k = A + jB$$

$$Z_{k+\frac{N}{4}} = X_k + W^{k+\frac{N}{4}} \cdot Y_k = C + jD$$

$$W = e^{-j\frac{2\pi}{N}}$$

$$X_k = a + jb$$
$$Y_k = c + jd$$
$$W^k = u + jv$$
$$W^{k+\frac{N}{4}} = - W^k = -u - jv$$

(a)

```
1.a
1.a+uc
1.a+uc-vd = A

1.a
1.a-uc
1.a-uc+vd = C

1.b
1.b+ud
1.b+ud+vc = B

1.b
1.b-ud
1.b-ud-vc = D
```

(b)

Fig. 7. (a) Butterfly-block implementation. (b) Butterfly-block microinstructions set.

samples are always stored in positions previously occupied by samples already processed. Analogously, the computed outputs are stored into the output memory (OM) at locations previously occupied by samples which have been already output.

The SPC is planned for use in the development of future research on speech analysis, synthesis, and recognition.

For this purpose the program of the Centro di Elaborazione Numerale dei Segnali (CENS) is directed towards the implementation of a network of mini- and microcomputers.

These units will be working in parallel performing different tasks and the SPC will be the acoustic terminal of the network. It will perform speech analysis for recognition or it will act as a vocal tract simulator in speech synthesis. The other units will be used for obtaining a phonetic transcription of a written text or for controlling the recognition of spoken sentences.

Particularly, for what recognition is concerning, the microprograms of the SPC will probably be extended for performing a pitch synchronous FFT and a spectral analysis based on linear prediction.

APPENDIX A

Time evolutions of some control variables corresponding to the computation of the state variables and the output sample for a fourth-order filter in the parallel form are shown in Fig. 8.

The first row represents the clock signal; each interval indicated by a roman number, has the duration of 100 ns and is labeled by an arabic number representing a particular set of binary values assumed by the variables of the set $\{\gamma_i\}$.

The remaining rows represent the time evolution of some of the control variables previously defined.

The equations to be implemented are

$$Y(nT) = C_1 W_1(nT) + B_1 W_1(nT - T) + C_2 W_2(nT)$$
$$+ B_2 W_2(nT - T) + FX(nT) \quad \text{(A1)}$$

$$W_1(nT) = X(nT) + D_1 W_1(nT - T) + E_1 W_1(nT - 2T)$$
$$\text{(A2)}$$

$$W_2(nT) = X(nT) + D_2 W_2(nT - T) + E_2 W_2(nT - 2T).$$
$$\text{(A3)}$$

During the intervals I and II the machine is waiting to start the computation of a new sample as soon as a conversion complete signal is issued by the A/D converter.

In interval III, as a "conversion complete" signal is received, the address counters are cleared and an input sample is stored in register ㉑ of Fig. 5.

During the time from IV to VIII the state variable $W_1(nT)$ is computed. First, the input sample is entered into the $AR1$ register while $AR2$ is cleared. Then a sequence of two multiplications and additions is performed

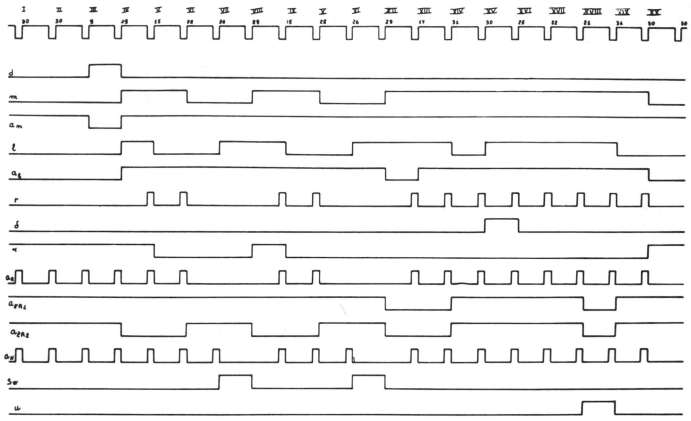

Fig. 8.   Time evolution of control variables.

(V and VI) and the two final addends are added and the result is stored into the SVM (VII). The same sequence is performed during the time from VIII to XII to compute $W_2(nT)$.

The instructions XII through XX allow the computation of the output sample in accordance with (A1). First $AR1$ and $AR2$ are cleared, then (A1) is computed by the following sequence:

$$B_1 W_1(nT - T) = P_1' + P_1''$$

(instruction XIV)

$$P_1' + P_1'' + C_1 W_1(nT) = P_2' + P_2''$$

(instruction XV)

$$P_2' + P_2'' + FX(nT) = P_3' + P_3''$$

(instruction XVI)

$$P_3' + P_3'' + B_2 W_2(nT - T) = P_4' + P_4''$$

(instruction XVII)

$$P_4' + P_4'' + C_2 W_2(nT) = P_5' + P_5''$$

(instruction XVIII)

$$P_5' + P_5'' = Y(nT).$$

(instruction XIX).

During the interval XV one of the input registers of AU is fed, through a multiplexer, the input sample. During the interval XX the computed sample $Y(nT)$ is stored in the D/A converter register and the computer stops to wait the start of a new computation.

It can be seen that the total time for computing an output sample and two state variables of a fourth-order digital filter is 2 μs; this time gives an idea of the speed of the microprogrammed processor.

ACKNOWLEDGMENT

The authors are grateful to Profs. R. Sartori and A. R. Meo for useful suggestions and criticisms. They are also indebted to G. C. Serra for his help in building the machine.

REFERENCES

[1] B. Gold, I. L. Lebow, P. G. Hugh, and C. M. Rader, "The FDP, a fast programmable signal processor," *IEEE Trans. Comput.*, vol. C-20, pp. 33–38, Jan. 1971.
[2] R. White and H. T. Nagle, "Digital filter realizations using a special-purpose stored program computer," *IEEE Trans. Audio Electroacoust. (Special Issue on Digital Filtering)*, vol. AU-20, pp. 289–294, Oct. 1972.
[3] L. Gilli and A. R. Meo, "A system for implementing digital filtering in real-time," in *Proc. Symp. Design of Logical Systems*, Brussels, Belgium, Sept. 1969, pp. 67–89.
[4] C. S. Wallace, "A suggestion for a fast multiplier," *IEEE Trans. Electron. Comput.*, vol. EC-13, pp. 14–17, Feb. 1964.
[5] R. De Mori and A. R. Meo, "Reduced parallel multipliers and errors involved," Centro di Elaborazione Numerale dei Segnali, Turin, Italy, Int. Rep., 1971.
[6] P. Calcagno, E. Garetti, and A. R. Meo, "Optimization and comparison of fixed-point implementations for first and second order digital blocks," *IEEE Trans. Audio Electroacoust.* (Corresp.), vol. AU-19, pp. 314–322, Dec. 1971.
[7] R. De Mori, "Suggestion for an I.C. fast parallel multiplier," *Electron. Lett.*, vol. 5, pp. 50–51, Feb. 1969.
[8] B. Gold and C. M. Rader, *Digital Processing of Signals*. New York: McGraw-Hill, 1969.
[9] F. Ciaffi and A. R. Meo, "On performing multiplication in

signal processing," in *Proc. 6th Int. Symp. Information Processing*, Sept. 1970, p. D2-4.

[10] J. B. Knowles and R. Edwards, "Effects of finite-word-length computer in a sampled data feedback system," *Proc. Inst. Elec. Eng.* (London), vol. 112, pp. 1197–1207, June 1965.

[11] B. Gold and C. M. Rader, "Effects of quantization noise in digital filters," in *1966 Spring Joint Comput. Conf., AFIPS Conf. Proc.*, vol. 28. Washington, D. C.: Spartan, 1966.

[12] G. B. Gerace, "Digital system design automation: A method for designing a digital system as a sequential network system," *IEEE Trans. Comput.*, vol. C-17, pp. 1044–1061, Nov. 1968.

[13] R. De Mori, S. Rivoira, and E. Rusconi, "Research of rules for generating the Italian language using a computer-controlled digital speech synthesizer," in *Proc. 44th Conv. Audio Eng. Soc.*, Rotterdam, The Netherlands, Feb. 1973.

Microprocessor Implementation of High-Speed Data Modems

PIET J. VAN GERWEN, NIEK A. M. VERHOECKX, MEMBER, IEEE,
HENK A. VAN ESSEN, AND FRED A. M. SNIJDERS

Abstract—This paper describes the application of a commercially available microprocessor (Intel 3000 or Signetics 3000) to a flexible data transmitter and data receiver for high-speed data modems. For the transmitter a quadrature modulation scheme is chosen; the receiver is based on phase-shift compensation techniques and coherent demodulation with an externally derived digital carrier. For the realization with the given microprocessor it has been necessary to adapt the way of executing the various operations (especially the multiplications for the digital filtering) to the available computational capabilities. The resulting microprocessor implementations are also suitable for application in the current medium-speed synchronous data transmission systems.

I. INTRODUCTION

IN RECENT years digital processing techniques have gained increasing ground in the field of data transmission. Nowadays they are used in most modern data modems since they are cheaper than analog processing methods and take up less

Paper approved by the Editor for Data Communication Systems of the IEEE Communications Society for publication without oral presentation. Manuscript received August 11, 1976; revised September 27, 1976.

The authors are with Philips Research Laboratories, Eindhoven, The Netherlands.

space. Usually the digital circuitry is implemented either in hardwired logic components or in the form of customer-designed large-scale integration (LSI) circuits. Such LSI circuits can be regarded as special-purpose digital processors. With the advent of the microprocessor a relatively cheap and powerful general-purpose digital processor has now become available. The application of these microprocessors in data transmission modems offers several advantages. First of all, the design of a software-controlled hardware structure yields a very flexible system. By means of mere software modifications all important functions of the data system, such as modulation, spectrum shaping, and demodulation, can be programmed.

Secondly, the general applicability of microprocessors will lead to mass production, so that a further fall in price is to be expected, in contrast to the special purpose IC's with their inherently smaller production series.

In recent literature [1], [2] a description is given of a multiple medium-speed data transmission system in which the functions of filtering, modulation, demodulation, and timing are performed by a special high-speed signal processing unit.

Reprinted from *IEEE Trans. Commun.*, vol. COM-25, pp. 238–250, Feb. 1977.

In this paper we show that, with the bit-slice type of microprocessor commercially available today, a general-purpose implementation of high-speed data modems can be realized. We describe how this microprocessor can be applied to perform the signal processing of the encoding, filtering, modulation, and demodulation of the transmitter and the receiver in real time. In order to achieve this it is necessary to adapt the way of executing the various operations (especially the multiplications for the digital filtering) to the computational capabilities of the microprocessor. This has been done by the derivation of suitable functional diagrams which specify the different functions that have to be performed. It will be seen that these diagrams are versatile in the sense that they are applicable to all current synchronous data transmission systems. However, in our opinion their application in high-speed modems (9600 bits/s and higher) with their relatively small production series offers the best prospects from an economic point of view.

Both our transmitter and receiver designs are based on the Intel/Signetics 3000 microprocessor series, to which we will also devote some general considerations.

II. CURRENT SYSTEMS

For synchronous data transmission over voice-grade telephone channels at data rates greater than 1200 bits/s various modulation formats have been standardized by the CCITT or are in discussion with that end in view. These modulation techniques can be broadly grouped into two classes [3]: single sideband (including vestigial sideband and double sideband (including phase modulation, phase and amplitude modulation, and quadrature amplitude modulation). All double-sideband systems and most practical single-sideband systems yield a transmitted signal $s(t)$ with a symmetrical spectrum. This signal $s(t)$ with symbol rate $1/T_b = \omega_b/2\pi$ can be represented mathematically by

$$s(t) = \sum_{k=-\infty}^{\infty} x_k h(t - kT_b) \cos \omega_m t$$

$$+ \sum_{k=-\infty}^{\infty} y_k h(t - kT_b) \sin \omega_m t \qquad (1)$$

where ω_m represents the center frequency of the spectrum of the transmitted signal, which is equal to the line carrier frequency ω_c for double-sideband systems and equals $\omega_c \pm \omega_b/4$ for single-sideband systems [4], [5]. Line carrier frequencies are typically 1700 or 1800 Hz for double-sideband systems and 2100 Hz for single-sideband systems. The spectral shaping of the transmitted signal is completely determined by the function $h(t)$ in (1). The exact relations between the binary input sequence $\{d_k\}$ of the transmitter and the sequence $\{(x_k, y_k)\}$ in (1) is given by the so-called coding rule, which is uniquely defined for each system. The set of all possible values (x, y) of the sequence $\{(x_k, y_k)\}$ determines the signal constellation [6] of the system, which is usually given in a two-dimensional representation. This is shown in Fig. 1 for a number of current systems [3], such as the following.

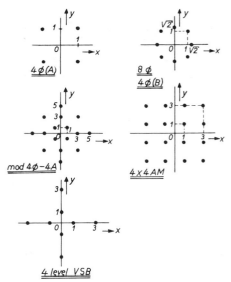

Fig. 1. Two-dimensional representation of signal constellations of several current systems for synchronous voice-band data transmission.

Medium-speed systems: Four-phase modulation of type A (4ϕ-A); eight-phase modulation (8ϕ), which is very similar to four-phase modulation of type B (4ϕ-B); and four-level vestigial-sideband modulation (4-level VSB).

High-speed systems: Four-by-four amplitude modulation (4×4AM); and modified four-phase, four-amplitude modulation (mod $4\phi/4$AM).

Although we are mainly interested in the high-speed systems, we will show that it is also possible to realize the medium-speed modems with the transmitter and receiver structures dealt with in this paper. As will be shown, this is due to the fact that for all systems of Fig. 1 both x and y can have only a very restricted number of different relative values ($0, \pm 1, \pm\sqrt{2}, \pm 3, \pm 5$). Moreover it is likely that systems with higher speeds than 9600 bits/s (e.g., 14.4 kbits/s or even higher) will become feasible in the near future. The signal constellations of these future systems will probably be an extension of the current ones. The inherent versatility of our structures will offer a good basis for the implementation of these newer systems, and therefore we will sometimes emphasize this versatility of our design models in the following sections.

III. DATA TRANSMITTER STRUCTURE

During the last few years several attempts have been made to produce a flexible design for various types of data transmitters by using digital techniques. An example is the principle of echo modulation, where the line signal is synthesized by generating signal elements in a time sequence [7], [8]. The number of required different signal elements, which to a large extent determines the overall complexity of the system, can only be kept small if certain relations between the signaling rate and the line carrier frequency are respected. Two identical systems that differ only in carrier frequency may therefore be very different in complexity when echo modulation is used. For example a two-phase modulation system with a symbol rate of 2400 Bd and a line carrier frequency of 1700 Hz requires six times the number of signal elements necessary for a

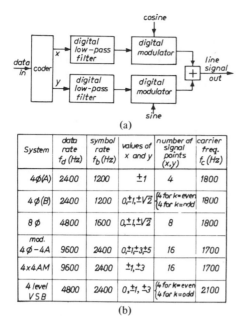

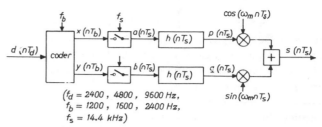

Fig. 3. Mathematical model of versatile data transmitter ($f_d = 2400$, 4800, 9600 Hz; $f_b = 1200$, 1600, 2400 Hz; $f_s = 14.4$ kHz).

the interpolation factor of the filter $h(nT_s)$ and is also an integer in our system, although it could have been taken to be any rational number [9]. The input signal $d(nT_d)$ of the transmitter is converted in the coder into signals $x(nT_b)$ and $y(nT_b)$. In order to describe the transmitter mathematically we have introduced the signals $a(nT_s)$ and $b(nT_s)$, which are given by

$$a(nT_s) = \begin{cases} x(nT_b/L), & \text{for } n = 0, \pm L, \pm 2L, \cdots \\ 0, & \text{otherwise} \end{cases} \quad (3a)$$

and

$$b(nT_s) = \begin{cases} y(nT_b/L), & \text{for } n = 0, \pm L, \pm 2L, \cdots \\ 0, & \text{otherwise}. \end{cases} \quad (3b)$$

Now the filter output signals $p(nT_s)$ and $q(nT_s)$ are given by the digital convolutions

$$p(nT_s) = a(nT_s) * h(nT_s) = \sum_{i=0}^{N-1} a(nT_s - iT_s)h(iT_s) \quad (4a)$$

$$q(nT_s) = b(nT_s) * h(nT_s) = \sum_{i=0}^{N-1} b(nT_s - iT_s)h(iT_s). \quad (4b)$$

The output signal of the transmitter is

$$s(nT_s) = p(nT_s) \cdot \cos(\omega_m nT_s) + q(nT_s) \sin(\omega_m nT_s) \quad (5)$$

which yields the analog signal $s(t)$ from (1) after digital-to-analog conversion and simple analog low-pass filtering. The digital filter $h(nT_s)$ is completely specified by the N successive impulse response sample values $h(0), h(T_s), \cdots h(NT_s - T_s)$ which constitute the filter coefficients of the system. Because the filter has an interpolation factor L we need only N/L multiplications for the calculation of each output sample. In our versatile design we like this parameter N/L to be the same for all systems, despite the fact that L varies with f_b at constant f_s. In this way the computational capacity of the microprocessor can equally well be exploited for each system. As an additional advantage, the filters in all systems give the same performance. We will illustrate this by means of Fig. 4, where a typical frequency characteristic $H(\exp\{j\omega T_s\})$ of the filter $h(nT_s)$ is shown. This filter characteristic can be specified by means of the ripple in the passband δ_1, the minimum attenuation in the stopband δ_2, the cut-off frequency f_g, and the roll-off factor $\rho = \Delta f/f_g$. For the modulation schemes[1]

Fig. 2. Versatile digital data transmitter. (a) Basic scheme. (b) Values of main parameters.

System	data rate f_d (Hz)	symbol rate f_b (Hz)	values of x and y	number of signal points (x,y)	carrier freq. f_c (Hz)
$4\phi(A)$	2400	1200	± 1	4	1800
$4\phi(B)$	2400	1200	$0, \pm 1, \pm\sqrt{2}$	4 for k=even, 4 for k=odd	1800
8ϕ	4800	1600	$0, \pm 1, \pm\sqrt{2}$	8	1800
mod. $4\phi-4A$	9600	2400	$0, \pm 1, \pm 3, \pm 5$	16	1700
4×4 AM	9600	2400	$\pm 1, \pm 3$	16	1700
4 level VSB	4800	2400	$0, \pm 1, \pm 3$	4 for k=even, 4 for k=odd	2100

(b)

similar system with a line carrier frequency of 1800 Hz. With the current high-speed systems the frequency relations are such that a straightforward implementation of (1) is more advantageous, especially when a microprocessor is used. The memory for storage of the system parameters (like filter coefficients) can then be smaller and the number of arithmetic operations comprised in the software of the microprocessor is hardly any larger. Fig. 2(a) shows the basic scheme of a straightforward digital implementation of (1). The binary input data are fed to the input of the coder at a rate of f_d bits/s. In the coder a signal conversion is performed in accordance with the coding rule of any particular system and the results are delivered as successive pairs of values (x,y) which appear at a symbol rate of f_b Bd at the two outputs. The possible combinations of values for x and y have already been given in Fig. 1. The output signals of the coder are applied to two identical digital finite impulse response (FIR) low-pass filters, the bandwidth of which directly depends on f_b. Finally the filtered signals are modulated in two digital modulators where they are multiplied by samples of a sine and a cosine signal and the resulting products are summed to yield the digital output signal of the transmitter. In Fig. 2(b) the values of the main parameters of both medium-speed and high-speed systems are given.

A mathematical model of the digital data transmitter of Fig. 2(a) with an output sampling frequency f_s is given in Fig. 3, where all digital signals have been labelled. A distinction can be made between three types of signal with respective sampling rates of $f_d = 1/T_d$, $f_b = 1/T_b$, and $f_s = 1/T_s$. In general we have

$$f_b = f_d/R = f_s/L \quad (2)$$

where $R = f_d/f_b$ is an integer indicating the number of bits per transmitted symbol which is closely related to the number of different signal points of the system. $L = f_s/f_b$ corresponds to

---

[1] Except four-level VSB, for which we have $f_g = f_b/4$.

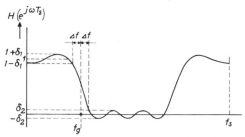

Fig. 4. Typical frequency characteristic $H(\exp\{j\omega T_s\})$ of digital low-pass filter $h(nT_s)$.

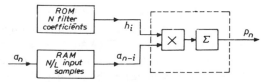

Fig. 5. Interpolating digital transversal filter implementation with multiplier/accumulator combination (interpolation factor = L).

of Fig. 2(b), we have $f_g = f_b/2$. Moreover we will choose the same value of ρ for the various systems. It has been shown [10, eq. 20] that for large values of the number of filter coefficients N a good measure of performance for a digital filter is given by the quantity D defined as

$$D = N \cdot \Delta F, \qquad \text{with } \Delta F = 2\Delta f/f_s \tag{6}$$

which in many cases depends only on δ_1 and δ_2. By substitution of

$$\Delta F = 2\Delta f/f_s = (\Delta f/f_g) \cdot (f_b/f_s) = \rho/L \tag{7}$$

we obtain

$$D = \rho \cdot N/L. \tag{8}$$

This means that for a constant number of multiplications N/L per output sample and a constant roll-off factor ρ, we can realize all modulation schemes[1] of Fig. 2(b) with the same filter performance (i.e., with fixed values for δ_1 and δ_2). In our transmitter design we have chosen $N/L = 20$ and $\rho = 0.125$, which corresponds to a value of $D = 2.5$.[2] With the Fourier approximation method we used in order to obtain Nyquist filtering (raised cosine shaping) this yields

$$20 \log (1 + \delta_1) = 0.1 \text{ dB}$$

$$20 \log \delta_2 = -40 \text{ dB}. \tag{9}$$

Due to the fixed output sampling frequency $f_s = 14.4$ kHz of our transmitter, the interpolation factor of the systems working at 1200, 1600, and 2400 Bd amounts to $L = 12, 9$, and 6, respectively [see (2)]. This in turn leads to a number of filter coefficients $N = 240, 180$, and 120 and specifies the coefficient storage capacity required for each system.

An obvious way of implementing the digital interpolating filters $h(nT_s)$ of Fig. 3 is shown in Fig. 5, where $a(nT_s)$, $h(nT_s)$, and $p(nT_s)$ are briefly indicated as a_n, h_n, and p_n, respectively. The most recent N/L nonzero input samples [see (3)] of the signal a_n are stored in a random-access memory (RAM), the contents of which are read out once in every T_s seconds. Each time a sample a_{n-i} appears at the output of the RAM, it is multiplied by a coefficient h_i taken from a read-only memory (ROM) to yield one of the products of (4). A total number N/L of these products is summed in an accumu-

lator to obtain one output sample p_n. As we want to be able to use only one interpolating filter for all modulation schemes of Fig. 1, the filter has to be able to handle nine different relative values of a_n, viz. 0, ± 1, $\pm\sqrt{2}$, ± 3, ± 5. In order to obtain a reasonable relative accuracy for the binary representation of these values, we need 8-bit samples at the input of the multiplier. This does not necessarily imply that the RAM also has to store 8-bit signal samples. It is possible to code each sample into four bits and store it into the RAM in this form, because each sample can have at most one of nine possible values. Between the RAM and the multiplier a simple decoder then has to be inserted that converts the sample into normal binary representation.

In the configuration of Fig. 5 the calculation of each output sample p_n requires a total number of N/L multiplications (8 by 8 bit) and N/L additions. This amount of computation can be reduced on the basis of the following observations.

1) From Fig. 2(b) we see that in each particular type of system under consideration x and y can have at most four different absolute values, two of which can differ from 0 and 1. We will call these A_1 and A_2. So in Fig. 5 this would mean $a_n = 0, \pm 1, \pm A_1, \pm A_2$.

2) Equation (4a) can be written as

$$p_n = \sum_{i=0}^{N-1} a_{n-i} h_i. \tag{10}$$

Now applying the obvious identity

$$a_n = |a_n| \cdot \text{sgn} (a_n) \tag{11}$$

with

$$\text{sgn} (a_n) = \begin{cases} -1, & \text{if } a_n < 0 \\ 0, & \text{if } a_n = 0 \\ 1, & \text{if } a_n > 0 \end{cases} \tag{12}$$

we can write (10) as

$$p_n = \sum_{\substack{i=0 \\ |a_{n-i}|=1}}^{N-1} h_i \cdot \text{sgn} (a_{n-i}) + A_1 \sum_{\substack{i=0 \\ |a_{n-i}|=A_1}}^{N-1} h_i \cdot \text{sgn} (a_{n-i})$$

$$+ A_2 \sum_{\substack{i=0 \\ |a_{n-i}|=A_2}}^{N-1} h_i \cdot \text{sgn} (a_{n-i}). \tag{13}$$

From (13) it appears that we can calculate p_n by means of N/L simple multiplications of filter coefficients with the value 1, 0, or -1, by three separate summations which are after-

[2] For the VSB system with $N/L = 20$ and $\rho = 0.25$ we can also obtain $D = 2.5$.

wards weighted with 1, A_1, and A_2 and by the final addition of the three resulting terms. We have called this method of calculation "weighting accumulation" (WA). The corresponding functional diagram is given in Fig. 6, where the sgn-function multiplier is symbolically indicated by a dot within a square. We have found that a considerable reduction of computation time is obtained by applying this method of weighting accumulation to our microprocessor implementation.

An overall functional diagram of our flexible data transmitter is shown in Fig. 7. It should be noted that only one RAM is used for storing the 4-bit representation of the signal points (x,y). The diagram has been divided into smaller parts indicated by roman numbers, which can easily be recognized in the flow diagram of the microprocessor implementation of the transmitter that will be presented in Section VI.

IV. DATA RECEIVER STRUCTURE

The main function of the receiver in a data transmission system is to effectuate the demodulation process by which the line signal given by (1) is converted into one or two baseband signals. From these baseband signals the original binary data signal is regained by means of decision and decoding circuitry. In high-speed data transmission, equalization is required in order to eliminate the distortion caused by transmission impairments. Equalization can be performed either before demodulation (passband equalization) or after demodulation (baseband equalization) and can be done manually or automatically. Because the demodulation process in all these situations can be identical it is useful to consider the demodulation and related filtering separately. In this section we will derive a functional diagram for these operations suitable for realization in real time by a microprocessor.

In high-speed data transmission the demodulation is frequently done coherently. After passing a bandpass input filter, the line signal is multiplied in two parallel branches by a cosine and a sine signal of carrier frequency. From the two resulting signals the required baseband signals are derived by two postdemodulation low-pass filters. We have chosen a different demodulator structure schematically given in Fig. 8. In this structure two FIR bandpass filters are present which are obtained from simple transformations of one common low-pass filter. (These filters need not be Hilbert transforms of each other as will become clear later on.) The two filter output signals are multiplied by both a cosine and a sine signal of frequency ω_m [see (1)] and linearly combined. In this way double-frequency terms generated by the multiplications are eliminated and no subsequent low-pass filtering is needed to recuperate directly the two quadrature baseband signals[3] $\hat{x}(nT_b)$ and $\hat{y}(nT_b)$.

In the Appendix it will be shown by means of the mathematical model given in Fig. 9 under what conditions the sig-

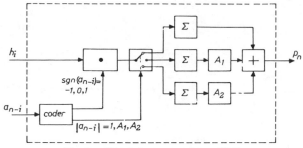

Fig. 6.   Weighting accumulator (WA).

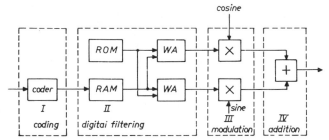

Fig. 7.   Functional diagram of flexible data transmitter for microprocessor implementation.

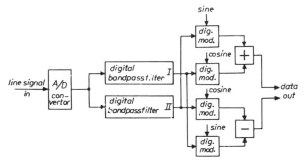

Fig. 8.   Versatile digital data receiver (basic scheme).

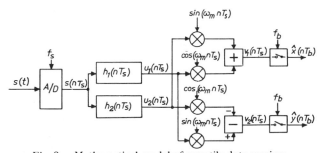

Fig. 9.   Mathematical model of versatile data receiver.

nals $\hat{x}(nT_b)$ and $\hat{y}(nT_b)$ correspond to the baseband signals $x(nT_b)$ and $y(nT_b)$ in the transmitter. In Fig. 9 $h_1(nT_s)$ and $h_2(nT_s)$ represent the impulse responses of the digital bandpass filters given by

$$h_1(nT_s) = 2h_L(nT_s) \cdot \cos(n\omega_0 T_s)$$

$$h_2(nT_s) = 2h_L(nT_s) \cdot \sin(n\omega_0 T_s) \tag{14}$$

where $h_L(nT_s)$ is a zero-phase digital low-pass filter[4], ω_0 is the

---

[3] In single-sideband systems $\hat{x}(nT_b)$ represents useful information only for n = even and $\hat{y}(nT_b)$ can then be disregarded. For n = odd only $\hat{y}(nT_b)$ represents useful information and $\hat{x}(nT_b)$ can be disregarded. Alternatively for single-sideband systems demodulation can be achieved by using sine and cosine signals of line carrier frequency $\omega_c = \omega_m \pm \omega_b/4$. In that case either $\hat{x}(nT_b)$ or $\hat{y}(nT_b)$ represents directly the demodulated data signal and the other one can be neglected [4].

[4] Although $h_L(nT_s)$, $h_1(nT_s)$, and $h_2(nT_s)$ are not causal here for simplicity of notation, they can easily be made causal by the introduction of a delay equal to half the length of the impulse responses.

center frequency of the bandpass filters, and $1/T_s$ is the sampling frequency of the receiver. The operation of the circuit in Fig. 9 can now be described completely by

$$v_1(nT_s) = \{s(nT_s) * h_1(nT_s)\} \cos \omega_m nT_s$$
$$+ \{s(nT_s) * h_2(nT_s)\} \sin \omega_m nT_s$$

$$v_2(nT_s) = \{s(nT_s) * h_1(nT_s)\} \sin \omega_m nT_s$$
$$- \{s(nT_s) * h_2(nT_s)\} \cos \omega_m nT_s \qquad (15)$$

and

$$\left. \begin{array}{l} \hat{x}(nT_b) = v_1(LnT_s) \\ \hat{y}(nT_b) = v_2(LnT_s) \end{array} \right\} \; L = f_s/f_b = \text{integer.} \qquad (16)$$

The demodulator structure in Fig. 8 is based upon phase-shift compensation techniques and therefore it is not very well suited for implementation with analog circuitry. For a digital implementation, however, this is not a drawback. On the contrary it has some important advantages, as we shall show. First of all, the zero memory of the multipliers constituting the modulators and the absence of filtering after multiplication make it possible to operate the digital multipliers at the same (low) sampling frequency f_b, which is sufficient to represent the output signals $\hat{x}(nT_b)$ and $\hat{y}(nT_b)$, and not at twice the highest frequency of the passband signals [11]. In our structure the multipliers are preceded by nonrecursive digital filters, and therefore these can also profit from this lowering of the sampling frequency. Although their input sampling frequency is f_s, as required by the analog-to-digital conversion of the receiver input signal, their output sampling frequency is f_b. This gives a considerable reduction in the number of computations required for the filtering operation at the cost of introducing a small buffer storage by means of which the change in sampling frequency is performed at the input of the filters. A second advantage of the digital implementation of Fig. 9 is the fact that both $h_1(nT_s)$ and $h_2(nT_s)$ can share the same storage registers for storage of their common input signal $s(nT_s)$. Moreover the storage capacity required for the filter coefficients is almost halved by choosing the center frequency ω_0 and the sampling frequency $1/T_s$ in (14) such that

$$\omega_0 T_s = \pi/4. \qquad (17)$$

Then (14) becomes

$$h_1(nT_s) = 2h_L(nT_s) \cdot \cos n\pi/4$$
$$h_2(nT_s) = 2h_L(nT_s) \cdot \sin n\pi/4. \qquad (18)$$

This can be rewritten as

$$h_1(nT_s) = 2h_L(nT_s) \cdot | \cos n\pi/4 | \cdot \text{sgn} (\cos n\pi/4)$$
$$h_2(nT_s) = 2h_L(nT_s) \cdot | \sin n\pi/4 | \cdot \text{sgn} (\sin n\pi/4). \qquad (19)$$

It can easily be seen now that, apart from the sgn-function [as defined in (12)] for each value of n, either $h_1(nT_s)$ equals

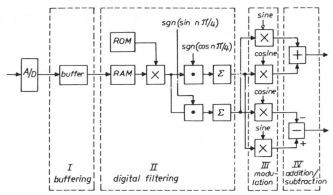

Fig. 10.   Functional diagram of flexible data receiver for microprocessor implementation.

$h_2(nT_s)$ or one of them is zero. So the nonzero values of $h_1(nT_s)$ and $h_2(nT_s)$ can be shared if the simple multiplications by -1, 0, and $+1$ required by the sgn-functions are performed separately. This is shown in the overall functional diagram of the demodulator stage given in Fig. 10. It is apparent how both bandpass filters use one common buffer, a RAM and a full-fledged coefficient multiplier. Only a simple sgn-function multiplier (again indicated by a dot within a square just as in Fig. 6) and an accumulator are provided for each of them separately. The symbol frequency and the demodulator frequency are derived from the incoming signal by means of synchronization circuitry, which is not shown explicitly. The receiver sampling frequency has a fixed relation with the symbol frequency, just as in the transmitter [see (2)]

$$f_s = Lf_b = 14.4 \text{ kHz,} \qquad L = \text{integer.} \qquad (20)$$

With this value of f_s a simple analog filter in front of the A/D converter suffices to limit the spectrum of the incoming analog signal so far that no unacceptable aliasing will occur afterwards. By selecting for L one of the values 6, 9, or 12, we can now maintain the same nominal sampling frequency for all usual values of the symbol frequency $f_b = 2.4$, 1.6, or 1.2 kHz. From (17) we also find for the nominal center frequencies of the bandpass filters $\omega_0/2\pi = 1.8$ kHz. For $h_L(nT_s)$ in (18) we have taken a Chebyshev approximation of an ideal low-pass filter with 51 filter coefficients. A Chebyshev approximation has been chosen because the (Nyquist) pulse shaping is performed at the transmitter and for the receiver filters we are therefore only interested in obtaining maximum attenuation in the stopband. For the application in double-sideband systems with $f_c = 1800$ Hz and single-sideband systems with $f_c = 2100$ Hz we have selected (see also Fig. 4) $f_{gL} = 1500$ Hz and $\Delta f/f_{gL} = 0.2$, which yields $20 \log (1 + \delta_1) = 0.1$ dB and $20 \log \delta_2 = -41$ dB. If double-sideband signals with $f_c = 1700$ Hz have to be included in the design, the low-pass filter has to be made somewhat wider because the center frequency of the bandpass filters must remain fixed at 1800 Hz. The resulting slight increase in noise bandwidth is considered to be acceptable. In that case we have chosen $f_{gL} = 1550$ Hz and $\Delta f/f_{gL} = 0.16$, which yields $20 \log (1 + \delta_1) = 0.13$ dB and $20 \log \delta_2 = -36$ dB.

Just as with the transmitter, the roman numbers in Fig. 10 indicate smaller parts that can easily be recognized in the flow diagram of the microprocessor implementation of the receiver, which will be presented in Section VII.

V. BASIC MICROPROCESSOR ARCHITECTURE

To implement the transmitter and receiver models described in the previous sections we chose the commercially available Intel/Signetics 3000 series. This bipolar microprocessor is microprogrammable and has a central processing array which consists of a number of identical central processing elements (CPE's). Each CPE represents a 2-bit slice, which may be arrayed in parallel to form a processor of any desired wordlength.

The basic block diagram of the microprocessor configuration used is shown in Fig. 11. There are five main parts: the central processing array (CPA), the microprogram control unit (MCU), the microprogram memory (MM), and external memory (EM), and the input/output devices. In the CPA all arithmetical and logical operations required for the digital signal processing are executed. These operations are specified in the microprogram, which is stored in the MM in the form of microinstructions. Via the F and K input buses a part of each microinstruction is fed to the CPA. The sequence in which the microinstructions are read from the MM (called the program flow) is determined by the MCU. To this end the MCU calculates the address of the following microinstruction on the basis of information about the current or previous conditions of the MM (input AC) and the CPA (input FI). The new address becomes available at the MA bus of the MCU. The MCU also has a direct output FO to the CPA, by which it can send one bit of information at a time to the CPA. The way in which the FI and FO signals are handled is dictated by the FC input to the MCU. On the MCU an extra input bus (X) is available through which the program flow can be influenced, e.g., by the contents of the external memory or by the input/output devices. The external memory in our applications is used for storing intermediate results and parameters of the data system, such as filter coefficients or carrier samples, which are presented to the input bus M of the CPA. Usually the input data of the system are fed to the I input of the CPA. After the execution of a microinstruction, the CPA can deliver the result at the D output, while the A output specifies whether this result has to be transferred to the output devices or at which location it has to be stored in the external memory.

For the practical application of the microprocessor the maximum speed of operation is of great importance. This determines the number of microinstructions which can be used for the calculation of one output sample. To characterize the speed of operation we can consider the time required for the execution of a typical microinstruction like the addition of two 16-bit words. Without special measures this will take about 400 ns in the worst-case situation. This time can be shortened by the introduction of a carry-look-ahead circuit which anticipates the carries occurring during addition. The worst case microinstruction time for the addition is then about 230 ns. The further introduction of pipeline circuitry reduces the worst-case time to approximately 150 ns due to the overlap of fetching and execution of microinstructions.

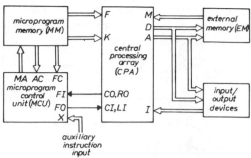

Fig. 11. Basic microprocessor configuration (Intel/Signetics 3000). *CPA connections:* F = function input; K = mask input; M = memory input; I = data input; CI, CO = carry input/output; LI, RO = shift right input/output; D = data output; A = address output. *MCU connections:* AC = address control input; X = auxiliary instruction input; FC = flag control input; FI = flag input; FO = flag output; MA = memory address output.

In the transmitter with an output sampling frequency f_s = 14.4 kHz, we can therefore use a maximum of 460 microinstructions for the calculation of each output sample. In the receiver the output sampling frequency is given by the symbol rate f_b, which at most amounts to 2400 Hz. So we must be able to calculate the two output samples $\hat{x}(nT_b)$ and $\hat{y}(nT_b)$ of (16) with less than 2760 microinstructions. In the following sections we will show how this has been accomplished.

VI. MICROPROCESSOR IMPLEMENTATION OF THE DATA TRANSMITTER

The functional diagram of the data transmitter given in Fig. 7 can directly be translated into the flow diagram of Fig. 12. In both figures the four main operations of coding, filtering, modulation, and addition can be recognized. These operations are performed in a cyclical way with a repetition frequency equal to the output sampling frequency (14.4 kHz). Each cycle starts with an interrupt pulse from a timing circuit. Because interpolation (with interpolation factor L) is applied in the digital signal processing of the transmitter, two different cycles are provided in the flow diagram. The longer cycle, including encoding and storing of new input data, is executed during the calculation of one out of each L output samples. During the calculation of the next $L - 1$ output samples no new input data are available and the corresponding operations are skipped. In both situations the calculated output sample of the transmitter is available before the occurrence of the next interrupt pulse by which a new cycle is initiated.

During the execution of the various operations given in the flow diagram, completely different signal flows occur between separate parts of the microprocessor. In order to obtain some insight into the physical configuration of the data transmitter it is useful to consider these signal flows separately. First we will describe the signal flow of the encoding operation. The encoding rules for the current data transmission systems are specified in CCITT recommendations. Very often these rules imply that the encoding of a group of input data bits into a signal point (x,y) depends partly upon the position of the previous signal point ("differential encoding"). To simplify the calculation of the new point from the previous one, the input

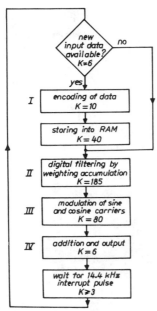

Fig. 12. Flow diagram of data transmitter (K = number of microinstructions).

TABLE I
CODING RULE FOR MODIFIED $4\phi/4A$ SYSTEM

$Q_2Q_3Q_4$	phase difference $\Delta\phi$	phase ϕ	Q_1	relative amplitude r
0 0 1	0°	0°, 90°	0	3
0 0 0	45°	180°, 270°	1	5
0 1 0	90°			
0 1 1	135°	45°, 135°	0	$\sqrt{2}$
1 1 1	180°	225°, 315°	1	$3\sqrt{2}$
1 1 0	225°			
1 0 0	270°			
1 0 1	315°			

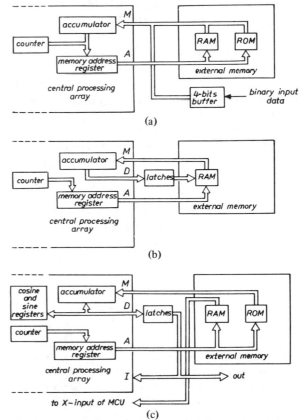

(a)

(b)

(c)

Fig. 13. Signal flows in data transmitter. (a) During encoding of new input data. (b) During storing of new signal point into RAM. (c) During filtering, modulation, and addition.

data bits should be converted into a more suitable representation. In our implementation this conversion is done by means of a ROM and the calculated signal points are stored in a RAM. The ROM and RAM together constitute the external memory of Fig. 11.

As an example we will consider the encoding operation of the modified $4\phi/4A$ system (see Fig. 1) in somewhat more detail. Now we do not characterize each signal point by its x and y coordinates but by its relative "amplitude" $r = (x^2 + y^2)^{1/2}$ and "phase" $\phi = \arctan(y/x)$.

The incoming data of the modified $4\phi/4A$ system are split into groups of four consecutive bits $Q_1Q_2Q_3Q_4$ (quadbits). The first bit (Q_1) in time of each quadbit is used to determine the relative amplitude r of the new signal point, while the other three bits determine the difference in phase $\Delta\phi$ between the old and new signal point. This is summarized in Table I [12].

The encoded signal points are stored in the RAM as 4-bit words $S_1S_2S_3S_4$, where S_1 is identical to Q_1 and the bits $S_2S_3S_4$ specify the phase ϕ as a multiple of 45° in normal binary representation. The bits $Q_2Q_3Q_4$ of each new input quadbit of the system are first converted into another 3-bit word representing the phase difference $\Delta\phi$ also as a multiple of 45° in normal binary representation. Mere addition (modulo 8) of this new word to $S_2S_3S_4$ of the previous signal point yields $S_2S_3S_4$ of the new signal point. The signal flow of the encoding operation is shown in Fig. 13(a), which corresponds to the right half of the configuration in Fig. 11. The 3 "phase" bits $Q_2Q_3Q_4$ of a new input quadbit are fetched from the input buffer and transferred as an address to the ROM via the accumulator register and the memory address register of the CPA. At the output of the ROM the converted 3-bit word appears, which is loaded into the accumulator register. Then the previous signal point $S_1S_2S_3S_4$ stored in the RAM is addressed by loading the memory address register from an internal counter and added to the contents of the

accumulator register. Finally, the result is provided with the "amplitude" bit Q_1 and the new signal point is available for storage in the RAM. That operation can be represented by a different flow diagram, which is shown in Fig. 13(b). The new signal point is temporarily stored in a few external latches while the previous signal point is transferred from the RAM into the accumulator register. Now the new signal is stored in the RAM at the address that has been used until then for the previous signal point. That signal point in turn takes the address of its own predecessor under the control of an internal decrementing counter. This procedure continues until all signal points have been shifted over one address position and the oldest one has been skipped from the RAM.

Now, the actual calculation (consisting of filtering, modulation, and addition) of a new output sample of the data transmitter is started. As explained in Section III, the filtering is based on the concept of weighting accumulation. This is realized as follows. From the RAM each of the stored N/L signal points is read sequentially and fed to the X-input of the MCU (see Fig. 11). From each of these signal points the MCU derives one of 16 possible starting addresses of a specific string of microinstructions (also called a macroinstruction) in the microprogram memory. Then a filter coefficient is read from the ROM of the external memory and put into the accumulator register of the CPA. In the CPA a stack of six registers (three for the cosine branch and three for the sine branch of the transmitter) is used in combination with the accumulator [Fig. 13(c)]. Depending on the particular macroinstruction specified by a signal point, the coefficient is multiplied twice by $0, +1$, or -1 (sgn-function multiplication) and added to the contents of one of the cosine registers and one of the sine registers, respectively. When all N/L signal points stored in the RAM have been processed in this way, the contents of each stack register are weighted with the appropriate factor $(1, A_1$, or $A_2)$. Next the three registers of the cosine branch are added together and multiplied by a sample of the cosine carrier fetched from the ROM. Likewise the contents of the three sine registers are summed and multiplied by a sample of the sine carrier fetched from the ROM. Finally the two modulated samples of the carriers are added to yield an output sample of the transmitter.

The filter coefficients, the carrier samples, and the output samples of the data transmitter are all represented as 8-bit words. In order to avoid accumulation of truncation errors during the processing, the intermediate results have to be expressed more accurately by using a larger wordlength, for which we have chosen 12 bits.

The complete microprocessor configuration of the transmitter is represented in Fig. 14 and the corresponding hardware is shown in the upper part of Fig. 15. The transmitter comprises a CPA consisting of 6 CPE's, an MCU, and an MM of 157 bytes of 32 bits each. Furthermore, the external memory consists of a ROM for storage of system parameters (356 bytes of 8 bits each for filter coefficients, carrier samples, and encoding rules) and a small RAM for storage of signal points (20 × 4 bits). Finally a few latches and a D/A convertor complete the system. In Fig. 12 the number of microinstructions K of each part of the flow diagram are indicated. In the worst-case situation, the calculation of an output sample requires 330 microinstructions, which is well below the maximum number of 460 we have derived in the previous section as a requirement for obtaining a 14.4-kHz output sampling frequency.

VII. MICROPROCESSOR IMPLEMENTATION OF THE DATA RECEIVER

The functional diagram of the data receiver in Fig. 10 can be converted directly into the corresponding flow diagram. This is shown in Fig. 16 for a high-speed system with a symbol rate of 2.4 kHz. Just as in the transmitter, the operations are performed in a cyclical way with a repetition frequency equal to the output sampling frequency, which here amounts to 2.4

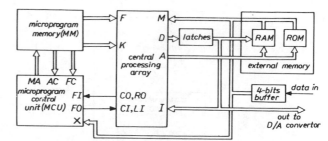

Fig. 14. Microprocessor configuration (Intel/Signetics 3000) for the data transmitter.

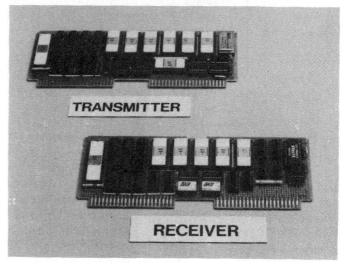

Fig. 15. Hardware of microprocessor implemented data transmitter and data receiver corresponding to Figs. 14 and 18, respectively.

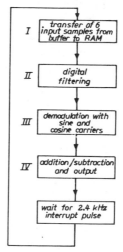

Fig. 16. Flow diagram of data receiver (for 2.4 kHz symbol rate).

kHz. Each cycle starts under the control of an interrupt pulse, which is derived from the received signal by means of an external symbol synchronization circuit. The same synchronization circuit also has to deliver a six times higher frequency of 14.4 kHz that serves as the input sampling frequency of the receiver. Because of the ratio of input sampling frequency and symbol rate, a number of $14.4/2.4 = 6$ input samples must be buffered during the calculation of each pair of output samples $\hat{x}(nT_b)$ and $\hat{y}(nT_b)$. At the beginning of a new calculation, the 6 samples stored in the buffer are transferred to the RAM con-

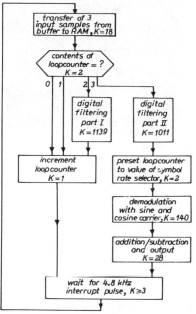

Fig. 17. Flow diagram of flexible data receiver suitable for symbol rates of 1.2, 1.6, and 2.4 kHz (K = number of microinstructions).

taining the 51 samples needed for the digital filtering, thereby replacing the 6 least recent samples. From the contents of the RAM 2 filtered samples are calculated by the procedure described in Section IV. Next the demodulation function is performed by means of 4 multiplications by cosine and sine carrier samples. Finally the 2 output samples of the receiver are obtained from pairwise addition and subtraction of the 4 demodulator output samples.

The flow diagram of Fig. 16 is based upon a cycle time determined by the interrupt pulse of 2.4 kHz. Actually we would have preferred a repetition frequency of 4.8 kHz because then the same flow diagram would have been applicable for all different symbol rates of the modulation schemes of Fig. 1, viz., 1.2, 1.6, and 2.4 kHz, thus yielding maximum flexibility. However the maximum speed of operation of the Intel/Signetics 3000 series does not allow all necessary calculations for one pair of output samples to be performed within 1/4800 seconds. Nevertheless it is possible to circumvent this problem. We found the solution in the combination of a computational cycle time of 1/4800 seconds and an output sampling frequency that can be chosen to be 1.2, 1.6, or 2.4 kHz by means of a manually controlled symbol rate selector. In this way 4, 3, or 2 computational cycles are available for the calculation of one pair of output samples and therefore the time-consuming operation of filtering no longer has to be executed within one computational cycle as will be shown. The resulting flow diagram is given in Fig. 17. Because of the halving of the cycle time, the length of the input buffer can also be halved. After each transfer of three new input samples from the buffer to the RAM, a decision must be made as to how many computational cycles have to be executed before the next output sample and, as a consequence, which processing steps have to be performed before the next interrupt pulse. To this end a loop counter is provided which can contain one of the numbers 0, 1, 2, or 3. If the contents at the decision moment is 0 or 1, this counter is only incremented with 1 and the next

interrupt pulse is awaited. If the contents of the counter is 2, a part of the filtering (viz., the handling of the first 27 coefficients) is executed, the counter is incremented with 1, and the interrupt pulse is awaited. Finally, if the loop counter contains the number 3, the remaining part of the filtering (handling of the 24 last filter coefficients) is performed, followed by demodulation, addition or subtraction, and output. Between these operations the condition of the symbol rate selector is read out to preset the loop counter to the value necessary for calculating the next pair of output samples of the receiver. This value is 0, 1, or 2 if the symbol rate of the system is 1.2, 1.6, or 2.4 kHz, respectively.

Just as in the transmitter, the filter coefficients, the carrier samples, and the output samples of the receiver are represented as 8-bit words. Moreover the input signal now is also expressed in 8 bits. In order to avoid accumulation of truncation errors during the processing, the intermediate results have to be expressed more accurately. This could again be realized by extending the CPE array. However, in the data receiver we have just enough computational capacity left to perform the crucial operations in two sequential steps instead of one, thereby obtaining improved accuracy with only an 8-bits wide CPE array.

The complete microprocessor configuration of the data receiver is shown in Fig. 18. The external memory can be considered to consist of the manual symbol rate selector and the external carrier recovery circuit which supplies the carrier samples. For the carrier recovery one of the usual methods applied in high-speed modems can be used if the carrier signal is made available in the required digital representation (e.g., by sharing the A/D converter already present at the input of the receiver). A completely digital solution could as well be envisaged. The filter coefficients of the receiver are stored in the ROM that constitutes the microprogram memory, so no separate ROM has been provided for that purpose. The total size of the microprogram memory of the receiver is 197 bytes of 27 bits each. The incoming signal samples from the A/D converter are presented to the CPE array via the input buffer and a RAM (51 × 8 bits). Because no preoperation like encoding as in the transmitter is performed upon these samples, the RAM is not considered as a part of the external memory but rather as a part of the input-output devices.

In Fig. 17 the number of microinstructions of each part of the flow diagram have been indicated. In the worst-case situation the calculation of one pair of output values with a symbol rate of 2400 Hz requires 2367 microinstructions, which complies with the maximum number of 2760 we derived in Section V.

The receiver hardware is shown in the lower part of Fig. 15 and an oscillogram of signal points $(\hat{x}, \hat{y})$ of the mod $4\phi/4A$ system is given in Fig. 19 (transmitter and receiver operating back-to-back).

VIII. CONCLUSION

In this paper we have described the microprocessor (Intel/Signetics 3000) implementation of main parts of both a data transmitter and a data receiver suitable for all synchronous

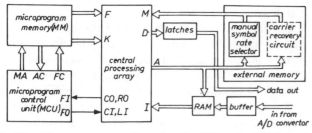

Fig. 18. Microprocessor configuration (Intel/Signetics 3000) for the data receiver.

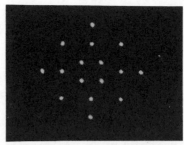

Fig. 19. Oscillogram of signal points $(\tilde{x}, \tilde{y})$ of mod $4\phi/4A$ (9600 bits/s) system. (Microprocessor-implemented transmitter and receiver operating back-to-back.)

voice-band data transmission systems currently recommended or discussed by CCITT. It has been shown how the microprocessor can be operated to do all necessary calculations in real time on the basis of functional system diagrams which are well adapted to the computational capabilities of the microprocessor. Although this paper is only intended to exemplify the application of the microprocessor to the field of data transmission, it is to be expected that this "component" will become a useful tool for the data transmission design engineer.

APPENDIX

MATHEMATICAL DESCRIPTION OF THE DATA RECEIVER

The operation of the data receiver modeled in Fig. 9 can most suitably be described in the frequency domain where any arbitrary digital signal $a(nT)$ is represented by its Fourier transform $A(\exp\{j\omega T\})$. From (5) we find, for the input signal of the receiver after A/D conversion in the absence of noise,

$$S(\exp\{j\omega T_s\})$$
$$= \tfrac{1}{2}P(\exp\{j(\omega + \omega_m)T_s\}) + \tfrac{1}{2}P(\exp\{j(\omega - \omega_m)T_s\})$$
$$+ \tfrac{1}{2}jQ(\exp\{j(\omega + \omega_m)T_s\}) - \tfrac{1}{2}jQ(\exp\{j(\omega - \omega_m)T_s\}). \quad (21)$$

The filter characteristics of $h_1(nT_s)$ and $h_2(nT_s)$ of (14) are given by

$$H_1(\exp\{j\omega T_s\}) = H_L(\exp\{j(\omega + \omega_0)T_s\})$$
$$+ H_L(\exp\{j(\omega - \omega_0)T_s\}) \quad (22)$$

and

$$H_2(\exp\{j\omega T_s\}) = jH_L(\exp\{j(\omega + \omega_0)T_s\})$$
$$- jH_L(\exp\{j(\omega - \omega_0)T_s\}). \quad (23)$$

At the output of these filters we therefore have

$$U_1(\exp\{j\omega T_s\}) = S(\exp\{j\omega T_s\}) \cdot H_1(\exp\{j\omega T_s\}) \quad (24)$$

and

$$U_2(\exp\{j\omega T_s\}) = S(\exp\{j\omega T_s\}) \cdot H_2(\exp\{j\omega T_s\}). \quad (25)$$

The demodulated signals $v_1(nT_s)$ and $v_2(nT_s)$ can now be represented by

$$V_1(\exp\{j\omega T_s\})$$
$$= \tfrac{1}{2}U_1(\exp\{j(\omega + \omega_m)T_s\}) + \tfrac{1}{2}U_1(\exp\{j(\omega - \omega_m)T_s\})$$
$$+ \tfrac{1}{2}jU_2(\exp\{j(\omega + \omega_m)T_s\}) - \tfrac{1}{2}jU_2(\exp\{j(\omega - \omega_m)T_s\})$$
$$(26)$$

and

$$V_2(\exp\{j\omega T_s\})$$
$$= \tfrac{1}{2}jU_1(\exp\{j(\omega + \omega_m)T_s\}) - \tfrac{1}{2}jU_1(\exp\{j(\omega - \omega_m)T_s\})$$
$$- \tfrac{1}{2}jU_2(\exp\{j(\omega + \omega_m)T_s\}) - \tfrac{1}{2}U_2(\exp\{j(\omega - \omega_m)T_s\}). \quad (27)$$

By straightforward substitution of (22)–(25) into (26) and subsequent simplification we find

$$V_1(\exp\{j\omega T_s\})$$
$$= S(\exp\{j(\omega + \omega_m)T_s\}) \cdot H_L(\exp\{j(\omega - \omega_0 + \omega_m)T_s\})$$
$$+ S(\exp\{j(\omega - \omega_m)T_s\}) \cdot H_L(\exp\{j(\omega + \omega_0 - \omega_m)T_s\}). \quad (28)$$

Substitution of (21) into (28) yields

$$V_1(\exp\{j\omega T_s\})$$
$$= \{\tfrac{1}{2}P(\exp\{j(\omega + 2\omega_m)T_s\}) + \tfrac{1}{2}jQ(\exp\{j(\omega + 2\omega_m)T_s\})\}$$
$$\cdot H_L(\exp\{j(\omega - \omega_0 + \omega_m)T_s\})$$
$$+ \{\tfrac{1}{2}P(\exp\{j\omega T_s\}) - \tfrac{1}{2}jQ(\exp\{j\omega T_s\})\}$$
$$\cdot H_L(\exp\{j(\omega - \omega_0 + \omega_m)T_s\})$$
$$+ \{\tfrac{1}{2}P(\exp\{j\omega T_s\}) + \tfrac{1}{2}jQ(\exp\{j\omega T_s\})\}$$
$$\cdot H_L(\exp\{j(\omega + \omega_0 - \omega_m)T_s\})$$
$$+ \{\tfrac{1}{2}P(\exp\{j(\omega - 2\omega_m)T_s\}) - \tfrac{1}{2}jQ(\exp\{j(\omega - 2\omega_m)T_s\})\}$$
$$\cdot H_L(\exp\{j(\omega + \omega_0 - \omega_m)T_s\}). \quad (29)$$

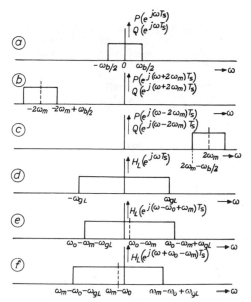

Fig. 20. Schematic representation of some Fourier transforms of signals occurring in the data receiver.

In Fig. 20 some of the preceding Fourier transforms are indicated schematically.[5] From this figure (lines *b*, *c*, *e*, and *f*) it can be verified that under the condition

$$-2\omega_m + \omega_b/2 < \omega_0 - \omega_m - \omega_{gL} \qquad (30)$$

or, equivalently,

$$\omega_{gL} < \omega_0 + \omega_m - \omega_b/2, \qquad (31)$$

the first and fourth term of (29) vanish and therefore (29) reduces to

$$
\begin{aligned}
&V_1(\exp\{j\omega T_s\}) \\
&= \tfrac{1}{2} P(\exp\{j\omega T_s\}) \cdot \{H_L(\exp\{j(\omega - \omega_0 + \omega_m)T_s\}) \\
&\quad + H_L(\exp\{j(\omega + \omega_0 - \omega_m)T_s\})\} \\
&\quad + \tfrac{1}{2} j Q(\exp\{j\omega T_s\}) \cdot \{-H_L(\exp\{j(\omega - \omega_0 + \omega_m)T_s\}) \\
&\quad + H_L(\exp\{j(\omega + \omega_0 - \omega_m)T_s\})\}. \qquad (32)
\end{aligned}
$$

Given a proper choice of $H_L(\exp\{j\omega T_s\})$ the second term in (32) will vanish and the first term will be reduced to yield

$$V_1(\exp\{j\omega T_s\}) = P(\exp\{j\omega T_s\}). \qquad (33)$$

This proper choice implies two conditions (see Fig. 20, lines *a*, *e*, and *f*):

1) $\omega_0 - \omega_m + \omega_{gL} > \omega_b/2 \qquad (34)$

and

$$\omega_m - \omega_0 + \omega_{gL} > \omega_b/2 \qquad (35)$$

[5] For single-sideband systems $\omega_b/2$ should be replaced by $\omega_b/4$.

which can be combined into

$$\omega_{gL} > \omega_b/2 + |\omega_m - \omega_0|; \qquad (36)$$

2) $H_L(\exp\{j\omega T_s\}) = 1$,

$$\text{for } |\omega| < \omega_b/2 + |\omega_m - \omega_0|. \qquad (37)$$

Combination of conditions (31) and (36) gives

$$\omega_b/2 + |\omega_m - \omega_0| < \omega_{gL} < \omega_m + \omega_0 - \omega_b/2. \qquad (38)$$

Summarizing we can state that under conditions (37) and (38), (33) holds. For the systems under consideration these conditions can be met adequately because ω_0 and ω_m have approximately the same value. This can be illustrated by a typical example with $\omega_b/2\pi = 2400$ Hz, $\omega_0/2\pi = 1800$ Hz, and $\omega_m/2\pi = 1700$ Hz. For these values we find, from (38),

$$1300 < \omega_{gL}/2\pi < 2300.$$

In a completely analogous way we can find from (27) under the same conditions

$$V_2(\exp\{j\omega T_s\}) = Q(\exp\{j\omega T_s\}). \qquad (39)$$

If $P(\exp\{j\omega T_s\})$ and $Q(\exp\{j\omega T_s\})$, which have been generated in the transmitter by means of the filter $H(\exp\{j\omega T_s\})$, satisfy the Nyquist I criterion, then the sampling frequency $f_s = M f_b$ of the digital signals $v_1(nT_s)$ and $v_2(nT_s)$ can directly be lowered to yield (see also footnote 3) the signals $\hat{x}(nT_b)$ and $\hat{y}(nT_b)$ given by

$$\hat{x}(nT_b) = x(nT_b) \qquad (40)$$

$$\hat{y}(nT_b) = y(nT_b) \qquad (41)$$

where $x(nT_b)$ and $y(nT_b)$ are the output signals of the coder of the transmitter (Fig. 3).

ACKNOWLEDGMENT

The authors would like to thank Dr. T. A. C. M. Claasen for his assistance in the design of the digital filters used in the systems described.

REFERENCES

[1] D. N. Sherman and S. P. Verma "System description of a programmable multiple dataset," in *Conf. Rec., Nat. Telecommun. Conf.*, New Orleans, LA, Dec. 1975, pp. 23/9–23/12.

[2] A. C. Salazar, D. N. Sherman, S. P. Verma, and J. J. Werner, "Implementation of voiceband modems on a digital signal processor," in *Conf. Rec., Nat. Telecommun. Conf.*, New Orleans, LA, Dec. 1975, pp. 23/13–23/16.

[3] International Telegraph and Telephone Consultative Committee, "Double-sideband modulation as a preferred technique for modems signalling at 9600 bits per second on telephone type leased circuits," COM Sp.A, 92-E, Geneva, Switzerland, Aug. 1974.

[4] H. C. van den Elzen, "On the theory and the calculation of

worst-case eye openings in data transmission systems," *Philips Res. Rep.,* vol. 30, pp. 385–435, Dec. 1975.

[5] R. D. Gitlin and E. Y. Ho, "The performance of staggered quadrature amplitude modulation in the presence of phase jitter," *IEEE Trans. Commun.,* vol.COM-23, pp. 348–352, Mar. 1975.

[6] C. F. Foschini, R. D. Gitlin, and S. B. Weinstein, "On the selection of a two-dimensional signal constellation in the presence of phase jitter and Gaussian noise," *Bell Syst. Tech. J.,* vol. 52, pp. 927–965, July–Aug. 1973.

[7] M. F. Choquet and H. J. Nussbauer, "Generation of synchronous data transmission signals by digital echo modulation," *IBM J. Res. Develop.,* pp. 364–377, Sept. 1971.

[8] —, "Microcoded modem transmitters," *IBM J. Res. Develop.,* pp. 338–351, July 1974.

[9] F. A. M. Snijders, N. A. M. Verhoeckx, H. A. van Essen, and P. J. van Gerwen, "Digital generation of linearly modulated data waveforms," *IEEE Trans. Commun.,* vol. COM-23, pp. 1259–1270, Nov. 1975.

[10] O. Herrman, L. R. Rabiner, and D. S. K. Chan, "Practical design rules for optimum finite impulse response low-pass digital filters," *Bell Syst. Tech. J.,* vol. 52, pp. 769–799, July–Aug. 1973.

[11] D. A. Spaulding, "A new digital coherent demodulator," *IEEE Trans. Commun.,* vol. COM-21, pp. 237–238, Mar. 1973.

[12] International Telegraph and Telephone Consultative Committee, "Report of rapporteur group meeting and draft recommendation," COM Sp. A, 148-E, Geneva, Switzerland, June 1975.

Part IV
Additional Reading

W. Dere and D. Sakrison (Elec. Eng. and Comput. Sci. Dep., Space Sci. Lab., Univ. California, Berkeley, CA 94720), "Berkeley array processor," *IEEE Trans. Comput.,* vol. C-19, pp. 444–447, 1970.

P. Gerwen and P. Van Der Wurf (Phillips Res. Lab., Eindhoven, The Netherlands), "Data modems with integrated digital filters and modulators," *IEEE Trans. Commun. Technol.,* vol. COM-18, pp. 214–222, 1970.

M. Bellanger and J. Daguet (Telecommun. Rad. et Tel., Plessis Robinson, France), "TDM/FDM transmultiplexer: Digital polyphase and FFT," *IEEE Trans. Commun.,* vol. COM-22, pp. 1199–1204, 1974.

A. Gibbs (Res. Lab., 59 Collins St., Melbourne, Victoria 3000, Australia), "SSB modulator for data signals using binary transversal filters," *IEEE Trans. Circuits and Syst.,* vol. CAS-22, pp. 820–826, 1975.

Author Index

Subject Index

343

Editor's Biography

A. C. Salazar (M'69) was born in San Juan Pueblo, NM, on December 7, 1942. He received the B.A. degree in mathematics and the B.S.E.E. degree in 1964, and the M.S. degree in electrical engineering in 1965, all from the University of New Mexico, Albuquerque. In 1967 he received the Ph.D. degree in electrical engineering from Michigan State University, East Lansing.

He joined Bell Laboratories, Holmdel, NJ, in 1967, where he has been engaged in projects involving data system planning and development. These include statistical evaluation of data set performance on the switched telephone network, digital systems planning, digital equalizer evaluation studies, digital filter design, and digital signal processor development for voiceband data transmission systems. In 1975, during a year's leave of absence from Bell Laboratories, Dr. Salazar was the U.N. International Telecommunications Union consultant in digital systems, stationed in Mexico City.

Dr. Salazar has been involved in IEEE activities concerned with digital signal processing, and has published many journal articles and presented conference papers in that field. At the 1974 National Telecommunications Conference he organized the first session in a major IEEE conference devoted exclusively to digital signal processors.